Further endorsements

"History is full of examples of complex scientific problems that are overturned after they were considered 'solved.' Cancer has proven to be more complicated than previously assumed, and even today the science is far from "settled." I applaud any researcher that looks at difficult scientific issues through a different lens and highlights the inconsistencies and proposes new ideas. Mark has done just that; his book is a sweeping and ̶ ̶ ̶ ̶ ̶ *examination of cancer biology that offers a novel theory on the cellular events that transform a normal cell into a cancer cell."*

Travis **Christofferson** MS – Author of *Tripping over the truth*

"This book navigates the complexity and mystery of cancer with remarkable dexterity, providing hugely useful insights into multiple aspects such as the different fuels that drive tumour growth, and how to curb them."

Dr Brigitte König PhD – Professor of *Medical Microbiology and Virology, Infectious Immunology and Infectious Epidemiology University of Leipzig*

"A lot is known about cancer as a symptom, much less about what causes it, although I'm not sure we should be surprised given we've not yet got consensus on what life really is! Mark Lintern's very thoroughly researched work drives a coach and horses through most of the prevailing theories of cancer causation – made more remarkable by him being a layperson and someone who had cancer – no doubt aided by his deep insights to the condition. Sometimes it takes someone from outside the field, who's on a mission – a life mission in this case – to trigger the greatly overdue rethink over what cancer is, why it's present in some and not others, and most importantly, how we can find solutions to it that work!"

Dr Rob Verkerk BSc MSc DIC PhD FACN – *Founder of the Alliance for Natural Health International*

"For over 2 decades we have evolved our Hallmarks of Cancer and yet still fall short of our understanding of and treatment for this shapeshifting disease. Mark Lintern's observations add another piece to the puzzle,

ACKNOWLEDGEMENTS

Janine, thank you for your patience, support and help with proof reading, Sorry for the late nights, and grumpy mornings.

To **Professor Thomas Seyfried** for taking the time to read an early version of my cancer model, and provide the guidance I needed at such an early stage. To **Dr Nasha Winters** for your feedback, guidance, and the incredible level of support you have provided, you've been a true beacon of light. To **Dr Robert Verkerk** for your amazing job at co-hosting the *Cancer Through Another Lens* event and everything you do at the **Alliance for Natural Health International**. To **Professor Michael Lisanti, Dr Ahmed Elsakka, Dr Will LaValley, Professor Brigitte Koenig, Dr Sean Devlin, Dr Penny Kechagioglou, Jane McLelland, Daniel Stanciu, Mark Sean Taylor,** for taking part as members of the expert cancer panel at the event and your ongoing support.

To **Mike Murphy**, and the **Love *from* Margot Foundation** for your financial support. To **Travis Christofferson, Patricia Peat, Brad** and **Maggie Jones,** and **Josephine Barbarino** for your correspondence, involvement in the *Cancer Through Another Lens* event, and ongoing support, and in particular **Gilian Crowther** for our wonderful conversations and help with progressing my ideas, and to the **Academy of Nutritional Medicine** for sponsoring the event. To **Versha Carter** and **Sophie Potten** from **Progressive Communications** for helping with the smooth running of the event, and general support for the project.

To **Kerri Summers** for your incredible organisational skills, to **Miquel Leon, April Ozlem Moss, Suzanne Johnson, Faye Sweet** and all the team at **Yes To Life** for your hard work and dedication, what an amazing team you are. And to **Robin Daly** for all the help and support in bringing this project to fruition, it was a pleasure working with you and continues to be a pleasure moving forward, I couldn't have done it without you.

To **Dr James Healy** and **Dr Cathy Goldstraw** for providing a GP's perspective.

To my **mum** for taking on the proof reading mantle at an early stage and battling my initial nonsensical prose and **Grandma Jean** for the comments provided.

To **Michael Hill, Laura Hammonds, Mike Devaney** and **Mark Curtis** for the feedback received, the interest shown and general support, also thank you for your design guidance.

To **Uncle Phil** and **Anthony Baskerville** for being two of the few who listened and had faith despite my many ramblings.

To the **doctors** and **nurses** who are on the front line, having to deal with the harsh realities of losing patients to the disease, all while doing their best with the limited tools they are provided; it can't be easy to see the devastation cancer causes day in and day out.

And finally to the funding put forward by investors and the hard work and brilliance of **scientists** and **cancer researchers** who have provided the evidence that has enabled me to join the dots and arrive at this compelling conclusion.

FOREWORD

The Somatic Mutation Theory (SMT – genetics as a cause of cancer) is still the dominant paradigm in which we have waged war on cancer for over 50 years with little progress. Despite the failure of this approach in which we can all agree that less than 10% of cancers are in fact, genetically driven, we are still far from a unified understanding of, and treatment for, this condition. In February 2023, a group of over 200 oncology experts along with 10 expert panellists made up of four scientists, three clinicians, and three patient experts from around the globe, spent six hours together exploring Mark Lintern's 8 years of research and inquiry into the origins of cancer.

Could it be that a non-science, graphic designer, pain to purpose, curiosity-driven, out of the box thinker, like Mark, might have something new to consider? Given over 200 cancer-centric people came together virtually on a weekend, nonetheless, to take part in such a discussion and exploration speaks volumes. Perhaps our inability to see the forest for the trees, is what hinders us from expanding our view instead of getting stuck in the same proverbial rut and Mark seems to be just the person to guide us onto another path.

Many of the innovations in medicine in the last few decades did not come from within the medical field. Biohackers, engineers, graphic designers, and systems thinkers in general have an ability to see things as part of a whole rather than separate parts, and seek root causes and possess keen problem-solving abilities often greater than what is dictated by our academic institutions. Our cognitive bias and over-reliance on using familiar tools and ideologies prevents us from identifying causes that could lead to more hopeful solutions.

As someone who has been trying to think beyond the tumor from a terrain perspective my entire career, when Robin Daly of the cancer care charity *Yes To Life* reached out to me, thinking Mark Lintern's work might be of interest, I was initially skeptical. The shortcomings of the mapping of the human genome, identifying an ever-growing number of hallmarks of cancer, the promise of precision medicine and 'moonshot' for cancer have left me feeling disappointed, and somewhat hopeless that a new perspective and new narrative in the cancer world could ever be obtained.

According to Mark, there is an interpretation of the disease that has not yet been considered. Indeed, providing a fresh perspective, Mark proposes that cancer is a result of *cell suppression* caused by parasitic pathogens that take advantage of damaged tissue, as opposed to the accepted theory that cancer is a disease of genetics resulting from cellular damage – *cell malfunction* if you will. And even more recently, with the growing interest and study of the Metabolic Theory of cancer, we have certainly gained ground, but still have a few gaps to fill. The Metabolic Theory asserts that aberrant energy metabolism in cells, lead to cancer cells seeking alternative metabolic pathways such as glycolysis and glutaminolysis, to meet their energy needs. This leads to altered nutrient uptake and utilization, and dysregulated signalling pathways that perpetuate the derangement leading to uncontrolled proliferation and survival of the cancer cells. Intriguingly, through his 'cell suppression' model, Mark also proposes an alternative explanation for the Warburg effect, highlighting – in lock-step with the Metabolic Theory – the significance of abnormal metabolism in cancer.

Following Mark's presentation to this group of oncology experts, I sought clarification of his well thought out and articulated theory. Did he believe that DNA damage is but one expression of cancer and not the beginning point? Does he agree that mitochondrial metabolic dysfunction is a precursor to DNA damage? And finally, does he suggest that mitochondrial metabolic damage is also not the beginning point, rather that an infectious agent is the culprit? In fact, he does propose that a pathogen is responsible for carcinogenesis, upstream from the Metabolic Theory, which is upstream from the Somatic Mutation Theory of cancer.

For me, it still begs the question of WHAT makes us susceptible TO the infection, if that is, the driver? I do caution the reader on being seduced by the notion of a single target and single treatment, and note that Mark addresses this point too, highlighting the need to treat the disease holistically. I so appreciate that Mark's theory is not the conventional view of infection (rapid infection, sepsis, transmission), rather one that is nuanced, in that the infection is opportunistic in nature and slow developing, which also suggests we can identify it and head it off at the pass.

In this book, Mark will walk you painstakingly through the hallmarks of cancer noting that most are well explained by the mitochondrial metabolic theory, much more so than the somatic mutation theory, however, he posits that there are a few discrepancies that can be better understood through a 'cell suppression' versus 'cell malfunction' lens, notably, providing an alternative explanation for the leading hallmarks associated with the disease.

What I love about Mark's process is it engages us in re-examining our beliefs and perceptions, begs us to ask more questions, which is the trademark of the scientific method, encouraging curiosity, an open mind and open dialogue, to continue to seek understanding, and therefore elicit actions in which to change cancer outcomes. I look forward to the discussions that will inevitably follow as this book makes its way into the world.

Dr Nasha Winters, ND, FABNO
Executive Director of Metabolic Terrain Institute of Health www.mtih.org

CONTENTS

QUESTIONING THE MAINSTREAM

THE PROPOSED CAUSE OF CANCER

A SIMPLE OVERVIEW

NATURE TO THE RESCUE

AN INFORMED APPROACH

Preface

On 12th February 2023 a landmark cancer event took place. It set a precedent – the creation of an open discussion platform for sharing ideas between medical professionals and patients, and set the ball rolling on a new way of looking at cancer that has the potential to greatly improve survival outcomes. In an online webinar organised by the cancer charity *Yes To Life*, a panel of 10 cancer experts – scientists, clinicians and patient experts – were assembled to critique a new model of cancer, along with an invited audience of just over 200 medical professionals from around the world. A list of the formidable expert panel, as well as details of the event, can be found on the *Yes To Life* charity website,[904] and in 'Appendix A' at the end of this book.

The event was called **Cancer Through Another Lens** and lasted six hours.[910] During that time a young chap called 'Mark' talked through three 40 minute presentations, complete with evidence. These presentations provided a new way of looking at cancer, based on the eight years of research he'd performed prior to the event. The goal was to assess this new model of cancer in an open and objective way, to see if it was credible and worthy of further consideration. That young chap was me.

Nothing like this had ever been trialled before, a lay person presenting evidence for a new model of cancer directly to a panel of experts, for it to be critically analysed in front of a live audience of medical professionals. I opened up my research, and myself, to scrutiny in a very public way, and was prepared to be grilled by some leading minds in cancer research to see if the new perspective of cancer I had developed could withstand critical analysis. It's one thing to have your ideas submitted for peer-review, it's another thing entirely to stand alone in an open forum and have your ideas challenged in full view of everyone present – for a brief moment, I wondered if I'd bitten off more than I could chew.

A year earlier I'd pitched my new model of cancer to the founder of the cancer charity *Yes To Life* in an extensive four hour internet video call.

Robin sat quietly and listened as I took him through the concepts of my cancer model. I only became aware of how long our meeting was taking, and how engrossed Robin had become, when a hand appeared to the right of the screen and passed him his dinner. Instinctively, he took hold of the plate full of food, thanked the hand, and remained transfixed upon his screen. Undeterred, I carried on while he munched on his meal. Once I'd finished, there was a short pause while Robin was formulating his response. He was impressed and intrigued, but expressed a sensible level of scepticism. He stated that if I truly had something of value to offer, something important to add to the cancer conversation worthy of consideration, then it would need to stand up to some serious scientific scrutiny, and there's no better way to do this than to have my ideas challenged in a very open and public way.

He proposed that I take part in a unique platform where leading cancer experts would consider my model and challenge it's concepts in an online debate. While this was an extremely daunting prospect, I knew that I could not shy away from such a proposition, good science is required to be rigorously scrutinised to check its validity – it isn't science if it can't be questioned. If I wanted to be taken seriously and my model accepted, I would need to allow the harsh, but necessary, method of scientific investigation to poke and prod my work, and the evidence that supports it. And so I agreed.

Fast forward to the 12th February 2023 at 2:55pm. There's five minutes left of the 10 minute intro video being played, where all the expert cancer panellists and me, are being introduced on screen to a live audience of over 200 medical professionals; each of which are eager to find out who I am, and what I have to say. I'm in a room alone at the *Yes To Life* head quarters about to give the most important set of presentations of my life – presentations that suggest that mainstream medicine has misunderstood the disease, and that there's a new way to interpret cancer. As you can imagine, I was a little nervous.

Those five minutes were the longest and most difficult to endure – knowing I was entering the lions den for all to see, and wanting to provide a good account of myself and my work, at a time when my blood pressure was rising fast. At this point my wife sent me a text message *"good luck husb, we're all rooting for you"* – and then a picture message showing my seven month old daughter watching the intro video on a laptop, back in my home town.

Janine Lintern 2023

Now I was becoming emotional with four minutes to go, when I needed to be focused. It had been such a struggle to reach this moment after eight years of research and hardship, and finally it was here. Everything I'd worked towards for the last eight years depended upon the outcome of this moment. Not only that, but it really mattered to me that family were watching, because I'd largely been alone in this journey up until this point, with some friends and family distancing themselves because they couldn't comprehend the enormity and significance of what I'd potentially achieved.

I slapped myself around the face several times, bounced on my toes while moving my head side to side as if I was about to enter a boxing ring, like in a *Rocky* movie, and then sat down at my desk, ready for what was to come. One minute to go...I had to focus...I had a job to do...

The proposition:

For the last 60 years, cancer has been said to arise when the DNA contained within the cell nucleus – which holds the genetic instructions for our development, functioning, growth and reproduction – becomes damaged or mutated. These mutations allegedly drive abnormal cell growth, resulting in a tumour. This is important to know because the latest data indicates that this established view of cancer is **incorrect**. This raises some serious questions: what does this mean for mainstream cancer treatments? Are there more accurate explanations of the disease? And could this mean there are more effective ways to treat cancer? This book addresses these critical questions and offers something unique to the cancer conversation: the proposition of viewing cancer through a different lens with suggestions for a more coherent interpretation of the mechanisms that give rise to, and drive this elusive disease. Simply put, the new perspective of cancer presented herein, has the potential to greatly improve the survival outcome for all cancer patients.

A little knowledge can go a long way:

Each cell within the human body (aside from blood cells) contains a copy of our DNA. There are approximately 21,000 DNA genes present within every cell. DNA genes control many important cellular functions including the creation of proteins. Damage to DNA genes can have adverse effects; for instance, if a gene that controls cell growth is compromised, this could lead to a mutation that causes the cell to duplicate itself uncontrollably, creating a mass of cells that we call a tumour. Further mutations in other essential genes may stimulate the abnormal growth of blood vessels and encourage cells to migrate throughout the body, potentially resulting in metastatic cancer.

Over the last six decades an immense amount of work and money has been invested in DNA-based cancer research to unlock the secrets of DNA. Scientists have made immense progress and greatly improved our knowledge of the human genome (all the genetic information of an organism). Recent advancements in technology have enabled scientists to study all the 21,000 DNA genes contained within a human cell, and in a relatively short time-frame. As a result, scientists have been working hard to identify the link between DNA mutations and tumour growth, by cataloguing the DNA genes that are found to be mutated in different cancer types. The scientific community were confident that, once these 'signature' mutations had been identified, we would be able to create cures by developing drugs to target, and inhibit, the combination of DNA mutations thought to be driving each cancer type, thereby stopping the disease in its tracks.

The concept of cancer being driven by DNA mutation forms the basis of the *DNA Theory* (also known as the *Somatic Mutation Theory*), which states that a clear pattern of up to 12 mutated DNA genes should be present to account for each step in cancer's progression[547] – abnormal cell growth, disruption of programmed cell death, stimulation of blood vessel growth, immune evasion, and so forth. A DNA gene related to each feature of cancer development is required to be mutated. But there's a major problem with this concept: despite six decades of research, and hundreds of billions invested, no conclusive link to DNA causing or driving cancer, has been identified. The predictable pattern of 'signature' DNA mutations that scientists were expecting to find doesn't appear to exist. Instead, the latest data is showing that DNA mutations are unrelated and random, which calls into question the entire mainstream view of the disease.

Most significantly, some cancers have been found to develop without any required DNA mutations being present at all. This begs the question: how can DNA possibly be responsible for driving cancer, when tumours form without the required DNA mutations? This indicates that DNA mutations bear no relation to the cause of the disease, and are more likely a symptom. Astonishingly, the DNA Theory that forms the basis of mainstream cancer treatment, lacks the evidence to support it:

> '...despite 65 years of research on the mutation theory [DNA Theory], there is still **no proof** for even one set of mutations that is able to convert a normal cell to a cancer cell.'
>
> *Genes* **2018**[611]

Despite these major discrepancies in the science, and many more besides, most of us are still under the impression that DNA mutations are driving cancer, because this continues to be the narrative relayed to us by our medical authorities, the doctors who follow these guidelines, and the media. To go against the findings of science in such a fundamental way is dangerously misleading, and threatens patient survival; not just because mutations appear to be random and unrelated, but because the DNA Theory that underpins mainstream thinking, and is often presented as being correct – is actually **unproven**.

This book will demonstrate that the underlying cause of cancer remains unknown and that the mainstream DNA Theory is unable to explain how cancer forms. While this may surprise you, it is a view that is well understood within the medical industry. Here, Professor Thomas Seyfried PhD. (Genetics and Biochemistry), *Professor of Biology* at *Boston College*, and author of a key textbook on the mechanisms of cancer, states:

> 'A major impediment in the effort to defeat cancer has been due, in large part, to the **confusion surrounding the origin of the disease. "Make no mistake about it, the origin of cancer is far from settled"**...

> ...Much of the confusion surrounding the origin of cancer arises from the **absence of a unifying theory** that can integrate the diverse observations on the nature of the disease...

> ...The somatic mutation theory [**DNA theory**], which has guided cancer research and drug development for over half a century, **is now under attack.'**

<u>*Cancer as a Metabolic Disease – Chapter 2* **2012**</u> [008]

This is of major concern, because if mainstream medicine has misunderstood the disease, then current cancer treatments are likely to be targeting the wrong 'cause', and so will inevitably be largely ineffective. And indeed, this appears to be confirmed by the latest treatment statistics.[018] Could this be why scientists have been unable to develop anything approaching a cure in over 60 years of targeting DNA? How can scientists claim a theory to be correct with so much certainty, and have the confidence to develop treatments based upon that theory, when it remains unproven by science and fails to explain the majority of the disease?

While this may be distressing to acknowledge, it's important to note that there are other theories of cancer, some of which can explain more about the disease. These include the *Cancer Stem cell Theory* (where a specific cell type is deemed responsible), the *Metabolic Theory* (in which a faulty energy system within the cell is seen as the cause), the *Tissue Organization Field Theory* (which cites the breakdown of surrounding tissue as the problem), the *Aneuploid Theory* (where damaged chromosomes are said to be driving the disease), the *Viral Theory* (proposing that tumours arise due to the influence of retro-viruses within the cell), and the *Atavistic Theory* (suggesting that cells regress to an embryonic state and grow out of control due to excess stress placed upon them). Each theory can explain the disease to varying degrees, significantly, **all** of them question the validity of the mainstream DNA Theory that has dominated medical science for so long:

> *"We argue that it is necessary to **abandon** the **somatic mutation theory** [DNA Theory]."*
>
> <u>Carlos Sonnenschein, Ana M. Soto</u> **2001** [915]

Further acknowledging the limitations in the mainstream approach to cancer treatment, Dr Robert Gatenby applied Darwinian evolutionary principles to his research, and developed the *Adaptive Theory*.[140] Looking at cancer from a different perspective, and drawing upon the notion of selective pressure in evolution, he's developed a strategy for improving the efficacy of conventional treatments, by utilising them in a different way to how they are currently administered to patients. This proliferation of fresh thinking that challenges the dominant narrative is exciting, because it creates the potential for new treatment avenues that offer improved survival outcomes over and above the limited options provided by the current medical system.

With the latest data calling the DNA Theory into question, we have arrived at a crossroads: do we continue viewing cancer as a DNA-based disease and carry on with the current narrative, hoping that better results will materialise after 60 years of limited progress? Or, do we re-assess the data and embrace the possibility that cancer could be caused by something else – and look towards identifying other potential causes outside of the favoured DNA paradigm?

In an effort to address this problem and ensure people with cancer are adequately informed, this book reviews the medical literature, providing a broad analysis of the latest science surrounding the origin of the disease, and does so in a manner that is easy for non-scientists to understand. But that's not all; it also presents a new model of cancer that offers a unique interpretation that provides a plausible explanation for all the key behaviours of the disease. In other words, this book provides a new interpretation of cancer that has the potential to improve survival outcomes, because there's a very real possibility that the underlying mechanism driving tumour growth has been successfully identified.

New discoveries that challenge the current consensus:

New technology has revealed the intriguing and crucial influence of the microbiome on cancer, and on health generally. The microbiome refers to the population of micro-organisms that live on, and within us. In patients with cancer, this microbiome is often dysbiotic (out of balance), meaning that certain disease-causing micro-organisms, known as *pathogens*, have become dominant.

Unexpectedly, this dominance has been shown to directly influence cancer; in fact, these pathogens have been shown to be driving tumour growth and facilitating the spread of the disease. Indeed, tumours harbour their own distinct population of micro-organisms, collectively known as the *tumour-associated microbiome*. This recent data has scientists scrambling to investigate, and make sense of, this emerging field of study. Significantly, this data is so new, that the established view of cancer does not take into account the influence of these unique microbiomes – tumours were, and often still are, incorrectly assumed to be sterile (free of micro-organisms). This indicates that the conclusions drawn from the majority of cancer studies, are wrong, because this micro-organism influence hasn't been taken into account:

> *'"The finding that [micro-organisms] are **commonly present** in **human tumours** should drive us to better explore their potential effects and **re-examine almost everything we know about cancer** through a 'microbiome lens,'"'*
>
> <u>*Inside Precision Medicine*</u> 2022 [858]

Supporting the notion that we've misunderstood the disease and that the science has been misinterpreted, the *National Cancer Institute* in America performed an extensive study into the accuracy of the science on cancer, and found that up to 80% of studies that form the backbone of the DNA Theory are incorrect, because they cannot be replicated.[018] This is discussed in Chapter 1. With this in mind, the new perspective presented within this book provides compelling evidence demonstrating that a particular type of micro-organism is driving the disease, and that its ongoing influence can provide a coherent explanation for every step of cancer development. Overlooking this infectious relationship with cancer may explain why 80% of DNA-based cancer studies have drawn the wrong conclusion and cannot be replicated. The micro-organism is generating the random DNA damage thought to be driving the disease, such damage is a symptom, not the cause – hence why tumour growth cannot be replicated using DNA damage alone.

It's important to note, that the kind of infection I am referring to is very different to the traditional type of infection that most of us are used to hearing about. With that in mind, some may dismiss my claim that infection is the underlying cause of cancer because micro-organisms have already been considered. In mainstream circles it's already acknowledged that some pathogens trigger the onset of cancer. Approximately 20% of cancers are officially accepted as being caused by infection, the *Human Papilloma Virus* (HPV) that's linked to cervical cancer, is one. *Helicobacter Pylori* bacteria that's linked to stomach cancer, is another. However, the interpretation of how these infections stimulate the disease is very different to the interpretation presented within this book.

The established view of infection causing cancer is based upon the principle of *cell malfunction,* where cell damage caused by the pathogen drives the disease, not the ongoing influence of the pathogen itself. Under this paradigm a bacteria or virus manipulates or damages DNA leading to mutations, which then go on to drive tumour growth. Challenging this interpretation, I'm proposing that a particular group of pathogens are directly driving cancerous conditions, not the cell damage they inflict. The pathogen itself is controlling the apparatus of the cell through a mechanism of *cell suppression* – cancer occurs and progresses because the infection is ongoing.

What's so interesting about the new model of cancer presented within this book, is that it's concept of **cell suppression** is unique and possibly the only concept for cancer causation yet to be explored. As I will show, all current mainstream theories fall under the same banner, which is that cancer is a result of **cell malfunction.** A faulty cell is thought to be responsible for driving the disease. My concept is radically different, in that I don't believe the cell is at fault or has developed a mind of it's own – your own body is not attacking you. Rather, that the cell's ability to control itself, and it's immediate environment, has been compromised by a foreign parasitic micro-organism that takes advantage of weakened and damaged cells. Could this one assumption, that cancer is a result of a faulty cell, be the reason why progress against cancer has stagnated, and why all mainstream theories are unable to fully explain the hallmarks of the disease? Are scientists viewing cancer through the wrong lens?

It is this fundamental shift in perspective of viewing cancer through a suppressive mechanism, coupled with the evidence that supports it, that has allowed me to build a coherent explanation for all key hallmarks of the disease. Through this cell suppression lens, cancer finally starts to make sense.

> *"The scientist is not a person who gives the right answers, he's one who asks the right questions." – Claude Levi-strauss*

The end game:

And here's where it matters in terms of surviving cancer. Most of the public are unaware that the cause of cancer is still up for debate. That many theories exist, and that cancer treatments are designed around the concepts and evidence that underpin each theory. For example, mainstream standard of care treatments are primarily based upon the concepts put forward by the DNA Theory. Treatments that seek to starve cancer of it's energy source and block energy pathways, are based upon the Metabolic Theory; the targeting of cancer stem cells is based upon the Cancer Stem Cell Theory, and so and so forth.

One would think that a combination of treatments from all relevant theories would be offered to cancer patients, unfortunately that isn't the case. Oncologists are not in the habit of offering a range of treatments that reflect the concepts, and science, behind each theory – it's not like your oncologist will offer you a round of DNA-based treatments, followed by metabolic treatments, followed by treatments that target cancer stem cells. This is because the medical establishment – quite unscientifically – favours, and promotes, the **unproven** DNA Theory above all others, as if it's concepts are already proven facts.

Placing your faith in mainstream oncology, therefore, means that you have inadvertently placed your faith in DNA-Theory-based treatments, because it is this theory that most of the mainstream treatments are based upon. The relevance of this is critical to understand, because the mainstream DNA Theory appears to be the least accurate at explaining the mechanisms driving cancer. This may explain why no cure has been forthcoming, and why these treatments are largely hit or miss in terms of efficacy. Determining the most successful treatment path to take then, comes largely down to knowing which theory, or theories, are the most accurate, and then applying specific treatments associated with those theories in relation to your individual situation.

This book goes some way to help you determine this given the detailed assessment of cancer it provides. This notion of understanding the accuracy of each theory, is especially relevant considering that the new model presented herein is the first to explain all key hallmarks of the disease, which indicates that this book provides the most accurate interpretation of cancer currently available. Moreover, it incorporates the Metabolic and Stem Cell Theories within it, because both appear to have identified key aspects of the disease. The question is, how credible is the new model of cancer that is presented within this book, does it shed light on the driving mechanism behind cancer?

Cancer Through Another Lens – post event analysis:

...Referring back to the *Cancer Through Another Lens* event that I mentioned at the beginning: after six hours presenting my ideas and answering the many questions that arose, this landmark event was drawing to a close. The panel of cancer experts were providing their conclusions, having well and truly put me through my paces. Thankfully, my eight years of research, and the hard work that Robin Daly and I had put into planning and executing the event, had paid off – the closing comments were good, they were very good. In fact, there was majority agreement that my proposition was worthy of serious consideration and that I'd presented a new and credible model of cancer. At the very least I'd added another crucial piece to the puzzle that may have serious implications for treatment, with the potential to improve survival outcomes. A link to the voting results from the event can be found on my website: *www.cellsuppression.com*.

That's not to say that everyone agreed with everything I had to say – I wouldn't expect them to. The new model I'd put forward would need to be rigorously tested and scrutinised in greater depth. But finally, after eight long years, my ideas had been accepted and validated. Commenting on the event, audience members *Dr Paul Ch'en* and *Bobby Sira* stated:

> *"Thank you Mark for the great talks and opening up the floor for further dialogue and re-thinking the cancer paradigm. Requires a lot of courage to be willing to be on the receiving end of feedback from* **world experts**. *So glad to have been able to attend such a stimulating session. Thank you to the organisers and those involved in the background who made it happen."*
>
> **Dr Paul Ch'en** – *M.BIOCHEM, D.PHIL, BM, MRCGP*

> *"Mark what an achievement. You truly have picked up the baton. I'm humbled by your presentation, dedication and* **eloquence of such complexity***. Thank you for continuing to challenge and bring remarkable people together for a fantastic conversation."*
>
> **Bobby Sira,** *BPharm, MRes*

In an article summarising the event on the *Alliance for Natural Health International's* website, Dr Robert Verkerk wrote:

> *'***Mark Lintern's** *desire to find rationality in a disease that so often appears deeply irrational is a big reason that his contribution is likely as important as it is. In the process, he's provided a* **well justified dismissal of the dominant dogma** *of the mainstream*

cancer establishment, the DNA or Somatic Mutation Theory of cancer.

*Now that it's been **rated as valid** by the majority of participants at the 'Cancer Through Another Lens' event last Sunday, it's due for imminent publication.'*

Alliance for Natural Health International **2023** [909]

The positive response from the experts attending the event surpassed my expectations, and means I have put forward a credible model of cancer that demands the same attention afforded to any other theory. While this is hugely positive, there is still a long way to go before it is acknowledged, let alone accepted, by the medical establishment, which appears to be very slow in acknowledging new information. For example, even though the Metabolic Theory has been around since the 1920s, has abundant evidence supporting it, and is, by all accounts, the most accurate mainstream cancer theory currently available, it has largely been ignored in favour of pursuing genetic research and treatments. This has occurred despite the DNA Theory being shown to be less capable of explaining the Hanahan and Weinberg Hallmarks of cancer.

Given that progress in medical science can be excruciatingly slow, especially when it comes to concepts that challenge long-established views, it may be a while yet before cancer patients get to hear about this new model of cancer from mainstream oncologists. The question is: do you have the time to wait for the medical establishment to recognise this new model, and update its treatment options to reflect the information presented here – which could take decades? Or, would you prefer to have the opportunity to view the evidence for yourself right now, so that you can decide whether or not the information contained within this book can help to improve your survival outcome?

Only by reviewing the evidence presented herein, and from other reputable sources, as well as conversing directly with your oncologist, will you be able to determine the most beneficial treatment path to take. Unfortunately, the onus is on you to learn all that you can about other perspectives, to ensure you acquire a balanced, well informed understanding of the disease.

While this is of course a daunting prospect, this book has been written to make this process as easy as possible for the lay person. It condenses eight years of research, with over 800 supporting references, into a book that can be read in less than a week. It aims to provide clarity in a sea of misinformation and a platform from which to do further research, should

xii

you need to. Crucially, the evidence is explained, as far as possible, in layman's terms. All the points raised are supported by evidence, which can be easily verified. Such a comprehensive and logical explanation of cancer has never been so accessible, and so easy to understand.

When all is said and done, the inescapable reality highlighted within this book is this: scientists are still attempting to make sense of a disease by analysing it through the lens of a theory that appears to be incorrect; meanwhile, well-intentioned doctors are forced to endlessly experiment with combinations of treatments because they are largely ineffective. This is precisely what we would expect to see from any theory that fails to address the underlying mechanism(s) that drive cancer.

This book aims to provide you with the additional knowledge and tools to better understand this terrible disease, and to allow you to make more informed decisions regarding the greater array of potential treatments available to you.

I

QUESTIONING THE MAINSTREAM

Introduction

It doesn't matter how many times you've heard it mentioned, or how much you've read on the subject – nothing can prepare you for a cancer diagnosis and it can be difficult to convey the emotions involved to someone who has never been diagnosed. The only way I can describe my experience, is that it's like waking up in an abandoned theme park on a cold and foggy morning, not knowing how you got there, only to find yourself strapped into a roller-coaster ride you never wanted to experience. After you finally give up on your futile attempt to struggle free, and as the ride slowly starts to pull away against your wishes, you notice the track ebbs and flows into a wall of fog with no ability to see beyond, or establish how the ride will end. Hearing the distant calls of encouragement and support from family and friends standing on the sidelines, you begin to realise you are completely and utterly alone on this journey – it's your life, and no one else's, that's on the line.

While oncologists may claim definitively that cancer is a genetic disease and that the treatments they provide are the most effective, the dull ache that has made its home within the pit of your stomach is made worse when oncologists highlight the limitations of the treatments they have to offer, and cannot directly confirm the exact mutations that gave rise to your tumour.

The inevitable feeling of dread a patient may feel may be increased further by noticing that the measure of success of mainstream treatments are based around 5-year 'survival rates' rather than 'cure rates'. Anxiety can peak when it's realised that oncologists are still experimenting with the toxic treatments they provide, and when it becomes worryingly clear that mainstream medicine simply does not fully understand the disease. The main concern in all of this, is the length of time it can take for the patient to acknowledge that this is the reality, before they start researching the disease for themselves, as well as the other treatment options available to them – time to undertake the research and apply it, is one luxury that is often limited for cancer patients.

Forgive me for laying it out on the line like this. My intention here is not to frighten you; it is to provide a realistic understanding of the situation you may find yourself in, and to highlight how ill-equipped mainstream medicine can be when treating the disease, especially for cancers that have spread. Dr Leonard Saltz, a colon cancer specialist at *Memorial Sloan-Kettering Cancer Center*, deals with misperceptions all the time:

> *"People too often come to us expecting that the newest drugs can cure widespread metastatic cancer [cancer that has spread]," Dr. Saltz said. "They are **often shocked** to find that the latest technology **is not a cure."***
>
> <u>The New York Times</u> **2009** [656]

Being aware of this reality and the limitations inherent within the medical system is critical when it comes to choosing the most beneficial treatment path to take. For many, a tumour will be caught early, and surgery under these circumstances can be very effective; but when cancer has spread, the outlook becomes much less favourable. Making quick decisions based on fear during a time of stress, and when little is known of the medical industry and its limitations, can reduce your treatment options and ultimately threaten your chances of survival. This is why I provide extensive information regarding chemotherapy, which is detailed in Chapters 3, 4, and 5. Every patient should be aware of this information before deciding whether or not to undertake this treatment option.

Often family and friends will encourage a patient to follow the instructions of medical practitioners, as they quite reasonably assume that oncologists know best, but while love and support are crucial in times like these, family and friends too, are usually unaware of the limitations of conventional treatments that I describe above. I would advocate therefore, for a more 'hands on' approach, where you and your family choose to play an active role in learning as much as possible for yourselves.

As time is of the essence, I have focused on keeping things simple and straight forward. My ultimate intention is to be able to remove that dull ache from the pit of your stomach and to fill it with knowledge, hope, and the resources you need to recover your health. In an ideal world, I would only present the positive aspects of the new model of cancer I am proposing, to keep the stress you experience to a minimum. But for you to acknowledge the potential shortcomings of some of the mainstream treatments being provided, I need to highlight the major flaws inherent within the dominant DNA Theory, which is being used as the basis for those treatments. I need to confirm that the medical industry has misunderstood the disease, as this will make it clear why some of the treatments they offer have the potential to do more harm than good – in particular, why steroids, antioxidant supplements, and poor dietary advice can fuel cancer growth.

This inevitably means that the early portion of this book will be dealing with uncomfortable information that challenges the perceptions many of us hold about cancer, which can be tough to accept at first, and stressful to acknowledge. For many, the safety net that we may feel the medical profession provides us with, will no longer exist once its significant flaws are exposed. But please do not be too dismayed, for I will be filling in the vacuum created, by dispelling illusions with positive information that is based on the latest science, and therefore of the most potential benefit. So, please be prepared for a critical evaluation of the dominant view of cancer and the treatments that are currently offered, but feel comforted by the knowledge that there is a silver lining weaving its way throughout the entire book.

Shall we begin?

It goes without saying that your choice of treatment will determine your survival outcome. While obvious, this is important to contemplate because there are many options available to patients besides the 'standard-of-care' treatments currently provided by conventional medicine. For example, the *Care Oncology Clinic protocol* uses a number of off-label drugs, these can be integrated into a conventional treatment regime. The clinicians at the *Care Oncology Clinic* work directly with NHS oncology units in the UK. Unfortunately, and for reasons I have yet to determine, this information is not common knowledge.

Unbeknown to the public, the medical industry presents a limited understanding of cancer, it is divided over the possible causes of the disease, and is many years behind implementing the latest scientific findings. So, if your oncologist fails to mention the Metabolic Theory and the ketogenic diet, does not explain how glucose, glutamine, and steroids feed cancer growth, neglects to highlight the danger and complexity surrounding antioxidant and iron supplements, doesn't supply you with a list of inflammatory food additives to avoid, and seems unwilling or unable to discuss the different fuels feeding your cancer type, then you are being woefully under-informed. Most importantly, if your oncologist is unable to explain how they intend to address the cancer stem cells present within your tumour, then it's crucial to find a doctor who can, because your survival is intimately entwined with the fate of these superior cancer cells.

Understandably, many will find it hard to accept that so many doctors and cancer scientists could be wrong, and that some standard treatments could actually risk feeding tumour growth. It is not the intention of oncologists to misinform, and they genuinely have your best interests at heart, believing the treatments they have to offer are the most effective currently available. The problem has more to do with their training, that results in their confidence in, and adherence to, the DNA Theory, despite the contradictory evidence that continues to emerge. It is the adherence to this theory that appears to be hindering progress, and blinding scientists to the possibility that a different mechanism is at play. So the question is, how could so many respected medical professionals be misinformed in this way? On the surface this seems like a ridiculous notion, until the major flaw in the way the cancer industry operates, is revealed.

The flaw in the established view:

In 1953, James Watson and Francis Crick famously discovered the structure of DNA. As DNA is thought to control most cellular functions, and as toxins can damage DNA, it wasn't long before influential scientists concluded that DNA damage must be responsible for cancer. The assumption that the cell has malfunctioned and is directly to blame for generating tumour growth came to dominate the way scientists viewed the disease. And so, from the 1960s onwards, the medical authorities presented DNA damage as the underlying cause of tumour growth, even though no significant evidence supporting this concept existed.

The medical authorities, institutions and influential scientists of the time (referred to hereafter as the 'medical establishment') then set about attempting to prove their assertions correct, by vigorously studying the disease from this DNA perspective, crucially, to justify the treatments being developed. And so, over six decades, an entire industry devoted to developing drugs that manipulate DNA was established, based on a theory that, to this day, remains unproven. The tragedy in all of this is that during this entire time, the medical establishment has unscientifically championed the DNA Theory as if it had already been proven correct. As a

4

result, critical research looking at other possible causes has been marginalised and ignored, because all of the attention and, importantly, the funding, has been ploughed into DNA research.

So, between the 1960s and the present day, the DNA Theory has become the dominant view, not because the evidence confirms it to be correct, but because medical students have been educated to view DNA damage/mutation as the underlying cause. The medical establishment has written the DNA theory into the medical curriculum, assuming it to be the most plausible. Even now, despite the latest evidence to the contrary, aspiring medical students continue to leave medical school convinced that DNA mutations are driving the disease. Naturally, all of their brilliance is therefore channelled into studying DNA, even though it hasn't been proven to be responsible.

Suddenly, it becomes easy to see how the majority of scientists could be misinformed when the DNA Theory they have all been taught to depend on is actually unproven, and potentially incorrect. An incorrect theory is an incorrect theory, regardless of the number of scientists who subscribe to it.

Indicating this to be the case, despite 60 years of attempting to prove DNA is to blame, scientists have failed to confirm that a single DNA gene is conclusively responsible for any part of the disease, while the treatments they have developed to target genetic mutations have been unable to provide a cure. In fact, the latest scientific data gained from *The Cancer Genome Atlas* project (discussed in Chapter 2) provides the most substantial evidence to date that DNA mutation is **not** driving tumour growth, much to the shock of the medical establishment. And yet, despite this recent conclusive evidence, the DNA Theory continues to be pushed as the correct view of the disease.

The danger in trusting the consensus:

Most of us support a majority view because we assume that when a consensus is reached, it is an indication that it is likely to be correct. In reality, this is often not the case; the consensus view is just the accepted establishment view of the time, based upon the limited data available, including any dogmatic beliefs that exist – if those beliefs and that data are incorrect, then the consensus view is wrong, the majority just don't realise it yet. Furthermore, we cannot ignore the influence of vested interests, who benefit from ensuring the status quo remains the dominant view:

*'Science is an ongoing search for truth & such truth has little to do with consensus. **Every major scientific advance involves challenges to a consensus.** Those who defend scientific consensus rather than specific experimental findings are not defending science but partisanship.'*

<u>Aaron Kheriaty MD</u> **2023** [919]

The key point here is to not fall into the trap of thinking that a consensus of opinion defines truth or fact, and shouldn't be challenged. In fact, if you were to side with the consensus view throughout history, you would have been incorrect the majority of the time. For example: the majority of scientists once believed the Earth was flat, that bloodletting would cure disease, and for almost 40 years it was denied, by the consensus, that the heart pumped blood around the body. And it is no different today. For instance, only recently was it finally accepted that bacteria cause stomach ulcers and that antibiotics can cure the disease, but not before almost two decades of the majority denying this treatment solution and ignoring the evidence.[464]

Our *microbiome* (which refers to the micro-organisms that live within us) is critical to our health, but current antibiotic drugs can kill beneficial bacteria leading to gut damage. The majority of doctors don't seem to understand how this increases long-term illness, when it should be common knowledge.

And even though the Metabolic Theory is substantially more accurate than the DNA Theory, over 70 years worth of evidence supporting this superior cancer theory continues to be largely ignored by the medical establishment – which explains why the majority of the public have never heard of the Metabolic Theory of cancer. As unbelievable as this next discovery may seem, in 2016 and 2018, two new organs were discovered within the human body – the *Mesentery* and the *Interstitium*.[695, 696] Both had been studied under a microscope for nearly a century without physicians knowing they existed. In other words, we still have a lot to learn and a majority view does not ordinarily indicate truth or fact, it would be unscientific to assume it does.

The danger, is that an appeal to the consensus, as opposed to the evidence, can generate an echo chamber where dominant opinion holds more weight than actual evidence, when, in reality, it is only the evidence that matters:

> *'Statements about the world derive their value from the facts and arguments that support them, not from the status and qualifications of the people who assert them.'*
>
> <u>*John Kay*</u> **2007** [920]

Shutting down free speech, debate, or the ability to question, is quite simply, anti-science. Scientific progress can only occur when the consensus is allowed to be challenged:

> *'The accomplished scientist is an original, an extremist, disrupting established patterns of thought. Good science involves perpetual,* **open debate**, *in which every objection is aired and dissents are sharpened and clarified, not smoothed over.'*
>
> <u>*John Kay*</u> **2007** [920]

Whenever we see an appeal to the consensus, where scientists are being 'cancelled' or ignored simply because they challenge the dominant narrative, or whenever you hear statements like 'trust the science', or 'the science is settled', you can be sure that 'science' is no longer being practised, as Michael Crichton once stated:

> *'Historically, the claim of consensus has been the first refuge of* **scoundrels***; it is a way to* **avoid debate** *by claiming that the matter is already settled...*
>
> *...Consensus is the business of* **politics***. Science, on the contrary, requires* **only one investigator who happens to be right, which means that he or she has results that are verifiable by reference to the real world***...Consensus is invoked only in situations where the science is* **not solid enough***...*
>
> *...The greatest scientists in history are great precisely because they* **broke with the consensus***. There is no such thing as consensus science. If it's consensus, it isn't science. If it's science, it isn't consensus. Period.'*
>
> **<u>Michael Chrichton</u> MD** [921]

Why it's important to question the status quo with cancer:

Clearly, there is a danger in following the established narrative; especially as the latest evidence indicates the mainstream view of cancer appears to be incorrect:

*'...despite 65 years of research on the **mutation theory**, there is still **no proof for even one set of mutations** that is able to convert a normal cell to a cancer cell.'*

<u>Genes</u> **2018**[611]

*'...**mutations** are **increasingly being questioned** as the causal event in the origin of the **vast majority** of cancers as clinical data show **little support for this theory**.'*

<u>Cell Physiology and Biochemistry</u> 2016[395]

*'Despite enormous efforts, the currently popular **gene mutation hypothesis** has **failed to identify cancer-specific mutations...** and **cannot explain why cancer occurs** only many months to decades after mutation by carcinogens.'*

<u>Proc Natl Acad Sci U S A.</u> 2000[165]

Regarding the clear evidence that challenges the mainstream narrative, Professor Thomas Seyfried does not hide his astonishment with the failure of the medical establishment to recognise the Metabolic Theory, as well as its unwavering support for the DNA Theory:

*'...the origin of carcinogenesis [origin of cancer] resides with the **mitochondria in the cytoplasm** [Metabolic Theory], **not** with the **genome in the nucleus** [DNA theory]. **How is it possible** that so many in the cancer field **seem unaware of the evidence** supporting this concept? How is it possible that so many in the cancer field have **ignored these findings** while embracing the **flawed** gene theory [DNA theory]?'*

<u>Cancer as a Metabolic Disease. Pg 204</u> 2012[008]

Professor Seyfried states that an abnormally functioning energy system is responsible for cancer, not any DNA mutations present within the nucleus. This interpretation of the disease is explained by the Metabolic Theory, which describes how a tumour cell's energy system appears to be faulty. In more recent times this theory has been referred to as the *Mitochondrial Metabolic Theory* (MMT), because the theory proposes specifically, that *mitochondria* – the energy factories within cells – appear to be faulty. For the purpose of simplicity, I'll continue to refer to it as the Metabolic Theory.

The involvement of the energy system is important to acknowledge because cell growth and cell death mechanisms are controlled by mitochondria, not just the DNA contained within the nucleus – meaning that a faulty energy system alone can potentially explain tumour growth, which challenges the DNA Theory. Indeed, evidence supporting the Metabolic Theory indicates that cancer is a metabolic disease, a disease that results from an abnormally functioning energy system.

It is this metabolic detail that the medical establishment seems reluctant to acknowledge. Could this be simply because it challenges the DNA Theory that so many have chosen to align with? Thankfully there continues to be a growing body of evidence confirming the interplay between the energy system of the cell and cancer – evidence that should encourage the medical establishment to eventually give it the attention it deserves. For example, a recent 2019 study into colorectal cancer confirms this metabolic relationship:

> *'Indeed, most core metabolic pathways [energy pathways], including **glucose, glutamine,** and **lipid** [fat] metabolism are exploited by cancer cells to **sustain their high rates of cell division**. Beyond cell proliferation, it is **becoming increasingly clear** that cellular **metabolism** [energy] is tightly associated with cancer cell fate...'*
>
> <u>Science Direct</u> **2019** [663]

Energy metabolism appears to play a crucial role in cancer, which is why the Metabolic Theory is heavily discussed within this book, and forms a key part of the new perspective it contains. Our medical authorities' failure to acknowledge the evidence for the Metabolic Theory, and to implement the changes in the medical system it calls for, has resulted in the limited view of cancer currently being taught to the majority of medical doctors. This has led to continued dominance of the DNA Theory, when it should have been side-lined long ago. This ultimately means that patients are ill-informed, and that oncologists are providing treatments that are potentially damaging and largely ineffective, simply because they are targeting the wrong functions of the cell. As stark proof of this – and while five-year survival rates have improved for some – in over 60 years no cure has been created for a single type of cancer, and there is still no sign of one on the horizon.

Conceivably then, a terminal diagnosis may not be terminal at all because such a diagnosis appears to be based upon a limited understanding of the disease. We mustn't allow ourselves to be condemned by a medical system that has limited itself, and the treatment options it provides, by its interpretation of cancer.

Diagnosis:

When a patient is first diagnosed oncologists will advise that DNA damage is responsible, that up to 12 DNA mutations gained over many years, has led to the disease.[547] However, patients aren't informed that this is based upon an unproven theory. There is no evidence to prove that a single DNA mutation is conclusively to blame for any part of the disease.[165, 395, 611] In fact, when attempting to discover the DNA gene assumed to be responsible for the spread of cancer, scientists were forced to conclude that this DNA gene didn't exist:

> '"Comprehensive sequencing was **unable to find a single mutation responsible** for the most important quality of cancer – the ability of cancer to spread and cause 90% of all cancer deaths".'
>
> **Travis Christofferson. Tripping over the truth 2014**[258]

Focusing heavily on DNA damage as the underlying cause, means that the notion of diet being able to treat cancer appears absurd, which is why it is often dismissed as nonsense. Viewing cancer from a DNA Theory perspective, nutrients alone can't revert mutated DNA back to its pre-existing state, or cause the damage needed to kill cancer cells, it, therefore, seems ridiculous to believe that diet can treat the disease when viewed from this limited DNA understanding.

However, as we have seen above, cancer does not appear to be caused by DNA damage or mutation. My proposal here is that a particular type of micro-organism is a central driver of cancerous conditions through the manipulation of key cellular pathways. Within this perspective, it is not mutated DNA that is affected by food but the elimination of the micro-organism that determines the outcome. As organic food and medicinal plants are high in antimicrobial compounds that can kill many common pathogens, the correct diet could have a beneficial, even curative effect, because these plant antibiotics target the driver of cancerous conditions by killing the micro-organism responsible. This is why the prospect of diet being able to treat cancer isn't ludicrous at all, and why there are thousands of studies that contradict the mainstream view by confirming that common food compounds selectively kill cancer cells, without harming healthy cells. The very fact that these studies exist indicates that the mainstream view is incorrect.

The micro-organism mimicking cancer:

When using the term 'micro-organism,' I am referring to bacteria, fungi and viruses; all three are microscopic organisms that can invade, damage and influence human cells. Not all micro-organisms cause disease; most are either benign or beneficial. Those that do cause disease are referred to as *pathogens*. In the first half of the book I refer to micro-organisms in general and only reveal the type of micro-organism proposed to be responsible for cancer halfway through. I have written the book this way as it's important to first demonstrate that micro-organisms are likely responsible, before discussing which specific type of micro-organism it may be. There are some critical points that need to be understood before jumping into the detail. These points can only be effectively made by referring to micro-organisms in their broader context; furthermore, there is already unjustified resistance to the notion that the micro-organism type in question, is responsible. This ill-informed sentiment may negatively influence your perspective if you've been subject to these ill-informed opinions, so for this reason, the identity of the micro-organism in question has been with-held until you've had a reasonable chance to study the evidence that confirms that micro-organisms could be driving the disease.

As you will discover, the volume of evidence supporting the new perspective contained within this book is substantial. A recent announcement made by the *Mayo Clinic*,[264] a top cancer research facility in America, has all but rubber-stamped one of these three types of micro-organisms as the cause of tumour growth. The Mayo Clinic has gone on record to state how a particular micro-organism has been found to create a 'palpable mass' in the GI tract. Stopping short of confirming it to be a tumour, Dr Vikram M.D admits that this mass mimics cancer to such an extent that he goes on to state that it's actually impossible to tell the difference; they appear to be one and the same thing.

Had this micro-organism not been identified within the tumour, it would have been categorised as cancer. In fact, initially it was, until further investigation confirmed a micro-organism was present. This mass was eventually not considered to be cancer, because many scientists are taught to think that only DNA can cause the disease, and so the potential cause is hidden in plain sight. Despite being equipped with the knowledge that a micro-organism can generate a mass that is indistinguishable from cancer, our medical authorities persist in believing that there's little evidence to link this particular micro-organism to the disease, which couldn't be further from the truth.

Current solutions offered:

As a result of targeting the wrong aspect of cancer, there is an obvious lack of progress being made with the current treatments provided. Outdated chemotherapy drugs created in the 1960s and '70s are still pushed as a primary solution today, even though death rates have remained relatively unchanged in over 55 years of their continued use. This means that your chances of being cured of metastatic cancer are not significantly better now than they were back in the 1960s. This is difficult to believe given the current hype about survival rates in the media; however, mortality figures confirm this to be the case (these figures are provided in Chapter 3).

This lack of progress has led scientists to present 'survival rates' instead of 'mortality rates' because mortality figures would paint a very gloomy picture. The survival rate refers to whether a patient is still alive after a certain period (normally five years).[701] The mortality rate actually confirms whether or not a patient has been cured. Here's a hypothetical example to highlight the difference: if all patients lived past five years only to die in the sixth year, the survival rate presented would be 100% because 100% of patients were still alive at the five-year marker. Cancer patients under immense stress can be forgiven for thinking that this implies that 100% of people are cured; however, the mortality data would confirm that all patients died from the disease in the sixth year. The 5-year survival rate clearly presents a picture of greater success, and obscures the reality, as data beyond the first 5 years is not included in these statistics.

Unfortunately, the focus seems to have shifted from attempting to cure cancer to measuring how many years we can keep patients alive for. This use of survival rates presents an exaggerated impression of efficacy because small improvements appear large when the measurement of success is based upon just the first five years of data. Professor Paul Davies highlighted this exaggerated perception of progress back in 2013:

> *"In spite of all the new promising drugs created over the last few decades, life expectancy has only improved by **4.1 weeks** on average for metastatic cancer [cancers that have spread]."*

***New Scientist Live* 2013** [018]

At the commencement of *The Cancer Genome Atlas* project in 2005 (which used new technology to study the DNA within cancer cells), there was hope that a cure could be found within a decade using this new data. But 18 years later, the hard work scientists have performed has failed to result in a single cure. Of the hundreds of cancer drugs designed to manipulate DNA, only one called *Gleevec*, shows any significant benefit. However, it's use is restricted to less than 2% of cancer patients, and it appears to work by manipulating the energy system of the cell, again indicating that it's the energy system that plays a critical role in tumour growth, rather than DNA (this is discussed in Chapter 2).[471] James Watson – made Nobel laureate for his co-discovery of DNA in 1953, and one of the most renowned scientists of our time – confirmed this lack of progress in 2013, with this astonishing statement:

> *'Targeted biological therapies [current cancer drugs]* **don't kill cancer cells**, *they are* **not curing cancer** *and it is unlikely that they can be made to do so in a practical or comprehensive way in the near future... We know the current approach is* **not working**, *because on the whole it has made* **no dent** *in* **cancer mortality** *[cancer death rates].'*

<u>*Cancer World.net*</u> **2013** [240]

The compelling results from recent research:

The latest results generated by The Cancer Genome Atlas project have challenged the DNA Theory, indicating that DNA isn't responsible for malignancy. This recent evidence (discussed in Chapter 2) has stunned the medical community. While some scientists have since turned their back on the DNA theory, many others are still scrambling to align the results so that they make sense within the DNA paradigm. Unfortunately, the public are largely unaware of this recent turn of events. If cancer patients knew of this, they would probably be widely questioning their oncologists' advice, because it would be apparent that the dominant narrative is falling apart.

But here's the most crucial point: leading scientists who we trust to make the correct decisions and draw the right conclusions, are struggling to accept that what they've been educated to believe as fact, is actually not true. Regarding this, Professor Thomas Seyfried's frustration with the unscientific basis for cancer treatment is apparent:

> *'...I attribute the absence of any real progress in the war on cancer over the last 40 years to the* **flawed concepts** *of the* **somatic**

[DNA] **mutation theory...** *this failure is an* **inexcusable tragedy** *ultimately responsible for the* **deaths of millions of cancer patients.**'

<u>**Cancer as a Metabolic Disease. Pg 204**</u> **2012** [008]

To compound this view, Professor Max Wicha, a leading expert on genetics and cancer stem cells, made the following statement supporting the notion that the dominant view is incorrect:

"... the **classical wisdom** *that comes from cancer research that has been led by the revolution in molecular genetics, has said that any cell in your body can become a cancer if it gets the right group of mutations...* **we now believe that this is wrong**... *we now think that only certain cells in your body are really prone to becoming* **malignant**... *we think that only populations of cells that have a property of* **stem cells** *called self renewal, are the cells that can become cancerous..."*

<u>**Professor Max Wicha**</u> **2013** [178 – 11:20]

Stem cells are superior to most of the cells within the body. They are mainly tasked with replacing damaged cells and creating all of the other cells our body contains; they can also regenerate themselves indefinitely under the right conditions. This ability to generate an unlimited supply of cells can be utilised to grow new tissue, which was famously demonstrated in 1997 when a human-looking ear was grown on the back of a mouse, known as the *Vacanti Mouse*. The ear was generated using stem cells.

While this has exciting implications for medical science, unlimited growth potential has a downside when it comes to cancer because tumours have been shown to contain cancer stem cells, giving them the ability to develop and continue to grow. Therefore, understanding cancer stem cell involvement is critical when it comes to treating the disease because it's this superior cell type that appears to make cancer so deadly.

Highlighting the danger in relying completely on mainstream treatments, the latest evidence confirms that chemotherapy fails to kill these deadly cancer stem cells and can even stimulate them to become more aggressive, eventually leading to a faster-growing tumour that ultimately develops resistance to the treatment:

"...this suggested to us that the **stems cells** *were* **resistant** *to* **chemotherapy**, *however it turned out to be even* **more frightening**

*than that, not only did the relative **proportion of them go up** with chemotherapy but the actual number of stem cells **actually went up**...*

*...It turns out the same thing happens in many other cancers when you **treat with chemotherapy**."*

<u>*Alfred Taubman Medical Research Institute*</u> **2013** [178]

In essence, we have arrived at a pivotal moment in medical history, which stands to demonstrate unquestionably that mainstream medicine has been channelling its resources in the wrong direction. While changing the dominant perception won't happen overnight, the latest studies are beginning to reveal the cracks, which means it's only a matter of time before this monumental error is consigned to the history books. The question is, how long will it take, and how many will continue to suffer before the science is finally accepted? On a positive note, we may have finally arrived at the point where we are in a position to re-evaluate the mechanisms of cancer, free from untenable assumptions, with the possibility of developing more successful treatment strategies.

Thirty reasons to take this new model of cancer seriously:

The 10 *Hanahan and Weinberg Hallmarks of Cancer* are a list of characteristics that all cancers share. Scientists use these hallmarks to analyse and understand the main factors that influence the disease. This helps with the development of drugs, and provides a framework in which to understand the disease. These hallmarks can also be used as a way of measuring the accuracy of any cancer theory. If a theory were capable of explaining all 10, that would strongly indicate that the underlying cause(s) has been identified. Only by correctly identifying the mechanisms involved can these hallmarks be fully explained. The hallmarks provide us with the most solid benchmark we have for evaluating any theory that purports to explain the disease.

In addition, I have identified at least 20 other conditions associated with cancer that are yet to be fully explained, but that have not so far made it into the official hallmark list. Combined into one list within the following table, provides an indication as to the accuracy of the theories presented.

QUESTIONING THE MAINSTREAM

The hallmarks of cancer explained by theory				
	New model	Metabolic Theory	Stem Cell Theory	DNA Theory
01 – Uncontrolled growth	✔	✔	x	x
02 – Growth signal failure	✔	✔	x	x
03 – Cell death failure	✔	?	x	x
04 – Limitless cell growth	✔	✔	✔	x
05 – Blood vessel growth	✔	✔	x	x
06 – Cancer spread	✔	✔	✔	x
07 – Faulty energy system	✔	?	x	x
08 – Immune evasion	✔	?	✔	x
09 – DNA damage	✔	✔	✔	✔
10 – Inflammation	✔	✔	✔	✔
11 – Glucose as fuel	✔	✔	x	x
12 – Glutamine as fuel	✔	✔	x	x
13 – Fat as fuel	✔	x	x	x
14 – Lactate as fuel	✔	✔	x	x
15 – Reverse Warburg effect	✔	x	x	x
16 – Arginine as fuel	✔	x	x	x
17 – Arginine auxotrophy	✔	x	x	x
18 – Role of Estrogen	✔	x	x	x
19 – Involvement of Iron	✔	x	x	x
20 – Involvement of Nagalase	✔	x	x	x
21 – Involvement of Galectin-3	✔	x	x	x
22 – Chemotherapy resistance	✔	✔	✔	x
23 – Methyl-deficiency	✔	x	x	x
24 – Aneuploidy	✔	✔	✔	✔
25 – Carcinogenesis	✔	x	x	x
26 – Failure of antioxidants	✔	x	x	x
27 – MDSC involvement	✔	x	x	x
28 – Macrophage involvement	✔	✔	x	x
29 – T-cell suppression	✔	✔	✔	x
30 – CYP1B1 universal marker	✔	x	x	x

Admittedly, this is my analysis of the data based upon the evidence available to me, others may dispute my interpretation regarding each theory, to some degree. Of particular concern, is that the mainstream DNA Theory fails to explain most of the disease, especially as mainstream treatments are based upon the concepts put forward by this theory. The Metabolic Theory, on the other hand, appears capable of explaining at least seven hallmarks, with a question mark against three. Professor Thomas Seyfried, who is the major proponent of this theory, claims that all 10 hallmarks are accounted for. However, while the mechanism put forward by Otto Warburg in the 1920s, and later updated by Professor Seyfried, can, in theory, provide a plausible explanation for each hallmark, there is contention over three of them. This is discussed in Chapter 9.

On the whole, most scientists appear to agree that none of the leading theories can explain Hallmark 7, which is arguably the most critical hallmark to account for, because most of the other hallmarks appear to occur as a result of hallmark 7. Putting these other theories aside, if we focus on the new model of cancer I propose, and if it is verifiably able to account for all 30 hallmarks/conditions depicted here, one could argue that this new model provides the most comprehensive explanation of the disease to date. This is exciting because any model of cancer capable of explaining this number of hallmarks/conditions, is an indication that it has identified a major driving mechanism responsible for cancer, if not 'the' mechanism that generates the disease. It goes without saying, that once the mechanism of cancer has been elucidated, the disease becomes far easier to treat.

Why am I presenting a new model of cancer within this book?

It may seem odd that I'm presenting scientific material directly to the public, rather than publishing it in a medical journal first. The reason for this is simple. As I've already alluded to, medical science is deeply biased towards supporting one perspective above all others (DNA as the root of cancer and synthetic drugs as the answer). My research has uncovered a well-documented side to the cancer 'industry' in which finance influences the science that is pursued, and where critical evidence is ignored if it doesn't support the preferred narrative.

Documented throughout history, there has always been a strong resistance to new, often better, evidence that brings the dominant consensus into question. Strict guidelines, vested financial interests, and the big egos at play within the 'business' of cancer, all play a part in stifling progress, because for some it is more advantageous to sustain the status quo. This conflict of interest is captured in a quote below from a recent investment report where the question: *"Is curing patients a sustainable business model?"* was answered in a manner that indicates, no:

> *"The potential to deliver 'one shot cures' is one of the most attractive aspects of gene therapy, genetically-engineered cell therapy and gene editing. **However**, such treatments offer a very different outlook with regard to **recurring revenue** versus chronic therapies..."*

> *"...While this proposition carries tremendous value for patients and society, it could represent a challenge for genome medicine developers **looking for sustained cash flow.**"*

> CNBC 2018 [867]

While this is a valid question for any business wishing to sustain itself financially, or investor looking to make the most profitable return on investment, it highlights that the goals of private enterprise can be diametrically opposed to the needs that can benefit society as a whole. Here, it is demonstrated that a cure represents a less profitable, and therefore less preferable outcome for investment interests. This is sadly the nature of capitalism.

As a result of this influence, new discoveries that should update our understanding about the world fail to be adopted in a timely manner, especially if they are not as financially rewarding, or challenge long-held views. Moreover, those scientists who do end up advancing science are often ridiculed or ignored for decades, before they are finally acknowledged.

This explains why it took Dr Barry Marshall nearly 20 years to convince the medical establishment that *Helicobacter pylori* bacteria cause stomach ulcers. It also explains why it took 40 years for the establishment to accept William Harvey's hypothesis that the heart pumped blood around the body. And we can begin to see why it required at least 50 years and thousands of studies, for it to conclusively be acknowledged that cigarettes cause disease and cancer. Now here we are, almost a century from the discovery of the Warburg effect – a crucial hallmark of tumour growth, and there is still significant resistance to accepting the overwhelming evidence that has accumulated to support the Metabolic Theory.

With this in mind, there is a high probability that the new perspective I am presenting will also be ignored, dismissed or side-lined, especially as it challenges the establishment view, and threatens the immense investment made in the DNA Theory. Therefore, it would be futile to present this fresh perspective through the official channels and expect any sort of objective analysis, particularly in view of the prevailing disinterest in the Metabolic Theory.

With the concern that family and friends could be misled by outdated and biased medical advice within the mainstream, and with a lack of trust in the willingness of the scientific community to provide the objective analysis my proposition demands, I made the decision to write this book so that this new interpretation of cancer, and the latest science supporting it, is accessible to, and is presented in, a format that can easily be understood by family and friends, as well as the general public – those most urgently in need of answers. This route places the resources required to make informed decisions firmly in patient hands, and has enabled me to provide those I care about with critical information that is otherwise very difficult to come by, but could mean the difference between life and death.

Achieving the inconceivable:

> *'Sometimes it is the people no one imagines anything of, who do the things that no one can imagine.'*
>
> *Alan Turing*

Understandably, many will be sceptical of the novel perspective of cancer I offer here. Some will dismiss it outright as unscientific 'quackery' without bothering to analyse the science supporting it. Radical new ideas are usually ridiculed by those who stand to lose the most from their recognition; this dismissive environment has been well documented throughout history. It is for this reason that I have relied upon scientific evidence to support all aspects of the new perspective being presented. Over 10 thousand hours of intensive study, spanning eight years of research, and supported by over 800 references, should not be equated to a few weeks' research on the internet, and dismissed so readily. While I welcome constructive criticism, those who unfairly attempt to dismiss my thinking are not just dismissing me, but the thousands of scientists whose evidence I have used to support every important point that I make.

Thinking differently:

Early in my research I became convinced that scientists had already created sufficient evidence over the years to be able to pinpoint the underlying mechanisms of tumour growth, and that all that was needed was a fresh pair of eyes to objectively re-analyse the scientific data and identify correlations that have been missed. As Nobel Prize winner *Albert Szent-Györgyi* once stated:

> *'Discovery consists of seeing what everybody has seen and **thinking what nobody else has thought.'***
>
> **Albert Szent-Györgyi**

If history has taught us anything, it's that those who defy the status quo by thinking differently, are often the ones who make the major discoveries that advance our civilisation. The majority simply adopt these new discoveries, but often only after decades of denial and ridicule:

> *'All truth passes through three stages. First, it is ridiculed. Second, it is violently opposed. Third, it is accepted as being self-evident.'*
>
> **Credited to Arthur Schopenhauer**

Dr Russell Ackoff, the pioneer of operations research, systems thinking, and management science, hit the nail on the head when he stated:

> *'...you see, **universities, colleges** and **public schools** are largely devoted to **maintaining the status quo, not to producing change**...'*
>
> <u>**Systems thinking speech**</u> **2015** [582]

We must always question new information as well as the established narrative, especially when such a view struggles to make any significant progress, as is currently the case with cancer. With this in mind, when **all** possible causes are considered, and the evidence is carefully analysed, a consistent pattern begins to emerge. As this consistency is brought to light – which is my intention within this book – the true drivers of cancer start to come into focus, illuminating exactly where we should place our attention, if we want to develop more effective treatment solutions.

CH.01

Questionable science

In recent times a worrying precedent has been set, one where authorities are insisting that we 'trust the science' they are presenting, or the opinions offered by select academics and institutions, as if a small group of appointed scientists know best and all other scientists implicitly agree. As I alluded to in the Introduction, sound science isn't based upon trust, or the opinions of one group or another, it's a discipline that is solely dependent upon evidence, evidence that is constantly evolving. Objective analysis of this evidence is crucial to ensure the data has been interpreted as accurately as possible. Moreover, evidence can be manipulated to serve certain interests, which occurs more often than we would like to believe, not to mention that scientists rarely agree, hence why at least eight different theories of cancer exist.

More concerning has been the censoring of those scientists who disagree with the mainstream narrative and a refusal to analyse the evidence they put forward.[259, 260, 263, 265] This is not how science should be conducted. Without objectivity or an ability to question the evidence, science becomes invalid. If the evidence is robust in support of the authority then it would stand up to scrutiny and allay any concerns – but when criticism is silenced, one has to question why; this would suggest that the evidence is not as robust as we are led to believe.

This is important to acknowledge because as this chapter will show, at least half of the medical science that has been created, in recent times, has later been found to be invalid or incorrect, especially when it comes to cancer. This highlights the inherent danger in 'trusting' one narrative, a chosen set of opinions, or a narrow interpretation of the data; what if the promoted narrative is formed from the evidence that is later found to be incorrect? Only good can come from continually questioning the science.

Gaining perspective:

The basic premise of this book is to highlight that, in our quest to understand cancer and create urgently needed treatments, we may have overlooked a key component of the disease and become slightly obsessed with studying one particular aspect to the exclusion of others, such as focusing primarily on cancerous DNA to the detriment of investigating cancer metabolism. With this in mind, the timeline below provides some context, indicating why we are struggling to solve cancer, through the realisation that not all avenues of investigation have been followed in equal measure:

1775 – Percival Pott discovers that soot from chimneys can cause cancer. This is one of the first known carcinogens (cancer-causing agents) to be identified.

1855 – Rudolf Virchow identifies that cancer is a result of uncontrolled cell growth, but he is unable to state why.

1890 – David Paul von Hansemann proposes that cancer is caused by abnormal chromosomes, which house our DNA. The structure and composition of DNA, however, isn't formerly identified until 1953.

1911 – Francis Payton Rous discovers that a virus can cause cancer, which challenges the chromosome (DNA) view, showing that there's a connection between cancer and micro-organisms.

1924 – **The Metabolic Theory is born**. Nobel Prize winner Otto Warburg, a close friend of Albert Einstein, discovers that cancer cells develop a faulty energy system. He proposes that cancer directly results from this defective energy system and not damaged chromosomes (DNA). The Metabolic Theory is born.

1953 – **The DNA Theory takes centre stage**. Professor James Watson and Francis Crick uncover the structure of DNA. This exciting new field of study creates a focus on DNA research, and it isn't long before DNA damage is claimed to be the cause of cell overgrowth and cancer. Certain toxins, called *carcinogens*, are proposed to cause

DNA damage leading to mutations that go on to drive cell growth. The DNA Theory is formed and continues to dominate our view of the disease today.

1966 – **The Metabolic Theory is sidelined**. An ageing Otto Warburg addresses scientists with his life's work on cancer. Unfortunately, the minds of many leading scientists are already made up: cancer is caused by DNA damage/ mutation, and nothing is going to dissuade the medical establishment from promoting this view of the disease. Warburg's Metabolic Theory is ignored and falls into obscurity.

1980 – Otto Warburg's Metabolic Theory is slowly revived with renewed interest from many notable scientists. This theory grows to directly challenge the DNA theory, although awareness of this rival theory is worryingly absent from the medical literature.

1994 – **The Cancer Stem Cell Theory is born**. Professor John Dick proves the existence of cancer stem cells, showing that this type of cell is linked to unlimited tumour growth and the spread of the disease.

1990 – **The Human Genome Project, 1990-2005**. Continuing to focus primarily on DNA, the Human Genome Project is created. It seeks to uncover all of the DNA genes present within a human cell in order to understand their function. It takes almost 15 years to catalogue them all, of which there are approximately 21,000. This means that up until 2005, scientists had never studied the entire DNA of a single cancer cell, let alone compared the DNA of different cancer types – which is needed to determine a link between DNA damage/mutations and tumour growth. In other words, it has been only after 2005 that scientist have been able to adequately analyse the DNA within a cancer cell to any meaningful degree, and the latests results are not as expected.

2005 – **The Cancer Genome Atlas Project begins**. For the first time, new technology allows scientists to analyse all 21,000 DNA genes found within a cancer cell and within a relatively short period. This new data allows scientists to compare all the DNA genes found in many different cancers, making it possible to identify the exact pattern of DNA mutations that are thought to cause and drive the disease. But when the pattern of DNA damage of over 6,000 tumour samples is analysed by 2013, the random pattern of DNA damage found to occur contradicts the predictable pattern of damage that the DNA

Theory asserts should exist. For the first time in history, evidence on a grand scale indicates that the DNA Theory is incorrect.

2023 – Reluctant to consider that DNA isn't responsible, scientists continue to assert DNA damage/mutation is the underlying cause even though the DNA Theory remains unproven. The DNA Theory is even amended to accommodate the unexpected randomness of the latest results, but alas, this amended theory is still unable to explain most of the key hallmarks of the disease. Despite its superiority, the Metabolic Theory has yet to take centre stage, while potentially effective metabolic treatments are rarely discussed with cancer patients.

While this timeline illustrates that the Metabolic Theory has been largely ignored, it also shows that little attention has been paid to the relationship between infection and cancer, not to mention the micro-organism I propose as the underlying cause. Could this overlooked relationship between infection and cancer represent the final missing pieces of the cancer puzzle?

A common misconception in science is that all possible causes of a disease are being investigated equally, and that if more resources are being poured into one particular area, then this is an indication that this area of study is likely to provide the most plausible answer to any given problem. While scientists are performing great work, the reality is that private investment is the largest driver of scientific investigation, and more often than not investment gravitates towards the most profitable path of enquiry, as opposed to the correct or most beneficial path of enquiry.

When investment accumulates within one area of research, another phenomena occurs – a majority develops which is then seen as a consensus of scientific thought. But is a consensus created by financial incentives the same as a consensus based on evidence? When such a consensus is reached, resistance can develop when that status quo is threatened by evidence.

In an example highlighting this inherent resistance to evidence that challenges the mainstream perspective, it took Doctor Barry Marshall almost 20 years to convince a dismissive majority that they were wrong about the cause of stomach ulcers. Dr Marshall was eventually able to prove that a bacteria called *Helicobacter pylori* was the root cause of this affliction, and he won the Nobel Prize in 2005 for this very discovery. The prevailing view was that no bacteria could survive within the highly acidic environment of the stomach. Desperate to confirm a dismissive majority wrong, Dr Marshall was forced to experiment on himself, and did so by drinking a broth full of the bacteria he'd been studying. Five days later he became ill and developed stomach ulcers. He cured himself with antibiotics, a solution not previously recognised. Had Dr Marshall not had the courage to experiment on himself, it is very likely that the medical establishment would not have acknowledged that *Helicobacter pylori* was a cause of this affliction, and patients would have continued to suffer from a disease that is now curable with a dose of antibiotics.[464]

Unfortunately, resistance to alternative perspectives still exist within the mainstream, especially in respect of cancer. Many factors are responsible, but it doesn't help that the medical curriculum has been written to include DNA mutations as the underlying cause of cancer, despite the theory being unproven. Wouldn't it be more scientific for the medical curriculum to acknowledge that the cause of cancer is unknown, and then encourage medical students to investigate the subject objectively with the emphasis on attempting to determine the underlying cause?

Alas, to this day medical students continue to leave medical school convinced that damaged DNA genes are the underlying cause of the disease, thus setting them on a biased course of research that inevitably leads to an abnormal focus on DNA and a dismissal of alternative perspectives. This unscientific devotion to the DNA Theory is still found in leading medical books used to educate medical students.[340, 482, 483] Studied the world over, these books unfortunately describe cancer as a DNA-based disease. There is little mention of the Metabolic Theory, nutrition, or alternative ideas, and neither is an objective approach to researching other possible causes encouraged. Without knowing anything about cancer one would think that this DNA-based interpretation is the only perspective worth considering.

How can we expect promising young scientists to correctly identify the origin of the disease when the subject they are studying is not taught or discussed objectively? It would appear that scientists have been so preoccupied with DNA that they've failed to stop and question whether charging down this route of investigation is the correct path to take. A positive example is set by Dr Siddhartha Mukherjee, who, despite publicly espousing the DNA Theory in his hugely popular book *The Emperor of All Maladies*, has now started to embrace other perspectives he has encountered. He is involved in a clinical trial that not only targets cancer metabolism through the use of a ketogenic diet (a metabolic therapy), but he is investigating how different diets affect patient outcomes to see if food can act as medicine. When discussing how diet can improve the effectiveness of cancer drugs he states:

> *'"If you combine them with a **diet** which [keeps insulin low], all of a sudden these **drugs become effective**," said Mukherjee, referring to the Nature study. "**The diet really works like a drug.**"'*

The Guardian **2018** [841]

Thankfully, many mainstream scientists are now beginning to acknowledge that there is more to cancer than previously thought, and that just targeting DNA may not be the correct approach after all.

Questioning the DNA Theory:

Many scientists are now turning their back on the dominant view, and new theories spring up every year. In the international scientific journal *Cell Physiology and Biochemistry*, a detailed analysis of the DNA Theory is expressed. This scientific paper titled *Somatic Mutation Theory – Why it's wrong for most cancers* not only proposes a new theory of cancer but explains in detail why the DNA Theory is incorrect. The *Somatic Mutation Theory* is another name for the DNA Theory. The study states:

> *'...**mutations** are **increasingly being questioned** as the causal event in the origin of the **vast majority** of cancers as clinical data show **little support for this theory**...*
>
> *...and it should be noted that some cancers are **not associated with any mutations whatsoever**.'*

Cell Physiology and Biochemistry **2016** [395]

Of critical importance from the quote above is that some cancers are not associated with any mutations at all. Such evidence confirms that DNA mutations are not the underlying cause; how can they be when cancer still develops without mutations occurring? This highlights that something else is responsible. With this in mind, it is worth repeating the following quote to hit home the reality being presented, that the mainstream view of the disease is incorrect; a 2018 paper analysing the DNA Theory concludes:

> *'...**despite 65 years of research** on the **mutation theory**, there is **still no proof for even one set of mutations** that is able to convert a normal cell to a cancer cell.'*

Genes **2018** [611]

In over six decades the DNA Theory has failed to identify any of the cancer-specific mutations that are deemed to be responsible and cannot explain why cancer occurs in the manner it does. Speaking of the errors with the DNA theory, an article published in the *Journal of the National Cancer Institute* reiterates that our medical authorities are wrong to be stating that DNA is the cause when it remains an unproven theory:

> *'The standard viewpoint that cancer is a genetic disease is often stated as a **fact** rather than a **theory**... why is this important? When a theory is treated as a fact, it **limits** the possibilities for **new research directions**.*
>
> *In the 1950s researchers hypothesized that cancer involved successive mutations interspersed with clonal expansions... However, this tidy picture **no longer holds**.'*
>
> <u>*Journal of the National Cancer Institute*</u> **2015** [403]

By presenting the DNA Theory as fact, the medical establishment is hindering progress as it prevents resources from being used to study other theories and other potential causes of the disease. Whether intentional or not, the public is being misled by a scientific community that has significantly failed to operate as it should – in an objective scientific manner. How can the medical establishment justify claiming a theory as fact when it hasn't yet been proven?

Speaking to the neurologist Dr David Perlmutter in a recent interview, Professor Thomas Seyfried, who is currently working on the Metabolic Theory, states that DNA damage is a red herring and that the majority of scientists are focusing on the wrong thing:

> *"...so the majority of the cancer field is focused on '**red herrings**', they [DNA mutations] are the effects, they are **not the cause of the problem**, the cause of the problem is the **damage to respiration** [cell energy] which then leads to a cascading series of events [DNA damage]..."*
>
> <u>*David Perlmutter MD and Dr. Thomas Seyfried*</u> **2017** [405]

It's rather shocking to think that so many scientists highlight significant flaws with the mainstream view, yet the medical establishment carries on regardless. The following scientific study, for instance, catalogues the successful response against an aggressive breast cancer using a therapy created from the Metabolic Theory that deals with the energy system of the cancer cell:

'This single case study presents evidence of a **complete** *clinical, radiological, and pathological* **response** *following a six-month treatment period using a combination of MSCT and a novel* **metabolic therapy** *in a patient with stage IV TNBC [Stage 4 Triple Negative Breast Cancer].*

Furthermore, this patient did **not experience** *the adverse effects that are commonly associated with the* **current standard of care** *[radiotherapy, chemotherapy] and this improved quality of life should also be considered...'*

***Cureus* 2017** [404]

Furthermore, the following study examined whether targeting mitochondria (the energy system of the cell) could be effective, it concluded that doing so can directly stop the spread of the disease:

'Collectively, these findings reveal **mitochondrial** *oxidative metabolism as a critical suppressor of metastasis and* **justify metabolic therapies** *for potential prevention/intervention of tumour metastasis [cancer spread].'*

Cancer Letters **2015** [645]

Defying the mainstream view, Jane McLelland treated her own terminal cancer with a concoction of off-patent drugs and a restrictive diet containing supplements.[449] Her research led her to target the energy system of the cell explained by the Metabolic Theory. Where the conventional approach would have failed her, here, an integrative approach that included energy restriction, was key to her defying the odds and becoming cancer-free.

The uncomfortable reality:

As I highlight in Chapter 2, it has only been since 2013 that we've had the data that indicates cancer is not DNA-based. The problem with this is that mainstream science is between 20 and 30 years behind adopting the latest evidence, not to mention that almost the entire cancer industry is built around the concept that DNA mutations are responsible. This translates into a medical establishment that is extremely reluctant to accept the possibility that the mainstream view of the disease is wrong.

The other problem seems to be the trust we have in our medical authorities. We assume they represent the voice of medical science as a whole and are objectively analysing all the data. In reality, the medical system is biased towards supporting an extremely narrow view of cancer and health in general, while favouring synthetic drug creation and DNA research over objectively researching all possible avenues. This means you aren't being given access to all the information you require – hence why most of us haven't heard of salvestrols, 3BP, the ketone diet, the microbiome, the Metabolic Theory, the involvement of glucose, glutamine and iron, as well as the views expressed above by leading cancer scientists.

As a result of focusing exclusively on synthetic drugs as the solution and insisting DNA damage is to blame, confusion and misinformation have become rife, which is a natural outcome in any situation where the data doesn't support the chosen narrative. For instance, the following acknowledgement from the *American Cancer Society* contradicts the impression most of us have been given in the media – that cancer runs in the family because we inherit bad DNA:

> *'**Inherited** mutations are **thought** to be a direct cause of only a **small fraction** of cancers… **Most cancers** are caused by **acquired** mutations.'*
>
> <u>*American Cancer Society*</u> ***2014***[202]

In other words, cancer is not inherited from our parents via DNA as it's often portrayed. Instead, it is an acquired disease, something that is determined by diet and lifestyle, something that is within our control. But this is not the view that some influential scientists are presenting to the public. The unexpected results generated by the latest data means that nothing appears to make any sense when using DNA to explain the disease. As a result, some scientists in support of the DNA Theory are now dangerously claiming that tumour growth arises due to bad luck and nothing more, because this is the only conclusion that can be drawn when attempting to align the data with an incorrect theory:

> *'Most cases of cancer are the result of "**bad luck**" rather than unhealthy lifestyles, diet or even inherited genes, claim scientists.'*
>
> *"…many forms of cancer are due largely to the **bad luck** of acquiring a mutation in a cancer driver gene **regardless of lifestyle** and heredity factors." said Professor Burt Vogelstein from John Hopkins University School of Medicine.'*
>
> <u>*MailOnline*</u> *2015*[498]

If cancer arises purely by chance, because that is what 'being unlucky' implies, we would not be witnessing the sustained and consistent rise in cancer incidence currently occurring. Luck and chance are random, not consistent. Logic dictates that there must be an underlying cause responsible for this consistent rise in cancer incidence.

Contradicting the mainstream view, *National Geographic* showed how diet plays an integral role in preventing the disease by conducting a two-year investigation into the healthiest places on earth. Five areas were discovered and were named 'blue zones'. It was found that these populations live, on average, 10 years longer than their European and American counterparts – well into their late 90s and early 100s – an age that should generate a higher incidence of cancer due to the increased potential for DNA damage. Yet, they have a much lower risk of developing the disease:

> *'Okinawans don't only live the longest, they are also extremely healthy into old age, with:*
>
> * *6-12 times fewer heart disease deaths than the United States*
>
> * *2-3 times fewer colon cancer deaths than the United States*
>
> * *7 times fewer prostate cancer deaths than the United States*
>
> * *5.5 times lower risk of dying from breast cancer than the United States*
>
> *Unfortunately, fast food and* **Western styles of eating** *have made it to the island, and younger generations are no longer reaping the health benefits of eating the traditional Okinawan way.'*
>
> **Bluezones.com 2017** [557]

The evidence surrounding diet helps to further highlight that this 'bad luck' narrative is incorrect. Studies clearly show a significant increase in incidence of some cancers by up to 30%, just through consuming an average daily intake of meat. A greater risk is found with other cancers:

> *'...increasing intakes of red meat were significantly associated with elevated risks of* **20% – 60%** *for cancers of the esophagus, liver, and lung.'*
>
> **PLOS 2007** [499]

On the other hand, studies into plant-based diets show a reduction of cancer across all cancer types of up to 50%.[558] Two themes consistently emerge, vegetables and fruit help to reduce risk, while meat, animal products, and other fatty foods are frequently found to increase risk:

> *'When analysing the association of specific vegetarian dietary patterns,* **vegan diets** *showed* **statistically significant protection** *for* **overall cancer incidence...**'
>
> <u>**Cancer Epidemiology, Biomarkers & Prevention 2013**</u> [559]

The relevance of diet can be seen with the Japanese diet, which has unfortunately undergone a major change. This change has led to a marked increase in cancer:

> *'...the Japanese diet has changed radically between the 1950s and 1990s, including a* **seven-fold increase in meat consumption.** *This coincides with a* **five-fold increase in colorectal cancer** *over the same period.'*
>
> <u>*Molecular Biology of Cancer, pg 253* **2012**</u> [483]

Such a difference in risk from diet alone surely confirms that cancer is related to the choices we make regarding the type of diet we consume and the lifestyle we choose to lead. Red meat, for instance, contains a kind of sugar that our cells are unable to process called *Neu5Gc* – this sugar causes inflammation.[074] Inflammation is recognised as an official hallmark of cancer. Increasing inflammation within the body generates consistent cell damage, leading to tumour growth. In another example, *carrageenan* is an additive found mainly in meat and dairy products that is proven to increase inflammation within the gut, and is directly linked to an increased stomach cancer risk.[075] Even a lack of basic vitamins has been shown to play a key role:

> *'Tumours were 80% larger on average in mice that were deficient in vitamin D compared with vitamin D-sufficient mice. Collectively, epidemiological and in vivo evidence suggest a link between* **vitamin D deficiency** *and* **increased cancer risk.**'
>
> <u>*Molecular Biology of Cancer, pg 270* **2012**</u> [483]

Cancer, therefore, is not due to bad luck but due to our reduced capacity to provide the body with the nutrients it needs to function optimally, and due to the increased damage we inflict upon our cells, damage that can be avoided. Like those who live in the blue zone areas of the world, we have a choice. We can either adopt a similar diet and lifestyle that protects our cells, dramatically reducing cancer risk, or we can pursue a lifestyle that generates persistent inflammation and cell damage that encourages it to occur. If we choose the latter, we mustn't kid ourselves into believing that cancer arose due to bad luck and is out of our control or sphere of influence.

The problem with presenting this bad luck narrative, is that it convinces the public that it doesn't matter what we consume or how we live our lives, because it implies that we will develop the disease regardless. This encourages a mindset of indulgence within the population that actually exacerbates the illness by facilitating its development.

Invalid science:

The idea that the mainstream view of cancer is inherently flawed may seem difficult for many to accept. But when we consider that scientists are basing their conclusions on an unproven theory, and that publication bias is also an issue, it becomes easier to acknowledge why the science being created turns out to be largely incorrect.[577, 657] To help us more readily accept this uncomfortable reality, some of the most distinguished scientists in the medical field openly acknowledge that a large portion of the science being created has been corrupted and is no longer valid or trustworthy – medical science itself seems to have slipped from the pedestal it once stood proudly upon. Dr Richard Horton is the current editor-in-chief of *The Lancet*, arguably the most prestigious medical journal on the planet. In 2015, he stated:

> '*The case **against science** is straight forward: much of the scientific literature, **perhaps half**, may **simply be untrue**. Afflicted by studies with small sample sizes, tiny effects, invalid exploratory analyses, and flagrant **conflicts of interest**, together with an obsession for pursuing fashionable trends of dubious importance, science has taken a **turn towards darkness**.*' – Dr. Richard Horton.

> '*...The apparent endemicity of **bad research behaviour is alarming**. In their quest for telling a compelling story, scientists too often **sculpt data** to fit their **preferred theory of the world**. Or they **retrofit hypotheses to fit their data**...*'

> **The Lancet.com 2015** [156]

This is an understanding shared by many but sadly not known by the general public. Mirroring this worrying reality, Dr Marcia Angell, editor-in-chief of the *New England Journal of Medicine*, had this to say:

> '*It is simply **no longer possible to believe much of the clinical research that is published**, or to rely on the judgement of **trusted***

physicians or authoritative medical guidelines. I take no pleasure in this conclusion, which I reached slowly and reluctantly over my two decades as an editor of the New England Journal of Medicine.'

PLOS 2010 [155]

In 2013, *The Economist* ran an article titled *How science goes wrong*. It discussed the incredible level of failure to produce valid science under the DNA model. Drawing on recent findings, the article states:

*'Last year [2012] researchers at one biotech firm, Amgen, found they could reproduce **just six** of 53 "landmark" studies in cancer research...'*[353]

In other words, 89% of the studies that form the backbone of the mainstream understanding of cancer appear to be incorrect, indicating that the DNA Theory is wrong. The article goes on to provide other examples:

*'...a group at Bayer... managed to repeat **just a quarter** of 67 similarly important papers. A leading computer scientist frets that three-quarters of papers in his subfield are bunk.*

*In 2000-10 roughly 80,000 patients took part in clinical trials based on research that was later **retracted** because of **mistakes** or **improprieties.'***

The Economist 2013 [353]

The *National Cancer Institute* also confirms this shocking failure of cancer science. They performed an extensive study of the medical literature and concluded that out of a million cancer studies performed so far, approximately 80% of them were wrong because they cannot be replicated.[018] This means that oncologists are advising patients based on research that is predominantly false. This should alarm every oncologist and cancer patient, and if ever there is a reason to question the DNA theory, then this is it.

An article in the *New York Post* points out there is a well-known phrase within the scientific industry that reflects the depth of the problem: it is referred to as the 'reproducibility crisis'.[365, 691, 689] If a study cannot be reproduced by other scientists, it is deemed to be incorrect. The article highlights that most studies cannot be reproduced and are therefore incorrect:

> *'For any study to have legitimacy, it must be **replicated**, yet only* ***half*** *of* ***medical studies*** *celebrated in newspapers hold water under serious scrutiny – and about* ***two thirds*** *of the "sexiest" cutting-edge reports… **are later dis-confirmed.**'[365]*

It's easy to gain a false sense of progress when the media is awash with positive stories of promising breakthroughs in cancer research. We constantly hear that advances are being made in the news; however, when most of these studies are shown to be wrong, we aren't made aware of it, so we are provided with a false perspective that implies significant progress is constantly being made, when in reality it isn't. In his book titled *Rigor Mortis: How sloppy science creates worthless cures, crushes hope, and wastes billions*, science correspondent Richard Harris states:

> *'For many years research on breast cancer was conducted on misidentified melanoma cells, which means that thousands of papers published in credible scientific journals were actually **studying the wrong cancer**. "It's impossible to know how much this sloppy use of the wrong cells has set back research into breast cancer," writes Harris.'* [365]

The article also refers to a paper written by Stanford Professor John Ioannidis titled *Why most published scientific research findings are false.* He found that:

> *'…out of tens of thousands of papers touting discoveries of specific [DNA] genes linked to everything from depression to obesity, only **1.2%** had truly positive results.'*

***New York Post* 2017** [365]

It is clear that much of the science currently being created is inherently flawed and cannot be trusted to be accurate, highlighting the pressing need for us to question our oncologists views and the treatments they provide. It is astonishing to think that the medical establishment continues to present the DNA Theory as fact and create treatments based upon this theory, when up to 89% of the science supporting it is incorrect, and the theory itself remains unproven.

The danger we all face – 50% expected to develop cancer:

Cancer rates are now reaching epidemic levels. It is on course to overtake heart disease as the number one cause of disease-related death. It is increasing at an alarming rate throughout all age groups, not just the elderly, as it is often implied.[143, 218] Although exact figures are hard to pin down, it's clear that cancer was not as prolific in the early 1900s as it is today.[142] By 2030, the *World Health Organization* estimates a further 70% increase in cancer incidence – that is, at least half of all family members will be expected to develop cancer in the decades to come, one-half of all men and one in three women are already expected to develop the disease.

The danger for the public is that most patients won't realise how ill-prepared modern medicine is to deal with the disease until it's too late. It's only when the standard toxic treatments have failed, caused irreparable damage and robbed us of precious time, that some patients become aware of this uncomfortable reality. It is at this point that some may start researching other possibilities. Sadly, the damage can sometimes be too significant for an alternative solution to be effective. The problem appears to be that cancer patients deemed to be terminal start the research into these other options too late, not having the luxury of time to acquire the knowledge needed to identify potentially effective solutions. Even so, there are many stories of patients with a terminal diagnosis taking another approach and having success. Bailey O'Brien, Kate Malvenan and Rosie Garrett are three perfect examples.

There is hope:

In 2010, doctors diagnosed Bailey with terminal cancer after conventional treatment had failed. They gave her seven months to live. Not prepared to give up, her family helped her research other potential solutions. After applying a number of non-conventional treatments and changing her diet to one that was organic and predominantly plant-based,[041] *Memorial Sloan Kettering Cancer Centre* provided her with some positive feedback:

> *'After what seemed like an interminable wait, the doctor came in and, looking at the floor, told Bailey she no longer needed his services. According to the scans, it looked like all the* **tumours were gone.**'
>
>

***Westchester* 2015** [349]

In 2015, Bailey passed the three-year threshold for recurrence. In 2023 she is already living 10 years longer than doctors forecast.

In 2018, Kate Malvenan was diagnosed with lung cancer which had spread. Three different specialists advised her that she had six to 24 months left to live. After discovering an alternative cancer centre in Mexico, she remortgaged her home to afford the three-week treatment. Following her first treatment in late October, Ms Malvenan was amazed after scans revealed that the apple-sized tumour had shrunk by 75% to the size of a grape.[411] As well as this, there were no longer traces of cancer in her lymph nodes and only limited cancer left in her liver:

> 'Treatments focused on heat, light and laser therapies – including **hyperbaric oxygen therapy**, full body hyperthermia, infrared lamp therapy, pulsed electro-magnetic field therapy...and **Intravenous vitamin C** therapy.
>
> She was also fed a strict **organic plant-based diet** while receiving treatment and continues to follow this eating plan to this day.'
>
> **MailOnline** 2019 [411]

Based on the limited understanding of cancer that the DNA Theory provides and the limited DNA-damaging treatments mainstream medicine endorses, Kate was considered terminal. However, within just three weeks of utilising several unconventional approaches combined with a strict organic plant-based diet, she was able to dramatically reduce her tumour and regress those that had spread. Kate is continuing with her treatment in the hope of fully eradicating it. These two success stories highlight how badly mainstream medicine misunderstands the disease and how to treat it.

In 2017, *The Telegraph* reported on Rosie Garrett, a 31-year-old who used a protocol of cheap over-the-counter drugs that targeted specific aspects of cell metabolism, she was given a terminal diagnosis, but has reduced her tumour and has far outlived the terminal diagnosis she was provided.[325] Rosie Garrett's story highlights the inescapable link to the Metabolic Theory and the cell's energy system.

There are many more stories of this nature, a few more are included within this book. Never before has it been so important to educate ourselves about this disease and look at all the options and evidence available. It would be detrimental to assume oncologists know best – especially as their medical education is limited to one interpretation of the disease, and to prescribe only the treatments that are based upon this limited interpretation.

CH 02

A glimpse of reality

Many high-profile scientists are acknowledging severe flaws in the dominant narrative. Unfortunately, the medical establishment has been extremely slow to address these issues and appears reluctant to change in accordance with the latest data. Thankfully, it would seem that positive change may be on the horizon because it is becoming increasingly hard to ignore the latest evidence indicating that the mainstream view of the disease is incorrect.

The Cancer Genome Atlas project:

The Cancer Genome Atlas project (TCGA) is the most extensive DNA sequencing project ever conceived regarding cancer, and its findings inadvertently challenge the DNA Theory. By 2003, new technology existed that allowed the sequencing of the entire cell DNA in a very short period of time – prior to this it took almost 15 years. By comparison, the TCGA project promised the sequencing of the entire DNA of multiple tumour samples within just one year. This meant that scientists could finally test many different tumours and catalogue the exact DNA mutations that occurred in each cancer type in order to compare them – this has the potential to prove that DNA mutations are responsible for tumour growth by confirming the consistent pattern of DNA mutations that generate the disease. Once uncovered, the promise of a cure becomes realistic.

This ambitious project was underway by 2005; all cancer research up until this point had been building towards this watershed moment. Scientists were so positive that the pattern of DNA genes responsible would be identified that it was predicted we would finally have a cure for cancer by 2013 – everything was converging on these new results. It would take over a year for the first to arrive.

By 2007, in-depth analysis became available from breast and colon cancers; but the results were unexpected. None of the mutations found were conclusively responsible for the origin of the disease.[258] Significantly, there was no clear pattern of DNA damage that could explain each cancer type's behaviour because the data showed random mutations, even within the same tumour. The utter randomness of DNA damage wasn't anticipated and didn't make any sense to the researchers; this meant there were no apparent targets for drugs to attack:

> 'When the first results of The Cancer Genome Project were reported, many scientists were **shocked** to learn that most patients, including those with the same type of cancer, **did not share the same cancer-related mutations**.... If the patients' tumours didn't contain the same oncogenic mutations, then they likely **didn't share the same drug targets.**'
>
> ISB 2021 [787]

Suddenly, the validity of DNA being responsible was thrown into question. For the first time, it was exposed on a large scale that cancer defied the rules of a genetic disease. Astonishingly, the same cancer cells from the same tumours showed random unrelated DNA mutations. How could separate DNA damage from the same cells be causing the same tumour? This meant that a drug targeted at one set of DNA mutations wouldn't be enough to kill the tumour, thus making targeted drugs pointless:

> 'In 2013 alone, there were more than 200 new cancer drugs developed and tested for clinical trials. However, a recent report on the pharmaceutical industry observed that about **93 percent** of cancer drugs **fail during development**. This is the **highest failing rate** among all drug discoveries. '
>
> ISB 2021 [787]

This failure is not surprising if we are open to considering that DNA may not be responsible. To this day, scientists are at a loss to explain the randomness of this DNA damage. Reluctant to accept that the mainstream theory could be wrong, some scientists fall into the trap of forcing the results to fit within the confines of their own world view and continue to insist that DNA is responsible.

To other scientists these new DNA sequencing results are clear; such unrelated random DNA damage cannot generate the same consistent conditions of cancer because genetic diseases are normally caused by the same DNA genes each and every time. According to the DNA Theory, up to 12 specific DNA genes would need to be damaged or mutated to cause cancer[547] – a consistent pattern of DNA mutation would need to be seen to explain the behaviour of each cancer type (e.g. the same DNA genes should be mutated in all skin cancers, lung cancers, and breast cancers of the same type), as this is how other genetic diseases manifest themselves.[194] It is the consistency of DNA damage that allows doctors to identify a genetic disease and treat it. Random damage would create vastly different illnesses that are unrelated to cancer, not the same disease each and every time.

The fact that we aren't witnessing different diseases as we would expect to see with random DNA damage, indicates that the cell itself is no longer in control; that cancer is potentially one disease caused by a consistency that has yet to be identified; in other words, random DNA mutations are just a symptom. As early as 1948 Cyril Darlington, a pioneer cytologist (the study of cells), had already drawn a similar conclusion. He claimed that the nucleus (DNA) didn't appear to be driving the disease because it no longer appeared to be in control:

> *'The development of unbalanced nuclei in tumours is without precedent in any living tissue… It implies a relaxation of detailed control of the nucleus… this in turn argues that the nucleus is **not itself directly responsible** for what is going on.'*
>
> <u>*The Plasmagene theory of Cancer. Pg 118* **1948**</u> [257]

Even Bert Vogelstein, a key proponent of the DNA Theory, admits there aren't enough mutations occurring for cancer to form, implying that the DNA Theory he believes in appears to be incorrect. Vogelstein is the lead scientist overseeing The Cancer Genome Atlas project, which is analysing the DNA within tumours:

*'In paediatric tumours the number of driver gene mutations is low (**zero to two**). In common adult tumours the number of mutated driver genes is often **three to six**, but several tumours have only **one or two** driver mutations. **How can this be explained**, given the widely accepted **notion** that tumour development and progression **require multiple, sequential** genetic alterations acquired over decades? **Where are these missing mutations?**'*

<u>*Tripping over the Truth – Travis Christofferson* **2014**</u> [258]

In many cases it is confirmed that there aren't enough DNA mutations to cause the disease. You might have thought that this would have drawn the conclusion that DNA is not driving tumour growth. But, in an attempt to keep the DNA Theory afloat Vogelstein claimed that invisible DNA genes must be responsible, even though the entire cell DNA had been sequenced and identified.

Taking the idea of dark matter from astronomy, Vogelstein concluded that some unknown matter must exist within cells, and this matter must be responsible.[258] This remarkable statement suggests that something other than the DNA we know about is causing the disease. This begs the question; why are we still targeting these DNA genes when they don't appear to be responsible? And does this explain why the treatments that target DNA appear largely ineffective? Continuing to label DNA as the cause seems to be a rather large leap of faith to take.

As a result of Vogelstein's dark-matter suggestion, Dr Charles Swanton set about attempting to find this dark matter hidden within DNA. After incredibly deep DNA sequencing and detailed analysis of the data, he concluded:

'I'm not sure we understand it – it's phenomenally complex.'

<u>*Tripping over the Truth – Travis Christofferson* **2014**</u> [258]

Consider this critical point: any problem will appear to be phenomenally complex if all attempts to solve it are focused on the wrong thing. Targeting the symptoms of any disease will never eliminate the root cause. The problem will never be solved and will forever appear phenomenally complex until it is acknowledged that the wrong factor has been blamed. With a reluctance to accept this probable reality, and a pressing need to explain the utter randomness of DNA damage, scientists chose to amend the DNA Theory to force the results to fit more readily, and even then the data still didn't align.

The amended DNA Theory:

In response to the unexpected randomness of DNA mutations, some scientists created the new 'systems' version of the DNA Theory in an attempt to better explain the disease.[258] Various driver genes, such as tumour suppressor genes, cell death genes and tumour growth genes, were grouped together and placed into three separate categories or 'systems', along with certain related pathways. Grouping genes and pathways in this way meant that scientists would only need to show that three mutations occurred instead of 12. If cancer formed without there being a mutation in any one of these three systems, this would indicate DNA was not driving the disease. All of the genes that are thought to cause cancer were included.

In 2008, more results from different cancer samples arrived from The Cancer Genome Atlas project. But even this modified theory could not account for them. Out of 22 brain cancer samples, only four had mutations in all three systems. Nine had mutations in two, five had mutations in one, and most significantly, one sample labelled Br20P,[258] had no mutations in any of the three categories. If DNA is responsible for cancer, then Br20P should not exist, and yet it turned out to be an aggressive brain cancer.

In 2013, the sequencing data from 100 breast cancer samples were released. But again, the results weren't as expected.[258] Of 100 samples, the maximum number of genes implicated in any one case of breast cancer was six, not the 10 to 12 required for the DNA Theory to be correct.[547] Significantly, 28 cases showed only one gene as the driver of the disease, but worst of all, there was little attention paid to the five cancers that showed no mutations at all. Let me just re-iterate that important point, five cancers formed without there being any driver mutations present at all.

Another study that discusses a new theory of cancer called the *Tissue Organization Field Theory*, which claims that DNA mutations are not the cause of cancer, confirms that many tumours develop without mutations being present in key genes that are assumed to drive tumour growth. Within a sample of 210 tumours, 518 key genes were analysed, 120 of which were classed as driver genes associated with cancer development; they found that:

> *'However, the distribution of mutations among tumours was quite uneven: i.e. 137 tumours showed DNA mutations, **while 73 had none...**'*

> *Bioessays* **2011**[309]

If DNA mutation is the cause of cancer, how is it possible for tumours to form without the required mutations occurring? Other scientific papers also confirm that tumours form without DNA being responsible:

> '...it should be noted that some cancers are **not associated with any mutations whatsoever.**'
>
> <u>Cell Physiology and Biochemistry</u> **2016** [395]

Four years into The Cancer Genome Atlas project, Professor Larry Loeb summarised what we had learned so far, questioning the validity of the mainstream theory, he asked:

> 'If cancer requires as many as **twelve** different mutations to arise... and the mutation rate is so low... **how can cancer possibly occur within the human lifetime?**'
>
> <u>Annual Review of Pathology</u> **2010** [547]

Professor Loeb confirms that the incidence of cancer does not coincide with the DNA mutation rate; there are not enough driver mutations to bring about the disease.

To compound this reality, scientists appear to have over-estimated the involvement of DNA. For instance, a tumour is thought to arise because the DNA gene known as p53, becomes mutated. The p53 gene controls cell death, so a mutation in the p53 gene would generate a tumour because cell death control is lost. Based on early research, scientists estimated that the p53 gene was mutated in over 60% of cancers.[070] For decades this estimation was hailed as proof that cancer was caused by DNA damage. But, according to the most recent results from the ongoing Cancer Genome Atlas Project, out of 13,508 cancer cases only 36% showed a p53 mutation.[357, 776] The Cancer Genome Atlas Project is an international database that is cataloguing the mutations found to occur in many different cancers. Scientists around the world are studying tumour mutations and then providing this information to be logged in this database.

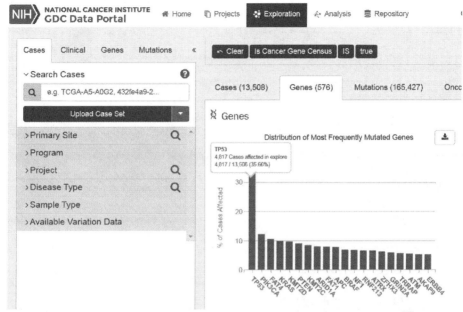

The Cancer Genome Atlas Data Portal **2022** [357]

While some cancers do have a higher rate of p53 mutations, a number of others show extremely low levels, contrary to the expectations of the mainstream DNA Theory. For a tumour to form shouldn't this cell death gene be mutated in 100% of cancers to account for the cell death mechanism failing in all cancers? More to the point, how did tumours still develop in the 54% of cases where the p53 gene was working normally? Surely this p53 gene would have initiated cell death preventing tumour growth, and yet tumours still developed.

Colorectal cancer is one of the significant causes of cancer death. Scientists postulated that a sequential accumulation of mutations in specific genes, such as 'p53', 'K-Ras' and 'APC' were responsible for driving the creation of the disease in line with the DNA Theory. K-Ras controls cell growth, p53 cell death, and the APC gene is involved in cell migration, so we would expect to see these three genes mutated in all samples of colorectal cancer to explain tumour growth and migration. But, when analysed, only 6.6% of samples were found to contain mutations in all three:

> *'The most common combination of mutations was p53 and APC (27.1%), whereas mutations in both p53 and K-ras **were extremely rare.'***

PNAS 2002 [819]

How can cancer be caused by DNA gene mutations when the required mutations don't occur in the majority of tumours and even within the same tumour? Surely for DNA mutations to be responsible all three should be mutated in all colorectal cancer samples? The cell death gene (p53) and the cell growth gene (K-Ras) would need to be mutated in order to explain tumour growth, and yet it was extremely rare to have both mutated together. Was Cyril Darlington correct in 1948 to conclude that DNA doesn't appear to be in control?[257]

Peto's paradox:

According to the DNA Theory, cancer develops as a result of the damage cells acquire over time, and is generally caused due to faults within the cell itself. It stands to reason then that the more cells there are in any living organism, the greater the probability that cancer will occur. This means that larger animals that harbour greater numbers of cells should have a higher risk of cancer. However, Sir Richard Peto, a professor of medical statistics and epidemiology at the University of Oxford, found that cancer incidence does not correlate with the number of cells in an organism and the organism's age, as the DNA Theory indicates it should. A blue whale living up to 80 years should develop cancer at a higher rate than humans because it contains at least 1000 times more cells which can potentially become malignant and develop the disease, but this is not the case:

> 'There appears to be **no correlation** between body size, longevity and cancer across species and the absence of such a relationship is referred to as Peto's Paradox.'

Trends in Ecology & Evolution 2011 [561]

Scientists are still attempting to explain this contradictory phenomenon across species. One argument suggests that it's all down to the number of p53 genes that we possess, humans have two. Elephants have approximately 50 p53 genes and rarely develop cancer, so it sounds plausible that the number of p53 genes is the deciding factor. However, this argument breaks down when we consider that the blue whale mentioned above, also has only two p53 genes like humans do. This indicates that the quantity of p53 genes is not the deciding factor. Cancer appears just as rare in blue whales as it does in elephants regardless of the number of p53 genes present.

Challenging the mainstream view:

One would think that an excellent way to prove the DNA Theory correct would be to transfer the damaged DNA from a cancerous cell into a healthy cell to see if that healthy cell would turn cancerous; or to grow animals from cancerous DNA, as we would expect to see abnormal tumour growth in these embryos given that DNA mutations allegedly drive the disease. Well, these DNA transfer experiments have actually been performed, and significantly, the results contradict the DNA Theory indicating that DNA mutations are not driving cancer. Regarding the studies, mice were cloned (copied) and grown from the DNA of cancerous mouse tumours. Scientists were expecting to see abnormal cell growth mimicking cancer, but in the majority of cases no tumours or abnormal growth behaviour developed, even though the DNA mutations thought to drive the disease were present. A report on one of the studies, where mouse embryos were cloned from the DNA of brain tumours, stated:

> 'Remarkably, **no malignancies** were observed in any of the recipient mice, and **normal** proliferation control [normal growth control] was observed in cultured blastocysts.'
>
> *Cancer Research* **2003** [253]

If DNA damage is the driver of tumour growth, tumours should form when damaged cancerous DNA is used to create new mice, but in these experiments this wasn't the case. This indicates that DNA is not in control of the cell. There are many more studies of this nature, but as these results cannot be explained by the DNA Theory, and stand to disprove it, they are given little attention.

In a recent interview for *The New York Times Magazine*, James Watson, who famously co-discovered the structure of DNA back in 1953, made a statement to the effect that DNA mutations are not driving the disease:

> '...locating the genes that cause cancer has been "**remarkably unhelpful**" – the belief that sequencing your DNA is going to extend your life [is a] "**cruel illusion**". If he were going into cancer research today, Watson said, he would study biochemistry rather than molecular biology.'
>
> *The New Your Times Magazine* **2016** [799]

The replication illusion:

Another contradiction worthy of mention relates to the speed at which cells replicate. Different cells of the body replicate at different rates. For instance, stomach cells replicate every 2-9 days; for skin cells, it's 10-30 days, and for fat cells, it's up to 8 years. It's assumed that a higher rate of cell replication increases the risk of cancer developing in specific cell types because DNA is at its most vulnerable to damage during the replication process, as highlighted in the image below:

Cell replication:

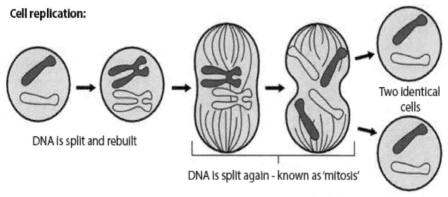

DNA is split and rebuilt

DNA is split again - known as 'mitosis'

Two identical cells

MajorEventsInMitosis.jpg

So, because DNA is more vulnerable when cells replicate, the DNA Theory asserts that cancer will develop more frequently in cells that replicate more often because their DNA is more exposed to damage. This seems logical; however, this is not actually the case.

Intestinal cells and stomach cells are two of the most rapidly dividing cells in the human body,[310] so we would expect to see these top the list of the most common types of cancers. But, even though prostate cells are fewer and replicate less frequently,[311] they are the leading type of cancer found in men by a considerable margin. Figures obtained from the *UK National Archives* in 2013 show that colorectal cancer (intestinal cancer) ranks 4th overall, and stomach cancer is ranked 15th.[312]

In a recent analysis compiled in 2016, there were more brain cancers than stomach cancers reported.[578] While stomach cells take approximately 6 days to replicate, the general consensus is that brain cells don't replicate at all, or if they do, it is only a few replications during an entire lifetime. If rapid cell division equates to a higher likelihood of cancer, how is it possible that brain cancers exist at all, let alone are more prevalent than stomach cancer?

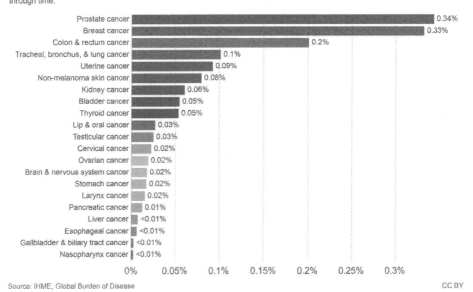

Share of population suffering from cancer types, United States, 2016

Share of total population with different forms of cancer, measured as the age-standardized percentage. This share has been age-standardized assuming a constant age structure to compare prevalence between countries and through time.

Source: IHME, Global Burden of Disease   CC BY

The mainstream view of how tumour development occurs via DNA damage is again contradicted.

Herceptin and Gleevec:

Herceptin and Gleevec are two drugs that have had some success against cancer, both are often cited as examples to support the DNA Theory and justify the current mainstream approach to cancer treatment. But when analysed, both appear to support the new cancer model presented within this book, rather than the DNA Theory itself.

Ready for use in the late 1990s, a decade later studies showed that Herceptin only extends life by an average of four months in the 20% of breast cancer patients it's supplied to.[258, 431] While four months is a lifetime for a cancer patient, it's certainly no cure. Ultimately, resistance develops, and cancer continues its formidable march.

Gleevec has had much greater success. It boasts an 85% five-year survival rate for Chronic Myeloid Leukaemia patients (CML), which is a remarkable result for the 1.5% who suffer from this rare cancer. However, while this sounds impressive, an article in *Science Daily*, which discusses the limitations of Gleevec (also known as *Imatinib*), provides a more sobering reality:

> *'...it soon became clear that the disease **almost always returns** without maintenance treatments of imatinib. Imatinib treatment **cures the disease in at best 5 percent of cases.'***
>
> <u>*Science Daily*</u> *2009* [470]

While it's excellent that Gleevec can help 85% of CML patients reach the five-year survival marker, it can only cure 5% at best. However, this is where it gets interesting. Gleevec seems to work by restricting glucose and by targeting the energy system of the cell,[298, 419, 471] as the following study confirms:

> *'The aim of this study was to investigate the effect on **glucose flux and metabolism...** after exposure to Imatinib [Gleevec]... These findings suggest that a **rapid decline in glucose uptake** following Imatinib treatment in GIST cells [cells of the intestinal tract] is **dependent** on **glucose transporter impaired anchorage** to the plasma membrane... '*
>
> <u>*American Journal of Biochemistry and Biotechnology*</u> *2005* [471]

This DNA drug inadvertently highlights the Metabolic Theory as being more relevant because it restricts glucose and the energy system. This indicates that glucose restriction is vital for treating cancer; incidentally, glucose is the primary fuel used by the micro-organism I propose as the underlying cause of the disease. Restricting glucose would also be detrimental to micro-organism survival.

Regarding the drug Herceptin, it was created to block the HER2 growth receptor,[308] which is stimulated in many cancer types. This generally inhibits tumour growth for a while. Intriguingly, studies also show that a particular micro-organism uses the HER2 receptor as a primary portal to invade the cell and does so by creating a protein called Als-3, tricking the cell into absorbing it.[255, 256]

Blocking the HER2 receptor prevents micro-organism invasion via this route, but the micro-organism uses other growth receptors and can invade a cell by other means. Is this why Herceptin only stalls cancer progression by four months on average? Does Herceptin just hinder the micro-organism until it adapts? This link between the HER2 receptor and micro-organism invasion would undoubtedly explain why Herceptin ultimately fails. It may also explain why a cancer cell's growth rate is increased because the micro-organism stimulates this growth receptor during cell invasion.

The Warburg Effect:

Of major concern is how out of touch the mainstream view appears to be with certain key features of cancer. For instance, the evidence confirming the role that glucose plays in feeding cancer is abundant, so too are the benefits of restricting this fuel. And yet the correlation between glucose and cancer is rarely discussed with the patient and it's ability to feed cancer is often denied by institutions we trust. This threatens patient survival because information that may benefit the patient is being misconstrued and in extreme cases denied, because it doesn't appear to fit with the approved narrative. To highlight this discrepancy and the need for us to be sceptical about the information we receive, it would be helpful to provide an overview of how energy is created within a cell, and show how this process directly relates to cancer.

Mitochondria (pronounced mito-kon-dria) are bacteria-like entities that live within our cells. Among other tasks, they produce the energy for our cells to function by combining glucose with oxygen. There are hundreds of them contained within each cell, and they are the preferred pathway used to create energy for the cell. This process of converting food to energy is known as metabolism, and is the focus of the Metabolic Theory in relation to cancer.

Cells also have a backup energy system that can create energy when mitochondria are unable to; this backup energy pathway is known as *glycolysis*. The interesting characteristic of cancer is that it uses glycolysis as it's primary energy source, **even when conditions favour mitochondrial energy creation**. This abnormal switch to glycolysis in cancer cells was discovered by a German scientist called *Otto Warburg* in 1924, and was termed the 'Warburg effect'. James Watson, who co-discovered DNA, had this to say about the Warburg effect:

> *'We still don't know the reason for the Warburg effect… If I had two billion dollars I would give it to 20 biochemists, give them $100 million each and tell them – go to it. You have to unleash* **biochemistry**, *and there is essentially* **no biochemistry left**, *because* **everyone moved into DNA**.'*

> *Cancer World.net* 2013 [240]

To understand the relevance of the energy system, below is a simplified explanation of how it operates within healthy cells.

Imagine a fried egg represents a cell. The yolk symbolises the nucleus, which houses our DNA. The egg-white symbolises the watery gel-like substance that makes up the rest of the cell, known as the *cytoplasm*. Mitochondria, which generate energy for the cell to function, live within the cytoplasm. A backup energy pathway exists directly within the cytoplasm that obviates the need to use mitochondria. These two energy systems work together, but either can work as the dominant energy state given the right conditions. They are referred to as:

1. **Aerobic respiration** – energy creation via mitochondria
2. **Glycolysis** – energy creation within the cytoplasm

The carbohydrate we consume is broken down into glucose and absorbed into the cell, where it is then converted into a substance called *pyruvate*. Pyruvate can be used in either of these energy systems. If mitochondria are healthy and oxygen is available, pyruvate will be transferred to mitochondria and combined with oxygen to produce energy. Cell energy is measured in units of ATP (*Adenosine Triphosphate*). This mitochondrial energy-generating pathway creates 36 units of ATP energy for every glucose molecule used.

If mitochondria become dysfunctional or oxygen is unavailable, pyruvate will not be transferred to mitochondria. Instead, it will stay within the cytoplasm where energy creation will be completed via glycolysis – the backup energy pathway. This results in only 2 ATP units of energy for every glucose molecule used, and generates lactic acid as a byproduct:

Cell energy creation

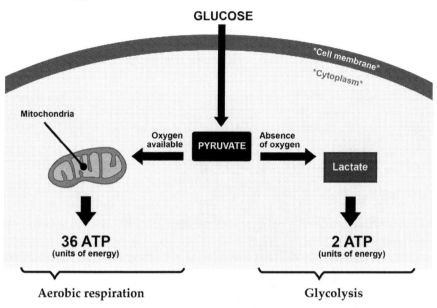

To sum up the differences between these energy-generating pathways: aerobic respiration requires oxygen, produces carbon dioxide and generates 36 ATP units of energy for every glucose molecule used, whereas glycolysis does not use oxygen, produces lactic acid and generates only 2 ATP units of energy for every glucose molecule used. In order to produce the same energy output as aerobic respiration, glycolysis would need to use at least 18 glucose molecules – this makes glycolysis a sugar-heavy energy pathway.[383] The more you rely on glycolysis (e.g. the more you sprint) the quicker you will reduce your glucose reserves.

The energy system of cancer:

Under normal circumstances, if an injury occurs and access to the blood supply is interrupted, the cell will temporarily switch to producing energy via glycolysis because the oxygen supply is lost – this happens because mitochondria are unable to generate energy without oxygen. This normal energy switch to glycolysis when oxygen is not available is referred to as *anaerobic glycolysis*. Anaerobic means 'without oxygen'. So, in this instance glycolysis is occurring because oxygen is not available – this is a normal everyday process.

The energy system of most cancer cells operates in an unusual manner. In contrast to healthy cells, tumour cells switch to using glycolysis **even when oxygen is available for mitochondria to utilise**. This is abnormal because mitochondria should be creating energy if there is enough oxygen available to do so. One possible reason for this could be that mitochondria have become faulty, and are no longer working properly, which would trigger the backup energy system even in the presence of oxygen. This was the reason proposed by Otto Warburg when he first observed the Warburg effect.

This abnormal energy switch is referred to as *aerobic glycolysis* because a switch to glycolysis is occurring even when oxygen is present. Aerobic means 'with oxygen'. It is important to acknowledge that the reason for this uncharacteristic energy switch to glycolysis in cancer is **unknown,** intriguingly, the 'mitochondria are faulty' assertion is in contention, because in many cancers they appear to be operating in a relatively normal capacity. This is one of the major pieces of the cancer puzzle yet to be explained. To summarise and clarify:

1. Aerobic respiration:
   - The main energy pathway of most healthy cells
   - Glucose and **oxygen** are combined within **mitochondria**
   - **36 ATP** units of energy produced per glucose molecule used
2. Glycolysis:
   - The backup energy pathway
   - Glucose is converted to **lactic acid** within the **cytoplasm**
   - **2 ATP** units of energy produced per glucose molecule used
3. Anaerobic glycolysis:
   - A switch to glycolysis occurs due to a **lack of oxygen**
   - This is normal and can occur due to cell damage
4. Aerobic glycolysis (the **Warburg effect**):
   - A switch to glycolysis occurs **in the presence of oxygen**
   - This is **abnormal**
   - This is the primary energy state of most cancer cells, the reason for this energy shift is unknown.

Since glycolysis generates only 2 ATP units of energy per glucose molecule, it is clear that cancer cells require more glucose than healthy cells, since they need at least 18 times more to generate the 36 ATP units a healthy cell generates by comparison through aerobic respiration:

> *'In the proliferating state, cells convert glucose to **pyruvate** through **glycolysis**... In this case, only **2 ATP** molecules are generated **per molecule of glucose**. Proliferating cells thus rely on a **high rate** of **glycolysis** and a **high glucose uptake** to support the doubling of their components during cell division.*
>
> ***Tumour cells*** *convert the majority of their absorbed **glucose** to **lactate**... and this dependency on a **high glycolytic rate** and **high glucose uptake** was termed the "**Warburg effect**".'*
>
> <u>*The FEBS Journal 2018*</u> [665]

This confirms that cancer feeds on sugar because most cancers rely primarily on glycolysis for their energy needs (sugar is converted to glucose). This indicates that starving the cancer cell of its energy source via glucose restriction could be an effective strategy.

To highlight this, recent studies into the diabetic drug Metformin have provided very positive results. Metformin reduces glucose levels in the blood, thus starving the cancer cell of the extra glucose it requires to function:

> *'Metformin has been prescribed to **lower blood sugar levels** of people with type 2 diabetes for over half a decade... **The drug can stop** or **slow down** particular types of **cancer** – including breast, prostate and pancreatic ...*
>
> *The research is centred on the power of metformin to **reduce blood glucose levels** through the liver.'*
>
> <u>*Diabetes.co.uk*</u> *2016* [330]

Of particular concern is that sugary foods are provided by hospitals to cancer patients alongside generally inappropriate dietary advice, with patients often being told just to ensure they consume enough calories. Such advice fails to highlight that calories gained from processed foods high in sugar can potentially fuel cancer growth. Even more concerning is that oncologists often provide steroids to increase the appetite of cancer patients. Steroids stimulate appetite by increasing glucose levels in the blood, ultimately promoting tumour growth by providing the tumour with access to the increased amounts of glucose it needs to proliferate.[407] Furthermore, steroids suppress the immune system (an undesirable side-effect common to many conventional approaches), which naturally benefits the cancer-causing micro-organism.

Sugar – feeding tumour growth:

Oddly, some of the most established cancer charities seem oblivious to this glucose link, with some actually promoting sugar consumption with the 'cake bake' theme they use to fundraise.[370] Given that medical science is awash with studies confirming that sugar feeds cancer, campaigns of this nature seem highly irresponsible.

Even more concerning, however, is that leading charities go to the extra lengths of muddying the waters on this subject by actually denying that sugar feeds the disease, against the weight of evidence. While scientists appear to be showing that there is a distinct relationship between sugar and cancer, this data appears to have been misinterpreted when presented to the public. In the below example the inference is that there is no evidence to show that sugar consumption (glucose consumption) has any effect on cancer cells, and yet as I will show, glucose consumption is critical to fuelling the disease and it's restriction can provide a benefit to the patient:

> 'Cancer cells usually **grow quickly**, multiplying at a fast rate, which takes a lot of energy. This means they need **lots of glucose...**
>
> ...Here's where the myth that sugar fuels cancer was born: if cancer cells need lots of glucose, then cutting sugar out of our diet must help stop cancer growing, and could even stop it developing in the first place. **Unfortunately, it's not that simple...'**
>
> CRUK 2020 [152]

> '...There's also **no evidence** that adopting a diet **very low in carbohydrate** will lower your cancer risk or help as a treatment...
>
> ...On the one hand, **sugar itself doesn't cause cancer**, and there's no way (at the moment) of specifically starving cancer cells of glucose without harming healthy cells too.'
>
> CRUK 2020 [152]

Within the first paragraph an immediate contradiction is clear, it's acknowledged that tumours require increased amounts of glucose to grow. Contradicting the statement made in the third paragraph, there is ample evidence to show that restricting glucose can benefit cancer patients (see the evidence that follows). Regarding the fourth paragraph, I don't think anyone is suggesting that sugar is a cause of cancer, rather, that it fuels its growth, and there is a scientifically proven way to restrict cancer cell's access to glucose without harming healthy cells, it's called ketosis. Ketosis can be achieved by adopting a ketogenic diet (low carb, high protein and fat diet). This diet has been documented within the medical literature for decades, and is often used as a form of treatment for people with epilepsy.[860]

It's very concerning that trusted institutions are making such claims, especially when the medical literature confirms that sugar feeds the disease, and that restricting glucose intake has been shown to be beneficial. Most notably, the PET scan highlights why these claims are misleading. A PET scan is designed to detect tumour location by analysing the increased rate of glucose absorption that tumours express; it specifically measures glucose accumulation within cells.

Before a PET scan is performed, the patient is injected with a radioactive glucose solution (a radiotracer). This solution accumulates selectively within malignant tissue due to their reliance on glycolysis and the increased glucose consumption this entails. The radioactive element of the radiotracer enables the PET scanner to register where tumours are located precisely because of their increased requirement for glucose. Pet scans rely entirely on the fact that cancer feeds on sugar. This is well known within the medical industry:

> 'A common use for PET is to measure the rate of consumption of **glucose** in different parts of the body.
>
> Accumulation of the radiolabelled **glucose**... allows measurement of the rate of consumption of **glucose**. One clinical use of this is to distinguish between benign and malignant tumours (malignant tumours **metabolise glucose at a faster rate** than benign tumours).'
>
> <u>**British Medical Journal**</u> **2003** [303]

> 'Positron emission tomography (PET) scans work on the basis that tumour cells exhibit **greater uptake of glucose** than most normal cells.'
>
> <u>**Molecular Biology of Cancer, pg 267**</u> **2012** [483]

To be clear, the studies below all confirm that cancer feeds on sugar (glucose) and it's consumption facilitates the disease, contrary to the claims being made by leading charities. The following study titled *Regulation of prostate cancer cell division by glucose*, highlights that glucose consumption increases prostate cancer growth and that this has been known for at least two decades:

> '...*high levels of glucose consumption* are required for *rapid proliferation* of androgen-independent prostate cancer cells...'
>
> <u>*Journal of Cellular Physiology*</u> ***1999*** [282]

This next study looks into the effects of sugar on breast cancer:

> '...*dietary sugar intake* has a *significant impact* on the development of *breast cancer*... We found that *sucrose* intake in mice comparable with levels of Western diets led to *increased tumour growth* and *metastasis*, when compared with a non-sugar starch diet.'
>
> <u>*Cancer Research*</u> ***2016*** [366]

A 2017 study into breast cancer found:

> 'Hyperglycaemia or diabetes mellitus (DM), which is characterized by *high blood glucose levels*, has been linked to an *increased risk of cancer for years*.
>
> In this study, we demonstrate that high glucose levels *promote the proliferation of breast cancer cells* by stimulating epidermal growth factor receptor (EGFR) *activation*...'
>
> <u>*Breast Cancer: Targets and Therapy*</u> ***2017*** [436]

One of the largest studies looking into the sugar cancer relationship even confirms the mechanism by which sugar stimulates cancer growth and mentions the Warburg effect:

> 'Our research reveals how the *hyperactive sugar consumption* of cancerous cells leads to a vicious cycle of *continued stimulation* of *cancer development* and *growth*. Thus, it is able to explain the correlation between the strength of the *Warburg effect* and *tumour aggressiveness*... This link between *sugar* and *cancer* has sweeping consequences.'
>
> <u>*Science Daily*</u> ***2017*** [653]

Given the study mentioned above regarding how the drug Metformin could inhibit cancer cells just by reducing glucose availability,[330] the science is clear. With this in mind, and regarding the other claim that there's no evidence of a beneficial effect using a low carbohydrate diet – studies into the effects of the ketogenic diet confirm the opposite:

> '*In summary, our results suggest that experimental brain cancer is manageable through principles of metabolic control where **plasma glucose levels are reduced** and ketone body levels are elevated.*
>
> ***Dietary energy restriction reduces tumour growth*** *through effects on angiogenesis, apoptosis, and inflammation… We contend that **dietary therapy may improve the clinical outcome of brain tumour patients** and enhance their quality of life.*'
>
> <u>British Journal of Cancer</u> **2003** [105]

To this end both Andrew Scarborough and Pablo Kelly are two case studies that confirm dietary glucose restriction can have a curative effect against incurable brain cancer, while having no detrimental effect on healthy cells. Both have overcome an otherwise terminal diagnosis by following a glucose-restrictive diet.[131, 348, 421]

Furthermore, there is an abundance of evidence showing how fasting can be beneficial against cancer on many levels and appears to improve chemotherapy treatment.[307, 336, 348, 676] Our bodies are designed to cope in situations of food scarcity and adapt. Fasting studies show an improvement in health and a re-stimulation of the immune system, positively affecting healthy cells. In a fasting state, old and poorly-functioning cells are removed and replaced with healthier cells – a process called *autophagy*. Given the evidence presented, the information being supplied by our leading cancer charities appears to be misleading in this regard when claiming that '*there's no way (at the moment) of specifically starving cancer cells of glucose without harming healthy cells.*' Glucose restriction performed under the guidance of a medical professional has been shown to be beneficial, not harmful to healthy cells,[159] and has clearly been shown to have a beneficial effect against cancer.

It's concerning that institutions we have grown to trust appear to be advising us incorrectly, especially when the medical tools they use to locate tumours (the PET scan) directly contradict the information they present, and when the evidence that they claim doesn't exist, is widely available. This dissemination of unsound information is made worse when trusted mainstream media news outlets repeat this misleading information without critical analysis, thereby reinforcing misinformation within the public domain.[331, 433, 434]

There doesn't appear to be any sound scientific reason why this fundamental biological mechanism of glucose fuelling cancer is being ignored and even denied by major scientific institutions, when the medical literature provides compelling evidence to support this concept. This, and the lack of evidence supporting the DNA Theory, highlights the urgent need for us to perform our own research, and question the information being presented by institutions we would reasonably expect to be able to trust.

Chemotherapy effectiveness

"Fifty percent of people will now survive" is the celebrated statement that is often presented in the media.[466, 246] Unfortunately, such statements provide the false impression that major progress is being made. This is largely because survival rates are being measured rather than cure rates. A 50% survival rate can be misinterpreted to mean that 50% of patients are cured, which is not the case at all. It simply means that across all cancers, on average, 50% of patients will still be alive 10 years after a diagnosis. The problem with this is that a significant percentage of that figure refers to patients where the cancer was caught early enough to have it removed via surgery. Furthermore, this 50% figure does not take into account how ill the patient is, or how far the disease has progressed, just that they were still alive for a particular length of time. What we really want to know, is how effective treatments are for people where the cancer is more advanced because this provides an indication of how well we understand the disease and how effective current drug treatments actually are.

Rather than using survival rates as a measure of success, a more accurate reflection of progress and treatment effectiveness is shown when we consider the cancer death rate, because the death rate provides a measure of the cure rate. When looking at this mortality data, it becomes clear that we are losing the battle against cancer and that tragically little progress in understanding the disease has been made.

Change in the US Death Rates* by Cause, 1950 & 2005

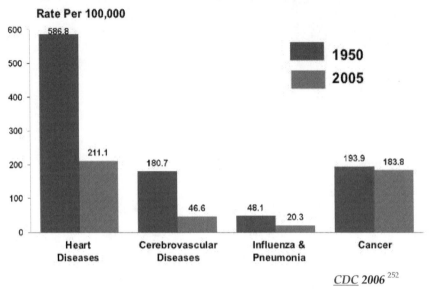

CDC 2006 [252]

Forgive me for using relatively old data here. The reason for this is because I have been unable to locate statistics that draw similar comparisons from 1950 up to the present year (2023). As current treatments are largely the same now as they were 15 years ago, it is likely that a similar trend would still be seen today. With this in mind, looking at the chart above, the cancer death rate has barely moved compared to other major diseases over the same 55-year period. Analysed as percentages, we can see that the death rate of each disease has been reduced by:

- **64%** for heart disease
- **74%** for cerebrovascular disease
- **58%** for influenza and pneumonia
- **5%** for cancer

While some progress has been made, this slight 5% improvement to the death rate for cancer can reasonably be attributed, in the main, to earlier diagnosis and surgery, not to targeted therapies or chemotherapy, which are said to attack the underlying cause. With technological and diagnostic improvements, a significant proportion of cancers are diagnosed early and surgically removed before they spread; these account for the main bulk of the 50% survival figure that is often presented. But when cancer has spread, the survival figure drops dramatically. To be able to cure these patients requires that we directly target the mechanism that drives cancer, which in turn requires an accurate understanding of this mechanism. Results clearly indicate that we are yet to correctly determine this mechanism and how to effectively treat it in advanced cancers.

Supporting the view expressed by James Watson, that very little progress is being made with the conventional drug approach, Professor Mel Greaves from the *Institute of Cancer Research* states:

> *'Talking about a cure in terms of elimination is just **not very realistic**...*
>
> *There are a few cancers that are curable but most are probably not including the common **carcinomas** in adults.*
>
> *You must have noticed that when you read reports about new target therapies, **isn't it odd** that they work dramatically, but three months later (cancer) is back with a bang. **It's almost always the story**.'*
>
> <u>**The Telegraph**</u> **2016** [244]

The carcinomas mentioned in the quote above constitute up to 85% of all cancers. Professor Paul Davies highlights that current cancer drugs have only increased life expectancy by four weeks on average for cancers that have spread.[018] Dr David Agus, who is Professor of Medicine and Engineering at *USC*, further confirms a similar lack of progress with the drugs that are being produced:

> *'...all these remarkable molecular targeting therapies work, but only for a **very short amount of time**... the challenge is to make a major impact on the disease, **but we're not doing that**...*
>
> *...we've got these drugs now for a **hundred thousand dollars** a year that **only give you an extra 2 or 3 weeks**...'*
>
> <u>**Fortune Magazine**</u> **2015** [266]

To highlight the gravity of the struggle that scientists face in treating the disease, it is helpful to view the five-year survival figures provided in the following table. 'Local' refers to a localised tumour that has not yet spread, while 'Regional' refers to a tumour that has spread to surrounding tissue, such as nearby lymph nodes. The 'Distant' category is what we want to focus on; it relates to cancers that have spread to distant parts of the body. This category reflects the effectiveness of radiotherapy and chemotherapy treatments because both treatments are used as the primary solution at this latter stage of progression (surgery is generally not applicable once cancer has spread). The effectiveness of the treatment is a reflection of the accuracy of the theory that underpins it. If the DNA Theory is incorrect, then mainstream treatments at this late stage will be largely ineffective, which unfortunately appears to be the case:

Table 8. Five-year Relative Survival Rates* (%) by Stage at Diagnosis, US, 2007-2013

	Local	Regional	Distant		Local	Regional	Distant
Breast (female)	99	85	27	Oral cavity & pharynx	84	64	39
Colon & rectum	90	71	14	Ovary	93	73	29
Colon	91	72	14	Pancreas	32	12	3
Rectum	88	70	15	Prostate	>99	>99	30
Esophagus	43	23	5	Stomach	67	31	5
Kidney†	93	67	12	Testis	99	96	73
Larynx	77	45	34	Thyroid	>99	98	56
Liver‡	31	11	3	Urinary bladder§	70	35	5
Lung & bronchus	56	29	5	Uterine cervix	92	57	17
Melanoma of the skin	99	63	20	Uterine corpus	95	69	16

American Cancer Society **2018** [215]

Unlike an antibiotic, which can, in most cases, provide a high cure rate against bacterial infection, chemotherapy treatment only offers a 27% chance that the patient will still be alive five years after diagnosis for breast cancer, this figure is only 5% for stomach cancer. Moreover, this doesn't reflect a cure; the diagnosis could still be terminal. These figures are a far cry from the generic 50% survival figure presented within the media that can be misconstrued as meaning 50% of people are cured.

An important question to ask is this: if we isolate chemotherapy treatment to assess its effectiveness, what contribution to this 50% overall survival figure does it provide; how good is this leading mainstream treatment? It's been challenging to find chemotherapy studies that assess the effectiveness of this treatment, but I did manage to track down four.

Collectively, the studies shown below confirm that, on average, the benefit that chemotherapy provides is meagre, at around 5%. That is, only 5 out of 100 people who are given the treatment will see a benefit, and crucially, by benefit, this doesn't mean cure. As one would expect from such a small level of improvement, all of these studies question its use, especially given the damaging side effects, the risk of organ failure, and the high costs involved.

I can imagine that reading this chapter may be very difficult for some of you who are already undergoing chemotherapy treatment, and you may feel like cancelling the therapy. Before making any decisions please ensure you consult your physician, as it may be more beneficial for you to finish the course of treatment you are currently undertaking. Chemotherapy can reduce tumour size upon initial administration, therefore, it may be able to provide some benefit in the short term or when administered at low doses – see the benefits of using low-dose combination chemotherapy as described by Dr Robert Gatenby and his adaptive treatment theory.[140]

It appears to be the prolonged use of chemotherapy that is problematic; too much toxicity can, and often does, trigger a survival response that encourages the tumour to become aggressive. This is explained over the following two chapters.

It's also worth noting that the human body is exceptionally good at healing, especially when supported by the correct diet and lifestyle, so if you've already had chemotherapy, please do not despair.

Regarding chemotherapy effectiveness, the study presented below looked at Australian and American chemotherapy success rates. It concluded that a negligible 2.3% and 2.1% improvement to the overall survival rate was found.[077] In other words, only 2.2 people out of 100 will see a benefit, 97.8 people out of 100 will not. This 2.2% figure doesn't represent a cure rate, just the percentage of patients who had a beneficial response to five-year survival:

> 'The overall contribution of curative and adjuvant cytotoxic chemotherapy to 5-year survival in adults was estimated to be **2.3%** in Australia and **2.1%** in the USA.
>
> ...it is clear that cytotoxic chemotherapy only makes a **minor contribution to cancer survival**. To justify the continued funding and availability of drugs used in cytotoxic chemotherapy, a rigorous evaluation of the cost-effectiveness and impact on quality of life is **urgently required.'**
>
> <u>**Clinical Oncology (Royal College of Radiologists) 2004**</u> [077]

The following study analysed at least 233 randomised studies and covered a total of 155,243 patients. It deals with adjuvant chemotherapy, which refers to chemotherapy that is provided alongside other treatment or is used after the successful removal of a tumour using surgery:

'There is solid scientific support from randomised studies that adjuvant poly-chemotherapy at 10 years will result in an absolute **mortality reduction** *for patients younger than 50 years by* **12%** *for node positive... and* **6%** *for node negative patients. For women aged 50 to 69 years, the corresponding figures for node positive and node negative patients are* **6%** *and* **2%,** *respectively.'*

Acta Oncologica 2001 [079]

Poly-chemotherapy refers to a combination of drugs. Compared with patients who had no adjuvant chemotherapy treatment, chemotherapy did show an absolute reduction in mortality of between 6-12% for patients below the age of 50. Or to look at it another way, 88-94% of patients who had chemotherapy saw no benefit in terms of mortality outcomes, and had to endure the toxic side-effects that occur. For older patients, who are the majority of people that develop cancer,[242] only a 2% to 6% reduction in mortality was found.

The next study deals with gastric cancer (stomach cancer) and highlights that surgery alone rarely cures this disease. In fact, between 50% to 90% of patients relapse even after surgery has been performed. The study aimed to see how effective chemotherapy was in preventing cancer from returning and killing the disease once it had returned. The study measured the five-year survival rate between 1,924 patients who were given both surgery and chemotherapy, and 1,857 patients provided with surgery alone. They found there was a slight improvement to patient survival with chemotherapy:

'Despite potentially curative resection of stomach cancer, **50% to 90%** *of patients* **die of disease relapse.**

Five-year overall survival increased from **49.6%** *to* **55.3% with chemotherapy.'**

Journal of the American Medical Association 2010 [595]

In line with the poor outcomes of other studies, chemotherapy provided a tiny 5.7% benefit. That is, 5.7% more patients lived a little longer with the disease than those who just had surgery. Chemotherapy didn't provide a benefit for 94.3% of patients who were given the drug. The other point to raise is that chemotherapy is supposed to be most effective against rapidly dividing cells because cells that replicate more quickly absorb more chemotherapy.[700] Gastric cells are some of the fastest dividing cells within the body, so if there is a type of cancer that chemotherapy should be highly effective against, it should be gastric cancer. Yet, it is only able to benefit, not cure, 5.7% of patients.

The final study relates to 7,000 patients and also deals with adjuvant chemotherapy. While the study appears to be in favour of the treatment, in the conclusion it states that although there is a beneficial effect for some, the toxic nature of the treatment means that its use is highly questionable given the small number of people who react positively:

> '...When data were pooled and plotted, significant differences in favour of chemotherapy were seen in OS (overall survival) in all seven sub-population, with a **relative benefit** of **7-12%** and an **absolute benefit** ranging from **2.5%** to **4.1%**.
>
> While significant differences are clearly found in this analysis, the **small magnitude of benefit** seen with this large population, especially when considering the number of patients needed for one to benefit, **raises important issues** when weighing risks and benefits of treatment for individual patients.'
>
> **<u>Lung Cancer</u> 2009** [080]

Again, in line with other studies, chemotherapy could only provide an absolute benefit between the range of 2.5% to 4.1%. In other words, only 4.1 patients out of 100 would see some sort of improvement to life extension when chemotherapy is used; furthermore, these statistics do not take into account any adverse side effects or whether the diagnosis was terminal.

Based on this data it would be reasonable to conclude that chemotherapy provides a benefit of 5% to survival, that is, only 5 people out of 100 will see a benefit from chemotherapy. Regarding the overall 50% survival figure mentioned earlier, chemotherapy likely contributes only 5% to that overall survival statistic. This is concerning considering the significant toxicity of the treatment.

Of course, the effectiveness of chemotherapy will differ in accordance with age, stage of progression and cancer type, so it's important not to apply this 5% rate of effectiveness to everyone; it is only an average statistic. Some cancers, such as testicular cancer for instance, show a 73% five-year survival rate even when it has metastasised, so one could argue that chemotherapy works for this type of cancer. A word of warning though: statistics can be misleading. The reason why 73% of these patients are still alive at the five-year marker is likely due to the slow rate of growth of this type of cancer, so it's not necessarily due to chemotherapy.

This slow rate of growth could simply mean that patients generally live longer with the disease, giving the false impression that chemotherapy has greater success with this cancer type. This is why the five-year survival figure can be misleading and why the death rate is a more accurate reflection of progress and effectiveness.

Childhood cancer, such as cancers of the blood and immune system (leukaemias and lymphomas), have seen a vast improvement in five-year survival from around 10% in the early 1900s to just over 80%, so it's not all bad news, and these improvements should be acknowledged and appreciated. Having said that, we mustn't assume that chemotherapy is effective for all based on the success with leukaemia – especially as this success doesn't tell the whole story. For instance, when an 80% five-year survival rate for childhood cancer is presented, we are often given the impression that 80% of children are cured and go on to lead normal healthy lives, but sadly this is not the case. When these children are followed over 30 years, the devastating effects of toxic chemotherapy treatment is revealed:

- **22% Survive at least 30 years** without suffering chronic health conditions
- **25% Survive at least 30 years** but suffer mild to moderate chronic health conditions
- **19% Survive at least 30 years** but suffer life-threatening or disabling chronic health conditions
- **34% die within 30 years**. 20% die in years 1 to 5, 14% die in years 6 to 30.

People against childhood cancer 2015 [219, 702, 703]

So, in reality, approximately 60% survive for 30 years but experience chronic illness. Only 20% go on to lead normal lives without suffering long-term debilitating side effects:

'60% of children who survive suffer **devastating late effects** such as **secondary cancers, muscular difficulties** and **infertility**.'

Cure Search 2020 [704]

The 80% five-year survival figure doesn't appear so appealing now that we see the long-term effect of using these toxic treatments. Moreover, chemotherapy dramatically increases the risk of secondary cancers forming:

> *'...children who were successfully treated for **Hodgkin's** disease [Hodgkin lymphoma] are **18 times** more likely to later develop **secondary malignant tumours**.*
>
> *Girls face a 35 percent chance of developing breast cancer by the time they are 40 – which is **75 times greater than the average.**'*
>
> *Tripping over the Truth – Travis Christofferson 2014* [258]

While every improvement in survival is welcome, we mustn't assume that an 80% five-year survival rate equates to a cure or a normal life without complications. There is a concern that patients may be given the wrong impression about chemotherapy effectiveness when its negative health impacts are not discussed, especially when positive outcomes with rare cancers are held up as examples of efficacy. This risks giving the impression that chemotherapy is generally more effective and less harmful than it actually is.

Even leading cancer charities appear to fall foul of using the positive outcomes associated with rare and slow-growing cancers (lymphoma, testicular cancer) in a vague manner that risks misleading patients by playing down its toxicities and embellishing it's effectiveness. While I understand there's a common human desire to place a positive spin on things, a balanced view is crucial if we are to avoid misleading patients. An example is this article which discusses how well chemotherapy works:

> *'With some types of cancer, **most people are cured** by chemotherapy. **With other types of cancer, fewer people are completely cured.***
>
> *Examples of cancers where chemotherapy **works very well** are **testicular cancer** and **Hodgkin lymphoma**.*
>
> *...the damage to healthy cells doesn't usually last. **Most side effects disappear once your treatment is over.**'*
>
> *CRUK 2020* [700]

To claim that *'most people are cured by chemotherapy'* in some types of cancer is extremely misleading because as we've seen with childhood leukaemia this isn't the case – an 80% improvement to five-year survival is not the same as *'most people are cured'*, especially when we take into account the increased risk of developing a secondary cancer. [258] The drug Gleevec may have increased five-year survival to 80% for Chronic Myeloid Leukaemia, but unfortunately studies show that only 5% are actually cured.[470] Hodgkin lymphoma has been a success story for patients younger than 60 with early stage disease, as five-year survival is around 90%, but this disease is rare and remains an outlier.[844] Hodgkin lymphoma affects less than 1%[844] of the population and is not a reflection of what happens in solid-tumour-based cancers – which account for the majority of cases.

While it's not incorrect to state that *'fewer people are completely cured'* in other cancers, that's a far cry from the reality, which is that most patients with metastatic disease are not cured with chemotherapy in these other cancer types. Surgery performed on cancers diagnosed early, accounts for the bulk of patients who are cured. It also appears disingenuous to state that *'most side effects disappear once your treatment is over'*. Regarding chemotherapy use on children, the long-term side-effects were well documented:

> *'It is now clear that damage to the organ systems of children caused by chemotherapy and radiation therapy may not become clinically evident for many years.*
>
> ***Thirty years*** *after a diagnosis of cancer, almost three fourths [75%] of survivors have a* ***chronic health condition***, *more than* ***40%*** *have a* ***serious health problem***, *and one third have* ***multiple conditions***. *The incidence of health conditions reported by this population* ***increases with time*** *and* ***does not appear to plateau.'***

> <u>*The New England Journal of Medicine*</u> **2006** [702]

Given that chemotherapy has provided no significant improvement in over six decades of clinical use, the significant toxicities involved, and with only a 5% contribution to the 50% overall cancer survival rate, it is perplexing to think that chemotherapy is still used, and championed, as a primary treatment solution for the majority of cancer types, and problematic that a leading cancer charity appears to imply that chemotherapy is far more effective, and far less damaging than studies have shown it to be.

Relative vs Absolute statistics:

It should be noted there's a crucial difference between 'relative' and 'absolute' figures in statistics, both of which are presented in the '*Lung Cancer 2009*' quote mentioned in the fourth study above. It is important to understand this difference otherwise there is a risk of being misled by the data. Often, by presenting the *relative* figure a drug or treatment can appear more effective than it actually is. Generally it's the *absolute* figure that is most relevant. Below is a hypothetical example that helps to clarify the issue:

Let's say, in *absolute* terms, a drug reduces heart attack risk from 2 in 100 people (a 2% risk) to 1 in 100 people (a 1% risk). This means that if you were to take the drug your risk of heart attack would be reduced from 2% to 1%; your overall risk reduction therefore is 1% if you take the pill – hardly anything to shout about. But, in *relative* terms, which applies to the relative difference between 2 and 1, this difference is 50% (1 is half of 2). This clearly sounds more impressive, the problem is that this relative figure doesn't reflect the broader context of the overall threat. And here's where the public may be mislead. Using the relative figure, a press release may state: *"New drug cuts heart attack risk by 50%"* because, in relative terms, a reduction from 2 to 1 is a 50% reduction. To the general public this sounds impressive, but it becomes less impressive when you realise we're actually talking about an overall risk of 2% being reduced to 1% – the pill reduces your overall risk of heart attack by just 1%.[785] This demonstrates how easy it is to misinterpret statistical information and the way in which treatments can be presented as being more effective than they actually are.

CH*04*

Chemotherapy and tumour aggression

If modern medicine has misunderstood cancer, then we must consider the possibility that the treatments being provided may actually be causing more harm than good. Given that the evidence indicates this to be true, I assume that oncologists are unaware of the information I am about to present, which would explain why they continue to provide chemotherapy as a treatment. This in turn only stands to highlight that oncologists are unfortunately not privy to the critical information they need to fully inform patients.

The most dangerous element of cancer – the cancer stem cell:

To fully appreciate the risks of treating cancer with chemotherapy I need to discuss the involvement of cancer stem cells. Broadly speaking, there are two types of cell: stem cells, which are superior cells that can create all other cells of the body, and regular cells, which stem cells create. Regular cells created by stem cells are referred to as *differentiated* cells or *daughter* cells, and make up the majority of cells within the human body, such as skin, lung and brain cells. They are cells that have become specialised and cannot create other cell types like stem cells can. To use an analogy, regular cells are like regular bees found in a hive that have specific tasks to perform, such as drone bees, worker bees, nursing bees and forager bees. Stem cells are like queen bees that produce all the different types of bees within the colony.

Stem cells are few in comparison and are located throughout the body. They are present in particularly high numbers within the liver and bone marrow. They also circulate throughout the bloodstream, stopping at areas that require new cells and aiding with cellular regeneration. It is the stem cell's job to create regular cells when needed, hence why regular cells are referred to as daughter cells.

The point of note here is that the majority of cells in a cancerous tumour originate from regular cells, while approximately 2% of a tumour is made up from cancer stem cells. This matters because it is the cancer stem cell that appears to be involved in tumour growth and its ability to spread. Significantly, cancer stem cells are able to replicate themselves indefinitely – in effect they are immortal – and can create a limitless supply of stem cells and daughter cells. Recognising the involvement of cancer stem cells is critical when it comes to understanding what cancer is, why a tumour appears to have limitless growth, how it evades the immune system, and how it spreads to other areas of the body. Of great concern is that the dominant DNA Theory, which the majority of oncologists have adopted, fails to take cancer stem cells into account, despite the fact that evidence confirms the pivotal role they play:

> *'There is increasing evidence that diverse solid tumours are hierarchically organized and sustained by a distinct sub-population of **Cancer Stem Cells (CSC)**. Direct evidence for the CSC hypothesis has recently emerged from mouse models of epithelial tumorigenesis...'*
>
> <u>**Nature Reviews Cancer**</u> **2008** [176]

Scientists found that when regular cancer cells were transferred into mice without cancer, no new cancers formed until cancer stem cells were introduced.[350] This confirmed that cancer stem cells are responsible for creating new tumours in other areas of the body. This explains why the DNA Theory cannot locate the DNA gene that causes metastasis (the spread of cancer) – because it doesn't exist. It is the cancer stem cell, or cells that possess stem cell properties, that are responsible for this deadly aspect of the disease.

When discussing this in a recent lecture, Professor Max Wicha reveals that many leading scientists are beginning to accept that the mainstream view is wrong:

*"... the classical wisdom that comes from cancer research that has been led by the revolution in molecular genetics has said that any cell in your body can become a cancer if it gets the right group of mutations... **we now believe that this is wrong**... we now think that only certain cells in your body are really prone to becoming **malignant**... we think that only populations of cells that have a property of **stem cells** called self renewal, are the cells that can become cancerous..."*

<u>A. Alfred Taubman Medical Research Institute</u> **2013** [178] [11:20]

Just to labour that point for a moment; leading scientists are now beginning to realise that the dominant view of the disease is incorrect. And yet, the DNA Theory is still used as the basis of new treatments, is still presented to the public as the most likely cause of the disease, and is still taught to medical students as the most accurate theory.

To help confirm the involvement of cancer stem cells and highlight why using chemotherapy for treatment is so questionable, here are some quotes taken from three lectures, where leading professors in cancer stem cell research detail the critical role these specific cell types play. Here I highlight the most relevant points made. I have included the time stamp for each quote, so you can locate it within the video. The first lecture *Cancer Stem Cells: The Origin of Cancer*[177] is by Irving Weissman, Professor of Pathology and Developmental Biology at Stanford University Medical Center (2009). The second lecture *Cancer Stem Cells*[178] is by distinguished Professor of Oncology Max Wicha M.D (2013), and the third lecture *Cancer Stem Cells: A New Target in the Fight Against Cancer*[179] is by Professor Robert Weinberg (2011).

Chemotherapy's major failing – cancer stem cells:

It is astonishing to think that chemotherapy is still used as a primary treatment for late-stage cancers when evidence confirms that cancer stem cells are resistant to the chemotherapy drugs supplied. And if this isn't bad enough, chemotherapy has also been shown to stimulate cancer stem cells to become more aggressive. This is partly because they possess a highly efficient pump that expels toxins. In his lecture, Professor Weissman was asked the question 'Aren't the drugs we have already killing the stem cells?' to which he replied:

"I wish I could say that they do, but in fact when we look carefully, the drugs that have been developed so far that shrink the tumour

> *down 90%; don't shrink 90% of the stem cells... we know that stem*
> *cells have pumps in them that **pump out drugs very efficiently**,*
> *their daughter cancer cells [regular cancer cells], which are killed by*
> *a drug, do not have this same pump."*
>
> <u>**Stanford University School of Medicine**</u> **2009** [177] [45:49]

Chemotherapy often shrinks the tumour after initial treatment, but this provides a false sense of efficacy. This is because it is mainly killing the regular cancer cells, leaving the cancer stem cells relatively unharmed; this allows the tumour to re-grow, ultimately leading to resistance. Unfortunately, as oncologists don't explain this critical detail, the patient is given confidence in continuing with a treatment that is destined to make matters worse in the long run. Regarding this very point, Professor Weinberg highlights why the mainstream view of the disease, and the use of chemotherapy, is so dangerous:

> *"For many kinds of therapy, the tumour will shrink, but the*
> *problem is the therapy is killing off the **non-cancer stem cells***
> *[regular cancer cells]; the **stem cells** [cancer stem cells] **many***
> ***of them will survive**. The cancer stem cells in that tumour are*
> *actually **more resistant to killing** by **many standard forms of***
> ***therapy**, and that creates a serious problem.*
>
> *If you look at the tumour as a whole, the oncologist **will declare***
> ***victory** because the tumour will have shrunk, **but there remains***
> ***the cancer stem cells**, and the reason why that's so bad is because*
> *obviously they survive, and weeks and months later they generate*
> *an entirely new tumour... **up until the last five years we***
> ***haven't understood the problem**."*
>
> <u>**Whitehead Institute for Biomedical Research**</u> **2011** [179] [40:00]

Since the 1960s, the medical establishment has been claiming to know the cause of tumour growth and has educated cancer scientists to believe the DNA Theory is correct. And yet, leading cancer specialists are now admitting that we haven't understood the problem.

Addressing this same issue, Dr Max Wicha, another leading scientist in the cancer field, confirms that chemotherapy increases the number of cancer stem cells and their aggressiveness, ultimately stimulating the disease to become more aggressive and deadly:

*"It turns out the same thing happens in many other cancers when you **treat with chemotherapy** – the **cancer stem cell number goes up.**"*

<u>*Alfred Taubman Medical Research Institute*</u> **2013** [178]

Adding to this irrationality is *Avastin*, a drug used in combination with chemotherapy to restrict blood vessel growth. Avastin also encourages stem cell growth and aggressiveness.[178] [37:57] Here, Professor Wicha presents clinical studies that show how regular cancer cells are killed, but cancer stem cells increase when the drug Avastin is used.[178 [39:14]]

At one point in time Avastin was taken off the market, but as Professor Wicha explains in his lecture, it was put back on the market due to a public outcry because the public thought it provided a benefit. It has now been banned for use with breast cancer but is still offered for other cancers. Regarding its recall, Diana Zuckerman of the *National Research Center* stated:

> '**The science is clear**, *breast cancer patients are more likely to be* **harmed** *than helped by Avastin.'*

<u>*Drugsdb*</u> **2012** [351]

When speaking of killing the entire tumour, Professor Wicha explains that we need to be using therapies that specifically target cancer stem cells, otherwise, chemotherapy and Avastin, which target only regular cancer cells, are useless:

> *"...All of these women getting treated with these agents [chemotherapy and Avastin], **and the fact that they don't work**, let alone the billions of dollars that are being used, are really* **wasted** *if you don't knock out the stem cells, all you're going to do is **stimulate the stem cells** with a variety of these agents."*

<u>*A. Alfred Taubman Medical Research Institute*</u> **2013** [178 [40:52]]

One such approach that may be worth considering when it comes to targeting both cancer cell types, is to utilise the off-patent drug *Metformin* (a diabetic drug that inhibits glucose metabolism), in combination with a chemotherapy drug, if conventional treatment is your preferred choice. Metformin appears to work synergistically with *Doxorubicin* (an anthracycline chemotherapy drug). According to one study, while Doxorubicin targets regular cancer cells, Metformin works in synergy by targeting cancer stem cells.[300] Aside from the *Care Oncology Clinic* in the UK utilising Metformin as part of their protocol, mainstream medicine does not include Metformin within chemotherapy regimes as standard. The shortcomings in mainstream standard of care treatments, which rely heavily on chemotherapy, are clear.

Aside from Metformin, there are many other agents, that appear capable of also targeting cancer stem cells, these agents are natural antibiotic compounds found in plants, herbs and spices. In his lecture, Professor Wicha confirms the potent ability of curcumin (turmeric) and a substance within organic broccoli called sulforaphane, to inhibit the cancer stem cells that chemotherapy fails to:

> *"...there are nutritional components that regulate stem cells...'Sulforaphane'* **found in broccoli,** *turns out to be a* **potent inhibitor** *of these stem cells... we've found that 'curcumin'* [**turmeric**] *also* **inhibits cancer stem cells..."**
>
> <u>*A. Alfred Taubman Medical Research Institute*</u> **2013** [178] [54:34]

Here we have a leading professor quoting scientific studies that prove certain food compounds effectively kill cancer stem cells. And yet, we are often advised there is no evidence to indicate plants provide any benefit. It would seem that the public, as well as oncologists, are not being fully informed.

CH*05*

Chemotherapy and tumour stimulation

Serious questions need to be asked about the use of chemotherapy, not just because of the risks already mentioned, but because it can actually cause the disease and facilitate cancer progression – although many oncologists dismiss these claims. So, to make sure there is no confusion, the *International Journal of Molecular Science* provides us with this critical information:

> *'...treatment agents can directly or indirectly damage DNA, or both. Ionising radiation **directly breaks the DNA backbone**, but it also produces **reactive oxygen species (ROS)** that damage DNA in multiple ways. This type of DNA damage has an impact on the fate of a cell by either causing cell death or by **being mutagenic, which can lead to diseases such as cancer**. In addition to this, DNA-damaging agents are **commonly used to treat cancer...** Ionising radiation is a physical agent that damages DNA and can **both cause and treat cancer.'***
>
> <u>*International Journal of Molecular Science*</u> **2014** [158]

In fact, in reference to alkylating agents (which are one of the most common types of chemotherapy drugs currently in use), the medical textbook *Molecular Biology of Cancer* also confirms that chemotherapy drugs are carcinogenic (cancer-causing):

> *'Mustard gas (sulfur mustard) is the most well known example of an **alkylating agent** because of its use and consequences observed during World War I. It is a bi-functional **carcinogen** that is able to form intra- and inter-chain **cross-links** on DNA directly.'*
>
> <u>*Molecular Biology of Cancer* 2012</u> [483]

Nitrogen mustards are a common type of alkylating chemotherapy drug used today; they are derived from the sulfur mustard referred to as a carcinogen in the quote above. These drugs are some of the most toxic DNA-damaging chemicals ever created:

> *'The **nitrogen mustards** are bifunctional alkylating agents that **damage DNA**... Mechlorethamine, bendamustine, melphalan, chlorambucil, ifosfamide and cyclophosphamide are the **nitrogen mustards most commonly used today.**'*
>
> <u>*International Journal of Molecular Science* 2014</u> [158]

Just to be clear, DNA damage is seen as the cause of cancer, and yet the chemotherapy treatments provided also cause severe DNA damage throughout the entire body when absorbed. Within the current mainstream paradigm, chemotherapy by definition, is a cancer-causing agent. This is also confirmed in the following journal article:

> *'Unfortunately multimodality treatment can come at a price, in particular **therapy-related malignancies** [cancer caused by the therapy].*
>
> *This has importance in that patients must be made aware of this **potential detriment from therapy**...'*
>
> <u>*Ulster Medical Journal* 2013</u> [465]

The article above confirms that chemotherapy caused cancer of the blood when used to treat a breast cancer patient. To further compound the cancer-causing properties of this treatment, a study discussed in *The Telegraph* confirms that chemotherapy actually increases the spread of the disease:

> *'Researchers in the US studied the impact of drugs on patients with breast cancer and found medication **increases** the chance of cancer*

*cells **migrating** to other parts of the body, where they are **almost always lethal**.*

*It is thought the **toxic medication** [chemotherapy] switches on a repair mechanism in the body which ultimately **allows tumours to grow back stronger**. It also increases the number of 'doorways' on blood vessels which allow cancer to **spread throughout the body**.'*

The Telegraph 2017[393]

What is actually being described here is the role of cancer stem cells, and how chemotherapy causes them to multiply and become more aggressive, as was confirmed in the previous chapter. Unfortunately, this critical understanding is misunderstood by many oncologists because the DNA Theory doesn't even acknowledge the presence of cancer stem cells. This highlights how outdated the mainstream view of cancer has become, along with the treatments being provided. The study within the article states:

*'...we show that chemotherapy **promotes distant metastasis** [spread]... suggesting that chemotherapy, despite decreasing tumour size, **increases the risk of metastatic dissemination**.'*

Science Translational Medicine 2017[394]

Even more concerning is that oncologists still don't fully understand how chemotherapy works or the extent of the damage it causes to the human body:

*'...**DNA-damaging** agents have a long history of use in cancer chemotherapy. The full extent of their cellular mechanisms, which is essential to balance efficacy and toxicity, **is often unclear**.'*

International Journal of Molecular Science 2014[158]

'Another limitation in the use of anticancer compounds arises from adverse toxicity to non targeted tissues [healthy tissue].

*While the mechanisms that underlie these side effects have been studied for years, our understanding **remains incomplete**.'*

Chemistry and Biology 2013[157]

But why are these drugs so toxic and cancer-causing? The reason is highlighted below, which, to the astonishment of many, confirms that some are derived from the chemical weapons sometimes used in warfare:

> 'The treatment of cancer is still largely based on the use of **chemotherapeutic drugs**... The first widely used cancer drugs were discovered in the 1940s as a result of studying **victims of chemical warfare** during World Wars I and II...
>
> ...Soldiers exposed to **sulphur mustard gas** were found to have depleted bone marrow and reduced lymph nodes. Subsequent testing in 67 patients with non-Hodgkin's lymphoma and leukaemia revealed marked tumour regression (Goodman et al., 1946).
>
> It was later noted that these **remissions were short-lived**, with **resistance** to the compounds **developing rapidly** [all the patients died].'
>
> <u>International Journal of Molecular Science</u> **2014** [158]

> '**Sulphur mustard** has been used as a **chemical weapon** since World War I. **Nitrogen mustard**, a **derivative** of sulphur mustard, was one of the **first chemotherapy agents** but never has been used in warfare.
>
> These agents cause blistering of exposed surfaces. **Both mustard agents** rapidly penetrate cells and generate a highly toxic reaction that disrupts cell function and causes cell death.'
>
> ***emedincinehealth* 2017** [001]

In 1946 cancer cells were indeed killed when exposed to these toxic chemotherapy compounds, but remissions were short-lived, with resistance to chemotherapy developing rapidly, leading to an aggressive cancer and the death of the patient. Nothing much appears to have changed because the nitrogen mustards currently used today are still derived from chemical warfare agents, and the central problem continues to be the resistance to the drug that often develops:

> 'A primary cause of **failure** of anticancer treatments is the intrinsic or acquired **resistance** of a tumour to the drug, which **often leads to disease re-occurrence.**'
>
> ***Chemistry and Biology* 2013** [157]

Put simply, the most common treatment offered is a highly toxic poison known to severely damage DNA and is provided even though its damaging effects are still not fully understood. This treatment has been used for over 55 years with little improvement in patient outcomes and can itself cause the disease, not to mention it stimulates cancer stem cells to become more aggressive and deadly. How many decades of using these toxic treatments without progress does the medical establishment need us to endure before it accepts that chemotherapy isn't the answer?

In 1986 the bio-statistician John Bailer assessed the effectiveness of cancer treatments. He evaluated all treatments used between 1950 and 1982, including chemotherapy. He concluded that only 4% of patients were cured,[258] and stated that we were losing the war against cancer, not winning it. It was clear back in the 1980s that cancer treatments were largely ineffective. And yet, nearly 40 years later, we continue to use the same drugs, hoping that the outcome will be different.

In addition to this, follow-up data regarding the long-term effects of chemotherapy treatment on children, found that:

> *'In addition to sharply increased risk of heart attack and stroke, the children who were successfully treated for Hodgkin's disease are 18 times more likely to later develop secondary malignant tumours.'*
>
> **<u>Tripping over the Truth – Travis Christofferson</u> 2014** [258]

The mainstream drug approach to treating cancer appears to be more detrimental to patient health than our medical practitioners care to let on. And yet, we are constantly presented with the notion that this toxic drug approach is the most effective, and therefore the only course of treatment worth undertaking. It is bewildering to think that such an ineffective and toxic treatment has been used for so long and is still the primary treatment offered today.

Oncologists do highlight that chemotherapy is toxic and explain that the goal is to poison the tumour hoping that any damage to the rest of the body will be repaired. The idea is that the tumour will die before too much damage is caused to vital organs. However, this explanation is rather vague and rarely highlights how damaging these toxins are, the type of damage they cause, and the long-term effects on the body.

There are many different chemotherapy treatments, so it would be wrong for me to tar them all with the same brush. Not all are derived from chemical warfare agents; however, most severely damage DNA and inevitably generate mutations. For example, *anthracycline* chemotherapy drugs are not based on sulfur mustards; they were originally derived from the toxins that *Streptomyces* bacteria produce. Even so, these toxic drugs damage DNA and the full extent of the damage they cause is still not fully understood:

> 'The mechanism by which **anthracyclines** inhibit cancer is still **not completely clear...**'
>
> <u>Chemoth.com</u> [380]

There seems to be serious shortcomings in the mainstream view of cancer, in that the DNA Theory appears to be incorrect, and the 'standard of care' treatments appear to be highly toxic, largely ineffective and can stimulate or even cause the disease.

How chemotherapy damages DNA:

Understanding how chemotherapy generates DNA damage will help us realise the error in mainstream thinking that makes using these treatments so contentious.

When chemotherapy toxins enter the cell, they are absorbed into the nucleus and bind to the DNA within. This can cause 'cross-links', bridges across DNA that shouldn't be present. Essentially, these toxins glue parts of our DNA together, preventing it from working correctly. This leads to mutations when the cell divides or when the cell DNA is incorrectly repaired.[158]

When highly toxic chemicals attach to DNA and create cross-links, this can result in 'double-strand breaks' (DSB) in DNA. It is the DNA repair mechanism that's actually causing this damage because it cuts away these parts of the DNA to repair it. To clarify, when toxins bind to DNA genes, glueing them together, the DNA repair mechanism cuts away all of the genes stuck together, essentially leaving a gap in the DNA ladder. It then attempts to repair the gap by rebuilding the DNA that has been cut away. But when the amount of toxin exposure increases to a critical level, the damage caused by the repair mechanism can be too significant for it to be fully repaired, especially if essential nutrients are lacking due to a poor diet. This can lead to mutations and excessive damage, as this study confirms:

> '**DSBs** can be cytotoxic but can also lead to insertions, deletions and chromosomal rearrangements. In one study, AS52 Chinese hamster

*ovary cells were treated with the bifunctional agent chlorambucil or a mono-functional chlorambucil analogue [chemotherapy]… the mono-functional analogue was shown to induce **point mutations** whereas the bifunctional chlorambucil induced **major genetic deletions.'***

<u>International Journal of Molecular Science</u> **2014**[158]

The contradiction is clear, chemotherapy contributes to the DNA mutations and DNA damage, that is claimed to cause cancer.

The chemotherapy contradiction:

As one would expect when using an incorrect theory to guide treatment decisions, major contradictions become apparent; this is especially the case with the DNA Theory and the chemotherapy treatment associated with it. For instance, for the human body to function efficiently cells need to be constantly dividing to replace the millions of cells every minute that reach the end of their life-span. To ensure new cells are viable, any DNA damage within a cell needs to be recognised so that it can be repaired – only once DNA is repaired will cells duplicate. When DNA damage is detected, the repair mechanism within the cell halts growth signals preventing cell duplication. Once DNA is repaired cell division continues and new identical cells can be produced. In other words, cells stop growing (dividing) when DNA damage is detected but resume growth activity once DNA has been repaired.

The premise behind how chemotherapy is thought to work is based upon this concept – that by damaging DNA with toxic drugs, the cancer cell will be prevented from dividing because it will be constantly stuck in a state of DNA repair; this should prevent cancer cell growth. Using chemotherapy to create constant DNA damage appears to be the goal because it is assumed that such damage will result in cell dormancy or cell death.[700] Unfortunately, there are several significant flaws with this concept:

1. This type of DNA damage can lead to mutations.
2. Chemotherapy can't be used indefinitely.
3. Healthy cells are more sensitive to DNA damage. This leads to extreme toxicities that damage organs and can result in the very mutations that are thought to generate the disease.
4. Cancer stem cells are resistant to chemotherapy.

These points aside, the primary contradiction in using chemotherapy as treatment is this: the efficacy of chemotherapy is reliant upon the cell repair mechanism working correctly – that is, the repair mechanism needs to recognise the DNA damage that chemotherapy causes, in order for it to cut out the relevant strands of DNA, leading to cell death or dormancy. However, and in contradiction, a tumour is said to arise because the repair mechanism no longer works – failure of cell repair allegedly leads to the mutations that generate the disease.[388]

So, if the repair mechanism is no longer working – which is required for cancer to form, then chemotherapy is rendered useless because it requires the repair mechanism to be fully functional in order for the cell to recognise the DNA damage chemotherapy causes. If, on the other hand, the DNA repair mechanism is working normally – which is required for chemotherapy to be beneficial, then a tumour would never form in the first place, because the DNA mutations initially thought to cause cancer would have been repaired by the normally-functioning repair mechanism. The mainstream view of a) how a tumour forms via a failed repair mechanism and b) how a functioning repair mechanism is required for chemotherapy to work, are mutually exclusive.

Therefore, it seems counter-productive to be generating DNA damage using chemotherapy to target a DNA repair mechanism that no longer recognises this DNA damage as a problem. Confirming this contradiction and the major flaw in using chemotherapy to treat the disease, researcher Caroline Schild-Poulter from the *University of Western Ontario*, states:

> *'One of the hallmarks of cancer is that the cells **don't initiate apoptosis** [cell death] **despite having defects** in their genetic material. In other words the damaged cells **do not commit suicide**, and this develops into cancer. **Failure to activate apoptosis** also makes it difficult to cure cancer. **You cannot kill these cells by causing DNA damage** to them **using chemotherapy** or **radiation**, because these cells **resist dying**.'*

> <u>*University of Western Ontario* **2009**</u> [428]

This is even outlined in the medical textbook *Molecular Biology of Cancer*, which states:

> *'Many tumours have **defective apoptotic pathways** (cell death pathways) and are **inherently resistant to chemotherapies**, regardless of whether or not they have been previously exposed to the drugs.'*

This medical book goes on to highlight how the DNA damage caused by chemotherapy can lead directly to mutations and the development of cancer itself:

> *'The lack of apoptotic effect in response to extensive DNA damage caused by these genotoxic drugs provides an opportunity for the accumulation of mutations.* **Consequently, the risk of carcinogenesis increases.** *Indeed, therapy-related leukemia, whereby a* **new cancer arises after the administration of chemotherapy,** *is a clinical problem.'*
>
> *Molecular Biology of Cancer. pg164* 2012 [483]

The continued use of chemotherapy appears absurd in light of the many contradictions that are apparent and the cancer-causing attributes of the therapy itself. All this helps to explain why chemotherapy only provides a 5% benefit and why the death rate hasn't improved in over 55 years of persistent chemotherapy use. It's clear that we must question the mainstream view of the disease and challenge the use of toxic chemotherapy treatments.

Promising solutions:

Thankfully it's not all doom and gloom, there are many brilliant scientists pursuing other avenues of research looking into promising solutions, many of which are naturally-based.

For instance, salvestrols, which are antibiotic plant extracts, have shown excellent potential against several cancers. The discovery of salvestrols and their use against cancer was discussed by Cancer Research UK as far back as 2007.[228] The BBC presented a news article in which Cancer Research UK commented on the Salvestrol discovery. The article highlights that a promising natural chemical called *Salvestrol Q40*, found in tangerine peel, can kill human cancer cells. It is present in all sorts of fruits and vegetables and is produced in abundance at the point of ripening. The lead researcher Dr Hoon Tan, commented:

> *'It is very exciting to find a compound in food that can* **target cancers specifically**... *it proved to be* **20 times more toxic to cancer cells** *than their healthy equivalents.'*

Salvestrols have been tested on cancer patients and show great promise. While these case studies are small, they highlight their enormous potential as an effective cancer treatment. Between 2007 and 2010, 15 cancer patients used Salvestrol supplements to fight the disease; all 15 were cured of their particular cancer type.[103] This result is remarkable and indicates that common food extracts could be used to help treat cancer.

The promise of 3BP:

Around 2001, the scientist Young Hee Ko, who was studying cancer metabolism, used a chemical compound called 3BP (3-bromopyruvate), which can inhibit the energy system of cancer cells. On her research website she highlights the exciting potential of this drug:

> *'In 2000, I discovered that the small molecule 3-bromopyruvate (3BP) is a **highly potent** and **effective anticancer** agent with **preferential selectivity for cancer cells**. 3BP works by targeting the most common property of cancer cells – their markedly elevated capacity to metabolize **glucose** and **glutamine**. It enters cancer cells quickly via mono-carboxylate transporters (MCTs) and **immediately targets** the **mitochondria**. It does all of this while leaving most normal cells **unharmed**.'*
>
> **_Kodiscovery.org_**[525]

The drug 3BP stands to provide a metabolic solution. To highlight its potential, James Watson paid homage to it in 2013. He wrote:

> *'3-bromopyruvate [3BP], the powerful dual inhibitor of hexokinase as well as oxidative phosphorylation, **kills highly dangerous hepatocellular carcinoma** cells [liver cancer] more than **10 times faster** than the more resilient normal liver cells and so has the capacity to **truly cure**, at least in rats, an otherwise highly incurable cancer.'*
>
> **_3BP and the metabolic approach to cancer_ 2013**[261]

The promise of curcumin:

To highlight the potential of natural compounds, in a 2003 review study that analysed the evidence surrounding the effectiveness of curcumin (a compound found in the spice turmeric), scientists concluded not just that curcumin was effective, but that it provides enormous potential in both preventing and treating the disease:

*'Evidence has also been presented to suggest that curcumin can suppress tumour initiation, promotion and metastasis. All of these studies suggest that curcumin has **enormous potential** in the **prevention** and **therapy of cancer**. Pharmacologically, curcumin has been found to be **safe**.'*

<u>Anticancer Research</u> 2003 [607]

This is just a tiny glimpse of the medicinal properties and cancer-killing abilities associated with certain medicinal plant extracts. These exciting properties are discussed in the latter half of the book where I cover the basics of nutrition as it relates to health, disease and cancer.

The promise of immunotherapy:

Some fantastic advancements have been made in this field. Scientists are now able to enhance the immune response. This has taken us into the realm of personalised cancer medicine. Most immunotherapies stimulate cancer-killing T-cells, which appear to have been suppressed in cancer. Checkpoint inhibitors can prime these T-cells to recognise cancer cells and this therapy has been shown to be very effective in some cancers for some people. While promising, it is early days for this treatment, and unfortunately these checkpoint inhibitors do not work in all patients. There is always a risk with over-stimulating the immune system given that it may attack healthy cells as we see in autoimmune disease:

*'However, the use of such "checkpoint inhibitors" **does not work in all patients** and we currently **do not understand why**. Furthermore, the use of checkpoint inhibitors, such as the combination of anti-PD-1 and anti-CTLA-4, causes **severe toxicity** in the **majority of patients treated**.*

*Toxicity depends on the individual and ranges from inflammation of the GI tract, the most common complication, to **autoimmune phenomena** affecting the thyroid, skin, liver, joints, pancreas, and brain...'*

<u>Frontiers in Immunology</u> 2017 [896]

I wonder, would immunotherapy work better against cancer, if these immune cells were enhanced to attack the particular micro-organism that I propose is driving the disease? This would reduce toxicity because the immune cell would not be overstimulated to target our own cells, as it is currently primed to do.

$$CH\ 06$$

Fantastic free radicals

Free radicals play a critical role in cancer. At present they are thought to cause the DNA damage that allegedly brings about the disease – free radicals are seen as a cause of cancer. Needless to say, there is confusion surrounding their involvement because the data doesn't align with the mainstream DNA Theory. When we view the disease through the lens of cell suppression and the involvement of a micro-organism, this data starts to makes sense. This new perspective highlights free radicals' greater role in preventing and curing the disease and in identifying a micro-organism as the underlying cause of tumour growth. To truly understand cancer, we must understand the relevance of free radicals and the role they play.

Free radicals are molecules (made up of atoms) that cause damage to cells, primarily because they harbour an unpaired electron and seek to steal an electron from other stable atoms. Atoms can be combined with other atoms to create different molecules or compounds. One example is water, which is comprised of two hydrogen atoms and one oxygen atom linked together (H_2O). Atoms contain subatomic particles called protons, neutrons and electrons. Protons are positively charged, neutrons have no charge and electrons are negatively charged. Electrons orbit the nucleus of an atom and can be shared between atoms. To make energy, cells can transfer electrons from one atom or group of molecules to another, this transfer generates energy. During this process atoms can be left with an unpaired electron rendering their electrons unbalanced, and this is where cell damage can occur and free radicals are formed. Primarily, atoms are stable (less reactive) when all electrons are paired and balanced. Molecules become unstable when they harbour unpaired electrons – there is essentially an imbalance in electrical charge, these atoms are known as free radicals. The damaging aspect of free radicals relates to the fact they seek to balance the missing electron by stealing it from another stable atom. This can destabilise molecules, essentially leading to damage.

This has particular relevance to the health of cells because free radicals can be generated during the creation of energy within mitochondria. This is because mitochondria are manipulating oxygen atoms and their electrons – oxygen is highly reactive. Mitochondria may accidentally produce free radicals during the process of energy creation.

To compensate for any accidental release of these damaging free radicals, mitochondria also produce *antioxidants,* which bind to free radicals neutralising their damaging effects by providing them with the missing electron they need. Hence their name 'anti' (against) 'oxidants' (oxygen). Essentially, antioxidants act like a shield or bullet-proof vest; they absorb the free radicals rendering them inactive and harmless. This is why antioxidants are hailed as being beneficial.

Based on the notion that free radicals can damage DNA, proponents of the DNA Theory propose that free radicals released by mitochondria during energy creation – known as 'metabolism' – are a major cause of the DNA damage that allegedly generates tumour growth. According to the *US National Library of Medicine* free radicals cause cancer:

> 'The process by which normal cells become progressively transformed to malignancy is **now known to require the sequential acquisition of mutations** which arise as a consequence of damage to the genome. This damage can be the result of endogenous processes such as errors in replication of DNA, the intrinsic chemical instability of certain DNA bases or from attack by **free radicals** generated during **metabolism.**'
>
> <u>Molecular Aspects Medicine</u> **2000** [064]

Specifically, it is the free radicals that arise from metabolism that are identified as the type of free radicals responsible for tumour growth. To re-cap, cells require energy to function. Part of the process of energy production requires the breakdown of glucose and oxygen within mitochondria. This energy-creating process is referred to as cell metabolism; the cell is metabolising (breaking down and combining) oxygen and glucose and manipulating the electrons they contain.

During this process, approximately 2% of damaging free radicals are accidentally released from mitochondria. It is this accidental release of free radicals during metabolism that is blamed for causing cancer. This is why free radicals generated via 'metabolism' are cited in the quote above as a cause of tumour growth. These metabolically-produced free radicals are thought to be damaging DNA, leading to the mutations that are believed to cause cancer.

Oxidative stress:

Here's the concern with the mainstream interpretation: researchers appear to be selective regarding the information they consider, often ignoring critical details that might lead to a different conclusion. For example, free radicals aren't only generated during normal energy metabolism; they are also created when the cell is threatened or damaged, such as when it absorbs a toxin or is attacked by a micro-organism. When threatened, the cell enters into a state of *oxidative stress*, which results in mitochondria intentionally producing far more free radicals than it would typically produce during regular energy metabolism. This increased free radical production is also referred to as *Reactive Oxygen Species* (ROS) – because oxygen free radicals are intentionally being released by mitochondria in reaction to a threat. These free radicals are created to kill the micro-organism invading the cell or to break down the toxin that is threatening the health of the cell. [769, 883]

As the state of oxidative stress produces far more free radicals than normal energy metabolism, oxidative stress has the potential to cause greater DNA damage, as illustrated by the following image:

Metabolism
Free radicals from normal energy production

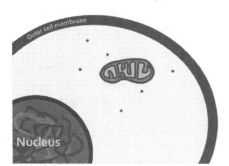

Oxidative Stress
Free radicals produced via toxin exposure

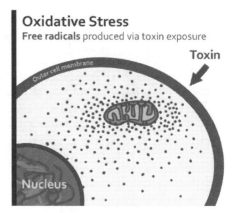

Intriguingly, we see this same oxidative stress response with chemotherapy, which highlights another contradiction within the mainstream treatment strategy, in that chemotherapy generates the very free radicals that are cited as causing the disease, further emphasising chemotherapy's cancer-causing potential:

> *'Chemotherapy-induced formation of **free radicals** is **well demonstrated** most notably with **alkylating agents...** and anti-tumour antibiotics...'*
>
> <u>*Jefferson, Myrna Brind Centre of Integrative Medicine* 2006</u> [065]

There is an important distinction to be made between the differing roles ascribed to free radicals in the inception of cancer. If metabolic free radicals are the primary form responsible for causing the disease, then this suggests that cancer is a result of the cell causing damage to itself, a process that is out of our control. This implies that everyone has the same odds of developing the disease regardless of how healthy they are because we have no control over the 2% of free radicals that are accidentally released during energy creation. From this perspective, cancer would be a result of bad luck, and indeed this has been the conclusion drawn by some prominent scientists.[498] On the other hand, if oxidative stress is responsible, this indicates that cancer is a result of external factors such as toxins or micro-organisms, and is not caused by an intrinsic fault within the cell itself. So, is the cell to blame, or are external factors responsible for generating the free radicals thought to cause the disease?

Is metabolism or oxidative stress to blame for cancer?

Contrary to the 'bad luck' assertion – that cancer develops randomly due to an inherent fault with how the cell operates – abundant data confirms that the risk of cancer differs greatly depending on diet and lifestyle choices. Some people have a substantially reduced risk of cancer, despite releasing 2% of free radicals via metabolism in line with everyone else. This indicates that metabolically-produced free radicals are not the primary factor driving the disease, and that some other factor must be involved.

We can also look at this from another perspective. Since the early 1900s the incidence of cancer has greatly increased:

> *'The lifetime risk of cancer increased from **38.5%** for men born in 1930 to **53.5%** for men born in 1960. For women it increased from **36.7** to **47.5%**'*

> *British Journal of Cancer* **2015** [674]

The quote above states that, between 1930 and 1960, the risk of cancer increased by 15% for men and 10.8% for women. Cancer Research UK confirms that between 1990 and 2020, the rate increased by 12%,[675] while the World Health Organization predicts a further increase in cancer cases of around 70% by 2030.[241] To account for this increase in cancer incidence in a way that supports the view that metabolically-produced free radicals are the primary driver of cancer, we would expect to see more free radicals being released via metabolism today than we have done in the past.

The problem with this proposition is that there doesn't appear to be any evidence to suggest that mitochondria are becoming less efficient and releasing a higher percentage of free radicals over time, or in subsequent generations. In fact, this concept of mitochondria becoming less efficient contradicts the theory of evolution, which asserts that our cells improve with each generation, not that they degrade. Life would not have developed to the complex level it has under conditions where cells evolve to become less efficient.

It seems highly unlikely that the 2% proportion of free radicals accidentally released by mitochondria today, would have been much lower just two generations ago. This would have to be a global phenomena to account for the rise in cancer incidence we are seeing across the entire planet. Moreover, studies show that antioxidants are released by mitochondria in correlation to the free radicals produced during metabolism, meaning that metabolism-based free radicals are neutralised before they can inflict the damage that is thought to cause cancer:

> '...up to **two percent** of the oxygen used in this process [metabolism] is transformed into superoxide, a **free radical** that is toxic to cells... However, **evolution** has equipped eukaryotic cells with comprehensive mechanisms that can **decompose free radicals which arise in the cell** and therefore **prevent damage** to the cell.'

> 'This tells us that cells can **predict** when the [free] radical production will rise and adapt their metabolism **before the free radicals are even produced.'**

Max-Planck-Gesellschaft 2011 [677]

This indicates that free radicals generated via metabolism cannot be responsible for the disease, or at the least, for the dramatic rise in cancer we are witnessing because they are neutralised as they are produced. This means that if cancer is caused by free-radical damage, it is more likely to be due to an increase in oxidative stress. If this is true, then it follows that the rise in cancer incidence is being driven by the ever-increasing levels of toxins we are now exposed to, not a decrease in the operational efficiency of our cells.

Approximately 100,000 synthetic chemicals have been introduced into circulation since the early 1930-40s.[705] They are regularly found within our food supply and adorn almost every surface and product found throughout our environment. This is the first time in our history as a species that we have encountered these new-to-nature compounds, and the rise in our exposure to them has been exponential. We've transitioned from a world where harmful chemicals were few and far between to one where it is impossible to avoid them. Rapidly rising levels of toxic exposure inevitably result in an increase in oxidative stress. This is highlighted by a study in Chapter 15, which found over one hundred toxins within the umbilical cord blood of newborn babies, many of which were carcinogenic. Although oxidative stress is more likely to be the cause of free radical damage that allegedly leads to cancer, there is contention over whether or not free radicals actually cause cancer, which adds weight to the notion that the mainstream view of the disease is incorrect.

Do free radicals cause cancer?

I have already proposed that the evidence indicates that DNA damage is not the underlying cause of tumour growth. If this is correct, it would follow that free radicals aren't a cause of the disease either. Has mainstream research misinterpreted the role they play? How can we reach any robust conclusions about this important question? Well, both exercise and antioxidant experiments can help shed light on the issue.

As we exercise we increase free-radical production. Our cells require more energy, therefore more oxygen is consumed and converted, leading to the potential for increased release of free radicals from mitochondria. Using conventional wisdom, an increase in free radicals from exercising should increase cancer risk, due to the extra DNA damage it is likely to inflict. However, contrary to the mainstream narrative, exercise reduces cancer risk rather than increasing it.[068] Discussing the latest evidence, the article below states:

> *'A growing body of evidence continues to support previous research about the cancer-fighting benefits of exercise and link between physical activity and cancer prevention.*
>
> *We now believe physical activity is a **primary component of preventing cancer**...*
>
> *A survey based on information collected over a 23-year period in a research project called the **Copenhagen Male Study** found that **regular exercise can help prevent intestinal cancer**.*
>
> *Several other studies have had similar results, and one can now say that **any doubt has been dispelled**.'*[068]

Citing further sources, the article goes on to state:

> *'A recent study revealed that physical activity prevents endometrial cancer and breast cancer according to a study involving 850 women. The **more the study subjects exercised, the less their odds of being diagnosed with cancer**, even if they were considered "at risk" for the disease.*
>
> *...other research found that moderately fit men had a **20 percent lower risk** of dying of lung cancer compared with men who were not fit. And men who were **highly fit had a 60 percent lower risk** than men who were not fit... This appeared true even after adjusting for smoking habits.'*[068]

The study also confirms that cancer is a systemic disease and not a local isolated issue as mainstream medicine appears to assert:

> *'The **fact that exercise** is now being shown to **prevent cancer** is important for one more reason: it **proves that cancer is systemic**, not local. In other words, cancer is a **whole-body failure, not just a specific tumour or lesion that can be surgically removed or targeted with radiation**.*
>
> *Because cancer is a systemic failure, **it must be treated holistically** – that is, the whole person must be considered: their physical health, immune system function, mental health, spiritual health, and of course their day to day activities such as eating and exercising.'*
>
> <u>*preventdisease.com*</u> **2020** [068]

The *National Cancer Institute* discusses the impact of exercise on breast cancer patients, highlighting similar outcomes:

> *"Women with breast cancer who met the minimum physical activity guidelines both before diagnosis and at the 2-year follow-up (after treatment) had a 55% reduced chance of their cancer returning and a 68% reduced chance of death from any cause (not just breast cancer)."*
>
> <u>**National Cancer Institute**</u> **2020** [923]

So, contrary to the conventional view, an increase in free radical production caused by exercise reduces cancer risk by up to 60%.

Antioxidants:

It is well established that antioxidants are good for our health, primarily because they bind to free radicals, which can neutralise their ability to cause cell damage. While mitochondria create these damaging free radicals, they also create the antioxidants used to neutralise them – this provides mitochondria with control over the use of the free radicals they produce to ensure limited damage is inflicted upon the cell itself. Some of these antioxidants include *glutathione, superoxide dismutase* and *melatonin*.

Depending on the quantity of free radicals being produced at any given time, our internal reservoir of antioxidants can be diminished, which can lead to an imbalance resulting in oxidative stress and cell damage. This is where the antioxidants within food and supplements come to the rescue. To stave off attack from micro-organisms and oxidative damage, plants create antioxidants too – some of these include vitamin A, C and E as well as beta-carotene, which is present within carrots for example. Dutch physician Christiaan Eijkman and British biochemist Frederick G. Hopkins shared the 1929 Nobel Prize in physiology and medicine for their work on vitamins. They confirmed that external vitamins (antioxidants), gained from food, are an additional requirement for optimum health.

With this in mind, under the premise that free radicals can cause the DNA damage that is thought to cause cancer, and based on the knowledge that antioxidants can neutralise free radicals, the medical establishment hypothesised that artificially increasing antioxidant levels within the human body through the regular supplementation of high dose antioxidants, would reduce free radical damage almost completely, and prevent tumour development. This makes sense if DNA damage is the underlying cause of cancer. To test this, many studies have been performed where high doses of antioxidants were supplied to mitigate free radical damage. Curiously, these studies consistently showed no benefit. In fact, some found that a reduction in free radicals – brought about by flooding the body with abnormal levels of antioxidants – actually increased the risk of cancer,[002] contradicting the mainstream view that free radicals, through DNA damage, generates the disease:

> *'...dietary antioxidants have* **consistently failed to reduce the incidence of carcinoma** *in prospective human clinical trials. Rather, some studies have* **even suggested a harmful effect of antioxidants** *in persons* **at risk for cancer.***
>
> *A recent study by Sayin and colleagues in genetically engineered mouse models that mimic human early non–small-cell lung cancer has confirmed that the* **antioxidants N-acetyl-cysteine and vitamin E actually increase cancer burden** *and mortality in a* **dose-dependent** *manner.'*
>
> *Medscape* **2014**[003]

The above article claims that these antioxidant studies refute the theory that free radicals cause cancer. Other scientists continue to confirm similar findings:

> *'For decades, health-conscious people around the globe have taken antioxidant supplements and eaten foods rich in antioxidants. Yet clinical trials of antioxidant supplements have repeatedly dashed the hopes of consumers who take them hoping to reduce their cancer risk.*

Virtually all such trials have failed to show any protective effect against cancer. In fact, in several trials, antioxidant supplementation has been linked with increased rates of certain cancers. In one trial, smokers taking extra beta carotene had higher, not lower, rates of lung cancer. '

Cold Spring Harbor Laboratory 2014 [004]

Two more studies further confirm that excessive amounts of antioxidants increase the risk of cancer incidence, and in some cases, actually encourage cancer to develop. [338, 339]

'Beta-carotene supplementation has not been shown to have any beneficial effect on cancer prevention. Conversely, it was associated with increased risk not only of lung cancer but also of gastric cancer at doses of 20–30 mg day.

In a randomized controlled trial (RCT) investigating the effect of an antioxidant supplementation containing beta-carotene, supplemented women had a significantly increased risk of skin cancer compared to women in the placebo group.'

International Journal of Cancer 2010 [339]

An article from the *National Cancer Institute* discussing these findings highlights some important points:

'"The findings support the idea that antioxidants, by reducing oxidative stress, [reducing free radicals] benefit tumour cells more than they benefit normal healthy cells," Dr. Morrison added. "The results also support the idea that treating patients with pro-oxidants might be a way to prevent metastasis," he said.'

National Cancer Institute 2015 [190]

Reducing free radicals using antioxidants seems to have the opposite effect by increasing the risk of cancer and encouraging its growth once it has developed. This contradicts the mainstream DNA Theory and the hypothesis put forward, which asserts that DNA damage generates the disease and ongoing DNA damage, caused by free radicals, furthers disease progression by generating more mutations. Rather, a reduction in free radicals and cell damage (fewer mutations) actually accelerates the progression of the disease. Not only does this indicate that free radicals aren't a cause of cancer, but it suggests that DNA damage isn't either because as DNA damage is reduced through a reduction in free radicals, the risk of cancer and it's progression seems to increase.

This is a significant finding, and one where we must be careful regarding any conclusions drawn. For instance, in light of this one could argue that it would be reasonable to conclude that antioxidants are actually bad for us and should be avoided at all costs. Indeed, Dr Bergo warns against taking antioxidant supplements based on this evidence:

> *'Based on the available evidence, Dr Bergo said "he was **extremely concerned** with the **aggressive marketing** of antioxidants to cancer patients."* He said *"And because there's **no strong evidence** that antioxidants are beneficial, cancer patients should be encouraged to **avoid supplements** after they have a diagnosis".'*
>
> <u>**National Cancer Institute**</u> **2015** [190]

But as with most things in life, it's never that black and white, this subject is extremely nuanced. On the one hand antioxidants are essential for health – they reduce free radical damage and inflammation – inflammation is the pre-cursor to many diseases including cancer; so in this respect antioxidants actually prevent cancer. And yet on the other hand in the studies above they appear to be detrimental. As always, the devil is in the detail. Determining why antioxidants increased the risk of cancer in these particular studies is essential to ensure we don't tar all antioxidants with the same brush, and lose sight of the benefits they can provide.

Putting the antioxidant supplement argument aside for a moment, how can these antioxidant studies be explained? Why do they appear to encourage cancer to form contrary to the established view? The reason for this is largely unknown but there are a couple of suggested hypotheses. One asserts that antioxidants are only targeting some free radicals and not others.[905] Another suggests that the free radicals that initially caused cancer, kill cancer cells once they've developed. And by reducing these cancer-damaging free radicals using antioxidants, the disease is able to progress more easily.[190] The issue with the latter claim is that it's not clear how this hypothesis fits with the contradictory notion that further free radical damage is required to generate the additional mutations that are needed for disease progression. The DNA Theory states that once cancer forms, additional mutations are required and occur over time due to increased cell damage from ongoing free radical insult. So, on the one hand the claim is that free radicals generate the disease and are then required to cause further damage to enable disease progression, but on the other hand the same free radicals that caused the disease and are required to promote the disease, are also killing it.

While both views should be taken into consideration, there is an entirely different perspective that can account for these results, and in a less contradictory manner. When we look at cancer through a micro-organism lens, a plausible explanation can be made. As I've already alluded to, the medical literature reveals that free radicals are intentionally used by mitochondria for both cell signalling purposes[907] and as a form of defence against invading micro-organisms.[191, 127]

When a cell is attacked by viruses, bacteria or fungi, mitochondria respond by producing free radicals via oxidative bursts, otherwise known as oxidative stress.[191, 127] The free radicals themselves are also referred to as *Reactive Oxygen Species* (ROS) because mitochondria are reacting to a threat by intentionally creating oxygen free radicals. An immune cell does exactly the same. It will ingest a pathogen and will then intentionally bombard it with a deadly burst of free radicals using an oxidative burst:

> *'Reactive oxygen species (ROS) can attack a diverse range of targets to exert antimicrobial activity, which accounts for their versatility in mediating host defence against a broad range of pathogens.'*
>
> *FEMS Microbiology Review 2013* [150]

Immune cells engulf pathogens containing them within hostile compartments called *phagosomes*, similar to the way that criminals are locked within a cage or a holding cell. The immune cell then bombards the pathogen with several deadly chemical compounds, one of the most effective anti-pathogen compounds are free radicals (ROS):

> *'ROS production by macrophages and neutrophils is a primary mechanism for killing internalized pathogens.'*
>
> *Frontiers in Cellular and Infection Microbiology 2016* [708]

Chemical warfare:

To understand more precisely why over-consumption of antioxidants appear to increase cancer risk, we must think on a cellular level. In the micro-organism world, toxins are created for defence, attack and invasion purposes. Bacteria and fungi are constantly battling for supremacy. Their primary method of attack comes in the form of damaging toxins. For example, the commonly prescribed antibiotic drug *Penicillin* is a toxin derived from a fungus called *Penicillium chrysogenum*. This fungal toxin kills bacteria and is one of the most common antibiotics prescribed today. Likewise, the anti-fungal drug *Nystatin* is created from a toxin produced by the bacteria *Streptomyces noursei* and is effective against fungal infections. Cellular and micro-organism conflict takes place largely through chemical warfare.

So, when a dangerous micro-organism attempts to attack and invade a cell, it will create an array of toxic poisons designed to interfere with cell DNA and disable its defences. As our cells are constantly under threat of attack from micro-organism chemicals, they have learnt to view toxins as a byproduct of these dangerous pathogens. So, when toxic chemicals are discovered by the cell, be it from a micro-organism, or equally a chemotherapy agent, synthetic drugs or antibiotics, mitochondria create free radicals en-masse to kill the invading micro-organism that is assumed to be responsible, and to break down the toxins causing the damage.[794] This is the oxidative stress response that modern medicine refers to. Free radicals, therefore, appear to be an essential part of our immune defence mechanism against invading pathogens and the toxins they create.

And here's the key point: flooding the body with abnormally high quantities of antioxidants to neutralise as many free radicals as possible, will likely dampen the free radical defence mechanism used by immune cells and mitochondria as a form of cell defence against invading pathogens. In other words, a key function of the immune response has been suppressed. Furthermore, as free radicals are used for cell signalling, the functionality of the cell will likely be inhibited. These conditions can benefit an invading micro-organism because it would encounter less resistance to the cells it intends to invade. This can explain why excessive use of antioxidants in the above studies have consistently shown no benefit and even an increase in cancer development – suppression of the immune system, and suppression of cell functionality, via suppression of free radicals, aids the process of pathogen infection.

The following 2015 article from the *National Cancer Institute* states that a reduction in free radicals (immune suppression) through the over-use of antioxidants, can increase tumour growth and metastasis:

> '*Evidence from two new studies in mice shows that antioxidants— dietary supplements commonly used in the belief that they may help prevent disease—**may actually promote tumour growth and metastasis.***

The new findings, authors from both studies said, suggest that cancer patients and people with an increased risk of cancer should avoid taking antioxidant supplements.'

National Cancer Institute **2015** [190]

The involvement of a micro-organism in the process of cancer development perfectly explains this conundrum. But what's more apparent and very telling from the evidence presented above, is that as free radicals and DNA damage is diminished due to antioxidants neutralising the free radical threat, cancer risk oddly increases. This appears to contradict the mainstream view, that free radicals and DNA damage are direct causes of cancer.

Caution – jumping to conclusions with antioxidants:

The concern in presenting these studies is that cancer patients will avoid antioxidants altogether. It's important to recognise that the use of antioxidants, especially during cancer treatment, is nuanced, because when used correctly, and under the right conditions, they can provide a benefit.

While the above experiments have shown a detrimental effect, this is likely due to the excessive levels, and synthetic versions, of antioxidants that were used. For instance, the synthetic version of vitamin E (*Alpha tocopherol*) was used in a number of studies. Synthetic compounds are often inferior to their natural organic counterparts.[905, 906, 908] Alpha tocopherol (the synthetic version of vitamin E) appears to block the cell's ability to absorb the natural version of vitamin E (*gamma tocopherol*).[908] One could argue that a fair trial of antioxidants has not been undertaken in these experiments, because natural vitamin E compounds may respond and react differently to that of synthetic derivatives.

It is my understanding that our cells utilise natural substances as and when they are needed, whereas synthetic compounds tend to block cell receptors and force themselves upon the cells that utilise them, cells seem incapable of using them selectively. If this is indeed the case, then this may explain why these studies increased cancer risk – these synthetic antioxidants were not being used by the cell in a controlled manner, leading to excessive suppression of the free-radical-based immune response. Therefore, it seems preferable to consume natural antioxidant compounds over and above synthetic compounds where possible.

In today's toxic and stressful world we produce far more free radicals through oxidative stress than we have done in the past. Arguably, our internal antioxidant reservoir is less capable of dealing with this increased and sustained free radical onslaught, and likely diminished more readily. This is not helped by conventional food, which, as I discuss in Chapter 16, contains at least 40% fewer antioxidants in comparison to the organic food that was once the norm. Furthermore, the processed foods we consume in the west also contain very little antioxidants while they tend to promote inflammation and oxidative stress, increasing the free radical burden. It would make sense then, to top up this depleted antioxidant reservoir with natural organic antioxidant supplements. Supporting this concept the following study states:

> *'...our endogenous [**internal**] antioxidant defence systems are **incomplete** without exogenous [**external**] originating reducing compounds such as vitamin C, vitamin E, carotenoids and polyphenols, playing an essential role in many antioxidant mechanisms in living organisms. Therefore, there is **continuous demand** for exogenous [external] **antioxidants** in order to prevent oxidative stress.'*

Oxidative Medicine and Cellular Longevity **2010** [908]

It is also worth noting that natural vitamins, as opposed to their synthetic counterparts, also possess other beneficial properties, they are not just antioxidants.

Another consideration is the dosage and how it is administered (orally or intravenously) – this matters because some antioxidants can become pro-oxidants by actually generating free radicals.[908] This can be beneficial depending on the type of treatment being undertaken, and can be used to a patient's advantage. For instance, chemotherapy generates free radicals; arguably this is the underlying reason for its potential effectiveness – it is a 'pro-oxidant' therapy. The goal of chemotherapy is to cause maximum damage to cancer cells. Before chemotherapy treatment starts, a potential strategy to improve it's effectiveness would be to temporarily deplete the body's antioxidant reserves, as this would allow chemotherapy to cause more damage (fewer free radicals would be neutralised during treatment). This can be achieved by using particular antioxidant supplements at high doses. This leads to a reduction of internal levels of antioxidants within the body through a pro-oxidant mechanism.[906, 908]

Some time after chemotherapy treatment has been administered, it may be beneficial to re-introduce antioxidants at lower doses to aid with the scavenging of the extra free radicals that pro-oxidant therapies produce. Thus the function of an antioxidant system is not just to remove oxidants (free radicals), but to keep them at an optimum level. This can be manipulated further by using antioxidants in a way that enables them to deplete antioxidant reserves with a view to improving pro-oxidant therapies. Furthermore, antioxidants themselves can be repurposed as pro-oxidant therapies, as we see with intravenous vitamin C therapy.

The take home message then, is that so long as natural antioxidants are being consumed at the correct dose and under supervision from a medical professional who understands the complexities involved, then antioxidant supplementation can be a useful tool in our battle against cancer. Given the nuances discussed here, it would be irresponsible to make any sweeping statement to the effect that antioxidant supplementation is bad, and should be avoided altogether, when antioxidants can be extremely beneficial if used under the right conditions.

II

KNOWLEDGE IS POWER

CH07

Making sense of it all

So far we've covered some uncomfortable realities that indicate we're still some way from understanding the disease and treating it effectively, despite the monumental effort made by scientists. It would now be helpful to spend a little time learning about key elements within our cells that are intrinsically involved in the development of cancer. Understanding these basic concepts will make it easier to converse with your oncologist and also help to clarify how and why the disease develops. Before we head into the detail it would be helpful to run through the basic life-cycle of a cancerous tumour:

- **Failure of cell death mechanisms:** Cell death fails to occur when it should. This causes cells to bunch together in the form of a lump.
- **Immune system evasion:** The immune system fails to recognise these rogue cells and does not kill them as it normally would.
- **Energy switch:** The energy system of these cells switches to glycolysis, leading to an increase in glucose and glutamine absorption and increased growth.
- **Loss of growth control:** Sustained glycolysis results in a proliferative state leading to perpetual cell duplication. As these

cells appear incapable of committing programmed cell death, a tumour slowly develops.

- **Blood supply increase**: The need for more nutrients stimulates new blood vessel growth to feed the expanding tumour.
- **Invasive expansion**: The tumour becomes invasive by expanding into the surrounding tissue.
- **Migration of cells**: Cells from the tumour migrate into the blood stream and re-settle at other locations within the body. This is known as *metastasis*.
- **New growth**: A new tumour forms at this distant site. The cancer has successfully spread, and the growth cycle continues.

The basic structure of a cell:

There are many factors and cell components worthy of mention when discussing cancer, which can make attempting to understand the disease a daunting prospect. These can be refined and simplified into a number of primary factors from which all other aspects of cancer arise. Let's start with the following three terms:

1. Nucleus
2. Mitochondria
3. Cytoplasm.

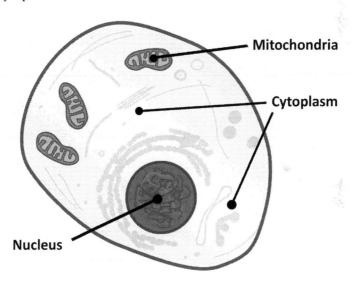

The nucleus is where cell DNA is stored. It's this DNA that is being referred to in the DNA Theory. Damage to these DNA genes are thought to cause cancer.

Surrounding the nucleus we find the cytoplasm, which is a clear gel-like substance that fills the void of the cell and contains all the other elements that operate within it. Energy needed for the cell to function can be generated directly within the cytoplasm itself. This process is known as *glycolysis*, which converts glucose into lactate, also referred to as 'lactic acid'. This is one of two main energy systems present within our cells – of the two glycolysis represents the backup energy system and features heavily in cancer.

The main energy system is found within mitochondria (pronounced mito-kon-dria), which are bacteria-like entities that float around within the cytoplasm. Mitochondria combine oxygen with glucose to create more energy than glycolysis can provide. The creation of energy via mitochondria is called *aerobic respiration*. A crucial difference between the two energy systems is that aerobic respiration – performed inside mitochondria – requires oxygen to produce energy, while *glycolysis* – performed within the cytoplasm – does not require oxygen (more on this a little later).

The role of DNA:

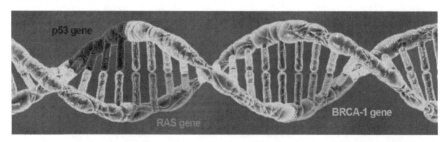

Regarding the DNA found within the nucleus, the image above depicts the familiar double-helix structure of DNA found in every cell of the body (except red blood cells). It's made up of the nutrients we obtain from food. Approximately 17 million cells die and are replaced every minute in the adult body. That means there are a lot of good-quality nutrients required to rebuild and maintain cells. Without those nutrients, DNA and cell functions will become damaged, leading to disease.

DNA is essentially an instruction manual of how to build and operate the cell. The ladder-like rungs of DNA represent different groups of genes, as is shown in the image above, which depicts the p53 gene (the cell-death gene), the RAS gene (the cell-growth gene), and the BRCA-1 gene (a DNA repair gene). There are approximately 21,000 genes within human DNA. These genes act like switches or levers; they control specific cell functions by switching them on or off and they issue signals to create specific proteins. These proteins are used for many tasks, including the building of cell structures.

When toxic chemicals are absorbed into the cell they can bind to DNA genes preventing them from working correctly. When this happens, the sophisticated DNA repair mechanisms cut away the affected area of DNA and replaces it with a new copy created from the nutrients we consume. This is why a good diet is critical for our overall health; without the correct nutrients, DNA cannot be repaired effectively, which increases the risk of mutations.

Each DNA gene has a specific role to play, so if a particular gene is damaged, it will cause a specific problem termed a 'genetic disorder'. This faulty or mutated gene will fail to produce a particular signal or protein when needed or may create an abnormal protein.

CHROMOSOME

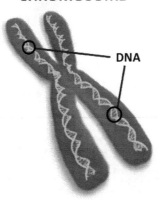

DNA

Our DNA is neatly packaged inside sausage-shaped containers called chromosomes, which are stored within the nucleus. Each human cell contains 23 complete chromosomes, which our 21,000 DNA genes are distributed between. Toxins can be absorbed into the nucleus of the cell and damage the DNA contained within these chromosomes and even damage the chromosomes themselves, which can further impair DNA function. Chromosomal damage is known as abnormal 'ploidy' or 'aneuploidy'. Aneuploidy is present within the majority of cancers.[897]

DNA and chromosomes aside, another fundamental aspect of cancer is abnormal energy activity. Mitochondria, which exist within the cytoplasm surrounding the nucleus, produce the bulk of energy in the majority of healthy cells.

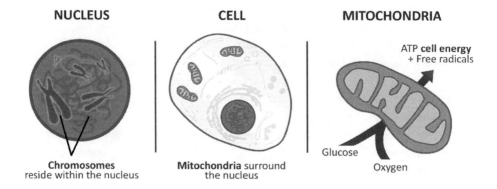

NUCLEUS	**CELL**	**MITOCHONDRIA**

ATP **cell energy**
+ Free radicals

Glucose

Oxygen

| **Chromosomes** reside within the nucleus | **Mitochondria** surround the nucleus | |

Cancer metabolism:

As previously discussed, mitochondria combine glucose with oxygen to produce ATP (Adenosine triphosphate) energy, which is used to power the cell. This particular energy pathway is known as *aerobic respiration*; it is the main energy system used within the cell. Effectively, the food we consume and the air we breathe are combined within mitochondria to create energy. The overall process of creating energy within the cell is referred to as *metabolism*. Cells are metabolising – breaking-down and combining compounds – to create energy. Combining a single glucose molecule with oxygen inside mitochondria generates an energy output of approximately 36 ATP energy units:

Aerobic respiration: Glucose + oxygen = 36 ATP

When oxygen is unavailable mitochondria can't produce energy. This causes the cell to switch to its backup energy system, where glucose is converted to lactate (lactic acid) instead, this pathway is called *glycolysis* or *fermentation*. This pathway only generates 2 ATP units of energy for every glucose molecule used, and it does not use oxygen. This backup energy system operates directly within the cytoplasm:

Glycolysis: Glucose > lactate (lactic acid) = 2 ATP[418]

Technically speaking, there are two parts to glycolysis which can be confusing if not understood; to clarify, I'll quickly explain this two part process.

At the start of energy metabolism, glucose is absorbed into a cell and broken down into a substance called *pyruvate*. This first stage of energy creation is also the first stage of glycolysis – this glucose breakdown to pyruvate needs to occur before any other step in the energy process is undertaken. So technically speaking partial glycolysis has occurred.

In the second stage, pyruvate will either be offered to mitochondria to generate energy using oxygen, providing oxygen is accessible and mitochondria are not defective, or, pyruvate will stay within the cytoplasm and be used in the second stage of glycolysis to complete the energy-creation process – this normally occurs when there is a lack of oxygen for mitochondria to use. If pyruvate stays within the cytoplasm for the energy process to be completed, this is when you could say that the full process of glycolysis has occurred:

Cell energy creation

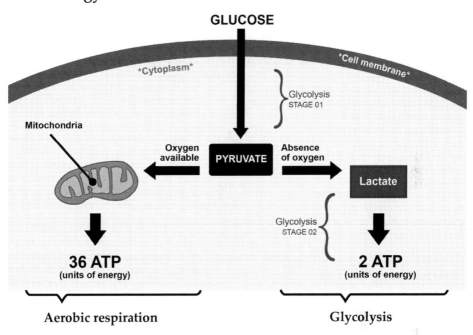

To clarify: when pyruvate is transferred to mitochondria and it is combined with oxygen to create energy, this process is referred to as **aerobic respiration**. That is, mitochondria are respiring (breathing if you will) using oxygen to create energy; remember, aerobic means 'with oxygen'. When oxygen isn't available, mitochondria cannot respire to produce energy, in this instance the energy process will be completed by the latter stage of glycolysis because it doesn't need oxygen to generate energy. The full name for this process is **anaerobic glycolysis**. Full glycolysis (stage one and two) has essentially occurred because oxygen is lacking. Remember, **anaerobic** means 'without oxygen'.

This energy switch to glycolysis is normal, and can occur as a result of cell damage – where the oxygen supply to mitochondria is temporarily lost, or to complement aerobic respiration in instances where we sprint, and cannot convert oxygen quick enough to meet the sharply increased energy demand.

To provide an analogy: imagine there are two chefs working in a kitchen, the head chef is called 'aerobic respiration' while the sous chef is called 'glycolysis'. Glycolysis prepares the food ready for cooking (glucose to pyruvate conversion), then asks aerobic respiration if they have the time to cook the food. Most of the time aerobic respiration will have time to do so (oxygen is available), but on other occasions they won't (no oxygen is available), so glycolysis will do the cooking instead, or, will help with the cooking to get the meal cooked faster, so both will work together (when we sprint).

Now here's the crucial distinction to understand with cancer: cancer cells will use glycolysis **even when oxygen is present** and available for mitochondria to use. This is abnormal because mitochondria should produce energy for the cell when oxygen is available. This is the equivalent of the head chef being available to cook the food, but being ignored by the sous chef who decides to cook the food themselves, without asking. The correct term to use in this instance – and this is where it can become confusing – is **aerobic glycolysis,** not 'anaerobic glycolysis', because glycolysis is occurring (glycolysis is cooking the food) even in the presence of oxygen (even when the head chef is available to cook). For simplicity, rather than referring to cancer cells using *aerobic glycolysis* for their energy needs, I will just use the generic term 'glycolysis', partly because it's easier to understand, and because tumour cells may be using both anaerobic glycolysis and aerobic glycolysis at any given moment in time – some areas of the tumour do not have access to oxygen, while others do. Regardless of whether its anaerobic or aerobic, the outcome is the same – lactic acid is produced as a byproduct, and only 2 ATP units of energy are produced for every single glucose molecule converted.

This reliance on glycolysis, especially in the presence of oxygen, indicates that something is wrong with mitochondria, that they appear to have become faulty. Since it was Otto Warburg who, in 1924, discovered this abnormal use of glycolysis in the presence of oxygen, it has been termed the 'Warburg effect'. So, when it comes to cancer, glycolysis and the Warburg effect refer to the same thing. And as glycolysis only generates 2 units of ATP energy per glucose molecule used, a cancer cell needs to consume at least 18 times the quantity of glucose molecules to match the 36 ATP units of energy that mitochondria can produce by comparison through aerobic respiration. This explains why cancer cells absorb far greater quantities of glucose than the healthy cells around them; they require increased amounts to function normally (glucose is obtained by breaking down sugar from food).

To put things into perspective, it helps to understand the way that cells operate by manipulating atoms to create new substances. Molecules form the basis of all the structures of life. They are made when two or more atoms are combined and stick together. For instance, an oxygen molecule (O_2) contains two oxygen atoms. One water molecule (H_2O) comprises two hydrogen atoms and one oxygen atom that bond together. One tiny droplet of water visible to the human eye contains approximately 170,000,000,000,000,000,000,000 of H_2O molecules. So when considering the size of cells, mitochondria, DNA, and micro-organisms, it helps to realise that these organisms are splitting atoms apart and re-combining them into different substances. This is why scientists cannot make concrete assertions on many aspects of cancer; our current technology simply cannot see to this level of magnification. It is a testament to the brilliance of scientists and the techniques they have developed that they can make any sense of this invisible world at all.

Free radicals:

Splitting two oxygen (O_2) atoms apart can result in the production of a free radical. Bonded together as pairs, oxygen contains an even number of electrons, so it is stable. But on their own, they contain an odd number of electrons – an unstable situation in which the odd unpaired electron seeks to bond with, or steal, an electron from other molecules. This can cause instability and tissue damage. It's important to note that mitochondria can create these single oxygen 'free radicals' by manipulating atoms and their electrons. In fact, mitochondria sometimes create and release free radicals as an unwanted byproduct of normal energy production; other times mitochondria create them intentionally for cell-signalling purposes or for defending the cell from invading micro-organisms (free radicals can be used to kill pathogens).[697] As previously noted, modern medicine currently views free radicals as the cause of the DNA damage that is thought to cause cancer, because it's assumed that the accidental release of free radicals during energy metabolism, damages DNA.

The take-home messages here are that free radicals can cause cell damage and can be created and controlled by mitochondria for specific purposes.

Antioxidants:

Antioxidants are molecules that can block free radical damage by providing them with the extra electron they seek; this neutralises their damaging effects, hence the name *anti* (against) – *oxidants* (oxygen). Plants produce antioxidants to stave off the damage caused by oxidation (reaction of fruit with oxygen). For example, soon after biting into an apple, it starts to go brown. This is the apple reacting to, and being damaged by, oxygen.

Like free radicals, antioxidants are also produced by mitochondria and are used to mop up any damaging free radicals that escape. Antioxidants are produced from copper, zinc and magnesium, as well as a few amino acids such as cysteine, which are found within our diet. When discussing cancer with your oncologist or researching the disease, you will find that free radicals and antioxidants are often mentioned.

Mitochondria and their separate DNA:

In early evolution, mitochondria appear to have been separate bacterial organisms that, at some point, merged with our cells. Before this merging of the two organisms, cells produced energy by converting glucose to lactate, the process we now refer to as glycolysis.[713] Mitochondria provided the cell with the ability to create energy by combining glucose with oxygen. This merging of the two organisms fuelled evolution because energy creation became much more efficient, requiring far less glucose to produce energy.

The important point of note here is that mitochondria have their own DNA separate from the DNA contained within the cell's nucleus. This separate DNA highlights that mitochondria were once an entirely independent organism. Essentially, our cells contain two different types of DNA code. And this is the critical point to understand: mitochondria communicate directly with the DNA contained within the nucleus, causing changes to this nuclear DNA:

*'...it is well known that the nDNA [nucleus] **interacts with** a physically and functionally separated genome, the **mitochondrial DNA** (mtDNA).*

*The interaction between these two genomes is **bidirectional**, meaning that there are both a flow of information from the nucleus toward the mitochondria and a mitochondrial **retrograde signalling pathway**.'*

Biomedical Research International 2014 [005]

Mitochondrial DNA is expressed as *mtDNA* in the medical literature, and the DNA contained within the nucleus is expressed as *nDNA* to help distinguish the two. It's important to acknowledge that mitochondria and the nucleus communicate directly with each other, and that two separate sets of DNA exist within our cells. When mitochondria are communicating with and influencing the DNA within the nucleus, this is referred to as *retrograde signalling*.

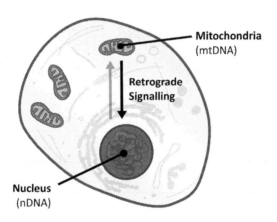

And here lies one of the major flaws within the mainstream understanding of cancer. The DNA Theory, which claims that DNA mutation is responsible for driving cancer, crucially ignores the mtDNA found within mitochondria, even though mitochondria are found to be dysfunctional in almost all cancers, can control cell death and cell growth mechanisms, and can directly influence nDNA. How can an accurate conclusion possibly be drawn when a huge chunk of the puzzle is not being taken into account? This arguably goes some way to explaining why scientists are struggling to make sense of the disease and produce effective treatments.

Cell death mechanisms:

The next aspect of a cell to cover is 'programmed cell death', also known as *apoptosis* (pronounced apop-toe-sis). This is a critical mechanism to understand because it's at the heart of tumour growth. Apoptosis has been engineered over millions of years as a fail-safe mechanism to protect the host organism from damaged cells that threaten its overall well-being. When irreparable damage occurs to the cell it triggers the 'self-destruct button' that leads to the cell's death and a replacement being produced. As the human body replaces millions of cells every minute, harbouring cells that don't die when they should can cause severe problems, such as tumour growth. Cell death mechanisms need to be working properly to prevent these growths from developing.

The DNA Theory asserts that defective DNA genes are the reason for the failure of cells to initiate apoptosis when required, which leads to an accumulation of cells (a tumour). But there are other mechanisms independent from nDNA that can instigate cell death. Mitochondria can also instigate apoptosis. In fact, they are pivotal to the process, perhaps more so than nDNA:

> *'Because mitochondria are also a central component of **apoptosis (programmed cell death)**, which is routinely used to rid the body of cells that are no longer useful or functioning properly, **mitochondrial dysfunction that inhibits cell death** can contribute to the **development of cancer.'***
>
> ### *Encyclopedia Britannica* [006]

Additionally, cell death can be initiated by immune cells using a different pathway. To achieve this, specific immune cells called *natural killer cells* (NK cells) bind to external connectors (called ligands) and trigger the cell death process.

These other cell death mechanisms are all part of a safety system designed so that the cell does not have to rely on one pathway alone. This indicates that cancer is unlikely to be a result of DNA damage, because even if the DNA-based cell death gene was mutated, there are other mechanisms that can instigate apoptosis.

Stem cells:

Another contentious factor is the cancer stem cell. Proponents of the DNA Theory often do not acknowledge their involvement, but, thankfully, many scientists do. The cancer stem cell is the last feature of the disease to appreciate in order to evaluate the mechanisms involved. Evidence indicates that these stem cells are responsible for infinite tumour growth, chemotherapy resistance, immune system evasion, and the spread of cancer cells to other areas of the body.

Stem cells are unique in that, under favourable conditions, they can replicate themselves indefinitely; they are effectively immortal. They can create all the other cells of the body, and have the capacity to generate a limitless supply. By comparison, regular cells have a limited life span and can only replicate themselves a certain number of times before they are programmed to self-destruct. Regular cells cannot create all types of body cells in the way stem cells can. For example, a skin cell can only create another skin cell, whereas a stem cell cancer create a skin cell, brain cell, or any other type. Cancer stem cells are covered by a different theory called the *Cancer Stem Cell Theory*:

> *'Emerging evidence suggest the existence of **cancer stem cells** (CSCs), a population of cells with the capacity to **self-renew**, differentiate and be capable of **initiating** and **sustaining tumour growth**.*
>
> *In addition, CSCs are believed to be responsible for cancer **recurrence**, anticancer drug **resistance**, and **metastasis** [cancer spread].'*
>
> **<u>Seminars in Cancer Biology</u> 2016** [273]

Effectively, before a normal cell dies, it sends out signals of its impending fate. These signals reach stem cells which create a replacement cell.[178] This is how most of our cells regenerate – stem cells replace dying cells as needed. The problem with treating a tumour is that approximately 2% of its mass is made up of cancer stem cells.[177, 178] These superior cell types are highly resistant to chemotherapy and can replenish the regular cancer cells that are killed by the treatment. The involvement of cancer stem cells helps to explain why many current treatments are largely ineffective at producing long-term remission, and why chemotherapy resistance occurs, because the tumour can be re-grown from these surviving cancer stem cells.

Microbiome:

The human body contains approximately 30 trillion human cells, dwarfing this is our microbiome which contains an estimated 39 trillion microbial cells including bacteria, fungi and viruses that live on and within us. Due to their small size, these organisms make up about 1-3 per cent of our body mass, but this doesn't make them any less influential.

Each of our cells contain around 21,000 DNA genes, but collectively, the sum of the DNA genes contained within the microbiome is potentially 500 times more.[859] Moreover, the ability of microbes to evolve quickly, swap genes, multiply and adapt to changing circumstances give them – and us, their hosts – remarkable abilities that we're only now beginning to fathom.[859]

The microbiome within our gut help to breakdown food, provide us with essential nutrients and protect us from harmful pathogens as well as toxins. Some of these micro-organisms can cause harm if they aren't kept in check by the more abundant beneficial bacteria. This collection of micro-organisms is known as the gut microbiome. There are various populations of micro-organisms living throughout the body, each organ, for instance, appears to harbour it's own unique microbiome population. Recent evidence confirms that all tumours also contain their own distinct population of micro-organisms – not only are scientists surprised by this, but they are at a loss to explain how these tumours became populated with these little critters.

We are only just beginning to understand this complex and dynamic relationship. Interestingly, studies show that the microbiome directly affects our immune system, aids in cell repair, can cause inflammation to occur, and can even inhibit or enhance the effectiveness of drugs.[821] They have a direct influence, almost to the extent that they appear to be managing our health similar to how a farmer tends to his crops. This is important to acknowledge because most mainstream theories, the DNA Theory in particular, do not take into account this micro-organism influence, especially when it comes to cancer. And yet our microbiome plays a pivotal role when it comes to our health. The question is, have we misunderstood cancer because we've overlooked, or misjudged, the influence of these micro-organisms?

Summary:

We've covered a lot of detail, so it might be helpful to quickly summarise this content:

- There are approximately 21,000 genes that make up our DNA.
- DNA resides within, and is shared between, 23 chromosomes, which are themselves contained within the cell nucleus.

- The DNA Theory asserts that damage to this DNA is the cause of cancer.
- Challenging this view is the involvement of mitochondria which create energy for the cell to function.
- Mitochondria have their own DNA which communicates bi-directionally with the DNA within the nucleus.
- Mitochondria are also involved with cell death and cell growth.
- The energy switch that occurs in all cancers points to the conclusion that mitochondria are defective. It would seem that the conditions of cancer are a direct result of this mitochondrial dysfunction rather than the random DNA damage that occurs within the nucleus.
- As part of the regular process of metabolism, mitochondria produce cell-damaging free radicals, as well as antioxidants to neutralise this free radical threat.
- The failure of the cell death gene found within the nucleus (commonly known as the p53 gene) is claimed to be the leading cause of tumour growth; however, there are at least three cell death mechanisms that all operate independently of one another.
- Apart from the p53 gene, cell death can be instigated by mitochondria as well as certain immune cells known as natural killer cells (NK cells). The DNA Theory is unable to account for why these two other mechanisms also fail.
- Stem cells are superior cell types that can create any other cells within the body, in any required quantity.
- Cancer stem cells make up approximately 2% of tumours, and are highly resistant to toxins such as chemotherapy.
- Cancer stem cells can create a limitless supply of cells and appear to be responsible for the growth of new tumours in other areas of the body.
- The microbiome refers to the trillions of micro-organisms that live on and within us, it is an emerging field of study. These micro-organisms directly interact with our tissue and our health is intimately entwined with theirs. Recent evidence confirms that all tumours harbour their own unique microbiome that appears to be directly influencing the disease.

Incidentally, proponents of the DNA Theory fail to recognise the relevance and involvement of cancer stem cells and all the attributes we find associated with them. They also fail to take into account the influence of the microbiome. In studies, scientists are drawing conclusions based on the incorrect assumption that tumours are sterile (free of micro-organisms). Furthermore, the Metabolic Theory, which recognises the cancer cell's abnormal energy state, is also largely ignored. This of course begs the question: how can mainstream oncologists assert their treatment solutions are the best, and that they are an authority on cancer, when a large number of factors critical to understanding the disease are missing, or simply not included, in their evaluation of the disease?

CH.08

How cancer forms

If cancer isn't caused by DNA mutation then what other factor(s) could be driving the disease? While there are many alternative theories describing different mechanisms involved, there is one that stands out. The 'Metabolic Theory' describes how the energy system of a cancer cell appears to be operating abnormally, and that it's a fault with this energy system that leads to cancer. In effect cancer cells require more energy to function and are sensitive to energy restriction. Based on this knowledge, Jane McLelland was able to successfully starve her cancer of the energy it needed to survive. Her approach to treating her own disease is detailed within her book *'How to Starve Cancer'* and can be adapted to suit different cancer types, but more on this later.

The discovery of a dysfunctional energy system in cancer cells was made in the 1920s by Otto Warburg, and has matured to become the most accurate mainstream cancer theory, although you wouldn't know it because the Metabolic Theory is rarely mentioned despite it's superiority – such is the devotion to the DNA Theory. If the Metabolic Theory is indeed more accurate, then we should be in for some exciting developments in the treatment of cancer. But how do we assess a cancer theory to determine its validity, how can we confidently make the claim that the Metabolic Theory is more accurate?

The hallmarks of cancer:

Cancer follows a predictable and consistent pattern of disease. Nearly all cancers share some fundamental attributes or behaviours, which have become known as the hallmarks of cancer. These hallmarks were identified and categorised by Douglas Hanahan and Robert Weinberg in the year 2000 and then updated in 2011. Their seminal paper has become the most cited medical paper ever published in the medical journal *Cell*. By identifying these hallmarks, Hanahan and Weinberg have provided scientists with a platform from which any cancer theory can be assessed. The accuracy of any theory, therefore, can be determined by the number of hallmarks it can account for.

There are 10 officially recognised hallmarks that are specific to cancer, which every cancer theory is attempting to explain – four more have recently been proposed by Professor Hanahan and are briefly discussed in Chapter 11. Until these other four are acknowledged as key hallmarks, these 10 remain the accepted hallmarks to explain. Any theory that can explain them all is likely to be the theory that has successfully identified the underlying cause of cancer, as it's highly unlikely that more than one factor could be responsible for generating all 10 hallmarks independently. That's not to say we should stop looking or investigating other potential causes when such a theory exists, I'm just highlighting the relevance, and potential benefit, of a theory that can explain so many factors related to the disease. Thanks to the work of these great scientists we can now directly compare the accuracy of different cancer theories by assessing them against these hallmarks.

Initially, Hanahan and Weinberg identified six characteristics that are now commonly accepted as the disease's main hallmarks, traits that are shared by all solid cancers. Lymphomas and leukaemias – cancers of immune cells and blood cells – are not classed as solid cancers. As such some hallmarks, such as 'extended blood vessel growth', do not apply because a solid tumour is required for this hallmark to occur. For an abnormal growth to be labelled as cancer, it was initially required to display just the following six specific hallmarks:

1. Uncontrolled cell growth
2. Resistance to anti-growth signals
3. Evasion of cell death signals
4. Limitless replication
5. Extended blood vessel growth
6. Invasion of local tissue and metastasis.

These came to be known as the *Hanahan and Weinberg Hallmarks of Cancer*. You may have noticed that an abnormal energy system isn't included as one of the hallmarks, even though a dysfunctional energy system is present within every cancer and is recognised in the medical literature.

Outraged at this, Professor Pete Pederson, who was working on the Metabolic Theory at the time, challenged Weinberg for choosing not to include the Warburg effect in the hallmark list and did this in a very public way. At a *National Institute of Health* seminar, Pederson announced:

> *'The hallmarks of cancer have been listed in a very well-known book now by Bob Weinberg of MIT, and he lists six hallmarks of cancer. One of these, the **first and most important one, he omitted**. This broadcast I understand is being broadcast throughout the world, so he'll get this probably in the mail tomorrow... many of us are aware of the list, but the one he omitted from this list is the **Warburg effect**. It is the oldest known property of cancer, and it is a **characteristic of every cancer**.'*
>
> **Tripping over the truth, Travis Christofferson 2014** [258]

A year after Professor Pederson's critical remarks in 2009, Professor Weinberg updated these hallmarks to include the Warburg effect – the faulty energy system that had been left out. Subsequently, these six hallmarks were increased to 10 in an update called *Hallmarks of cancer: The Next Generation*. The four added were:

7. Abnormal metabolic pathways (Warburg effect)
8. Evasion of the immune system
9. Genome instability (DNA damage)
10. Inflammation.

The abnormal energy system identified in the 1920s and explained by the Metabolic Theory was finally acknowledged a decade after the original hallmark list. However, this is not to say that much has changed from the patient perspective – the Metabolic Theory and it's associated treatments are rarely discussed. Nevertheless, now that scientists have agreed that these hallmarks represent 10 fundamental traits of the disease, we can use them as a way of assessing the accuracy of any cancer theory to determine its validity.

Hallmarks and the DNA Theory:

This would be a good moment to assess the validity of the DNA and metabolic theories, with the aim of gaining some clarity in the sea of complexity around cancer mechanisms. So, to claim the DNA Theory correct, and for mainstream medicine to justify creating the DNA-based treatments they are currently creating and using, scientists would need to show which DNA mutations account for each of the 10 hallmarks; after all, specific mutations are claimed to be responsible for generating and driving the disease. Identifying the pattern of DNA mutations for all 10 hallmarks would indicate that DNA is the underlying cause of cancer and that targeting these mutations with DNA-based drugs would be the correct treatment approach to take. But unfortunately when assessed, what we find is a worrying inability of the DNA Theory to explain most of these hallmarks. This finally gives us confidence in dismissing this theory to focus on more accurate theories that can help us truly understand the disease and how to treat it. With this in mind I only briefly discuss these flaws below, especially as it's already clear from previous chapters that the DNA Theory fails to explain cancer.

The primary DNA gene associated with tumour development is the p53 gene, as it controls the cell death mechanism. Prior to 2005, the p53 gene was assumed to be the most common mutation discovered in cancer. From a limited amount of data, it was estimated to be mutated in more than 60% of tumours.[070] But, according to *The Cancer Genome Atlas* DNA database, the p53 gene was found to be mutated in only 35% of samples analysed.[357, 776]

To try to explain this, scientists have suggested that many different mutations could cause the disease. But, when we look at other key genes that could be responsible, such as the p63 and p73 genes, these are rarely mutated.[204] The unlikelihood of DNA being responsible is further highlighted by the fact there are two copies of each DNA gene, and both need to be damaged for a tumour to grow. Given that between 8 to 12 mutations are said to be required for cancer to form,[547] this means that at least 16 to 24 DNA mutations are actually necessary for cancer to occur, and yet it frequently develops with only one or two mutations, and even without any mutations at all. This indicates that DNA damage is merely a symptom of the disease.

The RAS gene (which deals with cell growth) was estimated to be mutated in 25% of cancers,[201] but the latest data also shows this to be lower at around 18% in the samples analysed.[357] This is significant because if we are to explain how a tumour forms using DNA we would expect to see that both the RAS and p53 genes are mutated in 100% of cancers, but this isn't the case:

> *'Despite enormous efforts, the currently popular **gene mutation hypothesis** has **failed to identify cancer-specific mutations** with transforming function and **cannot explain why cancer occurs** only many months to decades after mutation by carcinogens...'*
>
> <u>*Proc Natl Acad Sci U S A*</u> **2000** [165]

> *'...**despite 65 years of research** on the **mutation theory**, there is **still no proof for even one set of mutations** that is able to convert a normal cell to a cancer cell.'*
>
> <u>*Genes*</u> **2018** [611]

Significantly, a 2008 study analysing data from The Cancer Genome Atlas project attempted to discover the genes responsible for the sixth hallmark: the spread of cancer (metastasis). The study couldn't find any genes responsible and was forced to conclude:

> *'Comprehensive sequencing was **unable to find a single mutation responsible** for the most important quality of cancer – the ability of cancer to spread and cause 90% of all cancer deaths.'*
>
> **Travis Christofferson. Tripping over the truth 2014** [258]

Consider also that no DNA gene has been found to be conclusively responsible for causing a faulty energy system, blood vessel growth, immune evasion, and that regular cancer cells cannot replicate themselves indefinitely. It then becomes clear that the DNA Theory can't account for eight out of 10 hallmarks – that's a failure to explain at least 80% of the disease. This appears to correlate with the American *National Cancer Institutes'* statement that up to 80% of cancer studies are estimated to be incorrect, because they can't be replicated using the DNA mutations claimed to be responsible?[018]

The two remaining hallmarks that the DNA Theory can partially explain are nine (DNA damage) and 10 (inflammation), but even these hallmarks are not themselves caused by mutated DNA. Carcinogens can account for both of them because they cause DNA damage and inflammation when absorbed into the cell. The DNA Theory, therefore, cannot account for the following eight hallmarks:

1. Uncontrolled cell growth
2. Resistance to anti-growth signals
3. Evasion of cell death signals
4. Limitless replication
5. Extended blood vessel growth
6. Invasion of local tissue and metastasis
7. Abnormal metabolic pathways (faulty energy system)
8. Evasion of the immune system.

The following two syndromes further indicate that DNA damage is not the root cause of the disease: *methyl-deficiency* (a lack of vitamin B12, B9 and choline) causes DNA damage and is an unofficial hallmark of all cancers. So too is *chromosomal damage*, which is directly associated with DNA damage. So, where we find both methyl-deficiency and chromosomal damage, we would expect to see cancer. However, the below study found the opposite:

> *'...children with **ICF syndrome**, a very rare **DNA methylation-deficiency** and **chromosome breakage syndrome**, have **not** been reported to have cancer.'*

> <u>*Oncogene*</u> 2002 [175]

Where these children exhibited similar DNA damage to that witnessed in cancer, it didn't generate malignancy, as the DNA Theory suggests it should – once again contradicting the mainstream theory. Furthermore, obesity is a primary risk factor for cancer, but as Dr Jason Fung points out: *'Being overweight or obese is **not mutagenic**. Having excess body fat **does not increase your risk of mutations**'*,[826] in other words, obesity underlines the lack of a relationship between DNA mutations and cancer.

Proponents of the more recent *Tissue Organization Field Theory* of cancer, who lay out the numerous flaws and contradictions present within the DNA theory, state:

> *'We argue that it is necessary to abandon the somatic mutation theory.'*

> <u>*Molecular Carcinogenesis*</u> **2000** [877]

The *Somatic Mutation Theory* is the official title of the DNA Theory. To summarise and consider other key points:

- In Chapter 2, I discussed the DNA transfer experiments where cancerous DNA was used to grow new mice – these experiments yielded normal growth instead of the tumour growth that was expected, indicating that DNA is not responsible.

- According to the DNA Theory, DNA mutations should be consistent, a clear pattern of DNA mutations would need to be present to bring about each cancer type. However, and contrary to the mainstream theory, DNA mutations are random, even within the same tumour.
- In many cases there aren't enough DNA mutations to actually cause the disease, if indeed mutations were the cause.
- In fact, some tumours develop without any DNA mutations being present at all. In these instances something other than DNA is unquestionably driving the disease.
- In Chapter 6, I discussed free radicals and the antioxidant experiments, which showed that when free radicals and DNA damage were reduced, the risk of cancer actually increased, the opposite of what the DNA Theory predicts should be happening.
- To compound this, the *National Cancer Institute* in America estimated that 80% of the million studies that currently form our understanding of cancer, are incorrect, because they can't be replicated.
- When analysed against the 10 hallmarks of cancer, the DNA Theory appears to only explain 20% of them, confirming that the mainstream theory remains unproven.
- As we would expect, given the above, DNA-based drug treatments have been largely ineffective, and have made no significant impact on cancer death rates.

Given these major contradictions it is reasonable to conclude that DNA damage/mutation is not the underlying cause of cancer, just as Cyril Darlington concluded, three quarters of a century ago, in 1948 (this was referenced in Chapter 2).[257] Surely then, isn't it time to consider other cancer theories and new perspectives?

BRCA1 – the inescapable link to mitochondria:

BRCA1 stands for 'Breast Cancer Type 1' and is a gene involved in DNA repair; it is implicated in breast and ovarian cancer. Oncologists often claim that a faulty BRCA1 gene increases the risk of mutations, suggesting that DNA is to blame for generating the disease. The problem with this assertion is that oncologists are ignoring other critical details that point in another direction entirely.

This gene mutation is known to adversely affect mitochondria, potentially leading to the faulty energy system alluded to in the Metabolic Theory. The BRCA1 gene is partly responsible for repairing the separate DNA found within mitochondria, which deal with energy production.[016,] [019] Is the increased cancer risk associated with the BRCA1 gene related to the mitochondrial dysfunction that it seems capable of causing?

As I discussed in Chapter 7, mitochondria were once a separate bacterial organism that merged with cells millions of years ago forming a symbiotic relationship. This is the reason mitochondria have their own DNA. This **mtDNA** (**mitochondrial** DNA) is separate from the **nDNA** (**nuclear** DNA) found within a cell's nucleus.

The BRCA1 gene (within the nucleus) creates a protein that travels outside the nucleus, across the cell, and into mitochondria. The purpose of the BRCA1 protein is to help repair damaged mitochondrial DNA because mitochondria cannot repair their own mtDNA, they rely upon the nucleus to do this job for them. Failure of the BRCA1 gene means that mtDNA is at risk of becoming damaged. When mitochondria become damaged, the energy system switches, eventually leading to cancer – according to the more accurate Metabolic Theory. Has a focus on nDNA led scientists to ignore other critical details, resulting in an incomplete interpretation of the mechanisms of cancer?

Hallmarks and the Metabolic Theory – energy is key:

Regarding the DNA transfer experiments that were discussed in Chapter 2 – which showed that mice did not become cancerous when grown from damaged DNA taken from a cancerous mouse tumour – Professor Thomas Seyfried, who is working on the Metabolic Theory, performed similar studies. Crucially, he tested the mitochondria present within the cytoplasm surrounding the nucleus, to establish the roll of the energy system as well. He found that cancerous growth did not form when damaged DNA was used to grow new tissue; but tumour growth did occur when this cytoplasm containing dysfunctional mitochondria were present, suggesting a central roll of the energy system in cancer:[007]

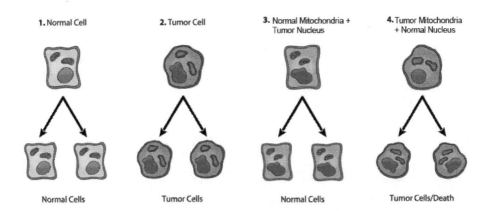

Illustration 1: <u>Oxford Journals – Carcinogenesis</u> 2014 [007]

Regarding the results, Professor Seyfried stated:

*'It is our view that all roads to the origin and progression of cancer pass through the **mitochondria**.'*

<u>Oxford Journals – Carcinogenesis</u> **2014** [007, 012]

Mitochondria's role in cancer:

Despite there being resistance to acknowledge the involvement of mitochondria, the scientific literature confirms that an abnormally functioning energy system plays a key role in cancer,[014] as stated by the following studies:

*'...**mitochondria play a key role in cancer**. In fact, **dysfunctional mitochondria** not only contribute to the metabolic reprogramming of cancer cells but they also modulate a plethora of cellular processes involved in **tumorigenesis** [**tumour development**].'*

<u>Current Genomics</u> **2013** [015]

This study also highlights the odd energy behaviour of cancer cells:

*'The **abnormal metabolism** of cancer cells is a **crucial feature** of tumours and provides promising therapeutic targets for cancer treatments. **Aerobic glycolysis** in cancer cells, termed the **Warburg effect**, is a highlighted characteristic of cancer-specific metabolism.'*

<u>Molecular Medicine Reports</u> **2015** [302]

Just so we are clear on this:

> *'Most cancer cells exhibit **increased glycolysis** and use this **metabolic pathway** for generation of ATP as a **main source** of their energy supply. This phenomenon is known as the **Warburg effect** and is considered as one of the **most fundamental metabolic alterations** during **malignant transformation.'***

<u>Oncogene</u> 2006 [788]

Clearly, abnormal metabolism (abnormal cell energy) is fundamental to the disease. So, how does a faulty energy system explain the hallmarks of cancer? How many hallmarks can the Metabolic Theory explain?

It can explain the majority of hallmarks according to proponents of the Metabolic Theory, which I will now explain in a little detail. In other words, scientists working on the Metabolic Theory have identified an absolutely key factor involved in cancer. So, what have they discovered?

It would seem that cancer is linked to the energy status of the cell, because most cancers develop an abnormally functioning energy system at some point in their life-cycle. Scientists postulate that mitochondria – which produce the bulk of cell energy – appear to be faulty, and that this malfunction leads to a switch in energy to the backup energy system known as *glycolysis*. This is categorised by an inability to create energy through the oxygen-based energy pathway within mitochondria, known as OXPHOS (Oxidative Phosphorylation). This results in a permanent switch to glycolysis that brings about, and explains, the remaining conditions of cancer.

Below, I briefly explain each hallmark in accordance with the evidence generated by the Metabolic Theory to show that mitochondria play a pivotal role in the development of the disease. With this new insight we can start to build a picture of how cancer operates and how to potentially treat it.

Tumour growth – Hallmarks 1, 2 and 3:

Crucially, the medical literature confirms that mitochondria are a primary controller of cell death and cell growth mechanisms:

> *'Because mitochondria are also a central component of **apoptosis** (**programmed cell death**), which is routinely used to rid the body of cells that are no longer useful or functioning properly, **mitochondrial dysfunction that inhibits cell death** can contribute to the **development of cancer.'***

Encyclopedia Britannica [006]

'Importantly, the mitochondria also participate in cell cycle control, ***cell growth*** *and differentiation, as well as play an important role in the induction of* ***apoptosis*** *[cell death].'*

The Human Protein Atlas [610]

So, as mitochondria are the hub of cell death and cell growth activity, and since they appear to be dysfunctional in cancer, their uncharacteristic behaviour can explain a tumour's development because the mechanisms that would normally control cell death and tumour growth have been lost. This suggests that the first three hallmarks are accounted for by the abnormally functioning energy system because this process appears to occur in all cancers:

1. Uncontrolled cell growth
2. Resistance to anti-growth signals
3. Evasion of cell death signals.

Blood vessel growth – Hallmark 5:

I will come back to the fourth hallmark in a moment. But first, it's important to explain the fifth hallmark, which relates to the way tumours develop their own blood supply, also termed *angiogenesis*. This will highlight how pivotal the energy system is to tumour growth and cancer progression.

Tumours develop their own blood supply, and as much as scientists have tried, supporters of the DNA Theory have been unable to explain this. And yet, how tumours acquire their own blood supply is easy to determine and just as easy to understand.

As I've discussed extensively, there are two main energy systems within a cell: aerobic respiration performed by mitochondria, and glycolysis undertaken within the cytoplasm. Mitochondria combine glucose with oxygen to make energy. Glycolysis is the backup energy system, and when used, it converts glucose into lactic acid, it does not require oxygen. In a situation where the oxygen supply is lost (such as tissue damage) mitochondria cannot produce energy, so glycolysis takes over until the oxygen supply is restored. Furthermore, a switch to glycolysis is needed in order to instigate an inflammatory response. The goal of this response is specifically to alert immune cells to a problem and to initiate the cell repair process. As part of this process blood vessels are grown to aid with cell repair by ensuring there is a supply of nutrients to the damaged cells. This simple switch to glycolysis, and the consequent lactic acid production, is a warning sign that something is wrong, that damage has occurred and that the blood supply has been lost. This is dangerous because cells die without access to nutrients.

In response to lactic acid accumulation, the body adapts to produce growth factors aimed at restoring the blood supply and aiding with cell repair. New blood vessels grow towards the cells that are producing excessive lactic acid, and once they succeed in resupplying oxygen to the cells, the energy system switches back to aerobic respiration allowing mitochondria to take over energy creation using oxygen. This halts lactic acid production because glycolysis is no longer needed; and, in turn, stops blood vessel growth as the lactic acid dissipates. Balance is restored.

This natural process of blood vessel growth, stimulated by excessive lactic acid production, can also be seen during prolonged physical exercise, although it is more subtle than when damage has occurred because lactic acid production is lower. Nevertheless, it still provides sufficient lactic acid to stimulate blood vessel growth.

Vigorous exercise, such as when we sprint, forces us to use glycolysis to support mitochondria in generating energy because the current blood supply cannot provide the amount of oxygen needed to fulfil this higher energy demand. The consequent increase in lactic acid, produced by the extended use of glycolysis, indicates to the body that more oxygen is required at this exercise intensity. Growth factors are stimulated to improve the blood supply in direct correlation to the amount of lactic acid being produced, which allows mitochondria to access more oxygen the next time exercise is performed at that same level of intensity. This is a clever system designed to improve our performance by alerting our bodies to when the oxygen supply isn't good enough for the current energy needs. Our physiology adapts to fix the problem based on the amount of lactic acid being produced. This is one of the reasons why we become fitter when we exercise and why the veins in athletes appear so prominent. The two studies below verify that lactic acid promotes blood vessel growth:

> '...the **release of lactate** [**lactic acid**] by cancer cells effectively contributed to the in vivo development of the **tumour vasculature** [stimulated **blood vessel growth**].'
>
> <u>Journal of Internal Medicine</u> **2012** [609]

'*It is well known that* **lactate** *is a* **key player** *in* **angiogenesis**, *cell migration,* **stimulation of VEGF**, *wound healing and repair. In cancer,* **lactate** *plays an important role in* **angiogenesis stimulating VEGF protein expression** *in endothelial cells.*

Lactate can enter tumour endothelial cells and **lactate** *released from tumour cells through MCT4 is enough to* **stimulate angiogenesis** *and* **tumour growth**.'

<u>Carcinogenesis</u> **2017**[771]

Now that we understand that glycolysis generates blood vessel growth as a matter of normal function due to its production of lactic acid, we can easily determine how a tumour is able to develop its own blood supply. This occurs because cancer cells rely on glycolysis for their energy needs, even in the presence of oxygen. This backup energy system is used as a cancer cell's primary energy source.[406, 529] This reliance on glycolysis generates a constant and unrelenting output of lactic acid, which is why the tissue surrounding a tumour is highly acidic.[009, 261] And as we now know, overproduction of lactic acid stimulates blood vessel growth.

This abnormal production of lactic acid tricks the body into thinking that the oxygen and blood supply has been lost, even when it hasn't, prompting new blood vessels to be formed. But, as lactic acid production doesn't stop in malignancy, neither does blood vessel growth. This is why the blood supply of a tumour is so substantial and disorganised. So, whether it's a natural switch in energy to glycolysis or an abnormal one, as we see occurring in cancer cells, lactic acid accumulation instigates blood vessel growth; this process is known as *angiogenesis*.[010]

For those interested in the pathways and genes involved, the Metabolic Theory explains them in more detail. For the purpose of this book and not to cause too much confusion, I will mention them only briefly here. You don't need to know the following abbreviations, but if your oncologist mentions them in the future, you'll know what they relate to.

A loss of oxygen (referred to as *hypoxia*), or dysfunctional mitochondria, stimulates the HIF-1a gene, which then stimulates the LDH gene (this switches on glycolysis and generates lactic acid). An increase in LDH gene expression stimulates VEGF production (Vascular Endothelial Growth Factor).[406] VEGF is the growth factor that stimulates blood vessel growth. This confirms that excessive production of lactic acid stimulates blood vessel growth via the instigation of VEGF.

Invasiveness and metastasis – Hallmark 6:

While lactic acid stimulates blood vessel growth, studies show that the corrosive nature of this acid also encourages the tumour to invade the surrounding tissue and increases the chance of cancer cells migrating into the bloodstream. This is due to the damage it causes, an overtly acidic environment leads to porous blood vessels, thus increasing the risk of cell migration. Lactic acid helps to explain the sixth hallmark – tumour invasiveness and metastasis:[010, 011, 334, 771]

> *'Scientists at the University of Arizona have found that culturing cancer cell lines in even a slightly acidic medium "**caused dramatic increases in both migration and invasion**".'*
>
> <u>*The Free Library*</u> **2013** [261]

In the below study lactic acid (lactate) is shown to stimulate migration of cells aiding with the spread of the disease (metastasis):

> *'In glioma cells, **lactate** induces the expression of transforming growth factor-β2 (TGF-β2), a key regulator of glioma cells **migration**. The addition of exogenous lactate increases cell motility and **random migration** of different cancer cell lines in a concentration-related manner. It has been also known for about **two decades** that **lactate level** is **highly correlated** with **metastasis** in different forms of cancers. '*
>
> <u>*Carcinogenesis*</u> **2017** [771]

The over-expression of lactic acid can help to explain the invasive nature of cancer and its ability to spread (metastasis), although there are other factors that also contribute, which are covered in Chapter 11. There is a third aspect to hallmark 6, which is its ability to grow a new tumour in a new location once it has spread. This cannot be attributed to excess lactic acid, but it can be explained via the involvement of cancer stem cells. It is the cancer stem cell, or cells that also harbour stem cell properties, that can migrate and grow tumours at distant sites. This is due to their capacity to generate unlimited cell growth and their enhanced ability to evade immune detection.

Retrograde signalling – Hallmarks 4, 6 and 8:

To fully explain hallmark 6 (cancer spread), as well as hallmarks 4 (limitless growth) and 8 (immune evasion), I need to discuss how cancer stem cells are created and how mitochondria are linked to this process. This is important because it is the cancer stem cell that explains all three of these hallmarks.

Mitochondria communicate with, and influence the DNA within the nucleus (nDNA). When this signalling becomes abnormally intense, it is referred to as *retrograde signalling*.[343] Retrograde signalling indicates that mitochondria are under severe stress and are attempting to change the cell's fate by stimulating nDNA to accommodate for whatever stress is occurring. Studies show that when mitochondria experience an extreme level of damage, they can trigger a change to occur within a regular cell – an 'epithelial' cell for example – that results in a transition back to a powerful stem cell state. This switch has also been shown to occur in cancer cells, leading to the creation of cancer stem cells. Essentially, mitochondria within an epithelial cell generate deadly cancer stem cells when they have become overtly damaged. These stem cells are sometimes referred to as *mesenchymal* stem cells:

> '*Metastatic breast tumours undergo* **epithelial-to-mesenchymal** *transition (EMT)… Notably,* **mtDNA reduction** *[damage to mitochondrial DNA] generates* **breast cancer stem cells**.'
>
> <u>Research Gate</u> **2017** [344]

This is a major discovery, because the way stem cells become involved has been a bone of contention for some time. For instance, the DNA Theory proposes that an *Epithelial-to-mesenchymal Transition* (EMT) occurs via random DNA mutations, however there's currently no pattern of DNA damage that can account for this – Professor Weinberg admits that the evidence for this is incomplete.[504] Rather, through the creation of cancer stem cells caused by excessive damage to mitochondria, the Metabolic Theory can fully explain hallmark 6: a tumour's ability to successfully spread and grow elsewhere within the body.

From an evolutionary standpoint this makes perfect sense. Naturally, damage of any kind risks killing any animal, plant or organism, so to recover, it stands to reason that cells, which have suffered a dangerous level of damage, should be capable of reverting back to a powerful stem cell state to help regenerate dying cells. This is likely a last resort survival response when an organism is faced with a high level of trauma. This process can be seen in some amphibians, which can regrow tails and entire limbs that have been lost. A jellyfish called *Turritopsis nutricula* provides another example: it can revert back to its early stem-cell polyp state when it becomes damaged, allowing it to regrow in order to evade death.

This universal ability to regenerate stem cells under stress can be seen in plants too.[476] Damage to a cut stem appears to instigate a stem-cell-like transition that enables roots to be produced where root cells didn't exist before, allowing the plant to survive severe trauma. This explains why chemotherapy appears to switch on a repair process that leads to resistance and increases tumour aggressiveness. The damage to mitochondria that chemotherapy causes triggers this survival mechanism, whereby an overtly damaged cancer cell transitions into a powerful cancer stem cell capable of regeneration – all due to the severe damage inflicted upon mitochondria. In other words, not only does chemotherapy stimulate cancer stem cells to become more aggressive, but it also potentially creates them:

> *'It is thought the toxic medication [chemotherapy] switches on a repair mechanism in the body which ultimately **allows tumours to grow back stronger.'***
>
> **<u>The Telegraph</u> 2017** [393]

As cancer stem cells are essentially immortal and can generate a limitless supply of new cells, damaged mitochondria via the creation of cancer stem cells, can explain hallmark 4: limitless growth. Based on this concept it wouldn't matter how many normal cancer cells are killed, if cancer stem cells remain, they will simply regrow the tumour indefinitely.

I must confess that I have taken a liberty here by including this ability of mitochondria to create cancer stem cells within this section of the book, because the main proponent of the metabolic theory – Professor Seyfried – doesn't mention how damaged mitochondria can generate cancer stem cells. He rejects the notion of an EMT being responsible for limitless growth and the spread of the disease. Although I note that his criticism relates to how the DNA Theory explains this EMT process via random DNA damage. It appears to be the DNA-based interpretation of an EMT that he is rejecting. In place of the role of cancer stem cells, he favours the hypothesis that macrophage immune cells – which have similar capabilities to that of stem cells – become corrupted by the cancer cells they attempt to destroy. This results in macrophage mitochondria becoming faulty, and is a consequence of a macrophage fusing with a cancer cell. The end product is a hybrid cell that now has additional properties allowing for limitless growth, suppression of the immune system, and the ability to spread.

While the macrophage fusion hypothesis is unproven, I can see, and accept, the potential involvement of both macrophages and cancer stem cells. Either way, whether it be cancer stem cell creation via damaged mitochondria, or macrophage fusion with cancer cells, faulty mitochondria have the potential to explain limitless growth, immune evasion and the process of metastasis.

Regarding immune evasion, the Metabolic Theory appears to fall short in its ability to fully explain Hallmark 8. As Professor Seyfried points out in his latest paper, macrophages can suppress the immune response,[866] and as I show in the quote below, cancer stem cells produce CD47, which hides them from the immune system:

> '...CD47 *thus serves as a* **"don't eat me"** *signal... CD47 has been found to be* **over-expressed** *on human tumours... enabling tumours to* **escape innate immune system surveillance**.'
>
> <u>*Journal of the American Academy of Dermatology*</u> *2016* [415]

The issue though, is that the involvement of cancer stem cells and this macrophage cancer cell fusion event, occurs during the latter stages of the disease, not at the beginning, which means that both events cannot account for how cancer cells are able to evade immune detection in early tumour development. Professor Seyfried doesn't seem to be able to explain how faulty mitochondria (specifically defective OXPHOS) – which is seen as the origin of cancer – enables cancer cells to evade immune detection at the onset of the disease and at its early stage of progression. The suppression of *Natural Killer* cells, and cancer-killing *T-cells* is not explained, and neither is the cancer-killing and contradictory cancer-promoting behaviour of *Myeloid-derived suppressor cells* and *neutrophils* explained through this 'faulty mitochondria' mechanism.

This indicates that the Metabolic Theory, through the corruption of mitochondria, can only partly explain Hallmark 8: evasion of the immune system.

Inflammation and DNA damage – Hallmarks 9 and 10:

Aside from the six hallmarks already accounted for, the Metabolic Theory can also explain two more – inflammation and DNA damage. Before a tumour develops, there will always be prolonged bouts of inflammation. This is likely due to the cell damage caused by the toxins we are exposed to within our diet or the environment. Toxic exposure instigates an oxidative stress response, where large quantities of free radicals are being created by mitochondria, and as we have seen, free radicals can damage cells. This free-radical damage can generate inflammation and the random DNA damage witnessed in cancer, explaining hallmarks 9 and 10: random DNA damage and inflammation.

This simple breakdown of the Metabolic Theory indicates that it seems to provide a plausible explanation for approximately 8 of the 10 hallmarks of cancer, because at some point in their life-cycle all cancer cells develop abnormal energy metabolism. This confirms that the energy system within a cell is a pivotal mechanism, if not 'the' pivotal mechanism, responsible for a large majority of conditions associated with the disease.

Hallmarks rearranged:

This new understanding highlights that the hallmarks of cancer, as they are currently listed, don't appear to be placed in any particular order reflective of the development or progression of the disease, or even of the hierarchical importance of each hallmark. Considering how central they have become to processing the data on cancer, it could be helpful to rearrange them. For instance, in light of the evidence presented, it appears that the Warburg effect (Hallmark 7) is the most important one of all, and a factor of the disease that occurs right at the onset of tumour growth. It seems logical, therefore, to place Hallmark 7 first.

The point at which cells become cancerous, is also not clear – exactly when does this transition occur according to the original list? How many, and which hallmarks are required for a cell to be defined as cancer?

Original hallmark list:

1. Uncontrolled cell growth
2. Resistance to anti-growth signals
3. Evasion of cell death signals
4. Limitless replication
5. Extended blood vessel growth
6. Invasion of local tissue and metastasis
7. Abnormal metabolic pathways (faulty energy system)
8. Evasion of the immune system.
9. Genome instability
10. Inflammation

In order to answer this we first need to know the current definition of cancer, which, according to the *National Institute of Cancer* in America: *'Cancer is a disease in which some of the body's cells* **grow uncontrollably** *and* **spread** *to other parts of the body'*. Cancers are also defined by 'stage', where 'stage one' refers to a small tumour that is still contained within the tissue it developed in, right up to 'stage four', which refers to a large tumour that has spread to other parts of the body. So, uncontrollable growth appears to be the point at which a growth is categorised as cancer. The spread of the disease is a hallmark behaviour that develops later, but is not required for out-of-control cells to be classed as being cancerous. With this in mind, I now provide a revised hallmark list that attempts to clarify the development of the disease. I propose the following change:

Hallmarks **REARRANGED**	
Initiation Pre-cancerous stage	1. **Abnormal metabolic pathways** *(Hallmark 7)* 2. **Chronic inflammation** *(Hallmark 10)*
Cancer	3. **Evasion of cell death** *(Hallmark 3)* 4. **Resistance to anti-growth signals** *(Hallmark 2)* 5. **Uncontrolled growth** *(Hallmark 1)*
Progression	6. **Immune evasion** *(Hallmark 8)*
Malignancy	7. **Blood vessel growth** *(Hallmark 5)* 8. **Limitless replication** *(Hallmark 4)* 9. **Invasion of local tissue and metastasis** *(Hallmark 6)* 10. **Genome instability** *(Hallmark 9)*

In the initiation pre-cancerous stage, we see a switch to the Warburg effect and chronic inflammation, which is, in fact, a common feature of damaged tissue. This is not yet cancer, because these first two hallmarks can potentially be resolved within the normal repair process. This highlights that while glycolysis is a requirement for cancer to form, it's initiation **doesn't necessarily result in cancer**. Only when chronically inflamed cells fail to commit programmed cell death and start growing out of control, can this abnormal cell behaviour be categorised as cancer. So, arguably, there is something – possibly a number of factors or stages – missing between *Chronic inflammation* and *Evasion of cell death* that enables the transition from a 'regular' cell, still capable of repair, to a cell that 'loses control'. Over the following chapters I set out to fill in this missing information and propose a yet-to-be considered mechanism that can provide a full explanation of this cancerous transition.

It is often suggested that we all have cancer, but are completely unaware of it, because the immune system deals with it before it gets out of control. For that reason 'immune evasion' comes next and signifies the progression phase of the disease, in which the immune response is no longer able to manage the situation. The remaining four hallmarks are symptoms of the immune system's ongoing inability to deal with the situation, and represents the malignant phase that ultimately leads to the deadly aspect of the disease – its ability to spread.

Genome instability appears last in this list of symptoms, which will no doubt be a bone of contention for some. But as the weight of evidence shows, driver DNA mutations do not occur at all in some cancers, highlighting that genome instability cannot account for carcinogenesis, or be the underlying mechanism that generates the disease. The DNA Theory is also unable to explain the previous hallmarks leading up to it. While some genome instability may exist in early tumour development, most is accrued as the cancer progresses; this, coupled with the inconsistencies associated with the randomness of the DNA damage that occurs, only stands to illustrate that genome instability appears to be an ongoing symptom, as opposed to a driving mechanism – hence why chemotherapies that target the genome have generally had little success.

When viewed from this perspective, the transition from a regular cell to a cancer cell, and the relevance of each hallmark in relation to disease progression, starts to become clear. The reasons for the shortcomings in the current approaches to treating cancer also become apparent. The majority of mainstream treatments appear to be targeting the symptoms of the disease by targeting 'genome instability', which is the last, and therefore least significant hallmark in the re-ordered list. Other drugs attempt to prevent blood vessel growth and metastasis, again, targeting the later symptoms of the disease and demonstrating a considerable lack of efficacy.

Immunotherapies that seek to harness the power of the immune system, target Hallmark 6, which again isn't a hallmark related to the underlying mechanism that drives the disease. By contrast, metabolic treatments, which are unfortunately not part of mainstream treatment protocols, target the first, and arguably the most important hallmark, which forms a core feature of cancer itself. The reasons for the shortcomings of the mainstream approach to treating the disease become immediately apparent, when viewed from this perspective: within 'standard of care' treatments, the most important hallmark, a key mechanism associated with the disease, is not addressed in any way.

III

THE ALL-IMPORTANT DETAILS

Chasing symptoms

From the perspective of attempting to solve cancer, the strength of the Metabolic Theory is great news, it's almost there. But, and yes, there's all too often a but, there appears to be a few caveats with the Metabolic Theory. Not only is there contention over Hallmark 8 – the ability to fully explain immune evasion, but there is also contention over Hallmarks 7 and 3 – the cause of abnormal metabolism, and failure of the cell death mechanism respectively.

This is critical, because in order for the Metabolic Theory to be correct, it needs to identify the mechanisms that can account for these remaining hallmarks; in particular, why cancer cells rely on glycolysis, which is arguably the most important hallmark to account for because the Metabolic Theory is based upon the principle idea that mitochondria are defective. This, it is thought, leads to the other hallmarks that occur – as mitochondria control apoptosis, defective mitochondria may be able to explain why this cell death mechanism fails to be triggered. Identification of a specific pattern of damage would need to established to account for this forced energy shift, and would need to be present in all tumours.

To clarify, Professor Seyfried proposes that defects within mitochondria, which restrict the oxygen energy pathway known as 'OXPHOS', are the underlying cause of cancer. This breakdown in aerobic respiration (OXPHOS) results in a reliance on the backup energy system of 'glycolysis' and another pathway that deals with 'glutamine fermentation'. This glutamine fermentation pathway is known as *Substrate Level Phosphorylation* (SLP), and as it occurs in mitochondria, a lowercase 'm' is included within the acronym: 'mSLP'.

Active glutamine fermentation (mSLP) within mitochondria, highlights that mitochondria are still operational, so already we can see that they are not entirely defective. That aside, the implication of defective OXPHOS, means that glucose and glutamine are the primary fuels feeding the disease. And as a reliance upon glycolysis and mSLP generates a proliferative state of being, a mass of duplicated cells accumulate – all because mitochondria and their OXPHOS pathway are deemed to be defective.

On an aside, glutamine fermentation seems to come into effect only after glycolysis has been activated and often only when glycolysis (glucose) fails to provide the energy and substrates needed for the cancer cell to proliferate, so it is secondary to glycolysis. For this reason I will just refer to glycolysis as opposed to mentioning mSLP as well, it will be implied that both are occurring. The use of glutamine in cancer is discussed several times in later chapters.

One possible mechanism that could validate Professor Seyfried's hypothesis, would be the presence of damaged DNA within mitochondria (mtDNA) – specifically the mtDNA that controls the OXPHOS pathway. This damage would be able to explain why mitochondria are no longer using the OXPHOS pathway to create energy. But in conflict with the Metabolic Theory, and as all good scientists should do, Professor Seyfried highlights a number of controversies, one being that no pathogenic mtDNA mutations are present that can confirm the OXPHOS pathway defective:

> '...the role of mitochondrial DNA (mtDNA) in the origin and progression of cancer is **controversial**. We were **unable** to find **any pathogenic mtDNA mutations** in a broad range of chemically induced and naturally arising mouse brain tumours (Kiebish and Seyfried, 2005)...
>
> ...Our studies were comprehensive in that we sequenced the **entire mitochondrial genome [mtDNA]** after first isolating and purifying the mitochondria from the tumour tissue.'
>
> **Frontiers in Cell and Developmental Biology 2015** [032]

While mtDNA damage does occur in cancer, the particular pathogenic mtDNA mutations that are required to confirm OXPHOS is defective, and a reliance upon glycolysis occurs, don't appear to be present. So, is there any other damage to mitochondria that could validate the claim that OXPHOS is defective?

Mitochondria contain a lipid membrane called *cardiolipin*. Cardiolipin contributes to the regulation of the OXPHOS pathway. In support of the Metabolic Theory this cardiolipin membrane does appear to be damaged in all cancers. So one could argue that damage to cardiolipin is the underlying mechanism that inhibits OXPHOS leading to a reliance on glycolysis, and thus cancer. However, in diseases that share the same cardiolipin and energy abnormalities, cancer does not form, indicating that an additional factor over and above cardiolipin abnormalities and a reliance upon glycolysis, is required for cancer to form.

Barth syndrome and cardiolipin abnormalities:

In Barth syndrome cells predominantly use glycolysis because they harbour abnormal cardiolipin composition, similar to cancer cells. As mentioned above, cardiolipin forms part of the membrane of mitochondria and is involved in the OXPHOS pathway (oxygen-based energy pathway), this is confirmed in the quote below:

> *'In addition to the ultrastructural abnormalities in mitochondria and MAM, **no cancer cell** has been found with a normal content or composition of **cardiolipin**, the cristae-enriched phospholipid that contributes to **OxPhos** function [energy function within mitochondria].'*
>
> <u>iScience</u> **2020** [769]

This is interesting because even though Barth syndrome patients and cancer cells share almost identical energy abnormalities, cancer is extremely rare in children who suffer from Barth syndrome, suggesting that cardiolipin abnormalities and a switch to glycolysis aren't responsible.[032] Professor Seyfried argues that cancer does not form in these children because they are hypoglycaemic – they have low blood sugar, so there is a lack of glucose to feed the tumour.[032] That would probably hold true if it wasn't for the fact that glutamine also feeds the disease, and as Professor Seyfried points out, cancer cells will utilise glutamine when glucose is scarce. This suggests that cancer should still form – if the cell is to blame that is – given that, in Barth syndrome, these cells compensate for this lack of glucose by also absorbing glutamine.[862] That cancer does not arise despite having access to glutamine and possessing the same energy abnormalities, indicates that faulty mitochondria (defective OXPHOS) and a reliance on glycolysis, are not the underlying mechanisms driving the disease.

Another major challenge to the defective OXPHOS hypothesis, is that there is growing acknowledgement that mitochondria within tumours are still operational. Not only is the TCA cycle within mitochondria still working (which I'll explain later), but OXPHOS itself is still being utilised:

> 'Nowadays it is **widely accepted** that a switch to a glycolytic metabolism (the Warburg effect) is a **core hallmark of cancer cells**. However, contrary with what was suggested by Warburg, we know today that mitochondria of tumours are **not defective** and therefore **are not the cause of the observed metabolic reprogramming**.'
>
>

The FEBS Journal 2018 [665]

> 'The revealed studies pointed out that **OXPHOS** was **not constantly suppressed** during carcinogenesis, it could be partly **restored** under nutrient shortage status...Clinically, 3-bromophyruvate (3-BP), a **potent glycolysis inhibitor** has been proved **not always helpful** in cancer patients.'
>
>

Oncotarget 2017 [716]

In one study, brain cancer cells were killed by specifically inhibiting the OXPHOS pathway, indicating that this pathway is operational, as it is required for cancer cell survival:

> 'Mechanistically, Gboxin was found to accumulate inside glioblastoma cell **mitochondria** and disrupt primary glioblastoma cell **metabolism**....Gboxin rapidly interacted with **OXPHOS** proteins, particularly **complex V**...
>
> ...In summary, this study has identified a novel small-molecule inhibitor of **oxidative phosphorylation** [OXPHOS] that exerts glioblastoma tumour-cell-specific toxicity.'
>
>

Nature Reviews Cancer 2019 [879]

Similarly, Professor Michael Lisanti from the *University of Salford* in the UK, has had some success against cancer stem cells using several antibiotic drugs that inhibit mitochondria. While Doxycyline targets the ribosomes within mitochondria, preventing mitochondrial biogenesis (propagation / function), the anti-parasitic drug *Pyrvinium pamoate* blocks OXPHOS, this combination was effective at inhibiting cancer stem cells, suggesting that OXPHOS is still active and required for cancer survival.[661]

Ketones are the energy molecules created by the liver when it breaks-down fat, this normally occurs when glucose is in short supply, such as when we fast, or consume a low carbohydrate diet. Professor Seyfried claims that cancer cells cannot use ketones because their mitochondria are defective. However, Professor Lisanti found that ketones can fuel tumour growth, which contradicts the assertion made by Professor Seyfried.[881] Moreover, within their investigations, Lisanti and colleagues also show that OXPHOS, and the TCA cycle within mitochondria, are active in breast cancer cells.[881]

But possibly the most telling evidence comes from studying *Oncocytomas*, which are rare benign tumours. These tumours are characterised by the accumulation of defective mitochondria, defective OXPHOS and the inability to produce ROS. These mitochondria harbour pathogenic mtDNA mutations in the genes that control OXPHOS, which explains why OXPHOS no longer works. Surprisingly, cells containing these defective mitochondria, and their reliance upon glycolysis, don't generate cancer, instead they form benign tumours:

> '*Primary oncocytoma cells are **defective for respiration** and **ROS production**, are **highly glycolytic**...suggesting that loss of respiration may activate a metabolic checkpoint that limits tumour growth to **benign disease**.'*
>
> <u>*Molecular Cell*</u> **2016** [883]

This suggests that, actually, defective mitochondria, in particular defective OXPHOS, is not the origin of cancer, rather, that cancer requires active mitochondria to aid with the absorption, and conversion of, nutrients – as this illustration from the study summarises:

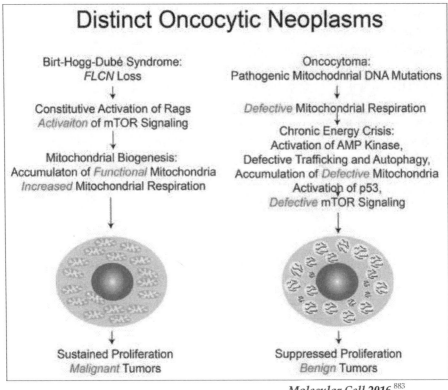

Distinct Oncocytic Neoplasms

Birt-Hogg-Dubé Syndrome:
FLCN Loss

↓

Constitutive Activation of Rags
Activaiton of mTOR Signaling

↓

Mitochondrial Biogenesis:
Accumulaton of *Functional* Mitochondria
Increased Mitochondrial Respiration

↓

Sustained Proliferation
Malignant Tumors

Oncocytoma:
Pathogenic Mitochodnrial DNA Mutations

↓

Defective Mitochondrial Respiration

Chronic Energy Crisis:
Activation of AMP Kinase,
Defective Trafficking and Autophagy,
Accumulation of *Defective* Mitochondria
Activation of p53,
Defective mTOR Signaling

↓

Suppressed Proliferation
Benign Tumors

Molecular Cell **2016** [883]

This supports the model of cancer I am proposing, that cancerous mitochondria are active, but suppressed, which gives the false impression that they are defective. This suppression occurs in the main pathways associated with pathogen survival, reducing mitochondria's ability to defend the cell from the controlling pathogens. This can explain why many challenge the premise behind the Metabolic Theory, that defective OXPHOS is the origin of the disease, and have found OXPHOS to be operational to varying degrees. This may also explain why Professor Seyfried was unable to identify pathogenic mtDNA mutations in the brain cancers he was studying; these missing mutations are suggestive of mitochondria that can still utilise OXPHOS.

In fact, the ability of cancer cells to produce abundant ROS (oxygen free radicals), has always sat uneasy with me because ROS production occurs within the *Electron Transport Chain* (ETC) – which forms part of the OXPHOS pathway. Surely, if OXPHOS is truly defective, ROS production via the ETC in mitochondria, should not be possible. Indeed, supporting this, oncocytoma evidence highlights that when OXPHOS is inoperative in these benign tumours, ROS cannot be generated. That ROS is produced in cancer cells, stands to confirm that OXPHOS is indeed active in cancer, seemingly contradicting the Metabolic Theory.

So, while a switch to the backup energy system (glycolysis) appears to be driving cancer, it doesn't seem to occur as a result of an inoperable OXPHOS pathway or defective mitochondria. Analysing this further, sustained glycolysis doesn't appear to be driving cancerous conditions either – an additional factor seems to be required.

Glycolysis in other cells:

If we look at endothelial cells (ECs) for instance, which are the cells that line our veins and arteries, we see that they primarily operate using glycolysis for their energy needs,[678] which is the same energy state that cancer cells use. And yet, despite this, cancer does not form as a matter of normal function in these cells:

> *'ECs are **highly glycolytic** (it has been calculated that up to **85%** of ATP [energy] in ECs is produced by **glycolysis**) despite the fact that they are in immediate contact with oxygen present in the blood.'*
>
> <u>*Frontiers in Immunology*</u> **2015** [639]

Quiescent fibroblast cells provide another example, these cells lie dormant and do not proliferate and yet they consume similar rates of glucose via glycolysis compared with proliferating fibroblasts:

> *'Fibroblasts in both proliferating and contact-inhibited states [dormant states] **utilize glycolysis extensively**.'*
>
> <u>*PLOS Biology*</u> **2010** [861]

The use of glycolysis doesn't appear to be a guarantee that cells will grow out of control, which makes the claim that a switch to glycolysis causes cancer, a hard sell. Similarly, stem cells also operate by primarily using glycolysis, but don't regularly develop into cancer:[212]

> *'Quiescent stem cells are **mostly glycolytic**... Outside the hypoxic niche, the oxygen levels begin to rise increasing the oxidative phosphorylation (OxPhos)...which stimulate the cells to proliferate and differentiate...*

*...During proliferation, stem cells **mainly rely on glycolysis** while still maintaining low OxPhos levels to fuel the cells with biosynthetic intermediates important for cell growth.'*

Cells **2020** [797]

Even though a healthy stem cell predominantly uses glycolysis (the preferred energy state of cancer cells) cancer does not regularly form in these healthy stem cells. Mitochondrial dysfunction, and a switch to glycolysis appear to be symptoms of the disease rather than the underlying cause of it. This suggests that an additional factor must be responsible for triggering Hallmark 7.

Hallmark 7 – one hallmark to rule them all:

We've now reached a critical moment in our quest to understand cancer, because Hallmark 7 (abnormal metabolism/Warburg effect) remains unexplained. This means that Hallmark 7 has become the most important hallmark to account for. Why? Because glycolysis is not only a proliferative energy state, but the lactic acid it produces appears to influence angiogenesis, tumour invasiveness and metastasis, key components of the disease. It also instigates inflammation, while inhibition of the cell death mechanism seems to result from this energy state as well. Essentially, it is a process that is at the heart of the disease – we just don't know why:

*'**We still don't know the reason for the Warburg effect**... If I had two billion dollars I would give it to 20 biochemists, give them $100 million each and tell them – go to it. You have to unleash **biochemistry**, and there is essentially **no biochemistry left**, because **everyone moved into DNA**.'*

James Watson, Cancer World.net **2013** [240]

Identifying the underlying cause of this abnormal energy state, should reveal the underlying cause of tumour growth. Whatever is driving the Warburg effect, is likely driving cancer.

This is exciting, because solving cancer may just come down to identifying, and then eliminating, the known factors that can possibly cause an abnormal energy switch to glycolysis. When I realised the relevance of explaining Hallmark 7, I was rather taken back by a lack of acknowledgement by the medical establishment, of how crucial this hallmark is to understanding the disease. But, I can see why such a crucial piece of the cancer puzzle has been overlooked. If scientists are already convinced that DNA mutation is driving the disease, why would they think to look elsewhere for its origin? The question to answer then, is this: what are the possible factors that can cause an energy switch to glycolysis? Some known factors include:

1. Faulty mitochondria (deficient OXPHOS)
2. DNA damage/mutation
3. Exercise
4. Hypoxia (a lack of oxygen)
5. Insulin resistance (associated with diabetes)
6. Inflammation
7. Iron overload
8. Glucose abundance (Crabtree effect)

Interestingly, all of these factors can be easily discounted. For instance:

1, 2 – Faulty mitochondria and **DNA damage/mutation** have not been confirmed to be the cause of Hallmark 7. While mitochondria are clearly damaged in many cancers, deficiency in OXPHOS remains in contention and there are a number of other anomalies where the Metabolic Theory is concerned; for instance, as mitochondria are deemed to be defective, this prevents apoptosis from occurring, because the 'kill switch' within mitochondria no longer works. Yet studies confirm that apoptosis does indeed occur in the presence of antibiotic plant compounds, as well as with honey and silver. This contradicts the notion that the failure of cell death in cancer is a result of defective mitochondria, because it can be re-instigated through the mitochondrial cell death pathway (more on this later). Furthermore, Children with Barth syndrome, and other cells that rely on glycolysis, rarely develop cancer despite having the same defects present in cancer. Regarding the DNA Theory, it is unable to provide evidence to show how DNA mutations may transform a healthy cell into a cancer cell, furthermore, its mutations are seen as being a downstream event of metabolic dysfunction. Therefore, we can discount both as a cause of Hallmark 7 at this stage.

3 – Exercise can increase the use of glycolysis, but when we analyse studies into exercise we notice that the risk of cancer is reduced significantly, by up to 60%. So a switch to glycolysis via exercise is clearly not responsible.[068]

4 – Hypoxia refers to a lack of oxygen, which does lead to an energy switch to glycolysis. However, cancer occurs even when oxygen is present and available – so a lack of oxygen cannot be the underlying cause of hallmark 7.

5 – Insulin regulates blood glucose levels by stimulating glycolysis. This forces cells to absorb more glucose, reducing levels of glucose within the blood. **Insulin resistance**, which occurs in diabetic patients, increases the use of glycolysis.[807] For insulin resistance to be responsible for causing hallmark 7, it would need to be present in all cancer patients to account for this energy switch. However, studies show that this is not the case. In a breast cancer study only 48% of cancer patients had insulin resistance,[805] while this figure was 66% in patients with endometrial cancer.[806] While it plays a role in cancer development, this indicates that insulin resistance is not the underlying cause, just the mechanism that facilitates glucose absorption and leads to dysregulated blood glucose levels.

6 – Inflammation is the cell's response to damage – it alerts immune cells to a problem and starts the process of cell repair. Whenever inflammation occurs, glycolysis is in use. However, a switch to glycolysis is required first in order to generate an inflammatory response, inflammation is an effect of glycolysis, rather than the cause of it.[881]

7 – Iron overload occurs as a result of prolonged cell damage, and refers to the release of iron into the surrounding tissue. Iron is normally stored away to prevent its release and used sparingly when needed. It is directly associated with cancer development and progression. It can instigate glycolysis by causing mitochondrial dysfunction – this could explain the energy switch in cancer.[491, 496] However, specific damage to mitochondria would need to occur for iron overload to be the underlying cause of hallmark 7, damage that scientists have been unable to find. Iron overload, therefore, cannot explain hallmark 7.

8 – Glucose abundance can stimulate a switch to glycolysis. This often occurs in laboratory experiments and is known as the *Crabtree effect*.[902] This artefact of the in vitro environment (test-tube environment) can give the false impression that mitochondria are faulty and the Warburg effect is occurring, because glycolysis is operational despite there being enough oxygen for mitochondria to use. This highlights that, in the presence of abundant glucose, glycolysis can become dominant even if there is nothing wrong with mitochondria. The question then is this: is glucose abundance responsible for cancer? While glucose fuels the disease, glucose abundance in and of itself, is not the underlying cause of cancer. There are many examples where cancer continues to thrive even when glucose is restricted. This is due to cancer's ability to utilise other fuels, such as glutamine. Some cancers, such as prostate cancer, utilises fat rather than glucose.

Furthermore, fibroblast cells and endothelial cells – the latter of which line our blood vessels – operate within an environment of glucose abundance, and primarily use glycolysis for energy. But they do not develop into cancer as a matter of normal function, which indicates that an additional factor to that of glucose is also required to instigate the Warburg effect and cancer.

The missing part of the puzzle?

Now that we've discounted the above factors – and I'm sure there may be others I've not considered – where do we go from here? Well, there is one other significant factor that is routinely overlooked, and crucially, it can explain the exact energy conditions found to occur in cancer.

Intriguingly, the study below confirms that cells react to instigate the Warburg effect when they are attacked by pathogenic micro-organisms. The process of infection essentially replicates the energy switch to glycolysis that is found in cancer. Under infectious conditions, a switch to glycolysis occurs even when oxygen is present. Infection makes it appear as though mitochondria have become dysfunctional. In other words, micro-organism infection instigates **aerobic glycolysis** (the Warburg effect), accounting for hallmark 7, and may explain why other theories are struggling to identify specific cell damage that can account for this hallmark:

> *'Infection triggers expansion and effector differentiation of T cells specific for microbial antigens in association with metabolic reprogramming...*
>
> *...transitioning from a reliance on mitochondrial oxidative phosphorylation [OXPHOS] to aerobic glycolysis...*
>
> *...This type of positive feedback circuit may also provide a mechanistic explanation for the Warburg effect observed in cancer cells.'*
>
> <u>Science</u> **2021** [774]

In another 2021 journal article titled *'Pathogens hijack host cell Metabolism: Intracellular infection as a driver of the Warburg effect in cancer and other chronic inflammatory conditions'*, the authors review the latest evidence of the link between infection and cancer:

> *'A number of hypotheses have been generated to explain why host cells in cancer... adapt a pathological Warburg-like*

*metabolism…an **under-explored** factor that can contribute to the altered metabolic state in chronic inflammatory disease is **intracellular infection**.*

*Many intracellular pathogens have evolved to either **hijack** the **Warburg metabolism** of activated host cells to **their own advantage**, or to infect and **"push"** host cells into a state of increased glycolysis.'*

Immunometabolism **2021** [816]

In other words, many infectious pathogens instigate the Warburg effect and take control of it, leading to the over-expression of glycolysis even when oxygen is available and mitochondria are capable of creating energy. These are the exact conditions found to occur in cancer. Moreover, this type of infectious relationship with cancer has been 'under-explored'. This very telling review study goes on to state:

*'Once acquired, many **Warburg-inducing pathogens persist** with the host **throughout life**. Indeed, induction of a Warburg-like state is central to the ability of pathogens to **persist in a manner** that can drive a range of **chronic symptoms**.'*

Immunometabolism **2021** [816]

Clearly the goal of these pathogens is to thrive within the host for long periods, the aim of which is likely to acquire nutrients from within the cell for improved survival:

*'These pathogens **hijack host cellular metabolism** in order to **redirect glycolysis and mitochondrial TCA cycle intermediates** towards the biosynthesis of lipid droplets, fatty acids, amino acids and nucleotides **required for their own nutritional and survival needs**.'*

Immunometabolism **2021** [816]

Does this explain why cancer is a slow-growing disease and why the Warburg effect is a prominent feature of cancer? Is glycolysis sustained because the pathogen persists? In Chapter 11, I present the evidence that confirms a particular type of micro-organism can generate the exact energy shift witnessed in cancer.

So, how much evidence is there to support the concept that a pathogenic micro-organism, or group of micro-organisms are driving cancer? As the following two chapters will reveal, the depth of evidence is compelling, so much so in fact, that the micro-organism in question can not only help to explain all 10 hallmarks to a better degree than all other current theories, but it's involvement can account for an additional 20 other cancerous conditions that scientists are still struggling to explain. Such evidence, I suggest, renders a micro-organism as the prime suspect for actually causing the disease.

If true, this means an effective solution for cancer is within immediate reach, using a combination of treatments that are deemed relatively safe and effective. Therefore, it's a case of identifying them and testing them in a clinical setting. This is something that can be done quickly and is relatively inexpensive. Reassuringly, an antimicrobial treatment approach can be added to any therapeutic regime as an additional option, meaning that patients may be able to see results straight away, without incurring the risks associated with stopping current standard-of-care treatments.

Obviously this would require a measured approach, plenty of research and a lengthy discussion with your oncologist or other medical professional. For information purposes only, I have provided a 'potential solutions' chapter at the end of the book that discusses a possible approach to treating the disease, based upon the evidence presented within this book. It covers some of the drugs currently in use that have already demonstrated some success, and importantly, explains why.

Clues that point towards micro-organism involvement:

Referring back to children with Barth syndrome, mentioned above, we begin to see how micro-organisms could be involved in cancer. The key point here was that even though these children shared a common energy abnormality with cancer cells (a switch to glycolysis and cardiolipin abnormalities), they rarely developed cancer. The reason for cancer developing in one situation and not the other seems to relate to the fact that children with Barth syndrome are hypoglycaemic – meaning they have extremely low blood sugar levels. This was something highlighted by Professor Seyfried who claims that a lack of glucose prevents cancer from developing because it means the cell is starved of the nutrients it needs to create new cells. However, and as I discussed above, during glucose scarcity cancer cells utilise glutamine to provide the substrates needed for proliferation and ATP energy via the TCA cycle within mitochondria, which suggests that glucose would not be as pivotal as Professor Seyfried is suggesting, as the cell can compensate by consuming glutamine.

What we do agree on, is that glucose appears to be the deciding factor that determines whether or not cancer develops. This reliance on glucose explains why studies have demonstrated that the drug Metformin can inhibit cancer and reduce tumour growth. Metformin generates the same hypoglycaemic conditions found in children with Barth syndrome by lowering glucose levels within the blood.

The question is, why would increased levels of glucose increase the risk of cancer, or why would a lack of glucose prevent it? If we work on the assumption that a micro-organism is responsible for the disease, an alternative explanation presents itself. The pathogen in question feeds on glucose and thrives within patients who consume large quantities of it – this is because up to 90% of its cell wall can be made up of carbohydrate, in essence, glucose is its primary food source.[047] A lack of glucose is the pathogen's achilles heal, which would explain why a lack of glucose in Barth syndrome appears to be so pivotal. Scarcity of glucose inhibits fungal growth preventing them from establishing themselves, which means cancer does not form even when these cells have access to glutamine. This would explain why fasting, and the drug Metformin, have shown promise against cancer, and why children with Barth syndrome rarely get cancer – the micro-organism does not have access to the abundance of glucose it requires to sustain an infection.

Another telling aspect of this Metformin interaction, which restricts the creation of glucose by the liver, is that when the drug was tested on certain micro-organisms, it was shown to also possess strong antimicrobial properties capable of killing the micro-organism in question (this detail is covered within Chapter 11 and 13). Does this additional antimicrobial activity explain why Metformin appears effective against cancer? It's not just restricting access to its primary food source, it's directly affecting the pathogen as well.

Very telling, is that the 'cardiolipin abnormalities' cited by proponents of the Metabolic Theory as a reason for the Warburg effect, has been shown to be a symptom of micro-organism invasion, particularly the toxins these micro-organisms produce.[791] Highlighted in a review study titled *Mycotoxins and oxidative stress: where are we?*[791] is the confirmation that micro-organism toxins damage mitochondria and generate the same cardiolipin abnormalities witnessed in cancer by generating NO free radicals (oxidative stress), which may explain why these cardiolipin abnormalities exist in all cancers.

The data seems to be aligning with the view that cancer may be caused by an external micro-organism that suppresses specific cellular functions.

The Warburg effect, a lack of consistent mtDNA damage needed to explain the disease, the cardiolipin abnormalities that exist, and the glucose connection, can all be attributed to infection.

Is the cell really at fault?

While the concept of cancer being caused by cell damage or cell malfunction is a plausible one, the data is failing to align with this concept. In this situation we are obliged to consider alternative perspectives. Could it be that cancer is not due to an error within the cell itself? All important theories seem wedded to this school of thought and attempt to draw conclusions based upon this cell-malfunction premise. Is it misguided to be placing all of our eggs in this one basket? As the data increasingly fails to align with this cell-damage perspective, we are witnessing an exponential rise in the perceived complexity of the disease. But when we stop to consider a different paradigm, one where the cell is not at fault but is suppressed, a more compelling conclusion can be drawn from the same data that allows us to make sense of the disease.

For instance, this assumption that the cell is to blame can be seen at work when scientists attempt to explain how a tumour forms. In reference to the Metabolic Theory, Professor Seyfried states that a tumour is thought to arise because the cell-death mechanism has failed. It is claimed that mitochondria, which control the cell death mechanism, are no longer working, that they have become defective:

> *'The **mitochondria** control **apoptosis** [**cell death**], mitochondria control the '**kill switch**' in the cell… but if you have cells that have defective **mitochondria** then the **kill switch doesn't work…**'*
>
> <u>*David Perlmutter MD and Dr. Thomas Seyfried*</u> ***2017*** [405]

Specific damage to mitochondria (yet to be revealed) renders it incapable of committing cell death. The same assumption is made under the DNA Theory, where a failure of the p53 gene (which also controls cell death mechanisms) is seen as the reason for tumour growth – essentially, the DNA kill switch is faulty, and no longer works. Cell death, therefore, cannot occur in the normal manner. So, according to both theories, tumours form due to a breakdown of the cell-death mechanism, known as *apoptosis* (programmed cell death). Damaged genes in either the mitochondria or nucleus are deemed to be incapable of instigating apoptosis. The error in this view becomes apparent when it is realised that under certain conditions, cancer cells can re-instigate apoptosis – the very mechanism that is claimed to be broken and no longer able to function.

Within the mainstream view, in order to kill a cancer cell, we need to damage it to the extent that the cell can no longer physically operate, or splits open and dies – which is the aim of toxic chemotherapy. This uncontrolled form of cell death is known as *necrosis*. Necrosis results in an unplanned release of the cell contents into the surrounding tissue, due to excessive damage. This generates inflammation. Apoptosis (programmed cell death), on the other hand, causes the cell to shrink into a small package that is taken away by an immune cell, with no resulting inflammation.[408] It is a planned, intentional and efficient form of ridding the body of damaged cells.

Interestingly, when bromelain (the antibiotic compound found in pineapple) is presented to cancer cells, instead of necrosis occurring, cancer cells willingly commit programmed cell death in the normal manner via *apoptosis* – indicating that this cell-death mechanism is not actually defective:

> '*Our study of MKN45 cells implicated different mechanisms in* **bromelain-induced cell death**. *While promoting* **apoptosis** *with involvement of the* **caspase system** *and extra-nuclear p53...*
>
> *...Leu et al showed that* **p53** *could interact with Bak, a pro-apoptotic* **mitochondrial membrane protein**, *resulting in release of* **cytochrome C** *from* **mitochondria**.'
>
> <u>*Oncology Targets and Therapy*</u> *2013* [093]

In the above study, the cell-death mechanisms referred to in the DNA Theory and Metabolic Theory, assumed to be damaged and inoperative, are both re-activated, allowing cell death to occur in the usual manner via apoptosis. More intriguing, however, is the following study where honey instigated mitochondrial-driven apoptosis in 3 cancer cell lines but not in a healthy epithelial cell line:

> '*The activation of caspase-3/7 and -9 was observed in all TH-treated cancer cells indicating the involvement of* **mitochondrial apoptotic pathway**.'
>
> <u>*Food and Chemical Toxicology*</u> *2011* [196]

The honey study is particularly interesting as the main constituent of honey is sugar/glucose – which is the primary food source of cancer cells.

And yet rather than feeding them, honey encourages a reaction where cancer cells choose to kill themselves by enacting a cell death pathway that is said to be inoperative – this highlights that the Metabolic Theory cannot explain Hallmark 3. Similar studies confirm that these crucial cell-death mechanisms still appear to be in working order, contradicting both mainstream theories. This occurs in many other experiments where plant compounds are introduced to cancer cells, and begs the question: if these cell-death mechanisms are still working, why does cancer still form?

While scientists have been unable to explain this conundrum, it begins to make perfect sense when the suppressive nature of a micro-organism is considered. When the antimicrobial properties of bromelain and honey kill the micro-organism within the cancer cell, the cell-death mechanism is no longer under the control of the pathogen. The cell is now free to perform the job it has been programmed to do whenever it is damaged beyond repair, apoptosis (programmed cell death) is subsequently initiated. Why else would these natural antibiotic compounds only affect cancer cells, while leaving healthy cells untouched? These plant antibiotics are clearly targeting something specific to cancer cells. Could this be the abnormal presence of a pathogenic micro-organism, which is suppressing these cell functions in order to ensure its survival?

Often modern medicine implies that a tumour forms because the cancer cell has developed a mind of its own and 'chooses' to survive by not committing cell death. However, the above bromelain study also blows this assumption out of the water because when bromelain is introduced, the cell initiates cell death, contradicting the view that the cell has 'gone rogue' and gained a mind of its own. Why would a rogue cell, intent on survival, choose to kill itself after being provided with the same nutrients that normally sustain healthy cells? It makes far more sense to consider an external influence.

It is clear that the DNA Theory is extremely flawed and that while the Metabolic Theory is far superior, having identified a key aspect of the disease that can account for the majority of hallmarks, this theory also struggles to explain Hallmarks 3, 7 and 8 – essentially the underlying mechanism driving tumour growth. Is it time to consider that we've been viewing cancer through the wrong lens? Are we incorrectly blaming the cell when we should be considering an external factor, such as the suppressing nature of a pathogenic micro-organism?

CH 10

Confirming micro-organism involvement

The notion that a micro-organism is responsible for cancer is nothing new, around 20% of cancers are already associated with infection. *Helicobacter pylori* is a bacteria linked to stomach cancer, while the *Human papilloma virus* (HPV) is linked to causing cervical cancer. But while viruses, bacteria and fungi have been associated with the disease, this concept hasn't gained much traction because DNA mutation has been the primary focus of cancer research for the last six decades. Moreover, when infection is discussed it is often dismissed as an indirect cause, playing a similar role to that of a carcinogen by causing cell damage. Ultimately, it is this cell damage that is seen as the underlying mechanism driving cancer, not the influencing attributes of the micro-organism per se.

Challenging this concept, I'm proposing that an opportunistic pathogen (disease-causing micro-organism) is directly controlling/suppressing specific cell functions and pathways to ensure its continued survival. Rather than damage instigating tumour growth, it is pathogen control over the cell that generates this proliferative state. The damage witnessed in cancer is a symptom of prolonged infection. This damage, as random as it may be, will have an indirect bearing on the disease and will add an extra layer of complexity when it comes to treatment.

This suppressive influence can explain why cancer does not form even when the DNA mutations thought to cause the disease are present, why cancer sometimes develops without DNA mutations occurring at all, and why up to 80% of cancer studies have been found to be incorrect[018] – cell damage and DNA mutation are side-effects, not the driving mechanism. So many studies are incorrect because scientists are not factoring in the influence of the micro-organisms when drawing their conclusions.

Micro-organism suppression forces the cell to operate on 'autopilot', which explains its counter-intuitive activity, and can account for why cancer cells choose to commit cell death in circumstances where anti-microbial compounds are introduced – the pathogen is killed relinquishing control of cell death mechanisms, which results in the cancer cell committing apoptosis (programmed cell death). This directly challenges the notion that this cell-death mechanism is broken beyond repair and that the cell has developed a mind of its own, which are the assertions often used to explain tumour growth and account for its seemingly erratic behaviour.

The idea that the cancer cell has gained autonomy, and is choosing to act in a selfish manner in order to thrive and determine it's own destiny, not only goes against millions of years of evolutionary programming, where cells operate in a commensal manner for the benefit of the organism, but such behaviour is more reminiscent to that of a parasitic pathogen attempting to survive and propagate within the tissue it has invaded. The conduct of the cancer cell is more likely a reflection of this pathogen's controlling influence, its desire to survive within these 'cancer' cells, and the **unbridled proliferation** that is the default state of micro-organisms.

While the behaviour of the cancerous tumour is contradictory to its own survival – in that it will also die when it kills it's host – this is not the case for micro-organisms. Once the host dies, these pathogens continue to thrive, given that the nutrients within cells becomes far easier to access now that the immune system and cell defences are no longer a barrier to invasion.[880] While it is more likely just an unfortunate result of unbridled micro-organism proliferation – one could argue that the death of the host is the ultimate goal of the pathogen, because it benefits from this outcome to a greater degree.

Moreover, if you imagine the full life-cycle of this event, what transpires is that particular pathogens experience the ability to control and thrive within a human host. Once death of the host occurs, these nutrients become easier to access – a time of abundance for micro-organism growth if you will. These micro-organisms re-populate the soil and may once again find their way into another human host in future. Only now they've evolved to become more efficient at thriving within us having learnt from their previous experience. Could this human and pathogen interaction explain the evolution of the disease and why the incidence of cancer continues to increase in each generation? Are these pathogens simply becoming more efficient at this process over time, while the toxic load on our immune system renders us less capable of defeating these pathogens before they can become established?

Significantly, this micro-organism-based cell-suppression concept of cancer is not incorporated into any current cancer theory. It is possibly the only remaining avenue yet to be explored in the search for the cause of the disease. So, as you move through this chapter and the next, keep this suppressive mechanism in mind, because when you start looking at cancer through this suppressive lens, many of the little-understood features of the disease will begin to make sense.

While I understand you are eager to discover which micro-organism I propose is responsible, discussing micro-organisms in their broader context allows me to highlight some critical points that need to be understood first. This sets the stage for the 'big reveal' in the chapter that follows.

Carcinogenesis – consistency is key:

Carcinogenesis refers to the process by which a carcinogen causes cancer to form. Scientists know that certain toxins stimulate tumour growth but the exact mechanism that converts a healthy cell into a cancer cell remains elusive. Attempts to replicate the DNA damage thought to cause the disease has led to a failure to reproduce cancer in most cases – the *National Cancer Institute* in America highlights that at least 80% of studies that form the backbone of our current view of cancer are incorrect because they can't be replicated.[018]

The carcinogenesis conundrum has scientists scratching their heads. In particular, the DNA damage witnessed in cancer appears completely random, which doesn't align with the DNA Theory. This is a problem for the mainstream view because this random damage is at odds with the consistency of tumour growth. For instance, carcinogens come in many forms; chemicals (liquid), radiation (waves) and even hard matter (particles) such as asbestos, and yet despite their obvious differences in composition, toxicity, and the type of damage they inflict, they all cause the same condition to form (cancer). How can so many different agents that affect cells in distinctly separate ways, generate the same consistent disease? How can randomness cause consistency? The answer is that it can't. So, for the consistency of cancer to occur – and by consistency I am referring to the 10 hallmarks shared by all cancer types – there must be a consistent set of symptoms that arise from the damage caused by all carcinogens. These consistent symptoms must be the catalyst that stimulates tumour growth, regardless of the randomness of damage inflicted. Uncovering these consistencies and then understanding how they contribute to cancer is the key to comprehending this process.

When we shift our thinking to include infection, carcinogenesis begins to make sense because several consistencies become apparent. No matter the damage caused, all carcinogens generate immune suppression, chronic inflammation, overproduction of lactic acid and iron overload. All four factors in combination encourage, stimulate, and facilitate micro-organism infection of damaged cells. Micro-organisms present at the site of injury, benefit from the conditions that carcinogens generate.

A weak immune system benefits pathogens because they encounter less resistance. Inflammation renders cells vulnerable to invasion while lactic acid and iron overload feeds the infection process. Additionally, iron overload and lactic acid suppresses the immune response at the site of injury, handing the advantage to the pathogen. This generates the very conditions that benefit invasive, disease-causing micro-organisms.

To a greater degree than the other three factors, immune weakness highlights the involvement of a micro-organism in generating tumour growth. In fact, the correlation between a weak immune response and cancer development is startling, which is why it's confusing that such an important correlation appears to have been overlooked for so long. This may explain why chemotherapy, which dramatically weakens the immune system, is still offered to patients as a primary treatment solution. Weakness of the immune system is not considered significant, because micro-organisms are thought to play an indirect role only, in a small number of cancers.

Consistency factor 1 – immune suppression:

Challenging the mainstream view, organ transplant- and HIV-based studies show that a four-fold increased risk of cancer is seen in patients with a weakened immune state, with some cancers increasing by up to 20-fold:

'We were **surprised** to find that this population is at increased risk for a large number of **different cancers**—32 **different types of cancer**, including some that we **don't commonly** associate with HIV and **immunosuppression.'**

<u>Division of Cancer Epidemiology and Genetics, NCI 2012</u> [045]

HIV patients are at risk because HIV weakens the immune system. A separate study confirms that the increased rate of cancer in HIV patients is not associated with viruses, which highlights that another type of micro-organism must be involved:

'HIV-infected persons are at particular risk for cancers with a known infectious cause, although the higher risk has decreased in the **antiretroviral** therapy era. Cancers **without a known infectious cause** are **modestly increased** in HIV-infected persons.'

<u>AIDS 2009</u> [187]

A four-fold overall increase was found in a different study from Sweden regarding organ transplant patients, with some cancers increasing in risk by 20-fold, simply due to a weakened immune state. The study even claims that this challenges the established belief that most tumours are non-immunogenic (not influenced by immune weakness). Organ transplant patients are at risk because they are provided with drugs that suppress the immune system; these are administered to prevent immune cells from attacking the newly transplanted organ in the weeks following an operation, this immune suppression is enough to encourage cancer to develop – the study states:

'...we found, significantly, **about 20-fold excess risk of cancer** of the vulva and vagina, **10-fold** of anal cancer, and **five-fold** of oral cavity and kidney cancer, as well as two- to four-fold excesses of cancer in the oesophagus, stomach, large bowel, urinary bladder, lung and thyroid gland. In conclusion, organ transplantation entails a **persistent,** about **four-fold, increased overall cancer risk.'**

<u>British Journal of Cancer 2003</u> [046]

According to the study above, cancers formed in areas of the body that weren't associated with the transplant. Given that drugs are supplied to suppress the immune system, this indicates that it was the immune system's weakness, and not the transplanted organ, which resulted in this increased risk. Another study states:

> *'HIV infection is associated with significantly increased risk for developing lung cancer, independent of smoking status.'*
>
> <u>*Clinical Infectious Diseases*</u> ***2007*** [186]

The following transplant study found that a two- to five-fold increased risk occurs due to immune suppression. The study even states that this supports the theory that cancer develops as a result of immune weakness:

> *'The theory that cancer may arise under conditions of **reduced immune capacity is supported** by observations of humans with **immune deficiencies** such as occur following organ transplants...*
>
> *...Significant overall **2- to 5-fold excess risks** in both sexes were seen for cancers of the colon, larynx, lung and bladder, and in men also for cancers of the prostate and testis. Notably high risks, **10-fold to 30-fold above expectation**, were associated with cancers of the lip, skin (non-melanoma), kidney and endocrine glands, also with non-Hodgkin's lymphoma, and in women also with cancers of the cervix and vulva-vagina...'*
>
> <u>*International Journal of Cancer*</u> ***2006*** [188]

And this final study states:

> *'We conclude that organ transplant recipients are at a **highly increased risk** for non-melanoma **skin cancer** and must be closely followed throughout their lives.'*
>
> <u>*British Journal of Dermatology*</u> ***2008*** [189]

Contrary to the DNA Theory and the view held by the majority of oncologists, a weakened immune system dramatically increases the development of cancer, which is highlighted by the lack of a direct correlation between immune weakness and the DNA damage that is thought to cause the disease. This points to micro-organism involvement, because disease-causing micro-organisms benefit from immune suppression due to the reduced resistance to invasion. Certain micro-organisms that lie dormant within us are known to turn pathogenic (disease-causing) when the immune system becomes weak, explaining why we are all susceptible to getting cancer and why a weakened immune system is directly correlated with an increased risk of cancer.

Men's complaint of 'man flu' might be justified after all:

Other evidence confirms this immune system correlation. The latest analysis of the data compiled by the *National Cancer Intelligence Network*, the *Men's Health Forum*, and *Cancer Research UK* shows that men are more likely to develop cancer and die from it:[268]

> *'The team found that when they looked at data from cancers that affected both men and women, the difference became even more striking. Men were* **60 per cent** *more likely to get cancer than women, and* **70 per cent** *more likely to die from it.'*
>
> Cancer Research UK **2009** [268]

But why? Are men's DNA genes less robust? Are their mitochondria weaker? Do they have inferior stem cells? As we might expect, the answer relates to the strength of the immune system. A study led by Dr Claude Libert from *Ghent University* states:

> *'Statistics show that in humans, as with other mammals, females* **live longer** *than males and are more able to fight off shock episodes from sepsis, infection or trauma...*
>
> *"We believe this is due to the X chromosome... several X chromosome-located strands of microRNA have important functions in* **immunity** *and cancer".'*
>
> Science Daily **2011** [269]

Women have two X chromosomes, but men only have one, with the other replaced by a Y chromosome. The study indicates that the X chromosome helps create a more robust immune system, and with one less X chromosome, men's immune systems are weaker.[269] Not only do men have to contend with lower immunity, but studies also show that testosterone suppresses the immune system. Regarding this, scientists from the Mayo Clinic state:

> *'Researchers and physicians have known for years that there is a* **difference in immunity between men and women...**'
>
> *'...What we are showing is that* **testosterone** *seems to* **impede immunity...** *When testosterone is removed, the immune cells come back strong and aggressive, ready to attack.'*
>
> Science Daily **2004** [270]

So, men are hit on two fronts: intrinsically weakened immunity and suppression of the immune system, both of which translates into an increased risk of cancer – as you would expect if a micro-organism is responsible. The study states that women's increased immunity is why they are more prone to developing autoimmune disease because women's immune systems are more sensitive and aggressive. This difference in immunity supports the studies above, and explains why men are at a higher risk of developing and dying from cancer.

In failing to factor in the role of a micro-organism, scientists supporting the DNA Theory are baffled by the increased risk seen in men:

> *'This particular gender gap is **mysterious** because there's **no significant biological reason** as to why men should be more susceptible to many types of cancer than women.'*
>
> <u>*Cancer Research UK*</u> ***2009*** [268]

Distracted by the consensus view that claims DNA damage is responsible, scientists overlook the biological significance of the immune system. As a result, confusion dominates, with the disease appearing far more mysterious and complicated than it possibly is.

Lack of sleep:

According to the latest research, not getting enough regular sleep has been acknowledged as a risk factor for cancer. Scientists are unable to explain why:

> *'Intriguingly, disturbance of sleep, particularly in shift workers and night nurses, has been linked to higher incidences of cancers, with night shift nurses having **a clear statistically higher incidence** of **breast cancer**.'*
>
> <u>*Genes and Development*</u> **2012** [381]

There is no direct correlation between a lack of sleep and the DNA damage allegedly required to form a tumour. But, when we consider the influence of a micro-organism, this relationship between sleep and cancer makes sense – because a lack of sleep suppresses the immune system:

> *'Prolonged sleep curtailment and the accompanying stress response invoke a persistent unspecific production of pro-inflammatory cytokines, best described as chronic low-grade **inflammation**, and*

*also produce **immunodeficiency**, which both have detrimental effects on health.'*

Pflugers Archiv **2012** [382]

Immune weakness and persistent low-grade inflammation renders cells more vulnerable to micro-organism invasion. Furthermore, we produce the hormone *melatonin* during the sleep cycle. Among the many benefits of melatonin, is its capacity to act as a powerful natural antibiotic that is highly effective at killing pathogenic micro-organisms.[532, 533] Less sleep produces less melatonin, which increases the odds of infection.

Vitamin D and immune weakness:

Incredibly something as simple as a lack of vitamin D has been associated with an increased risk of cancer:

*'Tumours were 80% larger on average in mice that were deficient in vitamin D compared with vitamin D-sufficient mice. Collectively, epidemiological and in vivo evidence suggest a link between **vitamin D deficiency** and **increased cancer risk**.'*

Molecular Biology of Cancer, pg 270 **2012** [483]

What is it about a lack of vitamin D that increases cancer risk?

*'Regulation of **immune function** continues to be one of the most well-recognized extraskeletal actions of **vitamin D**... There is strong evidence that vitamin D metabolic enzymes are expressed in virtually all cells in the **innate** and **adaptive** arms of the **immune system**.*

*At an innate level, intracrine synthesis of 1,25D [vitamin D] by macrophages and dendritic cells stimulates expression of **antimicrobial proteins** such as cathelicidin, as well as **lowering intracellular iron concentrations** via suppression of hepcidin.'*

JBMR Plus **2021** [777]

It is clear that the immune system plays a key role, which indicates that cancer is generated by a micro-organism that thrives within immune-compromised hosts. Of particular interest is how vitamin D regulates the expression of iron, reducing it in instances where iron has become freely available – this explains its positive effects against cancer because pathogens require iron to proliferate and sustain an infection.

Increased sugar consumption and immune weakness:

The link between high sugar consumption and cancer is indisputable,[282] yet mainstream medicine continues to question this link. Aside from the fact that glucose feeds micro-organism and tumour growth, studies looking at the role of sugar in the bloodstream found that high rates of sugar consumption also inhibits the immune system.[248, 249, 284] This helps to explain why sugar feeds the disease:

> *'"Research does show that consuming 75 to 100 grams of a sugar solution can **hinder** the body's **immune functions**," he said. "I should note that 75 grams sounds like a lot, and it's hard to think you may be consuming 75 grams of sugar, but really all it is is the equivalent of two cans of your soda."*
>
> *He added that the **suppression of the immune system** starts as soon as 30 minutes after the consumption of sugar and can last up to five hours.'*
>
> <u>*Huffington Post*</u> **2020** [767]

Neutrophils are immune cells that are tasked with killing micro-organisms. They identify pathogens by the glucose and carbohydrate structures contained within their cell walls – micro-organisms are essentially made from specific sugar structures. When we consume sugar in large quantities we confuse the immune system, which targets the sugar rather than the micro-organism.[249, 284] Furthermore, this sugar feeds the pathogen.

Fasting has been shown to improve the immune response because it depletes sugar within the body. This bolsters the immune system, allowing neutrophils to locate and target pathogens without being distracted. This is why studies show that fasting has a beneficial impact against cancer; the micro-organism that generates the disease is better targeted when immune cells are no longer being confused by the presence of excess sugar. [364, 770]

The glutamine immune suppression connection:

The link between cancer, immune weakness and micro-organisms can be seen with glutamine. Cancer cells consume high levels of glutamine, which would intuitively lead to a strategy of glutamine restriction to inhibit the disease. But the high consumption of glutamine by cancer depletes levels within the rest of the body,[432, 443, 444] and this results in several detrimental outcomes. One of these is suppression of the immune system, because glutamine is critical to immune cell function:

> 'Indeed, the provision of glutamine to patients following bone marrow transplantation resulted in a **lower level of infection** and a shorter stay in hospital than for patients receiving glutamine-free parenteral nutrition.'
>
> <u>Amino Acids</u> **1999**[442]

Depletion of glutamine aids the proliferation of micro-organisms and thus cancer. The drain on glutamine stores that occurs in cancer naturally weakens our immune defence over time, explaining why the illness becomes more aggressive as it progresses.

The antioxidant immune suppression connection:

In Chapter 6, I discussed how antioxidants suppress the immune system by reducing free radicals, which are used by cells to kill pathogens. Given that I'm claiming a micro-organism causes cancer, we would expect to see that suppressing the immune system using antioxidant supplements would increase cancer risk, and as I confirmed in Chapter 6, this is precisely what we see. On average, studies showed a 3-fold increased cancer risk, with some showing up to a 20-fold increase, simply because the immune system had been suppressed. This was exactly the opposite of what scientists expected to find. As the DNA damage caused by free radicals was reduced with antioxidant supplementation, cancer risk increased, indicating that neither DNA damage nor free radicals are responsible for generating or driving the disease.

In conjunction with the rest of the evidence presented in this chapter, this strongly indicates that micro-organisms are at the heart of tumour growth because immune suppression benefits pathogens by increasing their ability to invade cells and sustain an infection.

Consistency factor 2 – inflammation:

The second consistent factor brought about by carcinogen exposure that aids micro-organism infection and cancer development, is inflammation. In fact, inflammation is categorised as one of the 10 official hallmarks of cancer because it is recognised as a precursor to tumour development – wherever tumours occur, inflammation exists.

Inflammation is the reaction to cell damage. It is how a cell signals immune cells for help to repair any damage caused. When carcinogens are absorbed, inflammation results. But how could inflammation link micro-organisms to tumour development? When cells become inflamed they increase their permeability (the pores of the cell are opened); this makes it easier for immune cells and nutrients to enter the cell to aid in cell repair and the removal of toxins. Unfortunately, this simultaneously renders the cell more vulnerable to micro-organism attack, especially when the immune system is weakened. Inflamed cells increase the chance of micro-organism invasion:

> *'...the [micro-organism] is able to **exploit inflammation** stimulated through other mechanisms **to enhance its ability to colonize.'***
>
> <u>*Current opinion in microbiology*</u> **2011** [572]

This indicates that micro-organisms are involved at the initial stages of tumour development because tumours develop from the inflammation that micro-organisms exploit. Inflammation is also generated by the presence of pathogens themselves; when micro-organisms attack, the cell reacts by generating inflammation to alert the immune system to the infection. The presence of a micro-organism helps to explain why persistent inflammation exists within tumours and why inflammation is a hallmark of the disease. Add immune suppression to a state of persistent inflammation (persistent cell damage), and you have the conditions that encourage and facilitate micro-organism invasion of damaged cells.

Consistency factor 3 – iron:

The link between iron and cancer is rarely addressed and is certainly not factored into any mainstream treatment protocol, nor are patients advised about how iron, inflammation, immune suppression and tumour growth are linked, which is worrying, considering that iron plays such a critical role in cancer development.

Iron overload is an unofficial hallmark associated with the disease. Like many other aspects of cancer that cannot be explained by the DNA Theory, the involvement of iron is largely ignored. The disturbing apathy surrounding iron's role in cancer is highlighted in the study below, which confirms its central role in causing a tumour to form, and its ability to facilitate the progression of the disease:

> *'Substantive and transformative evidence... implicates changes in the uptake and management of **iron** as **crucial features of cancer**,*

*and suggests that **altered iron metabolism** is a key metabolic 'hallmark of cancer'.*

*Iron is **more deeply embedded** in tumour cell biology **than has been previously understood.'***

Nature Reviews. Cancer **2013** [488]

In fact, iron is now being considered as a carcinogen due to its ability to stimulate tumour growth:

*'...iron works as a double-edged sword, and its excess is a **risk for cancer**, presumably via generation of reactive oxygen species... Indeed, **iron is carcinogenic** in animal experiments.*

*Furthermore, a recent epidemiological study reported that **iron reduction** by phlebotomy [drawing blood] **decreased cancer risk** in the apparently normal population. These results suggest that fine control of body iron stores would be a wise strategy for **cancer prevention.'***

Cancer Science **2009** [496]

So, what involvement does iron have with micro-organisms, inflammation and immune suppression?

'Freely available iron** can severely damage or destroy the whole mechanism of **natural resistance**, leading to **rapid bacterial or fungal growth in tissue fluids.'

*Freely available iron is derived from **iron overload**, free haem compounds, or hypoxia in **injured tissue**. This can severely damage or abolish normal [defence] mechanisms in tissue fluids leading to **overwhelming growth** of **bacteria** or **fungi.'***

Journal of Medical Microbiology **2006** [489]

In other words, iron is a crucial compound released by damaged cells that specifically stimulates micro-organism growth and facilitates cell invasion whenever it is accessible. For this reason, access to iron is usually tightly controlled within cells. It is confined within storage proteins called *ferritin* and *transferrin*, only to be released as and when it is needed for cell growth. Iron is essentially kept under lock and key by the cell because cells know that micro-organisms pose a threat once they gain access to it. The danger occurs when persistent cell damage results in iron being released accidentally into the surrounding tissue. This is because iron is like rocket fuel to pathogens:[486, 487, 801]

> *'To successfully sustain an **infection**, nearly all bacteria, fungi and protozoa **require** a **continuous supply of host iron**.'*
>
> <u>*Biochimica et Biophysica Acta*</u> ***2009***[485]

While on the one hand iron fuels infection, on the other, freely available iron suppresses the immune system, specifically the immune cells that are present within the vicinity of damaged cells. The immune cells that would typically prevent micro-organism invasion are suppressed – the outcome of this goes without saying:

> *'Iron overload **adversely affects macrophage / monocyte** [immune cell] **function** directly and indirectly.*
>
> ***Iron excess** appears to cause alterations of **T-cell** (cellular immunity) and **B-cell** (humoral immunity) function.*
>
> *The ability of **excess iron** to cause a spectrum of **immune dysfunctions** is beginning to be understood and appreciated.'*
>
> <u>*Annals of Clinical & Laboratory Science*</u> ***2000***[490]

T-cells are the immune cells tasked with killing cancer cells. These specialised cells are also suppressed during malignancy, which is something that mainstream medicine is unable to explain. And yet, the involvement of iron highlights why T-cells are temporarily suppressed, allowing a tumour to develop. This suppression specifically aids micro-organism invasion at the site of injury and explains why early cancer cells containing the micro-organism are not killed by immune cells. It becomes easy to see why chronic inflammation and the subsequent iron release leads to cancer, when it suppresses immune cells while simultaneously stimulating pathogens and increasing their capacity to colonise damaged cells.

Further evidence confirming this link between iron availability and the inception of cancer emerged when scientists attempted to uncover the reason asbestos leads to tumour growth. They concluded that it was directly related to the freely available iron initially generated by asbestos damage:

> *'Few people expected that **asbestos**, a fibrous mineral, would be carcinogenic to humans.*

*Several lines of recent evidence suggest that the major pathology associated with asbestos-induced MM [cancer] is **local iron overload**, associated with asbestos exposure.'*

Redox Report 2013 [491]

Essentially, toxic substances increase iron availability in the surrounding tissue, due to the cell damage they cause. With this in mind, and as you would expect, we see this occurring with chemotherapy, which highlights yet another method by which chemotherapy increases the risk of cancer:

'Chemotherapy **can increase levels of freely available iron**. One study showed that 70 patients with acute leukaemia had raised levels of **transferrin saturation** (50–59%) before treatment.

This was increased to **96% or above** after treatment **with chemotherapy**...'

Journal of Medical Microbiology 2006 [489]

Consistency factor 4 – lactic acid (lactate):

When cells are damaged they usually lose their oxygen supply. This forces the cell to switch to its backup energy system, called glycolysis. In order to repair damaged cells an inflammatory response is instigated, and glycolysis is also required for this process. So where there is both cell damage and inflammation (as we see occurring with carcinogens) you will find glycolysis in use. As I've previously discussed, lactic acid (lactate) is the byproduct of glycolysis – this is important to note because like iron overload, excessive lactic acid accumulation feeds micro-organisms and suppresses immune function within the surrounding tissue:

'Monocytes are highly motile cells and precursors of tumour-associated macrophages. **Lactate inhibits monocyte migration** and release of cytokines tumour necrosis factor and interleukin-6 (IL-6). Furthermore, **lactate strongly inhibits the activation of T-cells** as well as the differentiation of monocytes to dendritic cells. **Lactate also inhibits natural killer cell function** directly...'

Carcinogenesis 2017 [771]

While immune cells are inhibited, lactate feeds the micro-organism in question and stimulates it to become less visible to the immune system:

> *'Notably, [the] **lactate-grown** [micro-organism] stimulated interleukin-10 (IL-10) production while decreasing IL-17 levels, rendering these [micro-organism] cells **less visible** to the **immune system** [compared to] glucose-grown [micro-organism] cells.'*
>
> <u>*Infection and immunity*</u> **2013** [712]

Re-defining carcinogenesis:

Once pieced together, these multiple strands of scientific investigation can be seen to form a homogenous whole – a plausible explanation for the onset of cancer. Just as when looking for a culprit, a detective will look for the person with the greatest motivation, so we too will find, in the following chapter, that the evidence points to a particular type of micro-organism as the offending cancer-causing agent, because it benefits so uniformly from the conditions that every carcinogen generates.

When taken together, carcinogenesis is the result of immune weakness, chronic inflammation, iron overload, and excessive lactate production, brought about by the chronic damage typically generated by carcinogens. These consistent conditions weaken and suppress the immune response, and facilitate infection by feeding the micro-organism responsible.

This consistency explains why so many different toxic substances can generate the same disease regardless of the DNA damage incurred. This explains why we are witnessing a consistent rise in cancer incidence in line with the rise in toxins we are exposed to, and why anything from a chemical toxin, to asbestos, sunlight and even a lack of sleep are risk factors for cancer. The battle between the pathogen and the immune system explains the unpredictability of the disease. But, of course, even when the favourable conditions that can give rise to cancer exist, a tumour may still not form. In this instance the cancer-causing micro-organism may not be present at all, or in sufficient quantity.

Over the last six decades we have been subject to toxins within the products we buy and the food we consume on an ever-increasing scale. This is progressively decreasing our ability to combat invasive pathogens, while stimulating the infection process. Even babies are now being born harbouring toxins at extreme levels never seen before in human history (this is covered in Chapter 15). This increasing cell damage is handing the advantage to the pathogens already present within us.

The link between micro-organisms and cancer becomes even more apparent when nagalase, silver, honey and galectin-3 are considered. I will discuss galectin-3 in the next chapter, as it identifies which type of micro-organism is likely responsible.

Nagalase confirms micro-organism involvement:

Nagalase is an enzyme that is highly expressed in cancer, so much so that it is classed as a universal marker of disease progression and is sometimes analysed by doctors to determine the severity of cancer development – as tumour growth increases, so do the levels of nagalase:

> 'Increased **nagalase activity** has been detected in the blood of patients with a **wide variety of cancers... Nagalase activity is directly proportional to viable tumour burden.**
>
> ... **Increased nagalase activity has not been detected in the blood of healthy individuals.'**
>
> <u>European Laboratory of Nutrients</u> 2020 [056]

An enzyme is a specific tool designed to target and break down particular molecules. The abnormal quantities of nagalase present within a cancer patient are significant because the nagalase enzyme is designed to break down certain glucose structures related to immune system defence. In other words, this over-expression of nagalase that is found to occur in cancer, suppresses the immune system by breaking down immune receptors and preventing them from working. Confirming this, and the link to micro-organisms, studies show that pathogens produce nagalase to target the glucose present within an immune receptor called *Macrophage Activation Factor* (MAF). This receptor is used to stimulate immune cells into action.[055 – 059, 503] Incapacitating this receptor improves the chance of cell invasion because the immune response is suppressed:

> 'There is abundant evidence in favour of the presence and role of **nagalase** in **different pathogens.** The pathogenesis of some viruses such as Influenza, HIV or Herpes Simplex Virus-HSV is attributed to **nagalase.'**
>
> <u>JBUON</u> **2017** [060]

> 'We conclude that tumour-derived alpha-NaGalase [nagalase] is **different** in biochemical characterization compared to normal alpha-NaGalase from normal Chang liver cells. In addition, tumour cell-derived alpha-NaGalase **decreases** the potency of GcMAF on **macrophage activation.'**

Comparative Biochemistry and Physiology **2002** [055]

Progressive invasion of cells by the cancer-causing micro-organism leads to nagalase being produced in greater quantities, which mirrors what we see occurring with cancer as it grows within the patient. The amount of nagalase present is a direct reflection of micro-organism infection and directly correlates with tumour growth. Immune suppression and micro-organism involvement appear to be at the heart of the disease.

The miracle of silver:

Silver is not needed for the body to function as it contains no nutritional value. It is also not toxic within the safe levels used in the experiments presented here.[104, 698] According to the mainstream view based on the DNA Theory, killing cancer cells using silver is an impossible outcome. And yet remarkably, silver has been found to selectively kill cancer cells without harming healthy cells. Here, colloidal silver refers to tiny silver nanoparticles suspended in a solution consumed by the patient. This intriguing study states:

> *'The overall results indicated that the **colloidal silver** has **anti-tumour activity** through induction of **apoptosis** in MCF-7 breast cancer cell line, suggesting that colloidal silver might be a potential **alternative agent for human breast cancer therapy.**'*
> *Journal of Experimental and Clinical Cancer Research* **2010** [104]

Another study comparing a cancer cell line and a healthy non-cancerous cell line against silver nano-particle exposure concluded:

> *'The above-mentioned findings show that the coated silver nanoparticles inhibit and **destroy cancer cells** at certain doses **where normal cells are not affected**. This strongly suggests that silver nanoparticles coated with natural resins could be a great candidate for consideration in future cancer therapy.'*
> *Journal of Toxicology* **2022** [885]

If silver offers no nutritional benefit and does not adversely affect DNA – how is it able to selectively kill cancer cells, when cancer cells are harder to kill? The answer may be found here:

> 'Silver has a long and intriguing history as an **antibiotic** in human health care. It has been developed for use in water purification, wound care, bone prostheses, re-constructive orthopaedic surgery, cardiac devices, catheters and surgical appliances. The **antimicrobial action** of silver or silver compounds is proportional to the bioactive silver ion (Ag(+)) released and its availability to interact with **bacterial** or **fungal cell membranes**.'
>
> <u>Current Problems in Dermatology</u> **2006** [293]

In other words, silver's effectiveness can be attributed to its potent antimicrobial properties, which is highly suggestive of a direct link to micro-organism involvement:

> '"We've never actually found a pathogen **we couldn't kill**," Moeller says. "That's why silver is being used all over. **It's an incredibly safe**, very broad-spectrum **antimicrobial agent**. It's naturally occurring, and it's just really effective".'
>
> <u>Environmental Health Perspectives</u> **2013** [699]

The correlation couldn't be any clearer. The main beneficial property of silver is its ability to kill viruses, bacteria and fungi. This micro-organism-killing ability results in the death of cancer cells with no adverse effect on healthy cells. If silver was damaging DNA, more healthy cells would die than cancer cells because healthy cells are more sensitive to DNA damage. The fact that healthy cells are not affected, strongly indicates that the death of cancer cells can be attributed to the antimicrobial properties of silver, and ultimately, the death of a micro-organism. Healthy cells are unaffected because they are not under the influence of an invasive pathogen, so no change occurs. Silver, therefore, indicates that one of these three micro-organism types is the cause of the disease.

Honey:

Honey is even more intriguing, because the main constituent of honey is sugar, which, as mentioned, is the primary fuel for cancer. We would, therefore, expect honey to promote tumour growth, and yet remarkably, honey selectively kills cancer cells:

> 'Honey is **highly and selectively cytotoxic against tumour or cancer cells** while it is non-cytotoxic to normal cells... It, therefore, can be considered a potential and **promising anticancer agent**

which **warrants further research**—*both in experimental and clinical studies.'*

Molecules **2014** [195]

Another study confirms that honey is effective against human breast cancer and cervical cancer cell lines:

'*This study shows that Tualang Honey has* **significant anticancer activity against human breast and cervical cancer cell lines.**'

Food and Chemical Toxicology **2011** [196]

How is it possible that a compound comprised of the very sugars that feed tumour growth can kill cancer cells? This doesn't make sense within the mainstream paradigm, only when you consider the involvement of micro-organisms:

'*Indeed, medicinal importance of honey has been documented in the world's* **oldest medical literatures**, *and since the ancient times, it has been known to possess* **antimicrobial** *property as well as wound-healing activity.'*

Asian Pacific Journal of Topical Biomedicine **2011** [511]

The antimicrobial properties of honey cannot be over-emphasised. Take away its antibiotic attributes, and we are left with various sugars, the very compounds that would normally feed cancer. As with silver, it is the pathogen-killing properties within honey that appear to be the active factor that leads to the death of cancer cells.

A primary active antimicrobial agent within some honey is hydrogen peroxide, which can react with iron in the body to form Reactive Oxygen Species (free radicals). One could conclude then, that as cancer cells contain freely available iron that can react with hydrogen peroxide to generate cytotoxic (cell-killing) free radicals, that honey kills cancer cells not by killing any pathogen, but through a reaction with iron that leads to excessive free radical damage. And this could certainly offer an alternative explanation for why honey is able to kill cancer cells. Such an explanation, it could be claimed, refutes the premise that a micro-organism is responsible for cancer. That would hold some validity if it wasn't for the fact that non-peroxide based honey, such as Manuka honey, can also kill cancer cells,[886] which highlights its potent effect against cancer cannot be attributed to the generation of free radicals in an iron reaction, rather, that its effectiveness can be attributed to its non-peroxide antimicrobial properties.

Involvement of micro-organisms confirmed:

With all this talk of a micro-organism influence, an important point arises that I'm sure you're eager to hear an answer to. If micro-organisms are responsible for cancer, then they would be required to be present within all cancers, and all tumours, to account for the conditions that I assert they generate. You'll probably be aware that it has long been assumed that tumours are sterile (free of micro-organisms), but as emerging evidence has confirmed, and contrary to the dogma that has persisted for the last six decades, scientists have recently discovered that all tumours contain influencing populations of intracellular pathogens, shattering mainstream assumptions, and going some way to validate my hypothesis:

> 'When the team published its work in 'Science' in September **2017**, it was one of the **first conclusive demonstrations** that a tumour outside the gut had [**a micro-organism**] **living within it**…
>
> …the overturning of the **tumours-are-sterile dogma** is thanks in large part to the development of the next-generation [DNA] sequencing.'
>
> <u>The Scientist</u> **2022** [821]

What mainstream science believed to be true for decades has now been overturned. The notion that micro-organisms play a direct, influencing role within cancer cells is now a very real prospect and one that is only just beginning to be explored:

> '…in less than five years since Straussman and his team revealed those findings, the evidence for the idea has exploded as various groups have **carefully documented** the **presence** of **cancer type-specific microbial communities**.
>
> …"What we found through this process…**no cancer type was sterile**; we were finding microbial DNA and RNA in **every** [cancer type].'
>
> <u>The Scientist</u> **2022** [821]

> 'No one really knows what microbes are doing in cancer, but recent results suggest it's not nothing.'

These revelations indicate that prior conclusions drawn from laboratory work on cancer cells are potentially incorrect, because the influence of these micro-organisms was not taken into account:

> *'"Everything that has to do with tumour biology can now be reexamined." said Ravid Straussman.'*

Further studies have provided more insight into the cancer-promoting potential of these micro-organisms, in a journal article discussing the findings, it states:

> *"Emerging evidence indicates that the host **microbiota** affect **tumour progression across various cancers**."*

The study found that specific microbes colonised tumours, promoted the spread of the disease, and were also present in high numbers within clusters of metastatic cancer cells as they spread throughout the bloodstream. They continued to thrive within the tumour once it had spread to another area of the body.[863] This confirms that these micro-organisms travel with the tumour as it spreads, and may explain why cancer continues to grow once it has metastasised. These micro-organisms continue to stimulate a proliferative state because they continue to reside within the newly-created tumour niche.

Susan Bullman and colleagues have taken their research a step further, by analysing specific interactions and locations that microbes inhabit within a tumour niche. An article in the journal *Science* discussing their findings states:

> *'Our bodies harbour countless microbes—and **so do our tumours**, it turns out. Over the past 5 years, researchers have shown cancer tissue contains **entire communities** of **bacteria** and **fungi**.'*

This particular study focused on the involvement of bacteria:

> *'Through functional studies, we show that cancer cells that are infected with bacteria invade their surrounding environment as single cells and recruit **myeloid** cells to **bacterial regions**.*

> *Collectively, our data reveal that the distribution of the microbiota within a tumour is **not random**; instead, it is **highly organized** in microniches with immune and epithelial cell functions that **promote cancer progression**.'*
>
> <u>*Nature*</u> **2022** [865]

Effectively, tumour-associated micro-organisms exist within specialised colonies. These colonies recruit 'myeloid' cells, which are cells of the immune system, such as macrophages; and they appear to control these cells and stimulate the conditions that promote the disease. This is interesting, because Professor Seyfried, a proponent of the Metabolic Theory, has established that macrophages appear to be recruited by tumours and then seem to act in accordance with the goals of the tumour, by promoting cancer progression and the spread of the disease. Professor Seyfried proposes that these macrophages fuse with cancer cells and become corrupted, choosing to later spread and grow elsewhere. Could this behaviour be explained through the influence of these micro-organisms?

George Miller, a cancer doctor and researcher at *Trinity Health of New England*, commented on the study:

> *'"This paper fills a critical gap" by showing that bacteria inside cancer cells **may alter the cells' behaviour**'*
>
> <u>*Science*</u> **2022** [864]

Other studies looked into other micro-organisms:

> *'Fungi often take up residence in tumours as well... Certain combinations of fungal species correlated with lower odds of survival in several types of cancers, most strongly in ovarian and breast cancer.'*
>
> <u>*Science*</u> **2022** [864]

Of note, breast cancer is the most common cancer in women. On the back of these revelations, Douglas Hanahan, co-author of the 10 hallmarks of cancer with Robert Weinberg, has added four more hallmarks to the list, one of which is a *Polymorphic microbiome*. This refers to – and is an admission by the medical establishment, of – the emerging evidence that confirms micro-organisms are present and directly influencing the development and progression of the disease. This new hallmark instructs scientists to consider this microbial relationship and investigate it further. In his recent paper, Hanahan states:

> *'...in a survey of 1,526 tumours encompassing seven human cancer types (bone, brain, breast, lung, melanoma, ovary, and pancreas), each type was characterized by a **distinctive microbiome** that was largely localized **inside cancer cells** and immune cells, and within each tumour type, **variations in the tumour microbiome** could be detected...'*

Cancer Discovery **2022** [811]

Crucially a review study also looking at the bacteria found within tumours states:

> *'...Importantly, intratumour bacteria identified by the team were mostly **intracellular** and were present in both cancer cells and **associated macrophage immune cells.'***

Immunometabolism **2021** [816]

Highlighted here, is that tumour-associated macrophages are also infected with intracellular pathogens, which may help to explain their odd cancer-promoting behaviour.

So, while it's accepted that pathogens generate the Warburg effect, accounting for Hallmark 7, and that they have been shown to be present in all tumours, and are present in migrating cancer clusters linking them to metastasis, this doesn't necessarily mean they are a cause of the disease, they could have simply colonised the tumour after it had developed. So, an important question to ask, is this: is there evidence to show that these pathogens are present before the onset of cancer? If there is, then this means it is indeed plausible that these pathogens can instigate the disease, significantly supporting my claim that they are the underlying factors driving cancerous conditions.

Crucially, *Toll-like receptor* (TLR) activation in cancer, supports my hypothesis. Toll-like receptors are a group of receptors found on the surface of cells and within them, significantly, they are highly activated in cancer. Activated TLRs stimulate inflammation, and trigger other behavioural changes, for instance, TLR 2 can trigger a metabolic shift to glycolysis.[916] As the established view asserts that a faulty cell is to blame for cancer, and that inflammation is a key hallmark that drives cell damage, it is thought that these TLRs are defective, leading to chronic inflammation – the precursor to cancer.

However, when viewed through another lens a different perspective comes into focus. Intriguingly, TLRs are pattern recognition receptors designed to identify pathogens when they are present, or attempting to invade cells.[913, 914] Upon detection of an infectious micro-organism, they initiate inflammation to trigger an immune response to stimulate immune cells to attack the offending pathogen(s). TLR activation in cancer, confirms infectious pathogens are present, because their primary purpose is to identify, and alert the immune system to, invading pathogens through the stimulation of inflammation. Chronic inflammation generated by the activation of TLRs is a sign that an infection persists and hasn't successfully been eliminated. This aligns with Ravid Straussmans work mentioned above, which confirmed that pathogens are present, and thriving, within all cancerous tissue and all tumours, as the immune system has failed to eliminate them. This also indicates that pathogens are present before the onset of cancer, suggesting that they instigate the disease, because they stimulate the inflammation that is then thought to initiate tumour development.

In Chapter 8 under the title 'Retrograde signalling', I discussed the hypothesis put forward by Professor Seyfried: that macrophage immune cells fuse with cancer cells providing the tumour with the abilities of unlimited growth and migration. And as I mentioned a moment ago, tumour-associated macrophages are also infected with intracellular pathogens, which is just another aspect of cancer that seems to have a microbial correlation. When we pause to think about how the evidence appears to align, it seems ever-more plausible that certain parasitic micro-organisms could be involved at every stage of the disease, and may be driving cancerous conditions directly.

Significantly, the medical establishment is only just beginning to acknowledge this concept – the notion that micro-organisms are directly influencing the disease. This means that it's likely to take at least a decade before these latest discoveries are transformed into a form of treatment that can improve patient outcomes. For instance, in studies that targeted the bacteria in pancreatic cancer, two year survival rates were doubled.[864] In light of this evidence, I find it quite remarkable that neither the two primary mainstream theories of cancer have considered the role that these micro-organisms clearly play, which means that both are missing a vital part of the cancer puzzle that can lead to better treatments and a more accurate understanding of the disease.

Heterogeneity:

It has long been acknowledged that cells within tumours are heterogeneous (very different from one another), and that this heterogeneity challenges the DNA Theory, which asserts that a specific pattern of DNA mutations causes the disease, and that most cancer cells should harbour similar characteristics. The involvement of micro-organisms appears to explain this:

> *'Overall, this shows that the cell-associated members of the intratumoral **microbiota** can drive **heterogeneity** in patient tumours at the single-cell level within immune and epithelial populations.'*

<u>*Nature*</u> **2022** [865]

Does the presence of so many micro-organisms, and the toxins they excrete, explain the vast differences between tumour cells (heterogeneity) and the utter randomness of DNA damage present? And does this highlight that the random DNA mutations thought to cause the disease are merely symptoms of infection?

Cancer Through Another Lens – cell suppression:

Stepping back from the detail we can begin to see an alternative perspective emerging, one that is unique both in concept and in it's ability to fill in the missing pieces of the cancer puzzle.

Below I provide a graphic to illustrate the unique distinction between this new perspective and that of others. To briefly explain, nearly all mainstream theories appear wedded to the same concept – the notion that the cell is to blame for cancer, that the cell has malfunctioned in some way. This malfunction may manifest as DNA mutations, chromosomal damage, or a faulty energy system. Based on this thinking, it could be argued that only one primary theory of cancer exists called the *Cell Malfunction Theory*, and that all current mainstream theories are sub-theories that fall under the umbrella of this cell-malfunction paradigm. Each theory differs only in context of which part of the cell is thought to be at fault, and driving the disease.

In contrast, the perspective I'm proposing is one of cell suppression, where external factors that are foreign to the cell invade and suppress specific cell functions in order to acquire key nutrients and thrive within human tissue. In this instance, the cell is not at fault or to blame for the disease, rather, a tumour arises from an infectious agent that takes control of the very cell functions that would normally prevent excess cell growth and control the orderly death of cells at the appropriate time. Therefore, you could argue that the new interpretation of cancer I'm proposing, falls under a separate primary theory. One could call this the *Cell Suppression Theory*. This new interpretation can be seen as a sub-theory within this suppressive category, where a particular type of micro-organism is singled out as being responsible for generating the disease. Others may later provide evidence for a combination of micro-organisms working synergistically, or a different micro-organism entirely.

In essence, only two separate concepts seem to underpin all current theories of cancer. The 'cell-malfunction' paradigm, which nearly all mainstream theories exist within, and the 'cell-suppression' paradigm, a unique alternative that has yet to be fully investigated. This distinction is best illustrated within the following graphic. Here it's plain to see that the mainstream view of cancer fails to explain the consistency of the disease. This is referred to as the *Oncogenic Paradox*[866] by Professor Seyfried, who is one of a small number of scientists to recognise the need to explain cancer's consistencies. And as I've previously discussed, Professor Seyfried cites a defective OXPHOS pathway within mitochondria as the common factor that causes cancer, in an attempt to explain this consistency. The only problem with his hypothesis, is that this OXPHOS pathway doesn't appear to be defective, which was discussed in Chapter 9.

On the other hand, the cell suppression model is the first perspective of cancer to explain the consistency of the disease, in particular, the Warburg effect, challenging the notion that the origin of cancer is multifactorial (has many underlying mechanisms driving it):

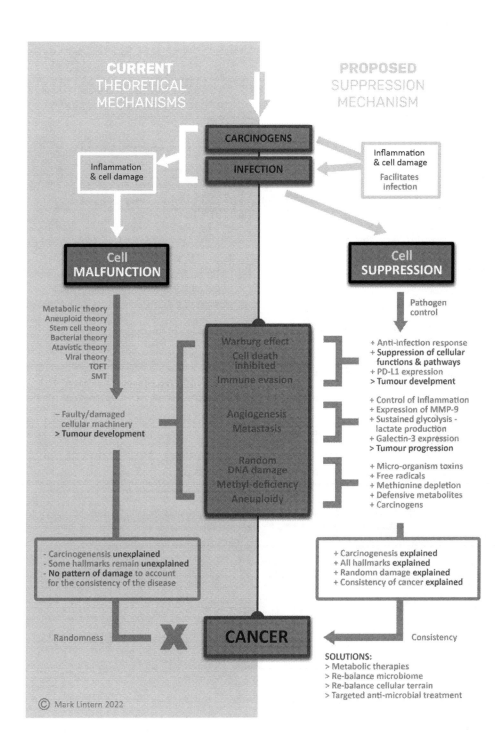

Susan Bullman[865] and Ravid Straussman highlight that not all cells within the tumour appear to be infected, that pathogens congregate within microbial niches. At first consideration this may appear to contradict my hypotheses, surely don't all cells need to be infected for the Warburg effect to be generated in all cancer cells? The study below alludes to the notion that cells are 'pushed' into a Warburg-like state:

> *'One explanation for why certain host cells enter a* **Warburg-like state in cancer**, *atherosclerosis, and related inflammatory conditions is that they are being* **"pushed" into a Warburg-like metabolism by external environmental influences**. *Indeed, most well-studied human viral, bacterial, and protozoan intracellular pathogens* **induce a Warburg-like or altered metabolic state upon infection**. *These pathogens* **hijack host cellular metabolism** *in order to* **redirect glycolysis and mitochondrial TCA cycle intermediates** *towards the biosynthesis of lipid droplets, fatty acids, amino acids and nucleotides* **required for their own nutritional and survival needs.'**

Immunometabolism **2021** [816]

In the following chapter I discuss how the Warburg effect is initiated in non-infected cells, and that this is a tissue response to infection in general, thus explaining why not all cells of the tumour harbour intracellular pathogens, this is discussed through the work of Dr Robert Naviaux.

How this would look in terms of the composition of a tumour, is depicted in the following illustration. These infectious micro-niches trigger the Warburg effect within infected cells as well as in surrounding non-infected cells. This ensures that glycolysis is sustained within this damaged tissue. A corrosive environment is generated via excess lactic acid and iron overload that suppresses the immune response, providing a barrier that protects the infection within the tumour itself. Stuck in the proliferative state of glycolysis, the infection expands with the growth of new cells as they are produced. These cells continue to operate using glycolysis until the infection is eradicated. As the immune system cannot eradicate these pathogens without help, this proliferative state results in the slow growth of a tumour mass, accompanied by the slow growth of the infection:

TUMOUR COMPOSITION
Cell suppression model

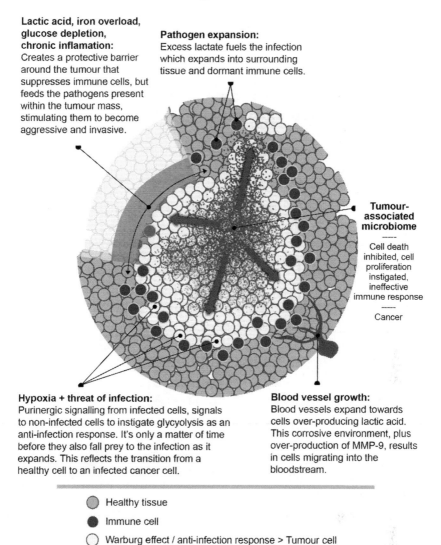

Lactic acid, iron overload, glucose depletion, chronic inflamation:
Creates a protective barrier around the tumour that suppresses immune cells, but feeds the pathogens present within the tumour mass, stimulating them to become aggressive and invasive.

Pathogen expansion:
Excess lactate fuels the infection which expands into surrounding tissue and dormant immune cells.

Tumour-associated microbiome

—

Cell death inhibited, cell proliferation instigated, ineffective immune response

—

Cancer

Hypoxia + threat of infection:
Purinergic signalling from infected cells, signals to non-infected cells to instigate glycyolysis as an anti-infection response. It's only a matter of time before they also fall prey to the infection as it expands. This reflects the transition from a healthy cell to an infected cancer cell.

Blood vessel growth:
Blood vessels expand towards cells over-producing lactic acid. This corrosive environment, plus over-production of MMP-9, results in cells migrating into the bloodstream.

- ⬤ Healthy tissue
- ⬤ Immune cell
- ◯ Warburg effect / anti-infection response > Tumour cell
- ⬚ Intracellular pathogens > Cancer cells

This cell suppression concept doesn't appear to be far-fetched at all, in fact, within the cell-suppression paradigm, a coherent solution could be as follows:

1. **Re-balance the cellular terrain** reducing toxin exposure and inflammation, while supplying nutrients for optimum cell and immune function.
2. **Re-balance the dysbiotic microbiome** that gave rise to pathogen dominance through diet and re-population of beneficial micro-organisms. Encourage beneficial micro-organisms that can also help to maintain the health of cells and control wayward pathogens.
3. **Inhibit the metabolic pathways** utilised by the cancer cell and the pathogen to restrict their primary fuel sources; namely, glucose and glutamine. This will weaken the pathogen and cancer cell.
4. **Target the cancer-causing pathogen** directly using a combination of anti-microbial drugs, off-label drugs that are also anti-microbial, and potent natural substances known to inhibit cancer cells as well as the pathogen(s) in question. Once the pathogen is eliminated its suppressive control over the cell should be relinquished, resulting in apoptosis.

Creating a hostile environment that is detrimental to both pathogen and cancer cell survival, would be the goal. Of course, exercise as well as mental and spiritual health are also paramount. Exercise to help deplete excess glucose levels, invigorate and increase the number of defensive mitochondria to help protect the cell and oxygenate the body. Being of a sound mental and spiritual state will reduce stress, inflammation and bolster the immune response.

Hallmarks revised:

Referring back to the hallmark list that I re-arranged in Chapter 8, we can now revise it with two additional hallmarks that help us to define the pre-cancerous processes:

Hallmarks REVISED	
Initiation Pre-cancerous stage	1. ***Tissue damage***
	2. **Abnormal metabolic pathways** *(Warburg effect)*
	3. **Chronic inflammation**
	4. ***Dysbiotic microbiome***
Cancer	5. **Evasion of cell death** *(Apoptosis)*
	6. **Resistance to anti-growth signals**
	7. **Uncontrolled growth**
Progression	8. **Immune evasion**
Malignancy	9. **Blood vessel growth** *(Angiogenesis)*
	10. **Limitless replication**
	11. **Invasion of local tissue and metastasis**
	12. **Genome instability**

Tissue damage is a pre-cursor to the Warburg effect and to inflammation, and is required for cancer to form and pathogens to take hold. And given the influence of micro-organisms highlighted within this chapter, a *dysbiotic microbiome* also appears to be a pre-cursor to cancer formation. Encouraged by several factors, including tissue damage and chronic inflammation, a dysbiotic microbiome is proposed as Hallmark 4, to account for the tumour-associated microbiome that develops.

Could it be that we've been viewing the disease from entirely the wrong perspective by assuming the cell has malfunctioned? Is tumour growth the result of cell suppression, with a micro-organism at the helm? And if so, which type of micro-organism or group of micro-organisms are likely responsible? Given that all cell-malfunction theories are struggling to explain the disease in full, and have potentially identified the symptoms that occur, is it time to consider a new paradigm – one that may have identified the underlying cause of those symptoms?

IV

THE PROPOSED CAUSE OF CANCER

The micro-organism responsible?

For the non-scientific readers amongst you, well done for getting this far; you've covered an incredible amount of information that can be difficult to take on board. Reaching this point in the book is no mean feat as we've dealt with concepts that are testing the boundaries of medical thinking. Finally, I can reveal the type of micro-organism that I'm proposing as the 'missing link' that's driving cancer. Within this chapter I discuss how it could generate tumour growth, using evidence to account for all of the 10 Hanahan and Weinberg hallmarks that define the disease, as well as another 20 additional associated-factors. Equally important are the following two chapters (Chapter 12 and 13), where I address the confusion surrounding the varying fuels that appear to feed tumour growth, and discuss the relationship between micro-organism involvement and a number of treatments that appear to show promise. After reading these chapters, the potential for improvements to the way we treat the disease will become apparent.

The case for a pathogen underlying the mechanism of cancer:

While studying cancer cells, distinguished scientist Dr Milton White made an interesting discovery. Upon detailed analysis, he documented that a particular micro-organism existed in all cases and had this to say:

*'cancer is a chronic, **intracellular**, **infectious**, biologically-induced **spore** transformation disease.'*

In a major paper on the subject, Dr White states:

*'Sufficient evidence exists to conclude that a cycle of sequential physiological events is the pathway contributing to the transformation of the mammalian cell to its malignant phase... A second factor requires the presence, **intracellularly**, of **conidia** derived from one of the various groups of the **anaerobic micro-organisms** known as **Ascomycetes**'*

*'These conidia as a **separate entity**, totally free of any part of their parental origin, constitute the **invasive agent** which, however, can or may lie quiescent at the onset.'*

<u>Medical Hypotheses</u> **1998** [193]

The Oxford dictionary definition of Ascomycetes is *'A **fungus** whose spores develop within asci (cylindrical sacs). They include most moulds, mildews, and yeasts'*. The Encyclopaedia Britannica states that *'Many **ascomycetes** are plant pathogens, some are animal pathogens, a few are edible mushrooms.'*

In another paper titled *Cancer: the role of oxygen in fungal-induced carcinogenesis*, Dr White concluded:

*'Our studies with supportive and tantalizing evidence indicate that cancer is due to the **intracellular** presence of an **invasive** obligate asexual **anaerobe micro-organism**.'*

<u>Science Direct</u> **2002** [361]

The compelling evidence presented over the following two chapters implicate **fungal pathogens** as the underlying driver of tumour growth and cancer progression. This micro-organism, which has become part of the human microbiome, invades cells when favourable conditions arise, triggering the initial hallmarks of cancer. Upon cell invasion the Warburg effect is sustained, and cell death mechanisms suppressed to ensure access to essential nutrients. This leads to the abnormal cell behaviour witnessed in cancer, including random DNA damage, and abnormal cell proliferation, which ultimately generates a tumour. Within this inflamed tumour niche, the intracellular infection is contained and protected by the now hostile extracellular environment through excess excretion of lactic acid and freely available iron, among other substrates and metabolites.

Sustained survival of the pathogen, and thus the cell, coupled with immune suppression and chronic inflammation, leads to a corrosive environment that generates blood vessel growth – feeding the infection contained within the tumour mass.

Just as a healthy person can fail to deal with a bacterial infection without the aid of antibiotics, the contained, and protected fungal infection may be impossible to eradicate without the aid of a more targeted anti-fungal approach. The difference between a bacterial and fungal infection is their rate of growth – the fungal infection is much slower, and probably won't be noticed for many years, until the tumour, which it inhabits, grows large enough for the patient to detect. At this point, it will be diagnosed as a cancerous tumour that has been caused by a malfunctioning cell – the result of DNA damage and mutation.

While fungi are difficult to treat once established, killing the fungal pathogen, or at least curtailing its dominance, becomes a primary goal within this new paradigm, alongside reducing inflammation and re-balancing the microbiome. While many alternative treatments aimed at reducing inflammation, restricting energy metabolism, and re-balancing the microbiome have been shown to be effective against cancer, the addition of a targeted anti-fungal approach is missing from both alternative and mainstream treatment protocols. Having said that, those that do appear to be effective seem to share an unexpected quality.

Notably, where re-purposed drugs are used against cancer with noticeable success – such as Metformin,[330, 718] statins[599, 823] and Mebendazole[783] – we find that they generally possess additional anti-fungal properties. This helps to explain why they provide such a positive effect against a disease they were not designed to treat. Metformin is a diabetic drug used to regulate blood glucose, Statins are fat-restricting drugs, while Mebendazole is an anti-parasitic drug; all of these possess anti-fungal properties. With this in mind, all that may be required to improve patient outcomes could be a more targeted anti-fungal approach to augment the metabolic treatments already in use.

With this in mind, if fungi are indeed an underlying driver of cancer, then we would expect anti-fungal drugs to be effective against a broad range of cancers in both pre-clinical and clinical studies. While the solution to cancer is more nuanced than just providing anti-fungal drugs, which can be extremely toxic and dangerous if not administered under professional guidance, this is precisely what the data is telling us.

The efficacy of anti-fungal drugs against cancer:

Studies show that anti-fungal drugs are effective against many different cancers, regardless of DNA damage, a result that should highlight fungal involvement:

> '...we identified the **azole** class of **anti-fungals** as inhibitors of tumour metabolism by reducing **proliferation**, **lactate production, glucose uptake** in GBM cells... Interestingly, several azole compounds were more potent at **killing GBM cells** in hypoxic conditions.
>
> In summary, the **azole** class of **anti-fungals** may represent a **new way** of targeting tumour **metabolism** in tumours dependent on **aerobic glycolysis.**'

<u>Neuro-Oncology</u> 2014 [033]

Ketoconazole and Clotrimazole are two anti-fungal drugs that have been shown to be effective against prostate, cervical, and lymphoma cancer cell lines:

> '...we coupled ruthenium (Ru) with the azole compounds ketoconazole (KTZ) and clotrimazole (CTZ), which are **well-known anti-fungal agents** that also display **anticancer properties.**'

<u>Cell Biology and Toxicology</u> 2013 [397]

Clotrimazole appears to restrict the energy system of the cancer cell, known as glycolysis:

> 'Another azole derivative which shows potentially useful anti-tumour activity is CTZ [Clotrimazole], recognized as a calmodulin antagonist and **inhibitor of glycolysis** and known to be the **primary energy source** in **most cancer cells**... CTZ induced **significant reduction in glycolysis** and ATP levels, which led to **tumour cell destruction** after 3 hrs.'

<u>International Journal of Cancer</u> 2004 [398]

Ketoconazole induces cell death in several cancer cell lines:

> 'In this study, we first demonstrated that the widely used oral anti-fungal drug, ketoconazole (KT), **can induce apoptosis in various**

type of human cancer cells and in a primary culture of rat liver cells.'

<u>*Toxicology and Applied Pharmacology*</u> *1998* [401]

The anti-fungal drug Miconazole also appears to be effective:

'In this study, we demonstrated that MIC [Miconazole] dose dependently arrested various human cancer cells...

...apoptosis occurred in tumour tissues treated with MIC... such results may have significant applications for cancer chemotherapy.'

<u>*Toxicology and Applied Pharmacology*</u> *2002* [400]

Another study states:

'Imidazole anti-fungals Miconazole and Econazole induce apoptosis in mouse lymphoma and human T cell leukaemia cells: regulation by Bcl-2 and potential role of calcium.'

<u>*Cell Death and Differentiation*</u> *1996* [402]

Econazole also induces cell death in colon cancer cells.[399] Another study found the anti-fungal drug *Itraconazole* to be effective in cancer patients with skin cancer:

'...a common anti-fungal treatment called Itraconazole, may be useful in treating basal cell carcinoma — the most common form of skin cancer...

Researchers at the Stanford University School of Medicine carried out a phase-2 clinical trial with 29 patients who had a total of 101 tumours. Within a month, the size and spread of tumours had decreased in most patients...'

<u>*Stanford medicine news centre*</u> *2012* [034]

These results are remarkable: a common anti-fungal drug dramatically affected the size and spread of various tumours in the majority of patients, highlighting that anti-fungal medications can work directly in cases of cancer.

There is now a push towards identifying effective drugs that weren't initially designed for cancer. The non-profit organisation *Global Cures* has identified 70 potential agents, and during testing, they also found Itraconazole to be effective:

> 'Clinical trials have shown that patients with prostate, lung, and basal cell carcinoma have benefitted from treatment with **Itraconazole**, and there are additional reports of activity in leukaemia, ovarian, breast, and pancreatic cancers. Given the evidence presented, Itraconazole warrants further clinical investigation as an **anti-cancer agent**.'

> eC*ancer Medical Science* **2015** [323]

Of particular interest is the following article, which highlights the effectiveness of Itraconazole when used directly on cancer patients and against many different cancer types:

> '...**Itraconazole** has been shown to induce tumour size reduction, e.g. pancreatic cancer and prostate cancer. However, there are **multiple reports** in literature indicating its relevance for **most types of cancers**...'

> *CancerTreatmentResearch.com* **2016** [512]

Cancer is said to be thousands of different diseases that require an individualised, targeted drug approach to combat each subset of random DNA mutations that occur. For this reason, it is asserted that one drug, or one approach, cannot possibly be effective against all of these different cancer types. Yet, contradicting this view, Itraconazole appears to be effective against most cancers tested. This indicates that cancer is one disease generated by a common factor or set of factors. If cancer was caused by many different combinations of DNA mutations, which would affect many different pathways, one drug that only targets a few pathways would not be effective against so many cancer types.

In an intriguing case, Itraconazole was used on a terminal pancreatic cancer patient to clear up a fungal infection that developed out of control. Interestingly, the tumour was reduced to a size that made it operable. As a result, the 64-year-old patient survived a terminal cancer diagnosis simply because he was provided with an anti-fungal drug. Pancreatic cancer is considered incurable using conventional treatment. The case report confirms that his incredible recovery was due to the anti-fungal medication:

*'After he received his nine-month course of Itraconazole to address the fungus infection, the pancreatic cancer was readdressed and found to be **resectable** [removable]. The tumour was resected and over the next several years, he showed no evidence of pancreatic metastases or relapse. The treating physicians assessed that the reduction in pancreatic tumour and inhibition of metastasis was **due to Itraconazole treatment**.'*

<u>*Journal of Oncology Pharmacy Practice*</u> **2016** [513]

The following study – which discusses the repurposing of anti-fungal drugs for cancer therapy – lists many of the cancers that are affected by a number of different anti-fungal drugs. This paper summarises, and confirms, how effective they are across a broad range of cancers. Clearly the promise of anti-fungal drugs against cancer indicate that fungal pathogens are directly involved:

*Increasing experimental and preclinical observations have demonstrated that anti-fungal drugs exert their antitumour properties via **off-site effects regardless of the original targets**.*

<u>*Journal of Advanced Research*</u> **2022** [890]

The study goes on to state:

*'Repurposing antifungal drugs in cancer therapy has attracted **unprecedented attention** in both preclinical and clinical research due to specific advantages, such as safety, high-cost effectiveness and time savings compared with cancer drug discovery. The **surprising** and encouraging efficacy of antifungal drugs in cancer therapy, mechanistically, is attributed to the overlapping targets or molecular pathways between fungal and cancer pathogenesis.'*

<u>*Journal of Advanced Research*</u> **2022** [890]

It's interesting to note the unprecedented attention now being afforded to the potential of anti-fungal drugs in relation to cancer therapy, and that their efficacy has surprised scientists, especially given the many aspects of cancer they appear to target – which may be a reflection of targeting the fungal pathogen that's controlling or inhibiting many different pathways within the cell.

Tamoxifen is a drug used in conjunction with breast cancer. It was initially designed to inhibit estrogen absorption into breast cells (estrogen is thought to stimulate breast cancer). However, this isn't its only effective property; recently, it has been discovered to possess strong anti-fungal properties:

> 'An FDA-approved drug used for **preventing recurrence** of breast cancer shows promise in fighting life-threatening **fungal infections** common in immune-compromised patients, such as infants born prematurely and patients with cancer. Some scientists suspected that Tamoxifen has **anti-fungal properties**; now new research from the University of Rochester Medical Center shows that it actually **kills fungus cells and stops them from causing disease.**'
>
>

News Medical Life Sciences 2009 [039]

So, how effective is it against breast cancer?

> 'Overall, the drug may lower the risk of: Breast cancer in the opposite breast by 50%. Breast cancer recurrence in premenopausal women by 30% to 50%. Breast cancer recurrence in postmenopausal women by 40% to 50%. Initial breast cancer diagnosis by up to 40%. Invasive breast cancer after the diagnosis of early-stage, non-invasive breast cancer (ductal carcinoma in situ or DCIS) by up to 50%.'
>
>

Cleveland Clinic 2020 [038]

Clearly, Tamoxifen has significant success; could this be because of its ability to kill a fungus that is potentially controlling the cancer cell? The article goes on to state how effective it is against fungi when used at the same dose that is effective at treating brain tumours:

> 'Tamoxifen is given to **prevent** breast cancer **from returning**. It is given orally, and often for months at a time. Scientists had known that Tamoxifen has **anti-fungal** properties in test tubes, but it was Krysan and his team, including Melanie Wellington, M.D., Ph.D. assistant professor of Pediatrics, that found that it kills yeast in mice with **Candida infections...** At high levels – about the same as those used, experimentally, to treat **brain tumours** – Tamoxifen **reduced yeast levels by 150 fold.**'
>
>

News Medical Life Sciences 2009 [039]

It appears that many anti-fungal drugs are successful at killing cancer cells, and many seem to affect the pathways that fungal pathogens manipulate, as we would expect. But here's the concern: having confirmed that anti-fungal drugs have a beneficial effect against many different cancers, these drugs are not offered by doctors as a potential treatment option.

CAUTION – anti-fungal treatment:

On a side note, you may be thinking at this point, that the solution to cancer, if caused by fungi, is to take a course of anti-fungal drugs and be done with it; I wish it was that simple. Fungi are incredibly difficult to treat once they have established themselves. One of the main reasons why – and I cannot emphasize this point enough – is due to the fact that anti-fungal drugs can be '**extremely toxic**', to the point that this toxicity may out-way any possible benefit. The reason for this toxicity will become apparent shortly, but to ensure I'm presenting information in a responsible manner, I need to re-emphasize the danger in thinking that an anti-fungal drug approach to treatment, is the answer to the disease.

Until we've been able to create non-toxic anti-fungal drugs, such an approach needs to be considered very carefully and under the supervision of a medical professional who understands the nuances and contraindications involved, as well as your personal circumstances and health status. For instance, if your liver is compromised, then taking an anti-fungal drug that is toxic to your liver may be more detrimental for you. Fungal 'die-off' is another serious consideration, which is, in itself, an extremely toxic event.

Furthermore, different anti-fungal drugs target different fungal pathogens. Not all fungal pathogens are affected by any one particular drug; in such a case, the damage caused by the drug may aid the progression of the particular fungal pathogen responsible for your cancer, especially if competing fungal pathogens are killed.

Moreover, resistance to the small number of anti-fungal drugs in use is already a problem, with some fungal pathogens resistant to them all. As fungal infection is extremely difficult to eradicate once it is established, a multi-pronged approach to treatment would be necessary to ensure the correct pathogens are being targeted with the least toxicity. For these and many other reasons, I must further emphasize that you must consult with your physician especially if you are intending to self-treat, they will be able to guide you through the complexities involved. For information purposes, I discuss some of the pro's and con's related to treating cancer within the 'Potential Solutions' chapter at the end of the book to highlight this complexity, and the need to be cautious with the treatments you agree to utilise.

Fungal infection mimics cancer:

In a recent video announcement, the Mayo Clinic all but confirmed fungi were responsible.[264] As I mentioned in the 'Introduction', when discussing the similarities between a cancerous tumour and a tumour created by the fungal pathogen *Basidiobolomycosis*, Dr Vikram M.D. admits that it is actually impossible to tell the two apart; they appear to be exactly the same thing. Had *Basidiobolomycosis* fungi not been identified within the tumours analysed, they would have been categorised as cancer, as indeed they initially were. But as fungi are not suspected of causing the disease, the diagnosis was changed to reflect a fungal infection rather than cancer. As was the case in the following two patients from a different study in Arizona:

> 'Case 1. In November 1998, a 37-year-old woman sought medical care at an emergency department for abdominal pain... She was hospitalized with a presumptive diagnosis of **gastric cancer** and underwent partial gastrectomy...
>
> Pathologic examination revealed an inflammatory mass involving the stomach and extending to the pancreas [tumour]... On the basis of histologic examination, **basidiobolomycosis** was diagnosed and she received **anti-fungal** therapy with **Itraconazole**. She is continuing her therapy and is **recovering**.'
>
> 'Case 2. In December 1998, a 59-year-old man sought medical care at an emergency department for abdominal pain... He subsequently developed colonic obstruction; probable **colon cancer** was diagnosed using barium enema and he underwent rectosigmoid resection in February 1999... **Culture** of surgical specimens grew **Basidiobolus ranarum** [fungi], and he was started on **Itraconazole**. He is continuing his therapy and is **recovering**.'
>
> <u>Centers of Disease Control and Prevention</u> **1999** [274]

In both cases, cancer was diagnosed, and surgery was performed to remove the tumour. Subsequent analysis of the tissue identified a known fungal infection as the cause of the tumour growth, leading to a down-graded diagnosis of fungal infection, rather than cancer. Another study titled *Fungal diseases mimicking primary lung cancer: Radiologic-pathologic correlation*, concludes:

> *'A variety of **fungal pulmonary infections** can present with radiologic findings that **mimic lung cancer**. Distinguishing between these infectious lesions [tumours] and lung cancer remains challenging.'*
>
> <u>Mycoses</u> **2013** [287]

While these radiological findings do not confirm that an infection causes cancer, it highlights that there is a clear correlation between what is perceived to be cancer, and that an infection can generate similar conditions. Further supporting the evidence presented by the Mayo Clinic, the *American Journal of Roentgenology* (radiology) states:

> *'..we would like to emphasize the relevance of **fungal infections** as an important **cause of pulmonary nodules and masses** that can **mimic lung cancer**... In addition to histoplasmosis... other fungal infections, such as coccidioidomycosis, cryptococcosis, aspergillosis, blastomycosis, and paracoccidioidomycosis can **simulate lung malignancy** as well.'*
>
> <u>American Journal of Roentgenology</u> **2013** [850]

A growing body of evidence now points to a clear link between cancer and fungal infection. While the relationship between micro-organisms and cancer is a field of study that's still in it's infancy, recent technological advancements have allowed us to detect these interactions.[793] The following study highlights this point:

> *'So far, **no attempts** have been made to explore the potential role of the oral **mycobiome** [fungal populations] in oral health and disease, including **oral cancer**. This is **surprising** given the **existing evidence implicating Candida albicans in oral carcinogenesis** [oral cancer development]...*
>
> *In fact, **candidiasis** [Candida infection] has for long been proposed as a risk factor for **malignant disorders**, including leukoplakia.'*
>
> <u>Journal of Oral Microbioligy</u> **2017** [792]

Leukoplakia are the white patches found within the mouth, these patches are associated with *Candida* infection and increase the risk of cancer. The study goes on to confirm a direct correlation between cancer and an unbalanced population of fungi, known as the mycobiome. *Candida* was found to be dominant in cancerous tissue:

> *'In conclusion, the current study uncovered a **dysbiotic mycobiome** characterised by lower species diversity and **increased C. albicans** relative abundance in association with OSCC [**oral cancer**].'*

Journal of Oral Microbioligy **2017** [792]

In another example, an oral tumour growth was suspected to be oral cancer, until analysis showed the presence of a fungal pathogen. The diagnosis was subsequently down-graded:

> *'A black 60-year-old man from a rural area was referred by the dentist to the Stomatology Clinic with a diagnostic hypothesis of **oral cancer**... the cytopathologic and histopathologic diagnosis was **paracoccidioidomycosis** [fungal infection].'*

Oral Surgery, Medicine, Pathology and Oral Radiology **2020** [820]

Are fungi driving cancer, or just along for the ride?

The following study found that *Candida* species were present in all biopsies of adenomas and attributes the growth of the adenomas to the fungal pathogen:

> *'...Candida species, another opportunistic fungal pathogen that rarely colonizes the gastrointestinal tracts of healthy subjects, were also discovered in our study at a relatively high abundance (2.8%) in **all biopsy samples**.*
>
> *Taken all together, these results further proved that the pathogenesis of the dominant fungus in intestinal mycobiota **may be common among patients with adenomas** and is also most likely involved in the **development of adenomas**.'*

Nature **2015** [822]

Adenomas are benign tumours – but can turn into cancerous adenocarcinomas. But correlation doesn't necessarily equal causation. So the question is, are fungi present as a consequence of cancer (just along for the ride), or are they directly influencing the disease? Is there evidence they drive cancer growth? In 2019, scientists studying pancreatic cancer made a very telling discovery. They confirmed that a particular type of fungal pathogen was actually driving tumour growth:

*'A new study, published Wednesday in the journal Nature, found that fungi can make their way deep into the pancreas... In mice and human patients with pancreatic cancer, the **fungi proliferate 3,000-fold** compared to healthy tissue — and one fungus in particular may make pancreatic tumours grow bigger.*

*The results show that **Malassezia** [fungus] was not only abundant in mice that got pancreatic tumours, it was also present in **extremely high numbers** in samples from **pancreatic cancer patients**.*

*Administering an **anti-fungal drug** got rid of the fungi in mice and **kept tumours from developing**. And when the treated mice again received the yeast, their tumours **started growing once more** — an indication, Dr. Aykut said, that the **fungal cells were driving the tumours' growth**.'*

The New York Times **2019** [642]

Not only did an anti-fungal drug prevent the tumour from growing, but it also reduced tumour size by 40%, within an otherwise incurable cancer:

*'The researchers also found that giving mice with the most common form of pancreatic cancer a strong **anti-fungal drug** could **reduce** their tumours by **up to 40%**.*

*"While past studies from our group have shown that bacteria travel from the gut to the pancreas,"... "our new study is the **first** to **confirm** that **fungi**, too, make that trip and that related fungal population changes, **promote tumour inception** and **growth**."'*

Medical News Today **2019** [667]

Interestingly, this fungal pathogen has also been linked to other cancers:

*'We have long known that **Malassezia fungi** — generally found on the skin and scalp [**and within the gut**] — are responsible for dandruff and some forms of eczema, but recent studies have also linked them to **skin** and **colorectal cancer**.'*

Medical News Today **2019** [667]

This study looking into the relationship between *Candida* and oral cancer, concluded:

> 'In this study we have shown that oral **candidiasis** [Candida infection] indeed **aids tumour progression...**'
>
> <u>bioRxiv</u> **2021** [810]

Ravid Straussman and colleagues, who created the first mycobiome atlas of tumours, (a register of fungal pathogens found to be present within tumours) had this to say about the preliminary data:

> 'It's possible, Straussman said, that fungi are somehow **aiding the tumour** to **form** or **grow**. "Bits of data here or there showed that fungi **correlated** with the **worst** or **bad prognosis**," he said.'
>
> <u>Stat News</u> **2023** [891]

What can the most common cancer type tell us?

Cancers are generally broken down into five categories depending on the type of tissue or area of the body they form within, as shown in the list below:

* Carcinomas = 85% (cells that cover surface areas)
* Lymphomas = 5% (immune system)
* Leukaemias = 3% (blood cells, bone marrow)
* Brain cancers = 3% (brain cells)
* Sarcomas = 1% (connective tissue, muscle, fat, cartilage)

> <u>Cancer Research UK</u> **2017** [069]

According to the data, 85% of all cancers form in the tissues that represent carcinomas. These relate to a specific type of cell called *epithelial* cells. These cells line the internal and external surfaces of bodily organs and other surface areas, including the skin. Their primary function is to provide a protective layer for the organ they enclose. Why is this relevant? Epithelial cells are the first type of cell to come into contact with fungal pathogens that cause disease. In other words, the majority of cancers develop in the type of cells that are regularly attacked by, and are the first line of defence against, fungal pathogens:

> 'The **epithelial** cells that comprise the majority of our mucosae play a crucial role in **preventing fungal invasion** across these surfaces. Their position at the outside surfaces of the body ensures that they

*are generally the **first host cell to come in to contact with the** overwhelming majority of fungi.'*

Virulence **2015** [564]

Is it just a coincidence that the cells most at threat of fungal attack end up forming 85% of all cancers? If random DNA damage was the underlying cause, surely we would witness a more even spread of cancer among different cell types? For instance, muscle tissue consumes large quantities of sugar, is highly insulin sensitive (insulin resistance increases cancer risk) and muscle produces higher amounts of free radicals that can cause DNA damage. All these features are linked to an increased risk of cancer, and yet despite this, muscle cells (sarcomas) only represent 1% of all cancers. The main correlation with the incidence of cancer appears to be the proximity of fungal pathogens to the target tissue, rather than the 'bad luck' associated with random DNA damage. Muscle cells are far less likely to be exposed to fungal attack, in comparison to epithelial cells. Does this account for the difference?

A recent review study looking at the correlation between *Candida* infection and its potential contribution to oral cancer is very telling. After highlighting that this common fungal pathogen can stimulate cell growth receptors, which could account for tumour growth, it states:

*'...Other observations **suggesting contribution to cancer development** include the ability for **C. albicans** to activate epithelial MAPK and ERK signalling pathways, which are associated with **growth** and **proliferation**; loss of E-cadherin and occludin, observed in **epithelial-mesenchymal transition** [cancer stem cell creation]; activation of **angiogenesis** [blood vessel growth] and pro-angiogenic factors; and the ability of Candida to enhance production of **known carcinogenic molecules** such as nitrosamines and acetaldehyde.'*

Immunology **2021** [809]

Significantly, in this study alone, just one common fungal pathogen is associated with a number of major hallmarks found to occur in cancer:

1. Increased cell proliferation (stimulation of EGFR growth factor)
2. Stimulation of new blood vessels (angiogenesis)
3. DNA damage
4. Loss of E-cadherin and occludin associated with cancer stem cell creation

5.   Stimulation of MMPs that can aid metastasis, along with
      angiogenesis and a loss of E-cadherin.

And when we take in to account the additional evidence within this
chapter that confirms the activation of other key hallmarks, it becomes
clear to see why the cancer-promoting processes alluded to above, help to
identify fungal pathogens as an underlying driver of tumour growth and
cancer.

Particularly interesting in this study, is the ability of *Candida* to
stimulate cell proliferation:

> '*C. albicans infection* **potently activates** *the EGFR (epidermal
> growth factor receptor)...Interestingly, the majority of these EGFR-
> associated cancers are located at sites where* **C. albicans
> commonly infects.**'

Immunology 2021 [809]

Given the key correlations mentioned, it might seem odd that
mainstream medicine appears to have overlooked this particular micro-
organism. However, the reason for this is not surprising when we study
key medical textbooks, because fungal infection is rarely mentioned. For
instance, on page 231, the *Molecular Biology of Cancer* lists micro-organisms
that are thought to facilitate cancer. This list includes five viruses and one
bacteria – not a single fungal pathogen is considered.[483]

This omission of a fungal relationship reflects the lack of attention
afforded to fungi, which would explain why such a relationship has been
overlooked:

> '*To date, there is increasingly* **strong evidence** *that suggests that
> the development of oral candidiasis [Candida infection] in oral
> tumour patients* **enhances progression** *events that could result in
> poor prognosis. Despite of this,* **no study has effectively
> investigated this phenomenon** *and characterized the potential
> underlying mechanisms for Candida enhancing OSCC [Oral
> cancer] development and progression.*'

bioRxiv 2021 [810]

> '*While we have made great strides in our understanding of bacteria,
> our understanding of fungal commensalism* **remains limited**...

> *...While bacteria comprise the overwhelming majority of biodiversity in humans, the shear **size of fungal cells**, relative to their bacterial counterparts, **compensate for this difference**. Previously, **fungi were considered to be irrelevant**...now we understand that fungal flora is **crucial** in maintenance, metabolism, and immunity of the microbiota and the host.'*

Frontiers in Microbiology **2021** [825]

In light of Ravid Straussman's pioneering work analysing the micro-organisms that are present within tumours, influential scientists are beginning to acknowledge how crucial this poorly understood micro-organism link is to cancer, which is refreshing to see. As a result, Professor Douglas Hanahan, who co-wrote the 10 Hallmarks of cancer in 2011, has recently (January 2022) proposed an update to this critical hallmark list. He has added four new hallmarks. Whereas micro-organisms didn't feature before, their influencing role in cancer has now been officially recognised.

Under the title *Polymorphic microbiome* scientists are now being encouraged to investigate the influencing role these micro-organisms appear to have regarding the development and progression of cancer.[811]

While this is a significant step toward the ideas presented within this book, and confirms that leading scientists are now recognising that micro-organisms may play a primary role in cancer, it may take a long while before this concept is accepted within the mainstream, given the ongoing support for the DNA Theory. Moreover, and in line with this theme of seemingly ignoring the fungal threat, while Professor Hanahan has recognised the link between cancer and micro-organisms, in his paper he mentions the word 'fungi' just once, identifying that they generally form part of the microbiome, but when discussing how micro-organisms can effect cancer in more detail, only examples of a bacterial influence are provided.

Hiding in plain sight:

My research indicates that fungal infection is gravely misunderstood, and the threat it presents to human health is largely misrepresented in the medical field.[152] In fact, fungal disease is growing more prevalent in society to the extent that previously non-disease-causing fungi are now being found to cause infection in humans:

'Today, fungi previously considered **non-pathogenic**, including mucoraceous genera (formerly called zygomycetes) and a variety of both hyaline and dematiaceous **moulds, are commonly seen** in **immune-compromised patients**. In addition, diagnosis of infection versus colonization with these fungi is a **frequent problem** that has important treatment implications.'

<u>Clinical Microbiology Reviews</u> 2016 [280]

A press release in the *British Journal of Cancer* highlights the link to fungi without either the author or scientists involved making the connection. The title of the press release reads: *How a plant's anti-fungal defence may protect against cancer*. It presents information about the work performed on the molecule found in red grapes called *resveratrol* and how this anti-fungal compound kills cancer cells. It states:

'A natural product which fights the **fungus** that can destroy grapes, mulberries, peanuts and bean-sprouts **may help prevent cancer**, according to a study published in the British Journal of Cancer...

..."**Resveratrol is a defensive molecule against fungus** in grapes and other crops, and is found at higher levels in those which have **not** been treated with man-made fungicides".'

<u>Cancer Research UK</u> 2002 [208]

Here, once again, scientists miss the relevance of resveratrol's anti-fungal properties because all the focus is on how the plant chemical interacts with DNA and cellular pathways.

Gaining perspective – the missing part of the puzzle:

Fungi appear to be the forgotten micro-organism. Unlike viruses and bacteria, their infection process is often slow and meticulous, which interestingly, mirrors cancer progression. Modern medicine has primarily focused on understanding and creating solutions for viral and bacterial infections due to their noticeably fast infection rate. We should praise the medical industry for the outstanding progress that has been made against these pathogens. However, they have struggled to address the growing fungal threat, mainly because the symptoms are mild and because fungal infection can be difficult to detect. And while advancements have been made, we need to recognise how little we understand about fungal disease, as to do so highlights the extent to which this micro-organism has been overlooked.

It is only recently that technological advances have enabled us to study this complex and elusive micro-organism in more detail. The severe lack of medical understanding, and the limited solutions available, are confirmed by this following study:

> *'Diagnosing and treating of systemic fungal infections can be a challenge for a doctor. Many of the symptoms are mild and vary greatly from person to person. Blood or skin tests exist for **only a few of these infections** and often are **inconclusive or fail** to find a fungus that really is there, a result called a false negative.'*
>
> **Human diseases and conditions** 2018 [203]

More than 600 fungal pathogens are currently known to cause disease in humans.[898] Despite this, we've only developed a few tests so far, and even these struggle to locate the small number of fungal pathogens we have designed them to recognise. The 2013 study below confirms how difficult fungal infections are to identify:

> *'Blood cultures are limited for diagnosing invasive **candidiasis** by **poor sensitivity** and **slow turn-around time**. New diagnostics are needed to complement cultures, in particular to identify the "missing 50%" of patients who are blood culture-negative.'*
>
> **Clinical Infectious Diseases** 2013 [275]

Highlighting the true extent of our lack of knowledge, researchers at the University of Leicester state that science has discovered approximately 150,000 micro-organisms. However, this is estimated to make up only 5% of all micro-organisms globally.[277] Only 10,000 species have been successfully grown in the lab.[461] Estimates do vary, recent studies suggest that only 120,000 fungi have been identified, but between 2.2 and 3.8 million exist.[899] To further highlight how little we know, scientists recently discovered 1,458 unknown bacterial species living within the belly buttons of patients.[430] While 3,000 previously undiscovered bacteria and fungi were found within the blood samples of patients.[816] So when contemplating how advanced modern medicine is, remember that up to 95% of micro-organisms are still unknown to science and that the diagnostic tools often struggle to find the 5% that we already know about. In fact, in a *Nature* article, when referring to the tiny proportion of microbial DNA that we've successfully scanned and analysed, compared with the proportion of DNA that potentially exists on the entire planet, it states:

> 'This means that the fraction of microbial diversity that we have sampled to date is effectively **zero**.'
>
> <u>Nature Reviews Microbiology</u> **2011** [900]

It's clearly unwise to dismiss fungal pathogens when there is still so much to discover. Having said that, scientists have already generated more than enough evidence to confirm that fungi play a direct role in driving the disease, by intensively studying a select number of fungal pathogens that affect our health.

The missing link to incurable disease:

To digress for a moment, it's important to highlight the extent to which fungi are a cause of disease in general. Doing so will emphasise the true threat that fungal pathogens pose to human health, and the degree to which this threat has been overlooked.

The deadly heart disease known as Kawasaki disease was found to be caused by *Candida* fungi.[132] *Aspergillus fumigatus* and *Candida albicans* are cited as the cause of another type of heart disease in an article within the *Brazilian Journal of Cardiovascular Surgery*,[133] but rarely is fungal infection acknowledged as being a cause of heart disease. An article in *Medical News Today* discusses research which found that Parkinson's disease is likely to be caused by a fungus.[134] Two American universities discovered a compound emitted by a mould called *1-Octen-3-ol*, which damages genes that transport dopamine. Dopamine is a chemical that's released by nerve cells to send messages to cells in the brain. A reduction in dopamine leads to a failure of neural signals to reach their intended target – hence why Parkinson's disease occurs. But despite this evidence, mainstream medicine continues to insist that the root cause of Parkinson's is still unknown. This is the case with many other disorders where fungi are heavily implicated.

The following study is a perfect example. It highlights the compelling correlation between multiple sclerosis and fungal toxins (another disease said to be incurable with an unknown cause):

> 'Multiple sclerosis occurs as a consequence of central nervous system neuronal demyelination [where the myelin sheath of neurons is damaged]. Decades of research suggest that the primary suspects

*(e.g., viruses, genes, immune system) are **associative** rather than **causative** agents, but a surprisingly coherent relationship can be made **between multiple sclerosis** and **fungal toxins**.*

*Specifically, certain **pathogenic fungi** sequester in non-neuronal tissue and **release toxins** that target and destroy CNS astrocytes and oligodendrocytes. Without these glial support cells, myelin degrades triggering the onset of **multiple sclerosis** and its associated symptoms.*

*We propose here that **fungal toxins are the underlying cause of multiple sclerosis** and thus may offer an avenue towards an effective cure.'*

<u>**Brain Research Bulletin**</u> **2010** [192]

More than a decade on from this study, has there been any progress on multiple sclerosis? No, is the simple answer. As of 2022, the NHS states that the cause of multiple sclerosis is still unknown, with no cure insight:

*'Exactly why someone develops multiple sclerosis (MS) **isn't known**. It's not caused by anything you've done and it's **not clear whether it can be prevented**.'*

<u>NHS UK</u> 2022 [313]

Rhizopus microsporus is the second most common pathogen belonging to the fungal group *Zygomycosis*. It is specifically responsible for skin and gastrointestinal infection and is predominantly hospital-acquired. The disease's onset is rapid and includes the invasion of blood vessels, causing thrombosis and tissue necrosis (tissue death). The infection can spread to whole body organs, causing meningitis and death within two to 10 days. Anti-fungal therapy alone is rarely curative.[294] Fungal meningitis can also be caused by *Cryptococcus, Histoplasma, Blastomyces,* and *Coccidioides* fungi that live within soil, and even *Candida*:

*'Meningitis results from the fungal infection spreading from the lungs to the spinal cord. Unlike the fungi above, **Candida**, which can also cause meningitis, is usually acquired in a **hospital setting**.'*

<u>**Centres for Disease Control and Prevention**</u> 2016 [321]

And yet, in the medical literature and public domain, you will be hard-pushed to find fungi listed as a potential cause of meningitis. For example, the NHS website has no mention of a fungal cause, giving the impression that meningitis is only caused by certain viruses and bacteria. A further danger that appears to be ignored is that of a toxin called *aflatoxin*. It is secreted by *Aspergillus* fungi, and its disease-causing potential is summed up by the study below:

> 'The diseases caused by aflatoxin consumption are loosely called aflatoxicoses. Acute aflatoxicosis results in **death**; chronic aflatoxicosis results in **cancer, immune suppression, and other "slow" pathological conditions.**'

> <u>Clinical Microbiology Review</u> **2003** [031]

Why is this relevant? Aflatoxin can be found within our food supply as it can contaminate grains, seeds, and nuts while in storage. Furthermore, *Aspergillus* fungi are ubiquitous within soil, and their spores are released into the air regularly, which means we are exposed to, and inhale these spores on a daily basis without realising it. Given that one of its byproducts is classed as the most dangerous naturally-occurring carcinogen known to us, you would think the public would be aware of the threat to health these fungi pose, yet rarely is fungal infection brought to our attention.

Aspergillus fungi have also been linked to asthma, pneumonia, and sinusitis, just to name a few – speaking of which, sinusitis is a perfect example of the way fungi are ignored and that a lack of understanding about fungal infection is present within the medical system. For instance, a study from the *Mayo Clinic* in 1999 confirms that fungi are the primary cause of almost all sinusitis problems,[539] yet as of 2023, the NHS website mentions nothing of fungi causing the disease.[540, 541]

Approximately 37 million Americans suffer from some form of sinusitis, which has dramatically increased in the last decade. An article discussing the Mayo Clinic study states:

> '"Fungus allergy was thought to be involved in less than ten percent of cases," says Dr. Sherris. "Our studies indicate that, in fact, fungus is **likely the cause of nearly all of these problems**. And it is not an allergic reaction, but an immune reaction".'

> "Medications haven't worked for chronic sinusitis because we **didn't know what the cause of the problem was**," says Dr. Ponikau. "Finally we are on the trail of a treatment that may actually work".'

Twenty three years on from this study that optimistically indicates that effective treatment is likely possible, no such solution exists. Neither are fungi even acknowledged as causing the disease.

Fungi even appear to play a significant role in causing diabetes. In the study below, fungal infection is shown to be the cause of chronic pancreatitis, which is linked directly to an increased risk of diabetes:

> *'The results show that cell culture contamination originates from an **original pancreatic tissue infection**, and that **Candida** can provoke an elevated level of **insulin secretion** in such patients, thus increasing chances for the onset of diabetes.'*
>

Of particular interest is that tumours were also present in the infected patients, thus directly linking prolonged fungal infection and inflammation to tumour development.

The latest science has confirmed a direct link between an inflammatory bowel syndrome known as Crohn's disease and the populations of fungi already living within the gut.[592] Phagocytes are immune cells that operate within the gut lining; when reduced in number or killed, fungal populations within the gut turn pathogenic and attack gut cells, causing inflammation and damage. While indicating the cause of Crohn's disease to be fungal in origin, the following study also highlights an effective solution:

> *'Anti-fungal drug treatment **significantly reversed** signs of the disease [Crohn's disease]... indicating that **fungal overgrowth had been the cause.**'*
>

And yet, as of January 2022, the latest information presented on the NHS website suggests that the cause of Crohn's disease is unknown, with lifetime management of symptoms being the only solution:

> *'The exact cause of Crohn's disease is **unknown**. It's thought several things could play a role, including: your genes, a problem with the immune system, smoking, a previous stomach bug, an abnormal balance of gut bacteria.*

*There's no cure for Crohn's disease, but treatment can help **reduce or control your symptoms**.'*

NHS **2022** [593]

Note that fungi aren't even suggested as a possible cause, even though it has been known for decades that disease-causing fungi live within the human gut. And as one would expect with a condition that increases inflammation and cell damage, and in which fungal pathogens are involved, inflammatory bowel disease greatly increases the risk of cancer developing:

'Inflammatory bowel disease is widely accepted as one of the important risk factors leading to colorectal cancer.'

World Journal of Gastroenterology **2014** [594]

Several fungal species are shown to cause various forms of arthritis.[617] However, the cause of arthritis is unknown, and the management of the inflammation using drugs is the only solution offered by doctors.

Many skin complaints such as psoriasis, eczema, dandruff, athlete's foot, and cracked heels are linked to fungal infection. In fact, a recent study of micro-organism populations living on the skin revealed between 12 and 20 different fungi that are persistently present, leading to many skin complaints. Highlighting the lack of understanding within the industry, the *National Institute of Health* states:

*'While humans have harnessed the power of yeast to ferment bread and beer, the function of yeast or other types of fungi that live in and on the human body is **not well understood**.'*

National Institute of Health **2013** [115]

Fungi produce a myriad of toxins that are linked to many diseases. Therefore, it is essential to have some way of measuring our exposure to these toxins, especially in the food we consume. Further highlighting our poor grasp of the threat that fungi pose, the limited research performed into these pathogens only enables scientists to track a few fungal mycotoxins deemed dangerous to our health. The worrying thing is, there are hundreds, if not thousands of mycotoxins that we are potentially exposed to. In general, just five fungal toxins are regularly screened for in food stores, providing some level of safety for consumers against exposure and contamination. However, the following study, which was set up to screen for toxin contamination, discovered that 139 different mycotoxins were found to be present in the food stock analysed:

> *'Legal authorities, food and feed industry alike acknowledge the importance of this issue and considerable effort is directed towards detecting and preventing **mycotoxin contamination**. However, of the 300–400 mycotoxins known to date, only a **very limited number** is subject to legal guidance and regular monitoring.*
>
> *A total number of **139 different fungal metabolites** were detected in the 83 feed samples. All of the samples were co-contaminated with seven to 69 different **mycotoxins**.'*
>
> *MDPI* 2013 [543]

Highlighting that we have a great deal more to uncover about the influence of micro-organisms, and that we've likely underestimated the role that they play in causing chronic disease, the study below uncovered over 3,000 previously unidentified micro-organisms present in the blood of immune compromised patients. Significantly, scientists concluded that these micro-organisms may be the cause of many of the chronic diseases, where the underlying cause is unknown – a conclusion I have drawn with cancer:

> *'...Kowarsky et al. used cell-free DNA sequencing to identify over **3,000** previously **unidentified** viruses, bacteria, and fungi in human blood samples obtained from immunocompromised patients.*
>
> *The team concluded that the **newly discovered microbes** and viruses "may prove to be the cause of acute or **chronic diseases** that, to date, have **unknown etiology** [an unknown cause]".'*
>
> *Immunometabolism* 2021 [816]

Is it time to channel more resources into studying the impact of fungal pathogens upon our health? Has a lack of urgency and funding led to an inadequate approach to monitoring fungal disease and the toxins they produce, and is this the reason why we suffer with so many incurable chronic illnesses? Could fungi, and the toxins they produce, be at the heart of many of them?

What threat do fungi actually pose?

The article below perfectly highlights the severity of the threat, in particular, how mycotoxins created by fungi can suppress the human immune system, kill immune cells, and even cause the DNA damage witnessed in cancer. Also note that fungi are highly adapted to grow specifically within human tissue. The next few pages are likely to be an eye-opener:

> 'Many mycotoxins are potent cytotoxins that cause cell disruption and interfere with essential cellular processes. Additionally, **some mycotoxins are carcinogens...** Commonly a **single mycotoxin** can cause **more than one type of toxic effect**. There are **hundreds of different mycotoxin.**
>
> Studies have shown that mycotoxins including patulin, penicillic acid, aflatoxin, T-2 toxin and satratoxins interfere with **macrophage** functioning [immune cell function] or **selectively kill macrophages...** other toxins may facilitate colonization of the airways of asthmatics leading to allergic bronchopulmonary aspergillosis (ABPA).
>
> Aflatoxins, produced by several members of the genus Aspergillus **are known carcinogens**. Aflatoxin B1 is known as the **most potent studied natural carcinogen...** Following ingestion exposure, this transformation occurs in the liver, and the result is **liver cancer.**
>
> Gliotoxin is produced during mycelial growth of Aspergillus fumigatus. **This toxin is known to cause fragmentation of DNA**. It is a potent **immunosuppressive** agent that stops phagocytosis actions of the macrophages and impairs induction of cytotoxic and alloreactive T-cells [**suppresses cancer killing immune cells**]. This toxin also disrupts the **normal attachment of epithelial cells** and fibroblasts, which allows fungal hyphae to **grow in human tissue**, causing a disease called aspergillosis.'
>
> <u>Environmental and Occupational Hazards</u> [027]

I would like to draw your attention to two critical points mentioned in the article above, because both help to explain key features of cancer that are unexplained by current theories. Firstly, *Gliotoxin* has been found to suppress the immune system by making cancer-killing T-cells dormant. One of the key features of cancer is that these T-cells are suppressed in cancer patients, but it is not known why; the presence of a fungal toxin can explain this. Secondly, the most dangerous feature of cancer is its ability to detach from the initial tumour site and migrate elsewhere within the body.

Fungal toxins have been shown to disrupt the bonds that hold cells together, indicating that fungal toxins could facilitate cancer spread.

Regarding the common opportunistic fungal pathogen known as *Candida*, this scientific article states:

> '*Candida albicans is part of the normal human microbiota,* **frequently colonizing** *the* **skin** *as well as the* **genitourinary** *[reproductive organs] and* **gastrointestinal** *tracts [gut]. Normally a commensal, this opportunistic pathogen is capable of causing* **overt disease** *(candidiasis), but usually only in hosts with defective immunity.'*

<u>Cell Host & Microbe</u> 2013 [425]

Note that this fungal pathogen is present in the areas of the body that are linked to the most common forms of cancer, and that they specifically cause disease when the immune system is weak. This is exactly what we discovered in the previous chapter, where I confirmed that a weakened immune system leads to an average 3-fold increased risk of cancer:

> '*The fungal pathogen Candida albicans colonizes basically* **all human epithelial surfaces,** *including the skin… Moreover, under conditions of* **immunosuppression,** *patients suffer from* **recurrent infections** *at* **multiple sites,** *highlighting the requirement of a* **functional immune system** *for keeping C. albicans in a* **nonpathogenic state.'**

<u>The Journal of Infectious Diseases</u> 2017 [758]

Candida pathogens are expert at colonising epithelial cells; is this why epithelial cell types form 85% of all cancers? The presence of fungi within the gut also allows them to gain direct access to the bloodstream, especially in patients where the immune system, and the balance of bacteria within the gut, has been compromised:

> '*The frequency of candidiasis has* **drastically increased in the last few decades** *due to an expanding population of* **immunocompromised** *patients… carrying* **unacceptably high morbidity** *and* **mortality rates** *even in patients treated with available antifungal agents.'*

<u>Cell Host & Microbe</u> 2013 [425]

Too large for inclusion here, one article worth reading highlights the many cancers that are directly linked to various fungal mycotoxins.[029] Of particular interest in another article, is how the fungal toxin *Aflatoxin* was found in breast cancer tissue, how *Cyclosporin* (a drug created from a fungal toxin) was found to cause breast cancer, and that breast cancer was reduced when treated with Tamoxifen – an estrogen-blocking drug that has strong anti-fungal properties.

Clear and present danger – hospital infections:

Many will be surprised to hear that life-threatening fungal infections are commonly acquired in hospital, somewhere you might think they wouldn't and shouldn't exist:

> *'Fungal infections are the **third most common hospital-acquired infection**, and have emerged as a **growing threat** to human health. They have **lethal consequences** for the growing population of patients immunocompromised with AIDS and leukaemias or therapeutically immunosuppressed. The two most common fungal pathogens are **Candida** and **Aspergillus species**: Candidiasis is the most common HIV-related fungal infection with **mortality reaching 49%**.'*[120]

The following study confirms how difficult it is to create anti-fungal drugs because of the commonalities that fungal cells and human cells share. This correlation places fungi as a prime suspect for causing cancer. Similarities in cell structure suggest the likelihood, and ease by which, fungi can control human cell functions and pathways:

> *'Developing effective therapies against fungi has been **more difficult** than for bacterial pathogens, given the **eukaryotic** biology **they share with humans**; as a result, **few effective anti-fungals are currently available**. Most of the existing drugs have **serious side effects**, and resistance to these compounds is an increasing problem.'*

> <u>Genome Research</u> **2005** [120]

Similarities shared between human cells and fungal cells means that few anti-fungal drugs have been developed because most of them are also toxic to humans. The limited number of drugs designed to target these pathogens has provided them with an advantage. Additionally, overuse of effective antibiotics that kill a plethora of bacteria – including the healthy ones – further encourages fungal dominance.

Fungi are incredibly sophisticated micro-organisms that have evolved to live almost anywhere. In particular, fungi create bio-films that, given our limited understanding, are practically impossible to eliminate in a hospital setting. These bio-films harbour viruses and bacteria, and appear to be part of the reason why 'super-bugs' are such a threat in hospitals.

> *'**Candida albicans** is the most prevalent human fungal pathogen associated with **bio-film formation** on **indwelling medical devices**. Under this form, Candida represents an **infectious reservoir** difficult to eradicate and possibly responsible for **systemic, often lethal infections**.*
>
> *Thus, it may be speculated that Candida bio-film can be a **reservoir of viruses too, posing a further health risk**.'*
>
> <u>*Virus Research*</u> **2014** [136]

These fungal bio-films cover instruments, tubes and appliances facilitating infection when inserted into the patient. This is troublesome, because the normal barriers that would protect us against fungal infection – such as the mucosal lining or the acid within the stomach – are bypassed. This provides these pathogens with easy access to internal organs.[135, 136] Of the difficulties faced, this study states:

> *'Risk factors, such as neutropenia, systemic **antibiotic exposure**, a **central venous catheter**, and a prolonged **intensive care unit stay**, predispose **individuals** to **invasive** and even **life-threatening systemic candidiasis**.'*
>
> <u>*Infection and Immunity*</u> **2012** [125]

Candidiasis is the term used to describe systemic infection by the fungal group known as *Candida*. It is acknowledged that fungal infections acquired in hospitals can lead to life-threatening fungal disease – a fact I'm sure most of us are completely unaware of. In fact, a new drug-resistant fungal pathogen has recently been identified in hospitals in America. Covering the story, STAT news states:

> *'Just five months after federal health officials asked hospitals and physicians to be on the lookout for an often-fatal, **antibiotic-resistant fungus** called **Candida auris**, 13 cases have been reported...*

*It is the first time that the fungus, which is easily **misidentified** in lab tests as a more common Candida yeast infection, has been found in the US, and four of the first seven patients with it have died.'*

STAT News 2016 [409]

In 2016, CNN ran an article titled *How fungi kill millions globally*. Referring to several scientific studies, it highlights a worrying reality that most of the public, and even medical practitioners, seem largely unaware of:

*'These tiny organisms can be fatal and kill an estimated **1.5 million people globally each year**. **It's a shockingly high figure** and is greater than the number of people who die from malaria, **more than twice the number of women who die from breast cancer**, and an equivalent number to those who die from tuberculosis, or HIV, each year, according to professor Neil Gow, President of the Microbiology Society.'*

*"Almost nobody has heard of **Cryptococcus**, **Candida**, or **Aspergillus**, but the three of those probably account for more than a million deaths every year,"..."Somewhere between **100** to **300** **spores** of a **fungus** called **Aspergillus** get in our lungs **every day**," says Gow.'*[458]

According to David Denning, Professor of *Infectious Diseases in Global Health* from the *University of Manchester*:

*'"These fungi are also some of the most **misdiagnosed infections** in **intensive care** units in the UK."..."Prevention is better than a cure," says Gow. "One of the things about fungi is that they're **quite difficult to dislodge** once they start to grow".'*

CNN 2016 [458]

Research from *Rice University* shows that 70 percent of all people are infected with *Candida*.[459, 684] When studies looked at how *Candida* moved throughout the body, they found:

*'The "remarkable pathogen" **Candida**, can cause infection in the body that is both superficial and systemic by penetrating **epithelial barriers**.'*

PLOS ONE 2012 [685]

When discussing how infectious *Candida albicans* can be, the following study highlights that it is adept at switching between its yeast and fungal forms. This ability to change form enables it to spread without being detected. It also highlights the way that *Candida* can resist being killed by the immune cells called neutrophils and how *Candida* can even kill macrophages, which are another type of immune cell:

> *'The yeast form is important for **dissemination through the bloodstream**, and adheres to **endothelial surfaces** [blood vessel cells]. The filamentous [fungal] forms, on the other hand, are more adapted for **invasion through the host epithelial tissue**, and also have a higher resistance to phagocytosis [resistance to being absorbed by immune cells] due to their morphology. Indeed, an engulfed C. albicans yeast cell **can destroy a macrophage** if filamentous growth is triggered after phagocytosis, and filamentous forms have a **higher resistance to neutrophil killing.'***
>
> **<u>Fungal Genetics and Biology</u> 2011** [549]

Clearly fungi are a greater threat to our health than most of us realise. As diagnostic tools are still woefully inadequate, and with most scientists focusing on DNA research, it may be a while before the general perception of fungal disease changes to accommodate the reality of the clear and present threat to human health that fungi pose. The current void in fungal knowledge seems to be directly reflected in our lack of understanding of many common diseases, that I believe will, in time, be realised as being fungal in origin – including cancer.

But what about cancer-associated DNA mutations?

Supporters of the DNA Theory will highlight that some cancers appear to be directly associated with specific mutations, and that such an association confirms that DNA is the underlying cause of the disease. For example, a mutation in the CDH1 gene increases stomach cancer [gastric cancer] risk by up to 70% for men and 83% for women.[569] A mutation in the APC gene increases the risk of colorectal cancer by 80%,[585] and a mutation in the BRCA1 gene increases breast cancer risk by up to 72%. These are significant correlations that need explaining. On the surface, this data appears to support the DNA Theory, because these gene mutations seem to lead to tumour formation. But to conclude DNA is the cause based on this association alone, is to overlook the intricate detail. Closer inspection reveals a consistency that benefits fungal pathogens.

To understand this, we need to discuss a protein called *E-cadherin*. E-cadherin enables cells to bind to each other through junctions within the cell wall. Studies show that a reduction of E-cadherin leads directly to tumour formation and the spread of the disease:

> 'Loss of **E-cadherin** *characterises the transition from benign lesions to* **invasive, metastatic cancer.**'
>
> <u>Cancer Cell International</u> **2003** [583]

This is significant, because both a CDH1 and APC gene mutation reduces the production of the E-cadherin protein that, as indicated above, is highly associated with tumour growth and cancer progression. This suggests that it's the reduction of the E-cadherin protein that is the issue, not the gene mutation itself:[570, 584, 585]

> 'Hereditary diffuse gastric cancer is caused by an inherited error (mutation) in the **CDH1 gene**. This mutation prevents the correct production of the **E-cadherin protein**.'
>
> <u>No Stomach For Cancer</u> **2020** [570]

> '**A mutation in APC** *in mouse intestinal epithelial cells can* **decrease the level of** *E-cadherin at the cell membrane...*'
>
> <u>Journal of Cell Science</u> **2007** [585]

So, a mutation in the CDH1 and APC genes leads to a reduction of the E-cadherin protein,[570, 583 – 585] but how is this related to fungi? E-cadherin acts as a barrier to prevent micro-organism invasion, so reducing it would increase the risk of infection.[571] In fact, studies show that the fungal pathogen *Candida albicans* intentionally degrades the E-cadherin protein to gain entry into the cell:

> 'Disruption of **E-cadherin** has a profound effect on the structural integrity of the epithelium and might **facilitate microbial invasion...** we demonstrated for the first time that **E-cadherin is degraded by C. albicans**. Furthermore, we obtained evidence which supports the hypothesis that **E-cadherin degradation** plays a role in the **invasion of oral mucosa by this pathogen.**'
>
> <u>Infection and Immunity</u> **2007** [571]

As well as this, *Candida* fungi create a protein called *Als-3* that mimics E-cadherin, which then tricks the cell into absorbing the fungus because the cell thinks it is part of the E-cadherin protein:

> *'**Als-3** is a fungal invasin that **mimics** host cell cadherins and induces **endocytosis** [absorption] by binding to N-cadherin and E-cadherin on oral epithelial cells.'*
>
> <u>*PloS Biology*</u> **2007** [256]

So, when the E-cadherin protein is inhibited – be it by fungi or by a gene mutation – it increases the risk of fungal invasion. As pathogenic fungi are already present within the GI tract, these mutations simply facilitate infection. When taken together, all these factors point towards fungi as the primary cause of tumour growth, especially where stomach cancer is concerned.

Highly significant, is that inflammation is a hallmark of cancer; and that persistent inflammation within the gut leads directly to tumour development. It is no coincidence that fungal pathogens are experts at taking advantage of inflammation when it occurs, because it also makes cells more vulnerable to fungal invasion:

> *'C. albicans is almost always found associated with humans or other mammals, typically in the **GI tract**, **genitourinary tract** or on **skin**… the organism is able to **exploit inflammation** stimulated through other mechanisms **to enhance its ability to colonize.**'*
>
> <u>*Current opinion in microbiology*</u> **2011** [572]

Candida can also take advantage of ulcers, as they too aid the process of fungal infection:

> *'**Candida** organisms **colonize ulcers**, particularly when the ulcers are large or perforated.'*
>
> <u>*Current opinion in microbiology*</u> **2011** [572]

Like inflammation, stomach ulcers are also seen as a precursor to stomach cancer; if you suffer from stomach ulcers, you are at a higher risk of developing the disease.[901] Furthermore, *Helicobacter pylori* (HP) is a bacteria that is linked to stomach cancer, but scientists don't know why. Significantly, to survive within the stomach, this bacteria actively reduces the acidity of the stomach:

> *'"Someone with **H. pylori** is actually less likely to have acid reflux and heartburn, because H. pylori **reduces the stomach's ability to produce acid** so it can survive," says Lynch. "Someone with heartburn likely doesn't have an H. pylori infection."'*
>
> <u>*MD Anderson Cancer Center*</u> **2021** [893]

This is important to know because colonisation of stomach tissue by *Candida* fungi, was more frequently observed in patients with low stomach acidity.[572]

This is why the bacteria *Helicobacter pylori* has been associated as a primary cause of stomach cancer. It attacks the stomach lining, generating persistent inflammation and stomach ulcers, while lowering the protective stomach acid barrier – all three conditions facilitate fungal infection.

Fungal dominance:

And this is where the role of the microbiome is so important, because it highlights the link between micro-organisms and the development of cancer generally – not just stomach cancer. Toxins, antibiotic exposure, and a poor diet and lifestyle not only result in cell damage, but microbiome dysbiosis – this is where an imbalance in micro-organism populations occurs that favours certain species, such as fungal pathogens. This fungal dominance may occur slowly over a long period of time, but appears to be a deciding factor in the development of disease. This dysbiosis enables fungal pathogens to take control and increases the odds of cell invasion and thus the formation of a tumour. Two good examples highlighting this, are oral cancer and stomach cancer (gastric cancer):

> *'Our previous study showed that the diversity of the oral **fungal microflora** of OSCC [oral cancer] patients is **remarkably different** from healthy individuals: the **fungal burden** and **diversity** of **yeasts** was **significantly higher** in patients with **oral tumours** compared to the oral cavity of healthy individuals.'*
>
> *bioRxiv* **2021** [810]

The conclusion drawn from the study is very telling indeed:

> *'In this study we have shown that oral **candidiasis** [Candida infection] indeed **aids tumour progression...** Thus, applying **antifungal treatment** simultaneously **with chemotherapy** might be recommended in this patient cohort.'*

bioRxiv **2021** [810]

A similar relationship has been found regarding stomach cancer:

> '*In this study, we described the fungal spectrum associated with GC* **[gastric cancer]... For the first time,** *we showed the characteristics of the* **fungal microbiome** *in the* **stomach tissues** *of GC patients, demonstrating* **imbalance** *of the* **fungi** *in the GC ecosystem.*
>
> *We...confirmed that* **C. albicans***, Fusicolla acetilerea, Arcopilus aureus and Fusicolla aquaeductuum were* **excessively colonized** *in the GC tissue.*'

Theranostics **2021** [824]

These two studies demonstrate that a dysbiotic microbiome favouring fungal pathogens is associated with cancer. The study also states that *Candida* even promote bacterial dysbiosis within the microbiome, enabling fungal dominance:

> '*Recently, Bertolini et al. confirmed that* **C. albicans** *induced mucosal* **bacterial dysbiosis** *and* **promoted invasive infection***.*'

Theranostics **2021** [824]

The study goes on to clarify that chemotherapy also promotes *Candida* infection, which would explain why chemotherapy appears largely ineffective against stomach cancer,[215] and appears to exacerbate the disease, as well as other cancers, when used long-term. Furthermore, it also confirms that the most common disease associated with *Candida* infection is the development of solid tumours:

> '*Since immunosuppression caused by cancer* **chemotherapy promotes C. albicans infection***, the relationship between* **C. albicans** *and* **cancer development** *or* **progression** *has been* **widely reported...**
>
> *...the most* **common underlying disease** *among patients with* **candidiasis** *[candida infection] is also* **solid tumors***.*'

Theranostics **2021** [824]

The study identifies the importance of re-balancing the microbiome as part of a cancer treatment strategy, by specifically targeting fungal pathogens:

> 'Our discovery that **C. albicans may have contributed** to the **pathogenesis** of GC not only lays a scientific foundation for the exploration of innovative therapies for GC but also provides a new idea for treating specific patients by **adjusting their intestinal microbial microbiome** as an adjuvant therapy or developing immunotherapies for targeted **control of fungal infections**, which is worthy of further study.'
>
> Theranostics 2021 [824]

In alignment with the oral cancer study already presented, an anti-fungal approach to treatment is recommended. This is an approach to treatment that aligns with the research I've preformed. Re-balance the health of the cellular environment and the microbiome, target cell metabolism and additionally address fungal dominance with several anti-fungal strategies.

Finally, this study concludes that fungal imbalance is associated with the development of gastric cancer:

> 'Our analysis clarified the **importance of fungal homeostasis** in the stomach and suggests that **fungal imbalance** is associated with the **occurrence** and **development** of **GC** [gastric cancer].'
>
> Theranostics 2021 [824]

Stepping back from the detail allows us to link all these factors together, to better understand why stomach cancer develops, and how fungal pathogens are integral to the process:

1. Constant irritation to the stomach lining caused by additives within the food supply in combination with HP bacteria living within the stomach, leads to persistent inflammation of stomach cells, the generation of ulcers and, importantly, a reduction in stomach acid.[573]

2. A dysbiosis of the microbiome occurs over time that favours fungal pathogens, aided by our over-exposure to antibiotics. Fungi, already present within the GI tract, take advantage of inflamed cells and the lower acidity of the stomach, and are drawn to the ulcers created by HP bacteria, making them easier to invade.

3. This cell damage releases iron and lactate into the vicinity, which further stimulates fungal invasion, while suppressing the immune response at the site of injury, handing the advantage to the fungal pathogen.
4. A 'CDH1' DNA gene mutation can suppress the production of E-cadherin in stomach cells. This can reduce the barrier to infection, further facilitating the fungal invasion process. Coupled with these other conditions, this DNA gene mutation simply increases the likelihood that fungal invasion will be successful, leading to an increased risk of tumour development, and ultimately, stomach cancer.

Bouts of illness such as the flu, a lack of sleep, a poor diet, or exposure to a carcinogen will also weaken the immune system, aiding the fungal pathogen still further. The involvement of fungi helps to explain why these mutations only result in cancer developing 80% of the time. In the other 20% of cases where this CDH1 mutation exists, but cancer does not form, the fungal pathogen may not be present, or in sufficient number to have any effect. One would expect that if DNA was to blame, and these genes were direct drivers of the disease, then tumours would form 100% of the time when these DNA genes are mutated, not 80% of the time as mentioned. Could the presence of a fungal pathogen, or lack thereof, account for the difference?

When we look at other factors that facilitate cancer growth we see a pattern emerging where E-cadherin is concerned. For instance, studies show that the HER2 receptor, which promotes growth, is stimulated in many cancer cells. Not only does this HER2 receptor act as a portal through which fungal pathogens can invade, but an increase in this receptor also correlates with a decrease of E-cadherin in much the same way a CDH1 and APC gene mutation correlates with reduced E-cadherin expression:

> *'It has been shown that over-expression of HER2 **down-regulates E-cadherin** expression in human mammary epithelial cells.'*
> <u>**Biochemical and Biophysical Research Communications** 2013</u> [587]

It would appear that a reduction in the E-cadherin protein is a key component in the development of the disease, and can be caused by several key DNA mutations. This helps to explain why so many random mutations appear to increase cancer risk – a loss of E-cadherin, caused by many combinations of DNA mutations, facilitates fungal invasion. Is it just a coincidence that fungi invade and stimulate this HER2 receptor, and that fungi also reduce E-cadherin during the invasion process?

As E-cadherin is used to bind cells together, the loss of E-cadherin also helps to explain why a cancer cell can break away and migrate. That fungi actively degrade E-cadherin only stands to underline that fungi are capable of stimulating the spread of the disease. That fungi stimulate the HER2 and EGFR receptors[803] indicates that these pathogens are responsible for increased cancer cell growth, because HER2 and EGFR are growth receptors.

Regarding the BRCA1 gene, this mutation leads to mitochondrial dysfunction because BRCA1 is responsible for mitochondrial DNA repair. This results in an energy switch that renders the cell more vulnerable to micro-organism attack because dysfunctional mitochondria are less able to defend the cell or control cell death mechanisms. Interestingly, the CDH1, APC,[583] HER2 growth receptor, and BRCA mutations are implicated in many other cancers. Rather than confirm that DNA damage is the underlying cause, the result of these mutations further underline the link to fungi, where, in conjunction with other factors, they help to facilitate fungal invasion encouraging a tumour to form.

Why are fungi the most likely culprit?

There are many reasons to suggest that fungi are the prime suspect for driving cancer. While bacteria and viruses can also cause some of the hallmarks associated with the disease, and no doubt contribute, there are anomalies that indicate they have an indirect influence as opposed to directly driving cancerous conditions.

First on the list is microbiome dysbiosis, leading to fungal dominance. The microbiome refers to the complete population of micro-organisms that live on and within us. Emerging evidence highlights that they play a primary role in health and disease. It may soon transpire that these little critters, found throughout the human body,[811] are the primary factors influencing many diseases with an unknown cause – including cancer (I cover the microbiome in a little more detail within Chapter 15).

A healthy body has a healthy microbiome containing microbial diversity, which largely consists of beneficial, protective bacteria. When this bacteria are able to keep pathogenic micro-organisms under control, preventing them from causing disease – the body is in balance. However, when we adopt a poor lifestyle with exposure to toxins, antibiotics and a poor diet high in refined sugar, we risk upsetting the delicate balance of this protective microbiome, which can result in fungal pathogen dominance, as was shown to be the case in the studies analysing oral cancer above. It is this dominance that renders fungi as a prime suspect in our investigations:

> 'In states of **dysbiosis**, the fungal and the bacterial biodiversity may be compromised…exposures to **antibiotics** or states of immunodeficiency may provide a selective pressure that leads to a **decrease in biodiversity** while allowing organisms such as **Candida** to **overgrow and proliferate**…
>
> …More research is needed to fully understand the interplay between **fungus, bacteria**, and the **host**, but it is evident that **fungus** can have a **profound impact** on **health and disease**.'
>
> <u>Frontiers in Microbiology</u> **2021** [825]

Of course, bacteria have also been linked to cancer, and while there is evidence to suggest they are also involved, the weight of evidence favours the fungal pathogen. In fact, fungal and bacterial pathogens have been shown to work together to the greater benefit of the fungus:

> "There is **compelling evidence** that **C. albicans** and C. dubliniensis form **tight associations with specific oral bacterial species**… Thus, when Candida infections arise, they often occur in **association with bacteria**… This is why factors that perturb the normal microflora, such as **antibiotic therapy**, or changes in hormonal or mucosal secretions, may encourage **C. albicans overgrowth**."
>
> <u>Polymicrobial Diseases</u> **2002** [840]

While bacteria may also be involved, and capable of aiding fungal colonisation in a synergistic relationship, it appears that fungal dominance results – which is not all that surprising given our over-exposure to antibiotics that kill bacterial species. While the majority of antibacterial drugs do not seem to be beneficial against cancer, this bacterial-fungal interaction would explain why a few antibacterial drugs are able to reduce tumours. By weakening the bacterial community that works synergistically with fungi, these drugs impede fungal colonisation.

Secondly, fungal cells share many similarities with human cells. They are the only micro-organism that do so. Both human cells and fungal cells are of the same cell type and contain similar pathways. These similarities suggest that fungi are more suited to influencing human cells.

Thirdly, these similarities render anti-fungal drugs more toxic – i.e. healthy cells will suffer more collateral damage from anti-fungal drugs – than antibacterials, meaning they are less likely to be used. There are also fewer anti-fungal options, fungal infection is more difficult to detect, and is often only suspected when antibacterial drugs fail to relieve a patient's symptoms. In other words, we are not addressing the fungal threat in the same manner, or with the same vigour, as we are in the case of bacteria, which provides fungal pathogens with a distinct advantage when it comes to establishing themselves within our tissue.

Generally speaking, life on Earth is made up of only two types of cell: *prokaryotic* cell types, which encompasses most bacteria, and *eukaryotic* cells, which include nearly all other living organisms, such as insects, animals, plants, humans and fungi. Viruses are not classed as living because they cannot replicate themselves; they can only do so by invading and utilising the machinery within prokaryotic cells (bacteria) or eukaryotic cells (plants, insects, animals and fungi).

A prokaryotic cell is a single-celled organism; it does not contain a nucleus or any mitochondria. Eukaryotic cells are single-celled or multi-celled organisms that do contain a nucleus and mitochondria. They are a more sophisticated type of cell containing more components that perform more complex tasks:

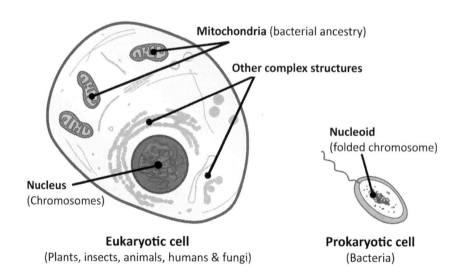

Eukaryotic cell
(Plants, insects, animals, humans & fungi)

Prokaryotic cell
(Bacteria)

Fungi share similar genes and pathways to that of human cells and contain mitochondria, being constructed of the same cell type. These shared characteristics are highlighted by the toxicity our cells also experience when we administer anti-fungal drugs:

> *'The main difficulty is that fungi, as **eukaryotes**, have cellular machinery **very close** to that of **humans**, making it extremely difficult to identify points that are lethal for the fungus but not the patient. Currently available anti-fungal agents are **toxic**... and **resistance** to these agents is **already an emerging problem.'***
>
> <u>*Clinical Microbiology Reviews*</u> **2004** [627]

An example of these shared pathways can be shown with statins, which are a set of drugs that are designed to inhibit fat production. *Lovastatin*, for instance, was initially designed to restrict an enzyme in human cells called *HMG-CoA*, which inhibits the creation of cholesterol (fat). But the drug can also affect fungal pathogens in a similar way by blocking the same HMG-CoA enzyme present within the fungus. This restricts the production of ergosterol, which is the fungal equivalent of human cholesterol.[599]

This indicates that fungi are highly capable of manipulating human cells because the structure of both cell types share similarities:

> *'...it is clear that human commensal yeast species such as **Candida albicans** have also evolved a range of specific factors that facilitate **direct interaction with host tissues**. The **evolution of virulence** across the **human pathogenic fungi** has occurred largely through very similar mechanisms.'*
>
> <u>*American Society for Microbiology*</u> **2011** [126]

We see this influence in many infection studies that show how fungi are capable of manipulating not only the cells of the body, such as epithelial or endothelial cells, but even the immune cells that are tasked with killing them.[851] Just one example of this comes in the form of a common fungal pathogen called *Cryptococcus neoformans*. This intracellular pathogen (a pathogen that can live within a cell) is so adept at invading and controlling human cells, that it is even able to survive within immune cells, laying dormant until conditions favour infection:

> *'The causative agent, **Cryptococcus neoformans**, has a remarkable ability to '**hide**' and **proliferate** within phagocytic cells of the*

human ***immune system***. *This intracellular phase is thought to underlie the ability of the pathogen to **remain latent for long periods** of time within infected individuals.'*

BMC Immunology **2007** [851]

In fact, this study highlights something else extremely interesting, this intracellular fungal pathogen is capable of transferring from one cell to another, while remaining intracellular. This not only allows them to evade immune detection, but highlights their ability to infiltrate tissue and turn infectious only when conditions become favourable, such as when carcinogens cause cell damage, leading to immune weakness. In this study *C. Neoformans* was able to cross the blood brain barrier (BBB – a highly robust defensive protection to safeguard our brain integrity) without damaging the blood vessel cells they were transferring between:

*'Yeast cells of C. neoformans adhered to and were **internalized** by the HBMEC [human brain microvascular endothelial cells], and they crossed the HBMEC monolayers via a transcellular pathway **without affecting** the monolayer integrity.'*

American Society for Microbiology **2004** [852]

In fact, *C. Neoformans* were shown to use a different 'Trojan Horse' approach to crossing into the brain, by hiding within infected immune cells:

*'Finally, we found that **Trojan horse crossing** enables CNS entry of **fungal mutants** that cannot otherwise traverse the BBB, and we demonstrate additional intercellular interactions that may contribute to **brain entry**. Our work elucidates the mechanism of cryptococcal brain invasion and offers approaches to study other neuropathogens.'*

mBio 2017 [884]

Could this ability to live within and transfer between macrophage immune cells, as well as cross the blood brain barrier, explain why macrophage immune cells appear to be involved in the spread of the disease, and why brain cancer occurs?

Bacteria:

As bacterial cells are fundamentally different, antibacterial drugs generally affect pathways that are not contained within human cells making these drugs less toxic. This has resulted in the over-use of anti-bacterial drugs within society:

> *'In a new study that surveyed* **91 rivers around the world***, researchers found* **antibiotics** *in the waters of nearly* **two-thirds of all the sites they sampled***, from the Thames to the Mekong to the Tigris.*
>
> *No continent was immune: They found traces of at least one drug in* **65 percent** *of all the samples they studied.*
>
> *In the Danube, the second-longest river in Europe, the researchers detected* **seven different types of antibiotics***. They found one— clarithromycin... in concentrations* **four times higher than "safe" levels.***'*
>
> <u>*National Geographic*</u> **2019** [588]

Additionally, over-prescription of antibacterials to patients, in combination with over-use of antibacterials within the meat and dairy industry, has meant that global populations have been, and continue to be, excessively exposed to these bacteria-killing drugs. With this in mind, if cancer was driven by bacterial infection, surely we would have seen a reduction in cancer prevalence in line with our increased exposure to antibacterial drugs? And yet cancer prevalence has steadily increased throughout the last few decades. Could this be due to the overgrowth of fungi that this overexposure of antibacterial drugs has encouraged?

> *'Abx treatment* **[antibiotic treatment]** *resulted in the* **overgrowth** *of a commensal* **fungal Candida species** *in the gut...'*
>
> <u>*Cell Host and Microbe*</u> **2014** [750]

Proponents of a bacterial cause for cancer highlight that a small number of antibacterial drugs, such as *Doxycycline* and *Salinomycin*, have been shown to kill cancer cells, and maintain that this supports their hypothesis; however, in both cases, the success of these drugs seems to be related to their DNA and mitochondrial-damaging effects,[854] as opposed to the killing of any particular bacteria:

*"Bacteria-free lymphoma patients administered a 3-week course of the acne antibiotic doxycycline showed complete remission of the disease, which indicates the therapeutic effects of the drug were **independent of infection**, the study noted."*

<u>*Pharmacy Times*</u> **2015** [853]

But most significantly regarding Doxycycline, studies have shown that it is also anti-fungal. Doxycycline has been shown to kill *Candida* fungal species.[926] So, just maybe the efficacy of Doxycycline, at least, can be attributed to its other hidden property, its ability to directly affect the fungal pathogen generating the disease.

Other antibacterial drugs appear to actually encourage cancer, possibly due to their damaging effects on mitochondria and other cell components, as well as by the reduction of beneficial bacterial populations. This indicates another type of micro-organism is in the driving seat.[855]

Moreover, as bacteria pose a serious and more immediate threat to any patient undergoing chemotherapy, due to their rapid infection rate, antibiotics are regularly prescribed to cancer patients – however, this regular exposure to antibacterial drugs does not result in any noticeable reduction in the tumour, indicating that bacteria are not the underlying micro-organism driving the disease:

*'**Infections** are typically the biggest complication of chemotherapy, and **antibiotics** are **commonly prescribed** to prevent and treat them.*

*"White blood cell counts can go so low that you have no defense against **bacteria**, and that overwhelming infection can be lethal."'*

<u>*Medical College of Georgia at Agusta University*</u> **2018** [889]

Furthermore, the use of antibiotics can kill the beneficial bacteria that would normally keep fungal pathogens under control – this is where these antibiotics actually aid the progression of cancer, and reduce the efficacy of cancer treatments:

*'"It is clear in animal models that if you wipe out the intestinal microbiota, like you do with antibiotics, it will attenuate the chemotherapy efficacy," says Zhou. "There is also emerging clinical evidence showing that for CTX-based chemotherapy, some patients who **also get antibiotics** for a longer period of time, seem to have **less optimal outcomes**."'*

By comparison, and as I presented at the beginning of this chapter, many common anti-fungal drugs have shown to be effective against a broad range of cancers, strongly indicating that fungal pathogens are the micro-organisms that have a primary influence over the disease. [889]

One misconception that may lead to a misunderstanding of my thinking, relates to the meaning of 'infection'. A traditional infection is generally seen as something that occurs rapidly and, if unchecked, will likely result in sepsis. This is reminiscent of bacterial and viral infections. But I'm not referring to a micro-organism that fits this description. The type of infection that I propose develops into cancer, is one that is opportunistic in nature, confined to a small area of damage/inflammation, stealthy and slow – which is more reminiscent of fungal infection.

Currently, *Helicobacter pylori* is the primary bacteria that is linked to cancer within mainstream circles, but as I presented a short while ago, it appears to play an indirect role by priming stomach cells for fungal infection by reducing stomach acid, generating inflammation and creating ulcers that fungi use to infiltrate tissue.

Recent efforts attempting to elucidate the roll of bacteria in tumours has shown that they do influence the disease. One particular study found that bacteria encouraged cancer metastasis, however, when the bacteria were eliminated they noted that this did not prevent tumour growth. [863] These results need to be taken with caution, as there are many bacterial species yet to be identified, although, while it indicates that pathogenic bacteria play a role in aiding the disease, it suggests they are not the underlying driver of cancers conditions, rather, that they facilitate fungal infection.

Viruses:

While viruses can contribute to cancer in an indirect manner that appears to aid fungal pathogens, they are relatively easy to dispel as an underlying cause. Viruses replicate within cells producing virons (baby viruses). When a critical mass of virons is reached, the cell often ruptures releasing its contents, which inevitably brings about cell death. This allows these newly-created virons to infect and replicate within other cells. This type of death is known as *cell lysis*. This begs the question, how can viruses be a cause of cancer when they often kill the cells they invade? A small number of viruses can reside within cells without killing them, as is the case with *Human Papilloma Virus* (HPV). This virus is claimed to be the underlying cause of cervical cancer, but as Professor Deusberg points out, evidence implicating HPV in cervical cancer is controversial, and many of the anomalies that contradict HPV involvement remain unanswered. [856]

A study looking into the relationship between a weakened immune state in organ transplant patients, and the increased risk of cancer, couldn't explain why immune suppression increased cancer risk. In the study they postulate that this could be due to the HPV virus being activated in various tissues – but they note that if this were true then immunosuppression would have led to greatly increased risk of cervical cancer, but no increased cervical cancer risk was found to occur, which further calls into question the link between HPV and cervical cancer, and viruses and cancer in general:

> 'However, if altered immune function entails activation of HPV infection and thereby increased viral load, an excess risk of **malignancies of the cervix should be expected, but no convincing excess was observed.'**
>
> <u>British Journal of Cancer</u> **2003** [046]

The study also stated:

> '...many of the excess risks we observed were **substantially higher** than those generally found in relation to **established risk factors** for the respective malignancies. '
>
> <u>British Journal of Cancer</u> **2003** [046]

In other words, none of the current accepted infectious causes of cancer – bacteria and viruses – can account for the increased cancer risk seen in organ transplant patients; another micro-organism, therefore, must be responsible.

There are around seven viruses associated with causing 12% of cancers.[894] These are classed as oncoviruses. Most are thought to cause cancer by damaging DNA in various ways. This link is indirect, because cancer appears to form a long time after the infection has been eradicated, which means that finding viral DNA in cancer, decades after the infection has passed, is an associative link at best.[856] Furthermore, DNA damage/mutation doesn't appear to be driving the disease, so viruses that allegedly cause cancer through this DNA-damage mechanism cannot be responsible. Furthermore, it's not clear how viruses could be deemed the underlying cause of cancer when they are only associated with 12% of the disease.

From this perspective it's a hard sell to claim that viruses are the underlying cause of cancer. I'd place viruses within the same category to that of other carcinogens, in that they are more likely to generate the conditions that facilitate fungal infection of damaged and inflamed tissue.

The tumour-associated mycobiome:

The increasing evidence linking micro-organisms to cancer has prompted further research. In a first of its kind, fungi were the focus of attention, and what scientists found surprised them. Together, the *University of California, San Diego* (UCSD) and the *Weizmann Institute of Science* in Israel, created an atlas of fungi that were unexpectedly shown to be linked to a range of 35 different cancers.[858]

It's the first time such an extensive evaluation of fungal-involvement in cancer has been performed. The study found that fungi were detected in all tumour types:

> *'Fungi were detected in **all tumour types** and demonstrated tumour-type specific profiles. Similar to bacteria, **fungi were visualized in both cancer** and **immune cells**. We found interesting **fungal-bacterial-immune cell associations**. In addition, we found specific fungi to be associated with **different clinical outcomes**,'*
>
> <u>*Weizmann Institute of Science*</u> *2023* [887]

As I've previously mentioned, macrophages play a huge role in cancer, they appear to integrate themselves into the tumour mass to become part of it – Professor Seyfried asserts that macrophages are a key part of a tumour and enable it to spread. Here, Ravid Straussman has shown that fungal pathogens were also found within the immune cells of the tumour:

> *'Imaging showed **most fungi** to be **intracellular within cancer** and **immune cells**... We also found significant correlations between specific fungi and age, tumour subtypes, smoking status, response to immunotherapy, and survival measures. Whether these fungi are correlated or causally associated is **yet to be determined**.'*
>
> <u>*Cell*</u> *2022* [857]

Does the interaction between the fungal pathogen living within the macrophage, explain it's behaviour? Does the macrophage become part of the tumour because it has been incapacitated by the fungal pathogen?

Another important point, is that most fungi were found to be intracellular – this explains why the Warburg effect is sustained, and why it's been so difficult for scientists to identify them when observing tumour tissue.

The point of note, is that scientists are only just beginning to link fungi to cancer, and that this whole area of investigation is in it's infancy. This field of study is so new, that at present, scientists are unable to determine the role that fungi play, stating that more studies are needed to establish this. The notion that fungal pathogens might be driving cancer no longer seems an outlandish concept. And while fungi may be present in smaller numbers when compared to bacteria, they are potent in their influence:

> 'We identified fungal-driven, pan-cancer "mycotypes" with distinct immune responses that stratified patient survival. Although our data do not establish causal relationships behind these clusters, they suggest that **fungi are sparse** but **immunologically potent**.'
>
> <u>Cell</u> 2022 [857]

This investigation into fungi and their interactions with cancer is in it's infancy. Very little research has been performed so far, not to mention that we have a long way to go in terms of identifying all fungi that exist – for example, within this study, 7.3% of the DNA contained within tumour tissue, was of 'unknown' origin. To put this in context, the bacteria and fungi that were identified represented only 1.2% of the DNA found to be present.[857] Discussing the findings in an article for *Stat news*, and highlighting that so much more is yet to be discovered, Ami Bhatt, an associate Professor of medicine and genetics at *Stanford University*, stated:

> '"It provides pretty compelling evidence there may be rare fungi within tumours...why and how they are there is a **head-scratcher**..."
>
> ...But once the fungi are there, if indeed they are alive and doing stuff, then **what exactly are they doing**? The experiments done thus far don't probe whether fungi in cancer are merely opportunistic bystanders or if they might be accomplices in cancer.'
>
> <u>Stat News</u> 2023 [891]

Regarding the potential influence of these fungal pathogens, Ravid Straussman states:

> 'It's possible, Straussman said, that fungi are somehow **aiding the tumour** to **form** or **grow**. "Bits of data here or there showed that

*fungi correlated with the **worst** or **bad prognosis**," he said. "It's hard to tell if it's just a correlation or if the fungi really contributed to the tumour."'*

Stat News **2023** [891]

The study also found that bacteria and fungi can work synergistically to improve their mutual ability to thrive within the unique environment of a cancers tumour:

> 'We observed strong positive correlations between fungal and bacterial diversities, abundances, and co-occurrences across several cancer types, suggesting tumour microenvironments (TMEs) may be **non-competitive spaces** for multi-domain **microbial colonization**.'

Cell **2022** [857]

Regarding this possible interaction, Ilana Livyatan – one of the postdocs working on the study, stated:

> '...since the fungi rarely exist in the body without bacterial neighbours, perhaps there are **interactions between fungi, bacteria, and the human body** that **drive cancer outcomes**.'

Stat News **2023** [891]

Professor Rob Knight from the *University of San Diego* expressed his surprise at the results:

> '"The existence of **fungi** in most human cancers is both a **surprise** and to be expected...It is **surprising** because we **don't know how fungi could get into tumours throughout the body**."'

Inside Precision Medicine **2022** [858]

Co-author Ravid Straussman summed up the study findings by stating:

> '"The finding that fungi are **commonly present** in **human tumours** should drive us to better explore their potential effects and **re-examine almost everything we know about cancer** through a 'microbiome lens,'"'

Inside Precision Medicine **2022** [858]

The implications of this are profound. This evidence indicates that current mainstream thinking on cancer is flawed, and likely incorrect because conclusions have been drawn based on incomplete data. None of the leading mainstream theories consider that micro-organisms play a direct role – most of these theories assert that a fault with the cell itself is the underlying cause of the disease. This has prompted Ravid Straussman to conclude that we need to **re-examine almost everything** we think we know about cancer, from a micro-organism perspective. How can oncologists be so confident in their assertions about cancer, and how best to treat it, when the data they consider is incomplete? How can one claim to have drawn a valid conclusion when important data is missing from that evaluation?

The study did highlight that 3% of tumours didn't harbour any fungi, which suggests that something other than fungi could be driving the disease. But, we need to be very careful how we interpret this data because this conclusion is based upon a database containing a record of only the fungal pathogens we know about. It is estimated that we have identified less than 5% of all micro-organisms on the planet. In the study out of 15,512 tumour samples, 97% registered positive for the fungi in this database. But 7.3% of the DNA analysed was of unknown origin (i.e. not human). This indicates that there are potentially many more cancer-related micro-organisms that are yet to be identified. Could the remaining 3% of tumours that didn't contain any known fungi, harbour fungal pathogens that are yet to be discovered?

Indeed it's worth repeating the following quote that highlights there is much more to be discovered. Upon analysing the blood of patients, researchers uncovered 3,000 previously unidentified micro-organisms. The authors of the study concluded that their involvement in disease is as of yet, unknown, and that they could well be a cause of many diseases we don't yet fully understand:

> '...Kowarsky et al. used cell-free DNA sequencing to identify over **3,000** previously **unidentified** viruses, bacteria, and fungi in human blood samples obtained from immunocompromised patients.
>
> The team concluded that the **newly discovered microbes** and viruses "may prove to be the cause of acute or **chronic diseases** that, to date, have **unknown etiology** [an unknown cause]".'
>
> <u>Immunometabolism</u> **2021** [816]

I think it would be naive to assume we know everything there is to know about the cause of disease in general, let alone to assume we've fully categorised and understood all of the micro-organisms that exist, and can cause disease. In reality we are only just scratching the surface.

Neutrophils and tumours:

Neutrophil immune cells accumulate in abundance around tumours. This is odd because neutrophils are not tasked with killing cancer cells.[706] Other than in response to inflammation, there is no reason for neutrophils to be present or accumulate in such a fashion, unless of course, a fungal pathogen is involved, because the primary role of this immune cell is to kill pathogens.

As it's assumed that DNA is the cause, the presence and role of neutrophils around tumours baffles scientists:[706]

> *'Controversy surrounds neutrophil function in cancer because neutrophils were shown to provide both pro- and anti-tumour functions. We identified a heterogeneous subset of low-density neutrophils (LDNs) that appear transiently in self-resolving inflammation but* **accumulate continuously with cancer progression.**[286]

This study goes on to confirm the role of neutrophils in killing micro-organisms:

> *'Neutrophils play a well-established role in host defence, where they phagocytose and kill invading* **micro-organisms** *by releasing activating cytokines, defensins, and reactive oxygen species [**free radicals**].'*
>
> <u>*Cell Reports*</u> **2015** [286]

Fungal-killing neutrophils[284] are present in ever-increasing numbers as cancer develops. This is in line with what we would expect to see if fungi are responsible and present within the tumour. The presence of neutrophils outside cells explains why there are no visible signs of fungi in the surrounding tissue. This, in turn, may go some way to explaining why scientists have been unable to identify fungi as a potential driver of the disease.

The confusion regarding neutrophil involvement stems from the fact they appear to provide both pro- and anti-cancer properties. In the latter stages of tumour development, some studies show that neutrophils increase cancer progression by helping it spread, while other studies show that they aid cancer cell death,[429, 706] which is counter-intuitive because neutrophils are not tasked with killing cancer cells. Could the killing of the fungal pathogen by neutrophils explain why they appear capable of killing cancer cells in the early stages of tumour growth?

The role of neutrophils in cancer progression explained:

When cells become damaged, they release chemicals such as interleukin 6, 8, and type-1 interferon, which generate an inflammatory response. This response signals neutrophils for help. Upon arrival at the site of inflammation, neutrophils combat the micro-organism or remove the toxin causing it. But their role doesn't end there; they also aid in tissue repair. It is in this act of attempting to repair cell damage that neutrophils aid cancer growth and the spread of the disease during prolonged bouts of inflammation.

Neutrophils produce enzymes called MMP, and in particular, they produce a distinct type known as MMP-9, which is designed to aid with cell repair.[423]

> 'Direct proof for **neutrophils** being the major tumour-associated leukocyte [immune cell] type expressing **MMP-9** was recently provided in a study employing human xenografts and syngeneic murine tumours.'
>
> <u>Journal of Immunology Research</u> **2015** [706]

This is important because MMP-9 has been implicated in aiding the spread of the disease and rendering tumours more deadly. In its general role, MMP-9 is used to control inflammation and aid in wound closure, by breaking down certain compounds no longer needed in the latter stages of the cell-repair process. This allows the wound to close and heal. MMP-9 also stimulates blood vessel growth to provide damaged cells with access to essential nutrients, and to facilitate the removal of damaged cells surrounding a wound. This allows new cells to be produced in their place.[706] It is MMP-9 that is used to help these damaged cells break away. It acts like molecular scissors, breaking the bonds that hold cells together.[423] The ability of MMP-9 to cause cells to break away from the wounded area and stimulate blood vessel growth, leads to cells migrating into the bloodstream.[424] While this usually benign process of cell repair inevitably aids the spread of cancer, MMP-9 is not intentionally being produced by the cancerous cell for this purpose, as scientists imply – rather, it appears to be produced in abundance as a direct result of prolonged damaged.

So, how can this be explained? In a normal situation, a pathogen will damage tissue, inflammation will occur, and neutrophils will arrive to kill the micro-organism. Following this, a complex repair process will take place. Neutrophils produce MMP-9, which removes damaged cells by breaking their bonds, allowing them to be released into the blood supply for easy removal from the site of injury. MMP-9 increases the blood supply as well as the delivery of nutrients that aid in wound healing. Temporary scaffold-like structures are created to aid tissue repair. In the latter stages of wound healing, these temporary scaffold-like structures need to be removed to fully close the wound. More MMP-9 is produced to break down these temporary structures, allowing wound closure. This normally ends the healing process. Once this is achieved, inflammation subsides, neutrophils move on, and the production of MMP-9 ceases.

The issue with cancer is that the production of MMP-9 never ceases, as cell damage and inflammation doesn't stop. This is due to a combination of factors such as fungal toxins, increased acidity, free radical damage and the continual expansion of the tumour into the surrounding tissue. It's only a matter of time before a cancer stem cell breaks away into the increased blood supply, resulting from an excessive production of MMP-9, which is being produced by neutrophils continuously attempting to heal the persistent damage.

Neutrophils are not acting to aid cancer; they are merely trying to fix tissue damage and reduce inflammation. I am proposing that it's the constant presence of the fungus that generates these conditions, which results in an accidental overproduction of MMP-9 by neutrophils attempting to close the wound.

Scientists are crucially missing fungal involvement, which is causing neutrophils to be present for longer than would otherwise be necessary. When neutrophils kill some fungal pathogens in early-stage cancer, they are seen as beneficial because cancer cells die as a result. However, as time goes by and overproduction of MMP-9 aids cancer spread, scientists conclude that neutrophils have 'chosen' to aid the disease. Scientists assume that neutrophils have been co-opted to join the tumour's cause. I take a more straightforward view: that neutrophils are just performing their regular duties of cell repair, and that abnormal levels of inflammation leads to increased expression of MMP-9, which in turn generates a corrosive environment that inadvertently aids cell migration.

The question is this: why don't neutrophils engage the fungal pathogen in late-stage cancer to prevent prolonged inflammation from occurring, as well as the overproduction of MMP-9 that ultimately aids the spread of the disease? The reason is likely due to the clever immune evasion strategies that fungi have developed, as I will now confirm by showing how fungi can be shown to be responsible for causing each hallmark of cancer.

How fungal interaction brings about cancer:

From this point forward the cancer hallmarks will be discussed with the appropriate evidence to show how fungal pathogens are linked to every stage of the disease, starting with the ways these versatile pathogens can evade immune detection and suppress the immune response.

Explaining Hallmark 8 – Immune suppression/evasion:

Immune cells fail to kill cancer cells and some appear to facilitate disease progression. The reason for this is largely unknown. Some claim that immune cells 'choose' to join forces with the tumour, as if they've developed an independent will, and moved over to the 'dark side'. This is highly speculative, to say the least. It's impossible at this time to evaluate the conscious thought processes of cells – if indeed they have any such capacity – to be able to draw such a conclusion. However, when we view this process through the lens of infection, a plausible explanation becomes apparent. It starts to make sense when the extent of fungi's ability to evade, suppress and even control the immune response, is explored and factored in.

To start with, some pathogenic fungi are *dimorphic*, meaning they can exist in two different states. They can change between their invasive fungal form and their non-threatening yeast form, in response to their environment. Our immune system sees yeast as less of a threat. Fungi use this strategy of switching between the two forms to infiltrate tissue in a manner that reduces its visibility to the immune system.[708] With this in mind, the study below highlights the virulence, adaptability and level of manipulation that the human fungal pathogen *Candida albicans* is capable of. Particularly impressive is its ability to adapt to almost any situation within the human host, and the way it can evade the immune system, and even modulate and manipulate the immune response by either activating or suppressing it:

> *'Candida albicans is a **serious agent of infection**, particularly in immunocompromised patients. The delicate balance between the host and this otherwise normal commensal fungus may turn into a **parasitic relationship**, resulting in the development of infection,*

*called candidiasis... The fungus is **not a mere passive participant in the infectious process...***

*...The **large repertoire of adhesins** displayed by this fungus may reflect the **variety of** host sites that it **can invade...***

*...Another important aspect of interactions with the host, with direct implications for pathogenesis, **is the potential of this fungus to modulate the immune response mounted by the host.***

*The capacity of cell wall constituents, including glucan, chitin, and mannoproteins, to modulate (**activate or depress**) the immune response is **well documented...***

*...**Approximately 80 to 90% of the cell wall of C. albicans is carbohydrate.**'*

Microbiology and Molecular Biology Reviews 1998 [047]

This fungal pathogen is incredibly versatile. Worthy of note is that up to 90% of the fungal cell wall is made up of carbohydrate. The fungal cell wall is basically made out of sugar. This is true of most fungi.[892] This can explain why the Western diet, high in refined sugar, is linked to a greater risk of developing cancer. Such a glucose-rich environment has encouraged the growth of fungi within us and makes them extremely hardy. Glucose aside, *Candida albicans* can avoid immune detection in another way:

*'Candida albicans can sense the immune status of host cells and adapt, **evading immune system defences.**'*

News-Medical.net 2012 [048]

Researchers determined that *Candida albicans* binds to the host immune signalling molecule, called Interleukin 17A (IL-17A),[048] which allows the fungus to navigate and tolerate the active immune environment of healthy host tissue. By exploiting IL-17A, the fungus not only survives but can cause disease to develop:

*"It's a bit like **the fungus is listening in to the conversations our immune system is having** so it can best determine how to react and **survive in our tissues.** This may also be a crucial step in determining when this opportunist decides to invade host tissue and*

cause **life-threatening disease** *in an immunosuppressed patient,"*
notes Dr. Palmer.'

News-Medical.net **2012** [048]

Fungi 'listens' to the immune system and then manipulates it for its
own ends. Another way *Candida albicans* can thwart detection is its ability
to block the Dectin-1 cell receptor, this prevents the cell from alerting the
immune system to the fungal threat: [052, 053]

> *'Chitin is a skeletal cell wall polysaccharide of the inner cell wall of*
> **fungal pathogens***... chitin is normally not exposed to cells of the*
> *innate immune system but is capable of influencing immune*
> *recognition by* **blocking Dectin-1***-mediated engagement with*
> *fungal cell walls.'*

American Society of Microbiology **2011** [051]

Evading Dectin-1 detection is one of the many strategies that allow
fungi to remain hidden while continuing to thrive within human tissue.
Gliotoxin is one of many mycotoxins produced by *Aspergillus* fungi. In a
study looking into the effects of gliotoxin on the human immune system, it
showed that the fungal toxin suppressed the immune cells known as T-
cells:

> *'...***gliotoxin***, the most abundant mycotoxin produced by AF*
> *(Aspergillus fumigatus), was able to* **suppress functional T-cell**
> **responses***...*
>
> *These studies suggest that the production of gliotoxin by AF may*
> *constitute an important* **immunoevasive mechanism***...'*

American Society of Haematology **2005** [129]

One of the main conundrums regarding the immune response to cancer
relates to why T-cells fail to kill tumour cells, and scientists are struggling
to figure out why. The study above provides an answer by showing how
fungal toxins are designed to suppress these cancer-killing T-cells, thereby
providing a rational explanation for why they don't attack.

Cryptococcus neoformans is one of the top three fungal pathogens of
humans. This particular fungus possesses some remarkable traits, not the
least of which is its ability to hide within the very immune cells tasked
with killing it, and then to transfer between immune cells without being
detected (*lateral transfer*):

*'We provide the first evidence for **lateral transfer** of a human **fungal pathogen**. This rare event may occur repeatedly during latent cryptococcal infections, thereby allowing the pathogen to remain **concealed** from the immune system and **protecting it** from exposure to **antifungal agents**...*

*...Finally, infected macrophage cells [immune cells] may travel widely throughout the host circulatory and lymphatic systems, where they interact intimately with one another and with other cell types through transient contacts. We speculate that internalised C. neoformans may use such transient contact in order to cross the **blood-brain barrier** by direct cell-to-cell spread from adherent infected macrophages to microvascular endothelial cells.'*

<u>BMC Immunology</u> **2007** [851]

Hidden within macrophages, *C. Neoformans* appears capable of infecting almost any area of the body that these macrophages travel to – this remarkable pathogen uses macrophages as a Trojan horse.

Earlier I discussed the findings by the Mayo clinic, where tumours formed in patients and were categorised as cancer and removed, only for their investigations to reveal a fungal pathogen was responsible for creating the palpable mass that perfectly mimicked the disease. This demonstrates that fungal pathogens are capable of evading immune detection to generate the same tumour-like symptoms that are more often diagnosed as cancer.

Immune suppression – Lactate (lactic acid):

When cells are damaged they become inflamed. The problem with inflammation, is that it renders cells more vulnerable to micro-organism invasion due to the histamine produced. Histamine opens up the pores of the cell to aid with cell repair, which leaves the cell open to infection. To aid with cell repair and instigate inflammation, a switch to glycolysis is required – this results in the production of lactate, also known as lactic acid. The problem with lactate is that it alerts pathogens to the conditions of cell damage. Upon detection of lactate, fungal pathogens trigger 'stealth mode' in preparation for cell invasion:

*'This represents the first description of active PAMP **masking** by a Candida species, a process that **reduces the visibility of the fungus to the immune system**...*

> *...This type of **immune evasion** is likely significant for **disease progression** in the host during periods of anaerobic metabolism [glycolysis] (when **lactic acid production is high**).'*
>
> **Nature Microbiology 2016**[613]

Not only does lactate trigger fungal pathogens to become less visible, but it can also inhibit the function of the immune cells that are designed to kill cancer cells:

> *'**Monocytes** are highly motile cells and precursors of tumour-associated macrophages. **Lactate inhibits monocyte migration** and release of cytokines tumour necrosis factor and interleukin-6 (IL-6). Furthermore, **lactate strongly inhibits the activation of T-cells** as well as the differentiation of monocytes to dendritic cells. **Lactate also inhibits natural killer cell function** directly...'*
>
> **Carcinogenesis 2017**[771]

Not only does lactate inhibit immune cells but it also improves the ability of the pathogen to kill immune cells because lactate feeds the pathogen:

> *'Lactate-grown [fungal] cells were taken up less efficiently by macrophages [immune cells], and those Candida cells that were phagocytosed [absorbed by the immune cell] were **more effective at escaping the macrophages** and **killing them**.'*
>
> **Infection and immunity 2013**[712]

Fungal pathogens are also stimulated to become invasive when there is a lack of oxygen (known as hypoxia), which is again a sign that damage to cells has occurred, and that an opportune moment for cell invasion exists. Under these hypoxic conditions, fungi adapt to evade immune detection:

> *'Our data suggest that C. albicans responds to **hypoxic niches [low oxygen niches]** by inducing β-glucan **masking...** thereby **modulating local immune responses** [evading immune detection] and **promoting fungal colonization**.'*
>
> **American Society for Microbiology 2018**[614]

Incidentally, hypoxic conditions increase the production of lactate. So, a lack of oxygen and increased lactate production are conditions that fungi measure, to determine the most opportune moment to invade cells. Both conditions trigger fungal pathogens to become stealthy and invasive, and are associated with tumours.

Immune suppression – Iron:

Prolonged inflammation and lactate production results in another detrimental outcome, the release of iron into the surrounding tissue. When normal control of iron is no longer possible, an overload of iron occurs. This is detrimental, because iron overload also feeds fungal pathogens and suppresses immune cells.

> '*Iron* overload *adversely affects macrophage / monocyte*
> [*immune cell*] *function* directly and indirectly.
>
> *Iron excess* appears to cause alterations of *T-cell* (cellular
> immunity) and *B-cell* (humoral immunity) function.
>
> The ability of *excess iron* to cause a spectrum of *immune
> dysfunctions* is beginning to be understood and appreciated.'
>
> <u>*Annals of Clinical & Laboratory Science* **2000**</u> [490]

> '*Freely available iron* can severely damage or destroy the whole
> mechanism of *natural resistance*, leading to *rapid bacterial or
> fungal growth in tissue fluids.*'
>
> Freely available iron is derived from *iron overload*, free haem
> compounds, or hypoxia in *injured tissue*. This can severely damage
> or abolish normal [defence] mechanisms in tissue fluids leading to
> *overwhelming growth* of *bacteria* or *fungi.*'
>
> <u>*Journal of Medical Microbiology* **2006**</u> [489]

> '*Iron* is an essential nutrient for *all microbes*. Many human
> pathogenic microbes have *developed sophisticated strategies* to
> *acquire iron from the host*... For example, in oral epithelial cells
> intracellular iron is bound to *ferritin*, a protein that is highly
> resistant to microbial attack... This study demonstrates that the
> pathogenic fungus *Candida albicans* can use *ferritin* as the sole
> source of *iron.*'
>
> <u>*PLOS Pathogens* **2008**</u> [487]

It becomes easy to see why immune cells appear ineffective against cancer, when both iron and lactate suppress them, while feeding the fungal pathogens' invasive behaviour.

Immune suppression – Glucose:

Intriguingly, glucose plays a role in immune evasion through the influence of the fungal pathogen. This is due to the insatiable appetite that fungi have for absorbing glucose. In the study below, *Candida albicans* killed the immune cell known as a macrophage by out-competing it for the glucose they both require. Fungi can actually disable immune cells by starving them of glucose, thus evading the immune response:

> *'We show that* **glucose competition by C. albicans** *is responsible for triggering death of* **infected macrophages.**'
>
> <u>*Cell metabolism*</u> **2018** [612]

Immune suppression – Glutamine:

Glutamine is a protein that helps to build muscle mass among other things. In particular, it is a crucial substrate for immune cell function:

> *'...***glutamine** *is considered as a* **"fuel for the immune system"**, *where a low blood concentration may* **impair immune cell function**, *resulting in poor clinical outcomes and increased risk of mortality.*
>
> *Currently,* **glutamine** *is routinely supplied as a component of clinical nutrition* **supplementation** *for pre-and post-operative patients, and also for many elite athletes to* **restore immune functions.**'
>
> <u>*Nutrients*</u> **2018** [829]

Suppression of the immune response occurs in cancer because glutamine is absorbed by cancer cells to a degree that depletes it from within the surrounding tissue; so much so, in fact, that it can induce the disease called *cachexia*, which is characterised by a loss of muscle mass (protein):

> *Accumulating evidence indicates that* **glucose** *and* **glutamine** *are the* **primary fuels** *used for driving the rapid* **growth** *of* **most tumours.**'
>
> <u>*ASN Neuro*</u> **2018** [798]

The high rate of glutamine absorption by the tumour contributes to immune suppression by starving immune cells of this critical substance. It's no coincidence that fungal pathogens also feed on glutamine, taking advantage of the cell absorbing it. In particular, fungi can convert glutamine directly into glucose via the *gluconeogenesis* pathway, which is present within the micro-organism itself.[616]

> *'To establish an infection, the pathogen* **Candida albicans** *must assimilate carbon and grow in its mammalian host. This fungus assimilates six-carbon compounds via the glycolytic pathway, and two-carbon compounds via the glyoxylate cycle and* **gluconeogenesis [conversion of glutamine to glucose].** *'*
>
> <u>*Cellular Microbiology*</u> **2006** [616]

Immune evasion – Estrogen:

It appears that estrogen increases the ability of certain fungal pathogens to evade immune detection:

> *'Here, we investigate how adaptation of C. albicans to estrogen impacts the fungal host-pathogen interaction.* **Estrogen promotes fungal virulence** *by enabling C. albicans to* **avoid the actions of the innate immune system.**'
>
> <u>*Cell Reports*</u> **2022** [842]

Evidence also confirms that estrogen stimulates pathogen virulence.[023] Could this explain why hormone-related cancers are so prominent in women?

And when we take 'nagalase' into account, it becomes clear to see why the immune system appears to be ineffective against both cancer cells and the fungus contained within them.

Immune suppression – Nagalase:

I touched on nagalase in the previous chapter, but here I provide a little more detail. Nagalase is an enzyme that is only found to be over-expressed in cancer cells, which means it can provide pointers to the underlying cause. It is directly related to tumour growth, and its presence increases as the size of the tumour increases:

> *'Increased* **nagalase activity** *has been detected in the blood of patients with a* **wide variety of cancers...** *For various types of tumours,* **various levels of nagalase activity were found.** *It*

*appears that the secretory capacity of individual tumour tissue varies among tumour types depending upon tumour size, staging, and the degree of malignancy or invasiveness… **Nagalase activity is directly proportional to viable tumour burden.***

*… **Increased nagalase activity has not been detected in the blood of healthy individuals.'***

European Laboratory of Nutrients 2020 [056]

So, what does the nagalase enzyme do? Why is it relevant? Nagalase plays a role in sugar metabolism by breaking down certain sugar structures. The form of nagalase expressed by tumours breaks down the sugar component of a receptor called GcMAF (Macrophage Activation Factor),[503] which is used to alert macrophage immune cells to a threat. Effectively, nagalase disables this immune receptor. This results in immune suppression, helping to explain why macrophages fail to kill the fungal pathogen and cancer cell.[055]

The beneficial form of nagalase normally generated by the cell itself appears to be different from the nagalase being excreted by the tumour: [057, 356]

*'Even though the intracellular (lysosomal) form of nagalase is vital for proper hepatic cell function [liver cell function], the **extracellular** form (secreted by cancer cells) seems to **only benefit the progression of cancer.'***

JBUON 2017 [060]

Could it be possible that something else could generate nagalase from within the tumour? It appears so. Studies show that common fungal pathogens produce nagalase to suppress the immune response during the process of infection.[058–060]

*'There is abundant evidence in favour of the presence and role of **nagalase** in **different pathogens**. The pathogenesis of some viruses such as Influenza, HIV or Herpes Simplex Virus-HSV is attributed to **nagalase**.*

*Although research about the presence of **nagalase** in **fungi** is limited, some studies show its presence in Aspergillus spp., Penicillium oxalicum, Streptomyces spp. and Acremonium spp.'*

JBUON 2017 [060]

Nagalase being excreted by the tumour indicates that fungi, as well as other micro-organisms, are directly involved. This aligns with the recent findings by Ravid Straussman who discovered that tumours contain their own unique population of micro-organisms, including the tumour samples used in laboratory experiments, previously thought to be sterile.[821]

But possibly the most defining link between immune evasion, cancer, and fungi is that of PD-L1, which is a protein that cells present on their outer surface to indicate to immune cells that they are healthy and friendly, and therefore not to attack. Upon encountering PD-L1 immune cells become passive. View it as like a check point system similar to the police asking for your identification to prove you are who you say you are. PD-L1 acts as your ID and confirms your status as a law-abiding citizen. The problem with cancer cells is that many over-produce this PD-L1 protein, essentially producing a fake ID that signals to immune cells that there's nothing untoward occurring. PD-L1 expression allows the cancer cell to evade detection.[845, 846]

Some scientists assert that cancer is a result of cell malfunction and that the cell has developed a mind of its own; as a result over-expression of PD-L1 is deemed to be a 'decision' made by the cell. Determining why PD-L1 is over-expressed would highlight an alternative explanation. However, as it is assumed to be a 'conscious choice' made by the cell, the focus for scientists is not on contemplating why, but on creating drugs that can inhibit the production of PD-L1. While there has been some success with this approach, effects are limited:

> *'Although PD-1/**PD-L1** blockade has brought about marvelous improvements in patients' clinical outcomes, only a **minority** of patients show a durable response to these therapies, and **intrinsic resistance** remains an intractable challenge.'*
>
> <u>*Nature Communications*</u> **2021** [847]

When we shift our focus and attempt to figure out why PD-L1 is over-expressed, we find a different conclusion can be drawn from the same data. And in line with the perspective presented within this book, evidence confirms that common fungal pathogens stimulate the over-expression of PD-L1 in epithelial cells during infection:

> *'**C. albicans** and heat-inactivated C. albicans **upregulated** the **PD-L1** expression in Cal27 [epithelial cells] and HN6 cells. Various signalling pathways involved in **PD-L1 regulation** were influenced by C. albicans infection.'*

Journal of Oral Pathology and Medicine **2022** [848]

Many fungal pathogens control the expression of PD-L1 – not just in epithelial cells, but in immune cells as well – in order to suppress them:

> *'Our findings show that a functional PD-1 pathway is essential for this fungal pathogen to progressively invade and kill the host. It is also extremely relevant that the pathogen itself can **modulate this pathway**. Our data show a substantial **up-regulation** of **PD-L1** on primary alveolar and peritoneal **macrophages** infected with Hc [Histoplasma capsulatum]...*
>
> *...Moreover, Hc infection also induces **up-regulation** of **PD-L1** on **other cell types**, such as DCs, CD4+, and CD8+T cells and B cells in the lung and spleen.'*

PNAS **2007** [849]

Does this fungal interaction explain why PD-L1 is upregulated in cancer? And does this help to explain why cancer cells are able to evade detection?

Immune evasion – advanced-stage cancer:

Both healthy stem cells and cancer stem cells produce a molecule called CD47,[658] which allows them to evade the immune system. This is one reason why the immune system appears to be ineffective against tumours. Through the expression of CD47, cancer stem cells become impossible to detect, and so they can regenerate the tumour regardless of how effective the immune system is. This is confirmed by the study below:

> *'...CD47 thus serves as a **"don't eat me"** signal... CD47 has been found to be **over-expressed** on human tumours... enabling tumours to **escape innate immune system surveillance**.'*

Journal of the American Academy of Dermatology **2016** [415]

The additional protective capabilities of stem cells, such as the efficient expulsion of toxins, means that any intracellular fungi are not just protected from the immune system but also from conventional therapies that can target them, rendering the infection more difficult to eradicate. Does this fungal interaction with specialised cells explain why tumours go unnoticed?

Explaining Hallmark 10 – Inflammation:

As I've just alluded to, inflammation precedes the development of all tumours and persists throughout a tumour's life cycle. Therefore, any theory needs to explain why it's directly linked to cancer. So, what is inflammation and is there a link to fungi?

Inflammation is how a cell signals that something is wrong, that damage has occurred, or when a pathogen is present. This alerts the immune system to the threat, and aids in cell repair. Anything that damages the cell can initiate inflammation, including physical injury, radiation, toxins and micro-organisms. Cells react to damage by expressing various chemicals, including histamine, which causes swelling. Histamine increases the flow of blood, nutrients, and immune cells to the site of damage, thus aiding the repair process. This is why inflammation causes swelling, heat and redness at the site of injury.

When fungal pathogens invade cells, an inflammatory response is normally generated. During the infection process, fungi can elicit an Interleukin 6 (IL-6) response. This instigates an inflammatory reaction within the cell alerting the immune system to the fungal threat:

> *'Our study demonstrates that TNF and **IL-6** are produced systemically during **C. albicans infection**...'*
>
> <u>*Infection and Immunity* **1992**</u> [413]

Not only is IL-6 expressed in response to fungal invasion, but it is also directly associated with cancer, indicating that IL-6 expression in cancer cells may reflect the presence of a fungal pathogen:

> *'A number of studies have shown that **IL-6** levels are markedly up-regulated in cancer patients... IL-6 expression independently predicts tumour **recurrence**, tumour **metastasis** and poor survival in head and neck cancer patients.'*
>
> <u>*World Journal of Otorhinolaryngology* **2016**</u> [414]

Inflammation – Toll-like receptors and fungi:

Cells utilise many different receptors that are present on their cell surface, and within the cell itself. Some are designed to specifically identify pathogens, triggering a response to an infectious threat. These particular receptors are known as *Toll-like receptors* (TLR). Once a pathogen is detected by a TLR it rings the alarm. Depending upon the receptor type (humans have 10 toll-like receptors that identify a range of viruses, bacteria, and fungi), an inflammatory response is elicited. Triggering a TLR also results in a switch to glycolysis, and the inhibition of cell death mechanisms, which is consistent with Dr Naviaux's *Cell Danger Response* model, where an infection triggers the Warburg effect (an energy switch to glycolysis) as it is a defensive response to infection. The result of this pathogen-TLR interaction, is inflammation:

> *'Various TLRs play a critical role in **innate immunity** by responding to the various PAMPs [pathogen-associated molecular patterns] (from the pathogenic bacteria, viruses, or fungi) which **drive the cellular response** producing **proinflammatory** cytokines, chemokines, and other mediators, thus playing an important role in **inflammatory reactions** and activation of the adaptive immune pathways as well.'*
>
> <u>Oncogene</u> **2014** [913]

And as we would expect to see if fungal pathogens are present and driving the disease, these TLRs are highly activated in cancer.[914] Their activation indicates the presence of pathogens within tumours, because their primary role is to detect infectious micro-organisms. This aligns with Ravid Straussman's work where he uncovered that tumours – which were previously thought to be free of micro-organisms – harbour distinct populations of intracellular pathogens. It also confirms that pathogens are present at the onset of the disease and indicates that they may drive tumour development, because they trigger the inflammation that is thought to be responsible for generating tumour growth.

In particular, activation of TLR 2 and 4 are associated with tumour promotion.[914] Significantly, TLR 2, 4 and 6 are primarily associated with fungal infections.[913] The other TLRs are stimulated in accordance with bacterial and viral infections, and appear to have an anti-tumour role.[914] Does the cancer-promoting role of activated TLR 2 and 4 confirm that fungal pathogens are driving the disease process?

Fungi also produce many toxins, all of which are damaging to cells to varying degrees. *Gliotoxin*, for instance, has been found to cause fragmentation of DNA.[027] These toxins naturally trigger inflammation because of the damage they cause. Furthermore, fungal pathogens have been shown to directly increase the production of a particular type of enzyme called MMP-9. This enzyme is corrosive and generates inflammation when produced in abundance. Might the presence of fungal pathogens explain why persistent inflammation exists in cancer?[346] There are many other factors that also contribute to, and drive, chronic inflammation.

Inflammation – Lactate (lactic acid) and fungi:

As I mentioned a moment ago, lactic acid is produced in abundance by tumours. This is due to cancer's reliance upon glycolysis because lactic acid is a byproduct of this energy pathway. When cell damage occurs, glycolysis is instigated so that an inflammatory response can be actioned. This becomes an issue when inflammation is prolonged, because reliance upon glycosides results in an over-production of lactic acid, which is corrosive. This creates an acidic environment in the surrounding tissue, leading to a 'feedback loop' that generates further inflammation. If this situation is not resolved – if the toxin/micro-organism is not removed or cell repair process completed – further inflammation will be generated within the surrounding healthy tissue. This will only exacerbate the conditions that favour fungal infection, because fungi feed on lactic acid.

Inflammation – Iron and fungi:

You may be noticing a pattern, where a few factors seem to generate the conditions that facilitate infection. Again we find ourselves referring to the involvement of iron. As I've previously discussed, iron plays a critical role in cancer development, as it can be released into the surrounding tissue during prolonged periods of cell damage. Why is this important? Aside from the fact that iron overload suppresses immune cells and feeds fungal pathogens, when iron is released, it generates further inflammation by creating damaging free radicals:

> *'However, iron is also biochemically **dangerous**; it can **damage tissues** by catalyzing the conversion of hydrogen peroxide to **free-radical ions** that attack cellular membranes, protein and DNA.'*
>
> <u>*Biomedicine & Pharmacotherapy*</u> **2001** [828]

Without damage and inflammation caused by toxins and other irritants, iron would not be released, which would make it harder for fungi to invade cells and sustain an infection. The human body is intelligent; it is aware of the threat of infection that iron release stimulates. It even attempts to restrict iron availability whenever inflammation or cell damage initially occurs to prevent micro-organisms from gaining access to it.[496] Scientists recognise this clever anti-infection strategy which has been given the nickname 'anaemia of inflammation', which translates as 'a lack of iron during inflammation' – iron is intentionally withheld.

However, this withholding of iron can only last for so long before persistent inflammation results in iron being released into cell and tissue plasma, where fungal pathogens can take advantage of its availability and damaging free radicals are produced, leading to further inflammation.[484]

Inflammation – Tumour development:

Understanding the inflammation process in more detail highlights why prolonged inflammation leads to tumour growth, and why fungal pathogens are likely to be found at the heart of this process.

During inflammation histamine is released to increase cell permeability (opens up the pores), this makes it easier for immune cells to enter the cell and remove any toxins present. The problem occurs when the toxic load becomes greater than the immune system's ability to deal with it. Inflammation only subsides when toxins are removed, and damage is repaired. Toxins that are not removed result in continuous expression of inflammation (the signal for help), which means the cell's pores remain open for extended periods, rendering it more vulnerable to fungal attack. So, while immune cells are distracted by dealing with toxins, fungal pathogens can take advantage of a cell that is easier to invade due to histamine production. Chronic inflammation, therefore, is a sign that the immune system is unable to cope with the situation, and that the cell is vulnerable to attack from pathogens.

When persistent inflammation exists, lactic acid is produced in abundance, because glycolysis is required to initiate inflammation and cell repair.[646] This leads to a corrosive acidic environment that promotes more damage and inflammation. Lactic acid has the additional effect of encouraging fungal pathogens to become invasive, while simultaneously suppressing the immune response, all while histamine keeps the pores of the cell open and vulnerable to fungal invasion. This dangerous situation is further exacerbated by the eventual release of iron, which also feeds the pathogen and suppresses the immune cells within the vicinity of the inflamed tissue. This can explain why chronic inflammation, coupled with immune suppression, culminates in cancer and is linked directly to the onset of the disease; fungi have free reign to invade a weakened and defenceless cell.

Again, this indicates that pathogens are present at the onset of tumour growth, because they can take advantage of, and are stimulated by, the initial stages of cell damage and inflammation that are generated from the outset – it is from this inflammation and cell damage that cancer develops.

This can explain why populations that live within the 'blue zones' of the world live longer and have a significantly reduced risk of developing cancer and many other diseases. Their lifestyle and diet support a robust immune system, and minimises toxin exposure, meaning that inflammation is reduced and that iron and lactate is less likely to be made available for micro-organisms to use to cause disease.

Explaining Hallmark 9 – DNA damage:

DNA damage is found to occur in most cases of cancer and forms the basis of the DNA Theory. So, can this random damage be explained by the presence of a fungal pathogen? Unequivocally, yes. The toxins and free radicals that fungi produce can cause random DNA damage.

According to the DNA Theory, the p53 gene is responsible for regulating cell repair and cell death and is the most frequently mutated DNA gene.[070] Potentially explaining why the p53 gene appears to be damaged so often in cancer, the following study highlights the role of fungal toxins:

> '...the relationship between **aflatoxin** exposure and development of human hepatocellular carcinoma (HHC) was demonstrated by the studies on the **p53** tumour suppressor gene. **High frequency of p53 mutations**... was found to occur in HHC collected from populations **exposed to high levels of dietary aflatoxin** in China and Southern Africa.'
>
> <u>*Johns Hopkins University 1999*</u>[071]

The type of DNA damage that occurs might directly reflect the type of fungal pathogen causing the disease, or the combination of pathogens present within the surrounding tissue. Gliotoxin, for instance (one of many mycotoxins produced by *Aspergillus* species), was found to fragment DNA:

> 'Gliotoxin is produced during mycelial growth of Aspergillus fumigatus. This toxin is known to cause **fragmentation of DNA**.'
>
> <u>*Environmental and Occupational Hazards*</u> [027]

> 'Mycotoxins are **carcinogenic toxins** that are produced by many **Aspergillus** and **Penicillium** [fungal] species growing on food commodities. Among the different mycotoxins, aflatoxin B1 has

*been reported as the **highest carcinogenic mycotoxin** and aflatoxin B1 can penetrate the cell membrane and attach to its DNA where it causes **irreversible mutations**.*

*In a study made to identify the DNA-attacking ability of carcinogenic mycotoxins... all [13] mycotoxins were found to have **destructive ability towards genomic DNA**.'*

Oncology Reports **2017** [707]

To further highlight the link between fungi and DNA damage, I need to briefly mention *aneuploidy* and *methyl-deficiency* because both of these conditions are present in people with cancer. Both are directly related to causing random DNA damage and need to be explained.[164, 297]

DNA damage – Aneuploidy:

As discussed previously in Chapter 7, chromosomes are the sausage-shaped capsules within the cell's nucleus that store our DNA. When chromosomes are damaged, there will be subsequent damage to the DNA contained within them, and is described as *Aneuploidy*. Aneuploidy (abnormal ploidy) is found to occur in most cancers.[897] To help explain this condition, the following study confirms that fungal toxins can cause it:

*'Fungi of the Fusarium species can infect food and feed commodities and produce the mycotoxins zearalenone (**ZEA**) and deoxynivalenol (**DON**).*

*It is concluded that ZEA and DON **can lead to abnormal spindle formation**, leading to less fertile oocytes and embryos with **abnormal ploidy**...'*

Biology of Reproduction **2007** [166]

Another study tested three different mycotoxins and found that two caused aneuploidy.[167] A third study highlighted that two more fungal toxins have been found to cause aneuploidy.[168]

DNA damage – Methyl-deficiency:

Methylation is a process in humans that can be likened to the process of oiling the mechanical parts of a machine, in order that it operates effectively. The pistons in the engine of a car would grind to a halt if they weren't lubricated with oil. In a similar way, proteins and DNA need to be methylated in order to work properly:

> *'In simple terms it [methylation] is a process in which certain chemicals called* **"methyl groups"** *are added to various constituents of* **proteins, DNA** *and other molecules. These are needed to keep them in* **good "working" condition**.*
>
> *If this process [methylation] does not happen your body is in for some* **serious trauma**.*

Healthier Talk.com [170]

A lack of methylation is known as *methyl-deficiency* or *hypomethylation* and results in DNA damage.[297, 363, 481] This is important to know because it is a key condition found in all cancers. Particularly interesting is that hypomethylation occurs in cells before they become cancerous; it appears to be an early symptom of the disease:

> *'It has been long known that global DNA* **hypomethylation** *is a general characteristic of cancer... DNA hypomethylation is an early event in the formation of cancer as it appears in* **pre-malignant tissue**.'*

Molecular Cytogenetics 2017 [830]

Methyl-deficiency can tell us a great deal about the underlying cause of cancer because it occurs right at the beginning – it seems to be a pre-cursor of tumour growth, and is a ubiquitous event. In other words, if we identify the cause of this methyl-deficiency, we'll identify the factor likely to be responsible for initial tumour growth.

To support the notion that fungal infection is generating tumour growth, there would need to be evidence to show that fungal infection can instigate methyl-deficiency, and this is exactly what we find in the medical literature. The two key factors involved are *vitamin B12* and a protein called *methionine*, both of which are required for healthy methylation to occur.

Methyl-deficiency can be caused by a deficiency in vitamin B12, because it forms part of the methylation pathway:

> *'Nutrient deficiency is one of the primary causes of* **impaired methylation**. *The two most* **important nutrients in methylation pathways** *are [vitamin]* **B12** *and* **folate**.'*

Kresser Institute 2017 [757]

Studies show that exposure to fungi, and the toxins they produce, can lead to vitamin B12 deficiencies:[169–172]

> 'Consistent vitamin B12 deficiency in chronic toxigenic **mould** exposures has been observed **in patients** exposed to chronic **toxigenic moulds** and **mycotoxins**... Since patients with chronic exposures to toxigenic moulds manifest **vitamin B12 deficiencies**, the role of **mycotoxins in vitamin B12 metabolism is recognized.**'
>
>

The Internet Journal of Toxicology 2007 [173]

Methionine is an amino acid (protein) that is also essential for methylation, without it, methyl-deficiency and random DNA damage results. A healthy cell can create methionine, but this process appears to be dysregulated in cancer, meaning that tumours can't create it. As a result, cancer cells are forced to rely on external dietary sources of methionine – this is referred to as *methionine dependence* or the *Hoffman effect*:

> 'Another example supported by recent evidence is the enzymatic **depletion** of the essential AA [amino acid], **methionine**. Cancer cell proliferation appears dependent on **exogenous methionine** and is known as **methionine dependence** or the **Hoffman effect.**'
>
>

Amino Acids 2021 [832]

Exogenous means 'external' to the cell, so, the Hoffman effect, mentioned in the quote above, refers to the fact that cancer cells are unable to create their own methionine, and are forced to rely upon external (dietary) sources. This exposes a weakness in cancer, where there's the opportunity to starve it of the methionine it requires by simply restricting methionine within the diet; and indeed, preliminary studies show promising results.[833]

The question is, why are these cells reliant upon external sources of methionine? Regarding the link to fungi, studies show that common fungal pathogens, such as *Cryptococcus Neoformans*, *Aspergillus* species and *Candida* species, all require, and consume, the methionine present within the cells they invade, because methionine is crucial for fungal survival and disease progression:

> 'Another mechanism for **amino acid–induced filamentation** in C. **albicans** is through **intracellular methionine metabolism** and the uptake of **methionine from the host** via CaMup1...

…This is supported by the concept that **A. fumigatus relies heavily** *on the amino acids' valine, isoleucine, and* **methionine** *as carbon sources* **during invasive aspergillosis.'**

<u>*Current Clinical Microbiology Reports*</u> **2019** [831]

Here it is shown that fungi deplete methionine present within the cell in order to implement invasive growth, which explains why the cell is then forced to rely on external sources of methionine. Furthermore, fungi have also been shown to inhibit methionine synthesis, through the expression of a toxin called acetaldehyde.[183] Moreover, *Candida albicans* can create mutagenic (capable of inducing genetic mutations) amounts of acetaldehyde during infection, which can account for the random DNA damage that exists.[184] This acquisition of intracellular methionine helps to explain why many tumours become methionine-dependent, and why methyl-deficiency occurs so early on in pre-cancerous tissue. Inflamed cells that harbour intracellular pathogens are unable to efficiently methylate their DNA because the substrates required to do so are in limited supply. The presence of a fungal pathogen, therefore, can help to explain why random DNA damage occurs in cancer, especially early-stage tumour growth.

Methyl-deficiency appears to be yet another symptom of cancer that not only explains why random DNA damage occurs, but adds to the abundant evidence linking fungal pathogens to the disease. That methyl-deficiency is present in pre-cancerous cells also stands to confirm that fungal pathogens are present right at the beginning of tumour formation, supporting the view that carcinogenesis is a result of fungal invasion.

Explaining Hallmarks 1 and 2 – Unregulated growth:

EGFR and HER2 are growth receptors that appear on the surface of cells. They are linked to generating a tumour because they increase the cell's growth rate, leading to faster replication. Cancer cells have increased numbers of these growth receptors. But how does this relate to fungi? Interestingly, fungal pathogens target these receptors to invade the cell, and promote receptor activation. In particular, studies found that *Candida albicans* produce a protein called Als-3, which mimics human proteins absorbed by the HER2 receptor. The cell is tricked into absorbing the fungus via a process called endocytosis:

*'Therefore, **Als3** is a **fungal invasin** that mimics host cell cadherins and induces **endocytosis** by binding to N-cadherin on endothelial cells and **E-cadherin** on oral epithelial cells.'*

PLOS Biology **2007** [256]

*'Here, we show that the EGF receptor (**EGFR**) and **HER2** function cooperatively to **induce** the **endocytosis of C. albicans hyphae**. EGFR and HER2 interact with **C. albicans** in an Als3- and Ssa1- dependent manner, and this interaction induces **receptor autophosphorylation** [activation].'*

PNAS **2012** [255]

Endocytosis means the action of a cell absorbing something – in this case, fungi and the Als-3 protein it produces. So, fungi cleverly gain access to the cell by fooling it into thinking it is something else, which stimulates these growth receptors in the process. That fungi gain entry through this receptor also highlights how tiny fungi are when they invade cells, rendering them extremely difficult to identify under a microscope.

In respect of EGFR growth receptor activation, *Candida* produce a toxin called *Candidalysin*. This toxin directly stimulates EGFR, encouraging cell growth upon invasion:

*'Recently, it was discovered that the invasive (hyphal) form of **C. Albicans** secretes a cytolytic peptide **toxin**, named **candidalysin**…*

*Candidalysin activates the **epidermal growth factor receptor** [EGFR] in epithelial cells…*

*The data indicate that **EGFR** plays a **central role** in mucosal **C. albicans infections**, with **candidalysin**-mediated activation of EGFR driving **MAPK**-based **immune activation**.'*

Current Opinion in Microbiology **2019** [803]

Furthermore, fungal invasion stimulates the 'MAPK' and 'PI3K/AKT/mTOR' pathways within cells. These two pathways control cell growth and proliferation, among other things,[634, 647, 803] thus helping to explain the increased growth that occurs in cancer. Further confirming this link to growth, in 2019, scientists discovered that a particular type of fungal pathogen was actually driving tumour growth in pancreatic cancer:

*'A new study, published Wednesday in the journal Nature, found that fungi can make their way deep into the pancreas... In mice and human patients with pancreatic cancer, the **fungi proliferate 3,000-fold** compared to healthy tissue — and one fungus in particular may make pancreatic tumours grow bigger.*

*"Administering an **anti-fungal drug** got rid of the fungi in mice and **kept tumours from developing**. And when the treated mice again received the yeast, their tumours **started growing once more** — an indication", Dr. Aykut said, "that the **fungal cells were driving the tumours' growth"**.'*

The New York Times **2019** [642]

As the corrosive acidic environment surrounding a tumour becomes worse – driven by glycolysis and it's byproduct, lactic acid – the integrity of nearby cells is lost. This diminishes the 'growth control' signals that normally suppress the growth of cells when they come into contact with each other, and different tissue. This helps to explain Hallmark 2 – why there's a failure of the normal growth suppression signals that would otherwise prevent abnormal growth in healthy tissue.

Increased growth – The hormone link:

Scientists acknowledge that some cancers are linked to hormones. Certain hormones, such as estrogen, have been shown to stimulate tumour growth; this is the case with breast cancer. Are fungi linked to these hormone-related cancers? Yes, it has been shown that fungi, *Candida albicans* in particular, are stimulated to become more aggressive, and grow, in the presence of estrogen. They have an estrogen-binding protein that can also generate hormone imbalances, linking fungi to breast and ovarian cancer:

*'Three Candida albicans strains were tested... All 3 test organisms showed **increased growth** in the presence of estradiol compared with estrogen-free controls.'*

Journal of Infectious Diseases **2000** [023]

*'Candida albicans is the most common etiological agent of vaginal candidiasis. Elevated host estrogen levels and the incidence of vaginal candidiasis are **positively associated**.'*

Eukaryotic Cell **2006** [024]

And as I've previously discussed, estrogen provides the additional benefit to particular pathogens of enabling them to evade immune detection.[842] Does access to increased amounts of glucose and estrogen help to explain why breast cancer is the leading cancer type in women by such a significant degree? This is especially significant considering these pathogens are well known to infect the reproductive organs. Fungal infection appears to stimulate cell growth – this interaction may account for the increased growth witnessed in cancer.

Explaining Hallmark 3 – Failure of the cell death mechanism:

A tumour forms because cells fail to die when they are programmed to – the cell-death mechanism no longer appears to be working. This is thought to be a result of DNA damage or damage to mitochondria, but as the evidence will show, there is an alternative explanation. One of the main routes through which a cell instigates cell death is via mitochondria when they release a chemical called *cytochrome c*. In healthy cells, a protein called *Bcl-2* blocks the release of cytochrome c, preventing cell death from occurring; it acts like a plug.

When programmed cell death is instigated, Bcl-2 is reduced, the plug is essentially removed, allowing cytochrome c to be released. The cell then collapses in a controlled manner, shrivelling down into a tiny package that is taken away by the immune system. This process of programmed cell death is called *apoptosis*.[417] An over-expression of the Bcl-2 protein (the plug) will prevent mitochondria from releasing cytochrome c; this can prevent cell death and lead to a tumour, especially if Bcl-2 expression cannot be reduced. Bcl-2 essentially controls the 'kill switch' within mitochondria:

> 'The **Bcl-2** family is the best characterized protein family involved in the regulation of **apoptotic cell death**.
>
> ...**Bcl-2** and Bcl-XL, **prevent apoptosis** either by sequestering proforms of death-driving cysteine proteases called **caspases**... or by **preventing the release** of **mitochondrial** apoptogenic factors such as **cytochrome c**.
>
> Thus, the **Bcl-2** family of proteins acts as a critical **life-death decision point** within the common pathway of apoptosis [programmed cell death].'
>
> <u>Genes to Cells</u> **1998** [295]

So, just as in finding the source of methyl-deficiency, finding the source of Bcl-2 control should indicate the factor likely to be responsible for tumour growth. Intriguingly, this next study confirms that fungi can indeed control Bcl-2 by either over-expressing or reducing it. This allows the pathogen to determine the fate of the cell; the path chosen depends upon which outcome benefits the pathogen the most:

> *'It has previously been shown that **C. albicans** was able to survive within macrophages… Several pathogens are known to interfere with host cell **apoptotic control** [cell death control]. Depending on their parasitic behaviour, differential triggering of cell **survival or cell death** is used by **microbes** to promote their [own] survival…*
>
> *…a **strong decrease in Bcl-2** staining was observed in cells that had ingested **C. albicans** yeasts…*
>
> *Intracellular pathogens have evolved diverse strategies to **induce** or **inhibit** host cell **apoptosis** [cell death], aiding dissemination within the host or facilitating **intracellular survival**.'*
>
> <u>*The Journal of Biological Chemistry* **2003**</u> [021]

In the study above, *Candida albicans* decreased Bcl-2 to kill the immune cell, highlighting its ability to control the cell death mechanism. And as the study states, *Candida* can either instigate cell death or suppress it depending upon which course of action facilities its survival.

Of particular interest is that anti-fungal drugs appear to reduce the very Bcl-2 protein that fungi have been shown to manipulate, indicating that fungi are the underlying cause of cell death suppression:

> *'Imidazole anti-fungals **Miconazole** and **Econazole** induce **apoptosis** in mouse lymphoma and human T cell **leukaemia** cells: regulation by **Bcl-2** and potential role of calcium.'*
>
> <u>*Cell Death and Differentiation* **1996**</u> [402]

We also see a similar response with the anti-fungal compounds found in food and medicinal plants. Here, the anti-fungal chemical bromelain, which is found in pineapples, is shown to kill cancer cells by also reducing the expression of Bcl-2:

> *'Our findings collectively indicate that **bromelain** exerts **cytotoxic** effects in a panel of human gastric and colon carcinoma cells… While promoting **apoptosis** with involvement of the **caspase***

*system and extra-nuclear **p53**, bromelain also appears to impair cancer cell survival by blocking the AKT pathway and **attenuating Bcl-2**... resulting in release of **cytochrome C** from **mitochondria**.'*

OncoTargets and Therapy **2013** [093]

Killing the fungal pathogen using bromelain could be predicted to have this effect on a cancer cell, especially if it has suffered extreme levels of damage. Once the cell has regained control, it is prompted to commit cell death – as it is programmed to do – in response to the damage already inflicted by the fungal pathogen, which renders it a danger to the host.

A separate study confirms that *Aspergillus fumigatus* intentionally suppresses cell death within lung cells:

> *'**A. fumigatus** conidia have been found to **suppress apoptosis** of type II pneumocytes [lung cells] induced by either tumour necrosis factor α (TNF-α) or staurosporine. **Inhibition of apoptosis is an active process** on the part of the conidia [fungus].'*

PLOS pathogens **2006** [562]

This is particularly interesting because we all inhale hundreds of *Aspergillus* fungal spores every single day. Aided by the damage to lung cells that smoking generates, could *Aspergillus* fungi be predominantly responsible for lung cancer?

> *'Upon inhalation of conidia, the fungus makes close contact with lung **epithelial cells**... conidia of **A. fumigatus** were able to **survive within epithelial cells**. This was due to the presence of DHN **melanin** in the cell wall of conidia...*
>
> *...melanised wild-type conidia were able to **inhibit** the extrinsic **apoptotic pathway in A549 lung epithelial cells** even for longer periods.'*

International Journal of Medical Microbiology **2014** [709]

Within the setting of the lung, the study below found that macrophage immune cells killed *Aspergillus fumigatus*; however, the pathogen survived undetected and went on to germinate without killing the lung cells it inhabited:

'Conidia [Aspergillus] are rapidly destroyed by murine macrophages but a significant percentage of internalized conidia persist and germinate in A549 epithelial cells [lung cells].

By 36 hours, the germlings were able to escape the phagosome and form extracellular hyphae without lysis [without death] of the host cell.'

Journal of Cell Science **2003** [714]

In terms of *Candida*, the following study confirms that it suppresses apoptosis upon successful cell invasion:

'...these findings indicate that epithelial apoptotic pathways are activated in response to C. albicans, but fail to progress and promote apoptotic cell death.'

Molecular Oral Microbiology **2012** [565]

The above quote highlights that the cell attempts to induce apoptosis but fails because the fungus overrides the cell death mechanism. The fungal pathogen *Cryptococcus neoformans* has developed several strategies designed to suppress and control cellular functions. In particular, studies show that this fungal pathogen suppresses mitochondria, causing mitochondrial dysfunction:

'C. neoformans has a multiple-hit intracellular survival strategy, resulting in the progressive deterioration of host cellular functions... The decreased mitochondrial potential results in the deregulation of fuel and energy requirements and in poor functioning of mitochondria.'

Frontiers in Cellular and Infection Microbiology **2016** [708]

Does this interaction explain why mitochondria appear to be defective in cancer cells? Another type of fungus has also been shown to suppress cell death mechanisms to sustain itself within the cell:

'We conclude that H. capsulatum induces an anti-apoptotic state on leucocytes [immune cell]... These facts may represent an escape mechanism for the fungus by delaying cell death and allowing the fungus to survive inside leucocytes.

It is advantageous for intracellular organisms to evolve strategies against apoptosis to ensure the continuous supply of nutrients *and protection from the host. In fact, some intracellular organisms, such as C. pneumoniae and virulent M. tuberculosis, **inhibit apoptosis**, as strategies to **survive and propagate in host cells**.'*

Scandinavian Journal of Immunology 2002 [563]

Moreover, upon infection, toll-like receptors (TLRs) are stimulated.[914] Not only are these same TLRs highly stimulated in cancer – indicating the presence of pathogens – but upon stimulation, these activated TLRs inhibit the cell death mechanism.[914] Through the direct activation of TLRs, fungal infection may have inadvertently prevented cell death from occurring.

It is clear that common fungal pathogens can suppress the cell death mechanism to keep the cell alive. This confirms that fungal pathogens can generate a tumour.

Explaining Hallmark 4 – Limitless growth:

There are many factors that contribute to the growth potential of cancer. As we've previously discussed, fungal pathogens can invoke cell growth signals through the activation of various growth receptors (EGFR, HER2). However, as regular cells can only replicate a limited number of times, unlimited tumour growth can't be explained in full by the stimulation of these receptors. Instead, this is the realm of cancer stem cells, or cells that acquire stem-cell-like properties, because it is the stem cell that has the potential for generating unlimited growth.

As discussed in Chapter 7, stem cells are superior cell types that have the ability to create regular cells, such as skin cells, liver cells, lung cells etcetera. When a regular cell is created, such as a skin cell, it foregoes its stem cell properties to gain a specific function relevant to the local tissue type – this process is called *differentiation* – the cell adopts a specific role, in this case the attributes of a skin cell.

In certain circumstances, where cells are damaged, regular cells can revert back to a stem-cell state re-acquiring the ability to create other cells and reproduce indefinitely. This reversal in role is called *de-differentiation* – the cell is relinquishing its specialist properties, to regain stem-cell qualities that can aid with cell repair. This reverse transition to a stem-cell-like state is known as an *epithelial-mesenchymal transition* (EMT), and generally occurs under stressful conditions where excessive cell damage and inflammation persists:

> *'...The behaviour of these cells provided one of the first indications that **epithelial cells** under **inflammatory stresses** can advance to various extents through an **EMT** [stem-cell-like transition]...'*
>
>

bioRxiv 2021 [810]

This is important because cancer stem cells can constitute up to 2% of the tumour mass, which would explain why tumours appear to possess the ability for limitless growth. This is also concerning because at present, many oncologists who subscribe to the DNA Theory either do not recognise the involvement of cancer stem cells, or are reluctant to acknowledge them, possibly because current chemotherapy treatments rarely kill cancer stems cells, and actually appear to stimulate them into becoming more aggressive. Regardless of the reason, the science is clear: cancer stem cells exist and are present in tumours.[811] Explaining their role is crucial when it comes to understanding and treating the disease. So the question is this: are fungi responsible for creating the cancer stem cells that appear responsible for the deadly aspects of the disease?

The previous section titled 'Explaining hallmark 9 – DNA damage', confirmed that fungi can inflict sufficient cell damage to trigger an EMT to a cancer stem cell. Additionally, studies show that damage to mitochondria can instigate a stem cell transition, which is not surprising given that mitochondrial DNA is more susceptible to damage than the more robust DNA contained within the nucleus:[013]

> *'Metastatic breast tumours undergo **epithelial-to-mesenchymal** transition **(EMT)**... Notably, **mtDNA reduction** [damage to mitochondrial DNA] generates **breast cancer stem cells.'**
>
>

Research Gate 2017 [344]

Studies show that fungal mycotoxins can cause mitochondrial dysfunction, accounting for mitochondrial damage, and driving this transition of a regular cell to a stem cell:

> *'Findings suggest that **mycotoxins** [fungal toxins] such as citrinin, aflatoxin, and T-2 toxin exert multi-edged sword-like effects in test systems causing **mitochondrial dysfunction**. Mycotoxins can induce oxidative stress even at low concentration/dose that may be one of the major causes of **mitochondrial dysfunction.'**
>
>

IUBMB Life 2018 [814]

When we specifically look at the markers used to identify stem cell creation, we find that the presence of a fungal pathogen can stimulate these same markers, indicating that the pathogen can stimulate stem cell creation. To clarify, there are several markers that need to be considered, these are: 'E-cadherin', 'P63' and 'Vimentin'. Firstly, a reduction in E-cadherin stimulates an epithelial-mesenchymal transition (cancer stem cell transition):

> 'Functionally, **E-cadherin** behaves as a tumour suppressor gene and plays diverse roles in regulating cell **polarity, differentiation,** migration and **stem cell-like properties.**'
>
> <u>Molecular Cancer</u> **2016** [812]

> 'The connection between **loss of E-cadherin** expression by cancer cells and passage through an **EMT** has been established by many studies. For example, induction of the c-Fos oncogene in normal mouse mammary epithelial cell lines **induces an EMT** and is associated with a **decrease in E-cadherin expression.**'
>
> <u>The Journal of Clinical Investigation</u> **2009** [813]

To reiterate, a loss of E-cadherin induces the creation of stem cells. Secondly, Vimentin and P63 are expressed by stem cells, so an increase in both indicates an increase in stem cell creation – both are used as markers to identify the presence of stem cells.[810]

And this is where the link to fungi is established. Studies analysing the interactions between fungi and oral cancer found that these exact conditions were generated by the fungal pathogen – E-cadherin was reduced and expression of Vimentin and P63 was increased:

> 'Oral **candidiasis** [Candida infection] **increases p63 and vimentin expression** and **decreases E-cadherin expression** in OSCC [oral cancer] histopathological specimens...
>
> ...We also found that oral candidiasis triggered by C. albicans enhanced the progression of OSCC in vivo through the induction of inflammation and overexpression of metastatic genes and markers of **epithelial-mesenchymal transition.**'
>
> <u>bioRxiv</u> **2021** [810]

This implicates fungal pathogens as a potential cause of the epithelial-mesenchymal transition (EMT) that results in the cancer stem cells that are present within tumours. The study concludes:

> 'Taken together, these results suggest that C. albicans **actively participates** in the complex process of OSCC [oral cancer] progression.'
>
>

bioRxiv **2021** [810]

In fact, a particular mycotoxin called *Ochratoxin A* (OTA) has been shown to directly stimulate an EMT, generating stem cells:

> 'Ochratoxin A (OTA) is a **mycotoxin** that occurs naturally in fungi such as Aspergillus spp and Penicillium spp. OTA is known to exist in a variety of food groups such as cereals, cocoa, coffee, nuts, milk, beer, and wine, which are frequently consumed in daily life... These results indicate that **OTA induces** EMT through the AhR-Smad2/3 pathway.'
>
>

Toxins **2021** [815]

A prolonged state of cell damage and inflammation, caused by the toxins and free radicals fungal pathogens generate, may explain why an epithelial-mesenchymal transition can occur in the chronically inflamed environment of a tumour mass. Suppression of cell death mechanisms by the fungal pathogen would expose the cell to an abnormal level of damage for an extended period of time, encouraging an EMT to occur. It would appear that prolonged fungal infection can explain the creation of cancer stem cells, and thus limitless tumour growth.

Explaining Hallmark 5 – Angiogenesis, blood vessel growth:

As a tumour grows, it requires increased access to nutrients to survive. Tumours adapt to this increased nutrient requirement by stimulating the growth of new blood vessels, a process known as *angiogenesis*. Once connected, these blood vessels are able to increase the flow of nutrients to the tumour, leading to more growth potential and rising tumour aggression. The question is: are fungi responsible for stimulating blood vessel growth? Yes, and on many levels.

Blood vessel growth is a multifaceted process involving several key stimulants, one of which is MMP-9, an enzyme that is over-expressed in cancer cells:

> *'Matrix metalloproteinases (**MMPs**) secreted by tumor cells... have been strongly implicated in multiple stages of the invasive and metastatic progression of tumor cells... In particular, **MMP-9** is important for tumor **angiogenesis** by enhancing the availability of vascular endothelial cell growth factor (VEGF) in malignant tumors.'*
>
>

<u>*Nature*</u> **2014** [804]

Essentially, MMP-9 stimulates blood vessel growth via the VEGF pathway. So, are fungal pathogens able to manipulate MMP-9 production, and therefore able to account for the blood vessel growth witnessed in cancer? *Candida* fungi have indeed been shown to increase the production of MMP-9 within the cell by inhibiting the production of TIMPs, which control MMP-9 production:

> *'... (**MMP**)-9 activity is controlled by the balance between MMP-9 and its major tissue inhibitor of metalloproteinases (**TIMPs**)... Our findings indicate that **Candida** can participate in tissue inflammation by **modifying the host's MMP-9** and **their inhibitors**.'*
>
>

<u>*Mycoses*</u> **2011** [346]

By inhibiting TIMPs, fungal pathogens directly increase the production of MMP-9, regulating inflammation and stimulating blood vessel growth.

On a side note, studies show that when cannabis is used on cancer cells, it decreases the production of MMP-9 by increasing TIMP-1 back to normal levels:

> *'Cannabinoids inhibit cancer cell invasion via **increasing** tissue inhibitor of **matrix metalloproteinases-1** (TIMP-1)...'*
>
>

<u>*FASEB J.*</u> **2012** [083]

This indicates that cannabis works by killing the fungus within the cell, because the plant extract affects the same pathways (TIMP-1 and MMP-9) that fungi have been found to manipulate. As we would expect, when the cannabis extract kills the fungus, TIMP-1 and MMP-9 revert back to normal levels.

Also forming part of this equation is that fact that fungal infection triggers glycolysis, which results in the overproduction of lactic acid – the evidence for this is discussed within the Hallmark 7 section that follows shortly. For now, it's important to recognise that lactic acid is expressed as a direct result of fungal involvement, and that this over-expression of lactic acid, caused by the pathogen, stimulates blood vessel growth.[612, 647] Very telling, is that *Candida* also produce a toxin called *Candidalysin*, which evidence shows can not only stimulate cell growth receptors such as EGFR; but blood vessel growth as well:

> '*Finally,* **candidalysin** *also induces FGF-2 secretion from human endothelial cells and* **drives angiogenesis** *during murine systemic infections. As to why candidalysin* **promotes angiogenesis** *is intriguing but it is notable that candidalysin also activates* **EGFR signalling**, *which is associated with angiogenesis.*'
>
> **_Current Opinion in Microbiology_ 2019** [803]

It is clear that fungal pathogens can directly and indirectly stimulate blood vessel growth, helping to explain why a tumour develops its own blood supply.

Explaining Hallmark 6 – Invasion and metastasis:

Invasion refers to the process of tumour cells expanding into adjacent tissue, while metastasis refers to the process of tumour cells disseminating into the bloodstream, and spreading to a different location within the body. Interestingly, studies show that there is a significant correlation between *Candida* infection and increased rates of metastasis. An increase in cancer within the kidneys and liver was matched by an increase in *Candida* severity.[028]

Invasion and metastasis – Fungi and MMP-9:

MMP-9 enzymes are normally used sparingly to aid with wound healing, due to their ability to breakdown and remove dead tissue, and to stimulate blood vessel growth. Excessive production of MMP-9, which occurs in tumours, becomes a problem because it creates a corrosive inflammatory environment that aids with tumour invasion, and ultimately metastasis, as this study confirms:

> '*Recent studies have reported that* **invasive cells** *express* **MMP-9** *at* **higher levels** *and that its expression is closely linked with* **vascular invasion** *and* **aggressive malignant phenotypes.**'
>
> **_Nature_ 2014** [804]

As I mentioned a moment ago, fungi can influence the production of MMP-9, which is also confirmed in the following study:

> *'C. albicans infection potently activates the EGFR [growth receptor]. Additionally, candidalysin can indirectly activate EGFR through a complex mechanism involving matrix metalloproteinases (MMPs) and EGFR ligands… Notably, MMP and EGFR ligand are each independently implicated in a number of cancers.'*

Immunology **2021** [809]

Here common fungal pathogens are implicated in the progression of oral cancer through the influence of MMP-9 and the stimulation of growth receptors. Moreover, I've demonstrated, and will further discuss the ability of fungi to stimulate the production of lactic acid. The excessive quantity of lactic acid generates a corrosive environment that encourages invasive growth because the cohesion of healthy tissue becomes compromised, while cells become damaged as the acidity of the tissue increases. This reduces anti-growth signals normally produced by healthy tissue, which ultimately facilitates the invasion of a tumour into adjacent tissue, all because of the ongoing influence of fungal pathogens.

Invasion and Metastasis – Macrophage involvement:

Another key factor involves cells of the immune system called *macrophages*. These immune cells gravitate towards tumours and appear to promote tumour growth and cancer spread. Scientists are at a loss to explain why.

This situation is critically important to acknowledge because macrophages can comprise up to 50% of the bulk of the tumour itself, meaning that these immune cells play a major role in promoting tumour growth and cancer progression. Explaining their involvement is crucial if we hope to successfully treat the disease:

> *'Tumours are complex tissues where cancer cells maintain intricate interactions with their surrounding stroma. Important components of the tumour stroma include **macrophages**, which are intimately involved in tumour rejection, **promotion**, and **metastasis**. In some cases, **macrophages** can comprise up to **50%** of the tumour mass, and their abundance is associated with a **poor clinical outcome in most cancers**.'*

Frontiers in Oncology **2018** [560]

While scientists are baffled by the behaviour of macrophages, the influence of a fungal pathogen can provide a coherent answer regarding their involvement. Macrophages generally have two roles to play and are present in two distinct forms. Some kill pathogens, while others repair cell damage. Pathogen-killing macrophages are known as 'classically activated M1 macrophages' (M1), and cell-repair macrophages are known as 'alternatively activated M2 macrophages' (M2).[560] This distinction between the two roles will help to explain why they appear to help tumour progression.

As I mentioned a little earlier, fungi can produce an enzyme called nagalase, which is also expressed within tumours. Nagalase disables the 'MAF' receptor that alerts M1 macrophages to a threat, such as a micro-organism.[503] This indicates that M1 macrophages (fungal-killing macrophages) are drawn to tumours to a lesser degree. Essentially, the fungus evades detection by inhibiting the activation of M1 macrophages. This influence explains why 'peaceful' cell-repairing M2 type macrophages are the dominant type within the vicinity of a tumour:

> *'Generally, Tumour-Associated-Macrophages acquire an **M2**-like phenotype that plays important roles in many aspects of **tumour growth** and **progression**.'*
>
> *Journal of Cell Physiology* **2013** [608]

Furthermore, *Candida* have also been shown to encourage M1 activated macrophages to switch to M2 type macrophages, which target cell repair, thus explaining why M2 type macrophages are the dominant form present within and around tumours:

> *'Further, there is evidence that **C.albicans promotes** the differentiation of M1 macrophages to **M2 macrophages** thereby enhance its survival rate.'*
>
> *Biomedicine & Pharmacotherapy* **2020** [751]

Persistent inflammation and the pathogen's manipulative influence draws an abundance of M2 cell-repairing macrophages to the tumour site. This inflammatory environment ensures that M2 macrophages remain for longer than necessary. The critical point of note, is that macrophages repair cells similarly to neutrophils by producing the corrosive enzyme MMP-9. Overproduction of MMP-9 generated by M2 macrophages attempting to repair this persistent damage, leads to a loss of cell cohesion and increased blood vessel growth. Ultimately this results in cancer cells breaking away into the bloodstream. As part of the repair process, M2 macrophages also increase IGF-1 and TGFB signals; unfortunately, both are growth factors that stimulate tumour growth.[560]

As the fungal threat is not dealt with, persistent cell damage and inflammation are continuous, resulting in the release of iron and lactate into the surrounding tissue. Not only does iron and lactate feed fungal growth, but both also disable macrophages and even the T-cells that are tasked with killing cancer cells:

> 'Iron overload **adversely affects macrophage / monocyte** [immune cell] **function** directly and indirectly.
>
> **Iron excess** appears to cause alterations of **T-cell** (cellular immunity) and **B-cell** (humoral immunity) function.
>
> The ability of **excess iron** to cause a spectrum of **immune dysfunctions** is beginning to be understood and appreciated.'
>
> <u>Annals of Clinical & Laboratory Science</u> 2000 [490]

So, fungi produce nagalase to suppress the immune response; and macrophages are encouraged to adopt an M2-like cell repair phenotype (posture). All while MMP-9 excretion, inflammation, lactate and iron release incapacitates the macrophages that are present. This explains why up to 50% of the tumour mass can be made up of these macrophage immune cells.

Furthermore, continued production of MMP-9 produced by neutrophils, fungi and now M2 macrophages, leads to cancer cells migrating into the bloodstream, and ultimately to the spread of the disease. This may explain why high numbers of macrophages found within a tumour are associated with a poor survival outcome.

Moreover, from the metabolic perspective, Professor Seyfried acknowledges the presence of macrophages. His take on their involvement centres around their stem-cell-like characteristics – their ability to move freely and generate new cells – and the manner in which they appear to fuse with cancer cells. This fusion results in the corruption of the macrophage and metabolic dysfunction, essentially converting the immune cell to a more cancerous way of behaving.[866] In effect it switches sides and is recruited to work for the tumour. This integration of macrophages into the tumour mass, and their ongoing involvement, can also be viewed from an infection perspective. Many common fungal pathogens of humans have become expert at not only suppressing macrophages, and changing their behaviour, but at surviving and even propagating within them, in a similar manner to how they are able to thrive within regular cells:

> *'All of the fungal pathogens described above have the genetic and metabolic machinery to* **survive** *and* **replicate within human macrophages**, *thus enhancing their pathogenicity and virulence. Many of the pathogens share common features associated with macrophage survival and replication…*
>
> *…reducing the antimicrobial activity of the macrophage and the utilization of* **alternative nutrient-acquisition pathways** *to enable* **survival within** *the* **nutrient-sparse macrophage environment**.'*

<u>*Cold Spring Harbor Perspectives in Medicine*</u> **2015** [878]

Could this interaction explain why macrophages become incapacitated and are absorbed into the tumour mass? Protected within the bulk of the expanding tumour, do these fungal pathogens expand into, and parasitise, these vulnerable macrophages? Indeed, this appears to be the case, as the latest evidence confirms that immune cells are also infected with intracellular fungal pathogens within the tumour environment:

> *'…we studied fungi in 35 tumour types…***Fungi were detected in all tumour types** *and demonstrated* **tumour-type specific profiles**. *Similar to bacteria, fungi were visualized in both cancer* **and immune cells**.'*

<u>*Weizmann Institute of Science*</u> **2023** [887]

And as I mentioned earlier, *Cryptococcus neoformans*, a common fungal pathogen of humans, has been found to infect and survive within macrophage immune cells:

> *'We provide the first evidence for* **lateral transfer** *of a human* **fungal pathogen**. *This rare event may occur repeatedly during latent cryptococcal infections, thereby allowing the pathogen to remain* **concealed** *from the* **immune system** *and* **protecting it** *from exposure to* **antifungal agents**…*

> *...Finally,* **infected macrophage cells** *[immune cells] may travel widely throughout the host circulatory and lymphatic systems, where they interact intimately with one another and with other cell types through transient contacts...'*
>
> *BMC Immunology* **2007** [851]

This also indicates that the intracellular nature of these pathogens enables them to infect other areas of the body by hiding within cells that circulate throughout the bloodstream. Indeed, migrating tumour cells have been shown to harbour intracellular pathogens that existed at the original tumour site. Effectively, these micro-organisms not only travel within these migrating tumour cells through the bloodstream, but they help stimulate tumour development at a distant site, once the tumour has spread:

> *'Our findings suggest that* **tumour-resident microbiota**, *albeit at low biomass, play an important role in* **promoting cancer metastasis**, *intervention of which might therefore be worth exploring for advancing oncology care. '*
>
> *Cell* 2022 [888]

While this study was only concerned with bacteria and did not screen for fungi, it would make sense that fungal pathogens would be included within the metastatic cancer cells travelling through the bloodstream, given that they also form part of the intracellular pathogens that exist within tumours. In fact, the expression of galectin-3 indicates that this is indeed the case.

Invasion and Metastasis – Galectin-3:

While helping to further explain how cancer cells can spread, the involvement of galectin-3 directly implicates fungi as the underlying cause. Galectin-3 is a sticky protein found in abundance on metastatic cancers (cancers that have spread).[895] It is this sticky quality that enables migrating cancer cells to attach to other cells within the body. But as scientists view cell malfunction as the cause of cancer, they assume that the DNA gene that controls galectin-3 has become faulty, or that the cancer cell purposely 'chooses' to produce this sticky protein, to help it migrate.

Missing the clues that highlight fungal involvement, scientists focus on the DNA gene that creates it (LGALS3) and attempt to block that gene with a targeted drug.[061] This solution appears to be misguided, because according to the IntOGen DNA database, the galectin-3 gene has only been found to be mutated in 0.1% of cancer samples analysed, confirming that DNA cannot account for the involvement of galectin-3.[356] Producing a drug to block this gene, therefore, will likely have limited success, as the gene doesn't appear to be the cause of the problem. So how does Galectin-3 confirm that a fungal pathogen is at the heart of cancer progression?

Galectin-3 is generated by cells to specifically recognise and kill fungal pathogens, one of which is *Candida albicans.*[063] Regarding this, the *Journal of Immunology* states:

> *'We found that **galectin-3 bound only to Candida albicans** species that bear β-1,2-linked oligomannans on the cell surface...*
>
> *Surprisingly, binding directly induced **death of Candida species.** Thus, galectin-3 can act as a **pattern recognition receptor** that **recognizes** a unique pathogen-specific oligosaccharide sequence...*
>
> *Thus, **we report a novel fungicidal activity for galectin-3**, suggesting that **galectin-3 participates in host protection against opportunistic fungal infections.'***

The Journal of Immunology 2006 [063]

The study points out that galectin-3 is expressed when fungal pathogens are present:

> *'Galectin-3 is expressed by epithelia lining the body surfaces that are **exposed to Candida colonization**, such as oral mucosa, corneal, and conjunctival epithelia, and intestinal epithelia, **that constitute the first line of host defence against Candida invasion.'***

The Journal of Immunology 2006 [063]

Galectin-3 is essentially an anti-fungal agent designed to be expressed in the presence of fungi. The over-expression of galectin-3, especially in metastatic cancer cells, signifies the presence of a fungal pathogen. As cancer progresses, so the expression of galectin-3 increases.[827] Is this in response to the expanding fungal infection, and the failure of the immune system to deal with the fungal threat? This sits nicely with the latest evidence looking into the microbes present with tumours, which was previously discussed in Chapter 10 and earlier in this chapter. It was found that microbes travel with the migrating cancer cells and remain within the tumour when it has successfully spread elsewhere.[863]

Very telling is the ability of fungi to directly influence the expression of galectin-3:

> *'...a recent report demonstrated that **C. albicans** infection of a macrophage cell line in vitro reduced expression of **galectin-3** by 3-fold, suggesting a mechanism for the pathogen to **evade the fungicidal effect of galectin-3**.'*

> <u>*The Journal of Immunology* **2006**</u> [063]

The spread of cancer may just be an unfortunate result of the body's natural defence system, where the release of galectin-3, which is intended to kill the fungus, inadvertently aids the metastatic process.

It's all about the hallmarks:

We've covered a lot of ground here, so it would be helpful to pause for a moment and summarise what we've established so far, to determine how many hallmarks have been explained.

It is clear that fungi can invade cells at will, control the immune response, evade detection, and suppress macrophages and cancer-killing T-cells at the site of injury (**hallmark 8**). They can generate the random DNA damage that is often present, including aneuploidy and methyl-deficiency (**hallmark 9**). Fungi are a direct source of inflammation (**hallmark 10**), and they have a high affinity for estrogen, linking them to the most common forms of hormonal cancers. These pathogens can manipulate pathways directly related to tumour growth (EGFR, HER2, MAPK, mTOR) and suppress cell death mechanisms (Bcl-2, mTOR), which ultimately leads to tumour formation (**hallmarks 1, 2 and 3**). Invasion of adjacent cells due to uncontrolled growth, lactic acid accumulation, the loss of E-cadherin and a rise in MMP-9, as well as the expression of galectin-3, explain the invasive nature and spread of the disease (**hallmark 6**); this includes the ability of a regular cancer cell to transitions into a cancer stem cell via an epithelial-mesenchymal transition (EMT), providing the tumour with the capacity for unlimited growth (**hallmark 4**). The overproduction of MMP-9 and lactic acid accounts for the chaotic blood vessel growth that is also experienced (**hallmark 5**).

So to clarify, using supporting evidence I have shown that intracellular fungal pathogens, through various invasion and cell manipulation techniques, are directly capable of explaining at least 9 of the 10 hallmarks of cancer, which are highlighted in bold within the list below:

1. **Uncontrolled cell growth**
2. **Resistance of signals to stop their growth**
3. **Evasion of cell death signals**
4. **Limitless replication**
5. **Extended blood vessel growth**
6. **Invasion of local tissue and metastasis**
7. Abnormal metabolic pathways (faulty energy system)
8. **Evasion of the immune system**
9. **Genome instability (DNA damage)**
10. **Inflammation.**

Hallmark 7 is the only one remaining, the hallmark that all mainstream theories are currently unable to account for. When we consider that the DNA Theory appears only capable of explaining two of these hallmarks, it is perplexing to think that so many in the medical field can so readily dismiss the Metabolic Theory, let alone the unquestionable influence of a fungal pathogen, and claim so definitively that DNA mutation is the cause of the disease.

The final piece of the puzzle:

Finally we come to the last and arguably the most important hallmark of all. According to proponents of the Metabolic Theory, hallmark 7 explains all of the other hallmarks, so uncovering the cause of this energy switch should enable us to identify the underlying cause of cancer. If the evidence aligns with the model of cancer being presented within this book, then I think we can begin to get excited, because this would provide us with a way of explaining all required hallmarks for the first time, which would indicate that the underlying cause has been identified. So, let's attempt to explain the unexplained.

Explaining Hallmark 7 – The Warburg effect:

Mitochondria require oxygen to create energy and the free radicals that can be used to kill pathogens. When oxygen is unavailable, the backup energy system known as glycolysis becomes dominant, and when this occurs mitochondria may appear dormant or even dysfunctional. This is particularly the case with cancer, where glycolysis appears to be the dominant energy state of most tumours. Even when oxygen is available, mitochondria fail to create energy in the normal way, which forces the backup energy system to remain dominant – this seemingly counter-intuitive behaviour is termed the 'Warburg effect'.

This has led scientists to conclude that mitochondria are no longer capable of utilising oxygen for normal energy creation – they are essentially faulty. But at present, no mainstream cancer theory has been able to fully explain why this energy switch occurs. While mitochondria are damaged to varying degrees, no specific and consistent pattern of damage has yet been shown to be capable of explaining why the same outcome occurs in all cancers, and neither can any DNA genes account for this energy transition in the manner it occurs in cancer. The ultimate question then is this: are fungi able to instigate and control the Warburg effect, could they be responsible for the abnormal metabolism witnessed in cancer?

In line with the evidence presented so far, studies show that common fungal pathogens can suppress the creation of free radicals (ROS) within mitochondria,[125] highlighting that they have the ability to block oxygen utilisation to cause an energy switch:

> *'C. albicans actively suppresses ROS production in phagocytes* in vitro, which may represent an important *immune evasion mechanism.'*
>
> <u>Infection and immunity</u> 2015 [130]

Notably, *Acetyl CoA* is a molecule used in the production of energy within mitochondria,[426] as can be seen in the image below:

Cell energy creation

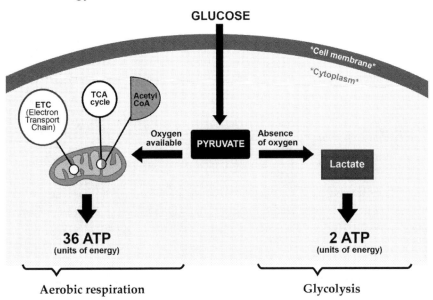

Any disruption to Acetyl CoA would inhibit the energy process. With this in mind, studies show that *Candida albicans* can produce a chemical toxin called *acetaldehyde*, which blocks the production of acetyl CoA.[186] This reduces oxygen utilisation within mitochondria, ultimately shutting off the oxygen supply:[581]

> 'Finally, he demonstrated **decreased respiration** in these tissues, **oxygen consumption falling** in parallel with the **declining level of acetyl CoA** as the concentration of **acetaldehyde increased**.'
>
> <u>Orthomolecular.org</u> [426]

Significantly, *Candida albicans* can produce DNA-damaging amounts of acetaldehyde:

> 'Candida albicans isolated from potentially carcinogenic oral diseases can produce **mutagenic** amounts of **acetaldehyde**.'
>
> <u>Journal of Oral Pathology and Medicine 2013</u> [184]

This indicates that fungi could instigate glycolysis through the production of a toxin. While this is a possibility, what we really want to see is direct evidence that fungi actually cause this energy switch.

Admittedly, I was astonished when I discovered the following, it took me a while to accept that this interaction has been overlooked by the majority of cancer scientists. But, by far the most compelling evidence implicating fungal pathogens as an underlying cause of cancer, is the evidence confirming that just the sheer presence of a fungal pathogen attempting to invade a cell triggers the Warburg effect, an energy switch to glycolysis:

> *'Collectively, these data show that* **C. albicans triggers** *the* **Warburg effect** *in macrophages...'*
>
> <u>Cell metabolism</u> **2018** [612]

Astonishingly, it is well known within immunological circles, that the Warburg effect is instigated by regular cells and immune cells as a form of defence against infection. Furthermore, a switch to glycolysis occurs even in the presence of oxygen. This seems to be a defensive strategy designed to starve the fungus of the glucose it needs to function. And as the study goes on to show, during the fight for survival between the fungus and a macrophage immune cell, in this case, the fungus can be victorious because of its insatiable appetite for glucose – the immune cell is killed because the fungus out-competes it for the glucose they both require to survive:

> *'We show that* **glucose competition by C. albicans** *is responsible for triggering death of* **infected macrophages.***'*
>
> <u>Cell metabolism</u> **2018** [612]

In fact, many intracellular pathogens are capable of triggering the Warburg effect in human cells, which you'd think would have placed pathogens, in particular fungal pathogens, at the top of the list for potential causes of cancer, not to mention Hallmark 7:

> *'Many intracellular pathogens have evolved to either* **hijack** *the* **Warburg metabolism** *of activated host cells to* **their own advantage***, or to infect and "***push'"** *host cells into a state of* **increased glycolysis.***'*
>
> <u>Immunometabolism</u> **2021** [816]

This is confirmed in many other studies where fungal pathogens are concerned.[634, 647] In the following study, monocytes (immune cells) intentionally switch to glycolysis when fungal pathogens are detected:

*'...these data confirm that **glycolysis** plays a **central role** in the induction of an effective **anti-C. albicans** host response both in vitro and in vivo:*

*...glycolysis-mediated mechanisms were demonstrated to be **crucial** for the **defence against the pathogen**.*

*Inhibition of glycolysis led to hosts that were significantly more **susceptible to the infection**.'*

PLOS Pathogens **2017** [634]

In the study above, drugs were used to suppress glycolysis, which prevented glucose from being depleted in the surrounding tissue. This resulted in increased rates of infection because the fungal pathogen was able to access the glucose it required.

Intentionally switching to glycolysis is clearly a defensive reaction that cells enact in direct response to the presence of an invasive fungal pathogen. This can explain why cancer cells switch to glycolysis even when oxygen is present: the cell reacts to the threat of fungal invasion and switches to glycolysis regardless of oxygen availability, perfectly explaining the Warburg effect witnessed in cancer.

Studies confirm that an energy switch to glycolysis is a critical component of trained immunity (defence against micro-organisms) – a switch in energy is required to kill fungal pathogens:

*'Trained monocytes display high **glucose consumption**, [and] **high lactate production**... reflecting a shift in metabolism with an increase in **glycolysis** dependent on the activation of mammalian target of rapamycin (**mTOR**) through a dectin-1-Akt-HIF-1α pathway.*

*'Our results indicate that induction of **aerobic glycolysis** through an **AKT-mTOR-HIF-1α** pathway represents the metabolic basis of **trained immunity**.'*

Science **2014** [636]

This is also confirmed in a recent study performed by *Memorial Sloan-Kettering Cancer Centre*, where they even noted that this offers an explanation for the Warburg effect in cancer:

*'**Infection triggers expansion** and effector differentiation of T cells specific for **microbial antigens** in association with **metabolic***

> **reprogramming**... *Naïve T cells are metabolically reprogrammed when they differentiate into T effector (Teff) cells, transitioning from a reliance on mitochondrial oxidative phosphorylation to* **aerobic glycolysis**...

> ...*This type of positive feedback circuit may also provide a mechanistic explanation for the* **Warburg effect** *observed in* **cancer cells**.'

<u>Science</u> 2021 [774]

A crucial point mentioned in the article below, is that glycolysis will remain as the dominant energy state until the fungal infection is eradicated, thus explaining why cancer cells (infected cells) continue to use glycolysis as their primary energy state:

> 'As for why activated immune cells would preferentially resort to this form of metabolism [the Warburg effect], Dr. Li suspects it has to do with the cells' need to produce ATP quickly to **ramp up their cell division** and **infection-fighting machinery**. The positive feedback loop ensures that once this program is engaged, **it will be sustained until the infection is eradicated**.'

<u>Memorial Sloan-Kettering Cancer Centre</u> 2021 [775]

Only once the fungal pathogen is killed, will the cell revert to a normal energy state, or commit programmed cell death if the infection has caused irreparable damage – which is exactly what occurs when cancer cells are exposed to anti-fungal drugs, or anti-fungal plant compounds.

This same glucose-restriction strategy occurs with tumours, exactly as one would expect if a fungal pathogen is driving the process. Here, tumours out-compete immune cells by absorbing so much glucose that they deplete it within the surrounding tissue – a reality that many oncologists often ignore:

> '...a similar mechanism of **immune cell evasion** to what we are proposing here for **C. albicans** has recently been demonstrated for tumours. **Tumours evade T cell-based immunity** by **increasing glucose utilization** due to the **Warburg effect**, leading to **competition between tumours** and **T cells for glucose** and **reduced immune function**.

> *This means that,* **while tumours have access to glucose to**
> **maintain growth,** *they are able to* **deplete glucose in the tumour**
> **micro-environment,** *leading to* **immune dysfunction.***
>
> <u>*Cell Metabolism*</u> **2018** [612]

This glucose-depletion can benefit the fungal pathogen due to the reduced immune response that clearly occurs, and helps to explain why these T-cells appear to be suppressed in cancer.

While this switch to glycolysis in human cells is clearly an intentional defensive response to the threat of fungal invasion, it can benefit the pathogen in a different way if the infection is not eliminated, which is likely to happen when the immune response is weak. Upon cell invasion, the pathogen gains access to the increased quantity of glucose the infected cell is now absorbing – which is at least 18 times more glucose to that of a healthy cell utilising aerobic respiration. This helps to explain how the pathogen benefits from indefinitely prolonging the life of the cell it infects – glucose is the pathogens primary food source. It's in the interest of the pathogen to ensure glycolysis is sustained.

Without access to large quantities of glucose, fungal pathogens become weaker and easier to kill. This is the premise behind the treatment approach of the Metabolic Theory – starving the cancer cell of the glucose it requires to function. The only difference here, is that I'm proposing that glucose starvation of cancer cells works by weakening the fungal pathogen, rather than directly acting upon the cell it has infected. This can explain why just starving a cancer of glucose may not always be effective, because the fungal pathogen is able to adapt, by acquiring it's energy from other sources, such as glutamine and fat, which I cover in detail in the following chapter.

To elaborate further, it is helpful to discuss pathways that mediate this energy switch, as doing so confirms that fungi are at the heart of this process. A key pathway that regulates cell energy is known as the *PI3K/AKT/mTOR* pathway. Where we see a switch to glycolysis in cancer, we would expect to see the activation of this pathway, and this is indeed what occurs:[635]

> *'***PI3K/AKT/mTOR*** signalling [a switch to glycolysis] has been*
> *implicated in the pathogenesis of various human cancers and is* **one**
> **of the most frequently** *deregulated pathways* **in cancer.** *Every*
> *major node of this signalling network is* **activated** *in a* **wide range**
> **of human tumours.'**

Predictive Biomarkers in Oncology **2018** [640]

'*Taken together, these results suggest that* **PI3K/AKT/mTOR** *signalling is* **indispensable** *for the regulation of* **aerobic glycolysis...**'

The Journal of Biological Chemistry **2015** [635]

Confirming a direct link to fungal infection, the study below confirms that this pathway is also stimulated in epithelial cells when the fungus *Candida* is detected:

'*PI3K/AKT/mTOR signalling may play a critical role in protecting* **epithelial cells** *from damage during mucosal* **fungal infections...** *PI3K/AKT/mTOR signalling may represent a common mechanism by which host cells protect against pathogen-induced damage.*'

The Journal of Infectious Diseases **2014** [647]

Epithelial cells – which function as a surface barrier and are the first to encounter an infectious pathogen – form the carcinomas that constitute up to 85% of all cancers. Does this fungal interaction with these cells explain why the Warburg effect is such a dominant factor of the disease? Below, the PI3K/AKT/mTOR pathway is shown to be stimulated in monocyte immune cells when they come into contact with *Candida* fungi:

'*Monocyte [immune cell] training with β-glucan, a ligand from* **C. albicans** *cell wall [fungal cell wall], has been reported to* **cause a switch from** *oxidative phosphorylation [mitochondria energy production]* **to aerobic glycolysis** *via activation of the* **PI3K/AKT/mTOR** *axis in human monocytes.*'

PLOS Pathogens **2017** [634]

Intriguingly, and in addition to this anti-fungal reaction, other studies confirm that stimulation of the PI3K/AKT/mTOR pathway also increases cell growth,[638, 664] and that, while utilising glycolysis, the cell death mechanism is suppressed.[072, 808] In other words, the act of fungal pathogens stimulating and sustaining glycolysis, can explain tumour growth through its ability to prevent cell death and stimulate cell growth – this is in addition to the ability of fungi to directly stimulate growth receptors and inhibit cell death mechanisms.

Further evidence supporting the role of fungi in cancer relates to another major pathway that is activated in cancer cells, the 'MAPK' pathway, which specifically controls cell growth and proliferation:

> *'The* **Mitogen-activated protein kinase (MAPK)** *pathway encompasses different signalling cascades of which the Ras-Raf-Mek-extracellular signal-regulated kinase 1 and 2 (ERK1/2) is one of the* **most dysregulated in human cancer.** *This pathway regulates multiple critical cellular functions including* **proliferation, growth** *and senescence.'*
>
> <u>*Expert Opinion on Therapeutic Targets*</u> **2012** [802]

And as we would expect to see if fungal pathogens are an underlying driver, when fungi invade cells they also stimulate this additional pathway. In fact, the MAPK pathway is stimulated first, and acts to identify the fungal pathogen as a threat, while the PI3K pathway becomes stimulated later in a defensive response, when the severity of the infection passes a certain threshold:

> *'C.* **albicans** *yeast cells modestly activated two main signalling pathways: the mitogen-activated protein kinase* (**MAPK**)*...it was also observed that OECs respond to the damage caused by C. albicans hyphae via the phosphatidylinositol 3-kinase (**PI3K**) pathway...*
>
> *...Thus, MAPK activation began to be viewed as a '**danger-response'** mechanism and PI3K [/AKT/mTOR] activation as a '**damage-protection'** mechanism, which together are* **critical** *for identifying when this normally commensal* **fungus** *has become* **pathogenic.'**
>
> <u>*Current Opinion in Microbiology*</u> **2019** [803]

In other words, the two most activated pathways in cancer that sustain the Warburg effect, are activated in cells when they become infected by common fungal pathogens. Activation of these pathways constitutes an anti-fungal response – strongly suggesting that fungal pathogens are the primary reason for the triggering of these pathways in cancer.

While confirming that stimulation of these pathways occurs in response to fungal attack, the studies below highlight something equally important; that the *Aspergillus* fungus can take control of the PI3K/AKT/mTOR pathway once it has invaded the cell. This allows it to sustain increased growth activity and prevent cell death (apoptosis) for extended periods:

> '...conidia of **Aspergillus ssp.** *[fungi]* **inhibit apoptosis** *of macrophages... Hence,* **mitochondrial cytochrome** *c release and caspase activation were* **prevented**. *Moreover,* **sustained PI3K/AKT/mTOR** *signalling in infected cells is an important determinant to* **resist apoptosis.**

> *For the first time, we show that* **melanin** *itself is a crucial component to* **inhibit** *macrophage* **apoptosis** *which may* **contribute** *to* **dissemination of the fungus within the host.**'

> <u>*Cellular Microbiology*</u> **2011** [637]

In other words, *Aspergillus* fungi are capable of generating abnormal cell growth and preventing cell death, and thus a tumour. Given that *Aspergillus* fungal spores are regularly inhaled – as I noted earlier –[458] does this explain why smokers are at a high risk of developing lung cancer? Confirming that control of the PI3K/AKT/mTOR pathway can lead to the development of a tumour, the next study states:

> '*The PI3K/Akt/mTOR pathway regulates several normal cellular functions that are also critical for* **tumorigenesis,** *including cellular* **proliferation,** **growth,** **survival** *and mobility. Components of this pathway are* **frequently abnormal in a variety of tumours,** *making them an attractive target for anti-cancer therapy.* '

> <u>*Anti-cancer Drugs*</u> **2005** [638]

Dr Naviaux's *Cell Danger Response* model:

Further supporting my cell suppression hypothesis, Dr Robert Naviaux explains this process in more detail through his *Cell Danger Response* model. Dr Naviaux has been studying the cell response to all manner of threats, and has established how a mitochondrial defensive response – that instigates a switch in energy to glycolysis – is used by the cell to protect from pathogen attack.[876]

There are three phases to the *Cell Danger Response* (CDR), which is illustrated in the following graphic taken from Dr Naviaux's paper.[876]

- **CDR1** represents the initial response to a threat in order to eliminate it, in this case a pathogen.

- **CDR2** represents the cell-repair phase, which is associated with increased cell growth and re-generation.
- **CDR3** represents a switching off of this process and a return to homeostasis (balance), the cell's original resting state.

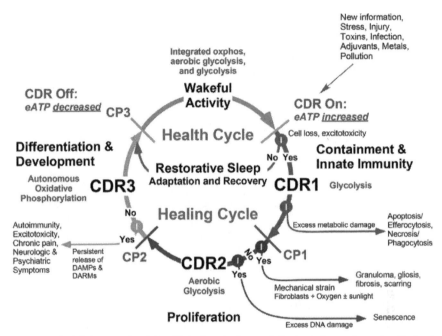

Source: Naviaux RK. Metabolic features and regulation of the healing cycle—A new model for chronic disease pathogenesis and treatment. Mitochondrion. 2018 August S1567-7249(18)30105-3

When we analyse this process, it becomes clear that mitochondria are not defective, but that initially the cell intentionally inhibits mitochondria in favour of glycolysis in order to combat the pathogen. Only in cancer, this backfires when the pathogen establishes itself, and glycolysis is sustained. So, let's have a look at how a cell reacts to a fungal threat in accordance with Dr Naviaux's model, and then compare this process to the Warburg effect in cancer, to see if we can draw any parallels.

Upon detection of an invading pathogen the cell enters the CDR1 phase. This results in several outcomes:

1. Mitochondria **intentionally inhibit** the **OXPHOS** pathway
    to flood the cell with oxygen, the aim of which is to restrict the
    pathogen's ability to construct RNA, DNA and proteins, inhibiting
    its ability to propagate.[876]
2. **Reactive Oxygen Species** (ROS) are generated (free radicals). Free
    radicals are used to attack and eliminate the pathogen.
3. A switch to **glycolysis** occurs **even in the presence of oxygen**
    As oxygen is used to combat the pathogen, mitochondria can no
    longer produce energy, so **glycolysis** is upregulated to generate
    the ATP energy required, and to instigate an inflammatory
    response.

Now, let's compare this anti-infection process to the Warburg effect
that occurs in cancer:

1. The mitochondrial **OXPHOS** pathway is **inhibited**
2. **Reactive Oxygen Species** (ROS) are generated (free radicals).
3. A switch to **glycolysis** occurs **even in the presence of oxygen.**

Both processes appear identical. Through Dr Naviaux's model, we are
provided with a little more detail on the inner workings of the cell. Where
proponents of the Metabolic Theory assert that OXPHOS is defective, here
it is shown that cells **intentionally** inhibit OXPHOS in response to a fungal
threat. It is not surprising that scientists have concluded that mitochondria
must be defective, when the initial presumption is that cancer is a 'cell
malfunction' disease, and especially when the influence of a micro-
organism has not been considered. Significantly, and as I'm hopefully
illustrating throughout this book, the data on cancer can be interpreted
through a different lens, and when it is, when an integral part of the
equation is factored in, a more plausible understanding presents itself.

This response to a fungal threat provides the first coherent explanation
for the Warburg effect in cancer, and can explain why there is contention
over the assertion that the OXPHOS pathway is defective, in particular,
where others have shown OXPHOS to be operational. This is because it
isn't defective, rather, the cell is intentionally restricting this OXPHOS
pathway to combat the pathogen. Moreover, once the pathogen establishes
itself, this pathway remains suppressed until it is eradicated. This battle
between the pathogen, the cell, and immune system can explain this
irregularity, and why an assumed-to-be defective and inoperative
OXPHOS pathway, can once again become active.

Sustained intracellular infection results in the cell becoming stuck between the CDR1 pathogen resolution phase, and the CDR2 proliferative cell growth repair phase of Dr Naviaux's cell danger response model – hence why a proliferative state is induced and a tumour forms.

This, coupled with all prior evidence, illustrates that infection, and fungal pathogens in particular, are capable of generating the abnormal energy switch to glycolysis that all cancers share, and in the exact manner expressed by cancer cells. This switch appears to be an initial defensive response to fungal invasion. The inability of the immune system to clear the fungal infection explains why glycolysis is sustained, it remains until the infection is eradicated. Prolonged reliance upon glycolysis results in increased cell proliferation, and inhibition of cell death mechanisms – resulting in the development of a tumour. This interaction perfectly explains the most important hallmark of all, hallmark 7 (the Warburg effect) – implicating fungal infection as an underlying driver of cancer, and the subsequent conditions associated with the disease.

And so we enter into uncharted water, where a new mechanism (referred to hereafter as *Cell Suppression*) can at last fully explain all 10 Hanahan and Weinberg hallmarks using supporting evidence. This indicates that an underlying driver of this terrible disease has been identified – could the origin of cancer simply be attributed to the suppressive and controlling nature of opportunistic, intracellular fungal pathogens that inadvertently force cells to adopt the proliferative state of the Warburg effect, or *aerobic fermentation,* as it is also known?

While, on the face of it, this is a great step forward, and if there wasn't so much resistance to new information within medical science, and such devotion to the DNA theory, I would feel confident in this new model of cancer being accepted and taken seriously within mainstream circles. However, I feel that even achieving something as unprecedented as this – explaining all 10 hallmarks – will not be enough for some. So, I decided to take my investigations several steps further to strengthen my model even more. During my eight years of research I noted that there were at least 20 additional cancer-related conditions that remain unaccounted for, and so I went ahead and explained these as well, using supporting evidence. Simply put, the more of cancer that can be accounted for, the greater the likelihood that such a model is correct. This provides a compelling case for fungi as an underlying cause of cancer that deserves the full attention of the medical establishment.

It's particularly exciting that the new Cell Suppression model of cancer presented within this book, can provide a coherent explanation for so many aspects of the disease – such an achievement further strengthens my hypothesis and raises the bar in terms of the criteria that other theories are expected to also explain. This is highly significant because most of these conditions remain unexplained by all mainstream cancer theories.

Significantly, 10 of these additional conditions have already been accounted for within the chapters already covered, which are highlighted in bold. The remaining 10 conditions, listed in light grey, will be explained within the second half of the book. Conditions 12 to 18 and 27 are covered in the following chapter:

11. **Glucose as fuel**
12. Glutamine as fuel
13. Fat as fuel
14. Lactate as fuel
15. Reverse Warburg effect
16. Arginine as fuel
17. Arginine auxotrophy
18. Role of Estrogen
19. **Involvement of iron**
20. **Involvement of nagalase**
21. **Involvement of galectin-3**
22. Chemotherapy resistance
23. **Methyl-deficiency**
24. **Aneuploidy**
25. **Carcinogenesis**
26. **Failure of antioxidants**
27. MDSC involvement
28. **Macrophage involvement**
29. **T-Cell suppression**
30. CYP1B1 universal marker

When speaking of the validity of any new concept, Dr Lev Ginzberg, who works in applied biomathematics, and Mark Colyvan, who is Professor of Philosophy at the University of Sydney, stated:

> *'An important test for any new theory is whether it is able to explain what was **not explained before**, and whether it is able to establish **new connections between theories**...'*
>
> **Ecological Orbits. Oxford University Press. Pg 10 2004** [686]

This Cell Suppression model seems to do just that – it can explain more about cancer than was previously understood, and links aspects of current theories together under a single umbrella.

Chapter summary:

By way of a summary, I now provide a short overview, detailing the key factors that drive the disease, explaining the entire process from initial tumour development right through to cancer progression. A couple of factors such as estrogen, lactate, and arginine are explained in fuller detail within the next chapter, but are included within the summary and graphic that follows.

How a tumour forms and cancer develops:

1. Carcinogens damage cells. Access to oxygen may be lost resulting in hypoxia. A temporary switch to glycolysis occurs and an inflammatory response is initiated. Lactic acid is produced and if the toxicity isn't dealt with, iron overload occurs. Sensing hypoxia and abnormal levels of lactic acid, opportunistic pathogens – present within the tissue microbiome – become invasive. Toxin exposure, excess production of lactic acid and iron overload suppresses the immune response at the site of injury, while lactic acid and iron feed the virulence of fungal pathogens. This creates a toxic niche that favours fungal infection. Upon detection of infectious pathogens, *Toll-like receptors* (TLRs) on the cell surface are triggered in an attempt to combat the pathogen. This consists of generating further inflammation and continues to maintain glycolysis, because both are anti-infection responses. Ongoing toxin exposure, inflammatory nutrients within the diet (excess omega 6), and a weak immune response, results in chronic inflammation exacerbating the situation. DNA mutations (such as CDH1 and APC), caused by cell damage, can aid with infection by inhibiting a protein called E-cadherin that would normally act as a barrier to invasion.

2. During the infection process, fungal pathogens initiate PAMP masking, and use various other means to evade detection, such as the production of nagalase, mycotoxins like gliotoxin, and manipulation of the dectin-1 receptor – just to name a few. The loss of glucose in the surrounding tissue further suppresses the immune response within the vicinity of the infection. One of the

primary invasion strategies of these pathogens is to gain access through stimulation of HER2 and EGFR growth receptors, through a process called *endocytosis,* where the cell is tricked into absorbing the pathogen. This helps to trigger cell proliferation. Once inside the cell the pathogen can upregulate PD-L1, which prevents the cell alerting immune cells to the presence of the pathogen, by making the cell appear normal – at this point, a good level of immune evasion has been established, and the infection has become intracellular.

3. Through *Purinergic signalling* – which is a form of communication between cells that I will explain shortly – uninfected cells within the surrounding tissue are made aware of the impending infection. In response, these cells switch their energy system to glycolysis if they haven't done so already – this is to deplete glucose in the surrounding tissue with the aim of starving the pathogen of the glucose it requires to function; the Warburg effect is initiated by localised cells that aren't yet infected. However, a toxic environment now exists that favours the fungal infection. In this environment the fungus out-competes damaged cells and weakened immune cells for the glucose they all require. This results in sustained cell invasion and further immune suppression. Incidentally this entire process stimulates the two primary pathways that are found to be upregulated in cancer, because both are used to establish an anti-infection response. The initial threat of infection stimulates the MAPK pathway (mitogen-activated protein kinase) which is an initial danger response to fungal infection.[803] The PI3K/AKT/mTOR pathway is then also stimulated as a damage-control response to the increasing damage caused by the pathogen.[803] Once established, fungi can now gain control of the PI3K/AKT/mTOR pathway. This pathway controls glycolysis and regulates cell growth as well as inhibition of cell death mechanisms – sustained use of this pathway, due to the presence of the pathogen, results in a proliferative energy state – which helps to explain why tumour cells grow out of control. The fungus monopolises the majority of glucose absorbed by the cell, along with many other substrates such as glutamine, methionine, and arginine, forcing the cell to absorb glutamine, fat, and even lactate to accommodate for the inevitable ATP energy shortfall, and the depletion of other nutrients by the pathogen. Reduction of these

compounds within the body over time further weakens the immune system because glucose, glutamine and arginine are all required by immune cells.

4. Cell death is suppressed through control of the PI3K/AKT/mTOR pathway and sustained use of glycolysis. The pathogen may also directly upregulate the Bcl-2 protein within mitochondria, inhibiting the mitochondrial cell-death pathway by preventing the release of cytochrome c. It will actively subdue free-radical production, including Nitric Oxide (NO) free radicals by depleting the amino acid arginine, while upregulating its own superoxide and glutathione antioxidant defence system. While certain aspects of mitochondrial control are suppressed, the TCA cycle within mitochondria continues to function, allowing glutamine, fat and lactate to be converted into ATP energy and other substrates needed for cell and fungal growth. This benefits the pathogen because it allows co-habitation, and generates the conditions that allow the fungus to thrive. Intracellular pathogen dominance results. The pathogen is now protected within the cell, while the corrosive, acidic, iron-saturated and glucose-sparse extracellular environment becomes increasingly hostile to immune cells. A fungal-dominant tumour-associated niche is established, where increased cell proliferation driven by sustained glycolysis within the infected cell and non-infected cells surrounding it, slowly generates a tumour.[831]

5. Sustained use of glycolysis depletes glucose within the surrounding tissue, which further suppresses immune cell function. It also generates large quantities of corrosive lactic acid (lactate), leading to a loss of cell integrity within surrounding tissue, and a reduction in cell growth suppression signals.

6. Overproduction of lactic acid stimulates blood vessel growth (VEGF), providing the tumour with its own blood supply. When different tissues are in close proximity to each other they normally act to suppress growth – but as lactic acid breaks cell bonds and the cohesion of surrounding tissue membranes, this growth suppression barrier is weakened. This allows fungi, and cancer cells, to grow into, and penetrate adjacent tissue, leading to invasive tumour growth. The fungal pathogen increases the expression of MMP-9, as do neutrophils and macrophages, which

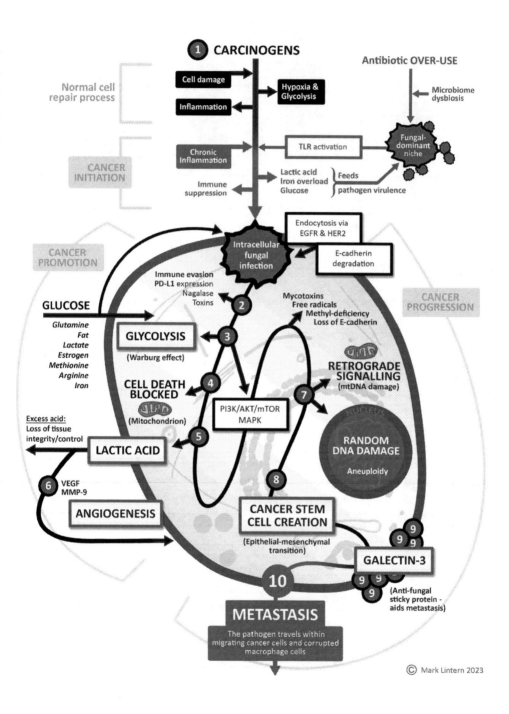

are attempting to use MMP-9 to heal the chronically inflamed cells of the tumour and surrounding tissue. This further stimulates blood vessel growth and tumour growth, and encourages cells to migrate.

7. Carcinogens, fungal toxins, methyl-deficiency, and oxidative stress generate random DNA damage. Without the ability to commit cell death, prolonged damage to mitochondria over time instigates *retrograde signalling* – which is when mitochondria actively attempt to change the cell's fate.

8. Retrograde signalling stimulates a 'regular' cancer cell to transition (dedifferentiate) into a deadly cancer stem cell, or cells that acquire stem-cell-like properties, via an *epithelial-mesenchymal transition*. This provides the tumour with limitless growth, improved immune evasion, chemotherapy resistance, and the ability to grow another tumour elsewhere within the body, once it has migrated. The tumour has become malignant and deadly.

9. The ever-worsening corrosive environment, with the build up of MMP-9, lactic acid and iron, leads to the inevitable break away of cancer stem cells into the bloodstream. The immune system makes a last-ditch effort to kill the fungus within these cells by attacking it with a sticky anti-fungal protein called galectin-3. However, if this fails, the sticky substance aids the migrating cancer stem cell to adhere to other cells at distant sites within the body.

10. With the help of galectin-3, MMP-9 produced by neutrophils and macrophages, the loss of the E-cadherin protein that binds cells together, and the over-expression of corrosive lactic acid, a cancer stem cell is able to migrate. Cancer, and the fungus within, have successfully spread.

The missing link:

Looking at the tumour as a whole, the following graphic illustrates how all the processes mentioned, come together to generate the disease, centering around the tissue response to intracellular infection. As shown, not all cells within the tumour mass are infected. Even so, these cells exhibit the Warburg effect, and represent adjacent cells in transition from a healthy cell, to a cancer cell – a non-infected cell, to an infected cell. Only a small number of fungal pathogens are required to elicit a response within the infected tissue – in other words, just a small number of fungal pathogens are required to generate a tumour:

'Although our data do not establish causal relationships behind these clusters, they suggest that **fungi** are sparse but **immunologically potent.**'

<u>Cell</u> **2022** [857]

The question is: why do non-infected cells switch to the Warburg effect? Dr Naviaux, mentioned a moment ago, explains this through the process of *Purinergic signalling,* which is a form of communication between cells. Through purinergic signalling, infected cells trigger the anti-infection Warburg-effect response in non-infected cells, even before they come into contact with the infection.[876] Cells work together to help eliminate the impending fungal threat. This switch to glycolysis occurs even in the presence of oxygen, enacting the very Warburg effect we see in cancer:

'Thus, a **sustained Warburg metabolism** *within a tissue may partly reflect the continual activation of immune cells recruited towards a* **relatively low biomass infection.** *In other words, signalling molecules released by a relatively* **small number of infected cells** *are capable of causing activation of* **neighbouring non-infected cells,** *triggering a* **feed-forward cascade of Warburg-like metabolism.**'

<u>Immunometabolism</u> **2021** [816]

From this instigation of the Warburg effect by surrounding cells reacting to the infection, we can see how a tumour expands. As the infection slowly expands throughout the damaged tumour – adjacent cells instigate the Warburg effect and proliferate adding themselves to the tumour mass.

Caught within the corrosive, immune-suppressing milieux of – lactic acid abundance, iron overload, glucose depletion, and hypoxia – it becomes only a matter of time before these non-infected Warburg-expressing cells succumb to infection, and to the suppressive influence of fungal pathogens as they spread throughout the damaged tissue. These cells are then absorbed into, and become part of, the tumour having lost control of key cellular functions to the controlling pathogens; adding their own cells to the mix as they proliferate. This explains the transition from a healthy cell to a cancer cell, and accounts for why all cells of the tumour are not required to contain an intracellular pathogen:

TUMOUR COMPOSITION
Cell suppression model

Lactic acid, iron overload, glucose depletion, chronic inflamation:
Creates a protective barrier around the tumour that suppresses immune cells, but feeds the fungal pathogens present within the tumour mass, stimulating them to become aggressive and invasive.

Fungal expansion:
Excess lactate fuels the infection which expands into surrounding tissue and dormant immune cells.

Reverse Warburg Effect:
Advancing infection stimulates the Warburg effect within the surrounding tissue. Peripheral tumour cells absorb the excess lactate as fuel.

Tumour-associated microbiome
(Fungal dominance)

Cell death inhibited, cell proliferation instigated, ineffective immune response
-----
Cancer

Hypoxia + threat of infection:
Purinergic signalling from infected cells, signals to non-infected cells to instigate glycyolysis as an anti-infection response. It's only a matter of time before they also fall prey to the infection as it expands. This reflects the transition from a healthy cell to an infected cancer cell.

Blood vessel growth:
Blood vessels expand towards cells over-producing lactic acid. This corrosive environment, plus over-production of MMP-9, results in cells migrating into the bloodstream.

○ Healthy tissue

● Immune cell

○ Warburg effect / anti-fungal response > Tumour cell

 Intracellular pathogens (fungal dominance) > Cancer cells

Mark Lintern 2022

303

It's clear that mainstream attempts to understand cancer are being hindered by a fundamental oversight: the failure to factor in the suppressive influence of intracellular pathogens that have been found to be present in all tumours.

The omission of a microbial influence within mainstream cancer theories means, that in all probability, the data has been misinterpreted, and so incorrect conclusions have been drawn, given that it's impossible to reach a valid conclusion based on limited or missing data; as Ravid Straussman alluded to when commenting on the link between micro-organisms and cancer: *"Everything that has to do with tumour biology can now be re-examined through a microbiome lens...?"*[821]

Given that up to 80% of studies that underlie the established interpretation of cancer, can't be replicated,[018] it's reasonable to suppose, that the abnormal behaviour of a cancer cell, is likely to be a reflection of the parasitic behaviour exhibited by particular pathogens that populate the tumour tissue.[821] These pathogens consume the nutrients intended for the cell, forcing it to absorb greater quantities of other nutrients to replenish those that have been depleted. This, coupled with the suppression of cell death mechanisms and sustained glycolysis, makes these cells **appear parasitic too**, because their forced behaviour imitates that of the parasitic pathogen, and seems to infer that the cell has developed a 'mind of its own'. The reason a cancer cell behaves like an alien invader is that an alien invader – a pathogen – has taken control of it, and is forcing it to serve its own agenda, rather than the host's agenda that it was created to serve.

Hallmarks refined:

With this new insight we can now refine the revised hallmarks that were amended back in Chapter 10, to include one last factor that appears to have been overlooked: the presence, and influence, of intracellular pathogens:

Hallmarks **REFINED**	
Initiation Pre-cancerous stage	1. Tissue damage
	2. Abnormal metabolic pathways
	3. Chronic inflammation
	4. Dysbiotic microbiome
Cancer	5. ***Intracellular pathogens***
	6. Evasion of cell death
	7. Resistance to anti-growth signals
	8. Uncontrolled growth
Progression	9. Immune evasion
Malignancy	10. Blood vessel growth
	11. Limitless replication
	12. Invasion of local tissue and metastasis
	13. Genome instability

Multi-factorial cause versus a singular cause:

Within this paradigm cancer is seen as a single disease driven by a common source, seemingly verified by the broad efficacy of anti-fungal drugs against a large array of different cancers. Sustained intracellular infection, the influence of which is predominantly fungal, triggers the symptoms of the disease – chronic inflammation, the Warburg effect, sustained proliferation, methionine dependence, glutamine upregulation, angiogenesis and so on and so forth.

Under the Cell Suppression model, the multi-factorial aspect of cancer only relates to the diverse array of factors – carcinogens, trauma, lack of sleep – that damages the cellular terrain and enables opportunistic pathogens a window through which they can take advantage of chronic inflammation and a weakened immune state, in order to propagate within this damaged tissue. Many factors can facilitate infection.

Conversely, and in light of it's perceived complexity under the established view of 'cell malfunction', and largely due to the randomness of damage witnessed, the origin of cancer is seen as being 'multi-factorial'. It is allegedly caused by any combination of damage and is seen as many different diseases that just coincidentally follow the same consistent path of progression. This is one of only two conclusions that can be drawn when the data doesn't align with any particular theory – that is, when no pattern of damage has been found to occur to account for cancer's initiation, promotion and progression, and where up to 80% of supporting studies fail to be replicated. The other conclusion, of course, is that the cell malfunction paradigm is wrong. But few seem willing to consider this as a possibility.

While scientists struggle to replicate cancerous behaviour based upon such randomness, the Cell Suppression model can provide a more plausible explanation that addresses the consistencies of the disease.

If, rather than being fixated on the random outcome of countless carcinogens, we pull back from the detail and re-focus on the common effects carcinogens generate, we can begin to see a pattern emerging that can then lead us to better identify the driving mechanism behind tumour growth. This produces a consistency that is coherent with the consistency of the hallmarks themselves, and sheds light on a common driving force. It indicates that cancer is actually one disease that develops within many different cells, generated by the same factors (the fungal pathogens) as they trigger the consistent symptoms that arise through the manipulation of the cell and it's local environment. The process that we call 'cancer' is simply the failed and ongoing response to a particular type of infection, one that is opportunistic and slow-growing in nature.

While fungal pathogens are often lumped into the same category as other carcinogens, they are, in fact, quite distinct. By this I mean that if you remove the fungal pathogen, **despite the presence of a carcinogen**, cancer will not form. This is because it is the fungal pathogen that ultimately drives the process – the carcinogen only provides the opportunity for the pathogen to establish itself.

Under the premise that the origin of cancer is multi-factorial, we can become lost in the detail. For instance, it is often suggested that prolonged emotional trauma correlates with the development of the disease – people with cancer often recall a traumatic experience from their past, such as a loss of a loved one, or extreme mental/emotional stress following a life event that occurred several years prior. It is suggested that this emotional stress has caused the disease and that an imbalance in 'life energy' has occurred, and that this disease process can be reversed using only the power of the mind. While I agree that it's vitally important to reduce stress and connect with yourself and others spiritually, and I'm open-minded to the concept of a direct mind-body connection to healing, the evidence for such a connection and ability to heal in this way is difficult to pin point and measure.

Sticking with the evidence available, there is a biochemical explanation for this correlation between emotional trauma and cancer. Simply put, prolonged stress not only weakens the immune system, but it generates low-grade chronic inflammation – this compromises the tissue terrain aiding pathogen colonisation of damaged tissue. Any number of other factors related to such trauma, such as regular comfort eating with processed and unhealthy foods, or other vices such as excess alcohol consumption, can aid pathogen colonisation and increase the risk of a cancer-type infection developing. It is, therefore, plausible to see why these life events can aid the infectious process that ultimately leads to cancer.

In conclusion: I propose that prolonged fungal infection of damaged cells can provide a coherent explanation for cancer development, and its progression to its malignant phase. Given the evidence, common fungal pathogens are likely to be a primary underlying cause of cancer, if not, all cancers. In this respect, random DNA mutations and random cell damage are likely to be symptoms of this fungal interaction, which would explain the seemingly impossible task of aligning this damage with the development of the disease.

CH 12

The fuels that drive tumour growth

There remains a crucial aspect of cancer that needs to be addressed, which has spread confusion within the cancer community. It relates to how glutamine, fat, lactate, methionine, arginine and estrogen also appear to be fuelling tumour growth. These alternative fuels are seen as a fly-in-the-ointment for the concept of glucose being the dominant fuel feeding cancer because sometimes they also seem to be driving its progression.[447, 626, 663, 710, 716] This appears to contradict the claim that glucose is key to understanding and treating the disease. There have been examples where glucose has been intentionally restricted, and yet cancer continues to progress, as was the case with Jane McLelland. Jane refers to these other fuels in her book *How to Starve Cancer*, which has done much to highlight the range of fuels that different cancer types appear to use to sustain their energy needs, as well as the pathways associated with them, and the drugs that can block these alternative energy pathways.

Understanding why tumours appear to fuel themselves differently needs to be explained by any cancer theory because it is critical to effective treatment. Unfortunately, mainstream medicine seems to ignore most of these fuels when it comes to treating cancer, possibly because scientists have been unable to make sense of this changeable behaviour. But once the involvement of a fungal pathogen has been factored in, it's possible to eliminate all the confusion, and to reach a coherent explanation of why tumours fuel themselves in the manner they do.

To fully understand the involvement of these fuels and the effect they have on cancer, I need to again shift your perception of the disease away from blaming the cell, or seeing the cell itself as the cause of cancer. Going back to this notion of 'cell suppression' as opposed to 'cell malfunction', the focus of attention falls on the fungal pathogen that is suppressing cellular pathways and absorbing critical nutrients. This influence forces the cell to adapt in ways that appear both abnormal and confusing, especially when viewed through a cell-malfunctioning lens.

All cells, including cancer cells, can adapt their energy system to accommodate different fuels,[663, 710, 716] and do so when certain nutrients are in short supply, so it shouldn't be a surprise to hear that cancer cells are also capable of adapting in a similar way.[882] They are, after all, the same as healthy cells, only with a few abnormal features. Cancer cells convert these other fuels into ATP energy via the TCA cycle (Tricarboxylic acid cycle) within mitochondria, as well as into other substances needed for the cell to function; healthy cells do this too.[522] The TCA cycle is a pathway within mitochondria that allows them to utilise carbohydrates, protein and fat. This pathway enables these substances to be converted into other substances as well – it acts like a chemistry lab – once processed, energy can be generated in an additional pathway called the *Electron Transport Chain* (ETC) where a reaction with oxygen occurs. The overall process associated with the TCA cycle and oxygen-based energy creation within mitochondria, is referred to as *OXPHOS* (Oxidative Phosphorylation) because nutrients are being oxidised (reacting with oxygen) to create energy.[762] There is another pathway known as the Fatty Acid Oxidation pathway (FAO),[871] which deals with oxidising fat inside mitochondria for energy. While fat can be synthesized from glucose within the cell, prostate, ovarian and even breast cancers, appear to utilise external sources of fat.[871] As all of these pathways are linked to the TCA cycle within mitochondria, I will use the singular term 'OXPHOS' when referring to mitochondrial activity where oxygen is used to create energy, just to keep things simple.[764]

I mention the OXPHOS energy pathway because when it is in use it signifies that mitochondria are active and utilising oxygen. In cancer, **glycolysis** is seen as the backup energy system that operates in place of OXPHOS. If OXPHOS activity is detected within a cancer cell, this would indicate that mitochondria are still functioning, which adds a new dimension to the disease and implies that glycolysis isn't the primary energy state i.e. that glucose isn't the primary fuel being used. This is important for two reasons: if OXPHOS is still active, it indicates that mitochondria are not dysfunctional, which challenges the Metabolic Theory; it is also important in terms of treatment – understanding which pathway is dominant will determine the optimal type of treatment to use, and its subsequent success. For example, Professor Michael Lisanti from the *University of Salford* in the UK, is currently testing a number of antibiotic drugs that target mitochondria to show that mitochondrial function is critical for the survival and propagation of cancer stem cells. In particular, the anti-parasitic drug *Pyrvinium pamoate* was effective at inhibiting cancer stem cells, Pyrvinium pamoate is a known OXPHOS inhibitor.[661]

He also went on to discover that ketones (the energy molecules derived from the breakdown of fat) stimulate tumour growth – which contradicts the claim made by Professor Seyfried who states that cancer cells cannot use ketones due to defective mitochondria.[881] Moreover, Lisanti and colleagues also found that OXPHOS, and the TCA cycle within mitochondria, are active in breast cancer cells.[881] And that Metformin, which is also effective against a broad range of cancers, inhibits OXPHOS by blocking *complex I* of the Electron Transport Chain within mitochondria.[661]

Furthermore, and as I discussed in Chapter 9, OXPHOS appears to be active in some brain cancers, because when it was targeted, cancer cell death occurred.[879]

That the OXPHOS pathway can be targeted in cancer stem cells, breast cancer and brain cancer, indicates that mitochondria are still active to some degree.[779] In fact, and if you recall, in Chapter 9 I presented a study that analysed benign tumours. It uncovered that dysfunctional mitochondria, where OXPHOS is fully impaired, led to a benign tumour not cancer, it concluded that malignancy requires that mitochondria be active.[883] As a result of these contentions, confusion exists over which fuels are actually driving tumour growth. For instance, in the Metabolic Theory camp, it is claimed that glycolysis is the dominant energy state in all cancers, and occurs due to an inability of mitochondria to generate energy via the OXPHOS pathway – mitochondria, therefore, are claimed to be faulty, or incapable of creating energy via OXPHOS. However, this doesn't appear to be the case:

> '*Cancer cells have* **upregulated glycolysis** *compared with normal cells, which has led many to the assumption that oxidative phosphorylation (OXPHOS) is downregulated in all cancers. However, recent studies have shown that* **OXPHOS** *can be also* **upregulated** *in certain cancers... and that this can occur even in the face of active glycolysis.*'
>
> <u>*Clinical Cancer Research*</u> **2018** [778]

This has also led some to claim that glycolysis isn't actually the dominant state, and therefore, that glucose isn't feeding cancer:

> '*Unlike the Warburg effect, some tumour cells exhibit* **high rates of OXPHOS**. *In these cells, glycolysis contributes 1% to 64% of ATP production,* **OXPHOS is still the predominant ATP supplier for cancer cells**. *Moreover, many studies show that OXPHOS and aerobic glycolysis are not always mutually exclusive, to some extent, they contribute differently to ATP production with the alterations in the tumour environment...*
>
> *...It implies that 'the Warburg effect' is* **not a general feature of all cancers**, *heterogeneous tumour cells [similar tumour cells that have different characteristics] exhibit* **flexible metabolic phenotypes** *[flexible energy-generation capabilities] even in a* **single tumour mass**.'
>
> <u>*Oncotarget*</u> **2017** [716]

So, while proponents of the Metabolic Theory claim that cancer is caused by faulty mitochondria – characterised by an inability of the cell to use OXPHOS to create energy – many studies appear to show that it's not quite as simple as that, in that the source of energy production varies between cancers and even within the same tumour; and that cancer cells still appear to be utilising oxygen.

This is where Dr Naviaux's *Cell Danger Response* and the involvement of pathogens, can help to explain the contested views expressed above, and make sense of the varying oxygen levels used by cancer cells.[876] This knowledge provides important insight into the mechanisms of cancer and how oxygen is utilised.

To clarify, Professor Seyfried argues that cancer results from damage to mitochondria, which prevents them from creating ATP energy using the OXPHOS pathway (oxygen-based energy pathway), this damage results in a reliance on glycolysis, leading to the rest of the conditions of the disease.

Others argue that oxygen use in cancer cells is high, and contend that this indicates that they still rely, to varying degrees, upon OXPHOS for ATP energy as well as using glycolysis.

I sit between both camps, in that my claim is that the OXPHOS pathway is not damaged to the extent proposed by Professor Seyfried, rather, it is suppressed due to a response to infection, and that this explains the disparity. Dr Naviaux explains that during the threat of infection, the cell danger response is instigated, this results in the intentional suppression of OXPHOS, by the cell, in favour of flooding the cellular environment with oxygen.[876] This is designed to inhibit invading pathogens. If you recall this was briefly discussed at the end of Chapter 11. As the use of oxygen is switched from creating ATP energy via OXPHOS to combating the pathogen, the energy system switches to glycolysis to provide the cell with the ATP it requires. And as I confirmed in Chapter 11, a switch to glycolysis forms part of an anti-infection response. This perfectly explains why OXPHOS is no longer used for ATP energy but is still active, why the cell switches to glycolysis, and why the cell continues to absorb high levels of oxygen – the cell is using it to battle an infectious threat.

Furthermore, the battle between the pathogen and the cell can also explain the random damage witnessed in cancer cells, particularly the damage caused by elevated ROS (reactive oxygen species) levels – otherwise known as 'free radicals'. The cell is using oxygen to combat the pathogen via an oxidative stress response, which unfortunately leads to further cell damage. The random damage inflicted upon the cell, therefore, is a symptom of this battle for supremacy between the pathogen, the cell, and the immune system, as opposed to this damage being the cause of the disease. This explains why it has been so difficult to identify a specific pattern of cell damage that could explain the odd behaviour exhibited by cancer cells.

Regardless of the various interpretations suggested by others, and the fact that OXPHOS still appears to be operational, evidence indicates that most cancers do primarily use glycolysis, increasing OXPHOS activity over time; some cancers operate the other way around – they primarily use OXPHOS and later rely on glycolysis, prostate cancer is one example. So how can this variation be explained?

The different rates of energy use largely are determined by nutrient and oxygen availability. Increased use of OXPHOS appears to occur in the latter stages of cancer progression, and is likely due to the fungal pathogen diminishing vital nutrients within the cell, including glucose. This forces the cell to adapt to nutrient scarcity, and so it 'rewires' itself to generate the ATP energy it needs from other sources, and to replenish lost nutrients. This is where glutamine, fat and other alternative fuels, such as lactate, are converted into ATP energy via the OXPHOS pathway within mitochondria. These compounds are also used to create other substances that aid cell growth and general operation; for instance, glutamine can be converted into *aspartate*, which can be used to create DNA and *arginine* – this conversion is performed within the TCA cycle present within mitochondria.

From the perspective of the fungus, it is beneficial to only partially suppress mitochondria, which is achieved by actively controlling cell defence mechanisms, such as free radical production via oxygen restriction; and programmed cell death, through over-expression of Bcl-2. This ensures pathogen survival and crucially enables co-habitation, allowing mitochondria to continue operating in an otherwise normal capacity, and thereby ensuring the fungus is provided with the nutrients it requires. When essential nutrients are depleted by the fungus, the cell will automatically increase OXPHOS activity to replenish these missing nutrients:

> 'The revealed studies pointed out that **OXPHOS** was not constantly suppressed during carcinogenesis, it could be **partly restored** under **nutrient shortage status** via metabolic reprogramming induced by LKB1-AMPK-p53 and **PI3K-Akt-mTOR** pathway.'
>
> <u>*Oncotarget*</u> **2017** [716]

This may explain why the OXPHOS pathway is active to varying degrees in different cancers at different stages of progression, and further indicates that mitochondria are not necessarily dysfunctional.

Importantly, OXPHOS is regulated by the very PI3K/AKT/mTOR pathway that fungal pathogens appear to control upon cell invasion, as I confirmed in Chapter 11. And here's the critical point to understand: regardless of the level of glycolysis or OXPHOS activity, the fungus will utilise the different fuels being absorbed by both energy pathways to create the glucose it requires to sustain itself. The fungus essentially adapts to utilise the glutamine, lactate, fat, methionine or arginine as they are absorbed into the cell.

Just to confuse matters, there is a third pathway, known as the *mSLP* pathway (Mitochondrial Substrate-level Phosphorylation pathway).[798] This pathway utilises the TCA cycle present within mitochondria, but is separate from the OXPHOS pathway in that oxygen is not required for it to generate energy, mSLP enables the fermentation of glutamine. Some scientists argue that it is the mSLP pathway that is operational within mitochondria, as opposed to the OXPHOS pathway. To a degree this distinction is immaterial, because regardless of whether mSLP or OXPHOS is in use, the fungus is able to acquire the fuel it needs to function, as each pathway absorbs these fuels as needed. The main issue is knowing which pathway to target and inhibit in any given situation – preventing the fungal pathogen from accessing this fuel is the goal.

So, contrary to the current universal assumption, the cell isn't intentionally using these fuels to survive; instead, the fungus is forcing the cell to absorb these fuels by artificially keeping the cell alive. Although it appears as though the cell is intentionally using these other fuels, in reality, the cell is working on autopilot – when certain nutrients are diminished, the cell automatically attempts to replenish them in order to restore balance – this is what the cell is programmed to do. The fungus is actually the driving force behind the disease, utilising these fuels for its own ends regardless of whether glycolysis, mSLP, or OXPHOS is the most dominant energy state or pathway being used. The cell's programmed job is to commit cell death when it becomes damaged to a level that threatens the host, but, the fungal invader prevents that from happening. Given the opportunity, the cell will commit cell death even when supplied with the nutrients that would normally sustain it – this is confirmed by the thousands of studies in which plant compounds have been shown to selectively kill cancer cells, by promoting apoptosis. If the cell itself was the driving force of cancer, it would utilise these plant nutrients to sustain it, not to consign itself to cell death.

With this in mind, it is important to distinguish between the energy requirements of the cell and the energy requirements of the fungal pathogen controlling the cell, and to separate them. This will allow us to better understand how these fuels drive the disease, and why these adaptations occur.

Glutamine:

Operating under the control of the fungus, the cell is forced to absorb increased amounts of glutamine. This is possibly due to the pathogen utilising the majority of glucose entering the cell, which prevents the cell from generating the amount of ATP energy it needs from glycolysis.[798]

Glutamine is absorbed in greater quantities and converted into ATP energy via the TCA cycle within mitochondria by utilising the mSLP or OXPHOS pathways; this is to make up for the ATP shortfall and to accommodate for the increased growth of the cell (glycolysis stimulates cell growth).[638]

> *'Ras activation [DNA activation] and hypoxia [a lack of oxygen] also strongly decrease glucose oxidation [decreases glucose-based OXPHOS energy creation within mitochondria]. Oxidative phosphorylation [OXPHOS], powered substantially by **glutamine-driven TCA turning**, however, **persists** and accounts for the **majority of ATP production** [glutamine-based OXPHOS energy creation is increased].*
>
> *Thus, **glutamine-driven** oxidative phosphorylation [OXPHOS] is a major means of ATP production even in **hypoxic cancer cells**.'*
>
> <u>Molecular Systems Biology</u> **2013** [875]

While this increased absorption of glutamine appears to be for the cell, and invariably some of it will be, it is primarily feeding the fungus. This is because the fungus can convert glutamine directly into the glucose it requires to thrive and sustain control.[616]

Not only does the liver convert excess glutamine back into glucose – via a pathway called *gluconeogenesis* – ensuring that glucose continues to be present within the bloodstream for the fungus to access, but the fungal pathogen can also convert glutamine directly into glucose via the same pathway, which is present within the micro-organism itself.[616]

> *'To establish an infection, the pathogen **Candida albicans** must assimilate carbon and grow in its mammalian host. This fungus assimilates six-carbon compounds via the glycolytic pathway, and two-carbon compounds via the glyoxylate cycle and **gluconeogenesis** [conversion of glutamine to glucose]. '*
>
> <u>Cellular Microbiology</u> **2006** [616]

So, while a patient may think they are cutting off the glucose supply to the tumour by restricting glucose consumption within their diet, the liver is working hard to replace the missing glucose in the bloodstream by converting available glutamine to glucose; this continues to feed the fungal pathogen. Furthermore, the fungus itself can directly convert the glutamine being absorbed by the cell, into glucose, which helps to explain why just restricting glucose within the diet may not work against some cancers.

On a positive note, the drug Metformin can block this glutamine-to-glucose conversion pathway within the liver and fungal pathogen[330] – hence why Metformin has been shown to inhibit and reduce tumours. Given that the drug targets this pathway within the fungus, we would expect Metformin to also be recognised as having anti-fungal properties – and indeed, this is the case. Metformin is essentially an anti-fungal drug, which can now explain why it appears so effective against cancer:

> 'Metformin active at 500 µg/ml, showed very good antimicrobial activity against most of the bacterial strains... The tested fungi are **Candida albicans** and **Aspergillus niger**. The tested drug showed **very good anti-fungal activity** with an average 13-17 mm zone of inhibition.'
>
> <u>Int. Archives of BioMedical and Clinical Research</u> **2018** [718]

From a treatment perspective, this indicates that combining dietary glucose restriction, with exercise, alongside Metformin to block this glutamine-to-glucose conversion pathway via the liver and within the fungus, could be an effective strategy for most cancer patients. This is because these two fuels (glucose and glutamine) feed the majority of cancers and fungal pathogens – 85% of cancers are carcinomas, which are highly glycolytic, they primarily utilise glucose and glutamine.[798]

On a cautionary note, please consult your physician before considering this approach as every person's situation is different. This approach may not work for your cancer type at its current stage of progression. You may have a fat-dominant cancer, so targeting glucose and glutamine may not be an effective strategy to employ. Please also view the *Potential Solutions* chapter at the end of the book for more details, before making any treatment decisions.

Fat:

What about cancers that appear to feed on fat? Surely fungal pathogens don't convert fat to glucose? Well, actually they do. When glucose is in short supply, fungal pathogens, such as *Candida* species, convert fat directly into glucose via a fat-to-glucose conversion pathway called the *glyoxylate cycle*.[597, 598, 605, 606, 708] This pathway is not present in human cells but has evolved within fungi as a way of enabling them to survive in hostile environments where access to glucose is restricted:

> '...the **glyoxylate cycle** *enables micro-organisms to grow on acetate or* **fatty acids** *[fat] as the sole carbon sources, reflecting the important adaptation of pathogenic micro-organisms such as Mycobacterium tuberculosis and* **C. albicans***. Micro-organisms that are able to achieve this cycle can* **produce energy** *and* **grow in lipid-rich** *[fat-rich] environments such as* **host cells***.'*

> <u>Molecular & Cellular Proteomics</u> **2007** [605]

> *'The* **glyoxylate cycle**... *is able to bypass the* **TCA cycle** *to achieve* **fat-to-glucose** *interconversion.'*

> <u>Lipids in Health and Disease</u> **2008** [606]

So, even when the only fuel being absorbed by the cell is fat, fungi can gain access to the glucose they need to sustain control over the cell, by directly converting it into glucose. The success of the fungal pathogen is determined by its ability to adapt quickly to the fat fuel source, as well as by the cell's ability to adapt quickly to the requirement for fat.[764] If the fungus cannot engage the glyoxylate cycle in time, or if the cell doesn't adequately adapt to absorb fat, the ensuing glucose deprivation may be sufficient to weaken or kill the pathogen. This can explain why glucose deprivation is beneficial for many, but not necessarily all cancer patients. This ability of fungi to convert fat into glucose also helps to explain why obesity is linked to cancer. Aside from fat cells producing estrogen – which stimulates fungal virulence, and generates low-grade inflammation – an excess of readily available body fat may help to create a supportive environment in which fungi can thrive.

Acquisition of glucose by any means is pivotal for the fungus, because up to 90% of the fungal cell wall is made out of carbohydrate, and carbohydrate is made from glucose:

> *'Approximately* **80** *to* **90%** *of the cell wall of C. albicans is* **carbohydrate**...'*

> <u>Microbiology and Molecular Biology Reviews</u> **1998** [047]

The survival of the micro-organism heavily depends upon the amount of glucose it has access to. It therefore has multiple pathways to provide for this, all of which need careful consideration in the search for effective treatment strategies.

Statins confirm fungal involvement:

Jane McLelland explains how she used the statin drug *Lovastatin* to block fat from entering fat-dependent cancer cells, which successfully inhibited tumour growth, promoting cell death. As this use of Lovastatin led to cancer cell death, many have naturally concluded that fat must be directly fuelling cancer cells, because the role of the fungus is not acknowledged, understood, or taken into consideration. If we analyse exactly how Lovastatin works, we can begin to see why it was so effective for Jane. In fact, by doing so, all the pieces of the puzzle align perfectly to support the Cell Suppression concept that explains how fungi and glucose are the core drivers of the disease.

Lovastatin blocks fat production in humans by restricting an enzyme called HMG-CoA (*Hydroxy methylglutaryl coenzyme A*), which inhibits the creation of cholesterol (fat). As fungal cells and human cells share many features, the drug affects both the cell and fungal pathogen in a similar way. Lovastatin works against the fungus by blocking the same HMG-CoA enzyme present within the pathogen. This inhibits the production of ergosterol, which is the fungal equivalent of human cholesterol. When ergosterol is blocked within the fungus, it dies. In other words, in addition to its intended purpose, Lovastatin – like Metformin – features effective anti-fungal properties:

> '**Statins** are interesting as they have **effective anti-fungal potential** against both yeast and filamentous fungi… The growth inhibition effect of statins on yeast cells is related to the decreasing **ergosterol** level, which occurs because of the inactivation of **HMG-CoA** reductase…'
>
> *World Journal of Clinical Infectious Diseases* **2011** [599]

It can be suggested that Lovastatin was effective for Jane because it attacked the fungus directly, and prevented it from generating the glucose it required to sustain itself, from fat. A pattern appears to be emerging, one in which effective treatments appear to not only target the energy system, but are also anti-fungal in nature.

Lactate as fuel – the Reverse Warburg effect:

The next fuel to explain is *lactate*, which is also referred to as lactic acid. Some cancer cells, particularly those on the periphery of the tumour, use lactate to fuel their energy needs instead of glucose. This has generated confusion because random DNA damage cannot explain why. Still, where the DNA Theory fails, the involvement of a fungal pathogen perfectly explains this conundrum. There are two distinct sources of lactate that need to be addressed for this to be understood:

1. Lactate created by the cancer cell itself
2. Lactate created by cells outside of the tumour

Point 1:

Excessive use of glycolysis results in a build-up of lactate in the surrounding tissue because lactate is a byproduct of glycolysis. Healthy and cancerous cells, can adapt to use this lactate by converting it into energy via the TCA cycle within mitochondria.[716, 872] This is nothing new; cells will adapt to use whichever fuel source is most accessible, especially when glucose is in short supply.

With little access to the primary fuels required, some cells within the tumour will be forced to adapt to take advantage of the lactate that is now abundantly available in the surrounding environment. This is why some cancer cells use lactate as fuel:

> *'This study showed that **breast cancer cells** tolerate and **use lactate** at clinically relevant concentrations in vitro [test tube experiments] and in vivo [live animal models].'*

<u>*PloS One*</u> **2013** [872]

But what's the relationship between lactate and fungi? How does lactate benefit this micro-organism? It turns out that lactate directly feeds fungal pathogens[712] – no conversion to glucose is even needed. Along with glucose, lactate directly fuels fungal energy needs. Not only that, but lactate increases the virulence (ability to infect) of *Candida* and increases its ability to evade immune detection. This helps to explain why cancers become more aggressive as they progress, because, over time, more lactate is produced:

> *'We have shown that the cell wall architecture of **C. albicans** is dramatically altered after cells are **grown on lactate** rather than glucose...*
>
> *...Overall, the observed upregulation of IL-10 and downregulation of IL-17 might suggest that **lactate-grown C. albicans** cells are **more virulent** than glucose-grown cells. This is in close agreement with in vivo studies [studies within animals] showing that lactate-*

*grown [fungal] cells are **more virulent** in both vaginal and systemic infection.'*

Infection and immunity 2013 [712]

Regarding how fungi use lactate to evade being killed by the immune system, the study states:

*'Lactate-grown [fungal] cells were taken up less efficiently by macrophages [immune cells], and those Candida cells that were phagocytosed [absorbed by the immune cell] were **more effective at escaping the macrophages** and **killing them.'***

Infection and immunity 2013 [712]

So, the abundant availability of lactate in circumstances where glucose is in short supply, provides fuel directly for the fungus, as well as the cell, which converts it into ATP energy. The fungus takes advantage of the cell's need to absorb lactate, which ensures that fungi can access the fuel for their energy requirements and aggressive behaviour – thus helping to explain why lactate appears to fuel cancer and increase tumour aggression.

Point 2:

Regarding the external source of lactate that cancer cells have been shown to utilise as fuel, scientists claim that cells surrounding the tumour – such as *fibroblast cells* – are recruited by the tumour to aid its progression by providing it with lactate.[716] This external source of lactate, generated from non-tumour cells in the surrounding tissue, is absorbed by cancer cells and used to create energy.

This process of tumour cells being fed lactate by the non-cancerous cells surrounding it, is termed the *Reverse Warburg Effect*. This is because it appears to be the opposite of the Warburg effect. The Warburg effect describes a process where glucose is used as fuel and lactate is created as an unwanted byproduct, whereas the Reverse Warburg effect describes the process of cells actually using lactate as fuel instead of glucose.[710, 716]

Based on the notion that our cells are to blame for cancer and have developed a mind of their own, scientists have attempted to explain this. They've concluded that tumour cells bully these external cells into aiding its cause by intentionally damaging the mitochondria contained within them, this is achieved by using free radicals. This free radical assault renders fibroblast mitochondria dysfunctional, leading to a switch in energy to glycolysis – essentially forcing fibroblasts to produce lactate, which is the byproduct of glycolysis. Viewing this process through a cell suppression lens, the question that springs to mind is: are external fibroblast cells being encouraged to feed lactate to the tumour and conforming, or, are they simply defending themselves from fungal attack, which results in an energy switch to glycolysis and over-production of lactate?

As I confirmed in Chapter 11, cells intentionally switch to glycolysis when under attack from fungal pathogens. This switch is an anti-fungal defence mechanism. Significantly, studies show that fungal pathogens can instigate this switch to glycolysis in fibroblast cells:

> *'...[fungal] infection increases the expression in the lungs of proteins related to energy metabolism, leading to activation of the **glycolytic pathway**. In the same study, these authors confirmed the activation of **glycolysis** in human pulmonary **fibroblasts**, culminating in the **Warburg effect**.'*
>
> <u>Frontiers Research Topics</u> **2022** [817]

Based on Dr Naviaux's work, I posit that, through purinergic signalling, external fibroblast cells are alerted to the expanding fungal infection by infected cells within the tumour mass. Once alerted, fibroblasts switch to glycolysis even in the presence of oxygen, enacting the very Warburg effect that we see in cancer:

> *'Thus, a **sustained Warburg metabolism** within a tissue may partly reflect the continual activation of immune cells recruited towards a **relatively low biomass infection**. In other words, signalling molecules released by a relatively **small number of infected cells** are capable of causing activation of **neighbouring non-infected cells**, triggering a **feedforward cascade of Warburg-like metabolism**.'*
>
> <u>Immunometabolism</u> **2021** [816]

Alternatively, this occurs due to direct contact with fungal pathogens that likely expand out into this external tissue, using the lactate already present to fuel their aggressive behaviour. This would explain why lactate is being produced by these external fibroblast cells. In line with this, we see that fibroblast cells do indeed switch their energy system to glycolysis in relation to cancer,[818] exactly as we would expect if a fungal pathogen were present. The study in question states:

'*Cancer cells induce oxidative stress in **neighbouring fibroblasts** by secreting reactive oxygen species (ROS), triggering aerobic **glycolysis** and production of high energy metabolites, especially **lactate**...*'

<u>*Oncotarget*</u> **2017**[716]

Unaware of a fungal influence, scientists postulate that free radicals are created by the tumour to purposefully damage the mitochondria contained within surrounding fibroblast cells, and that this renders them dysfunctional. It is this interaction that allegedly forces fibroblasts to switch to glycolysis.[772] This has led to the conclusion that fibroblasts are intentionally feeding lactate to the tumour, manipulated into doing so by the tumour itself.

To confirm their hypothesis – that free radical damage is causing fibroblasts to act in this way – in the study, *N-acetyl-cysteine*, *Metformin* and *Quercetin* were the antioxidants used to reduce the Nitric Oxide (NO) free radicals that the tumour is said to be utilising during this process. As well as these, a NO free radical inhibitor called *L-NAME* (nitro-L-arginine methyl ester) was also used. These, it is claimed, would reduce free radical damage inflicted upon these fibroblasts, resulting in a reversal of the energy switch away from glycolysis, thus reducing the lactate being produced. And indeed this did occur. Understandably, the conclusion drawn was that the tumour is intentionally using NO free radicals to inflict damage in order to force fibroblast cells to use glycolysis, and therefore produce lactate for the tumour to consume.

However, as always, there is another conclusion that can be drawn from the same data. And that is, that all three of the antioxidants used, as well as the NO inhibitor L-NAME, possess the additional property of being anti-fungal in nature. All of them are effective at killing human fungal pathogens.[765, 766, 925]

Could it be that using four anti-fungal compounds within their experiment, inadvertently provided them with the result they were looking for? Was it possibly nothing to do with a reduction in free radical damage, but due instead to the elimination of the fungus that was initially triggering the Warburg effect in fibroblast cells? Could this have been the reason why the fibroblast cells returned to a normal energy state – these cells regained control and no longer required the use of glycolysis to combat the pathogen? Certainly, a reduction in free radicals did occur, which understandably led to the conclusion that aligned with their initial hypothesis, but was this a red herring?

Now that we've covered the four main fuels used by cancer cells, I can summarise how they all interact to ultimately feed the intracellular pathogen to a greater degree than the cell that's absorbing them. Included within the graphic are *estrogen* and *arginine*, which are discussed over the following pages.

The fuels that feed cancer

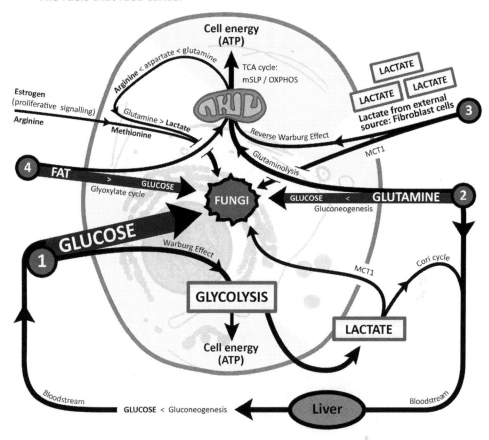

Mark Lintern 2022

Explaining the different ratios of fuels used by cancer cells:

While it is acknowledged that 80-90% of cancers primarily use glucose to fuel their energy needs,[710, 449] some appear to use glutamine, fat and lactate to varying degrees. Most cancers seem to use glucose initially and then adapt to using glutamine, fat, or lactate later in their development.[449] A few cancers operate the other way around, using fat initially, and later switching to glucose, as appears to be the case with prostate cancer.[603, 641]

In a 2021 study, scientists analysed the energy requirements of tumours more deeply, and found that the type of fuel consumed varied amongst different tumour cells. While confirming that glucose and glutamine were the two primary fuels being utilised, they noted that immune cells – which can constitute up to 50% of the tumour mass – consumed the most glucose, while cancer cells consumed a higher rate of glutamine:

> 'The team used two different PET tracers, one to follow **glucose** and one for the nutrient **glutamine**, and six different tumour models including colorectal, kidney and breast cancer. In each case, they found that myeloid **immune cells** (primarily macrophages) had the **highest uptake of glucose**, followed by T cells and cancer cells. Cancer cells, in contrast, had the **highest glutamine uptake**.'
>
>

EurekAlert **2021** [765]

Regardless of the varying fuels being absorbed by different cells, the fungus will use all four to ensure its energy needs are met. Within the disabled macrophage cells that can make up 50% of the tumour mass, the fungus will utilise the glucose being absorbed – macrophages rely on glycolysis during fungal infection. And as I highlighted in Chapter 11, one of the three most common fungal pathogens of humans, *Cryptococcus neoformans*, is an expert intracellular pathogen of macrophage immune cells, not only surviving within in them, but capable of transferring between them without needing to exit the cell.[851] Glutamine and fat being absorbed by cancer cells will also be converted into glucose by the fungus.

Fungi are opportunistic by nature; they will take advantage of whatever fuel is most abundant and easiest to access. This helps to explain why 80-90% of cancers are fuelled by glucose – 85% of all cancers form in epithelial cells (carcinomas), and most of these are highly glycolytic (glucose dominant). This energy switch to glycolysis is the easiest route from which fungi can obtain an abundance of glucose, given that at least 18 times more glucose is absorbed directly into the cell using this energy pathway.

Acquiring glucose from fat takes more effort and requires the fungus to adapt to use the glyoxylate cycle, a change that only appears to be implemented by fungi in situations of extreme stress, when other sources of glucose are difficult to come by:

> 'The most likely explanation for the induction of the **glyoxylate cycle** in bacteria and **fungi** upon phagocytosis is that activation of

this pathway represents the response of these micro-organisms to
nutrient starvation...'

Eukaryotic Cell **2002** [597]

In early tumour development the fungus will utilise the glucose within our diet. When this is restricted, it will rely upon the glucose created through the pathway known as *gluconeogenesis* – which is where the liver, and to a lesser degree the kidneys – convert substances, such as glutamine or lactate, back into glucose for cells to use. When gluconeogenesis is restricted – as can be achieved using the drug Metformin or the plant extract berberine – the fungus will utilise the glutamine that the cell absorbs to compensate for the lack of glucose; the fungus can directly convert glutamine into glucose. Alternatively, lactate can be utilised by the fungus, which is produced as a byproduct of glycolysis and readily available within the surrounding tissue. Only when glucose, glutamine and lactate are hard to come by will fungi adapt to generate glucose directly from fat, by activating the glyoxylate cycle – providing the cell is absorbing sufficient fat at the time.

This explains why the majority of cancers only use fat in advanced stages of the disease – when its energy requirements are much higher and energy sources have become scarce – and why advanced cancers tend to spread to areas where adipose tissue (fat tissue) is abundant. At this late stage, the fungus has had time to adapt to use the glyoxylate cycle. This may signify the transition of cancer to its malignant phase, when the fungal pathogen can use all four fuels to ensure its survival, and the acquisition of glucose is guaranteed. This is why glucose restriction via diet and using the drug Metformin may not work as well in advanced cancers.

Confirming that fungi can adapt to use many different fuels, the study below shows that this micro-organism utilises glycolysis (glucose), gluconeogenesis (protein-to-glucose conversion) and the glyoxylate cycle (fat-to-glucose conversion) when it is engulfed by an immune cell:

> *'During the early stages of a systemic infection, C. albicans activates the* **glyoxylate cycle** *and* **gluconeogenesis** *in response to phagocytosis [immune cell absorption].*
>
> *In the latter stages of an infection, when the fungus is* **colonizing tissue**, **glycolytic** *metabolism predominates [the glucose energy system is preferred]. Presumably, this increases the biological fitness of this pathogen within its host.'*

Cellular Microbiology 2006 [616]

The conditions within the patient, the diet being consumed, the number of immune cells surrounding the tumour, the cancer type and its stage of progression, will all determine the ratio of fuel being consumed by the cell and the fungus. Early tumours may have a ratio of 70% glucose (70% glycolysis), 20% glutamine and 10% lactate (30% OXPHOS). That ratio is likely to change as the tumour progresses and will also depend upon the cell's location within the tumour. For instance, cells at the outer edge of the tumour may absorb a ratio of 50% lactate, 30% glutamine, 5% fat (85% OXPHOS), with the remaining 15% being generated by glycolysis. Cells within the middle of the tumour that have direct access to the blood supply may consume higher quantities of glucose and much lower levels of lactate (90% glycolysis, 10% OXPHOS). Ultimately though, regardless of which fuel is being absorbed, the fungal pathogen will either convert it into glucose or will directly consume lactate or arginine, which can enhance its survival prospects.

Other fuels that are crucial to consider:

Aside from the four primary fuels mentioned above, there appear to be a few other fuels that specifically feed tumour growth, which, when inhibited, can lead to the death of cancer cells. Some cancers, for instance, utilise *estrogen*, while others appear to be very sensitive to the amino acids *methionine* and *arginine*. Determining why this sensitivity occurs has always been a bone of contention. Therefore, it is important to attempt to explain their involvement because if fungi are at the heart of cancer, we would expect to see that these compounds benefit fungal pathogens, by improving their ability to colonise and sustain tumour growth. Of particular importance is that estrogen-dependent cancers are the most common cancers in women, and that the most aggressive cancers appear to be deeply entwined with methionine and arginine. So, understanding the relevance of all three is critical when it comes to patient survival.

Estrogen – stimulating breast cancer:

Estrogen is predominantly a female sex hormone, although it is also found in men. It is a chemical that regulates many factors within the body, including energy metabolism. It is not a fuel in the context of fat, protein, and glucose, rather, it is a signalling molecule that acts like a messenger; it can stimulate a desired response such as cell-proliferation.[868] There is no doubt among scientists that estrogen fuels many types of breast cancer:

> '...clinical evidence link cumulative and sustained exposure to **estrogens** with **increased risk** of developing **breast cancer**. However, there is **no clear understanding** of the mechanisms through which **estrogens cause cancer**.'
>
> <u>J Steroid Biochem Mol Biol.</u> **2006** [621]

This seems to be corroborated by the use of hormone replacement therapy (HRT), which is found to increase the risk of breast cancer, mostly because of the extra estrogen that the treatment provides the patient.[387]

While scientists acknowledge the link between tumour growth and estrogen, they cannot explain why the hormone fuels the disease or describe the exact mechanism involved. Could this once again be because they are not factoring in the involvement of a fungal pathogen? Is estrogen fuelling the cell, or the fungus? It turns out that certain fungal pathogens are stimulated by estrogen and have estrogen-binding receptors:[023-024]

> 'Three **Candida albicans** strains were tested in the presence of 17-β-**estradiol** [estrogen] for increased growth and for enhanced survival during incubation... **All 3** test organisms showed **increased growth** in the presence of **estradiol**.'
>
> <u>The Journal of infectious Diseases</u> **2000** [023]

Estrogen, presented above as estradiol, stimulates fungal pathogens making them more aggressive. Bolstered by glucose and estrogen, does fungal involvement explain why breast cancer is the most common cancer in women?

Estrogen and fat:

Notably, fat cells produce estrogen. The greater the level of fat we store, the greater the amount of estrogen that is produced and circulates throughout the body, which has the undesirable effect of stimulating fungal infection:

> '**Estrogen is also produced by fat cells** and the adrenal gland... Overweight men are more commonly affected by low sperm count due to estrogen because there is more adipose tissue in the obese, which can set off the **creation** of **excess estrogen**.'
>
> <u>Live Science</u> **2017** [662]

Could this link between fat and estrogen, with fungi utilising both, help to explain why obesity is a risk factor for generating cancer? And does this also explain why advanced cancers tend to migrate to areas of the body where fat tissue is abundant?

Methionine – and fungal proliferation:

Methionine is a critical protein used in the methylation cycle. For DNA to work properly it needs to be methylated, and methionine is a primary protein required to facilitate this process. Without methionine, DNA damage occurs leading to a poorly functioning cell. Cells cannot proliferate effectively without it.

The confusion surrounding methionine in cancer, stems from the acknowledgement that some tumours – generally those that are aggressive – become methionine-dependent; they seem to be reliant upon high quantities of external sources of methionine. These cells appear to have lost their ability to create methionine internally, and are forced to acquire methionine from the diet and surrounding tissue:

> 'Another example supported by recent evidence is the enzymatic **depletion** of the essential AA [amino acid], **methionine**. Cancer cell **proliferation** appears dependent on **exogenous** [external] **methionine** and is known as **methionine dependence** or the **Hoffman effect**.'
>
> <u>Amino Acids</u> **2021** [832]

How is a reduced level of intracellular methionine, and reliance on external methionine explained? As I detailed in Chapter 11, fungal pathogens acquire intracellular methionine for purposes of increased virulence and proliferation. This depletes intracellular methionine levels, forcing the cell to rely on external sources of methionine, and leading to methionine-dependence:

> 'Another mechanism for **amino acid–induced filamentation** in **C. albicans** is through **intracellular methionine metabolism** and the uptake of **methionine from the host** via CaMup1...
>
> ...This is supported by the concept that **A. fumigatus relies heavily** on the amino acids' valine, isoleucine, and **methionine** as carbon sources **during invasive aspergillosis**.'
>
> <u>Current Clinical Microbiology Reports</u> **2019** [831]

Does this explain why methionine restrictive diets have been shown to kill methionine-dependent cancer cells?[833] In these cells the fungal pathogen is unable to access the methionine it requires, leading to a loss of fungal cell integrity and the death of the pathogen.

Arginine – the fuel of aggressive cancers:

Like glutamine and methionine, *arginine* is a protein that appears to feed cancer. It is needed for growth, wound healing, blood vessel control, and cell defence. It has a complicated relationship with tumours that scientists are struggling to understand, mainly because it can both feed and kill cancer cells. Importantly, arginine is linked to aggressive cancers, which makes understanding its role a necessity.

Much of the confusion centres around an enzyme called 'ASS1' (Argininosuccinate synthetase 1). This ASS1 enzyme is used to create arginine within the cell. Some cancers over-express ASS1, creating increased quantities of arginine that appear to feed the disease, while many other aggressive cancers don't express it at all:

> *'[A] common metabolic alteration observed in many cancers is the* **silencing** *of the* **ASS1 gene**... *the metabolic pathway responsible for... the* **biosynthesis of arginine**.*
>
> **Loss of ASS1 expression** *leads to* **dependence** *upon* **extracellular arginine** *for continued cell growth, proliferation, and survival.'*
>
> <u>Cell Reports</u> **2016** [711]

A loss of ASS1 expression means that arginine isn't being produced by the cell. This is important, as it highlights a potential weakness, because it means that the cell is reliant upon external sources of arginine found within the diet. This failure to create arginine within the cell is termed *arginine auxotrophy* and opens up the possibility that these aggressive cancers may be susceptible to arginine starvation therapy, in which arginine is restricted within the diet:

> *'...tumours* **proliferated** *and* **metastasized** *when mice were fed with* **arginine**; *however, [they]* **shrank** *and* **failed to metastasize** *when* **depleted** *of* **dietary arginine**.'*
>
> <u>BioCancer</u> **2020** [719]

But not all aggressive cancers are killed when arginine is restricted. Some react to become even more aggressive – and this is where the confusion begins:

> 'Arginine **deprivation** causes cell death in **some cancers**, but others **gain resistance** by **expressing ASS1** after a starvation response is induced.'
>
> <u>Drug Resistance Mechanisms in Cancer</u> **2019** [723]

Further complicating matters, some cancers die when supplemented with arginine, which is the opposite of what we would expect, given that arginine is thought to feed the disease:

> '**L-Arginine** supplementation significantly **inhibited tumour growth** and prolonged the survival time of mice.'
>
> <u>BMC Cancer</u> **2016** [727]

So, supplementing with arginine can both feed tumours and kill them, while depriving tumours of arginine can both kill them or make them even more aggressive – no wonder so much confusion exists. With this in mind, can fungal control of the cell explain this otherwise incomprehensible behaviour? Is there a link between arginine and the aggressiveness of fungi, that could explain why arginine is associated with aggressive forms of cancer? And can fungi explain this ASS1 defect? In a word, yes. As is consistently the case, we find that fungi are at the very heart of the issue.

Arginine and fungal aggression:

It turns out that arginine is critical for fungal aggression. It's needed for the fungus to transform from its benign yeast form, to its invasive fungal form, in which it develops protrusions called *hyphae*. These protrusions enable the pathogen to penetrate cell barriers, kill immune cells and spread more easily. Without arginine, fungal pathogens are limited in their ability to invade cells and sustain an infection:

> 'Taken together, these data suggest that in response to the oxidative burst generated by macrophages following phagocytosis, C. albicans specifically induces **arginine biosynthetic pathway genes** to **promote filamentous growth** within macrophages.'
>
> <u>Eukaryotic Cell</u> **2013** [715]

In the study above, *Candida* fungi used arginine to quickly stimulate hyphal growth (filamentous growth), which enabled them to become invasive, and to evade being killed by the macrophage. When arginine was restricted, the pathogen could not change into its aggressive form and was killed by the immune cell.

Aspergillus fungi require arginine to produce *siderophores*, which are used to chelate (extract) iron from host cells.[725] Iron is needed for micro-organisms to proliferate and turn aggressive. Without access to arginine, iron is harder to acquire; without iron, fungal pathogens are unable to sustain an infection:

> '*Arginine biosynthesis* is intimately linked to the biosynthesis of *ornithine*, a precursor for *siderophore production* that has previously been shown to be *essential* for *virulence* in A. fumigatus.'
>
> <u>MDPI 2020</u> [724]

> '*High-affinity* *iron acquisition* is mediated by *siderophore-dependent* pathways in the majority of pathogenic and non-pathogenic bacteria and fungi.'
>
> <u>Microbiology and Molecular Biology Reviews</u> **2007** [725]

So, gaining access to arginine stimulates fungi to become aggressive, and aids in their ability to sustain an infection. This explains why arginine is associated with aggressive cancers.

Gaining control of arginine is important for another reason, cells use arginine to create *nitric oxide* (NO),[723] which is a free radical that cells use to kill invading pathogens. It is therefore important for a fungal pathogen to control this process and suppress it:

> '*Nitric oxide (NO)* defends against *intracellular pathogens…* During infection, macrophages *import extracellular arginine* to *synthesize NO*. Later, [when] *extracellular arginine* is *depleted*, *ASS1 expression* allows macrophages to *synthesize arginine…* to *sustain NO output*.'
>
> <u>Cell Host and Microbe</u> **2012** [726]

To clarify, during infection an immune cell will use arginine present in the surrounding tissue to create nitric oxide – a free radical capable of killing pathogens. When this source of arginine is depleted, the cell itself will increase ASS1 expression, allowing it to create arginine internally to ensure the cell can continue to produce NO in defence against pathogens. Gaining control of arginine, is therefore, critical for fungal survival because doing so will allow the suppression of NO free radicals reducing this threat. Indeed, fungi can suppress NO free radicals,[050] by depleting arginine within the cell via the control of another enzyme called *arginase-1*.

This allows the fungus to divert arginine away from NO production and utilise it for its own ends. This consumption of arginine stimulates the fungus to become aggressive, which is explained in the study below and detailed in the following graphic:

'We show here that the human opportunistic fungal pathogen **Candida albicans** influences **L-arginine availability** for **nitric oxide** [NO] production by induction of the substrate-competing host enzyme **arginase-1**. This led to a **reduced production** of **nitric oxide** and, moreover, **reduced eradication** of the fungus by human macrophages...

C. albicans modulates **L-arginine** metabolism in macrophages during an infection, **potentiating its own survival**.'

mBio **2017** [722]

The following graphic shows that the compounds *citrulline* and *aspartate* are converted by the ASS1 enzyme into arginine, which is then used to create NO free radicals that can kill the fungal pathogen. It also illustrates how the fungus prevents this process by expressing arginase-1, which depletes arginine within the cell:

Arginine acquistion - Nitric Oxide free radicals are suppressed via arginase-1

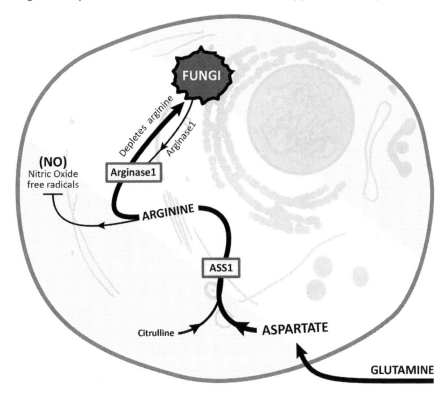

Mark Lintern 2022

So, arginine acquisition is vital for blocking cell defence, enabling the fungus to become invasive and sustain an infection. As with all other fuels that appear to be feeding cancer, this new perspective illustrates that arginine is fuelling the fungus, not the cell itself. Now that we understand the relationship between arginine and fungal pathogens, we can start to piece together the other elements of the puzzle:

1. Why arginine can feed cancer growth
2. Why arginine supplementation can kill cancer cells
3. Why arginine starvation can reduce tumour size
4. Why arginine starvation can stimulate tumour aggressiveness

1 – Why arginine can feed cancer growth:

This is simple to explain; an increase in arginine availability feeds the virulence of the fungal pathogen. In some aggressive cancers, the ASS1 enzyme, which creates arginine, is over-expressed, which means that the fungal pathogen has access to increased levels of arginine, stimulating it to become more aggressive:

> '*Argininosuccinate synthetase 1 (**ASS1**) expression is **increased** in gastric cancer [stomach cancer]. **Arginine depletion** significantly **inhibited** cell migration in the gastric cancer cell line. In conclusion, our results indicate that the ASS1 protein is required for cell migration...*'
>
> Scientific Reports 2015 [743]

> '*In contrast, several... tumours, including primary ovarian, stomach and colorectal cancer, are characterised by **ASS1 over-expression** [arginine creation].*'
>
> International Journal of Cancer 2010 [744]

> '*...we found that **ASS1** is **up-regulated** in 3D and also in mesothelioma. This result was unexpected because, in the literature, mesothelioma has been described as an ASS1-deficient tumour. Thus, there appear to be two groups of mesothelioma, those with ASS1 deficiency and those with **up-regulation of ASS1**.*'
>
> PLOS ONE 2016 [745]

So increased production of arginine by an overly-expressed ASS1 enzyme within the cell, feeds the fungal pathogen ensuring that the process of cancer is sustained. But why is this ASS1 enzyme over-expressed in the first place? ASS1 over-expression occurs because the fungus depletes arginine levels within the cell. This prompts the ASS1 enzyme to become excessively active in order to replenish the arginine that is lost.

Aspartate, created from glutamine, is the primary compound needed to make arginine. This explains why late-stage cancers absorb high quantities of glutamine, because it is required to create aspartate, which is then utilised by the ASS1 enzyme to replenish the arginine that the fungal pathogen is consuming. The involvement of a fungal pathogen explains why this ASS1 enzyme is over-expressed, why glutamine is absorbed in such high quantities by tumours, and ultimately why late-stage tumours appear to become aggressive when they have unrestricted access to arginine.

2 – Why arginine supplementation can kill cancer cells:

The reason why supplementation of arginine can kill cancer cells, as opposed to feeding them, relates to the function of immune cells. Immune cells that repair damaged cells deplete arginine within the surrounding tumour tissue, because they use it to aid with the healing process. This depletion of arginine suppresses the cancer-killing immune cells also present around the tumour because they require arginine to function as well – naturally, this benefits the tumour. But, when arginine levels are increased via supplementation, these cancer-killing immune cells are re-activated and regain their ability to kill cancer cells; resulting in tumour reduction. This is why arginine supplementation can kill cancer cells in certain situations. To confirm that this is indeed the case, this is discussed in more detail below:

Research confirms that immune cells called *myeloid-derived suppressor cells* (MDSCs) are present in abundance around tumours – these cells specifically deal with tissue repair.[730] The problem is that they use arginine to repair cell damage:

> *'MDSC [cells] may represent a **normal process** triggered by tissue damage with the aim of protecting the integrity of the tissues and 'healing' the initial injury. A demonstration of this mechanism was described in the late 1980s by Albina et al. studying the healing of surgical wounds.*
>
> *This infiltration would be followed by [MDSC] cells expressing **arginase I**, which would metabolize **l-Arginine** to ornithine and to **proline**, which in turn would trigger the synthesis of **collagen** by **fibroblasts**, ultimately leading to the **healing of the surgical wound**.'*
>
> <u>*Immunological Reviews*</u> **2008** [733]

Using arginine within a normal situation, such as to heal a surgical wound, is not a problem because once the wound is healed, MDSCs disperse, and arginine is no longer depleted from the surrounding environment. The problem in cancer is that the tumour is generating persistent inflammation and cell damage as it continues to expand. This results in MDSCs remaining for longer than is necessary, which results in the depletion of arginine within the tissue surrounding the tumour:

*'In cancer or chronic infections, tissue damage would trigger a similar response with the proliferation of **fibroblasts** producing **collagen** aimed at isolating and **healing** the **damaged tissue**.*

*As a matter of fact, many tumours are surrounded by dense fibrous tissue... The major difference between the disease processes (surgical wound versus malignant tumour) would be that the surgical wound would **heal**. In contrast, the malignant tumour would not stop growing and destroying tissue (**would not 'heal'**), which would trigger a **chronic inflammatory** process mediated by MDSCs that would ultimately lead to the **depletion** of l-Arginine from the micro-environment.'*

<u>Immunological Reviews</u> **2008** [733]

This arginine depletion results in the suppression of other immune cells, specifically the *T-cells* that are tasked with killing cancer cells:

*'**L-arginine** is a conditionally essential amino acid that is **fundamental** for the **function** of **T lymphocytes** [cancer-killing T-cells]. Recent findings in tumour-bearing mice and cancer patients indicate that increased metabolism of l-Arginine by myeloid-derived suppressor cells (**MDSCs**) producing **arginase I** **inhibits T-lymphocyte responses**.'*

<u>Immunological Reviews</u> **2008** [733]

Re-introducing arginine re-awakens these T-cells allowing them to kill cancer cells, explaining why arginine supplementation can kill cancer cells:

*'**L-Arginine** treatment **inhibited tumour growth** and prolonged the survival time of 4 T1 TB mice... the numbers and function of macrophages, CD4+**T-cells**, and CD8+**T-cells** [cancer-killing T-cells] were **significantly enhanced**.'*

<u>BMC Cancer</u> **2016** [727]

*'**Elevating L-arginine** levels induced global metabolic changes... in **activated T-cells** and promoted... **higher survival capacity** and... anti-tumour **activity**.'*

<u>Cell</u> **2016** [735]

Supplementing with arginine works against some cancers because it stimulates cancer-killing T-cells to reactivate, leading to the death of cancer cells. This is likely to be effective in early- to middle-stage tumours, when a large number of T-cells are present and relatively healthy. But why doesn't arginine supplementation work in late-stage cancers?

The number of healthy T-cells are diminished over time due to many factors, such as toxin and iron exposure, as well as the scarcity of naturally-occurring nutrients. The low numbers of cancer-killing T-cells in late-stage cancer means that when arginine is supplied, too few tumour cells are killed to make any noticeable difference to a larger and faster-growing tumour. At this late stage, the benefit bestowed by arginine falls towards the fungal pathogen, and the tumour, rather than the diminishing number of remaining T-cells – hence why arginine supplementation can reduce tumours in certain instances but feed the disease in others.

Misunderstanding MDSC involvement in cancer:

As part of the narrative in which some cells are recruited by tumours and start 'intentionally' aiding the spread of the disease – the equivalent of defecting in a war – there is a widespread belief in the scientific community that these MDSC immune cells have been 'turned to the dark side', and are choosing to work with the tumour:

> *'Our understanding of the role of **myeloid-derived suppressor cells** (MDSCs) in cancer is becoming **increasingly complex**. In addition to their role in **suppressing immune responses**, they directly support **tumour growth**, **differentiation**, and **metastasis** in a number of ways that are only now beginning to be appreciated.'*
>
> <u>*The Journal of Clinical Investigation*</u> **2015** [730]

As a result, the proposed solution to this problem is thought to be to target and kill these MDSCs, essentially attacking the body's own immune cells and normal repair mechanisms:

> *'The myeloid-derived suppressor cell (MDSC) is the **'queen bee'** of the tumour micro-environment. MDSCs protect the cancer from the patient's immune system, make the tumour resistant to immunotherapy, and allow the tumour to thrive while the patient withers away. **Eliminating MDSCs** should improve response rates to cancer therapy and patient survival.'*
>
> <u>*Trends in Pharmacological Sciences*</u> **2018** [747]

But does attacking our own defence system really make sense? MDSCs specifically engage in cell repair and are not interested in killing pathogens or cancer cells.[731, 732] So, killing MDSCs will likely have a detrimental outcome on the rest of the body. But why do scientists feel the need to target them? As well as suppressing cancer-killing T-cells by consuming arginine, MDSCs also produce MMP enzymes aimed at wound healing in a similar manner to that of neutrophils and macrophages (as I discussed in Chapter 11). This stimulates cell growth signals, blood vessel growth and encourages cells to break away into the bloodstream when they are produced to excess – which is the most dangerous aspect of cancer:

> '*MDSCs were demonstrated to promote tumour invasion and metastasis by...* **elevated production** *of multiple matrix metalloproteinases* (**MMPs**), *playing a major role in matrix degradation.*'
>
> <u>*Vaccines*</u> **2016**[732]

When viewed from the perspective that MDSCs are intentionally aiding cancer, it seems plausible to attack them. But, as with neutrophils and macrophages, scientists seem to have misinterpreted this cell-repair process in relation to the role of MDSCs, because they are not taking into account the influence of the fungal pathogen, which is generating cell damage and inflammation for an abnormal length of time. In essence, immune cells are just performing their regular duties of cell repair. The problem is that their prolonged presence depletes essential nutrients (like arginine), and generates abnormal levels of other substances (like MMP-9), which become corrosive and end up inadvertently aiding with tumour growth and migration. The abnormal growth of the tumour simply hijacks this normal healing process:

> '*Therefore, it is our hypothesis that tumours '***hijack***' a* **normal healing process.***'
>
> <u>*Immunological Reviews*</u> **2008**[733]

The intention of these immune cells is simply to attempt to repair the ongoing damage. They have not developed a mind of their own, nor are they intentionally working to help the tumour. Killing the fungus is the answer to the problem, as this will eliminate the cancer cells and the persistent inflammation, thereby enabling the immune cells to complete their job of repairing tissue damage; following which they will then disperse. Attacking our own immune system will inevitably impair essential immune function, while having a limited, short-term effect on the tumour.

3 – Why arginine starvation can reduce some tumours:

Arginine starvation can be effective against aggressive cancers because many contain a particular defect. As mentioned a moment ago, an enzyme called *ASS1* is often silenced and seemingly no longer functional in many tumours – these cells appear incapable of creating arginine internally. This means the cells are forced to rely on external sources of arginine found within the diet, supplied via the bloodstream. This reliance on dietary arginine places the fungus, and the cancer cell, in a vulnerable position by making them both susceptible to arginine starvation therapy, in which dietary arginine is restricted:

> *'ASS1 is a key enzyme in **arginine biosynthesis**, and its abundance is **reduced** in **many solid tumours**, making them **sensitive** to **external arginine depletion**. ASS1 was either low in abundance or absent in more than **60%** of 149 random **breast cancer biosamples**, suggesting that patients with such tumours could be candidates for **arginine starvation therapy**.'*
>
> <u>Science Signalling</u> **2014** [720]

> *'Extrinsic (dietary) arginine, which is non-essential in non-cancerous human cells, becomes **critical to the survival of cancer cells**, a condition known as **arginine auxotrophy** [inability to create arginine internally]. A **defect** in **arginine synthesis** is one of the **most common**, yet **under-recognized**, metabolic **vulnerabilities** in cancer.'*
>
> <u>Communications Biology</u> **2018** [721]

Restricting access to arginine within the diet has been shown to kill highly aggressive cancer cells. As mentioned above, the cell is not creating arginine internally, so cutting off other dietary sources results in the fungal pathogen also being starved of arginine. Furthermore, arginine restriction appears to affect the cell's ability to generate energy through glycolysis, which has the knock on effect of reducing glucose availability to the fungus – starving it of its primary food source:

> *'We found that pharmacologically induced **arginine depletion** causes... **decreased aerobic glycolysis**, effectively **inhibiting** the **Warburg effect**.'*

Cell Reports **2016**[711]

This explains why arginine starvation can have a beneficial effect in arginine auxotrophic (arginine deficient) cancers – the pathogen is weakened and ultimately killed due to an inability to access arginine.

4 – Why arginine starvation can stimulate tumour aggressiveness:

While restricting arginine can be beneficial in some instances, it can also prime the tumour to develop resistance, turning cancer more aggressive; this behaviour has baffled researchers. Thankfully this confusing process can now be explained. To make sense of this, we need to uncover why the ASS1 enzyme is acting so erratically. In particular, why in some instances it is over-expressed, and in others it is not expressed at all; and why it can be stimulated into action once again, after long periods of inactivity.

Critical to cell growth is the ability to synthesize DNA. When cells divide, DNA needs to be created for the new cell – the development of any organism is restricted by its ability to create new DNA. DNA is primarily synthesized from chemicals called *pyrimidines* and *purines*.[740] These are stored in equal amounts within cells and are used in equal quantities to form new DNA bases when cell growth/division occurs.[739]

This is important because fungi also require these same chemicals; the acquisition of pyrimidines and purines allows for increased fungal growth, because they are also needed to create new DNA within the pathogen. And as you might expect, fungal pathogens have become expert at obtaining these critical compounds from the cells they invade. This is significant, because it explains the unpredictable behaviour of the ASS1 enzyme that continues to puzzle researchers:

> '*In vitro, C. albicans actively takes up the* **purines** *guanine and adenine within a few hours from the growth medium. The concentrations of* **purines** *within the vacuole of the cell became* **supersaturated***, suggesting that when* **purines** *are* **available***, the fungus* **scavenges all it can***.*
>
> *Scavenging purines from their environmental niche likely confers a selective* **advantage** *to* **A. fumigatus***,* **C. albicans** *and* **C. neoformans** *[the three primary fungal pathogens of humans].*'
>
> *Microorganisms* **2017**[736]

Fungi also scavenge pyrimidines:

> *'The uptake of cytosine, thymine and uracil [**pyrimidines**] into both **C. glabrata** and **C. albicans** was linear for 30-60 seconds at all concentrations of **pyrimidines** examined.'*
>
> <u>Journal of General Microbiology</u> **1990** [737]

So, as with many other critical substances, fungi absorb pyrimidines and purines depleting them from within the cell. The cell responds by attempting to replenish these missing compounds. The crucial point of note here is that it is the chemical 'aspartate' that is required to create these pyrimidines and purines:

> *'Beyond its role as an amino acid in proteins, **aspartate** is required for conversion of IMP to AMP in de novo **purine synthesis** and provides the carbon backbone for de novo **pyrimidine synthesis**.'*
>
> <u>Cell</u> **2016** [739]

This loss of pyrimidines and purines, caused by the fungus, creates a dilemma for the cell: not only is aspartate required to replenish pyrimidine and purine, but it is needed to create arginine via the ASS1 pathway. And so we arrive at a critical point in our understanding that helps explain why the ASS1 enzyme appears to be faulty in aggressive cancers, and why it acts unpredictably.

As you can see in the following graphic, aspartate can be used to create arginine via the ASS1 pathway, while pyrimidines and purines are created when aspartate is shuttled into the pathway known as *CAD* (*carbamoyl-phosphate synthase 2, aspartate transcarbamylase, and dihydroorotase complex*). Both are on opposite ends of the scale, and both cancel out the process of the other, depending on which pathway is required to be used.[741] They are mutually exclusive. This is confirmed by the study below:

> *'**ASS1 deficiency** in cancer cell lines was associated with upregulation of **CAD**, **increased pyrimidine synthesis** and **proliferation rate**, and more **rapid tumour growth** in vivo.*
>
> ***Over-expression** of ASS1 in ASS1-deficient cancer cells was sufficient to induce diversion of **aspartate away from pyrimidine synthesis** and to **decrease proliferation**.'*
>
> <u>Cancer Discovery</u> **2016** [738]

To clarify, aspartate is the pivotal substance needed both for the creation of arginine, and for the creation of pyrimidine and purine used to create DNA – cells that are proliferating need to create new DNA.

Aspartate is shuttled between the two depending on which compounds need replenishing the most, or are needed the most given the conditions that arise. It is the expression of the ASS1 enzyme that determines which pathway gets to use aspartate:

> 'ASS1 levels **regulate aspartate** availability for **pyrimidine synthesis.**'
>
> <u>Molecular Cellular Oncology</u> **2016** [741]

From this, we can determine the reason why ASS1 appears to be defective in aggressive cancers, and where the confusion lies in circumstances where it is re-activated. Simply put, the fungal pathogen depletes levels of pyrimidines and purines within the cell – this enables the fungus to synthesize its own DNA in preparation for fungal growth and expansion. With the normal supply of pyrimidine and purine depleted, the cell is forced to replenish this critical DNA-creating resource. So the cell responds by reducing ASS1 activity, which allows the majority of aspartate to be used to create pyrimidine and purine via the CAD pathway. This gives the false impression that the ASS1 pathway has become faulty, because the cell no longer creates arginine. As far as the cell is concerned, this is not usually a problem because arginine can be acquired externally from dietary sources. The cell, therefore, doesn't need to create it from aspartate, and so it silences the ASS1 enzyme in favour of using aspartate to replenish the missing pyrimidines and purines, which has become the priority, as illustrated in the following graphic.

ASS1 is downregulated so that Aspartate can replenish Pyrimidine and Purine

Mark Lintern 2022

So, the drop in ASS1 enzyme activity is directly tied to the loss of pyrimidines and purines caused by the fungal pathogen, and the availability of external sources of arginine. This results in the cell utilising aspartate to replenish these depleted compounds. To do this, the cell suppresses ASS1 activity to shuttle aspartate into the CAD pathway. This explains *arginine auxotrophy* (reduced ASS1 activity) found to occur in many aggressive cancers, and indicates that the ASS1 enzyme is not actually defective. Confirming this to be the case, when arginine starvation therapy is implemented in arginine auxotrophic cancers, studies show that some re-stimulate ASS1 expression. This demonstrates that the mainstream view that the ASS1 enzyme is defective, is in fact incorrect:

> '*Some ASS1-deficient cancers undergo cell death when starved of arginine... but many others gain **resistance** to arginine deprivation. The most obvious pathway to resistance is **up-regulation** of ASS1*

*expression. Indeed, this is the only cellular long-term resistance mechanism that has been **confirmed** to occur...*

*This path is open to nearly every **ASS1-deficient cancer**, as **mutation** or deletion of ASS1 is **rare**...'*

<u>Cancer Drug Resistance</u> **2019** [746]

Note that a mutation or deletion of ASS1 is rare, meaning that the DNA Theory cannot account for the odd ASS1 activity witnessed. Now that this relationship is understood, we can determine why some tumours increase ASS1 expression and become more aggressive when starved of arginine.

Starving the cancer cell of dietary arginine switches the balance within the cell. The requirement for aspartate now shifts from replenishing pyrimidine and purine, back to the creation of arginine. Arginine has become the number one priority, as it is now the primary limiting factor. Since, in advanced cancers, arginine has already been depleted in the surrounding tissue, largely by immune cells, the only way for the cell to acquire it is by converting aspartate via the ASS1 pathway. The cell, therefore, increases the expression of the ASS1 enzyme to shuttle aspartate away from pyrimidine and purine creation, and into arginine creation. This is why the ASS1 enzyme, which is thought to be defective, is reactivated in arginine auxotrophic cancers (cancers where the ASS1 enzyme appears inactive).

In some instances, this transition may be too slow, which will result in the death of both the fungal pathogen and the cancer cell, because not enough arginine is available. This may also be due to low glutamine levels, because the aspartate required to create arginine is derived from glutamine. If glutamine is in short supply, or the cell has not increased the rate at which it absorbs glutamine to accommodate the sudden requirement for arginine, then internal levels of arginine will also become scarce. With this in mind, using a glutamine-blocking drug (*6-Diazo-5-oxo-L-norleucine* referred to as 'DON')[780] in combination with arginine starvation therapy, may prove beneficial against aggressive cancers where the ASS1 enzyme appears inactive.

This aside, if the cell can adapt quickly, and sufficient glutamine is being absorbed, then adequate amounts of arginine will once again be created and become available for the fungus to utilise to sustain the infection. This leads to a more aggressive cancer, because the cell is now forced to adapt to the depleted levels of arginine, pyrimidine and purine, caused by the fungus. So the cell increases its demand for glutamine to enable it to create the extra aspartate needed to replenish these depleted compounds. In doing so, the cell becomes more efficient at absorbing the very fuel that allows the pathogen to thrive. This explains why arginine starvation therapy can cause the cell to become addicted to glutamine:

> *'Arginine deiminase **resistance** [arginine starvation therapy resistance] in melanoma cells is associated with metabolic reprogramming, **glucose dependence**, and **glutamine addiction**.'*

> *...all ADIR cell lines showed elevated ASS1 expression... suggesting that **elevated ASS1** is the major mechanism of **resistance**.'*

> <u>*Molecular Cancer Therapeutics*</u> **2013** [742]

Factor in the increase in glucose absorption (confirmed in the study above) alongside the increased absorption of glutamine, and it is clear why the tumour becomes aggressive. The cell's adaptions inadvertently increase its support of the pathogen by taking in vastly increased quantities of the key fuels that sustain fungal proliferation. The depletion of essential nutrients by the fungal pathogen appears to be responsible for the changes in ASS1 enzyme activity witnessed in aggressive cancer. The demands of fungal proliferation provide a coherent rationale for this confusing situation.

Target the fungal pathogen and repair the terrain:

Ultimately, the solution must be to eradicate or control the fungal pathogen responsible. The fate of the fungus is determined by its access to certain nutrients, that, if inhibited and combined with anti-fungal treatments, should restore balance and control; thus eliminating damaged cancer cells as the influence of the pathogen is reduced. Certain fuels, such as glucose, glutamine, and lactate as well as the cell-growth-stimulating hormone estrogen, appear to be central to fungal survival and are seen to play a significant role in the early development of cancer. Fat seems to be a key factor in late-stage aggressive cancers, as is arginine – which is not surprising, given that arginine stimulates fungal aggression and improves its ability to cause new infections, while fat cells produce the estrogen that also stimulates pathogen aggression.

But, there is more to this than simply attacking the pathogen – a quick fix will never address the underlying conditions that gave rise to fungal dominance and tumour growth in the first place. Failing to address the inflammation, cell damage, iron overload, poor nutrition and excess consumption of glucose will almost inevitably result in cancer returning. The dysbiosis of the microbiome would continue to favour fungal pathogens. All terrains within the body need to be addressed to restore harmony and balance so that healthy defensive biological systems can be effective once more. It may sound like a cliché, but a healthier diet and lifestyle really does need to be adopted – ultimately this is the only way to live healthily and ensure fungal pathogens are kept in check. To this end, and at the very least, I recommend reading the book *The Metabolic Approach to Cancer* by Dr Nasha Winters. She addresses the ways in which diet and lifestyle can heal the terrain of the body, to bring balance back to tissue, cell metabolism, and the microbiome, now understood to be crucial to cancer prevention and our overall survival.

This simple approach isn't radical or dangerous, because the fuels that feed these fungal pathogens are exactly the same fuels that the science cites as fuelling cancer itself. Targeting both makes complete sense. An internal terrain characterised by toxins, inflammation and microbiome imbalance is ideally suited to supporting the fungal dominance that drives the disease. It makes sense then, to approach cancer by targeting these fuels, by re-establishing a healthy terrain that is hostile to fungal pathogens, and additionally by employing an anti-fungal treatment relevant to the dominant pathogens responsible.

CH 13

Drugs that support the Cell Suppression paradigm

Analysing current drugs on the market paints a fascinating picture. Listed below are some of the most effective drugs used to treat various cancers. I have indicated some of their additional properties, outside of the primary mechanism attributed to their efficacy. You may notice some recurring themes as you glance over them:

- Gleevec – glucose restrictor
- Herceptin – inhibits fungal invasion via HER2
- Tamoxifen – anti-fungal/estrogen inhibitor
- Arimidex – anti-fungal/estrogen inhibitor
- Abiraterone – improves immune function/testosterone inhibitor.

There are several drugs that have been proven to kill cancer cells:

- 2-DG – glucose restrictor
- DON – glucose and glutamine restrictor
- Metformin – anti-fungal/glucose restrictor
- Itraconazole – anti-fungal/glucose restrictor
- Clotrimazole – anti-fungal/glucose restrictor
- Ketoconazole – anti-fungal

- Miconazole — anti-fungal
- Econazole — anti-fungal
- 3BP — anti-fungal/glucose restrictor
- Melatonin — anti-fungal/glucose restrictor
- MP1 — anti-fungal
- Lovastatin — anti-fungal/fat restrictor[599]
- Fluvastatin — anti-fungal/fat restrictor[599]
- Atorvastatin — anti-fungal/fat restrictor[599]
- Mebendazole — anti-fungal/anti-parasitic
- Artemisinin — anti-fungal/free-radical generator
- Doxycycline — anti-fungal/anti-bacterial/energy restrictor[926]
- Amiloride — anti-fungal/pH regulation NHE1 inhibitor.

There are alternative approaches that have been shown to be effective at killing cancer cells:

- Exercise — glucose restrictor
- Ketogenic diet — glucose restrictor
- Fasting — glucose restrictor
- Hyperbaric Oxygen therapy — anti-fungal/free-radical generator/improved immune function
- Colloidal silver — anti-fungal
- Plant chemicals — anti-fungal/improved immune function.

When grouped together, an interesting picture emerges that highlights the link between treatment success and anti-fungal agents, as well as energy restriction.

The sugar and energy system relationship:

Gleevec,[298, 471] **Metformin,**[300, 330] **3BP,**[261] **2-DG,**[302] **exercise,**[068] **Clotrimazole,**[398] **Itraconazole,**[033] the **ketogenic diet,**[105] **Doxycycline,**[450, 926] **Melatonin,**[533, 535, 545, 546] and **fasting**[307, 336, 676] have all shown remarkable results at killing cancer cells in laboratory studies. While they seem to independently target many pathways within cancer cells, they all have the property of inhibiting glucose metabolism through various means. Most are capable of affecting fungal pathogens too.[299, 301, 302, 304]

Melatonin is interesting. It's a hormone that aids with sleep and is referred to as the master hormone because of its many benefits over other hormones. It is also a natural antibiotic. Significantly, studies show that melatonin is highly effective at killing micro-organisms, including fungi,[532, 533] which is one reason why sleep is so beneficial; the pineal gland floods the body with melatonin at night. In line with the Cell Suppression model, melatonin has been shown to kill cancer cells, and like all other effective solutions, it appears to restrict the energy system and glucose absorption.[545, 546]

Doxycycline is a well known, and well tolerated, anti-bacterial drug. It has proven effective at targeting cancer stem cells.[450] The *Care Oncology Clinic* use it as one of four off-patent drugs to target the metabolism of cancer cells.[781] Intriguingly, Doxycycline also possesses anti-fungal properties and is capable of killing *Candida* fungal species,[926] which may explain why it is one of only a few bacterial drugs that appear effective against cancer.

Fasting is interesting because its purpose is to deplete excess glucose. This simple restriction process has beneficial effects against cancer, highlighting the relevance of the energy system. Fasting has been shown to reduce insulin-like growth factor-1 (IGF-1), which reduces cell growth signals.[307, 676] It has also been shown to protect from the damaging effects of chemotherapy by reigniting the immune system, enabling stem cells to regenerate white blood cells (immune cells).[106, 306, 676]

In a review article titled *Sugar-free approaches to cancer cell killing*, published in the medical journal *Oncogene*, the authors refute the establishment view that glucose does not feed cancer:

> *'Tumours show an **increased rate of glucose uptake** and **utilization**. Up-regulation of **glycolysis**… promotes tumour growth** and has also been shown to **interfere with cell death at multiple levels**…*
>
> *Glucose deprivation** and **anti-glycolytic** drugs **induce tumour cell death**.'*
>
> <u>Oncogene</u> **2011** [305]

This study demonstrates the way that major institutions seem to be selective in the research findings they listen to. While these same institutions assert that cancer does not feed on sugar, and that its restriction has no beneficial effects, the study above confirms that restricting glucose, and blocking energy pathways using anti-glycolytic drugs, leads to tumour cell death. This highlights why it is so important to question the mainstream narrative.

6-diazo-5-oxo-L-norleucine (DON) is a glutamine inhibitor. It was shown to block both glutamine and glucose energy pathways in cancer cells,[769] which highlights the unmistakable link to cancer and energy metabolism. Glutamine inhibitor drugs have the potential to also block *arginine*, the fuel used by aggressive cancers, since arginine is created from *aspartate*, which is produced from glutamine. Blocking aspartate by inhibiting glutamine may also block DNA synthesis (aspartate is required to help create new DNA). This can potentially inhibit both fungal and tumour growth, because cells cannot duplicate without creating new DNA (this was covered in Chapter 12).

The fungal relationship confirmed:

Herceptin blocks the HER2 growth receptor found on the membrane of cells.[308] Fungi have been shown to use the HER2 growth receptor and other growth receptors as a portal to invade the cell.[255, 256] Blocking this receptor restricts access to the cell, halting fungal progression, at least for a while. This provides an explanation for the initial success of the drug, and the reason why it ultimately fails.

Tamoxifen is used against breast cancer as a hormone inhibitor – it blocks estrogen from entering breast cancer cells, and is effective at reducing breast cancer re-occurrence.[038] Fungi also have a high affinity for estrogen and contain estrogen-binding receptors; the hormone stimulates fungal growth and can aid in immune evasion.[023–024] Tamoxifen also possesses strong anti-fungal properties,[039] which could help to explain much of its success with breast cancer. However, it should also be noted that outside of breast cells, Tamoxifen acts like estrogen, and this actually fuels other estrogen-receptive cancers, such as uterine and endometrial cancer.[768]

While estrogen has been shown to stimulate fungal growth, it also orchestrates cell proliferation in healthy cells, so it is not surprising that when uterine and endometrial cancer cells view Tamoxifen as estrogen, they are stimulated to proliferate.[868] The reason why fungi are not killed by Tamoxifen in uterine and endometrial tissue remains to be uncovered, but may have something to do with fungi's adaptive abilities to utilise estrogen to generate resistance to certain drugs.[023]

This increased cancer risk for different cancer types should be considered whenever contemplating its use. The positive anti-fungal effects appear to be reduced in these other cancers, possibly due to the increase in estrogen the drug generates in this other tissue, and due to the resistance that naturally occurs when drugs are over-used. The problem with Tamoxifen appears to be its over-use – prolonged use of Tamoxifen as a preventative agent increases the risk of this resistance occurring.

Lovastatin kills cancer cells and is a powerful anti-fungal drug.[599] Lovastatin also blocks fat absorption, preventing fungi from generating glucose from fat.

Atorvastatin is the statin drug used by the *Care Oncology Clinic* as part of their protocol to treat cancer. Not only does it restrict fat, but it's also an effective anti-fungal drug in its own right.[599, 823]

Itraconazole kills cancer cells[033] and is also an anti-fungal drug. It inhibits hexokinase 2,[261, 033] a metabolic enzyme involved in glucose uptake, and so reduces glucose absorption. Once again, glucose, fungi, and the cell's energy system appear to be the key components involved.

Clotrimazole is an anti-fungal drug that kills cancer cells. Not only does it kill the fungus directly, but it also restricts the energy system by reducing glycolysis – which could simply be the outcome of the drug killing the fungal pathogen.[398]

Ketoconazole,[401] **Miconazole,**[400, 402] and **Econazole**[399] are three more anti-fungal drugs that have been shown to be effective against cancer.

Metformin kills cancer cells and is also an anti-fungal drug.[717, 718] In particular, it has been shown to kill the most common forms of human fungal pathogens: *Candida* and *Aspergillus* species, all while restricting glucose availability. Like Mebendazole mentioned below, Metformin also forms part of the anti-cancer treatment protocol being trialled by the *Care Oncology Clinic* in the UK.

Mebendazole, is an anti-parasitic drug. Intriguingly, Mebendazole is effective at killing common fungal pathogens:

> '*Lansoprazole, verapamil, albendazole and* **mebendazole** *showed* **significant anti-fungal activity** *at the tested concentrations against* **Aspergillus** *niger, Aspergillus flavus, and fluconazole resistant* **Candida albicans** *and Non- albicans Candida.'*
>
> *IASJ* **2012**[783]

Colloidal silver kills cancer cells.[104] This directly indicates that cancer is caused by a micro-organism, because killing micro-organisms is its primary property – it provides no nutritional benefit. In particular, silver is effective at killing fungi.[296, 544, 699]

MP1 has been shown in recent studies to selectively kill cancer cells.[272] MP1 is the venom taken from a particular wasp – and is a potent anti-fungal compound.[271]

3BP is a highly significant metabolic drug that reveals a great deal about both the energy system of a cancer cell, and the relationship between fungi and cancer. As fungal and human cells share many similarities, it would stand to reason that a drug that inhibits cancer cell energy pathways would also inhibit similar pathways within fungal cells – and this is exactly what we find:[550, 551, 556]

> *'... 3-BP toxicity in **yeast** is strain-dependent and influenced by the **glucose-repression system**. Its toxic effect is mainly due to the **rapid depletion** of intracellular **ATP** [cell energy].*
>
> *These findings may help to better understand the toxic activity of 3-BP and improve its effectiveness as an **anticancer** and **anti-fungal** drug.'*
>
> Oncotarget 2016 [552]

3BP not only blocks the energy pathways within the cell, but also within the fungus itself, providing a dual effect. 3BP also depletes antioxidant levels by reducing glutathione. This makes the cancer cell and fungal pathogen, more vulnerable to free radical damage, since glutathione provides protection from free radicals by neutralising them. Not only does 3BP increase cell vulnerability to damage by free radicals, but it also simultaneously ramps up the production of free radicals by stimulating this damage response, thus making 3BP a highly effective cell-damaging and fungal-killing drug:[553]

> *'...a significant decrease in GSH [**glutathione**] concentration is observed inside **micro-organisms** as well as **tumour cells**.'*
>
> *Moreover... the drastic **decrease** in the **ATP level** [energy] and GSH [**glutathione**] concentration, and the **increase** in the amount of ROS [**free radicals**] caused by 3BP, ultimately results in **cell death**.'*
>
> Oncotarget 2016 [555]

3BP has the potential to be a cure-all cancer drug because it appears to work on six levels. It inhibits the energy system of both cancer cells and fungal cells, making it both an anti-cancer drug, and an anti-fungal drug. It also decreases antioxidant levels within the cell and the fungus, making both more vulnerable to free radical attack. At the same time, it increases the production of free radicals, allowing for extreme levels of damage to be inflicted upon both the cancer cell and the fungus, without harming healthy cells to the same degree. [554, 555] Does this synergy in its capabilities against both cancer and fungal pathogens help to explain its notable efficacy?

Artemisinin is an anti-malarial drug that's in common use today. In pre-clinical studies it has been shown to kill cancer cells selectively. It appears to achieve this by reacting with the excess iron contained within the tumour. Peroxide within Artemisinin reacts with iron to form free radicals;[493, 494] healthy cells do not contain the level of freely available iron present within cancer cells, and so they aren't affected. A free radical reaction in cells containing free iron will likely kill intracellular pathogens. Additionally, Artemisinin shows anti-fungal activity in studies with the common fungal pathogens *Cryptococcus neoformans* and *Candida albicans*.[873, 874] Artemisinin appears more effective against C. neoformans,[873] which highlights why some treatments may not be universally effective – treatment success will depend upon the dominant fungal pathogen present, and whether or not it is already resistant to the anti-fungal treatment in use.

Hyperbaric oxygen therapy (HBOT) is a therapy used to saturate the body with oxygen. It has been used extensively in medicine for wound healing and dealing with a number of common infections:[834, 835, 836, 837]

> *"Hyperbaric oxygen therapy has been in medical use for half a century. Its mechanisms of action in the healing of chronic wounds include promoting neovascularization and **decreasing inflammation**. Clinical studies have demonstrated its efficacy in treating various conditions, and it is currently used for 14 different indications."*
>
> <u>*Advances in skin and wound care*</u> **2017**[834]

HBOT is shown to be effective at treating infections, even when standard anti-microbial treatments have failed:

> *'Antimicrobials and aggressive surgical procedures seem to be **ineffective** to date. Here we report a **successful treatment without antimicrobials**, only with HBO[T] and local care.'*
>
> <u>*IDCases*</u> **2016**[835]

In particular, HBOT has been shown to treat common fungal infections.[836, 837] And in line with this outcome we see that HBOT studies show a suppressive effect against cancer:[838]

> 'Mice exposed to HBO[T] showed a significant reduction in tumor volume, with no effect on body weight. ' While conventional wisdom might suggest that increased oxygenation of tumors would promote tumor growth, the results of the present study indicated otherwise.'
>
> <u>Cancer Biology and Therapy</u> **2010** [839]

Amiloride is an inhibitor of *NHE1*, which is a proton transporter within the cell that controls cellular pH levels.[917] Scientists have documented that, while the extracellular space around cancer cells is highly acidic, the intracellular pH levels are alkaline. It has been hypothesised that this change in pH is driving the Warburg effect.[917] To support this hypothesis scientists introduced the drug *Amiloride*, which inhibits NHE1. This reduces the alkalinity within the cell leading to apoptosis (programmed cell death). The use of Amiloride has led scientists to conclude that the pH of the cancer cell might be driving the disease. However, there is an alternative explanation that supports the fungal hypothesis: not only do fungal pathogens increase intracellular pH of infected cells to a more alkaline pH[831] – thus explaining why cancer cell pH is more alkaline – but it turns out that Amiloride is also a potent anti-fungal drug, and is effective at killing human fungal pathogens.[918] Again, a different interpretation of the data can be made that indicates the success of Amiloride to induce apoptosis was not necessarily due to it's ability to reduce intracellular pH, but due to it's fungal-killing properties. The pH of the cell decreased and apoptosis was instigated because the fungal pathogen, that regulates both, was killed.

Plant compounds:

All natural plant chemicals that are effective against cancer, such as curcumin (turmeric), garlic, ginger, bromelain (pineapple), sulforaphane (broccoli) and the cannabinoids found in cannabis, are strong plant antibiotic chemicals capable of killing fungi.[043, 044, 081, 082, 091–094, 101–103, 107, 110, 112, 178, 195, 197, 273]

Hormones:

Hormone Replacement Therapy (HRT) is offered to women undergoing menopause, a change which reduces estrogen and progesterone. HRT provides women with extra estrogen, to suppress menopausal symptoms. However, as estrogen stimulates fungal virulence,[023–024, 456] and cell proliferation in general, it comes as no surprise that HRT is linked to an increased risk of developing hormone-related cancers:

> *'Breast cancer was first shown to be associated with combined HRT treatment in 2003, when a large US trial found that the risk of developing breast cancer was **1.26 times higher** for women taking HRT than those who weren't. Then a UK study found a **doubled risk of breast cancer** in women taking HRT.'*
>
> <u>New Scientist</u> **2016** [387]

Abiraterone[384] and **Arimidex**[385] are interesting because both are associated with the most common cancers found in men and women, respectively. Both are hormone disrupters. Abiraterone inhibits testosterone production, while Arimidex inhibits estrogen production. When testosterone is reduced by Abiraterone, the male immune system increases in strength. Seen through the cell suppression lens, we would expect this response to be detrimental to tumour growth, because it would result in greater fungal death – as appears to be the case.[386]

Arimidex (also known as Anastrozole) is a drug designed to suppress the estrogen produced by fat cells. This is to prevent estrogen-sensitive cancers, such as breast cancer, from accessing the estrogen that fat cells produce. On the other hand, Tamoxifen specifically blocks estrogen from being absorbed into breast cells, as opposed to preventing fat cells from producing it. This is interesting because studies have shown Arimidex to be more effective than Tamoxifen at reducing the risk of breast cancer re-occurrence in women over the age of 50,[451, 452] which seems odd for several reasons: firstly, it's not just fat cells that produce estrogen, meaning that breast cancer cells will still have access to estrogen, albeit at a reduced rate, whereas Tamoxifen specifically blocks estrogen entering breast cells – from this perspective we would expect Tamoxifen to be more effective. Secondly, a side-effect of Arimidex is that it can severely suppress the immune system, which would typically aid the disease.[453, 579] And thirdly, Tamoxifen possess anti-fungal properties. It's reasonable to expect that, suppressing estrogen from fat cells alone, while impairing immune effectiveness would not provide more of a benefit than Tamoxifen, especially if a fungal pathogen is the driving mechanism. So, what other property does Arimidex possibly have that can explain why it seems to out-perform Tamoxifen in breast cancer tissue?

Arimidex is derived from the Triazole class of drugs. Triazole drugs are powerful anti-fungal drugs,[454, 455, 681] meaning that Arimidex must also be a strong anti-fungal drug, more so than Tamoxifen – the anti-fungal properties of which were an unexpected side-effect of the original drug's purpose. The powerful anti-fungal drug Itraconazole (mentioned above) is also a Triazole derivative. Although I haven't been able to locate studies that specifically test Arimidex to confirm its anti-fungal status, if true, this would certainly account for its overall effectiveness above that of Tamoxifen.

The anti-fungal nature of the majority of the drugs mentioned in this chapter appear to be at the heart of their efficacy, hence why it makes sense to use them, and consider other anti-fungal compounds when formulating a treatment strategy.

V

A SIMPLE OVERVIEW

CH 14

Development and progression of cancer: a summary

Reaching this stage of the book means that you've successfully completed the most challenging chapters; well done. The rest of the book is less demanding. While I have already covered how cancer develops by providing the evidence that supports the Cell Suppression model, I can now provide a clear overview of the disease in a short explanation condensed into this single chapter, without the need to present the evidence. In the latter half of the book I also discuss other critical details related to cancer treatment, toxin exposure, chemotherapy resistance, the conventional versus organic debate, and health as it relates to the disease, culminating in the answer to the ultimate question: can cancer be treated naturally?

Furthermore, there are some critical questions that every cancer patient should ask their oncologist after a diagnosis has been given. This essential list of questions is presented in the *Potential solutions* chapter at the end of the book. This provides a useful guide that can help you develop a strategy to tackle the disease.

For simplicity, over the following chapter I will be discussing the disease from the cell suppression perspective, as if it were correct; this allows me to talk definitively based upon this perception of the disease. To be clear, the Cell Suppression model is still theoretical, while it's based on sound science, it is not yet proven – as is the case with all mainstream cancer theories.

Cancer seen through the lens of cell suppression:

Supporting evidence indicates that a tumour is caused by a fungal pathogen that invades and suppresses specific cell functions under favourable conditions. This is an uncertain, time-consuming process due to the ongoing battle between the fungus, the immune system, and the beneficial micro-organisms that form part of our microbiome – hence why it can take years for cancer to develop. As such, there is no guarantee that fungi will take hold and cause a tumour to form; it all depends on several other factors that help facilitate fungal infection, and the strength of the immune response. Excessive toxin and antibiotic exposure, cell damage, prolonged inflammation, overproduction of lactic acid, iron release, immune suppression, nutrient deficiency, microbiome imbalance, a lack of exercise, over-consumption of glucose, and a high fungal burden, are the main factors that increase the risk of fungal infection and of a tumour forming.

In essence, when you consistently damage your inner terrain (cellular environment) and cause an imbalance in the population of micro-organisms that protect you (imbalanced microbiome), you are creating conditions that favour invasive fungal species that are already a part of your microbiome. These variables explain why cancer is so unpredictable, why it's not guaranteed to form even when the DNA mutations thought to cause the disease are present, and why almost anything from a lack of sleep to smoking is a risk factor for the disease.

Immune suppression, inflammation, iron release and excessive lactic acid exposure are the four consistent factors that facilitate the initial steps of tumour formation (carcinogenesis), because they aid fungal invasion in a variety of ways – all four are generated by all carcinogens. This consistency explains why random damage from so many different carcinogens can cause the same type of cancerous tumour regardless of the DNA damage inflicted. This consistency is the missing part of the puzzle that explains carcinogenesis and confirms that cancer is one disease generated by a number of consistent factors, not hundreds of different diseases generated by random damage that appears unrelated from one cancer cell to the next.

Cancer risk:

Micro-organisms live within us and upon our skin as part of our natural micro-organism population. This composition of bacteria and fungi is known as our microbiome. It is largely made up of beneficial bacteria, but also contains many known bacterial and fungal pathogens that are capable of causing disease under the right conditions. Up to 80% of our immune system resides within the gut, and is comprised of beneficial bacteria.

As we all have a sub-population of yeast and fungi present on and within us to varying degrees, and as we are exposed to fungal spores inhaled from the air due to exposure to dust and soil, we are all prone to developing cancer via fungal infection. A healthy body expresses minimal cell damage and inflammation while damaged cells are routinely removed through the process of programmed cell death known as *apoptosis*. Iron is kept under lock and key, preventing pathogens from accessing it, and the immune system remains strong enough to deal with any attempted infection. These natural processes reduce the risk of cancer. It is only when excessive toxin exposure is experienced, resulting in cell damage, chronic inflammation and immune weakness, as well as the release of iron and lactate, does the risk of infection and cancer increase.

The increased risk in modern times:

Non-organic food lacking in nutrition and containing pesticides as well as additives, generates a persistent state of cell damage and low-grade inflammation within the body, which places greater stress upon the immune system over time. This harmful situation is exacerbated by the harsh chemicals we apply to our skin, as well as the multitude of other chemicals found within our everyday environment.

Over-prescription of antibiotics and the antibiotics fed to factory-farmed cattle (present within non-organic meat and dairy), weakens the beneficial gut bacteria that constitute our first line of defence. Microbiome dysbiosis (imbalance) occurs because the beneficial protective bacteria are diminished allowing fungal pathogens to dominate. This encourages a disease-enabling state, where fungal dominance leads to damage of the gut lining, providing pathogens with access to the bloodstream, as well as an increased state of inflammation throughout the body. This is brought about, in part, by the myriad of fungal toxins (mycotoxins) being produced in greater quantities. Naturally, this weakens the immune response still further.

Antibiotics also affect the cell's energy system by impairing mitochondrial function,[629] this is because mitochondria are ancestrally related to bacteria. This also means that immune cells are weakened by antibiotics too, because their energy systems are also inhibited.[628] This helps to further compromise cell defences, leaving them more vulnerable to fungal attack on a more consistent basis. In this compromised state, fungal pathogens attack the first set of damaged cells they come into contact with, which are most commonly the epithelial cells that line the surface areas of our organs. This may explain why 85% of cancers form in these cells (carcinomas), these cells provide the first line of defence against invading pathogens.

In a recent study, scientists uncovered over 200 man-made toxins present within the umbilical cord blood of newborn babies, 180 of which are known carcinogens; this highlights the unprecedented exposure to harmful chemicals we currently endure (this study is presented in Chapter 15). This alarming level of toxin exposure has the same detrimental effect to that of carcinogens, only on a less potent scale; they damage cells, cause systemic inflammation, make iron and lactic acid easily accessible, and consistently weaken the immune system. A lifetime's worth of toxin accumulation stored within fat, accompanied by a decreased ability to deal with this toxic load, exacerbates these conditions when fat is broken down for fuel, which further aids fungal invasion.

This is why cancer is predominantly a disease of old age, and also why it is related to obesity. As we grow old we are less able to deal with the toxins we are exposed to. Our immune system becomes weak and the fungal burden within the body increases, fuelled by a poor diet and overconsumption of refined sugar. Populations of beneficial gut bacteria and all the protective functions of cells and organs diminish, rendering iron more easily accessible. While the body is slowly in decline and less able to protect us from fungal attack, the growth of fungal pathogens steadily increases.

The Western diet high in refined sugar has fuelled the rise in fungal populations that live within us because fungi are largely carbohydrate in their structure, and glucose is their primary food source. High sugar intake also suppresses the immune system, adding to the problem. Obesity and diabetes are known health risks for cancer because increased consumption of sugar and fat results in insulin resistance,[601] and also due to the increased fat stores present for toxins to accumulate in. Insulin resistance forces the pancreas to generate more insulin than usual, potentially leading to diabetes over time. This insulin resistance increases blood sugar levels, which helps to feed fungal populations,[602] thus increasing the risk of tumour development. Furthermore, fat cells produce estrogen, which stimulates fungal proliferation. This can explain why breast cancer is the most common cancer in women, glucose and estrogen fuel fungal growth in breast tissue more so than in any other tissue, because both are available to the pathogen and utilised for its survival.

It's easy to see why cancer risk increases when all the above is taken into account. Most of us are oblivious to our modern diet and lifestyles' negative impact upon our health. Chapters 18-20 provide some much-needed perspective, confirming why organic produce is superior to conventional food and why our lifestyles need to change.

The development of a tumour:

Toxins damage cells, leading to inflammation and hypoxia (lack of oxygen); this temporarily forces an energy switch to glycolysis because mitochondria cannot generate energy without oxygen. Glycolysis is also needed to generate an inflammatory response and aid with cell repair. This energy switch produces lactic acid, and if toxins persist, prolonged inflammation can become an issue where iron overload occurs. Cells absorb iron during bouts of inflammation, retaining it within specific proteins, such as *transferrin*. This is performed to restrict iron availability to pathogens and prevent it from becoming freely available as it can be reactive, especially with oxygen. Unfortunately, prolonged inflammation leads to the inevitable release of iron. Both iron overload and excess lactic acid, incapacitates immune cells within the vicinity of the damaged tissue, suppressing the immune response. Additionally, iron and lactic acid stimulate fungal infection – both are like rocket fuel to pathogens. This prolonged inflammation hands the advantage to opportunistic pathogens.

Sensing the fungal invasion, cells trigger *Toll-like receptors* (TLRs), that are designed to specifically alert cells, and then immune cells, to a micro-organism threat – this is why TLRs are highly stimulated in cancer. TLR activation triggers further inflammation and sustains glycolysis, because both are anti-infection responses. This leads to chronic inflammation if the pathogen is not eliminated. Inflammation also occurs within the surrounding tissue leading these cells to switch their metabolism to glycolysis, in order to combat the infection – as cells work together in a communal manner, infected cells also alert non-infected cells to the presence of the pathogen via purinergic signalling, this also triggers the

Warburg effect to occur in adjacent non-infected cells, ensuring that glycolysis is sustained.

Chronic inflammation generates histamine, which opens up the pores of cells, and under conditions of weakened immunity, this renders cells vulnerable to further infection, aiding fungal invasion to a greater degree. Particular DNA mutations can breakdown the E-cadherin protein, which would normally provide a barrier to infection; this increases the potential for infection, priming the cell for easier invasion.

This whole process occurs almost instantaneously. Viewed from a metabolic standpoint: upon detection of the impending fungal attack, mitochondria intentionally restrict the OXPHOS energy creation pathway in order to flood the cytosol (the body of the cell) with oxygen, this is an anti-infection response aimed at inhibiting the pathogens ability to synthesize RNA, DNA and proteins within the cell. This leads to a reliance upon glycolysis to generate the energy the cell needs to defend itself, and later to repair any damage caused. Such a response is designed to deplete glucose within the surrounding tissue, aimed at starving the fungus of its primary food supply. A switch to glycolysis occurs even when oxygen is available for mitochondria to use – this provides an explanation for why the *Warburg effect* occurs in cancer.

In conditions that are sufficiently toxic to favour the fungal pathogen, this glucose restriction and oxidation strategy fails, allowing cell invasion to occur. Cells continue to mount an oxidative stress response as best they can by producing free radicals en-masse, aimed at killing the fungal pathogen. This results in random DNA damage over time. In response, fungi increase their antioxidant defence and suppress mitochondria's ability to produce free radicals. Intracellular dominance is on the cards, which enables the fungus to sequester essential nutrients from within the cell, such as glucose, glutamine, arginine, pyrimidines and purines, and methionine.[831]

Methionine is required to further the progression of the infection.[831] To this end, the pathogen secretes ammonia to increase the pH within the cell, rendering it more alkaline,[831] and thus creating favourable intracellular conditions for pathogen development. This can explain the new area of study into the pH of cancer cells, where it has been found that the intracellular pH is more alkaline. Scientists are noticing a correlation between intracellular alkalinity and cancer progression, and have posited that this alkalinity is driving cancer[917] – it seems that intracellular fungal pathogens are responsible for this variation in pH.

The loss of methionine renders the cell reliant upon extracellular dietary sources of methionine, explaining why most cancer cells are methionine dependent. This loss of methionine results in *hypomethylation*, also known as *methyl-deficiency*. Poorly methylated DNA results in further random DNA damage, helping to explain why random DNA damage occurs in cancer, and why the mainstream approach of inhibiting DNA with drugs is destined to fail.

Acetyl CoA and *arginine* may be restricted by the pathogen – both are used to create the free radicals that kill pathogens. This ensures oxygen usage is reduced, and that damaging free radicals, ROS and NO (nitric oxide), are suppressed – so that cell defences are further diminished.

Through various signalling pathways, fungi over-express Bcl-2, which blocks the internal cell-death mechanism. The fungus further bolsters its dominance by gaining control of the PI3K/AKT/mTOR pathway, which stimulates cell growth and ensures that glycolysis remains the dominant energy state operating within the cell – the *Warburg effect* is sustained by the pathogen once it has established itself. Sustained use of glycolysis also blocks cell death mechanisms.

Fungi actively upregulate PD-L1 within the infected cell, which acts as a 'don't eat me' signal to the immune system. This enables the cancer cell, and the fungus, to evade immune detection. Fungi also release mycotoxins that cause further random DNA damage and incapacitates immune cells, such as T-cells and macrophages. The dectin-1 pathway is blocked, and nagalase is produced to evade immune detection and to further stifle the immune response. Incapacitated macrophages are subsequently invaded by the expanding infection, and added to the tumour mass.

With the key defensive apparatus suppressed and access to an abundance of glucose, iron, lactate, methionine and arginine, the perfect conditions are achieved for the fungal pathogen to thrive within this small niche. As glucose is its primary food source, it is in the pathogens best interests to sustain access to this food supply by keeping the cell alive. This sustained absorption of glucose by the tumour further suppresses the immune response by depleting glucose within the surrounding tissue – immune cells require glucose to function.

A diet lacking in nutrients, and a sedentary lifestyle coupled with exposure to a myriad of toxins, ensures that the immune system is constantly stressed and weakened, rendering it incapable of dealing with the opportunistic infection that is now protected within the corrosive niche of the damaged tumour tissue. Now that cell death mechanisms have been suppressed, growth receptors stimulated, and control of glycolysis established, an inflammatory proliferative state has been established – the stage is set for the abnormal growth of cells, and thus the slow growth of a tumour, where it will be noticed many years later.

Angiogenesis – development of a tumour's blood supply:

The continued use of glycolysis results in an overproduction of lactic acid a 'waste product' of the process. This promotes various growth factors such as VEGF (vascular endothelial growth factor), leading to blood vessel growth (angiogenesis). This is a natural reaction to excessive lactic acid accumulation. Over-expression of lactic acid tricks the body into thinking that cells have lost their oxygen supply; new blood vessels are grown in response. As fungi are artificially generating these conditions, lactic acid production does not stop, and neither does the growth of blood vessels. Fungi influence the production of MMP-9, which also stimulates blood vessel growth.

The varying quantity (but constant output) of lactic acid and MMP-9 from cells at different stages of suppression, means that blood vessels grow haphazardly. This is why blood vessel growth in tumours appears so disorganised. Angiogenesis helps feed cancer growth further, by increasing the supply of essential nutrients to both the cancer cell and fungal pathogens contained within them.

Invasion of local tissue:

Invasion of local tissue and metastasis (cancer spread) are the deadly aspects of the disease; when this occurs, a tumour is categorised as 'malignant'. Sustained lactic acid production damages the healthy cells surrounding the tumour, making it easier for fungi to invade and encroach upon adjacent cells. Normally, cell growth is restricted by the proximity of other cells within surrounding tissue. When different cells come into contact with each other, there are additional growth suppression mechanisms designed to prevent invasive growth.[309] For a while, this can prevent the tumour from growing into other tissues; however, constant expression of corrosive lactic acid and MMP-9 leads to damage and a loss of cell integrity. This ultimately breaks down this separate tissue barrier, and weakens the growth suppression signals that healthy cells were previously producing.

The abundance of lactic acid produced, and the chronic inflammation that develops in the surrounding tissue, encourages the pathogen to invade adjacent stromal cells such as *fibroblasts*. Prior to this, cells within the tumour signal to these surrounding fibroblast cells that an ongoing infection persists – through purinergic signaling, these non-tumour cells react to the threat of fungal invasion by switching to glycolysis in a defensive anti-fungal response, the goal of which is to deplete glucose and so prevent infection. This increases lactic acid output within the fibroblast cells surrounding the tumour, which continues to aid the pathogen and further suppress the immune response. An extracellular environment lacking in glucose, but abundant in lactic acid now exists. While fungal pathogens feed on lactic acid, the tumour cells are also forced to adapt to do the same, as lactic acid is the only food source left available to the expanding cancer cells at the periphery of the tumour mass. This lactic acid is then absorbed by the tumour itself, and converted into pyruvate to be used by the cell – this process is known as the *Reverse Warburg effect* – lactic acid is used for energy instead of it being expelled as a by product of glycolysis. Lactic acid can also be consumed by the fungus and used as fuel.

Extracellular acidity stimulates the expansive nature of the now aggressive fungal pathogen, while external cell barriers are broken down and chronic inflammation aids the invasive process. It becomes only a matter of time before the tumour expands into the surrounding tissue, aided by chronic inflammation, lactic acid and the inevitable release of iron into the damaged tissue. This corrosive environment also weakens the bonds that hold cancer cells together, such as E-cadherin, facilitating expansion into adjacent tissue, and priming cells to break away from each other.

Metastasis:

As fungi consume the vast majority of the glucose entering the cell, the cell is forced to adapt to acquire its ATP energy from other sources. This results in an increase in OXPHOS activity (mitochondrial energy creation), where glutamine, lactate, and fat are absorbed in increased quantities and converted into energy. This further helps to feed the fungus, which converts both glutamine and fat into glucose and can consume lactate directly. As glutamine availability is reduced, so too is the immune response because glutamine is also required by immune cells.[829] The sustained growth of the tumour is inevitable and unstoppable under these conditions. Killing the fungus by rebalancing the microbiome, removing toxins, restricting fuels such as glucose, glutamine and methionine, and repairing the cellular terrain, are all crucial to creating an environment hostile to the fungal pathogen, and ultimately reversing tumour growth.

If conditions do not change, chronic inflammation caused by the ever-expanding tumour draws MDSC immune repair cells (Myeloid-derived suppressor cells) to the tumour site. In an attempt to heal the chronically inflamed tissue, MDSCs deplete *arginine* from the surrounding environment because it is a protein used to repair cells. This stimulates fibroblast cells to create collagen for cell repair. Unfortunately, arginine depletion results in further immune suppression, because cancer-killing immune cells also require arginine to mount an effective immune response. Unwittingly, the attempt by MDSCs to repair this chronically inflamed environment aids tumour growth by inadvertently suppressing the immune response of cancer-killing T-cells.

Fungi also up-regulate the production of a group of enzymes called matrix metalloproteases (MMP-9) within the cell.[345, 346] These enzymes are efficient at breaking down cell walls, and they increase the stimulation of new blood vessels. Neutrophil and macrophage immune cells, along with MDSCs, also over-express MMP-9 in a unified attempt to heal the chronically inflamed cancer cells, a condition caused by the persistent presence of fungi and the toxins they produce. This combination further increases blood vessel growth and creates a corrosive environment that encourages cells to break away into the now easily accessible bloodstream. MMP-9 and lactic acid overproduction specifically render blood vessels 'leaky', enabling this process.

Up to 50% of the tumour mass can be comprised of macrophage immune cells, which are subdued by the lactic acid and iron that is released, as well as the depletion of glutamine, glucose and arginine from the tissue surrounding the tumour. This leads to the fungal pathogens invading these vulnerable macrophage immune cells. A loss of E-cadherin, which is a protein used to bind cells together, weakens cell-to-cell connections, making it more likely that a cell will detach over time and migrate into the bloodstream. This is the beginning of the process of metastasis, which is the spread of cancer to other organs.

Malignancy:

The involvement of cancer stem cells, the ability of fungi to generate glucose from fat, and access to the amino-acid arginine, play a key role in the malignancy of a tumour.

Cancer stem cells can be created by the excessive damage inflicted upon the cell by the persistent presence of a fungal pathogen. Fungal toxins, free radicals, and the lactic acid produced as a byproduct of glycolysis, inflict a critical level of damage to mitochondrial DNA over time. An inability to commit cell death results in excessive damage. When this damage reaches a certain magnitude, mitochondria can enter into a state of intense *retrograde signalling*, which is where mitochondria are influencing the DNA contained within the nucleus of the cell, the intention is to change the fate of the cell. This influence can force the cell to transition into a cancer stem cell via a process known as an *epithelial-mesenchymal transition* (EMT). An 'epithelial' cell is a regular cell, a 'mesenchymal' cell is a cell that has stem-cell-like qualities, so an EMT is the transition of a regular cell to a cell with stem cell properties. Fungal infection can lead to a reduction of *E-cadherin* and an increase in stem cell markers such as *p63* and *Vimentin*. These cell markers are commonly associated with an EMT transition, indicating that fungal pathogens can instigate the creation of stem cells. This is the point at which the tumour has become malignant (deadly). This is because cancer stem cells over-produce a protein called *CD47*, which protects them from immune attack – it acts as a 'don't eat me signal'. Stem cells can also generate an unlimited supply of cells, in this case, cancer cells, not to mention that they are resistant to most conventional treatments because they are proficient at expelling toxins. Once this transition occurs, the tumour becomes more aggressive and much more difficult to eliminate with conventional treatments – all due to the suppressive and damaging influence of intracellular fungal pathogens.

Inevitably, a cluster of cancer cells, including cancer stem cells, migrate into the bloodstream accompanied by the intracellular infection. The immune system is alerted and reacts to the fungal threat by producing galectin-3, an anti-fungal protein designed to kill fungal pathogens. For various reasons this strategy fails. This is likely due to the protection afforded to the intracellular pathogens by the cluster of circulating cancer cells, the hardy nature of the fungus, and a weakening of the immune system generally.

The sticky nature of galectin-3, now present on the surface of the migrating cluster of cancer cells, helps it to adhere to other cells within the body, enabling it to generate a new tumour in a different location, mainly stimulated by the ongoing infection. Exosomes released from the initial tumour site can also help to stimulate the growth of new cells at the distant site, and so a new tumour forms. Exosomes are small packages that contain nutrients and RNA instructions, among other things. These capsules are used by cells as a means of communication between distant cells. Cancer cells also produce exosomes allowing communication with distant cancer cells. At this point, the tumour has successfully metastasised.

By this late stage, the fungus has adapted to utilise the glyoxylate cycle, which allows it to convert fat directly into glucose. This makes the pathogen extremely hardy because it can gain the glucose it needs from several sources, even when glucose and glutamine is strategically restricted through diet, or through a drug. Additionally, the fungal pathogen feeds upon lactic acid, glutamine and arginine, while estrogen stimulates fungal proliferation.

Inevitably, the fungal pathogen depletes essential nutrients from within cancer cells. This prompts a response that forces the cell to work harder to replace these missing nutrients, culminating in upregulated receptor activity that increases the absorption of all the fuels and nutrients that feed fungal growth, particularly glucose, glutamine and arginine. This results in a weakened immune system, nutrient and protein deficiencies, and ultimately cachexia – which is described as a muscle-wasting disease; both glutamine and arginine are amino-acids essential for the creation of protein (muscle). Unless the fungal pathogen is killed, microbiome balance restored, and the immune system strengthened, the outcome will not be favourable, especially if cell-damaging and immune-weakening drugs are used, such as chemotherapy.

Cancer in a nutshell:

For the sake of simplicity, I will now summarise the entire process and why it occurs, over two paragraphs:

Carcinogens generate the conditions that favour fungal infection. Fungal invasion triggers and sustains the Warburg effect (*aerobic glycolysis* aka *aerobic fermentation*). This energy switch prevents cell death and stimulates cell proliferation. The fungal pathogen also suppresses the cell death mechanism. A tumour forms. The corrosive nature of lactic acid, produced as a byproduct of glycolysis, feeds the fungus and damages the surrounding tissue destabilising cell to cell growth restriction signalling. This acid degrades adjacent cells producing favourable conditions for fungal and tumour expansion, it also stimulates angiogenesis. Cell barriers are broken down while blood vessels become damaged and porous.

Increased numbers of immune cells are immobilised by fungal toxins, iron overload, lactic acid accumulation, and the depletion of glucose, glutamine and arginine within the surrounding tissue. It becomes only a matter of time before this corrosive environment leads to cells breaking away into the new 'leaky' blood vessels created in response to the overproduction of lactic acid. Suppressed by the pathogen, and unable to commit apoptosis, extreme damage occurs to mitochondria and DNA within the nucleus. This results in retrograde signalling and the creation of cancer stem cells as a primal survival mechanism. These cancer stem cells are invisible to the immune system, create limitless tumour growth, and are resistant to chemotherapy treatment. This continued corrosive environment, along with the increase in MMP-9 stimulated by fungi, enables cells, as well as the infection, to breakaway into the bloodstream.

The fungal pathogen is carried with the migrating cancer cells, whereupon settling within another organ, cancer stem cells form a new tumour. Cancer has spread, and this proliferative process continues, all due to the suppressive influence of intracellular fungal pathogens, and the immune system's inability to eliminate the opportunistic infection. The abnormal metabolic profile and many abnormally altered pathways activated in cancer, can be attributed to the influence of this parasitic behaviour.

Speed of tumour growth:

Some key factors that can determine the speed of tumour growth are:

1. The type and population of fungal pathogen(s) present
2. The influence of other micro-organisms
3. Conditions that favour opportunistic fungal pathogens
    * Level of inflammation
    * Level of immune weakness
    * Carcinogen/toxin/heavy metal exposure
    * Extent of emotional and physical stress
    * Lack of sleep
    * Level of exercise/physical fitness
    * A diet lacking in key nutrients
    * A diet high in sugar
    * Glucose availability
    * Access to freely available iron
    * Access to lactate
    * Access to arginine

- Estrogen levels
- Antibiotic exposure
- DNA damage that benefits infection (CDH1, APC, HER2 – causes a reduction in E-cadherin)

4. Loss of tissue cohesion
   - Lactic acid accumulation
5. Tissue growth rate
   - Angiogenesis stimulation
6. Number of cancer stem cells present
   - Level of damage inflicted upon the tumour (stimulates cancer stem cell activity to replenish lost cells)
7. Fungal use of gluconeogenesis (glutamine-to-glucose conversion)
8. Fungal use of the glyoxylate cycle (fat-to-glucose conversion)
9. The level of mitochondrial damage, which can lead to cancer stem cell creation or senescence (cell dormancy)
10. Over-stimulation of the ASS1 enzyme and subsequent production of arginine.
11. The health of the surrounding tissue and it's ability to restrict growth of the tumour as well as the growth of the tumour-associated microbiome.

A benign tumour:

Oncocytomas are rare benign tumours that occur in epithelial cells. These tumours are interesting because the reason for their benign status seems to be related to the health of their mitochondria. Interestingly, their mitochondria appear to be defective. In contradiction to the Metabolic Theory, it is this mitochondrial dysfunction that appears to render the tumour benign:

> *'Primary oncocytoma cells are **defective for respiration** [OXPHOS] and **ROS production**, are **highly glycolytic**... suggesting that loss of respiration may activate a metabolic checkpoint that limits tumour growth to **benign disease**.'*
>
> <u>*Molecular Cell*</u> *2016* [883]

According to the Metabolic Theory, defective OXPHOS (defective respiration) should result in cancer, however, this study shows that defective mitochondria result in benign, not cancerous, growths. According to the authors of the study, mitochondria need to be active in order to generate cancer, thus contradicting the Metabolic Theory. So how does this fit with the new cell suppression perspective being proposed?

Mitochondria are the workhorse of the cell, they not only provide energy by converting glucose, protein and fat into ATP, but they also create new compounds that the cell requires to function and proliferate. Glutamine and fat, for instance, can be utilised by the TCA cycle within mitochondria to produce other substances essential for cell growth. If mitochondria become defective they cannot produce the myriad of compounds that the cell needs to function and grow. This will generate nutrient shortage within the cell, which is not a beneficial outcome for intracellular pathogens that also require those same nutrients to thrive and grow. This will naturally result in greatly reduced growth for both the cell and the fungal pathogens that are present.

As these pathogens are protected within the core of the tumour they inhabit, their expansion is limited to the rate of expansion of the cells they invade. Fungal pathogens are more susceptible to the immune system if they stray outside of the protective tumour mass they inhabit.

As a result of reduced growth, due to limited access to key nutrients, a benign tumour will likely produce much less lactic acid. It is lactic acid that stimulates blood vessels, suppresses immune cells, and fuels the expansion of the infection into the surrounding tissue, because lactic acid feeds fungal virulence and can cause inflammation in adjacent cells. Inflammation aids fungal invasion of damaged cells. So, until blood vessels can be stimulated, or these pathogens can expand out into the surrounding tissue without incapacitating the mitochondria of newly infected healthy cells, a tumour will remain benign. The presence of a dysbiotic microbiome dominated by fungal pathogens within the benign tumour, explains why these tumours can turn malignant at a later date.

Defective mitochondria may not be capable of an epithelial-mesenchymal transition that can generate the cancer stem cells required for malignancy. In these instances the extreme damage caused by the invasion process may have inadvertently incapacitated mitochondria, hindering the entire cancerous process – these pathogens may have been victims of their own success.

Chemotherapy resistance:

In early diagnosis, surgery to remove the tumour is currently the preferred treatment offered by oncologists. While it can be effective, surgery will not eliminate the conditions that gave rise to the fungal threat, or address any fungal pathogens still present. The tumour initially created was the most prominent threat, but it was not the underlying problem. Cancer is classed as a systemic disease due to its ability to return even after surgery and chemotherapy. This is because the fungal threat and the lifestyle that supports it have not been addressed.

In late-stage diagnosis, when cancer has spread or is too large for surgery to be performed, chemotherapy is often the treatment of choice. Some claim that chemotherapy is beneficial because it appears to have a dramatic effect in reducing the tumour initially. While this is often the case, this result is misleading, because it hides the reality of what is occurring: chemotherapy appears to facilitate cancer progression in the long run, in part by stimulating cancer stem cells, causing systemic inflammation, iron and lactic acid release, and by weakening the immune system – the same consistent conditions caused by carcinogens.

Chemotherapy's limited success is often attributed to the DNA damage it causes by binding to DNA, but this is not entirely true. In reality, it is mainly due to the oxidative stress reaction it incites – the mass creation of free radicals the toxin generates as it damages the cell. This is an important distinction to make because it helps us to understand why chemotherapy appears to be beneficial initially, but then ultimately fails with prolonged use:

> *'**Oxidative stress** has long been implicated in cancer development and progression... **pro-oxidant** therapies [**free radical** producing therapies], including ionizing **radiation** and **chemotherapeutic agents**, are widely used in clinics.'*
>
> <u>Oxidative Medicine and Cellular Longevity</u> 2013 [389]

This is why the study below concluded that antioxidant supplements should not be provided during chemotherapy treatment, because doing so would neutralise the free radicals that chemotherapy generates:

> *'The fear is that antioxidant vitamins **may protect normal** and cancer cells against **free radicals that are generated by chemotherapy** and **radiation therapy**...'*
>
> <u>Jefferson, Myrna Brind Centre of Integrative Medicine</u> 2006 [065]

Therefore, the reduction of a tumour by chemotherapy is due to the mass production of free radicals it generates within cells, not the DNA damage it causes by binding to DNA directly. This mass creation of free radicals is a natural response produced by mitochondria when damaged by the toxin. Such abundant free radical production can damage DNA and compromise cell integrity, leading to cell death – which is the aim of chemotherapy and why it is deemed so toxic. The study above acknowledges this by advising not to prescribe antioxidants during chemotherapy treatment because doing so can neutralise the free radicals being produced, and thus, the potential damage that this process is designed to cause.

Initially, chemotherapy treatment appears effective because it produces an abundance of free radicals that kill a large proportion of the fungal pathogens residing within the tumour by stimulating a mitochondrial stress response. As approximately 98% of a tumour comprises regular cancer cells that absorb the drug, and as the initial creation of free radicals is extensive, a high proportion of fungi are killed. Subsequently, many cancer cells are once again able to commit programmed cell death (apoptosis) in the normal way, because fungi are no longer suppressing the cell death mechanisms within these cells. The tumour shrinks dramatically upon initial treatment. Chemotherapy appears effective, and so the oncologist claims a victory and provides more of the same treatment. However, this gives a false sense of efficacy for several reasons:

1. **Stem cell resistance** – Minimal free radicals are produced in cancer stem cells, making it harder to kill the fungus contained within; this is mainly because they are highly effective at expelling toxins.

2. **Increased stem cell aggression** – Chemotherapy stimulates cancer stem cell aggression. When a normal cancer cell dies, it signals the cancer stem cell of its impending fate. A new 'daughter' cell is created to replace the dying cell. So, when rapid and abundant death of regular cancer cells occur, as happens when chemotherapy is used, a huge request to replenish millions of dying cells is issued to the small number of cancer stem cells present within the tumour. Faced with the prospect of replacing an enormous quantity of dying cells in such a short space of time, cancer stem cells react by duplicating themselves to cope with the increased workload. Furthermore, the damage caused stimulates remaining cells to undergo an epithelial-mesenchymal transition (EMT) which results in the creation of new cancer stem cells to cope with the trauma caused. The result is an increase in cancer stem cell number and an increased rate at which replacement cancer cells are being created. The tumour has just become

infinitely more aggressive. Resistance to chemotherapy will shortly occur as more cancer cells are being produced by the now aggressive cancer stem cells than can be destroyed by the diminishing effects of the treatment.

3. **Fewer free radicals** – Initially, chemotherapy treatment creates a high volume of free radicals due to the damage it inflicts upon mitochondria. Unfortunately, the damage caused by the therapy incapacitates a large majority of the mitochondria that created the initial free radical burst. This inevitably reduces the number of mitochondria that can generate free radicals in the future. Therefore, further chemotherapy treatment induces less oxidative stress as an increasing number of mitochondria are incapacitated – meaning that fewer fungal-killing free radicals are created the more chemotherapy is used. The effectiveness of the treatment becomes dramatically reduced over time, due to the damaging nature of the treatment itself.

4. **Increased antioxidant defence** – Fungi are taken by surprise from the initial chemotherapy treatment, which generates large swathes of free radicals. But after the first round of treatment, the micro-organism responds by increasing its antioxidant defence in anticipation of another free radical assault. Fungi do this by increasing the production of superoxide dismutase and glutathione within their cell wall, which are natural antioxidants that neutralise incoming free radicals; essentially, fungi increase the strength of their defensive shield. The result of improved defence against a weakening free radical attack means that the effectiveness of chemotherapy is rapidly diminished over time. And there is worse to come.

5. **Weakened immune system** – Chemotherapy dramatically weakens the immune system because it is the immune system that must remove these toxic treatments from the body, and most immune cells are killed in the process. The effect of this goes without saying; fungi encounter less resistance from the immune system because the longer chemotherapy is used, the weaker the immune system becomes.

6. **Iron overload and lactate** – Chemotherapy increases the level of freely available iron and lactate due to the damage and inflammation it generates.[489] Both further suppress the immune system and have the added disadvantage of stimulating fungal pathogens to become more aggressive and invasive – lactate feeds

the pathogen while iron is essential for micro-organism proliferation. This encourages cancer to form in other areas of the body that become damaged by the treatment.

7. **Weakened microbiome defence** – As chemotherapy destroys the immune system and increases iron levels by damaging cells throughout the body, the threat of bacterial infection increases. Antibiotics are therefore supplied to the patient. Unfortunately, these antibiotics destroy the last line of defence by killing the beneficial bacteria that comprise 80% of the immune system. Rapid fungal infection ensues due to unfettered access to the bloodstream of the immune-suppressed patient. Antibiotics also damage mitochondria, which further reduces the number of free radicals that can be produced, and weakens their pathogen-fighting capabilities. Furthermore, chemotherapy itself, has even been shown to reduce the protective bacteria that normally keep fungal populations at bay.[793]

8. **Steroids feed cancer** – As chemotherapy can reduce a patient's appetite, oncologists provide steroids with a view to re-stimulating it. Steroids achieve this by increasing blood sugar levels, effectively feeding cancer in the process, and stimulating increased infection within the patient.

When chemotherapy fails to have any effect, new tumours rapidly appear in other areas of the body, normally the stomach, lungs, liver and bones; this is because all of these areas are easily accessible to fungal pathogens, and are already damaged by the treatment, laying the groundwork for fungal invasion.

As cancer generally takes between five to 10 years to grow, oncologists are confused by the sudden appearance of many other cancers in different parts of the body with prolonged chemotherapy use. Often, they conclude that there must have been other tumours that went unnoticed at the time of the original diagnosis – not taking into account that they have been using a potent carcinogen for treatment. Oncologists conclude that the tumour has developed resistance to the drug due to DNA mutations, and there is nothing more that can be done. But in reality, DNA mutations have very little to do with it; instead, chemotherapy has facilitated the onset of the disease by destroying all defence mechanisms that can combat malignant cells and fungal invasion, and by causing the damage that facilitates infection.

In some instances chemotherapy has been effective at curing cancer. This may be due to a slow-growing tumour that contains very few cancer stem cells that were caught early. Initial bouts of chemotherapy may have created enough free radicals to kill the fungi present, causing remission of the tumour or even killing the tumour completely. However, this is rare, given that chemotherapy has been shown to only benefit approximately 5% of patients with metastatic disease. While there can be some benefit to initial chemotherapy treatment due to it's ability to reduce some tumours, using chemotherapy alone and for prolonged periods seems to cause resistance and lead to a terminal diagnosis in most cases – born out by the fact that metastatic disease is often fatal, and that only 5% of patients undergoing chemotherapy treatment for metastatic disease appear to benefit.

The glutamine connection:

Glutamine is an amino acid used by the body to create protein. Its involvement in aiding cancer growth is acknowledged within the medical literature but is rarely discussed with patients or incorporated into treatment protocols:

> *'Substantial evidence exists documenting an important role for glutaminolysis and **glutamine** in cancer...Since the 1950s, it was recognized that tumours require **large amounts** of **glutamine** for **growth** and **survival**...Several decades later, it was recognized that **glutamine** is a **major energy source** in tumour cells.'*
>
> <u>ASN Neuro</u> **2018** [798]

Glutamine can aid cancer by being converted into lactate, which helps feed the fungus directly. Furthermore, excess glutamine and lactate are converted into glucose via the *gluconeogenesis* pathway, which occurs via the liver and kidneys, and within the fungus itself. So, even if a patient is limiting the amount of glucose in their diet, cancer cells (and the fungus within) can still access glucose for fuel by converting glutamine into glucose.[432]

You'd think the solution would be to block glutamine production, but glutamine is a double-edged sword; on the one hand it feeds cancer, and on the other, it supports the defence mechanisms that fight cancer. A reduction in glutamine in the rest of the body (caused by tumours monopolising it) results in immune suppression, a poorly functioning gut, and cachexia – a muscle-wasting disease. This creates a dilemma because so many beneficial functions need glutamine to fight tumour growth. What to do about glutamine is discussed in the 'Potential solutions' chapter at the end of the book.

Cachexia (weight loss):

As glutamine is used to build protein and muscle, and as tumours have been shown to absorb it at high rates,[798] cancer patients often experience cachexia;[442] categorised by excessive weight loss, or loss of muscle mass. Oncologists don't appear to know why cachexia occurs in cancer patients[445] (even though glutamine depletion explains this condition) and is detailed in the medical literature:

> *'It is caused by a combination of reduced food intake and abnormal metabolism, seemingly induced by tumour- and host-derived factors. It is **not known** precisely **how or why cancer** so frequently develops in such a way as to induce **cachexia.**'*
>
> <u>Cell Metabolism</u> 2012 [448]

Weight loss and the subsequent loss of appetite caused by chemotherapy lead doctors to supply steroids to re-stimulate appetite. Unfortunately, steroids achieve this by increasing blood glucose levels. In effect, oncologists are feeding tumour growth by supplying the fungus with the glucose it needs:

> *'...because you get sick from the chemotherapy, doctors often provide **steroids** to increase your appetite, but steroids **raise the blood sugar** fuelling the tumour cells...'* [407 [18:00]]

Worse still, steroids suppress the immune system, further aiding fungal infection.[623] By following mainstream medical advice, cancer can become stronger and more able to resist chemotherapy.[446]

Glutathione and chemotherapy resistance:

Glutamine is also used to create glutathione within mitochondria.[389] Glutathione is the body's master antioxidant. Glutathione protects cells from harm because it neutralises free radical damage, helps to remove toxins, and is used to create T-lymphocytes (T-lymphocytes are immune cells that kill cancer cells).[390, 391] A decrease in glutathione within the body results in weaker cell defences and a weaker immune response. On the flip side, as tumours contain an abundance of glutamine and, therefore, glutathione, they are protected from toxic damage and free radical attack.

This has serious implications for chemotherapy, in that it renders the treatment less effective against tumours but more damaging to healthy cells:

> *'...ionizing **radiation** and **chemotherapeutic agents**, are widely used in clinics, based on the rationale that a **further oxidative stimulus** [further creation of **free radicals**]... should cause the collapse of the antioxidant systems, leading to cell death.*
>
> *However, this latter approach has provided **unsatisfactory results** in that many primary tumours **over-express antioxidant enzymes [Glutathione]** at very high levels, leading to a **resistance of cancer cells to drug doses.'**

<u>*Oxidative Medicine and Cellular Longevity*</u> *2013* [389]

Our cells naturally resist toxic substances, so it's counter-productive to use poisons to cure disease. We should be working in unison with the body's natural defences rather than against them, because the body always reacts protectively to limit the damage inflicted. Cancer cells protect themselves in the same manner healthy cells do. The only difference is that cancer cells absorb much higher amounts of glutamine, which provides them with the ability to create more glutathione, resulting in a stronger defence against toxic substances. This is one reason why chemotherapy appears largely ineffective.

In light of this, the medical establishment believes that the solution is to reduce glutamine levels within the patient, so cancer cells can no longer use glutathione to protect themselves against toxic chemotherapy treatment. But, reducing the protection of glutathione, in general, will mean that healthy cells will have even less protection than they do now. This threatens to make chemotherapy far more toxic and damaging to healthy cells, vastly increasing the threat of organ failure, which will hamper the overall effectiveness of chemotherapy because less can be used.

Scientists working on the Metabolic Theory appear to have already solved this problem. As I previously discussed, Young Hee Ko has been testing a potential cancer drug called 3BP, which reduces glutathione levels in cancer cells, all while increasing free radical damage, making it highly effective against cancer without being as toxic to healthy cells. It is also a potent anti-fungal drug, which is likely why it is so much more effective at killing cancer cells than healthy cells. 3BP has the potential to be a cure for many cancers because early studies show that it works in the same way as chemotherapy by creating damaging free radicals, only in a more targeted manner and with far less toxicity.

It's unfortunate and concerning that the medical establishment, and key funding parties, have shown little interest in this potentially ground-breaking drug, and that Young Hee Ko has struggled to find funding for something that, in all likelihood, could benefit the majority of people with cancer.

Alternative treatments – potential dangers, effects and outcomes:

Many claim that alternative treatments fail too, and that this is proof they don't work – but this view is short-sighted and is often used to mislead. There is no human clinical trial evidence supporting natural solutions to confirm they do work, but that's the underlying problem, there is no evidence to confirm they don't work either because they haven't been tested in large-scale human clinical trials. So it seems disingenuous to dismiss alternative approaches based on a lack of evidence – there is only a lack of evidence to support or dismiss these treatments because the studies haven't been performed.

With this in mind, there are four main reasons why alternative treatments may fail a patient attempting to use a non-conventional approach:

1. Like oncologists, patients are unaware that it is a fungal pathogen causing the disease, so they are working blind. Some solutions, such as antioxidants and steroids, can actually facilitate fungal growth, but patients will use them under the false premise presented quite generally that they are always beneficial. The antioxidant dilemma was covered in Chapter 6. Regarding steroids, they increase blood glucose levels, and as we now know, cancer and fungi feed on glucose.
2. Many are also unaware of the role the energy system plays as well as the many different fuels that feed the disease – mainly due to mainstream medicine ignoring these critical details.
3. Often, a patient undertaking an alternative approach will not closely monitor known cancer markers. Without monitoring progress, patients will not know if the treatment is providing a benefit or causing harm, and may fail to adapt accordingly.
4. The public are generally unaware of how to administer treatments. Often, the approach taken is to bombard cancer from all angles by

consuming everything that is thought to be effective all at once. But, combining so many treatment protocols together can have a negative impact, by increasing toxicity or by cancelling out the effects of other drugs or treatments.[519] Furthermore, two people with the same cancer can react differently to the same treatment. These potential hazards need to be well researched and considered, but are not often understood.

Misinformation is rife, both in the alternative and conventional medical sphere, which also makes it difficult to know what to do. Many will attempt to adopt a plant-based diet, but fail to switch to consuming organic produce; conventional produce contains lower amounts of natural anti-fungal compounds, and much higher quantities of cell-damaging toxins. Patients may remove refined sugars, but will still consume carbohydrate through pasta, rice and potatoes, which can feed fungal growth when consumed regularly, and in amounts that cause glucose level 'spikes' (carbohydrate is broken down into glucose). Patients may also be unaware that the liver can create glucose via gluconeogenesis, which will continue to feed glucose to the fungus within the cancer cell, even when glucose is restricted within the diet.

Many other foods are consumed because they are thought to be beneficial, such as using vegetable oil instead of animal fat; however, most vegetable oils contain cell damaging ratios of omega-3 to omega-6. A higher ratio favouring omega-6 can cause systemic inflammation, which weakens the immune system, leads to iron release, and renders cells vulnerable to fungal invasion, thus aiding the disease. Fish is seen as healthy, but we have polluted the oceans to such a degree that toxic levels of mercury accumulate in the largest fish we consume, at levels detrimental to our health. Chicken is also seen as the healthiest meat; however, chicken has been known to harbour dangerous bacteria, which risks causing infection and weakening the immune system, at a time when a cancer patient needs to be in optimum health.

Chocolate, sweets and alcohol are consumed as little treats, but these sugary 'rewards' can undo weeks or months of progress, allowing fungi to regroup. Regular bouts of illness such as the flu or common cold will also set the patient back, and allow the fungal infection to regain a foot-hold. Antibiotics damage mitochondria and kill the beneficial bacteria that keep fungal infection at bay; these are taken without understanding the risks they pose to mitochondria and the microbiome. Consuming non-organic meat and dairy, which contain antibiotics and growth hormones, will damage the protective bacteria that live within the gut and stimulate tumour growth. Moreover, many fungal strains can likely cause cancer to form, and not all solutions will be effective at killing all species of fungi. Some may already be resistant to the limited anti-fungal drugs available.

So, without knowing what we are up against, and with all the misleading information presented in the media that predominantly champions a limited, and likely incorrect, understanding of the disease, it's difficult to stay focused and implement the most effective solutions. It would be wrong to believe that natural solutions are ineffective based solely on the public trying to treat themselves. That so many people have claimed to have survived cancer using alternative treatments, despite a lack of medical training and despite all the misinformation, indicates that alternative solutions are likely to be effective when administered correctly under the proper supervision. Naturally, there will be varying degrees of success and failure when dealing with an unseen and misunderstood foe.

CH 15

Answers to important questions

Which factors determine where cancer develops?

A combination of a weakened immune system, persistent inflammation, the level of cell damage, the amount of iron released, along with the fungal burden within the afflicted area, will determine if cancer develops. The strength and type of carcinogen and the length of exposure will determine which cells are damaged and in which area of the body tumours form. Here are a few examples:

1. **UV radiation from the sun** damages skin cells when exposed to excess. This leads to inflammation and provides the fungal pathogens already living on the skin with access to lower skin layers. Iron and lactate is released at the site of damage leading to immune suppression. Both also stimulates fungal growth, increasing the likelihood that an opportunistic infection will take hold – skin cancer is noticed many years later after a long battle with the immune system.

2. **Asbestos and smoking** damages mouth, throat and lung cells, leading to persistent inflammation. Iron and lactate are released, which feeds fungal infection and leads to immune suppression at the site of injury. Fungal spores are inhaled daily and are

stimulated by iron and the inflammation generated. Lung and upper GI tract cancers develop many years later.

3. **Alcoholic toxins** filtered by the liver induce regular bouts of inflammation and oxidative stress in liver cells. Mitochondrial impairment follows, coupled with a consistent weakening of the immune response at the site of injury. Iron and lactate levels are increased, yeast turns pathogenic, and fungal attacks increase in that tissue – liver cancer develops many years later.

4. **Endocrine disrupters,** such as BPA found in plastic, cause inflammation, hormone imbalance and suppress the immune system. With stimulation of fungal virulence by estrogen, and the ability of fungi to directly influence hormone production, fungi can generate further immune weakness and take advantage of the rise in freely available iron and lactate, given that fungal pathogens regularly populate the human reproductive tract. Successful invasion of a cell ensues, and hormone-related tumours develop many years later.

5. **Stomach irritants and Helicobacter pylori bacteria** cause persistent inflammation of the stomach lining,[054] leading to ulceration, lactate and iron release and a reduction of stomach acidity. Fungal invasion ensues aided by periods of immune suppression. Fungal invasion in this instance, can be bolstered by a mutation in the CDH1 gene, which reduces the production of E-cadherin, a protein that fungi inhibit as a means to aid in cell invasion. Stomach cancer develops many years later.

Many other factors can draw fungal pathogens to the site of injury, and then facilitate infection. These factors make it easier for them to invade cells due to the inflammation and immune suppression that inevitably occurs. This is why almost anything that can cause cell damage appears to be able to generate cancer.

Why is cancer predominantly a disease of old age?

Most cancers are diagnosed in people over the age of 65. This is thought to be due to an increased accumulation of DNA damage over time. This would seem to make sense; the longer we live, the greater the potential for DNA damage to occur, and thus the greater the likelihood that cancer will form from the accumulation of mutated DNA genes.

However, *The Cancer Genome Atlas* project has shown this to be incorrect. It highlights that cancer develops even when the mutations assumed to be responsible do not occur. In fact, the latest data shows that tumours can form with only one mutation and some with none at all, indicating that the level and type of DNA damage is unrelated to the disease. And as I will later show, cancer incidence is increasing at a higher rate in younger age groups, even though younger generations haven't had the time to accumulate the DNA damage synonymous with old age.

The more logical conclusion would be that, as we age, our immune systems become weaker, cell integrity is more easily compromised, and cell defences are less effective, due to the accumulation of toxins and cell damage that has occurred throughout our lives. While our defences are in decline, the fungal burden within us can increase, although this is dependent on our lifestyle and the health of our microbiome. Exposure to antibiotics and a diet high in refined sugar will slowly decrease our protective bacteria and increase the fungal burden, which improves the odds of successful cell invasion by opportunistic pathogens. As we age, we also tend to exercise less. Exercise has been shown to reduce cancer risk by up to 60%. This is likely due to the strengthening of the immune system, the increased number of mitochondria it generates, increased tissue oxygenation, and the depletion of excess glucose within the body, which essentially reduces the food supply of the fungus.

Weakened cell defences and increased cell damage, coupled with an increasing fungal burden, results in a greater likelihood that cancer will develop the older we become.

Why does cancer seem to run in the family?

To understand this, we need to know about our microbiome and its role in gut health. The microbiome refers to the trillions of bacteria and fungi that live on and within us, most of which are beneficial. Fungi and yeast in particular, live on our skin, in our gut, and often in our reproductive organs.

Every person's microbiome is unique: it is our micro-organism 'fingerprint'. It has only been within the last decade, or so, that technology has allowed us to study these elusive micro-organisms. We know very little about this ecosystem because up to 80% of it cannot be grown in a laboratory setting. But thanks to improved DNA sequencing, we can now catalogue many of the micro-organisms that make up our unique micro-organism population, to better understand the role they play.

Tasha Sturn took an image of her son's hand print. She placed it on a petri dish in order to culture any micro-organisms that were present. After a week, a combination of bacteria and fungi grew and were visible, providing a colourful sample of bacterial and fungal growth in the shape of her son's hand. While the vast majority of micro-organisms do not cause disease, for those that do, this reminds us that these micro-organisms are ever-present, and that their battle for supremacy occurs around the clock. Oh, and that it would be a good idea to wash our hands before breakfast, lunch and dinner. The iconic image can be found on her website *www.everythingmicro.blogspot.com.*

Unseen, these micro-organisms permeate every surface that supports life and form the backbone of our immune system. When referring to our immune system, most people think of white blood cells, which are the immune cells running around our bloodstream. But these only make up 20% of our overall immune defence. Unknown to many, our beneficial microbiome, primarily our gut bacteria, makes up the other 80%.[538] This is important to understand because the primary location where disease-causing micro-organisms gain access to our blood supply is our gut.

Bacteria within the small and large intestine control and kill pathogens that are consumed via food. In particular, *Lactobacillus* bacteria have been shown to bind to the toxins that pathogens create, protecting us from their damaging effects.[119] They are our first and most powerful line of defence against disease. Not only do they protect us from pathogens, but they protect us from the other diseases these pathogens can generate:

> *'Recent advancements in laboratory techniques have revealed functions of the human gut microbiota related to **immunity** and the **gastrointestinal, brain, and cardiovascular systems**. Research has also suggested a profound effect of the human gut microbiota on **host cells** and **genes**. This extensive interaction has suggested that the microbiome functions effectively as a **separate organ**.'*

> *'An imbalance of the gut microbiota has been linked with gastrointestinal conditions such as **reflux, peptic ulcers, irritable bowel syndrome, non-alcoholic steatohepatitis** [liver disease], and **inflammatory bowel disease**.'*[673]

The latest evidence confirms that most diseases can be traced back to the health of the trillions of bacteria living within us. This is a monumental discovery that is going to revolutionise medicine. It is also being shown that our gut bacteria produce many of the nutrients we require to live healthy lives:

> *'Gut microbiota are crucial for adequate vitamin levels in the human body. Menaquinone, folate, cobalamin, and riboflavin (ie: vitamins K, B9, and B2) are* **produced by gut microbes.** [673]

It seems that diet plays a crucial role in determining the health of our microbiome and whether we encourage a micro-organism population that is beneficial or exacerbates disease:

> *'The difference in gut microbiota composition between individuals consuming a vegan/vegetarian and an omnivorous diet is well documented...*
>
> *The available literature suggests that a* **vegetarian/vegan diet** *is effective in promoting a diverse ecosystem of* **beneficial bacteria** *to support both human gut microbiome and overall health.* [673]

A meat-heavy diet has been shown to encourage microbes that increase disease by producing harmful byproducts known as TMAO's:

> *'Trimethylamine N-Oxide [TMAO] is a microbial metabolite [microbial excretion] believed to be associated with* **cardiovascular** *and* **neurological disorders.** *Carnitine and choline are the precursors of TMAO and are primarily found in foods of* **animal origin** *(eggs, beef, pork).*
>
> *Higher TMAO levels have also been observed with* **red meat intake,** *increasing risk for* **cardiovascular disease** *and* **inflammatory bowel disease.** *Vegetarians have a* **different gut microbiota composition** *than omnivores with a diminished capacity to produce trimethylamine (TMA), the precursor to TMAO.'*
>
> **Frontiers in Nutrition 2019** [673]

A balanced microbiome, consisting mainly of beneficial bacteria, is critical to our overall health, and its composition is determined by the food we consume. And yet, doctors regularly prescribe antibiotics that kill these helpful bacteria, weakening our immune defence, and allowing fungal populations to increase and cause damage to the gut lining. This simple realisation highlights that there's something intrinsically wrong with modern medicine, in that its understanding of disease appears limited and outdated.

Sadly, this new understanding of the microbiome has yet to be adopted by the medical establishment and taught to medical doctors, who continue to prescribe antibiotics that damage our beneficial micro-flora. The over-use of antibiotics is a leading cause of leaky gut syndrome and many other gut-orientated diseases that generate further long-term health issues.

Reducing beneficial gut bacteria through the overuse of antibiotics has significant implications for our health, by reducing our ability to remove toxins from the body and create the vitamins we need. A lack of vitamins, large amounts of toxin damage and increased fungal attack will never end well. Now that we understand a little about the protective nature of the microbiome, I can discuss how this relates to cancer running in the family.

A shared microbiome:

A mother's microbiome is passed down to the baby at birth because the baby ingests the micro-flora from the mother's birth canal during the birthing process. This provides the baby with its first inoculation of protective microbes that go on to populate the gut. The problem occurs when this beneficial microbiome is weakened or replaced by pathogenic bacteria and fungi that cause disease. When an unbalanced microbiome harbours higher populations of pathogens, such as yeast, it is passed down from mother to child. This makes the infant more vulnerable to fungal attack, which only damages the gut during early development – could this explain why childhood food intolerances and autoimmune diseases are dramatically increasing?

Toxins that accumulate over time are also passed down from parent to child during pregnancy. This increases the burden on the immune system and causes inflammation, making cells easier to invade – increasing the likelihood that cancer will develop within the family line.

By not looking after our microbiome, we, as parents, are unwittingly setting our children up with weaker defences and stronger enemies because we are destroying the beneficial bacteria and encouraging the growth of fungal yeast colonies during birth. In effect, the child's life starts with a handicap that predisposes it to greater fungal infection, increased gut damage, an increased risk of developing food intolerance, and ultimately a predisposition to cancer. Unless this is reversed through the correct diet, the next generation of children will receive an even more unbalanced inoculation of dangerous cancer-causing fungi, which exacerbates the problem for their children... and so forth.

Another major factor that encourages cancer to run in the family relates to shared lifestyle and dietary habits; families generally eat the same diet and can be equally inactive. If family members follow a similar diet, for example one that is high in refined sugar, lacking in nutrients, full of toxins and additives, and that they share a similar dysbiotic microbiome burdened with opportunistic fungal pathogens, then all of them will simultaneously encourage cell damage, immune weakness, and fungal dominance. This will predispose all members to a greater risk of intracellular fungal infection and subsequently, cancer. It's worse if a family are collectively unfit because exercise helps deplete glucose stores which fungi feed upon, and increases the strength of defensive mitochondria – hence why studies into exercise show a reduction in cancer risk by up to 60%.[068, 923]

Why does cancer occur in children?

Mainstream medicine views cancer as a disease of old age, so why are children increasingly diagnosed? The answer to this, is that it's closely tied to the microbiome that children are provided with at birth, and the strength of the immune system.

We see the effect of the microbiome in determining the health of a baby delivered by caesarean section. Children born in this way haven't ingested their mother's beneficial bacteria via her birth canal. Instead, the first micro-organisms that have access to the baby's gut are dangerous pathogens found on the surface of the parent's skin. Because of this, C-section babies are more prone to develop complications and disease later on in life. This is confirmed in the study below, which highlights that our immune strength is mainly dependent upon the initial supply of good or bad micro-organisms provided to us at birth:

> '"We have shown, for the first time, that **Caesarian sections** can constitute a joint risk factor with **several immune disorders**."
>
> In the study, recently published in the journal Pediatrics, Bisgaard and colleagues examined the correlation between C-sections and immunological disorders in two million Danish children born over a period of 35 years between 1973 and 2012.
>
> "It's the biggest study I've ever seen that finds a **correlation between Caesarian delivery** and **asthma and tissue-immune disorders**".'
>
> <u>Science Nordic</u> **2014** [116]

There is a marked difference in health trajectories between the two types of delivery. Something as simple as this highlights how important the gut microbiome is, and how it can encourage disease if the wrong micro-organisms populate the GI tract.

The following study shows how we have evolved a symbiotic relationship with our microbiome, where we each rely on the other to stay healthy. For instance, some of the sugar in mother's milk is not actually intended for the baby itself, but is formulated to aid the growth of a beneficial microbiome within the gut:

> *'Raising an infant is an act of **ecosystem engineering**. You're not just caring for a baby, but an entire world.*
>
> *Right from birth, babies are colonised by **legions of microbes that set up shop in their guts**, skin, and more. **These are vital**. They help the growing human to digest its food, and to **keep harmful microbes away**. They are so important that **newborns temporarily suppress their own immune system** to give their microbial partners a chance to establish themselves.*
>
> *Mum helps too. Her **vaginal secretions** provide her child with a **starter pack of microbes**. And her **breast milk** contains **special sugars** that seem to **selectively nourish the gut bacteria** that infants need.'*
>
> <u>*National Geographic*</u> *2014* [117]

Note that the baby purposefully suppresses its own immune system for a short while to help develop these good bacteria; this immune suppression is key to understanding why childhood cancers exist. Remember, in Chapter 10 it was shown how a weakened immune system vastly increases the risk of cancer developing.

If a mother has an unbalanced microbiome, has developed a systemic fungal infection, or has given birth via caesarean section, her child will likely be born with a microbiome imbalance favouring pathogenic fungi. Not only is a baby's immune system under-developed during its early development, but when the baby is born, it suppresses its immune system to aid the development of the beneficial bacteria attempting to colonise the gut. Moreover, new born babies are often provided with a course of antibiotics at birth or early in their development, following the threat of a possible bacterial infection – naturally this enables fungal colonisation to a greater degree. If populations of fungi are present and toxins abound, this suppression of the immune system provides fungi with an opportunity to invade cells, particularly the vulnerable and active stem cells found in the bone marrow that create red and white blood cells. Within five years (the average time for cancer to form), the child is diagnosed with cancer. Is this why 'four' is the most common age for children to develop cancer and why the most common cancer types in children are leukaemias and lymphomas; cancers of the blood (red blood cells), and the immune system (white blood cells), cancers that are rare in adults?

The importance of gut health is further highlighted in a recent study undertaken by Melanie Rutkowski from the *University of Virginia*. This study found a direct relationship between a weakened gut microbiome, cancer development and the spread of the disease. An article reporting on the study states:

> *'Altering the* **microbiome***, the collection of micro-organisms that live in the gut and elsewhere, had dramatic effects in the body,* **priming the cancer to spread***.*
>
> *In this inflamed environment, tumour cells were much more able to disseminate from the tissue into the blood and to the lungs.*
>
> *Ultimately, based upon these findings, we would speculate that an* **unhealthy microbiome contributes to increased invasion** *and a* **higher incidence of metastatic disease***.'*
>
> <u>*newswise*</u> **2019** [596]

A lack of protective bacteria means that fungal pathogens are free to damage the gut lining, which allows fungi, and the toxins they produce, access to the bloodstream. The health of our microbiome is critically important and is compromised further by the ever-increasing toxins we are exposed to.

The toxic world in which we live:

To demonstrate this, a recent study of the blood of newborn babies revealed a disturbing reality – the presence of over 200 toxins, 180 of which are known carcinogens:

> *'...researchers at two major laboratories found an average of* **200 industrial chemicals** *and pollutants in umbilical cord blood from* **10 babies** *born in August and September of 2004 in U.S. hospitals.*
>
> *Among them are eight perfluorochemicals used as stain and oil repellents in fast food packaging, clothes and textiles — including the Teflon chemical PFOA... dozens of widely used brominated*

flame retardants and their toxic byproducts; and numerous pesticides.

*Of the 287 chemicals we detected in umbilical cord blood, we know that **180 cause cancer** in humans or animals, 217 are **toxic to the brain** and nervous system, and 208 cause birth defects or abnormal development in animal tests.'*

EWG 2005 [392]

This exposure to toxic substances is unprecedented in human history, let alone in newborn babies. Mixed together, these chemicals act as mild carcinogens in that they damage cells, cause systemic inflammation, iron release and immune suppression.

With this in mind, the increase in childhood cancer that we are witnessing is due to increased toxin exposure, combined with a weak microbiome passed down from mother to child, and is facilitated when the baby suppresses its own immune system for the benefit of its newly acquired microbiome. It is during this time of weakness that fungi take advantage of the inflammation present, due in large part to the myriad of toxins that babies are now exposed to:

*'C. albicans... is able to **exploit inflammation stimulated through other mechanisms to enhance its ability to colonize.'***

Current opinion in microbiology 2012 [572]

Why cancer incidence and disease in general is increasing:

With the ever-worsening Western diet, exposure to an unprecedented level of toxins and increased levels of antibiotics, each generation is being provided with a greater toxic load, less nutritious food, and an imbalanced microbiome burdened with evermore fungal pathogens. This increases the likelihood that successful fungal invasion will occur in each new generation, leading to the increase in cancer incidence we are witnessing across all age groups.

One under-reported issue relates to the level of antibiotics we are exposed to, and how this negatively affects our beneficial gut bacteria leading to an increase in fungal burden:

*'Abx treatment [**antibiotic treatment**] resulted in the overgrowth of a commensal **fungal Candida species** in the **gut** and increased plasma concentrations of prostaglandin E2 (PGE2), which induced M2 macrophage polarization in the **lung**... Thus, Abx treatment*

> *can cause **overgrowth of particular fungal species in the gut**
> and promote **M2 macrophage activation** at distant sites to
> influence systemic responses including **allergic inflammation**.'*
>
> <u>Cell Host and Microbe</u> **2014** [750]

In the study above, antibiotic use not only increased the population of fungal species within the gut, but resulted in *Candida* fungi manipulating distant macrophages, stimulating an allergic inflammatory reaction in the lungs – *Candida* were able to generate disease at a distant site within the body. This highlights that fungal pathogens can contribute to many different diseases; and that the health of the gut microbiome plays a pivotal role in our health.

The over-use of antibiotics is a critical issue, because they appear to be causing an imbalance in our microbiomes that facilitates fungal infection, and disease in general. This is important, because antibiotics also damage mitochondria leading to weakened cell defences. And as we now know, when mitochondria are damaged they may switch to glycolysis, which is the primary energy system utilised by cancer cells.

The extent to which we are exposed to antibiotics is much greater than many of us realise, and is highlighted by the latest scientific studies that have tested the world's rivers for these chemicals:

> *'In a new study that surveyed **91 rivers around the world**,
> researchers found **antibiotics** in the waters of nearly **two-thirds
> of all the sites they sampled**, from the Thames to the Mekong to
> the Tigris.*
>
> *No continent was immune: They found traces of at least one drug in
> **65 percent** of all the samples they studied.*
>
> *In the Danube, the second-longest river in Europe, the researchers
> detected **seven different types of antibiotics**. They found one—
> clarithromycin... in concentrations **four times higher than "safe"
> levels**.'*
>
> <u>National Geographic</u> **2019** [588]

Not only is this exposure contributing to increased gut damage, but it is generating a rapid increase in antibiotic-resistant bacteria, which threatens to promote other deadly illnesses.[589] When the reality of this antibiotic over-use is realised, it suddenly becomes clear why so many gut issues are arising within the population: we are destroying our protective microbiome through the consistent exposure to vast quantities of antibiotics, often without realising it. Purchasing a water filter capable of removing pesticides is a worthwhile investment, so too is switching to organic food.

Antibiotics aside, farming with toxic pesticides has also added to the cancer burden, through to the persistent inflammation that these toxins generate within the human body. These chemicals benefit fungal populations due to immune suppression and the inflammatory damage they cause to cells, resulting in the release of iron that further stimulates infection. Essentially, we are unwittingly creating a carcinogenic environment within the human body, by accumulating toxins to such a level that their collective presence is sufficient enough to facilitate fungal infection and generate tumour growth. Given the way we currently continue to pollute the world at an alarming rate, this situation can only worsen.

With this in mind, looking at the graphs below highlights the correlation between increased toxin exposure and increased cancer rates. The results are plain to see; as we changed from organic farming to farming with pesticides in the 1940s, cancer mortality rates dramatically increased:

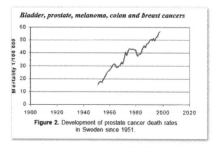

Figure 2. Development of prostate cancer death rates in Sweden since 1951.

Figure 3. Skin melanoma mortality in Sweden since 1912.

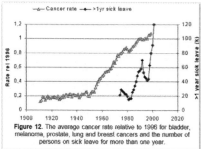

Figure 12. The average cancer rate relative to 1996 for bladder, melanoma, prostate, lung and breast cancers and the number of persons on sick leave for more than one year.

Journal of Australian College of Nutr. & Env. Medicine 2002 [142]

There have been at least 100,000 synthetic chemicals created since the early 1900s due to advancements in chemistry.[705] These toxic chemicals are present in everything from computers, toys, clothes, carpets and furniture, to cleaning products and aerosol sprays, cosmetics and, of course, food. Approximately 1,000 new chemicals are introduced each year. The above report makes for some fascinating reading. It discusses how incidences of other diseases, such as asthma and allergies, also soar around the same time, following the same trend. This indicates that fungi are at the heart of many of these diseases, aided by the toxic environment we are now unwittingly forced to endure.

Is age to blame?

Many attempt to play down the toxic nature of our environment by claiming the rise in cancer is simply due to living longer – the older we are the greater the accumulation of DNA damage. If this were true, statistics would show that the increase in cancer incidence would be associated almost entirely with the elderly, with hardly any increase in cancer incidence occurring within younger generations; however, this is not the reality. The latest statistics in the UK, which looked at age-related cancer incidence between 1993 and 2015, found that the greatest increase in cancer incidence was found to be within the youngest generations:

- 24% in the 0-24 age group
- 20% in the 25-49 age group
- 13% in the 50-69 age group
- 15% in the 70-79 age group
- 11% in the 80 and over age group.[474, 475]

In Britain, childhood cancer incidence rates increased by 38% between 1966-2000.[143] Cancer incidence is rising at a faster rate in the very young rather than in the elderly, which highlights that the disease is not simply related to lifespan. This worrying trend indicates that our diets, lifestyle and the toxins we are now exposed to, as well as the destruction of our protective microbiome, are all contributing to the rise in cancer we are witnessing – all of which have the potential to collectively benefit opportunistic fungal pathogens that are already present as part of our microbiome.

VI

NATURE TO THE RESCUE

CH 16

Food, lifestyle and cancer

'Anytime you eat or drink you are either feeding disease or fighting it.'

Heather Morgan MS, NLC

It may seem evident that nutrition is important. Yet, many of us are unaware of how unhealthy our seemingly healthy diets have become and how beneficial the correct diet and lifestyle can be, especially for preventing and healing disease. There appears to be a notable disconnect between what is *thought* to be healthy and what actually *is* healthy. It hasn't helped that we've been born into a world that feeds us the notion that we can eat whatever we like, because if something breaks down, we can just pop a pill to solve the problem. But masking symptoms with toxic drugs is not fixing the underlying issue; it's papering over the cracks.

In reality, the modern food we consume is actually causing disease, due to the dangerous combination of unseen toxic additives and its reduced nutritional content. The pills we assume are fixing the problems that result from this inadequate diet, are merely masking the damage caused and exacerbating poor health in the long run. A lifetime's worth of tissue damage caused by a poor diet cannot be reversed overnight, especially not with a pill lacking in any nutritional content, and is itself, toxic.

With this in mind, it's recognised that the Western diet, which is mainly produced using pesticides, herbicides, fungicides, fertilisers and more, is linked to a higher incidence of disease, including cancer. It's also noted that a lower incidence of cancer correlates with the consumption of organic fruit and vegetables.[209]

Professor Gerry Potter is a distinguished scientist from *De Montfort University*. Along with Professor Dan Burke, Professor Potter performed extensive studies into food compounds and discovered that certain natural plant chemicals can kill cancer cells. They called these medicinal compounds *salvestrols* and noted they were produced in organic food as a result of micro-organism infection – they are antibiotic compounds produced by plants to combat pathogens. They found that salvestrols are barely present in foods grown with pesticides, which is, unfortunately, the food that most of us now consume in Westernised societies.

The global cancer map below catalogues cancer incidence around the world. In line with the view presented by Professor Potter, it shows that cancer is a disease of affluence; it is far more prominent in modern, Westernised countries as opposed to poorer developing nations. The World Health Organization acknowledges this correlation in their global report on the disease.[113]

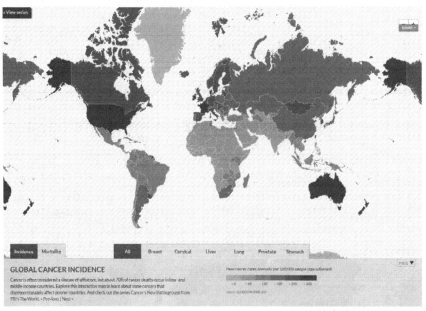

Globalcancermap.com

Cancer prevalence is clearly related to the diet and lifestyle choices we have adopted in the West. Could the reduction in Salvestrol within the food supply, explain why such geographical disparity with cancer exists?

Blue zones – National Geographic:

Significantly, Dan Buettner from *National Geographic* performed a two-year study that looked into the healthiest places on earth – areas of the planet where people lived the longest, had minimal disease and significantly reduced cancer incidence. They discovered five such areas, which they named 'blue zones'. They discovered that these zones all share very similar traits and follow a diet and lifestyle with many key commonalities. The existence of these blue zones confirms that cancer is greatly influenced by lifestyle, diet, and the surrounding environment. So, why is modern medicine failing to learn from these excellent examples? What are the beneficial factors unique to these blue zones that are often dismissed by mainstream medicine?

1. **Fresh organic food** – The consumption of highly nutritious, freshly picked and locally grown organic foods that are free of pesticides and high in anti-fungal chemicals.
2. **Predominantly plant-based diet** – Plenty of fresh vegetables, whole grains, and the correct balance of omega oils from seafood. Meat is consumed in small quantities and not very often. The meat is organic and not pumped full of growth hormone or antibiotics.
3. **No refined sugars** – Just natural sugars from fresh whole foods, such as fruit and honey.
4. **Plenty of exercise** – Whether it is Tai Chi, walking regularly, or tending to crops, these people live an active lifestyle.
5. **Fresh air** – An outdoor lifestyle with minimal pollutants and plenty of fresh air.
6. **Less mental stress, greater happiness** – These people are happier, slower pace of life. In most cases, it's more physically demanding. However, they have time for each other, have developed a great sense of community spirit and are far less mentally stressed than those of us in the West who often feel trapped and alienated by our hectic lifestyles.

The overall theme appears to be to consume nutritious organic foods, predominantly acquired locally and from plant-based sources, in combination with a lifestyle that encourages and supports a robust immune system. This approach reduces inflammation, toxins, mental stress, and promotes a good level of moderate exercise. Minimal consumption of refined sugar makes it hard for a fungal infection to take hold. These simple factors are enough to prevent the disease and are all the factors that support the *Cell Suppression* model. A life without cancer appears to be as simple as re-learning how to be healthy, not just physically but mentally too.

Consuming nutrient-deficient food that constantly generates inflammation and cell damage will only result in a weakened immune system and vulnerable cells. This will inevitably lead to increased bouts of infection and disease caused by micro-organisms that take advantage of the damage generated, and the iron released. Popping a pill will do nothing to address a lifestyle that encourages these unfavourable conditions.

The food you thought was good for you:

But aren't we healthier than we have ever been before? Although it might appear that way, sadly this isn't the case. While many claim there is no difference between conventional and organic produce, in reality, evidence confirms that conventionally grown food is less nutritious and contains higher quantities of cell-damaging toxins. So, to help dispel this myth, I will discuss why conventional food is feeding disease and why organic food fights it.

Toxins:

It is only in the last 70 years or so that the normality of eating organic has been replaced by non-organic food grown using poisons (pesticides, herbicides and fungicides). This change in agriculture started around the 1940s and has profoundly affected the quality of food we consume, to the extent that the organic produce, which has been the staple of all diets globally since time immemorial, is now seen as a fringe consumer product. The following article links to a study that lists the percentage of pesticide residues found to be present within some non-organic foods:

- 98% of oranges
- 97% of flours
- 97% of pears
- 93% of pineapples
- 91% of grapes
- 91% of apples
- 81% of dried grapes

- 76% of raspberries
- 74% of bread
- 73 % of carrots
- 70% of peppers

Natural News 2013,[123] ***Pesticide Action Network*** [477]

It is known that toxins are stored within the body and build up over time. When the body cannot remove them, they are stored in fat, only to be released once again when fat is burnt for energy. We are often assured that this accumulation of different toxins is safe, even though no studies have been performed to determine the effects of all these different toxins when combined. The UK government's expert committee on *Pesticide Residues in Food* (PriF) provides a yearly report. They found that 63.5% of fruit and vegetables sampled from the UK food chain contained pesticide residues, and 72% were found in starchy foods and grains.[463]

A recent study showed that switching from a conventional diet to consuming organic food, reduced the pesticide levels found within the human body:

> *'The consumption of an **organic diet for one week significantly reduced OP pesticide exposure in adults.**'*
>
> *Environmental Research* 2014 [144]

A lack of media exposure regarding the multitude of toxins found within everyday food, and its reduced nutrient content, has fostered apathy towards the dangers generated by modern food production. As a result, most of us are oblivious to the negative impact a seemingly healthy diet is having upon our health.

Nutrient content:

Toxins aside, there are other factors to consider, one of which is related to the nutrient levels within the food we now consume. The study below, from 2003, found that non-organic food was 35% to 80% less nutritious, and in some cases, vitamins were missing completely, when compared to organic food consumed in the 1940s. Organic food was also found to contain at least 40% more plant antibiotics – the natural medicinal compounds in plants that have been shown to kill cancer cells in countless studies.

To look at it another way, our cells receive approximately 60% less nutrition and 40% fewer plant antibiotics than would normally have been received prior to 1940. Not only that, but food now comes packaged with inflammation-causing and cell-damaging toxins, and even growth hormones that can stimulate tumour growth signals. As Dr Nasha Winters points out in her book *The Metabolic Approach to Cancer*, growth hormones are fed to cattle precisely to increase the growth of the animal for obvious reasons – the larger the animal and the quicker it reaches that larger size, the more profit that can be made. The problem, is that the consumer is also exposed to these growth hormones, which have been shown to increase tumour growth markers.[922] If you have developed an abnormal tumour growth, it's not going to be beneficial to stimulate its growth further by consuming growth hormones.

Is this why cancer incidence has increased at such a phenomenal rate since the 1940s – which is roughly when pesticide farming and other additives began to be introduced? This, coupled with a reduction in nutrient content, and we've developed a very profitable but deficient food system that is placing undue strain on the body – this is not the healthy and clean organic food that our bodies are used to, and require to function optimally. The study below confirms this worrying loss of nutrition in the conventionally grown food most of us now consume:

> '*Analysing food tables prepared by government scientists between 1951 and 1999… researchers found that **potatoes had lost 100% per cent of their vitamin A** and **57% of their vitamin C**…'*
>
> *…**potatoes appeared to have lost 47% of their copper, 45% of their iron** and **35% of their calcium** while **carrots showed even bigger declines**. Broccoli – suffered an **80% drop in copper** while calcium content was a quarter of what it had been in 1940, **a pattern repeated in tomatoes**… You would need to have eaten **10 tomatoes in 1991** to have obtained the same **copper intake as from one tomato in 1940**.*
>
> *Unlike minerals, vitamins and antioxidants are not supplied by the soil… so you cannot add them using fertilisers. They are produced by the plants themselves and are natural pest-defence compounds, part of a range of chemicals we are just beginning to understand. Studies have shown that levels are up to **40% higher in organic produce**. If you're using artificial pesticides, plants don't have to produce these protective chemicals.'*
>
> **The Guardian** 2005 [124]

This hasn't just affected vegetables, but animal produce too:

- **Beef** contained 38% less iron and 84% less copper
- **Chicken** contained 15% less potassium, 26% less phosphorous and 69% less iron
- **Turkey** 71% less calcium and 79% less iron
- **Cheddar cheese** 38% less magnesium, 35% less potassium, 33% less copper and 47% less iron.
- **Whole milk** had 21% less magnesium and 63% less iron.

Natural Health News **2015** [128]

This can explain why so many chronic and auto-immune diseases are increasing on a global scale. Without realising it, the vast majority of the population consume food that contains far fewer nutrients than were consumed in the past.

A recent study that monitored 70,000 people for seven years, found that an organic diet alone reduces the risk of cancer by 25% when compared with a similar non-organic diet:

> *'The study found **25% lower rates of cancer** diagnosis among those with the **highest organic food consumption**. The difference remained significant when the typically healthier lifestyles of organic consumers were taken into consideration in the statistical analyses.*
>
> *...this study suggests that reducing exposure to pesticides by making organic food more widely available **should be given greater attention in cancer prevention**.*
>
> *Supporting organic food and farming is also a positive response to widely held concerns about **animal welfare**, reducing resistance to antibiotics and **the climate impact** of our diets.'*

Soil Association **2018** [527]

Further supporting the organic argument, an international team of experts led by *Newcastle University* looked at the difference between organic and conventionally grown food:

> *'**Organic crops** are up to **60% higher** in a number of key antioxidants... Cadmium, which is one of only three metal contaminants along with lead and mercury for which the European Commission has set maximum permitted contamination levels in food, was found to be almost **50% lower in organic crops** than conventionally-grown ones.*

*Professor Leifert added: "The organic vs non-organic debate has rumbled on for decades now but the evidence from this study is **overwhelming** – that organic food is high in antioxidants and lower in toxic metals and pesticides".'*

Newcastle University 2015 [528]

Thankfully, major studies are beginning to recognise the dangers of pesticide farming and the need to revert to a sustainable and organic agricultural model. Unfortunately, this message is not filtering through to our authorities or into the public domain, leading many to incorrectly claim there is no difference between conventional and organic food other than the price.

Why organic is superior:

Micro-organisms, especially fungi, live within the soil. Certain fungi form a beneficial symbiotic relationship with the roots of plants and trees, helping them to absorb more nutrients. In exchange for breaking down nutrients in the soil that the plants cannot access, and providing these nutrients along with water via the plant's roots, the plant rewards fungi with its primary food source – glucose.[121] Both the plant and fungi benefit from this shared, symbiotic relationship:

*'Fungi are central to the health of terrestrial ecosystems, and they have played a foundational role in the evolution of life on land... **The symbiosis between fungi and plants plays a crucial role in protecting plants from disease and facilitating nutrient uptake**; 95% of all plant families have associated mycorrhizal fungi.'*

Genome Research 2005 [120]

Foods grown with pesticides, herbicides and fungicides have soil devoid of fungi and beneficial bacteria because these chemicals kill them. This symbiotic relationship is lost, which means that the plant no longer receives the extra nutrients that the fungus was previously providing. As a result, the mineral content of the plant is reduced. Fewer minerals mean that plants create less vitamins, generating a weaker plant, and providing the consumer with food that contains less nutritional content. The organic vs non-organic argument appears to be clear cut; organic produce is far more nutritious. And when we additionally consider plant antibiotics and soil nutrient depletion, this claim is undeniable.

Plant antibiotics:

With organic farming, plants are attacked by pathogenic fungi that live within the soil. When this happens, the plant learns the cellular composition of this invader and creates a unique anti-fungal chemical to combat it. The plant does the same for bacteria and viruses that attack it. In other words, plants make medicinal chemicals that only target disease-causing micro-organisms, leaving the beneficial micro-organisms alone. In effect, organic plants especially, are antibiotic factories. These chemicals are the vitamins, polyphenols, salvestrols and phytoalexins plants produce. They are medicinal because they benefit us when we consume them, by helping to kill the same micro-organisms that cause disease within us.

So, when we eat an organic plant containing natural anti-fungal chemicals designed to kill *Aspergillus* fungi, we flood our body with plant compounds that kill the *Aspergillus* fungi that also cause disease within us. This is demonstrated by Dr Greger when, in his book *How not to die*, he discussed how sulforaphane (the antibiotic compound found in broccoli) was found to be present in breast tissue when it was removed and analysed after surgery (this is discussed in Chapter 18).[643]

Other studies confirm that plant antibiotics, such as polyphenols, help to boost beneficial gut bacteria and encourage them to produce helpful anti-pathogenic compounds that protect us from disease-causing micro-organisms:

> '*Polyphenols*, or naturally occurring plant metabolites [*plant antibiotics*], in plant foods increase 'Bifidobacterium' and 'Lactobacillus' abundance, which provide *anti-pathogenic* and *anti-inflammatory* effects and cardiovascular protection. Common polyphenol-rich foods include fruits, seeds, vegetables, tea, cocoa products, and wine.'
>
> <u>**Frontiers in Nutrition**</u> **2019** [673]

Non-organic plants, on the other hand, are grown in soil devoid of the pathogens that would usually attack them. Without this micro-organism threat, conventionally grown plants have no need to create any form of antimicrobial defence, so they don't make the phytoalexins, salvestrols, and polyphenols (the antibiotics) that also support our immune system. This was discussed earlier in an article presented by the BBC:

> '*However, the compound [Salvestrol Q40] tends to be produced at higher levels when infection levels [of micro-organisms] among*

*crops are high. Therefore, the use of **modern pesticides** and **fungicides**, which have cut the risk of infections [in crops], have also led to a **drop in Salvestrol levels in food**.'*

BBC 2007[228]

Add to this the toxic pesticides present, and the difference is clear to see – conventional food is less nutritious, it provides fewer minerals, fewer vitamins, and fewer plant antibiotics. It also contains toxic residues that damage cells, cause inflammation, and weakens the immune system.

Soil nutrient depletion:

Furthermore, using pesticides in a continuous drive for greater profit, creates a lack of bio-diversity that damages entire ecosystems and results in over-used soil – where the nutrient density of the soil is depleted over time. The negative impact of this land abuse is compounded by the fact that less fungi are present within the ground to break down rotting plant matter to replace depleted nutrients. While farming with pesticides can provide greater yields initially, and while the food looks good in the shop window, it has reduced nutritional content. Continued use of pesticides will produce ever-weaker plants over time, because essential nutrients are continually depleted the longer the land is over-used in this way. The result of such unsustainable farming practices is that, conventional crops cannot survive without being supplemented with increasingly potent pesticides the longer the land is farmed, as they are no longer hardy enough to fend off micro-organism attack:

*'Organic systems **enhance soil composition** as well as **prevent soil erosion** due to the greater amount of plant material and biomass in the soil.*

*Compared to sustainable farming, conventional crops are **terribly inefficient** at maintaining the integrity of agricultural landscapes.'*

Stony Brook University 2019[660]

Aside from the reduced nutritional content that this land abuse leads to, the over-use of pesticides means that as micro-organisms gain resistance, the quantity of pesticides used on crops will need to increase. This means that, as time progresses, the consumer will inevitably be exposed to ever-rising levels of toxic chemicals within the food they consume.

This is likely to result in pathogenic bacteria and fungi developing resistance to pesticides, since there is a limit to the number of pesticides that can be used on plants before the food itself is considered unfit to eat. When this happens, there is the potential for the collapse of crop yields across the entire globe, because these plants have no inherent defence against the now drug-resistant micro-organisms that attack them. In fact, the medical literature is now awash with reports warning us of pesticide-, antibiotic-, and GM-resistant weeds and pathogens that threaten crop production. If ever there was a reason to support organic farming, then this is it:

> *'...according to a number of scientific reports, **super-weeds** that are **immune to Monsanto's pesticides** have **spread to millions of acres** in more than 20 states.*
>
> *...Bill Freese, a science policy analyst for the Center for Food Safety in Washington explained that "the biotech industry is taking us into a more **pesticide-dependent agriculture**... **we need to be going in the opposite direction**".'*
>
>

Forbes **2011** [624]

> *'The germs are multiplying so rapidly that the number of deaths caused by **drug-resistant infections** could outpace those caused by **cancer** in the next three decades, according to a study funded by the **British government**. More than **10 million** people worldwide could die from drug-resistant infections in 2050, surpassing the eight million projected to die from cancer.'*
>
>

Organic Consumers Association **2019** [625]

According to the latest UN report on bio-diversity, we are rapidly approaching a dangerous period regarding global agriculture, especially if we fail to switch to organic practices:

> *'The plants, animals, and micro-organisms that are the bedrock of food production **are in decline**... if these critical species are lost... it places the future of our food system under **severe threat**.'*
>
>

BBC **2019** [567]

While the general public seems oblivious to this looming threat, scientists are warning of this impending catastrophe, and that our collective health is actually in decline, not improving as we have been led to believe. We must realise the importance of organic food and switch accordingly.

Organic farming practices rely on the quality of the soil to provide plants with the nutrients that enable them to grow strong, and to fight off infection and disease. Greater care is taken of the soil, because its quality is critical to a good harvest. This increased care results in nutrient- and mineral-dense land, healthy crops, and improved bio-diversity that supports other wildlife. Organic produce is grown in soil containing micro-organisms that increase nutrient uptake, and force the plant to create natural antibiotic compounds that we utilise when they are consumed. Overall, organic farming encourages a healthy environment and ensures the quality of the soil is not depleted over time, producing healthy plants rich in nutrients, that can stand on their own two feet – so to speak.

Conversely, non-organic produce is weak food that requires toxins or synthetic antibiotics to survive, as with its reduced nutritional status it would never thrive in an organic (natural) setting. Conventional food grown using synthetic pesticides is significantly inferior.

Conventional meat and dairy:

Non-organic factory-farmed animals, which sadly provide the majority of the meat we consume, fare no better. These animals are so sickly from the poor conditions they are forced to endure, and from the genetically modified food many are fed,[574] that farmers are forced to pump them full of antibiotics to stave off disease. The danger in giving animals antibiotics as a matter of course is that we are then exposed to them within the meat and dairy products we consume. This damages our beneficial gut bacteria, which constitutes up to 80% of our entire immune defence. Furthermore, cattle are often injected with growth hormone, which risks stimulating tumour growth signals in humans when their meat and dairy produce is consumed.

Unfortunately, many people turn their nose up at organic produce because of the elevated cost, but if non-organic food is half as nutritious, then surely a consumer would need to at least double the price or eat twice as much conventional food to gain the same nutritional content, which makes organic food cheaper by comparison. This is not to mention, of course, that twice the amount of non-organic food would come with double the quantity of cell-damaging and immune-weakening toxins, growth hormones and antibiotics, creating a toxic time bomb that will only lead to ill health.

The negative impact of conventional food:

A recent UN report on worldwide toxins confirms that pesticides aren't needed to feed the growing population, which is often the central argument for their use. In fact, the report states that pesticides do not provide any benefit in this regard but are incredibly damaging to the environment and human health, with over 200,000 deaths attributed to pesticide poisoning annually. Reporting on the study, *The Guardian* ran the title *UN experts denounce 'myth' pesticides are necessary to feed the world*, and states:

> *'Chronic exposure to pesticides has been linked to **cancer**, Alzheimer's and Parkinson's diseases, hormone disruption, developmental disorders and sterility.*
>
> *"**It is a myth**", said Hilal Elver... "Using more pesticides has **nothing to do with getting rid of hunger**... Production is definitely increasing, but the problem is poverty, inequality and distribution."*
>
> *...many of the pesticides are used on commodity crops, such as palm oil and soy, not the food needed by the world's hungry people: "**The corporations are not dealing with world hunger**"...'*
>
> <u>*The Guardian*</u> **2017** [355]

In one of the most extensive studies to date, and in support of the benefits a plant-based diet can provide, the latest science confirms that rejecting meat and dairy will not only improve human health but will be the greatest single change that anyone can make to positively impact the environment, and correct the damage that the meat and dairy industry is causing to the planet:

> *'Avoiding meat and dairy products is the **single biggest way** to **reduce your environmental impact** on the planet, according to the scientists behind the **most comprehensive analysis to date** of the damage farming does to the planet.'*
>
> <u>*The Guardian*</u> **2018** [510]

While meat and dairy are essential for some communities to survive, and while I wouldn't advocate for animal products to be abolished from our diet, the over-consumption of meat and dairy we currently see globally – sourced from non-organic animals that are kept in poor conditions, are not needed to feed the world. Furthermore, animal agriculture, in its current factory-farmed form, is one of the primary causes of deforestation, ocean acidification and produces most of the CO_2 that we are pumping into the atmosphere.[510, 530, 531]

This short-term profit-led approach of creating food using pesticides, growth hormones and antibiotics, is not sustainable long-term, the consequences of which are already affecting our environment, the quality of our food, and the quality of our health.

The living longer myth:

There is an attempt to dispel the notion that disease is increasing and that population health is deteriorating by suggesting that the reason disease appears to be increasing is because we are living longer. Unfortunately, we forget that our grandparents (who we are basing this 'living longer' conclusion on) grew up in a period before genetically modified food, mass-produced synthetic chemicals, and the introduction of pesticides. Their diet consisted primarily of organically-grown, nutrient-rich foods, dense in plant antibiotics. Our grandparents were, by default, more connected to nature and exposed to far fewer synthetic chemicals.

Today, most of us are consuming less nutritious food that is devoid of plant antibiotics. Despite this difference, we attribute the old age of our grandparents alive today, to the synthetic drugs and toxic agricultural practices that we now have available. As a result, we assume our health will only get better, completely unaware that the quality of our food is in decline and that we have become perilously detached from our natural environment.

In reality, human health has peaked and is on an undeniable downward trajectory. Obesity is reaching epidemic levels, antibiotic resistance is at an all-time high, while the quality of our food is continually diminishing. Current drug solutions merely mask the ever-increasing symptoms of a poor diet and the toxins we are now exposed to.

It will be in the generations born after the 1970s that we will truly see the damaging effects of this drug- and pesticide-ridden culture. Already we are witnessing a rise in food intolerances and chronic disease on a scale never seen before in human history.

Often the blame is placed on genetics (DNA) as if the responsibility isn't ours and our health is something out of our control – 'just bad luck'. This view encourages a further reliance on drugs that inhibit damaged genes, as these are seen as the answer, rather than the nutrients that support correct DNA repair. And so, the downward spiral continues, in which we become more reliant on a failing medical system that is exacerbating the problem, by not dealing with the underlying causes.

Evolution has created extremely proficient cells that improve over time. Still, there is a point at which our repair mechanisms can no longer cope with the levels of toxins they are exposed to, especially in an environment in which nutrient quality has been diminished. We are now reaching this toxic limit. Given the study that found over 200 industrial chemicals in the umbilical cord blood of newborn babies,[392] it is evident what a perilous situation we are in. A body full of good quality organic nutrients and devoid of toxins will rarely get sick, as the blue zones of the world confirm.

CH 17

Can cancer be treated naturally?

This is a contentious issue, mainly because the big players who fund scientific research are reluctant to test natural extracts in human clinical trials, which could provide a definitive answer to the question above. No large-scale double-blind random controlled trials have been performed on humans when it comes to testing natural substances and cancer, which exposes the bias within the medical industry, where the majority of research appears associated with solutions are those that are most profitable, as opposed to the research that is most beneficial to humanity as a whole. These trials are the gold standard of testing and are needed to prove whether natural substances are effective.

The problem isn't just the reluctance to test plant chemicals in their natural state to establish their medicinal efficacy, it is the unscientific manner in which these substances are dismissed without supporting evidence to justify such claims. Cannabis is a perfect example. Scientists regularly state that 'no evidence exists' when dismissing its potential effectiveness in treating cancer. This is often said in a manner that implies that this lack of evidence proves it isn't effective. In reality, no evidence simply means that the relevant human clinical trials haven't yet been performed – meaning that cannabis could very well be effective.[422, 440]

If testing found that cannabis didn't work, there would be evidence to that effect, which would lead scientists to state 'evidence confirms that cannabis is ineffective', not that 'no evidence exists at all'. In other words, cannabis could be beneficial as a treatment, we just won't be able to scientifically confirm this until the relevant human clinical trials are undertaken – which is extremely frustrating because there doesn't appear to any interest in doing so.

This is highlighted in instances where drug trials in support of creating synthetic drug-based cannabis solutions, are funded, but similar trials for cannabis in its more natural form are not funded or do not progress to the latter stages despite showing great promise.[422]

In other words, the trials to create a profitable drug get preference over those that could prove the natural extract effective. This is particularly concerning because the latest pre-clinical studies confirm that the natural cannabis extract, which contains over 100 different cannabinoid compounds, is far more effective than the singular, isolated THC or CBD compounds that are currently being used to create synthetic drugs.[760]

Confirming this to be the case, Dr Cristina Sanchez, who has a PhD in molecular biology, presents the latest data regarding cannabis.[760] In a recent seminar Dr Sanchez summarised the evidence that confirms the whole cannabis extract is far more effective at inhibiting cancer than the THC extract alone, that is often used for synthetic preparations:

> *'...the pure THC produces this anti-tumour reaction,* **but the extract** *is* **more potent** *than the pure cannabinoid...So the take-home message is that all breast cancer subtypes are sensitive to cannabinoid anti-proliferative action and that the extract is* **more potent** *than the pure compound [THC]'.*
>
> <u>CanMed</u> **2018** [760]

When compared against Tamoxifen, the whole cannabis plant extract was shown to be as effective, without any of the side effects attributed to Tamoxifen.[760] When commenting on the potential of natural products as treatments, it would be more accurate for scientists to admit that the relevant studies have not been performed, thus helping us to draw more accurate conclusions. But to state this would be to admit that scientific investigation isn't being pursued objectively, and that would damage the reputation of medical science as a whole.

The grandfather of cannabis research:

Professor Raphael Mechoulam is known as the grandfather of cannabis research. He has been the recipient of over twenty international awards for his pioneering work on the cannabis plant, and was the first to isolate the active medicinal ingredient, 'THC'. In a recent documentary highlighting the point that medical science isn't always operating objectively, Professor Mechoulam discussed the effectiveness of the plant as medicine, the urgent need to test it in its natural form in human clinical trials, and the worrying level of disinterest to do so:

> 'Obviously, mice can be treated with cannabinoids for cancer, mice can be treated for many other diseases, but in humans the answer is **"No, it has not been tested".**'

> The Scientist 2015 [469]

The documentary also features an interview with Professor Guzman – one of Spain's leading experts on cannabinoids. When asked about cannabis in relation to cancer, he states:

> 'Classical cannabinoids [natural cannabis extracts] are the ones that **work best** at inducing **cell death in cancer cells**. Now we know that cannabinoids exert **anti-tumour activities in animals,** not only in brain tumours but in **many different types of tumours.** We also know that cannabinoids tackle not just cell death but **other processes of cancer cell growth.**'

> The Scientist 2015 [469]

Professor Mechoulam discusses a study he undertook that showed how cannabinoid extracts prevented seizures in epileptic patients, but he notes that nothing has happened 34 years after publishing the research. There has been no interest in studying this further to benefit patients.[469]

The utter lack of interest in pursuing research into the impressive natural medicinal qualities of cannabis is alarming. Why the resistance? Especially when many examples are showing its benefit within the population.

To highlight its potential in humans, in 2017, *The Mirror* reported on Deryn Blackwell, a 14-year-old boy who was fighting two cancers, one a rare form of blood cancer. After chemotherapy had placed his cancer into remission, Deryn's fourth bone marrow transplant failed to take hold, which meant his diagnosis was now terminal, as he had no immune system left to fight infection. He was given two weeks to live and placed in a hospice to see out his final days. But something incredible happened. Deryn started to recover from his terminal diagnosis. After a month, he left the hospice in good health with his bone marrow transplant successfully grafted – an impossible outcome, according to doctors. So what happened?

His mother had started to administer cannabis oil in secret to relieve his pain and suffering. The family were shocked to realise that cannabis was having such a positive effect – Deryn's mother even stopped the cannabis treatment briefly to see if it was responsible. Sure enough, when she did, Deryn's white blood cell count dropped, so she continued the treatment. Speaking to the press, Deryn's mother stated:

> *'I'm not here to say cannabis can cure cancer or is a miracle drug…*
> *But it did help Deryn and so I think we need to ask, could it help*
> *others too?'*

Mirror.co.uk 2017 [362]

This incredible story is also captured in a book written by the family, called *The boy in 7 billion*. And while cannabis may not have directly cured Deryn's cancer in this example, it was able to bring him back from the brink of death, when the medical system could do nothing more to help him.

In a recent example of the direct benefit of using cannabis oil against cancer, Lin Coxon is attempting to share her personal success with the UK government, to urge them to fund medical trials testing cannabis oil on patients. Reporting on her miraculous experience, the *Daily Record* states:

> *'…while waiting for her treatment to start in August the 69-year-old*
> *read how, in some cases, cannabis oil had been found to help treat*
> *cancer so she bought some and began taking it.*
>
> *Incredibly her last scan revealed the cancer has **completely gone**
> **from her lymph nodes** and the tumour is **hardly visible**.*
>
> *She said doctors at the hospital are **fascinated** by her case and are*
> *continuing to monitor her progress even though she isn't going*
> *ahead with the chemotherapy as they originally suggested.'*

Daily Record 2017 [437]

Dr Wai Liu, senior research fellow at St George's University of London, commented:

> *'Cannabidiol, which is just one element of the cannabis plant and*
> *one that does not have any psychoactive effect on people, has been*

shown to target communication signals that are malfunctioning in cancer cells.

*Although our data has mainly been laboratory based, we have a **growing** and **large collection of testimony from patients using cannabidiol**, usually in a cannabis oil type product, who report **positive effects** on their battle with this dreadful disease... Lin's story is one that adds to this growing list...'*

Daily Record 2017 [437]

Dee Mani was diagnosed with triple-negative breast cancer in 2017, which is deemed the deadliest form. She turned down chemotherapy and radiotherapy after losing her sister to cancer, following her choice to take the chemotherapy route. Dee started taking one drop of cannabis oil a day. According to her follow-up scan just over four months later, it was confirmed the tumour had melted away and no longer existed:

'Alongside taking the cannabis oil, I also changed my everyday diet and started meditation too.'

Metro 2018 [472]

In another case, discussing his eight-month-old patient in an online interview with the Huffington Post,[473] Dr William Courtney confirms that the child's brain cancer had disappeared within four months with cannabis treatment alone. Within eight months, the brain had fully restored itself. This is particularly important, because brain cancer is classed as incurable within conventional medicine. Regarding cannabis, Dr Courtney states:

"Currently the child is being called a miracle baby, we should be insisting this is front line therapy for all children, before they [doctors] launch off on medications that have horrific long term side effects..."

Cannabis News World 2018 [473]

Regarding the misinformation being presented in the media about the potential of cannabis he states:

*"...there's a lot of information out there that has been built up with the **intent to cause confusion...** the non-psychoactive element of the plant facilitates a lot of its benefits because it allows elevated doses."*

Cannabis News World 2018 [473]

The evidence is available, and there is every indication that it could be extremely effective as a treatment against cancer in humans. There doesn't appear to be a justifiable reason not to test cannabis in human clinical trials in its raw extract form; after all, *G.W Pharmaceuticals* have been given a licence to grow and test cannabis in the UK to produce the synthetic drug Sativex,[088, 655] as well as other synthetic cannabis-based products. It is clearly not illegal to pursue cannabis research. It seems a flawed premise that medicinal plant compounds only become medicinal when they are isolated, weakened, synthetically re-created and then packaged into a pill.

Food as medicine:

Plants survive by creating highly effective antibiotic, anti-fungal, and anti-viral chemical compounds that kill the micro-organisms that attack them. These same pathogens also attack humans. Millions of years of consuming these plants have meant we've evolved to utilise these beneficial chemicals to kill the similar set of pathogens that cause disease within us. Furthermore, the nutrients that plants provide aid in cell repair, and strengthen the immune system, making food an all-round medicinal substance.

Humans and other animals need these compounds to maintain life functions and prevent disease. Around 15 different vitamins are necessary to meet the nutritional needs of humans. In 1897, Dutch physician Christiaan Eijkman found that something in the husks of rice (the B vitamin thiamine) not present in the polished grains prevented beriberi (a disease that affects the nerves, the digestive system, and the heart). Soon after, British biochemist Frederick G. Hopkins fed a synthetic diet of fats, carbohydrates, proteins, and minerals (but no vitamins) to experimental rats. The rats showed poor growth and became ill, leading Hopkins to conclude that some 'accessory food factors' were necessary in the diet. Eijkman and Hopkins shared the 1929 Nobel Prize in physiology and medicine for their work on vitamins.

Gundula Azeez, policy manager for the *Soil Association*, highlights the importance of vitamins and antioxidants found in organically grown produce:

> *'Unlike minerals, vitamins and antioxidants are not supplied by the soil,'... They are* **produced by the plants themselves** *and are* **natural pest-defence compounds**... *Studies have shown that levels are up to* **40 per cent higher in organic produce**. *If you're*

*using **artificial pesticides, plants don't have to produce these protective chemicals.***'

The Guardian 2005 [124]

Given that all animals are colonised by trillions of micro-organisms, good and bad, it would seem that we have evolved to consume the antibiotics that organic plants create, in order to stave off the diseases caused by many of these pathogens. In fact, an exciting discovery has recently been made regarding plant extracts and cancer. Scientists have identified a mechanism by which cells convert plant compounds into medicine within humans, confirming the potential for cancer to be treated naturally.

Salvestrol and CYP1B1 – the medicine and the mechanism:

In Chapter 5, I touched on the role of salvestrols and how effective pre-clinical studies have shown them to be against a small number of cancers in humans. Salvestrols are a class of naturally-occurring substances, such as the phytoalexins, vitamins and phytonutrients, that are created by plants to defend themselves from bacterial and fungal attack.[648]

Salvestrols were discovered as a result of research being performed on an enzyme called CYP1B1. This enzyme converts chemicals into other substances that can be used by the body. As a result of this discovery, scientists are attempting to create drugs designed to exploit the function of this enzyme; for instance: prodrugs are toxic drugs being developed that can be consumed without harm. They only become toxic when they are metabolised (converted) by the CYP1B1 enzyme within the cell. This can lead to cell death, but only when these toxins are converted by this particular enzyme – the enzyme needs to be active.[649] With this in mind, there is a good reason why there is so much excitement and interest in CYP1B1 within the cancer community – it is active in all cancers:

> *'**CYP1B1** has been found to be expressed in **all cancers**, regardless of oncogenic origin [DNA origin], while being **absent from healthy tissue**. It is now widely regarded as a **universal cancer marker**.'*

Journal of Orthomolecular Medicine 2012 [648]

This is a major breakthrough because scientists have discovered an enzyme associated with cancer that can be targeted directly, meaning that a drug can be created to kill cancer cells without harming healthy cells;

this provides the potential for creating a single, all-purpose cancer drug. As a result, there has been interest in creating synthetic drugs that can exploit this CYP1B1 enzyme.

While undertaking this research, some scientists recognised that the chemical structure of the drugs being created to exploit CYP1B1, were almost identical to the structure of chemicals found naturally in certain plants and food.[649] Intrigued by this, a search was undertaken to locate them, which led Professor Gerry Potter and Professor Dan Burke to discover defensive chemicals within plants that held the same chemical structure. And when they were used on cancer cells, they were also converted by the CYP1B1 enzyme into toxic substances, leading to the death of cancer cells. They re-categorised these exciting plant compounds as *salvestrols*:

> '*This relationship between* **Salvestrols** *and* **CYP1B1** *results in a* **highly targeted, dietary rescue mechanism** *for* **killing cancer cells**... *Specifically, CYP1B1 metabolizes Salvestrols to produce a metabolite within the cancer cell that* **induces apoptosis** *[cell death].*'
>
> <u>*Journal of Orthomolecular Medicine*</u> **2012** [648]

The anti-cancer properties of resveratrol, a natural substance found in grapes and red wine, are widely known and were discussed in Chapter 7. Up until recently, the mechanism associated with this activity was unknown. Here, the following study confirms that resveratrol is converted by the CYP1B1 enzyme into a substance that specifically kills cancer cells:

> '*We report here that the* **cancer preventative** *agent* **resveratrol** *undergoes metabolism by the cytochrome P450 enzyme* **CYP1B1** *to give a metabolite which has been identified as the known anti-leukaemic agent* **piceatannol**.
>
> *This observation provides a novel explanation for the* **cancer preventative properties** *of resveratrol. It demonstrates that a* **natural dietary cancer preventative agent** *can be* **converted** *to a compound with* **known anticancer** *activity by an enzyme that is* **found in human tumours**.*'
>
> <u>*British Journal of Cancer*</u> **2002** [752]

With this discovery, science has now confirmed that plants provide medicinal substances that are converted within our cells to specifically kill diseased cells, particularly cancer cells. Scientists noted that these cancer-killing salvestrols were abundantly present within organic produce but scarce within conventional fruit and vegetables grown using pesticides.[648] This may explain why some patients have had no benefit when changing their diet – they may have been consuming non-organic food lacking in salvestrols and other anti-microbial plant compounds.

While there has been little interest in funding human clinical trials to prove whether salvestrols are effective, three small human case studies have been conducted, which confirmed salvestrols have enormous potential against many cancers. In total, 15 out of 15 cancer patients became free of their various cancers after using the salvestrol supplements supplied.[103] You would think this result would have governments and charitable institutions eager to provide the funding necessary to test salvestrols in the human clinical trials – but yet again, we see an endemic reluctance to support research into non-patentable natural compounds that offer limited profit potential.

There is a further issue. As cancer is assumed to be a result of the cell malfunctioning, this increased CYP1B1 activity in cancer, is seen as a cause of the disease rather than a reaction to it. Some assert that the CYP1B1 enzyme must be faulty and causing tumour growth, which could potentially lead to a misguided approach to treatment, where inhibiting CYP1B1 activity is viewed as a solution:

> *'CYP1B1 is known to show high frequency expression in a wide variety of cancers. These findings **suggest** that the **regulation of CYP1B1 expression** can act as a therapeutic strategy... An increasing number of CYP1B1 **inhibitors** have been developed and patented.'*
>
> **Pharmacology & Therapeutics 2017**[756]

But blocking the action of CYP1B1 with a drug is likely to have a detrimental effect, as it will prevent the salvestrols within our food from killing cancer cells.

It's heartening then, that other scientists do recognise the beneficial function of CYP1B1. The only issue is that they cannot explain why these plant nutrients kill cancer cells. Nonetheless, it is acknowledged that these plant compounds, found in many fruits and vegetables, can exploit this CYP1B1 enzyme to stop cancer in its tracks. This not only confirms the mechanism by which food can be converted into medicine within the cell, but that science now supports the concept that cancer can be treated naturally. So, when someone declares that food or diet has no beneficial or medicinal effect against cancer, you can now cite the evidence surrounding the CYP1B1 enzyme and salvestrols, in response, to help put this myth to bed.

Providing an answer?

Crucially, the question that needs to be answered is this: why is the CYP1B1 enzyme only over-expressed in cancer cells, and can the Cell Suppression model explain it? I'm sure by now that you have guessed the answer, and as you would expect, fungi appear to be at the heart of the process.

Essentially CYP1B1 is directly involved in an anti-fungal response. When fungal pathogens attack cells, the Interleukin-13 (IL-13) cell receptor triggers CYP1B1 activation, which stimulates the PPARy signalling pathway.[650] This pathway controls inflammation in response to a fungal threat. When fungal pathogens are present, the CYP1B1 enzyme is activated because it forms part of the pathway involved in a PPARy anti-fungal response:[650]

> *'...our experiments established that the interaction between **Dectin-1** and **Mannose Receptor** is important to orchestrate the host **anti-fungal defence...***
>
> *...the expression of these two receptors was increased by **IL-13** through the activation of the nuclear receptor **PPARy**, suggesting that **PPARy** could be a therapeutic target to **eliminate fungal infection**.'*
>
> <u>PLOS Pathogens</u> **2010** [651]

> *'Overall, these data demonstrate that **IL-13** or **PPARy** ligands attenuate [reduce] **C. albicans infection** of the GI tract through **PPARy activation** and hence suggest that PPARy ligands may be of therapeutic value in esophageal and GI candidiasis [**Candida infection**] in immunocompromised patients.'*
>
> <u>The Journal of Immunology</u> **2008** [755]

While these studies confirm that the activation of PPARy can be a result of a response to fungal attack, the following studies confirm that CYP1B1 forms part of this anti-fungal PPARy defence pathway:

> *'We demonstrate that LRH-1 is induced by **IL-13** via a STAT6-dependent mechanism, which in turn induces the transcriptional **activation** of CYP1A1 and **CYP1B1**, two enzymes involved in the generation of 15-HETE **PPARy ligand**. Finally, we also*

*demonstrate the importance of intact LRH-1 signalling in the **anti-inflammatory** and **anti-fungal functions** of alternatively activated macrophages [M2]...*

*...Taken together, these data provide in vivo evidence that LRH-1 is involved in the **PPARγ**-dependent **anti-fungal functions** elicited by IL-13 through CYP1A1- and **CYP1B1**-induced 15-HETE production.'*

Nature Communications 2015 [650]

As shown in the study above, CYP1B1 activation is needed to generate 15-HETE, which is required to activate the PPARy anti-fungal response. In the following study, a reduction in CYP1B1 activity caused suppression of PPARy, confirming that CYP1B1 and PPARy are linked:

*'A recent study revealed that **CYP1B1** disruption altered the expression of 560 liver genes, including **suppression** of peroxisome proliferator-activated receptor γ (**PPARγ**).'*

Pharmacology & Therapeutics 2017 [756]

In other words, the over-expression of the CYP1B1 enzyme, found to occur in all tumours, occurs as a direct response to fungal attack, which is characterised by the increase in a PPARy anti-fungal response. CYP1B1 is activated as part of an anti-fungal defence mechanism.

Coupled with the activation of *Toll-like receptors* that occurs before cancer develops – which are pathogen detection receptors – this indicates a fungal pathogen is present in all instances of the disease, and substantiates the proposition that fungi could be the underlying cause of tumour growth. It may be the interaction with a fungal pathogen that stimulates the increased CYP1B1 activity that is found to occur in **all** cancers.

Now that we know the CYP1B1 enzyme can be stimulated by fungal infection, we can at last understand why salvestrols, and other anti-fungal plant nutrients, are able to selectively kill tumour cells, through this CYP1B1 mechanism.

The CYP1B1 enzyme utilises these plant compounds by converting them to express their toxic anti-fungal nature, leading to the death of the fungal pathogen that is suppressing the cell death mechanism. In the study below the anti-fungal Salvestrol compounds react with CYP1B1 leading to cell death:

> *'Specifically, CYP1B1 **metabolizes** Salvestrols to produce a metabolite within the cancer cell that **induces apoptosis** [cell death].'*
>
> <u>*Journal of Orthomolecular Medicine*</u> *2012* [648]

This is also confirmed by resveratrol (found in red grapes), which was shown to be converted by CYP1B1 into *piceatannol* in a study mentioned earlier in this chapter. Both possess strong anti-fungal properties:

> *'Compared with resveratrol, **piceatannol** is a **more potent anticancer agent** and preferable agent with other biological activities like antioxidant activity… Both resveratrol and piceatannol are very important naturally occurring polyphenolic **stilbenes**, produced by plants in response to **fungal infection**.*
>
> *In bladder cancer, it has been reported that **piceatannol** induces **apoptosis**. Its **pro-apoptic** activity has been observed in various cancer cells.'*
>
> <u>**Blood Disorders and Transfusion**</u> **2014** [753]

> *'Here, we report for the first time the potential of resveratrol as an apoptosis inducer in the human pathogenic fungus **Candida albicans**… In summary, **resveratrol**… is a potential agent for **treating human fungal diseases**.'*
>
> <u>*Current Microbiology*</u> *2014* [754]

In fact, Professor Dan Burke, who co-discovered salvestrols and identified the interaction with the CYP1B1 enzyme, confirms that salvestrols are created by plants to specifically target fungal pathogens:

> *'Plants have a very sophisticated chemical defence system against pathogens, against insects, against microbes, but in this case **against fungi – fungal infection, blight, mould**.*
>
> *It turns out the **Salvestrol** compounds are a very important part of a plant's chemical **defence** against **fungal infection**. And a key characteristic of the Salvestrols turns out to be that they are made by the plant **primarily** in **direct response** to **fungal attack**.'*
>
> <u>*Natural Medicine World 2017*</u> [590 [38:43 – 39:30]]

This confirms the specific mechanism by which human cells appear to convert plant compounds into medicinal chemicals, and in particular, that compounds specifically designed to kill fungal pathogens are the ones that are effective at killing cancer cells. This supports the proposition that killing the fungal pathogen is potentially the solution to treating cancer.

Over millions of years our cells have evolved to utilise the antibiotic chemicals that plants create for our benefit, and have incorporated them within cell defence mechanisms that target these same pathogens; hence why we have developed the enzymes needed to use these compounds.

Unfortunately, modern living has led to a reduction in the consumption of organic foods that contain these essential medicinal plant antibiotics. Our immune systems are no longer supported by the food high in salvestrols that would typically aid in killing the fungal pathogens that cause a tumour to form. Does this explain why cancer incidence has dramatically increased since the 1940s, the same time that the Salvestrol content found in food started to dramatically decrease?

Not only does this confirm that food provides medicine, but that organic food in particular, which is naturally high in anti-fungal Salvestrol compounds, has the potential to be useful against cancer cells in a targeted, non-toxic manner. This counters the myth that cancer can't be treated naturally or that food has no medicinal benefit, and highlights the urgent need for funding to be provided to test salvestrols in the human clinical trials that matter, so that we can determine their potential as an effective treatment, as soon as humanly possible. This helps to confirm why eating a healthy balanced organic diet is so important, especially one as natural and unprocessed as possible. It would be great to be able to indulge in many of the tasty processed- and convenience-foods that are prevalent in society, and just to take a pill to fix the body when it starts to falter. Unfortunately that's not how it works. The body is a complex ecosystem that requires the correct nutrients to function optimally on countless levels. Once that complex ecosystem is compromised, a simple pill will not be able to provide that ecosystem with the nutrients it needs to repair itself and thrive.

In response to a worrying level of apathy towards the potential of salvestrols to effectively treat cancer, Professor's Gerry Potter and Dan Burke have created Salvestrol supplements, allowing patients to add them to their cancer treatment regime, and to document the results themselves.

CH 18

Plants and drugs

The drive for profit has unfortunately distorted our understanding of what constitutes medicine, by creating a culture in which profitable drugs are viewed as the answer to almost every health issue, rather than looking to the medicinal properties contained within food and plants. Listen to the news, and you'll soon realise that the words, 'medicine' and 'drug' are seen as interchangeable, completely precluding consideration of natural solutions to health. In an extension of this over the last three years, the notion of 'natural immunity' appears to have also dropped off the radar, as if it's been replaced by vaccines and drug treatments.

Drugs do have their place, and some are celebrated medicines that have greatly advanced human health. However, the promise of financial return seems to be the driving force determining which drugs are deemed 'effective', or which research is deemed 'relevant'. For instance, there are plenty of off-label drugs that show immense promise in the fight against cancer. Just ask the *Care Oncology Clinic* (COC) and Jane McLelland. The COC utilise four off-patent drugs in a protocol for cancer patients that appears to be having great success. Whereas Jane's remarkable research highlights the many off-patent drugs, and natural compounds, that can be used to target specific metabolic pathways within cancer cells, to the extent that she cured her own cancer. The problem is, that these drugs are not the focus of mainstream treatments, quite possibly because they are no longer profitable. I touch on these drugs in Chapter 13 and in the *Potential Solutions* chapter that follows. I think it's important to recognise that the treatments provided by mainstream medicine are not necessarily the most effective, that there are other options available. Furthermore, that there are vested interests who shape the course of research and treatment, the goals of which don't necessarily align with the needs of the patient. How the medical industry operates is beyond the remit of this book, but is something that the public should be aware of, if only to gain a greater understanding of the fallibilities that exist within medical science. For this reason I highlight some further resources within 'Appendix B', which provides insight into how the medical industry operates, and why 'the science' being promoted, can't always be trusted.

As investment underpins the direction of research, the medical education system has been built around the drug-based, profit-driven paradigm that has given rise to the current emphasis on drug-based solutions within conventional medicine. We all understand the concept of being nutrient deficient, but never can it be said we are drug deficient – although that seems to be the message pharmaceutical companies want us to believe. 'A pill for every ill' is a common phrase these days. This narrative strengthens the view that only synthetic drugs provide medicine, which, is a ludicrous notion when you pause to think about it – our cells are not made out of the synthetic chemicals present within drugs, furthermore, they are devoid of the nutrients that sustain life and repair cell damage.

Part of the problem is that the medical curriculum presents synthetic drugs as the primary solution to most of our ills; hence why doctors prescribe them for almost every ailment. As a result, they are misled just as much as everyone else. The public are also born into this world view; most of us see drugs as the answer to our health issues, rather than a healthy diet and lifestyle. In fact, many scoff at the idea of treating our ailments with natural products, mainly because we've been conditioned to see them as ineffective. In reality, science confirms that plants have exceptional medicinal properties, which is why up to 60% of cancer drugs on the market are currently produced from plant sources. Many are unaware, that the compounds within plants kill a plethora of disease-causing micro-organisms, not to mention they are essential for healthy cell function. Many are also unaware that drug companies extract these natural compounds to use as the basis for the synthetic drugs they intend to profit from.

One could argue that pharmaceutical companies aren't doing anything wrong. Even though they may be denying the effectiveness of natural remedies, they may genuinely feel that a successful synthetic solution can be created that mirrors the medicinal properties of these plants, and that having taken the financial risk to fund the necessary trials, these companies deserve to be financially rewarded. While I can partly understand this point of view, the unpalatable truth is that people are dying because critical information is being denied for financial gain. No amount of money can justify this approach.

So, to help dispel the myth that natural plant compounds have no beneficial effect against cancer, I present a scientific study below, using a medicinal plant we are all familiar with: aloe vera. This study is just a glimpse of what plants have to offer, and just one of many studies included within this book.

The magic of aloe vera:

The aim of the aloe vera study below was to investigate the potential for preventing cancer from forming in people who are often exposed to carcinogens in the workplace. To start with, the study acknowledges how drugs of plant origin are promising against cancer, because they possess anti-tumour properties without the toxicities associated with synthetic drugs. It states:

> *'Chemo-preventive drugs of **plant origin** are a **promising strategy** for cancer control because they are generally non-toxic or less toxic than synthetic chemo-preventive agents, and can be effective at different stages of carcinogenesis. The present investigation was undertaken to explore the antitumour **activity of topical treatment with aloe vera…'***
>
> <u>*Environmental Pathology, Toxicology and Oncology*</u> *2010* [112]

The study divided mice into four groups. In each group, the mice were given two carcinogens to generate cancer. Group 1 was assigned both carcinogens without being provided with any aloe vera, this was the 'control group' – i.e. the group used as a benchmark with which to compare the efficacy of the chosen intervention, aloe vera in this instance. The other three were given topical aloe vera gel, aloe vera orally, and the last group of mice were assigned both together. If aloe vera has no effect, then all the results should match the control group – all groups should develop cancer at the same rate. The data showed:

- *A 100% incidence of tumour development was noted in Group I, which was decreased to 50%, 60%, and 40% in Groups II, III, and IV, respectively.*

- *Also in Groups II, III, and IV, the cumulative number of papillomas was reduced significantly from 36 to 12, 15, and 11; and tumour yield from 3.6 to 1.2, 1.5, and 1.1.*

*We conclude that **aloe vera protects mice against DMBA/croton oil-induced skin papillomagenesis.'***

<u>Environmental Pathology, Toxicology and Oncology</u> 2010 [112]

While the human body may react differently, these results are astonishing as a model of potential effectiveness. In the fourth group, where both the topical gel was applied, and oral aloe vera were taken together, the number of skin tumours (papillomas) that developed were reduced by two thirds. Bear in mind that two potent carcinogens were used, yet aloe vera reduced tumours from forming by up to 60%.

Despite having the perfect conditions for a tumour to grow, cancer is finding it harder to form in the presence of aloe vera. How can this be explained? According to the study, its effectiveness is assigned to the antioxidants contained within the plant. The presumption is that these antioxidants have neutralised the free radicals that cause the DNA damage that's thought to be responsible for cancer. A reduction in free radicals would mean a reduction in DNA damage, and thus a reduction in tumour development – if DNA mutation was the underlying cause, of course.

However, the study presented in a moment confirms that aloe vera is also effective at killing cancer cells, not just preventing them from developing. This matters because it indicates that antioxidants are not the only factor at play, because antioxidants have no beneficial effect once cancer has already formed, as they can only prevent damage from occurring. Some other property of aloe vera is killing cancer cells. The following study confirms this very point: that an extract from aloe vera – labelled as 'AE' – is effective at killing cancer cells:

*'Here we report that AE... has a specific in vitro and in vivo **anti tumour activity**... The cytotoxicity mechanism consists of the induction of **apoptosis** [cell death]... AE might represent a conceptually **new lead antitumour drug**.'*

Cancer Research **2000** [111]

Considering that antioxidants cannot kill cancer once formed, how does modern medicine explain this? Well, they can't, and generally don't – instead, scientists document the changes that occur within the cell, but the reason for the reaction remains unknown.

Attempting to explain this using the DNA Theory highlights how out of touch the medical industry appears to be. If we adopt the mainstream view, we must assume the plant can specifically target the damaged DNA that scientists claim is the cause cancer. If this is true, we are forced to conclude that aloe vera must have knowledge of human DNA; through some miracle, the plant is able to create chemicals that recognise and specifically fix the random DNA damage witnessed from person to person, animal to animal and even tumour to tumour, at any given moment in time. Or else, the plant must be capable of causing the specific DNA damage required to kill cancer cells, without harming healthy cells in the same way. But to believe this is to believe in magic, because what we are suggesting here would be similar to drinking a magic potion that is miraculously able to fix whatever damage has occurred, regardless of the randomness of that damage, or affect relevant pathways, all while having no effect on the same DNA genes, or pathways, in healthy cells. How could a non-intelligent compound accurately affect only the pathways and DNA contained within cancer cells?

So, based on what is now suggested, that the potential cause of cancer is fungal in origin, we can more easily, and more logically, establish why aloe vera appears so effective and can be selective. When viewing any plant-based study, it's often the antimicrobial chemicals found within the plant that are shown to effectively kill cancer cells; it is these substances that synthetic drug manufacturers are attempting to replicate. With this in mind, it's more logical to conclude that these antimicrobial chemicals are killing the fungal pathogen responsible for controlling the cancer cell. This would perfectly explain why the same aloe vera compounds can prevent cancer from forming, and kill it once it has developed. In both cases, it acts directly upon the fungal pathogen, by providing a barrier to cell invasion, and by killing it, once the tumour has formed and the pathogen has established itself.

As I have previously discussed, plants respond to infection by creating antimicrobial chemicals, which we often refer to as the vitamins, polyphenols and salvestrols that we consume. As these human fungal pathogens are also found to be pathogens of plants,[692, 693, 694] we are provided with these anti-fungal plant compounds when we consume them. Once absorbed, they are used by cells to aid in resisting pathogen attack. This correlates with the Salvestrol and CYP1B1 enzyme discovery discussed in the previous chapter, where the mechanism that converts plant antibiotics into cancer-killing agents, was explained. So, given that tumour growth is instigated by a fungal pathogen, it is not surprising to see beneficial results against tumours when plant antimicrobial chemicals are used or consumed.

With this in mind, Dr Michael Greger wanted to know whether these effective cancer-killing plant compounds are absorbed by cancer cells when we consume them as food; do they reach the area of the body we want them to affect, do these food compounds, when ingested, directly fight cancer? Discussing the effectiveness of the compound called *sulforaphane* found within broccoli; on page 221 of his book *How Not to Die*, Dr Michael Greger refers to a study performed by *John Hopkins University*. They found that when they fed cancer patients broccoli before they were due to have surgery, and then tested the removed cancerous breast tissue, significant amounts of sulforaphane was found to be present. Regarding this, Dr Greger states:

> *'In other words we now know that the cancer-fighting nutrients in broccoli **do find their way to the right place when we swallow them.'***
>
> **<u>Michael Greger M.D. 'How Not to Die' 2015</u>** [643]

This is great news, because we can have some level of confidence that these medicinal anti-cancerous food compounds are capable of reaching their intended target when we consume them. The only dilemma is knowing how much organic food to consume, to ensure the requisite amount of these beneficial substances to have a positive effect. In 'Appendix B – Further reading' I refer to a book written by Ann Cameron, where she explains how she was able to cure her cancer by juicing and consuming a specific quantity of carrots, daily. While this is anecdotal, and may sound far-fetched, in Chapter 19 I explain why this approach was likely effective for Ann. Her book also contains many well-researched references to support the approach she took.

The protective blood of vegans:

We can see the benefits of plant compounds at work within the human body. Discussing his book *How Not to Die* at Google's headquarters in New

York City, Dr Michael Greger speaks of the latest scientific studies regarding cancer and a plant-based diet. When making a comparison with that of a meat-based diet, he states:

> *"If you drip the blood of those eating a standard American diet onto cancer cells growing in a Petri dish, the cancer growth rate is cut down by 9%. But if you put people on a plant-based diet for a year... dropping the blood on the same cancer cells produces nearly* **eight times the stopping power** *when it comes to* **suppressing cancer growth...**"*
>
> <u>**Dr. Michael Greger talking at Google**</u> [225] [11:00 – 11:50]

The study he is referring to concludes:

> *'...since there is a significant rate of recurrence following any conventional treatment for prostate cancer, our findings may encourage some patients to make changes in* **diet** *and* **lifestyle** *as an adjunct to conventional treatment in the hope of decreasing the risk of recurrence.'*
>
> <u>**The Journal of Urology**</u> **2005** [226]

Dr Greger mentions that this study was replicated in breast cancer cells, first using the blood of women while on a meat-based diet, and then using the same women's blood after being on a strict plant-based diet for just two weeks. The study found that even in such a short space of time, the same women's blood showed a significant 12% improvement in cancer growth reduction,[227] indicating that diet plays a key role.

In 2012 the non-profit organisation *Getting to Know Cancer* enlisted 180 leading cancer specialists on one of the most extensive research projects ever undertaken. These scientists were looking for a new broad-spectrum approach to cancer treatment; this collaboration was called the *Halifax Project*. This initiative was setup because scientists recognise that the tumour environment is highly complex and that current conventional treatments, which tend to target single elements within tumours, are not targeting enough of this complexity:

> *'In spite of the importance of targeted therapies now used in treatment and currently in development, it is clear that most cancers* **cannot be successfully addressed** *solely with* **single-target therapies**. *The history of cancer treatment has taught us the importance of drug resistance.'*

Seminars in Cancer Biology **2015** [759]

The Halifax Project's goal was to establish a more effective approach to treatment by uncovering agents that could target many of the hallmarks related to the disease. The resounding conclusion drawn was that natural substances worked against many aspects of cancer and have the potential to be more effective, and far less toxic, than the current synthetic treatments provided by modern medicine:

> *'**Plant-derived** compounds, **phytochemicals**, are in many cases **better tolerated** than the synthetic analogs used in cancer therapy today. Furthermore, they often exhibit **broader mechanisms of action** and sometimes **even higher affinity** against important cancer targets **compared to the synthetic alternatives.'***

Seminars in Cancer Biology **2015** [759]

Medicine's reliance on medicinal plants:

Continuing to highlight the importance of nutrition in medicine, and also that plants possess superior medicinal properties, the journal article below discusses the implications regarding the extinction of medicinal plants, and how this threatens drug discovery. It illustrates that plants possess medicinal properties, and points out how much the medical industry relies upon them to create synthetic drugs. It even highlights how much better the medicine that nature provides is – and most strikingly, it confirms that over 60% of cancer drugs in testing, or on the market today, are actually derived from plant sources:

> *'Although early drugs came from plants—**aspirin** from willow tree bark, **morphine** from poppies, **digitalis** from foxglove, penicillin from mould… natural-product experts who **continue to develop cancer drugs from plants** and other natural products insist that **nothing beats nature for finding drug leads**. They note that **more than 60% of cancer therapeutics** on the market or in testing **are natural product based.'** [213]*

Just to make sure we are clear on this point, Josh Rosenthal states:

> *'**Cancer** has a long history of **depending on natural products for drugs**… Cancer therapeutics from plants include paclitaxel, isolated from the **Pacific yew tree**; camptothecin, derived from the **Chinese** "**happy tree**," combretastatin, derived from the **South African bush willow**.' [213]*

The former director of the *National Cancer Institute's* natural products branch, Gordon Cragg, PhD, states:

> '*Nature has produced wonderfully complex molecules that **no synthetic chemist could ever dream up**... These molecules evolved over millions of years as **chemical defences** by plants, animals, and micro-organisms, enabling them **to survive attack by fungi, viruses, and other threats**. An estimated **50,000– 70,000 plant species alone** are thought to have medicinal qualities.*'

Journal of the National Cancer Institute 2008 [213]

In the example below, a tropical herb was found to be as effective as a synthetic anti-fungal drug, when tested on patients under the same conditions, but with much less toxicity:

> '*To date, **few randomized clinical trials** of **plant antimicrobials have been performed**.*
>
> *Giron et al. compared an extract of **Solanum nigrescens** [a tropical herb] with **Nystatin** [an anti-fungal drug], both given as intravaginal suppositories, in women with confirmed C. **albicans** vaginitis. **The extract proved to be as efficacious** as Nystatin.*'

Clinical Microbiology Reviews 1999 [507]

While there is a vast difference between pre-clinical (lab and animal testing) and clinical trials (testing on humans), there are numerous studies showing the efficacy of natural plant compounds in comparison to synthetic drugs, and in particular, their ability to target cancer. [043, 044, 081, 082, 084, 089, 090, 091, 092, 093, 094, 095, 097, 099, 100, 101, 102, 103, 104, 137, 139, 195, 196, 197, 198, 199, 205, 206, 229, 230, 231, 232, 233, 234, 235, 236, 238, 239, 296, 316, 327, 329, 511, 544, 604, 607, 619, 632, 633, 652]

Natural substances hold great potential with regards to combating cancer, and appear to be more effective than the current approach of synthetic drug creation that modern medicine is pursuing. One has to question why synthetic drugs are preferred over natural-based compounds that show just as much, if not more, promise.

Questionable motives:

Regarding the aloe vera study previously discussed, the intentions of the industry are laid bare. Rather than testing the plant extract to determine its effectiveness on humans in its natural form, the conclusion of the study states:

> *'...AE might represent a conceptually **new lead antitumour drug.'***
>
> <u>**Cancer Research**</u> **2000**[111]

The priority appears to be to acquire profit through synthetic drug creation. This is not an isolated incident. In almost all studies that find plant chemicals effective against cancer, the conclusion drawn is to isolate an active ingredient, disregard the natural product, and to create a synthetic version that can be sold for profit. But isolating a single chemical from a plant often weakens the original substance's effectiveness, potentially leading to an inferior drug solution, a trajectory that was highlighted by Dr Christina Sanchez in the previous chapter regarding cannabis. Plant extracts contain many different anti-microbial compounds that all work in synergy to create a more potent microbe-killing response. Using only one of these chemicals, reduces the overall potency of a medicine.

Another downside of manufactured drugs is that our cells are not familiar with synthetic chemicals and find them toxic, leading to drug resistance, which further reduces their efficacy. Highlighting this, the following study confirms three critical points:

1. Cancer stem cells are the cell type that need to be targeted
2. Chemotherapy is ineffective at killing cancer stem cells
3. Natural antibiotic chemicals found in everyday food are effective at killing cancer stem cells:

> *'Despite the development of newer diagnostic methods... breast cancer **recurrence, metastasis** and **drug resistance** are still the **major problems** for breast cancer.*
>
> *Emerging evidence suggest the existence of **cancer stem cells** (CSCs), a population of cells with the capacity to **self-renew**, differentiate and be capable of **initiating** and **sustaining tumour growth**.*
>
> *In addition, CSCs are believed to be responsible for cancer **recurrence**, anticancer drug **resistance**, and **metastasis** [cancer spread].*

*Naturally occurring compounds, mainly **phytochemicals** [plant antibiotics] have gained **immense attention** in recent times because of their wide safety profile, ability to target heterogeneous populations of cancer cells as well as **cancer stem cells**, and their key signalling pathways.*

*...we summarize our current understanding of breast CSCs and their signalling pathways, and the **phytochemicals** that affect these cells including **curcumin, resveratrol, tea polyphenols, sulforaphane, vitamin E, retinoic acid, 6-shogaol,** pterostilbene, isoliquiritigenin, celastrol, and koenimbin.*

*These phytochemicals may serve as **novel therapeutic agents** for breast cancer treatment and future **leads for drug development.'**

<u>**Seminars in Cancer Biology**</u> **2016** [273]

The food compounds highlighted in the article above were so effective at killing cancer stem cells that researchers concluded they could be used for breast cancer treatment and should be researched further. Each compound refers to the antimicrobial substances found in food, which are shown in the list below. This confirms it is the antibiotic micro-organism-killing compounds found within the plant that are the active ingredients killing cancer cells, thus highlighting the link to micro-organism involvement. Once again, the solution suggested is to create a new drug, instead of informing the public of the cancer-fighting ingredients already present within our food cupboards:

1. Curcumin: found in turmeric
2. Resveratrol: found in grapes, berries and peanuts
3. Sulforaphane and indole-3-carbinol: found in cruciferous vegetables such as broccoli
4. Genistein: found in organic soybeans
5. Quercetin: found in vegetables, fruit and grains such as capers and radish leaves
6. Shogaol: a pungent constituent of ginger
7. Isoliquiritigenin and Glabridin: found in licorice
8. Pterostilbene: found in almonds, grape leaves and blueberries.

I encourage you to read the study to learn more about each food type and how effective the study found them to be. Regarding the effectiveness of Resveratrol, it states:

'*Resveratrol is extensively studied for prevention and treatment of various diseases including cancer. The compound showed* **anticancer activity against multiple cancer types** *and inhibited cancer initiation, proliferation, metastasis as well as induced* **cancer cell death***, cell cycle arrest, and inhibited various signalling pathways.*'

Seminars in Cancer Biology 2016 [273]

This study goes on to highlight how effective these food chemicals are against cancer stem cells in pre-clinical trials:

'*We have indicated important phytochemicals such as curcumin, resveratrol, sulforaphane, and green tea polyphenols etc. that can be* **useful for targeting breast cancer cells as well as breast CSCs.** *These phytochemicals reduced cell proliferation, induces cell cycle arrest and cell death (by inducing apoptosis or autophagy)...*'

'*...***there is no question** *that the repertoire of* **anti-cancer natural compounds is high** *and we have but found* **only a handful** *of these...*'

Seminars in Cancer Biology 2016 [273]

In 2020, a study found that many natural compounds were effective against breast cancer cells:

'*A promising approach for treating* **BrCa** *[breast cancer] involves* **natural compounds***, which are chemical substances derived from living organisms. Various natural compounds* **reverse** *the effects of* **drug resistance** *and* **affect various targets***, demonstrating that they have* **therapeutic benefits.**'

Tetrandrine *[present in the Chinese herb, Stephania tetrandra] displays a preventive effect against the growth of inflammatory and breast tumour-initiating cells by* **killing these cells***... tetrandrine* **reverses drug resistance of tamoxifen.**'

HNK *[derived from the plant, Magnolia grandiflora] shows potential as an agent for* **treating BrCa***. The compound suppresses the growth of the BrCa cells and enhances the efficacy of other drugs against these cells.*'

Frontiers in Bioscience **2020** [728]

The following study sums up the situation nicely:

> '... *although we have gone to a purifying active principle mode for drug discovery [creating single isolates], nature appears to be the* **best combinatorial chemist** *and has developed excellent defensive mechanisms. There is definitely no question that* **the whole is better** *than any* **one individual part**, *and we should probably think about* **going back** *to* **developing extracts** *[of plants] as therapeutic and preventive modalities.'*

<u>Seminars in Cancer Biology</u> 2016 [273]

This review study acknowledges that plant compounds in their complexity are superior to the single isolates used in synthetic drugs. It even suggests that heading back to using plant extracts in their natural form is the direction medicine should be taking.

Acknowledgement of the science that confirms the medicinal qualities found in plants is what is lacking; the science is available, it just isn't being presented to us, or being embraced by our medical institutions, who seem intent on only pushing a synthetic drug narrative. This is extremely odd considering that Hippocrates, who is seen as the father of medicine, understood this concept more than 2000 years ago, and is often quoted as saying:

> *'Let thy food be thy medicine and thy medicine be thy food.'*

VII

AN INFORMED APPROACH

$$\text{CH} 19$$

P otential solutions – Part 1

Disclaimer:

*The information contained in the following two chapters is **not** intended to be used as personal medical advice, instruction, or for treatment, it is purely for information purposes. This information is not an advertisement to sell treatment products, nor does the author guarantee that such information will lead to a cure. Any decision to implement treatment based upon the information presented is made at your own risk. The author and publisher are not liable for any harm you may incur that results from acting upon the information presented; continuing to read this chapter and the next is your admission of full responsibility. You should not undertake any action affecting your health without consulting a qualified health professional. The author and publisher are not doctors, medically qualified or health care providers. All current cancer theories, including the DNA Theory that forms the basis of mainstream treatments, are currently **unproven**. The following information is based upon the evidence supporting the Cell Suppression model presented within this book, which concludes a common fungal pathogen, or group of fungal pathogens, are responsible for driving the disease.*

Where to start?

Researching cancer and how to treat it can be daunting, especially when considering a non-conventional approach, as there is an incredible amount of information to consider. This chapter aims to cut through all the noise and simplify this information to provide you with a clear picture of your options, and other resources that can help. The intention is to allow you to make informed decisions moving forward.

Now, some may claim that targeting fungi as a method to treat cancer is a fool's errand, because my model of cancer is currently unproven. Firstly, I should point out that my work does not indicate that you should just target fungi. Secondly, while the *Cancer Through Another Lens* event, held on the 12th February 2023, confirmed that I have written a plausible and credible theory of cancer, it does still need to be validated via relevant testing to demonstrate conclusively that particular fungal pathogens are driving the disease. However, this is does not undermine my hypothesis – far from it. This is the natural course of validation that every theory is required to undertake. To put this in context, all current mainstream theories are in the same boat: like my proposition, they are all currently unproven, including the DNA Theory that forms the basis of current mainstream treatments. The important point of note, is that the accuracy of each theory varies substantially: my metric for this assessment is the number of hallmarks of cancer that each theory is required to explain. This needs to be taken into account when deciding on a treatment path to take, because the rationale behind each treatment is based upon the evidence that supports any given theory.

This is a crucial point to appreciate. For instance, the DNA Theory forms the basis for the vast majority of mainstream cancer treatments that most conventional oncologists have to offer, because the dominant view of cancer in mainstream medical circles, is that cancer is a genetic disease. Metabolic therapies, which are slowly being adopted into the mainstream, are based upon the concepts put forward by, and evidence supporting, the Metabolic Theory – within this theory cancer is considered a metabolic disease, so targeting energy pathways is key. The Cancer Stem Cell Theory highlights the need to target cancer stem cells, but by and large, the mainstream chemotherapy treatments that are based upon the DNA Theory, do not target these cancer stem cells. As far as I am aware no conventional oncologists supportive of the DNA Theory, is in the habit of also offering Metabolic or Stem cell therapies.

Put simply, the effectiveness of any treatment that you choose to undertake, in all likelihood, will depend upon the relative accuracy of the cancer theory that underpins that treatment. To that end – while some may contend the analysis I have performed – evidence indicates that the DNA Theory can only account for two of the 10 Hanahan and Weinberg

Hallmarks of cancer. By this same measure, the Metabolic Theory can account for at least seven. Significantly, and worthy of consideration, is that the Cell Suppression model I have put forward, can, at present, account for all 10 Hallmarks and is the first model of cancer to do so. Furthermore, an additional 20 conditions that mainstream theories are struggling to account for, are also explained. This indicates that, while all theories still need to be validated, the Cell Suppression model is the most accurate when assessed against the Hallmarks of cancer, as well as other conditions associated with the disease.

At present then, it appears as though the treatments that are provided by mainstream medicine are based upon the least accurate of these theories, which may explain why conventional treatments are largely ineffective and no cure has been forthcoming.

Based on this analysis, it would be fair to conclude that adopting a treatment approach in line with the conclusions drawn from the proposed Cell Suppression model, is likely to be more effective than the limited treatments offered by a mainstream theory that appears to have misinterpreted the origin of the disease, and the mechanisms that drive it. Worthy of note, is that the Metabolic and Stem Cell theories of cancer, are also recognised by, and form part of, the Cell Suppression model – treatments that target cancer stem cells, and cancer cell metabolism, are considered of prime importance. Incidentally, most metabolic treatments are also anti-fungal in nature, while many factors that target cancer stem cells, are again, anti-fungal in nature, indicating that all roads to the development of cancer lead back to the influence of opportunistic fungal pathogens.

With all this talk of fungi driving the disease, I must stress an important point. It would be dangerous to jump to the conclusion that all that is needed to treat cancer is a course of anti-fungal drugs. While targeting fungal pathogens is crucial in my opinion, I do not advocate for the sole use of anti-fungal drugs to treat the disease, because they can be extremely toxic. Incorrect use of anti-fungal treatment may have an adverse effect. The health status of the patient, and the use of any other medications, need to be taken into account. Not all fungal pathogens are effectively killed by the anti-fungal drugs currently in use, furthermore, resistance to these drugs is an emerging problem. There is a level of complexity to cancer, as well as the treatment of fungal infections, that needs to be understood in order to enable safe and effective use of these toxic treatments. Once established, fungi are incredibly difficult to treat, moreover, the specific fungal pathogens that are possibly responsible for driving the disease, are not yet known.

The essential first steps:

The first step in tackling your diagnosis is to understand the type of cancer you have and it's stage of progression. From here you'll gain a general understanding of your options and your survival outcome in relation to the treatments offered by mainstream medicine. If your diagnosis is unfavourable there are still sound reasons to remain hopeful. Remember that, a conventional diagnosis is based upon an unproven theory that seems to misinterpret the underlying mechanisms that drive the disease, and can only offer limited treatments associated with that limited interpretation. As I've previously discussed, there are many who have survived a terminal diagnosis by adopting a non-conventional approach, even after conventional treatments have failed. This is not to say that conventional treatments are uniformly ineffective – surgery can be very effective when applicable, and some drugs have a good survival profile; the key is to keep an open mind, and do your own independent research.

Once you understand the type of cancer you have and its level of progression, you may wish to research, or contact others, who have survived the same disease to gain insight into the approaches they took. This may highlight an effective treatment strategy; you may uncover a correlation with certain drugs, or lifestyle approaches, that seem to provide a benefit. Others may find this prospect simply too daunting and may prefer to seek out expert help from practitioners with a good understanding of cell suppression and metabolic mechanisms – the *Yes To Life* cancer charity are setup to aid patients with locating the required resources. Even for those who choose to do their own research, since cancer is such a complex disease, validation of your study material and the conclusions you've drawn, by an expert, is always highly advisable.

Focusing on a solution is a good start – but to truly defeat any disease, and tailor treatments for the greatest effect, it's essential to understand the underlying cause of the disease itself. If we don't know what's driving it how can we be sure we are targeting the correct mechanism? It makes sense then, to study the leading cancer theories currently available, paying particular attention to the one that seems the most accurate. The more accurate the theory, the greater the likelihood that the underlying cause of the disease is being targeted, and that treatments associated with it will have the greatest effect.

And as I mentioned a moment ago, the new perspective of cancer presented within this book shows promise, as it appears to provide the most accurate account of cancer to date. Furthermore, this new model also incorporates the Metabolic Theory and key aspects of the Cancer Stem cell Theory within it, both of which are the next two most accurate theories respectively. While it must be kept in mind that the Cell Suppression model has yet to be proven through any form of trial, those without the luxury of the time to wait for the results of studies, may want to consider ways in which they can safely address the reasonable possibility of its accuracy. In a nutshell, a degree of confidence can be drawn from an approach that includes targeting relevant fungal pathogens, associated energy pathways (metabolic pathways) within the fungus and cancer cell, cancer stem cells, and re-balancing of the microbiome and cellular terrain, because the weight of evidence indicates that these are the key factors associated with cancer.

Once you've researched the drugs and solutions used by other cancer survivors, you could then cross-reference this data to see if it aligns with the Cell Suppression, Metabolic and Stem Cell theories mentioned above. You may be able to identify a pattern that supports the notion that cancer is caused by a fungal pathogen, and that targeting energy pathways and stem cells is the way to go. For instance, as Jane McLelland highlights in her book *How to starve cancer*, she used the fat-inhibiting drug *Lovastatin*, which she claims helped her to combat her cancer. Looking at this through a Cell Suppression lens, it's noteworthy that Lovastatin also possesses strong anti-fungal properties, which may help explain why its use was so effective in Jane's case. Many drugs that show promise may not be described as anti-fungals, but that doesn't mean that they don't possess anti-fungal qualities. For instance, the diabetic drug *Metformin* and the anti-parasitic drug *Mebendazole*, both show a benefit against cancer. While one is designed to restrict glucose and the other to combat parasites, studies show that both are also effective at killing common fungal pathogens (see Chapter 13). The anti-fungal properties of drugs is not always obvious, so be sure to thoroughly research the additional properties they possess – you may find that off-patent drugs that appear effective against cancer, also have anti-fungal or metabolic restrictive qualities. This will increase confidence in your chosen therapeutic approach.

Research as many perspectives and treatments as possible because even within any one perspective there are nuanced views that can be of benefit. For instance, Dr Nasha Winters is a cancer expert, clinician, and survivor who eloquently details her view of cancer from a metabolic perspective. In her book *The Metabolic Approach to Cancer*, she elaborates on the relationship between cancer and the microbiome, placing emphasis on the need to re-balance this microbiome and repair the cellular terrain. It is also imperative that you converse with your oncologist and build a positive relationship. Despite the likelihood that the mainstream view they support is incorrect, conventional therapies can still be helpful under particular circumstances, notably surgery. Ultimately, medical professionals only want to help and have a wealth of knowledge and support networks that are crucial to your recovery. The key is to stay open-minded and consider all options while being sensitive to the opinions expressed by medical experts, who may not respond well to a patient challenging their views. Should you choose to use a conventional treatment approach, be sure to ask for evidence to support the effectiveness of any treatment being offered by your oncologist, and insist on knowing exactly how the treatment works – a list of essential questions to ask your oncologist are presented shortly. In essence, research, research and then research some more.

Stress negatively affects decision-making:

The sheer stress of a cancer diagnosis can be overwhelming and may compromise our ability to make rational decisions. As a result we may be more susceptible to relinquishing responsibility, and more likely to accept whatever treatment oncologists are offering immediately following a diagnosis.

Please note that in most cases you will have plenty of time to digest your diagnosis and choose a relevant treatment path; cancer doesn't occur overnight. Most tumours are very slow-growing taking between five and 10 years before they become noticeable. So unless you are in an immediately life-threatening situation, you will have time to gather your thoughts, perform research, and plan your treatment strategy. The worst response would be to rush into a treatment decision under duress. Your oncologist should be supportive of your need to take a week or two to process the information. Do not allow yourself to be pressured into accepting treatments through fear and the demand for an immediate response, especially given the limitations of the interpretation of cancer that mainstream medicine is working within.

A critical, though often overlooked aspect to consider, is the mental stress associated with a cancer diagnosis, and how this immense emotional upheaval can be addressed. My research led me to read *The Cancer Whisperer* written by Sophie Sabbage. Sophie draws on her experience as a motivational therapist to focus on dealing with the emotional aspects of cancer. Her deep understanding comes from firsthand experience of the disease, having developed brain cancer herself. I cannot rate this book too highly. Until recently, the emotional aspect of cancer has largely been ignored, but it forms an essential aspect of healing, and ensuring patient survival. Sophie's writing is inspirational and she eloquently provides practical advice on how to turn a cancer diagnosis into a platform to positively affect every aspect of your life.

Initial overview:

Some of the most effective treatment options on the market, as well as some promising options currently undergoing clinical trials, appear to share similar traits. They all either restrict the cell's energy system by disrupting glucose absorption, block other key fuels that feed fungal pathogens, such as glutamine, fat, and lactate, or they are anti-fungal agents that target fungal pathogens directly.

All plant compounds – such as salvestrols – which are shown to be effective at killing cancer cells, contain strong anti-fungal compounds. These compounds are regularly confirmed to be the active medicinal ingredients killing cancer cells.

Regarding the potential of natural solutions, there is a fantastic little book called *Curing Cancer with Carrots*,[671] which details how Ann Cameron cured herself of cancer by juicing 5lbs of carrots daily. This was achieved after surgery had failed, with tumours returning and spreading to her lungs. Ann refused chemotherapy and radiotherapy after doing her own research, and after stumbling across this notion of using carrots to cure the disease, she remains cancer-free to this day.

This initially seems like a far-fetched claim, but when the two primary compounds within carrots are highlighted, curing cancer with carrots becomes a reasonable concept. Both *falcarinol* and *luteolin* are two well-studied compounds proven to be effective against cancer cells. Additionally, both have been shown to be highly effective against fungal pathogens.[669, 670] Falcarinol in particular, is created by the carrot to defend its roots from fungal attack. Given my proposition that cancer is caused by a fungal pathogen, the anti-fungal compounds found in carrots can explain why this protocol has the potential to be so effective, particularly when consumed in such large quantities. Obviously the success of such an approach will depend on your overall diet and lifestyle.

The conventional approach:

It's worth reminding ourselves of the approach offered by conventional medicine, as this will provide perspective. Conventional treatment pivots around surgery, chemotherapy drugs, and radiotherapy. Some immunotherapies are also available. The benefit of the conventional approach is that these treatments have been extensively tested. The downside, is that despite this, most of these treatments are ineffective long-term, providing only short-term gains if at all. Aside from surgery, which can be very effective against early-stage cancers, these treatments are not only toxic, but, in many cases, can also cause cancer themselves. When considering a conventional approach, always insist on viewing the evidence that corroborates the effectiveness of the treatment being offered, as well as learning of the side-effects that diminish its usefulness and efficacy.

Moreover, standard of care treatments generally work against the body's natural healing abilities, by using toxic substances to cause cell death through a mechanism of severe cell damage. By poisoning both the body and the tumour, it is hoped that the tumour will be caught in the cross-fire and that the body will recover quicker than the tumour is able to. Since with every conventional treatment there is a risk, this needs to be weighed against any potential benefit, always considering the resulting quality of life. To aid us make an informed decision, it's worth re-iterating some of the many shortcomings of the mainstream approach:

1. Cancer fails to recognise DNA damage as a problem, which would normally result in programmed cell death once a damage threshold has been reached. As these cells resist dying, it seems counterproductive to target a cancer cell by attempting to further damage DNA with toxic drugs.

2. As healthy cells do recognise DNA damage, the toxicity of chemotherapy can affect all healthy cells of the body that absorb it. This has the potential to lead to mass cell death, mutations, a risk of organ failure, and even the development of cancer itself, in these once healthy cells.

3. Cancer stem cells appear to be resistant to most chemotherapies, which calls into question its usefulness as a treatment.
4. Chemotherapy has been shown to increase cancer stem cell growth and aggression by switching on a repair mechanism that can make tumours deadly.
5. The efficacy of chemotherapy rapidly diminishes over time, likely due to the damage it inflicts upon mitochondria, which produce free radicals. The longer chemotherapy is used, the fewer free radicals are generated, and the less effective the treatment becomes. The toxicity of the treatment also risks weakening the immune system, damaging cells, and is known to damage our microbiome. This could aid fungal infection and may increase cancer growth, by effectively creating the same conditions as are generated by carcinogens.
6. Chemotherapy can reduce a patient's appetite, contributing to cachexia (muscle wasting disease). To counter this, steroids are often supplied to stimulate appetite. The problem, is that steroids unfortunately increase blood glucose levels, which risks feeding tumour growth, and are immune suppressive.
7. On average, studies have found only a 5% benefit to five-year survival from chemotherapy for cancers that have already metastasised. Naturally, the actual benefit in a given case will differ with cancer type and the age of the patient.
8. The conventional approach rarely targets cell energy metabolism.
9. The conventional approach rarely recognises the role of glucose, glutamine, lactate, and fat in feeding cancer growth.
10. The conventional approach rarely addresses the involvement of cancer stem cells.
11. Chemotherapy use hasn't significantly improved the cancer mortality rate in almost 55 years of persistent use.
12. Chemotherapy and radiotherapy can themselves cause cancer.
13. Apart from increasing the risk of developing future cancers, chemotherapy and radiotherapy may cause other long-term debilitating complications.
14. The toxic nature of chemotherapy drugs can result in a failure to complete the full course of treatment. This will greatly reduce the effectiveness of the treatment.
15. Scientists still don't fully understand how chemotherapy drugs work, and the extent of the damage they cause.

16. This next point may surprise you, but is crucial to acknowledge: medical doctors are not educated about the science of nutrition and how the medicinal properties in food can aid against the disease.[223, 224, 376, 377, 378] The medical curriculum focuses primarily on drug treatments as a solution to our ailments, not on teaching doctors how food and nutrition effects health,[379, 478, 683] which is odd given that food is the cornerstone of health. As a result, oncologists can only provide simple diet advice, such as to ensure you're consuming enough calories – which is extremely vague, and may encourage disease progression if patients are still consuming refined sugar. In my opinion, diet should be front and centre in any treatment strategy. As doctors are not qualified to provide diet advice, they often refer patients to a dietician or qualified nutritionist. The key point here is to ensure your nutritionist, or dietician, is aware of the Metabolic Theory to account for the abnormal metabolic needs of cancer cells, and the new Cell Suppression model presented within this book, to account for the fungal influence. And of course, there should be an insistence on using only organic produce.

On a positive note, initial chemotherapy can dramatically reduce the size of the tumour allowing it to be removed via surgery. It may also slow-down the progression of the disease for a while, allowing time for other solutions to be researched and implemented. Although this seems rarely applicable to late-stage cancers that have spread. One must also take into account chemotherapy's ability to stimulate cancer stem cells and weaken the immune system, both of which have been shown to be detrimental with long-term chemotherapy use.

Important questions to ask your oncologist:

All oncologists are highly-skilled hard-working scientists. Unfortunately, they have been confined to work within a medical system that restricts the outlook they present, as well as the treatments they can provide. While most are well-intentioned and dedicated to their patient's well-being, some can be irritated by patient's questions and suffer from a terrible 'bedside manner'. It is important to remember that the view of cancer they present, and the treatments they are allowed to offer, are limited, and based upon an unproven theory. Hence information or questions that are based on an entirely different view of the disease are likely to fall on deaf ears, or even get rejected outright.

The relevance of the microbiome, medicinal plants, and the ways nutrition can benefit the patient are at best, poorly addressed, but more usually, never mentioned. Furthermore, cancer metabolism and cancer stem cells are seldom discussed, and rarely form part of a conventional treatment strategy. Even less likely is that your oncologist will consider the involvement of a fungal pathogen when determining which treatments to provide. Any notion of a fungal cause – should you ever mention it – would almost certainly be dismissed. Please be mindful of this when conversing with your oncologist, as they may become hostile in response to information that challenges their medical beliefs. Like all good scientists, the best oncologists will be open-minded and respectful of your opinions and intentions, analysing any evidence you present as objectively as they can, and taking the data seriously. However, bear in mind that this is an ideal scenario that is often in contrast to actual experience.

You should never feel intimidated or under pressure to do as your oncologist requests. You have every right to ask as many questions as possible and to refuse any treatment being recommended, if you feel uncomfortable with it, or feel the risks outweigh any alleged benefit – this is, after all, your life and body on the line, not theirs. It's important to understand everything that is being discussed, and the risks involved regarding the treatments being proposed, as the toxicity of the treatment itself can be fatal.

Make a note of everything important, and research it in your own time before committing. Digitally record your meeting with your oncologist (but with their knowledge, not covertly) so that you can replay the information to ensure you took it all in. You'd be surprised at how much detail we fail to absorb when under stress. Always take someone with you. Their support is vital, and they can help ensure you don't misunderstand important details.

With this in mind, there are some key points to consider, and some crucial questions that any person newly diagnosed with cancer should ask. The response to these questions will indicate whether you need to gain a second opinion or switch to a different oncologist entirely. Be sure to find answers to these questions, especially if your oncologist fails to:

1. **Ensure** you understand the exact type of cancer you have, right down to the correct spelling, as well as its stage of progression and how aggressive it is.

2. **Ask** for confirmation of the dominant fuel or ratio of fuels feeding the tumour (glucose, glutamine, lactate, fat, arginine, methionine or hormones that stimulate cell proliferation, such as estrogen) – this is critical, as it will determine the type of treatment approach to take.

3. **Clarify** the use of the terminology being used – the word survival can often be confused with the word cure. Is your oncologist referring to five-year or 10-year survival? How about disease-free survival? A five-year disease-free statistic provides the likelihood that you will be cancer-free after five years. A five-year survival statistic only refers to whether you will reach the five-year mark regardless of disease progression.

4. **What** is the end goal of the treatment? A cure, to reduce tumour size, to extend life, or is it simply palliative?

5. **Understand** the treatment options being offered, and the likely success rate of the treatment for your age group, ethnicity and gender – and insist on seeing the evidence that supports these success rates.

6. **How** is the treatment understood to work? By damaging DNA, creating free radicals, stimulating the immune system, blocking specific pathways, fuels or genes; or by causing necrosis (forced cell death via extreme cell damage)? And how will it affect healthy cells?

7. **What** are the short-term and long-term side-effects, will kidney function be lost, can it damage the heart, what are the chances of liver failure or infertility, and are there other life-long debilitating outcomes?

8. **What** are any suggested drugs derived from – synthetic chemicals, micro-organism toxin, plant toxin, etc...?

9. **What** are the chances of cancer spreading, or returning when using the treatment offered?

10. **Can** the treatment cause cancer, and what are the odds of this occurring?

11. **How** will the treatment affect my quality of life?

12. **What** is the likelihood of resistance to the drug developing?

13. **What** is the likelihood that I won't be able to endure the full course of treatment? And what would it mean for my survival chances if the treatment is stopped early?

14. **What** is the percentage improvement in five- and 10-year survival over and above doing nothing? Ensure you are provided with the 'absolute' risk reduction/improvement figure, not the 'relative' risk reduction/improvement figure, as it can be very misleading (the difference between these two figures was discussed in Chapter 3).

15. **Do** your treatment recommendations target cancer metabolism; specifically, glucose, glutamine, lactate and fat metabolism?

16. **Is** the iron connection to cancer being addressed? In particular increased iron metabolism of the tumour, iron overload, and anaemia of inflammation that patients often experience?[924]

17. **Is** the cancer *arginine* sensitive? If so, are you able to provide arginine starvation therapy and what's the success rate?

18. **Do** your treatment recommendations target cancer stem cells, and can you provide evidence of efficacy in this respect?

19. **Should** I change my diet and lifestyle – is there anything I can do to increase my chances over and above the treatments you recommend? (The answer should be 'yes', and include specific recommendations, such as tackling glucose and glutamine intake in relation to curbing cancer metabolism. Reducing inflammatory markers, with an organic whole foods diet approach, coupled with increased exercise. Just maintaining sufficient calories is wholly inadequate, and fails to acknowledge the link between diet feeding the metabolic needs of the tumour).

20. **Are** you willing to discuss non-conventional solutions if I present evidence for their efficacy, and would you support me in adopting lifestyle or complimentary approaches?

21. **Are** you aware of the *Care Oncology Clinic* and how it uses off-label drugs to target cancer cell metabolism? Are you able to offer a similar approach?

22. **Do** I have time to postpone the treatment you are offering to trial other solutions? If so, how many months grace do you think I have, before you recommend starting conventional treatment?

23. **Do** your treatment recommendations address the health of the microbiome and its dysbiotic relationship within cancer, specifically the tumour-associated microbiome? As well as take in to account the microbiome's contribution to drug resistance?[821]

24. **The** recent *Cell Suppression model* of cancer indicates that intracellular fungal pathogens are driving cancerous conditions

through a suppressive mechanism, including the initiation of the Warburg effect. Are you familiar with this new interpretation cancer, Ravid Straussmans work in identifying intracellular fungal pathogens in all cancers, and the evidence highlighting that fungal pathogens are directly influencing the disease? (provide your oncologist with a copy of this book). With this in mind, are you prepared to support me in working out an anti-fungal strategy that can work in synergy with any treatments you are offering?

This last point should only be pursued if your oncologist appears open-minded. They would need to digest this new information ready for your next appointment. But be mindful that until oncologists are aware of this new interpretation of cancer, they will likely respond dismissively, probably claiming there is no evidence to support a fungal-led view of the disease.

Answers to these questions should provide you with the understanding you require, and highlight how supportive your oncologist is. If most of your questions cannot be answered adequately, then it may be time to change your oncologist, or adopt a different approach to that being offered.

Going it alone – a word of warning:

Most of the public are not trained in how to safely administer treatments. Some people reading this book might be tempted to apply all the solutions that could be effective at the same time, thinking that it's best to kill cancer as quickly as possible by attacking it from all angles. While a broad-spectrum approach is likely to be the most effective, bombarding the body with too many chemicals that haven't been researched can be extremely dangerous for several reasons:

1. Applying too many solutions at once can do more harm than good. It can be difficult to determine which approach is or isn't working when so many are being used. Drug interactions need to be considered. When combined, they could either cancel out the effectiveness of one another, or result in a toxic outcome that can damage vital organs, such as the liver or kidneys. The website '**www.drugs.com**' provides information about adverse drug interactions and contraindications.

2. When fungi are killed, they release toxins. This needs to be taken into account, killing fungi too quickly may place an added burden

on the liver. With this in mind, feeling worse immediately after treatment can be a positive sign that the fungal infection is being killed. So be careful not to be too hasty in changing your protocol, while staying mindful of what led to you feeling a particular way. It is a good idea to keep a diary to monitor your progress. And to log any issues that arise.

3. The human body is complex and will react differently from person to person. This can be due to many factors such as the type of tumour, the stage of progression, the patient's age, genetics and ethnicity, the amount of DNA damage that has been inflicted, the health of the gut microbiome, and even the patient's blood type. There are slight differences in how we all metabolise drugs/chemicals. This subtle difference can result in the failure of a treatment that worked for someone else.

Key points to consider:

It would be preferable to undertake a similar approach to that of a medical doctor; that is, to incrementally introduce solutions while assessing the reaction. Of course, listening to the advice of your doctor is also paramount to allow you to weigh up the benefits and risks. Unfortunately, having identified fungi as the cause of cancer doesn't mean that the solution is straightforward, for several reasons:

- **Fungal type** – The type of fungal pathogen potentially causing tumour growth is unknown. In fact, there may be several involved, which means it's unclear which anti-fungal drug would be the most effective. For example, Itraconazole can kill the fungal pathogen *Aspergillus fumigatus*, whereas Fluconazole and Ketoconazole do not.
- **Drug resistance** – Fungi may already be resistant to the limited number of anti-fungal drugs that are available. In particular, *Candida* has been shown to use estrogen to increase their resistance to the azole class of anti-fungals.[023] As a result, an anti-fungal drug approach to breast cancer may not work.
- **Fuel type** – While most cancer types absorb high rates of glucose, many use glutamine and lactate, with some even reliant on fat – such as prostate cancer. Some appear to be stimulated by estrogen, such as breast and uterine cancers. It is therefore imperative that you discover the dominant fuel type being absorbed by your particular tumour. This will determine the type of drugs to use to

treat the disease. For instance, Lovastatin can block fat absorption and possesses effective anti-fungal properties, while Metformin can inhibit glucose production, and also possesses anti-fungal properties. Restricting glucose when you have a fat-dependent cancer may not be very effective. Jane McLelland sets out the different fuel types in her book *How to Starve Cancer*, and provides a guide to the drugs that can target energy pathways to restrict cancer metabolism. Keep in mind though, that most advice is not coming from a background that acknowledges fungi as a potential cause, so you may want to keep the role of the fungal pathogen in mind at all times.

- **DNA mutations** – DNA damage may reduce the effectiveness of some drugs or plant-based solutions. For example, some cancer cells may not absorb cannabis due to defective cannabinoid receptors. Human biology is varied and complex, even without the random DNA damage that occurs in cancer.

- **Tumour associated factors** – It's not just the cancer type that matters, but other factors and conditions associated with it. Stomach cancer, for instance, can make it difficult for patients to consume the nutrients needed to kill cancer cells, especially if the stomach is highly inflamed. Up to 90% of the mucous layer that protects the stomach lining from stomach acid is water, so a concerted effort to rehydrate may help increase this mucous barrier and reduce inflammation, making it easier to consume certain foods. Just be sure not to drink water too close to consuming food, as this may reduce the acidity of the stomach, which can reduce the ability of the stomach to break down food. Food additives such as carrageenan have been shown to irritate the stomach lining – removing these types of additives from one's diet is critical. *Helicobacter pylori* bacteria can live within the stomach and appear to play a role in stomach cancer progression, due to the persistent cell damage and inflammation they inflict upon stomach cells. If you have stomach cancer or stomach ulcers, you should consider testing for the presence of this bacteria. When it comes to brain cancer, the blood-brain barrier needs to be considered, because not all drugs can penetrate it.

- **Liver health** – The liver is of paramount importance – you only have one. It is the primary organ that deals with removing toxins, and it regulates other critical aspects of the body, such as glucose metabolism and fluid retention within the bloodstream. When the liver is compromised, treating cancer becomes far more complicated. Its health will need to be considered as part of your overall strategy. Unable to efficiently expel toxins means that the body becomes burdened with damage and inflammation, which will only benefit fungi and cancer. Using toxic drugs for treatment can cause more liver damage, hampering its ability to function, which leads to a multitude of other issues that risk cascading out of control. Artemisinin, for instance, is the anti-malarial drug that creates damaging free radicals when it comes into contact with iron. While this can be effective against many cancers, it may be dangerous to use when the liver is compromised, because the liver stores an abundance of iron, making it particularly susceptible to damage when Artemisinin is used.[493, 494] It is critical to support the liver with a nutritious toxin-free organic diet to aid with cell repair – the liver is the only organ that can fully repair itself.

It's important to acknowledge the complexity involved, consider different options when required, and try not to get too despondent if some strategies don't appear to work straight away. Fungi are clever; they adapt well to new stimuli, are opportunistic in nature, and thrive by invading inflamed and damaged cells. They are also expert at developing resistance to drugs,[729] which is why they are difficult to dislodge once they've established themselves. A combination of anti-fungal approaches that work synergistically may help to eliminate fungal infection more effectively, and with less toxicity.[729]

A patient may not see the results expected if they are indecisive and switch from one protocol to another too quickly, or relax a regime too soon. Targeting cancer requires a well researched and carefully measured approach that places the least amount of strain on organs such as the liver and kidneys, and considers the danger of potential drug interactions.

With this in mind, presented below is an evidence-based approach that you may wish to consider. Bear in mind I am not a nutritionist or medical practitioner. I am simply presenting information based on the available data I have to hand, in conjunction with the Cell Suppression model. Health, nutrition and human biology is complex, there is no one-size-fits-all approach, and many scientists disagree with one another; so you will need to approach your research objectively, looking at several sources of information and above all converse with a medical professional.

An evidence-based approach for the majority of cancer patients

The original Hanahan and Weinberg Hallmark list was written to gain insight into the main mechanisms of the disease, both for the purpose of understanding cancer, and identifying targets for drug creation. For instance, in the original list, Hallmark 5 referred to blood vessel growth, known as *angiogenesis*. The identification of this hallmark has prompted scientists to study this process in detail, and then attempt to develop anti-angiogenic drugs to suppress the growth of blood vessels in cancer. Unfortunately this list does not appear to be arranged in any particular order that represents the progression of the disease, so in earlier chapters I rearranged it and then added in the hallmarks I felt were missing. This new categorisation enables us to better assess the likely effectiveness of treatments, as we can better determine whether they are targeting a fundamental feature driving the disease or just a symptom that occurs.

When viewed through the lens of the refined hallmark list in the following table, we see that mainstream treatments don't appear to target the underlying mechanism that drives the disease, but instead focus on downstream hallmarks that are less foundational and more symptomatic. Logically, targeting earlier hallmarks in the list should produce better outcomes. For example, commonly used chemotherapy and radiotherapy treatments target Hallmark 13, *genome instability*, which seems to be one of the least relevant aspects of the disease. Given that abundant evidence indicates that DNA mutations are symptoms of the disease, as opposed to the mechanism driving it, it's not surprising that the success rates with these treatments are rather poor.

Anti-angiogenic drugs target Hallmark 10 by attempting to restrict the tumour's ability to stimulate new blood vessel growth. While this can be effective in the short-term, it is found to be largely ineffective as a long-term. Patients using these drugs generally don't live any longer, and develop an increased risk of their cancer becoming more aggressive; this is not to mention the fact that the toxicity of these drugs renders their use for any length of time, impossible.

Immunotherapies that attempt to enhance the immune system target Hallmark 9. While theoretically these therapies show promise, so far they have failed to have a significant impact, probably due to the fact they are not addressing the underlying mechanism driving the disease.

At the other end of the scale we have metabolic therapies that target Hallmark 2 – the abnormal energy behaviour shown to be exhibited by all cancers. These therapies show great potential and have certainly been effective for incurable brain cancer, as Pablo Kelly, Andrew Scarborough and Professor Ben Williams can attest.[131, 322, 324 348, 421] This is probably because these therapies are targeting a key underlying mechanism that is directly driving the disease. It's tragic that the medical establishment continues to resist investing in a metabolic therapy approach – which only underlines why cancer patients might reasonably consider taking matters into their own hands.

Hallmarks refined – with associated treatments:

Hallmarks **REFINED** & associated treatments	
Initiation Pre-cancerous stage	1. Tissue damage
	2. Abnormal metabolic pathways (***Metabolic therapies***)
	3. Chronic inflammation
	4. Dysbiotic microbiome
Cancer	5. Intracellular pathogens
	6. Evasion of cell death
	7. Resistance to anti-growth signals
	8. Uncontrolled growth
Progression	9. Immune evasion (***Immuno-therapies***)
Malignancy	10. Blood vessel growth (***Anti-angiogenic therapies***)
	11. Limitless replication
	12. Invasion of local tissue and metastasis
	13. Genome instability (***Radio- and Chemo-therapies***)

When we consider the proposed treatment approach that aligns with the *Cell Suppression* model, not only are metabolic therapies included and Hallmark 2 being targetted, but treatments that target Hallmarks 1, 3, 4 and 5 are also considered to be paramount – which are arguably the hallmarks that represent the totality of the mechanisms that initiate and drive the disease. Targeting the first five hallmarks will inevitably have a knock-on effect against the remaining hallmarks, which largely represent the symptoms that occur as a result of the first five hallmarks. This indicates, that by following a treatment approach aligned with the evidence supporting the *Cell Suppression* model, survival outcomes are likely to be vastly improved.

Looking at cancer treatment through a cell suppression lens, and given the evidence presented within this book, the following approach appears coherent and logical.

Repair the cellular terrain and re-balance the microbiome:

It makes sense to eliminate the life-style factors that encouraged the disease. Modern farming has reduced the nutritional content of foods, providing the body with fewer nutrients and rendering it less capable of fighting disease. The use of pesticides has reduced the protective anti-fungal compounds that plants would normally create, and loaded them with toxic residues. These accumulate within the body, ensuring that cell damage, inflammation and immune weakness occur consistently, aiding cancer development (fungal infection).

A diet high in refined sugar feeds fungal populations and cancer cells. Most meat and dairy produce is factory-farmed, non-organic, from animals fed genetically modified feed,[754] and raised with growth hormones and antibiotics. The latter two risk stimulating tumour growth signals and have been shown to diminish the diversity and quantity of protective gut bacteria that make up 80% of our total immune defence. As this diet and lifestyle can promote cancer, it makes sense to change these conditions.

Adopting an organic, whole-food plant-based diet, topping up vitamin D and vitamin B12 levels, and eliminating refined sugar should be your number one strategy. Not only will this starve cancer (i.e. the fungus) of the refined glucose that, in all likelihood, has been promoting it, and reduce toxins that cause cell damage, but it will supply greatly increased quantities of critical nutrients, along with the anti-fungal phytoalexins, salvestrols, and polyphenols that have been shown to kill both cancer cells and fungal pathogens. Vitamin B12 deficiency, which occurs with most cancers, pre-disposes the cell to excessive DNA damage and generally to poorly functioning cells, while vitamin D regulates immune function.

Regularly fasting at this crucial time can also provide great benefit. It will rid the body of old and damaged cells, re-ignite the immune system and further help to starve both the fungal pathogen and cancer cells of the elevated levels of glucose they require. Dr Nasha Winters covers this in depth in *The Metabolic Approach to Cancer*, as does Jane McLelland in *How to Starve Cancer*.

Moderate exercise has been shown to be an effective strategy for preventing cancer, so this is also paramount. A regular fitness routine will again deplete the body of excess glucose, and will rejuvenate mitochondria, improving cell defence and your all-round immune health.

In support of natural plant compounds in relation to cancer, the *Halifax Project* was a research initiative set up to investigate more effective avenues of treatment. It enlisted an international task force of 180 scientists to explore therapeutic agents that can simultaneously target multiple aspects of cancer, because its assessment of the industry found that current treatments don't sufficiently account for the levels of complexity inherent in the disease. After extensive research, they concluded that plant compounds should be considered, because they were capable of targeting many genes and pathways within cancer cells, and to a greater degree than many synthetic drugs:

> '***Plant-derived*** *compounds,* ***phytochemicals****, are in many cases* ***better tolerated*** *than the synthetic analogs [drugs] used in cancer therapy today.*
>
> *Furthermore, they often exhibit* ***broader mechanisms of action*** *and sometimes* ***even higher affinity*** *against important cancer targets* ***compared to the synthetic alternatives****.'*

<u>*Seminars in Cancer Biology*</u> **2015** [759]

Adopting these lifestyle changes will not only weaken fungal pathogens, but will also reduce toxin exposure, inflammation, instigate repair processes, strengthen the immune system, and aid with gut microbiome health; while diminishing the level of growth hormones, toxins and antibiotics present within your body. Furthermore, it will help tackle obesity at its root – reversing many of the key factors that lead to the disease. Implementing a healthier lifestyle, and consuming organic food that retains more of its nutrients and anti-fungal compounds, is a logical foundational strategy for cancer.

Target metabolism and fungal pathogens:

Given the evidence, there is a compelling case for undertaking the following approach in the majority of cancer cases:

- Inhibit *glucose*
- Inhibit *glutamine, arginine* and *methionine* (proteins)
- Inhibit *lactate* (lactic acid)
- Increase vitamin D intake
- Adopt an anti-fungal approach
- Target freely-available iron.

Eighty five percent of cancers (called carcinomas) form in epithelial cells. Carcinomas predominantly use glucose, glutamine, and lactate to fuel their energy needs. So, for the majority of people with cancer, targeting these fuels seems to be a sensible course of action:

> 'Accumulating evidence indicates that **glucose and glutamine** are the **primary fuels** used for driving the rapid **growth** of **most tumours**...simultaneous **restriction** of these **two substrates** or inhibition of mSLP **should diminish cancer viability, growth,** and **invasion.'**
>
> <u>ASN Neuro</u> **2018** [798]

The great thing about restricting glucose and glutamine is that lactate will also be restricted. This is because lactate is a byproduct of glycolysis, a process which is inhibited when glucose and glutamine metabolism is restricted:

> 'We hypothesize that **lactagenesis** [lactate production] for **carcinogenesis** is the explanation and purpose of the **Warburg Effect**. Accordingly, **therapies to limit lactate exchange** and signalling within and among cancer cells should be priorities for discovery. '
>
> <u>Carcinogenesis</u> **2017** [771]

Here scientists highlight that lactate is an important metabolic substrate in cancer. Validating my proposal, the conclusion drawn in the study is to inhibit lactate production in order to inhibit cancer. This can be achieved by restricting glucose, which will inhibit glycolysis and thus the production of lactate. Significantly, and crucial to the point, these are the same three primary fuels used by fungal pathogens. By starving the cancer cell of the fuels known to feed it, you will also be directly starving the fungus.

Furthermore, reduction of lactate through inhibition of glycolysis,[790] is likely to reduce blood vessel growth (angiogenesis) because lactate production stimulates blood vessel growth. Inhibiting angiogenesis will restrict nutrient availability, weakening both cancer cells and fungal pathogens.

Glucose restriction can be achieved through diet, fasting, exercise and the use of specific anti-glycolytic drugs. Metformin, or the natural plant compound *berberine*, can block the glutamine-to-glucose conversion pathway known as *gluconeogenesis*, which is present within the liver and within fungal pathogens. Metformin specifically reduces blood glucose levels by blocking this conversion. Combining Metformin with a diet that restricts the glucose we consume, such as a ketogenic diet, may be a beneficial strategy to discuss with your oncologist. Furthermore, both Metformin and berberine possess potent anti-fungal properties, so they will act directly upon fungal pathogens as well.

It should be noted that Metformin only stops glutamine from being converted into glucose; it doesn't prevent glutamine from entering the cancer cell. This is important because glutamine is converted into many other substances within the cell, such as *aspartate* and then *arginine*, which is used to aid cell growth, and is absorbed by the fungal pathogen for the same reason. These compounds fuel fungal and cancer aggression. So, you may want to consider a glutamine inhibitor drug that blocks the cell from absorbing glutamine, such as *6-diazo-5-oxo-L-norleucine* (also known as 'DON').[780] Confirming the potential effectiveness of blocking glucose and glutamine in the manner I've described, other medical professionals have recently suggested a similar approach:

> 'It is *well recognized that **most, if not all**, tumour cells are dependent on **glucose** and **glutamine** for growth... The dependency of tumour cells on **glycolysis** and **glutaminolysis** will also make them **resistant** to **apoptosis** and **chemotherapeutic drugs**. The activity of the p-glycoprotein, which **protects** cells from **toxic chemotherapy**, is driven by glycolysis...*
>
> *...**6-diazo-5-oxo-L-norleucine** (DON), not only **inhibited glutamine metabolism** but also **inhibited glycolysis** and **related pathways**, thus disabling the **Warburg effect** and significantly reducing tumour growth.*

> *...As **glucose** and **glutamine** are the **prime fuels** for **driving tumour growth**, therapeutic strategies that can simultaneously target the availability of these fuels should have potential in improving progression-free and **overall survival** for **most patients with cancer.**'*
>
> *iScience* **2020** [769]

Using DON to block glutamine has the potential to also block *arginine*, which is the fuel used by aggressive cancers. This is because arginine is created from *aspartate*, which is produced from glutamine. Crucially, fungal pathogens require arginine to instigate their invasive behaviour, so blocking glutamine will have the added benefit of inhibiting fungal pathogens as well.

Blocking aspartate by inhibiting glutamine may also prevent DNA synthesis, which is required for cell growth. This is because aspartate is required to create new DNA. Potentially, this can inhibit tumour growth, because cells cannot replicate without making DNA (this was covered in Chapter 12). Fungal pathogens also need to synthesize DNA in order to grow. They do this by stealing the compounds that the cell uses for this purpose. If the cell can no longer create these compounds due to a lack of aspartate and glutamine, then the fungal pathogen also won't be able to create new DNA either, this will ultimately inhibit fungal growth.

Furthermore, glutamine is used by cancer cells to create glutathione, which is a powerful antioxidant that can protect cancer cells from drugs. So, using DON (or other glutamine inhibitors) has the potential to weaken cancer cell defence mechanisms by reducing its ability to create protective glutathione, which would normally provide protection from the damaging effects of free radicals.

Methionine is the third amino-acid to consider, as it's use is increased in cancer cells. An amino-acid is the medical term used to describe proteins. As with arginine, cancer cells don't appear to be able to create their own methionine; instead they are forced to rely on dietary sources.[832] This makes cancer cells vulnerable to arginine and methionine starvation therapy.[833] Moreover, methionine is a key protein that fungal pathogens need to sustain an infection, so restricting it will also inhibit fungal activity. Confirming that inhibiting glutamine, arginine and methionine has therapeutic value against cancer, the following study states:

> *'One such vulnerability exhibited by cancer is an increased demand for **amino acids** (AAs), which often results in a dependency on*

*exogenous [external] sources of AAs... Examples of other successful strategies include the exploitation of **arginine deiminase** and **methioninase**, nutrient restriction of **methionine** and the inhibition of **glutaminase**.*

Nutrient restriction**, enzymatic depletion and enzymatic inhibition of AA [amino acid] metabolism have all demonstrated **success** in **preclinical** and **clinical models**, supporting these therapies as **viable strategies for cancer treatment**. These alternative approaches have the **potential** to **revolutionise standard clinical practice.'

Amino Acids **2021** [839]

Alongside a protocol to restrict cancer metabolism, is to supplement with vitamin D. The reason for this is three-fold. While vitamin D is required for optimum immune function,[777] it additionally appears to restrict iron availability, thus starving both cancer cells and fungal pathogens of the iron that they both need to survive (remember that fungal pathogens require iron to sustain an infection, and become aggressive once they gain access to it). Furthermore, in many cancers, vitamin D has been found to also suppress both glycolysis and glutamine metabolism – the same two primary fuel systems that we are attempting to target and suppress with drugs:

*'At an innate level, intracrine synthesis of 1,25D [**vitamin D**] by macrophages and dendritic cells stimulates expression of **antimicrobial proteins** such as cathelicidin, as well as **lowering** intracellular **iron** concentrations via suppression of hepcidin.*

*Vitamin D is **suppressive** of **glycolysis** in multiple cancers. For highly glycolytic cancer cells, this inhibition of glucose metabolism is detrimental, resulting in **loss of proliferation** and **increased apoptosis**...*

*It has also been reported that 1,25D is able to **suppress glutamine** metabolism in breast cancer cells, partially through inhibiting transcription of the **glutamine transporter**.'*

JBMR Plus **2021** [777]

A *Cancer Research UK* article discussing a 2019 study, which analysed the effect of vitamin D on melanoma cells, states:

> *'The researchers from the University of Leeds discovered that **vitamin D** influences the behaviour of a signalling pathway within melanoma cells, which **slowed down their growth** and **stopped** them **spreading to the lungs** in mice.'*
>
> <u>Cancer Research UK</u> **2019** [784]

The approach I've just described above is largely the one that is supported by proponents of the Metabolic Theory, so you can be confident that these are strategies that are supported by the latest science. Additionally, and quite possibly a game-changer, is to include an anti-fungal approach to treatment, especially as evidence confirms that anti-fungal drugs appear to be effective against most, if not all cancer types. Complementing these drugs with natural anti-fungal options – such as salvestrols, cannabis oil or curcumin – would likely provide even more benefit, especially if combined with an organic plant-based diet. As I highlighted with Dr Michael Greger's research in Chapter 18, the anti-cancerous/anti-fungal compounds found in organic food, do find their way into tumour cells when we consume them – so we know that these beneficial compounds are getting to where we want them to be. Just be mindful of the toxicities that accompany current anti-fungal drugs.

Other drugs such as statins, which block fat creation and are also anti-fungal, can have a beneficial effect, especially with cancers that appear to rely on fat for their energy needs. Moreover, statin and anti-fungal combinations should be considered, because studies have shown improved efficacy against common fungal pathogens, when specific combinations of both drugs are used.[599]

Again, in line with the approach I have presented, the *Care Oncology Clinic* (COC), a private cancer clinic in the UK working alongside the NHS, is actually treating cancer patients using Metformin and a statin drug Atorvastatin, as well as using two other drugs: Doxycycline and Mebendazole.[781] These four drugs have been selected for their combined ability to specifically target cancer metabolism (the energy system of the cancer cell):

> *'Launched in 2013, the Care Oncology Clinic (COC) was established to provide a new kind of cancer treatment – a combination of oral medications specifically designed to target the **metabolism of cancer**, depriving cancer of the nutrients it needs to grow and spread.*

*The treatment, which uses **existing drugs**, prescribed **off-label**, aims to complement and enhance standard of care cancer therapies.*

*Delivery of this **metabolic treatment programme** in a clinic setting with data collection and analysis is what makes it unique.'*

<u>Care Oncology Clinic</u> **2021** [773]

Set up by medical professionals and utilised by NHS oncologists, the goal of COC is to show that existing cheap, and safe drugs can be re-purposed to effectively target the energy system of the cell. This is similar to the approach advocated by Jane McLelland in her book *How to Starve Cancer*, that helped her defeat the disease.

So why do these off-label drugs appear to be effective? Aside from the metabolic restrictive capabilities of Metformin and Atorvastatin (glucose and fat restriction), very telling is that all four seemingly unrelated drugs possess anti-fungal properties. Metformin,[718] Atorvastatin,[599, 823] Mebendazole[782, 783] and Doxycycline,[926] all actively affect common fungal pathogens. The efficacy of the COC protocol my be due, inadvertently, to the targeting of fungal pathogens. As always, there appears to be this common fungal theme running through most, if not all, treatments that show efficacy against the disease. On a side note: it might be worth highlighting the anti-fungal properties of the COC's protocol to your oncologist, if they seem open to the notion of fungal pathogens playing a role in cancer.

Of particular interest, when Doxycycline is used in combination with anti-fungal drugs against fungal pathogens, it dramatically increases the effectiveness of the treatment. In two separate studies, Doxycycline vastly improved the fungal-killing ability of the anti-fungal drug Fluconazole when both were used together.[795, 927] This also occurs when Doxycycline is used in conjunction with a number of other anti-fungal drugs.[796]

This *Care Oncology Clinic* drug combination is similar to the treatment approach that my research indicates would be effective. It's foreseeable that the COC might have greater success by introducing a more potent anti-fungal strategy, such as including the anti-fungal drugs Itraconazole or Fluconazole within their protocol, or even natural anti-fungal compounds such as salvestrols, curcumin, berberine and cannabis oil. Regardless of which combinations are used, it is clear that targeting energy metabolism has great potential, especially when combined with vitamin D supplementation, and an anti-fungal strategy.

Additional considerations:

Given Doxycycline's additional anti-fungal properties,[926] it has also been shown to be effective when combined with other drugs or protocols, such as with vitamin C.[450] Another aspect of the disease to target comes in the form of the iron overload that often occurs in tumours. In order to take advantage of this excess iron, it might be worth considering intravenous vitamin C therapy or the drug *Artemisinin*. Both these approaches produce peroxides that can react with iron. This reaction generates damaging free radicals, and is recognised as a *pro-oxidant* therapy. In studies, these therapies appear to produce sufficient free radicals to kill only cancer cells. In healthy cells, iron is stored safely within proteins that prevent such reactions occurring, so very little damage to healthy tissue occurs (this is explained in the following chapter). Potentially, therefore, this is a targeted, non-toxic therapy. To confirm that pro-oxidant therapies are an accepted approach to treatment, note that chemotherapy is a pro-oxidant therapy, it works by generating free radicals, although there is an important difference: rather than selectively targeting cancer cells, chemotherapies tend to damage all rapidly dividing cells of the body, including healthy cells, generating a free radical reaction in healthy cells too. Artemisinin and intravenous vitamin C, while producing a similar toxic free radical reaction, do so in a highly targeted and far less toxic manner.[493, 494]

Hyperbaric Oxygen Therapy (HBOT) is used to increase oxygen saturation within tissue, which allows for an increased free radical reaction (most free radicals are generated from oxygen). HBOT has been shown to kill cancer cells,[838] moreover, HBOT is effective at controlling common fungal infections.[836, 837]

These treatments in particular are *pro-oxidant* in nature, that is they encourage the generation of free radicals. The aim here is to cause damage, preferably selectively, to cancer cells. Please note that, there is considerable complexity to this type of treatment, especially in relation to the use of antioxidants. Antioxidants are protective against free radical damage, so their involvement in cancer and treatment is key to an effective outcome. Not only do they protect healthy cells, but they can also protect cancer cells from the free radical damage that pro-oxidant therapies are attempting to generate.

This is a complex area to understand, and antioxidants can be either beneficial or detrimental to treatment outcomes, if the nuances involved are not appreciated. For instance, antioxidant supplementation can be used in a pro-oxidative manner to improve the effectiveness of other pro-oxidant therapies. This complexity was discussed in more detail in Chapter 6 under the heading 'Antioxidants', found towards the end of that chapter. Before utilising antioxidant supplements as part of any treatment strategy, I would recommend re-reading this section, as well as consulting a medical professional who understands the complex relationship between free radicals and antioxidants. Daniel Stanciu Ph.D has accumulated a wealth of information on this topic that can clarify the complexities involved. His website 'cancertreatmentresearch.com' provides a good foundation from which to perform your own research, and will give you confidence in discussing this crucial topic with your oncologist.

Remember that applying these strategies may not work for everyone. Variations in tumours and the health status of individual patients need to be considered, and there are many other variable factors involved. In particular, the condition of the liver must be taken into account. More aggressive and late-stage cancers may be more reliant upon the amino-acid *arginine*, so arginine starvation therapy may need to be considered. Some cancers are stimulated by estrogen, and there's always the potential for random DNA damage to render the cell resistant to specific treatments. Furthermore, some fungi may already be resistant to particular anti-fungal drugs.

A cautionary note regarding the use of glutamine inhibitors such as DON: many beneficial biological functions require glutamine to operate, and if restricted, may provide an advantage to cancer cells. A reduction in glutamine can impair beneficial gut bacteria, cause issues with gut repair, and suppress cancer-killing immune cells. It may be preferable to use glutamine inhibitors sparingly, in short bursts at key points during your treatment strategy. In her book, Jane McLelland refers to the 'pulsing' of medications intermittently in what she describes as 'kill phases', essentially exposing the patient to a drug for short periods. This may be worth considering for these glutamine inhibitors, to allow the gut and immune system a chance to recover.

It is evident that a detailed strategic approach to treatment needs to be considered and meticulously planned, one which is finely tuned to your individual circumstances. It is also clear that there are many other less toxic options available besides those provided by mainstream medicine, options with greater potential efficacy, because they are targeting key factors that drive the disease, as well as the fungal pathogens that I propose are the cause of the disease.

We mustn't allow our outlook to be restricted by the limitations of the view presented by the medical establishment. Asserting that DNA mutation is the cause of cancer, and therefore the only factor worth targeting, is a narrow and frankly, unscientific attitude to take. There is now abundant evidence indicating that DNA mutations are not driving the disease, and my research demonstrates that a targeted metabolic/anti-fungal approach holds great promise. We only have to look at the lack of efficacy of mainstream treatments to realise it is unwise not to consider a broader range of options and information – objectivity is key in science and to making genuinely informed treatment decisions.

While working with your oncologist, it may also be beneficial to seek out an 'Integrative Doctor', a 'Nutritional Therapist' (specialising in cancer support) or 'Functional Medicine Practitioner'. These medical professionals tend to provide a more holistic view and are open to using lifestyle and complementary treatments. They will be able to test vitamin and mineral levels, and assess the health of your microbiome, which constitutes up to 80% of your immune defence. A list of practitioners can be found in the *Yes To Life* Directory, which can be accessed at the following link: www.yestolife.org.uk/life-directory/

It would also be wise to partner with a personal trainer to oversee your exercise plan, and to keep you motivated.

To help you, I have prepared a '7-step action plan' that summarises some of the detail we've just covered. It will guide you through the process of creating a personalised treatment strategy with your oncologist. Following this, I list 35 key factors to help guide your research. It provides you with a foundation from which to undertake further research, and create a strategy that caters for your individual needs.

A 7-step action plan

Step 1: Diet and lifestyle:

Adopt the new lifestyle approach described above. The idea here is to support your body's natural healing abilities, reverse the toxic conditions that encouraged cancer to develop, and create an internal environment that is hostile to both cancer cells and fungal pathogens.

Adopt an organic, whole-food plant-based diet: This will help remove toxins, reduce inflammation, remove the growth hormones and antibiotics found in meat and dairy, and will provide you with cancer-fighting anti-fungal plant compounds, all while reducing your refined sugar intake, starving the tumour/fungus of its primary food source. The organic nutrients will support cell repair and immune function. Be mindful of consuming too many carbohydrates though, as these are also converted to glucose. You should consider reducing your intake of carbohydrate-rich foods, such as bread, potatoes, pasta and rice, and ensure you avoid refined white versions. As bread is associated with yeast, and gluten (which can damage the gut lining and cause inflammation), it may be preferable to eliminate it altogether. Sweet potatoes are preferable to white potatoes, and wholegrain brown rice is a far better choice than white rice. Consult a qualified Nutritional Therapist to create a safe diet plan that will obviate the glucose spikes that feed tumour growth.

Develop an exercise regime: This will help to eliminate excess glucose, oxygenate the body, and strengthen cell and immune defences.

Supplement essential nutrients: Consume vitamin B12, vitamin D3 and vitamin K at the very least, but be wary, not all supplements, such as antioxidants, are beneficial in all circumstances. You can monitor your nutrient intake with a diet app on your phone, which can reveal other nutrients you may be deficient in, such as *iodine* and *selenium*.

Eliminate toxins and inflammation-causing additives: These can be present within food, e.g. *carrageenan*, and also within personal care products. Look towards using organic products that contain natural extracts, as opposed to synthetic chemicals. Make a concerted effort to eliminate your exposure to mould within the home and workplace – fungal moulds secrete toxins, which can suppress the immune system.

Establish a de-stress routine: Reduce stress hormones and support your immune system by practicing meditation, yoga, forest bathing or other relaxing activities. According to the latest Japanese studies, forest bathing (the act of spending time within woodland areas) has been shown to improve immune function and activate cancer-killing immune cells.[630, 631]

And fast: Fasting can quickly reduce excess glucose, help to remove old and dying cells, and re-stimulate the immune system. Fasting for more than 30 hours has been shown to greatly benefit immune function, and provides protective properties against chemotherapy, but be mindful of your physical state and ease your way into this practice. Supervision by an expert in the field is highly advisable, particularly if undergoing conventional treatment, such as chemotherapy.

Step 2: Establish the fuels being used and stage of progression:

This is critical when deciding which treatment choice to make, because it will determine the types of approaches you should use. To discover the dominant fuel being absorbed by your cancer, open a search engine on your computer and simply enter: 'your cancer type + metabolic phenotype', for example: 'Endometrial stromal sarcoma metabolic phenotype'. This should bring up several articles discussing the dominant fuel types known to be used with your cancer type; have this verified by your oncologist. It is also paramount that you get answers to all the questions mentioned at the beginning of this chapter, from your oncologist. This is the foundational information that will determine your course of treatment.

Step 3: List the potential treatments for your cancer type:

Make a list of all the potential drugs and natural compounds that appear to have potential. While your doctor or pharmacist may not be able to prescribe some of the treatments you wish to undertake, they can interpret the data from blood tests and advise you regarding known drug interactions. The key is finding a doctor or pharmacist who is supportive of your decision to treat yourself using an integrative approach. Locate support groups and others who have successfully treated the same cancer, cross-referencing their information with your independent research.

Step 4: Research drug interactions and side effects:

Research the contraindications associated with the drugs and natural compounds on your list. Choose the most effective medications with the least side effects. Ensure they act upon the fuels your tumour is consuming and include compounds that are anti-fungal in nature. Keep the health of your liver in mind at all times. Seek medical guidance – but be mindful that medical doctors will generally be dismissive of the concept of a fungal pathogen being responsible for driving the disease, and may even reject the concept of targeting cell energy pathways, let alone fungal pathogens.

Step 5: Apply the strategy religiously:

Draw up a plan of how to administer the treatment you have researched, and make sure you involve your oncologist, to ensure you are not simply over-doing it, or using combinations that interact badly with each other. Encourage your family and friends to help you when you hit low points, or are doubting yourself and the treatment you are using.

Ensure that you are strict and refrain from falling into bad habits such as consuming treats like chocolate and alcohol that feed the disease. Establish other treats that can benefit you and not the disease. Include a diet plan and an exercise regime, and stipulate time for relaxation, breath-work and mindfulness practices. Follow your strategy for a reasonable length of time, unless, of course, it is clearly detrimental. Be wary of jumping from one protocol to the next or of constantly changing your mind; you may inadvertently stop using a treatment that is actually working.

Step 6: Monitor your progress using blood tests:

Analyse your blood for known cancer markers so that you can check your progress and adapt accordingly. Arrange scheduled blood tests with your oncologist. Also, keep a day-to-day journal, recording how you feel and the responses that occur throughout your treatment. This will allow you to identify problems or benefits in relation to the particular treatments you are using. You can then discuss these with your oncologist. I cover the basics regarding blood tests and what to look for in the following chapter.

Step 7: Re-address your strategy, adapt accordingly:

Cancer cells and fungal pathogens are good at adapting to new stimuli and can be difficult to kill once they've established themselves. Depending on your blood results, you may need to rethink your strategy. A fungal pathogen may be resistant to a drug you are using, DNA damage may have rendered a solution ineffective. Your blood type and the health status of your microbiome can have a significant influence on the efficacy of a drug. Despite our similarities, our bodies are remarkably individual. Your gut microbiome and blood type can determine how well you absorb and utilise drugs and other treatments. If your current approach is not working, then return to stage 3 and repeat the process.

This 7-step approach also applies to conventional treatment should you choose to undertake this route. Adopt step 1 and 2. In step 3, establish whether or not the treatments offered target the fuels feeding your cancer type, and the cancer stem cells generating tumour growth. Also, determine if anything else can bolster the effectiveness of the treatments, or reduce their side effects. Fasting, for example, has been shown in several studies to reduce the side effects of chemotherapy, and strengthen the immune response. Particular antioxidant supplements taken in the correct manner and at the correct time can benefit pro-oxidant therapies, and help you to recover form them. It may even be beneficial to have the composition of your microbiome analysed, which can be achieved by sending a stool sample to a relevant lab offering this service; a practitioner such as a Nutritional Therapist can arrange this. This may lead to a better functioning gut and improved immune function. In step 4, double-check side-effects and drug interactions, and then apply steps 5, 6 and 7.

35 key considerations

Due to the complexities involved, I have created a list of 35 critical factors to consider when researching which approach to take – this will aid in the decision-making process when creating your strategic plan of attack. Some of these have already been mentioned. This is by no means an exhaustive list, so please do as much research as you feel is necessary.

1. Adopt an organic, whole food plant-based diet:
If you didn't apply this initially, consider applying this now. Include raw juices of fruit and veg and spices that contain known medicinal compounds and anti-fungal chemicals. These include bromelain (pineapple), sulforaphane (broccoli) and curcumin (turmeric), which have been shown to inhibit cancer stem cells. This produce should be as fresh as possible, and preferably local because the anti-fungal salvestrol compounds present within the food, are at their most abundant at the point of ripening, and degrade during storage. Essentially, the aim is to change your diet and lifestyle to reverse the cell-damaging and inflammation-causing habits that may have led to the disease in the first place.; and to create a healthy environment in which the tumour, and fungal pathogen, will struggle to grow.

2. Agree to non-invasive surgery where applicable:
If the tumour can be safely removed without being intrusive, it makes sense to remove it. While there is a chance of cancer spreading during surgery, the greater threat is the tumour mass and the concern that it may generate cancer stem cells. Therefore, it would be wise to also adopt an organic, whole-food plant-based diet and an exercise regime to help kill any remaining cancer cells. You may wish to consider other options such as cannabis or salvestrol supplements for a while after surgery, and even an anti-fungal drug for a short period.

3. Research the fuel that is feeding the disease:

Uncovering the dominant fuel type will determine which treatments you need to adopt. As always, converse with your doctor, do your own research, and read Jane McLelland's book *How to Starve Cancer* to learn about these fuel types and the compounds that can be used to target these metabolic pathways. Keep in mind though, that fungal involvement is not likely to be considered within most protocols suggested by others. Learn about the drugs that can inhibit the fuel your tumour is absorbing, with a view to it being the fungus that is actually utilising this fuel. Choose your medications based upon their anti-fungal capability, as well as their fuel restricting properties. Lovastatin is an excellent example of an anti-fungal drug that inhibits fat absorption; Tamoxifen is an example of an anti-fungal drug that restricts estrogen (but only in breast cancer). Metformin blocks the glutamine-to-glucose conversion pathway and is also anti-fungal.

4. Support sleep patterns and the immune system with melatonin:

Naturally, your sleep will be affected, which will negatively impact your immune system. We create melatonin when we sleep, and broken sleep patterns reduce the amount the body produces. Melatonin is essential because it is a potent antimicrobial hormone capable of killing fungal pathogens,[532, 533] and has been shown to kill cancer cells.[533, 534] For this reason, and due to its ability to improve sleep,[535] if insomnia becomes an issue, it may be beneficial to take melatonin supplements before going to bed. The benefits of melatonin against cancer appear to be remarkable and well worth researching. It's of particular interest that melatonin restricts glucose absorption and cancer cell energy creation.[545, 546] Please consult your physician regarding safe dosage, and when it is best to take these supplements, but be aware not to rely heavily on melatonin supplements to get you to sleep; too much reliance on an external source can mean your body will stop producing it naturally.

5. Supplement with vitamin D and K:

Vitamin D is critical to immune function and to the absorption of calcium. Vitamin D regulates calcium within the blood and is used to help alert immune cells to the risk of fungal infection. Vitamin D deficiency is an under-diagnosed condition that is directly related to many diseases, including cancer. Ensure the supplement used is the D3 form and not the synthetic D2 form, which doesn't appear to be as effective. Vitamin K works in unison with vitamin D and is needed to ensure calcium is absorbed into your bones and removed from soft tissue. MK-7 appears to be the preferred version of vitamin K to take. As with any vitamin, there is a limit to the benefit it provides. Overdosing on vitamins will not provide ever-increasing levels of benefit; past a specific dose, some vitamins can do more harm than good, so always be mindful of the quantity you are taking.

6. Supplement with vitamin B12:

All cancer patients develop a level of methyl-deficiency, which is largely caused by a reduction in Vitamin B12, but also dysregulation of methionine metabolism. Vitamin B12 is required to keep DNA functioning normally, and depletion adversely affects every cell of the body. A plant-based diet won't supply the vitamin B12 needed, unless B12-fortified foods are consumed. This is increasingly the case for a standard meat-based diet as well, because most cattle bred for consumption are factory-farmed, and no longer acquire vitamin B12 from eating grass in open pastures. It is the consumption of the bacteria present in the soil that creates this vital vitamin. It is important to regularly monitor vitamin B12 levels within the blood.

7. Restrict glucose and lactate via diet:

Glucose is the primary food source of cancer cells and fungi. Cancer cells absorb it at approximately 18 times the rate of normal cells due to the switch in energy to glycolysis that occurs. Furthermore, glycolysis generates lactate (lactic acid), which fungi also use as fuel. This makes glucose restriction a particularly promising strategy, because it depletes the two primary fuel sources of the cancer cell and the fungus. Eliminate all refined sugars from your diet. Refined sugar is not bound to fibre, so it's absorbed into the bloodstream extremely quickly, providing the fungus and tumour with the abundance of glucose both need to thrive. Try to consume foods containing a low GI rating. The Glycaemic Index (GI) of a food indicates how quickly sugar from it is absorbed and converted within the body. Depending on your cancer type, you may also want to consider the ketogenic diet, which is specifically designed to restrict glucose. Please note that the ketogenic diet generally incorporates meat consumption; red meat, in particular, can generate inflammation.[074] This diet is also lower in plant anti-fungals to that of an organic plant-based diet. There is a plant-based version of the ketogenic diet worth considering.

8. Restrict glucose via exercise:

Exercise will deplete glucose stores and strengthen mitochondria, which are part of your natural cell defence system. Within a month of starting a moderate exercise programme, the number of mitochondria within each cell can almost double; this provides cells with an increased ability to defend against invading fungal pathogens. Exercise has been shown to prevent cancer from forming by up to 60%, which is a remarkable figure, so it should be an essential part of any treatment regime. Don't overdo it though, as excessive exercise can weaken the immune system. I wouldn't recommend performing exercise immediately after consuming a meal either, as some advocate. It's thought that exercising immediately after food consumption will help burn off any sugar consumed. However, this may be detrimental, as diverting considerable resources to exercise will be likely to reduce the stomach's capacity to absorb the essential nutrients that are needed to support the immune system and kill the fungal infection; it can also lead to cramps and nausea. There are much better ways to restrict the amount of sugar that tumours can access, such as limiting the glucose you consume at meal times.

9. Restrict glutamine-to-glucose conversion:

If dietary glucose restriction doesn't appear to be working, this could be due to the liver generating glucose from lactate and glutamine via *gluconeogenesis*. This means that glucose is still being supplied to tumours via an internal glucose-creation mechanism that keeps blood glucose levels normal in spite of glucose restriction within the diet. Critically, fungi can also convert glutamine into glucose when glucose is scarce by utilising this same gluconeogenic pathway that is present within the fungus itself. Thankfully, the drug Metformin and the plant extract berberine can block this conversion from occurring in both the liver and the fungus. The only downside to using berberine is that medical science hasn't tested it on humans in clinical trials to determine how much berberine is needed for it to be effective. The drug Metformin has been tested and is known to be effective at restricting the liver's ability to create glucose. It is used by diabetics, so has a long proven safety profile; however, it comes with side effects and can be toxic to the liver. Metformin also has anti-fungal properties.[717, 718]

10. Restrict cell energy pathways using off-label drugs, such as DON:

Patients have reported great successes with a multitude of off-patent drugs that restrict cell energy creation. These include Jane McLelland,[449] Rosie Garrett,[325] and Professor Ben Williams.[322, 324] Jane McLelland provides a detailed account regarding which cellular pathways each of these over-the-counter drugs affect. I highly recommend reading her book, *How to Starve Cancer* and understanding her 'Metro map'. You may also want to consider a glutamine inhibitor drug, such as *6-diazo-5-oxo-L-norleucine* (also known as 'DON')[780] that directly prevents glutamine from being utilised by cancer cells (Metformin does not block glutamine absorption, just the conversion of glutamine into glucose via the liver). Successfully blocking glutamine absorption may also block aspartate, arginine creation and DNA synthesis, which fungi rely upon for growth (aspartate is created from glutamine and used to create DNA and arginine). It may also sensitise the tumour to damage because the cell will be inhibited from making the protective antioxidant glutathione (which is also created from glutamine). Just ensure the glutamine inhibitor drug of choice does not adversely affect the gut and the immune system (both require glutamine to function). With this in mind, it may be preferable to use glutamine inhibitor drugs sparingly and pulse them in 'kill phases', allowing the gut and immune system to recover between bouts of the treatment.

11. Consider anti-fungal medications:

Itraconazole, Clotrimazole, Ketoconazole, Miconazole, Econazole and Fluconazole are anti-fungal drugs that have shown efficacy at killing cancer cells and reducing tumour size. I cannot emphasize enough that caution needs to be taken with these drugs, because they are extremely toxic. The advice is always to research the medication you plan to use, and consult a medical professional. Depending upon your overall health status and any other medications you may be taking, anti-fungal drugs may result in a detrimental reaction. Furthermore, the fungal pathogen(s) proposed to be responsible are currently unknown, and not all anti-fungal drugs kill all fungal pathogens. For instance, while Fluconazole is available over the counter and can be effective at killing *Candida* fungal species, it is ineffective against *Aspergillus* fungi – if *Aspergillus* infection is driving your cancer, the toxicity of Fluconazole may worsen your outcome and aid these *Aspergillus* species. Itraconazole, which is only available with a prescription, kills both *Candida* and *Aspergillus* species as well as many others. It's broad-spectrum efficacy may explain why Itraconazole appears to be more effective against a broader range of cancers than Fluconazole.

12. Consider fat restriction in combination with anti-fungal drugs:

If you have a fat-dominant cancer, choosing a statin help. Statins work on several levels. They restrict the cell from absorbing fat and act upon the fungus directly by preventing the fat-to-glucose conversion pathway present within the fungus. Statins are exciting because they can also be used in combination with the azole class of anti-fungal drugs to markedly increase their effect.[599] When combined with Fluvastatin, the anti-fungal effects of Itraconazole are improved, allowing lower dosages, and so reducing toxicity.[599] Lovastatin works in synergy with Fluconazole, improving its anti-fungal effects.[599] Both combinations are effective against *Candida albicans*. A word of caution – there are different types of statins. According to Jane McLelland, the *lipophilic* type appears to be effective, but the *hydrophilic* type of statin appears to aid the disease, as she explains in her book (pg 333 under the heading *mevalonate*). Please research this carefully.

13. Consider medicinal plants and essential oils:

Consider cannabis oil, but be aware of local laws. The oil should be natural, not synthetic, and from a reputable source, preferably grown in organic conditions. All of our cells contain two cannabinoid receptors, allowing the medicinal and anti-fungal elements of cannabis to be absorbed directly and immediately into cells. This is why cannabis appears to be so effective and acts so quickly. All essential oils extracted from plants have shown promising effects against cancer in pre-clinical studies, and they all contain powerful anti-fungal compounds. These potent essential oils should be as pure as possible and taken only after researching how to safely administer them.

14. Consider taking colloidal silver:

Silver was widely used as an antibiotic before the creation of synthetic antibiotics. Colloidal silver refers to tiny silver nano-particles that are suspended in a solution, which is then consumed. Studies confirm that it selectively kills cancer cells in a dose-dependent manner. But as with any substance, toxic levels can be reached if consumed to excess.

15. Eradicate systemic fungal infection:

Anti-fungal drugs can kill the initial infection, but they may not completely eliminate fungi within the body. If a lifestyle change is not adopted, then the previous lifestyle that encouraged fungal infection will again promote tumour growth, only next time, the fungus may be resistant to the previous anti-fungal medication used. So it's not wise to just rely on anti-fungal drugs alone. There are many diets that purport to eliminate or mediate unwanted fungal infections.

16. Consider plant-based anti-fungal supplements:

Salvestrol supplements contain condensed plant antibiotics and have been shown to treat 15 cancer patients in three small human trials. The two professors that identified and created them made salvestrol available as nutritional supplements. This was in response to the lack of interest to fund human clinical trials that could establish the efficacy of salvestrol. In particular, science confirms that salvestrols are converted by the CYP1B1 enzyme into toxic substances that only kill cancer cells.

17. **Factor in fungal die-off**:

Fungi release toxins when killed. These 'mycotoxins' are released into the bloodstream, causing systemic inflammation that can result in severe reactions. This can make the patient feel like they are getting worse, and place an extra strain on the liver, which deals with toxin removal. Patients should keep this in mind when attempting to treat cancer, so as not to overload the liver by killing the fungus too fast. Blood tests should be taken, and cancer antigen markers should be closely monitored to see if tumour volume decreases. You may also wish to monitor 'nagalase', which can indicate the extent of infection within the body, and is a reflection of the tumour burden.

18. **Reduce your exposure to fungi:**

Remove mould-fermented produce from the diet, such as cheese, alcohol, and yeast associated foods such as bread. Regularly wash bed linen and avoid dampness in the home and work environment that can encourage fungal growth. Consider wearing a surgical mask when outside or in public, not only to protect yourself against germs passed on by others that risk weakening your immune system but because, on average, we inhale up to 300 fungal spores a day via the air we breathe. An N95 rated mask can filter out most fungi, bacteria and some viruses. Just be mindful that wearing a mask for too long can have adverse effects on your carbon dioxide and oxygen consumption, and if over-used there is a risk of the mask harbouring toxic levels of the bacteria and fungi you breathe out. Please note, not all fungi are pathogenic, in fact, some are medicinal, such as *Trametes Versicolor* (also known as turkey tail*)*, which has actually been shown to inhibit cancer cells, so mycotherapy should also be considered.[548]

19. **Consider restricting methionine and arginine:**

Both methionine and arginine are consumed by fungal pathogens and are required for their continued survival. Studies show that in cancer, levels of both are abnormal and increased consumption of methionine and arginine occur. Restricting both has been shown to have a beneficial effect, especially in aggressive cancers that rely on dietary sources of methionine and arginine.[833]

20. **Use iron to your advantage – Artemisinin:**

Artemisinin is an anti-malarial drug that's in common use today. In pre-clinical studies it has also been shown to kill cancer cells selectively. It appears to achieve this by reacting with the excess iron contained within the tumour. Peroxide within Artemisinin reacts with iron to form free radicals;[493, 494] healthy cells aren't affected, as they do not contain the level of freely available iron that is found to be present within cancer cells. Artemisinin is, therefore, a targeted form of treatment that only kills cancer cells, and of course, free radicals also kill fungal pathogens. Iron supplementation during the use of Artemisinin has been shown to increase the potency of the drug. In studies, Artemisinin was shown to be more effective than chemotherapy at killing cancer cells and a great deal less toxic.[495] The condition of the liver should be considered before opting for this approach because the liver stores large quantities of iron. While Artemisinin should be fine to use with a healthy liver, freely available iron will be present in a damaged liver, which may react with the drug, causing further damage to this critical organ.

21. High-dose intravenous vitamin C therapy:

Recent studies have confirmed that high-dose intravenous vitamin C therapy (IV-C) can selectively kill cancer cells because hydrogen peroxide reacts with the freely available iron present within cancer cells, in much the same way as Artemisinin. This produces a large quantity of damaging free radicals. IV-C therapy is also being tested in clinical trials, as the free radical damage it generates seems to sensitise cancer cells to chemotherapy.[520] Before this recent landmark study was conducted, high-dose IV-C therapy was deemed controversial and ineffective. But this previous view of the therapy was based on studies that were set up incorrectly: scientists should have been measuring the effectiveness of *intravenous* vitamin C, but instead measured high-dose vitamin C given orally in supplement form – this provided a completely different reaction.[520] High-dose vitamin C taken intravenously generates free radicals that kill cancer cells by reacting with iron. But when vitamin C is taken in pill form, it is metabolised to create antioxidants that neutralise the free radicals that kill fungi, and it increases iron absorption, with potentially the opposite effect of supporting the fungal pathogen.[654]

22. Eliminate inflammation:

Wherever inflammation is found, cancer too may be found. Inflammation is not the cause of the disease; it is the warning sign that damage is being caused by either a toxin or micro-organism or even both. Many chemical toxins in conventional foods and everyday products will cause irritation and inflammation (cell damage). Personal care products often contain toxins, even carcinogens. Processed foods can contain additives such as carrageenan, and many vegetable oils have the wrong ratio of omega-3 to -6; all these should be avoided because they all generate persistent inflammation. There are many more everyday products and food additives that need to be avoided. I cover some of these in Chapter 20.

23. Avoid endocrine disrupters (such as BPA):

These are found in plastics, and many common household items, including fizzy drinks cans, tin cans that store food, and even bottles used to feed babies. They create hormonal imbalances that weaken the immune system and generate inflammation. Some products are now BPA free and are advertised as such, although the BPA has often been replaced by some other compound that is as yet, untested for its effects.

24. Carefully consider antioxidant supplements:

The issues surrounding antioxidant supplementation is complex. Some studies, which are limited in scope due to their reliance on synthetic antioxidants, indicated that antioxidants in high doses can encourage cancer growth. Antioxidants are essential for healthy cell function in order to control damaging free radicals. They can also be used to aid with pro-oxidant therapies. How you utilise antioxidants will depend on your health status, and the treatment strategy being deployed. Given the nuances involved, discussing your choices with a medical professional who understands the complexity associated with free radicals and antioxidant interactions, is critical to ensuring antioxidant supplements are being used in a beneficial manner.

25. Avoid exposure to antibiotics where possible:

Antibiotics destroy the beneficial bacteria of our microbiome, and also damage mitochondria. If antibiotics cannot be avoided, you should consider supporting the gut microbiome with probiotics and prebiotics during and after medication. Probiotic tablets designed to bypass the acid within the stomach are available to purchase at most health food stores. But please consult a medical professional who appreciates the complex interactions between probiotic supplements and the microbiome, as this is a relatively new area of study; our understanding of the intricate relationship between the microbiome and our health is in its infancy.

26. Reduce your exposure to growth hormone:

Growth hormone is found in animal products, especially milk and factory-farmed meat. It is injected into cattle to artificially increase growth. These hormones stimulate growth signals in cancer cells too, increasing the risk of driving tumour aggression. If purchasing meat or dairy products, always opt for organic and grass fed.

27. Remove cosmetics containing known irritants:

SLS, parabens, parfum and other synthetic chemicals will irritate the body and cause inflammation as well as cell damage. Most cosmetics contain some, if not several of these toxins, so take the time to research brands that specifically market their products as being free from them, look for the Soil Association organic mark, and beware of 'greenwashing' – where appealing language and natural-looking packaging is used to make a toxic product appear 'cleaner' than it really is.

28. Consider glutamine supplementation:

Glutamine depletion throughout the body (caused by tumours absorbing it in quantity) causes side effects that benefit cancer cells. A lack of glutamine results in immune suppression, weakening of our defensive microbiome, and cells that are less able to defend themselves. Glutamine depletion also leads to cachexia (a wasting disease resulting in muscle loss). Studies show that, on balance, glutamine supplementation may provide a greater overall benefit to the patient rather than the tumour.[460, 462] This needs to be carefully considered, and the best choice will depend on your health status; it is also contrary to one of the options previously suggested, which is to restrict glutamine absorption. The option you choose will depend entirely upon your particular circumstances, whether a pro-oxidant treatment is being used, and the stage to which the cancer has progressed. With a pro-oxidant therapy you would want to reduce glutamine temporarily in order to reduce the antioxidant 'glutathione', so that the treatment is more damaging.

29. Hyperbaric oxygen therapy (HBOT) and breathing techniques:

This therapy increases the oxygen within the body, which can have many beneficial effects. Hypoxia (a lack of oxygen) causes an increase in acidity as it promotes the activation of glycolysis, which generates lactic acid as a byproduct;[489] lactic acid feeds the aggressive nature of fungal pathogens, which also prefer hypoxic conditions. Hyperbaric oxygen therapy can help reverse this process, reducing the amount of lactic acid being produced, as well as the levels of freely available iron. Increasing oxygen levels within the body has been shown to improve resistance to infection from micro-organisms,[489, 834, 835] in fact, studies show that HBOT is anti-fungal and can treat common fungal infections,[836, 837] which aligns with the Cell Suppression model. Could this be why HBOT has been shown to have a positive effect against cancer?[838] With this in mind, you may wish to consider implementing specific breathing methods into your daily routine, such as the 'Wim Hof' breathing method, which effectively increases oxygen saturation within the cells of the body. Wim Hof and his breathing technique have been studied in a scientific setting, so there is good evidence to support its health benefits. Home HBOT chambers are now available, although these are costly. A more economic alternative may be available at a nearby MS Therapy Centre, which usually have a chamber, and often allow cancer patients access at low cost.

30. Alkalising the body:

This is seen as controversial because acidity is a symptom, not the underlying cause. However, studies confirm that reducing acidity levels can inhibit cancer invasiveness. The controversy seems to be associated with how best to alkalise the body. Rebalancing body pH levels appears to be a beneficial strategy; however, it can facilitate cancer growth if applied incorrectly. Luckily, a plant-based diet seems to be metabolised within the body to generate alkaline conditions. This is covered in more detail within the next chapter.

31. Stay well hydrated by drinking filtered water:

Dehydration will diminish your body's natural repair mechanisms. Good hydration will expedite the excretion of toxins and pathogens and ensure the body is working at its optimum. According to Dr Batmanghelidj, most of us are unaware that we are chronically dehydrated, and that undiagnosed dehydration is a major player in many diseases, given that the body cannot function effectively without being adequately hydrated.[314] Consider using a gravity-fed ceramic water filtration system capable of removing chemicals such as fluoride, pesticides and heavy metals from the water supply. Cheaper common household water filters can't remove most toxins; a more robust ceramic gravity-fed filtration system should be used.

32. Resist treats that will support fungi and weaken the immune system:

Its extremely tempting to reward ourselves with treats such as confectionery or alcohol, as we all deserve to let our hair down.

Unfortunately, refined sugars found in confectionery suppresses the immune system and feeds fungal and cancer cell growth. Consuming these treats will undo the progress you have made because it will allow fungi to re-group, as will alcohol.

33. **Research how others have treated the same type of cancer**:
Speak to other cancer survivors – you are not alone. Don't just rely on close friends and family for support. They may not have any experience of cancer and will likely push you to choose conventional treatment, because they are unaware of the state of the industry, and understandably, believe that doctors know best. Jane McLelland has a great Facebook group for cancer patients, as do many others, such as Mark Sean Taylor's group 'Patient Led Oncology Trials'.

34. **Join support groups and seek out other health professionals:**
While family and friends will support you as best they can, they may not have the experience to deal with your illness emotionally. Support groups can provide an extra level of understanding, which will help take a little pressure off you and your family. Look for groups interested in researching all options and integrative care, such as Yes To Life's Wigwam groups. Seek out an Integrative Doctor, Nutritional Therapist (who specialises in supporting people with cancer), or a Functional Medicine Practitioner, as they provide a holistic approach and are open to using a broad range of treatments. They will be able to look at your vitamin and mineral levels, including the health of your microbiome.

35. **Be friendly towards your oncologist**:
Most medical professionals genuinely want to help and are just following the mainstream training they have been provided with. In most cases, they are restricted by the profession and cannot legally provide the unconventional treatments you may wish to pursue. But be wary of pushy and rude doctors who aren't supportive of your views and concerns, as dealing with them can be undermining and can sap valuable energy you need to pursue your health and well-being. This is your body, not theirs.

This is by no means an exhaustive list; there are other approaches presented by people who have experience of successfully treating their cancer, so please continue your research, and consider checking out the other resources listed in Appendix B.

CH.20

Potential solutions – Part 2: the extra detail

Surgery:

Depending on the surgery required, I would advocate having surgery if the tumour is small enough to operate on. While there is a risk of the cancer spreading, the risk is low. If the tumour is local and contained and the surgery not too invasive, it seems logical to have it removed. Often oncologists will offer chemotherapy as an adjunctive treatment after surgery; the idea is to kill any cancer cells they may have missed. While initial bouts of chemotherapy can be effective at killing cancer cells, be mindful that chemotherapy damages healthy cells in ways that can help promote the disease.

There are less toxic ways of generating the same free radicals that chemotherapy creates, such as using Artemisinin or intravenous vitamin C therapy – both of which are far less damaging to healthy cells. Changing your diet and lifestyle is one of the best adjunctive regimes to undertake because it works with the body in a non-toxic manner by boosting immune strength and the body's natural healing abilities, as well as creating an environment that is hostile to fungal infection and cancer growth.

Blood tests – monitoring your progress:

Monitoring your progress is one of the most crucial aspects of any treatment protocol; it will identify whether the treatment you are using is proving beneficial. You are then in a position to modify the treatment protocol if need be. As a species, we are remarkably different from one another, as witnessed by our varied responses to healthcare interventions. A drug that may work for most may not work for you. This difference can be due to many factors, including genetics, age, lifestyle, ethnicity, microbiome health, and even your blood type. You are unique; the subtle differences we each embody, mean that we need to monitor our progress individually to discover what works best for our particular circumstances and body type. It would be beneficial for you to at least monitor the following:

* Vitamin D and K
* Vitamin B12
* Blood glucose levels
* Infection levels
* Anaemia – caused by low iron levels and low red blood cell count which can be attributed to liver damage
* Nagalase levels – indicates infection level and is a marker of tumour growth
* Cancer-specific antigens – measuring these antigens will highlight the size of the tumour and indicate whether it is growing or diminishing
* Liver function/iron levels – testing for the following markers will indicate the functionality of the liver (normal levels are shown in square brackets):[514, 515]

Bilirubin	= [00 – 24 umol/L]
Albumin	= [34 – 50 g/L]
Alanine amino transferase (ALT)	= [05 – 50 IU/L]
Aspartate amino transferase (AST)	= [07 – 40 U/L]
Alkaline phosphatase (ALP)	= [20 – 130 U/L]
Gamma glutamyl transferase (GGT)	= [10 – 71 IU/L]
Ferritin	= [30 – 400 ug/L]

* Complete blood count (CBC) – a complete blood count will determine levels of vitamin B12, whether the patient is anaemic, potential micro-organism infection levels, and provides detailed

analysis of red and white blood cell counts. White blood cells represent the strength of the immune system.

* Inflammation markers – such as C-reactive protein (CRP) will indicate the level of cell damage and infection within the body, which, if too high, will only aid disease progression. You should aim to reduce these markers.[903]

* Jane McLelland provides additional details in her book (*How to Starve Cancer*) regarding other specific cancer markers you should also consider testing for.

Liver function and iron analysis:

ALT (Alanine amino transferase) and **AST** (Aspartate amino transferase) levels, indicate the degree of inflammation within the body. Amino transferases are enzymes present in liver cells that leak into the bloodstream when liver cells are damaged. These levels are usually high in patients with hepatitis (inflammation of the liver) and can be up to 20 to 50 times higher than normal. The ALT value is more specific to the liver than the AST value; the AST value may indicate muscle damage elsewhere in the body. Ratios of these enzymes can help determine whether you have NASH (non-alcoholic Steatohepatitis) or alcohol-related liver disease. If you have NASH, you have inflammation and liver cell damage, along with fat in your liver.

Alkaline phosphatase (ALP) is an enzyme found mainly in the bile ducts of the liver. Increases in ALP and another liver enzyme called Gamma GT (GGT) can indicate obstructive or cholestatic liver disease. GGT levels are a potential indicator of your alcohol intake.

Bilirubin is formed from haemoglobin and the main pigment in bile (a yellow/green substance made by your liver). An increase in bilirubin causes jaundice, which is a yellowing of the eyes and skin in liver disease.

Albumin is an essential protein that helps keep fluid pressure within the body stable and acts as a carrier for other important substances. Albumin may decrease in chronic liver disease, particularly as the disease gets worse, but may be reduced for other reasons such as a protein deficiency.[516] Reduced albumin levels can lead to a condition called *ascites* where fluid congregates in places it shouldn't – the stomach and legs may swell with fluid. This can also lead to low blood pressure, which increases the risk of fainting.

Ferritin is a measure of how much iron is stored in your body and can be used to diagnose anaemia or iron overload.

There are a lot of variables when evaluating a liver function test. Each result should be viewed in the context of the rest of the data; it is not wise to view these results in isolation. To ensure you are interpreting the information correctly, it would be preferable to seek the guidance of a health professional who can accurately analyse the data for you.

The glutamine dilemma:

Tumours absorb large quantities of glutamine. This is due in part to a reduced capacity of the cancer cell to acquire ATP energy from glucose, even if the cancer cell is absorbing it – from the Cell Suppression perspective, this is because it is the fungus that uses the majority of the glucose absorbed. This results in glutamine being used to create the ATP energy needed to fuel the cell.[710] As the cell divides and grows, it requires many other nutrients. Glutamine is also needed to create some of these essential nutrients. *Aspartate* is one, *glutathione* is another – the former aids with cell growth, and the latter is an antioxidant that generates resistance to toxic chemotherapy treatments.

Furthermore, both the liver and the fungus can convert glutamine into glucose, via a pathway called *gluconeogenesis*. This is where the drug Metformin is effective against cancer; it inhibits the gluconeogenesis pathway present in the fungal pathogen, but also in the liver, starving both of the glucose they require. So, should we restrict our glutamine intake or increase it?

To make the correct judgement, we must consider that glutamine also plays an essential role in supporting the immune system, supporting our gut microbiome, and creating glutathione in healthy cells, which protects them from toxin and free radical damage. When glutamine is depleted throughout the body – as generally occurs with cancer – it weakens the integrity of healthy cells and the gut lining, and suppresses the immune response, which aids the disease.[829] This puts us in a dilemma, because glutamine appears to feed cancer but is also needed to support the mechanisms that can fight cancer. The important question is: does glutamine supplementation benefit the tumour more than the patient?

Studies show that increasing glutamine through supplementation may have more of a beneficial effect for the patient than for the tumour.[460, 462] These studies indicate that when glucose is restricted and glutamine availability increases, the tumour's rate of growth does not increase. The effect of improving the immune system, cell defence, and cell repair, seems, on balance, to provide the patient with an advantage against the disease. This may reflect the fungal pathogen's reliance on glucose and its need to convert glutamine into glucose. Supplementing glutamine while treating with Metformin will provide the gut and immune system with the glutamine they require, while simultaneously restricting the ability of fungi to convert this glutamine into the glucose they need. This appears to be the crucial point.

Oncologists will probably disagree with increasing glutamine levels. This is because doing so reduces the effectiveness of the pro-oxidant chemotherapy treatments they wish to provide, and then there is always the concern that, as tumours consume glutamine, providing more to the patient could fuel the disease, but as I've just discussed, this doesn't appear to be the case. Regarding pro-oxidant therapies, cancer cells use glutamine to create glutathione, which is the antioxidant that protects them from toxin exposure and the free radicals generated by chemotherapy. From an oncologist's perspective, reducing glutathione is the goal, because this makes cancer cells more susceptible to chemotherapy damage, and so reducing glutamine is the preferred objective. If you decide to undertake a conventional pro-oxidant therapy, you may wish to consider using a glutamine inhibitor drug such as 'DON',[769] to restrict glutamine, and when used correctly, certain antioxidant supplements, especially in high doses, can aid pro-oxidant treatments by conversely diminishing antioxidants such as glutathione – the nuances of using antioxidant supplements were covered in Chapter 6.

The concern with a pro-oxidant approach, where glutamine and the antioxidant glutathione are restricted, is that healthy cells also become more vulnerable to toxic damage, because their glutamine and glutathione levels are also reduced. This increases the risk of organ failure and cachexia, which may render chemotherapy treatment less effective, simply because less of it can be tolerated. This isn't helped by the fact that restricting glutamine weakens immune cells and the gut microbiome.

Sugars from fruit:

As sugar is broken down into glucose, and glucose feeds cancer growth, there remains an important question to ask: is it safe to consume fruit? There is an abundance of evidence confirming how plant compounds, including fruit, effectively kill cancer cells. Organic pineapples appear to be effective due to the highly potent anti-fungal compound *bromelain*, which they contain. Honey, which is almost pure sugar, is also effective against cancer cells, demonstrating that some sugars appear beneficial. So what's the difference between fruit sugars and refined sugars? It appears to be the anti-fungal compounds found within these organic fruits that render the danger of consuming this sugar negligible. In fact, it is the very willingness of the cancer cell to absorb the sugar which aids in the delivery of these potent anti-fungal compounds into the cell, thus enabling them to interact with the intracellular fungus, and kill it. On the other hand, refined sugar does not contain any anti-fungal properties. This appears to be where the difference lies, it feeds the fungus without harming it. Honey, a substance that is primarily made of sugar, is capable of killing cancer cells instead of feeding them, as it is highly anti-fungal – this is particularly the case with non-peroxide honey, such as Manuka honey.

The key seems to be to ensure you consume organic produce, as it contains higher levels of plant antibiotics when compared to conventional food grown with pesticides. Besides this, conventional food also contains toxins that damage the cell, increasing inflammation and iron availability, aiding fungal invasion and cancer growth.

Diet:

Diets designed to kill fungi, such as the *anti-Candida* diet, and diets focused on repairing a damaged gut, such as the GAPS diet, should also be considered. The ultimate aim here is to weaken and remove fungal infection and make it very difficult for fungi to invade new cells. Supporting the immune system and reducing inflammation is imperative. Always consult a qualified dietician or Nutritional Therapist.

Genetically modified food will likely cause inflammation, given that the body won't recognise these modified molecules. GM foods are devoid of the plant antibiotics required to kill fungal infections, so should be avoided. Furthermore, GM foods are usually designed to withstand toxic pesticides sprayed on crops, meaning that many GM foods contain high levels of toxins. Organic produce contains the highest levels of nutrients and plant antibiotics without the toxic load.

Alkalising the body – the acid connection:

This needs to be thoroughly researched before attempting this strategy. I'm mentioning it here because it is one of the many alternative treatment approaches being bandied around the internet, and it could, potentially, be dangerous to adopt. The presumption seems to be that cancer forms because of an acidic environment within the body (consuming too many foods that turn tissue acidic once metabolised). Alkalising cancer tissue is seen as a way to inhibit the disease and even cure it. This conclusion is based on the fact that the tissue surrounding the tumour is highly acidic. While tumours do reside within an acidic environment, which can aid fungal infection and cancer progression, this acidity is not a cause of the disease but a symptom of tumour metabolism.

Lactic acid is produced as a result of the switch to glycolysis that occurs. It is a byproduct of an already cancerous cell, so it stands to reason that alkalising the body will not cure the disease.

However, neutralising the acid surrounding a tumour will be beneficial, and studies confirm that doing so inhibits tumour invasiveness and its ability to spread. Lactic acid is corrosive, so any reduction in acidity is a good thing.

Changing the pH balance within the body should be done with caution, and can be dangerous if adopted without professional guidance. Some advocate changing the pH of the blood, while others advocate drinking bicarbonate of soda to reduce the body's acidity level. Consuming bicarbonate of soda will neutralise the digestive acid within the stomach, and this may have adverse effects on digestion and absorption of vital nutrients. Weakened stomach acid will also fail to kill any dangerous micro-organisms consumed with food, increasing the risk of infection. Furthermore, blood pH is tightly regulated to stay at a constant pH of around 7.4, which is slightly alkaline anyway. Drinking bicarbonate of soda will not change blood pH levels – changing blood pH is not the goal here. It is the tissue pH that is the target of change, not the pH of the blood. Many media commentators incorrectly refer to changing the pH of the blood when speaking of alkalising the body.

Other points to consider:

1. **Prebiotics and probiotics** – A cancer patient's microbiome should be supported because these beneficial gut bacteria make up 80% of our overall immune defence. Consuming prebiotics – a form of dietary fibre that feeds beneficial gut bacteria – may be helpful in sustaining balance within the microbiome and promoting health. Probiotics refer to bacteria that are consumed to help repopulate the gut when bacterial populations have been diminished. Research still needs to be conducted to determine the many nuances associated with this complex field of study. Fermented foods, such as sauerkraut, are especially effective at helping to re-

establish good bacteria within the gut; difficult-to-digest cabbage enables some beneficial bacteria to bypass the acid within the stomach. It may be preferable to replenish the gut microbiome through natural means. Be sure to obtain unpasteurised sauerkraut, as the heat of pasteurisation can kill the beneficial bacteria within the product. Please also ensure a medical professional is consulted before applying any probiotic regime. We are still in the very early stages of understanding the microbiome, so all intake of probiotics should be cautious, and always for the short term only.

2. **Juice daily** – Juicing is the easiest and quickest way to obtain plant nutrients. Less strain is placed on the digestive system, because most of the hard work of breaking down the food has already been done, meaning that essential nutrients are more easily absorbed. But be wary of consuming too much sugar from fruit that isn't organic.

3. **Consider drinking antimicrobial herbal tea** – Pau d'Arco and green tea are two good examples that appear to possess anti-cancer properties, but be wary of consuming too much caffeine as this is a known urinary irritant. As always, ensure you do the relevant research.

4. **Milk** – This breakfast staple is not needed in the human diet. We are the only species that drinks it beyond early childhood and the only species that drinks milk from another species. Milk that is intended for a larger animal contains greater quantities of growth hormones that risk stimulating tumour growth in humans. In addition, cattle are often injected with artificial growth hormones and antibiotics, and many are fed genetically modified feed, the long-term health effects of which are unknown. This is surprisingly true of Europe, while cattle and crops are not allowed to be genetically modified, European law does not prevent GM crops from being fed to cattle.[574] Without realising it, Europeans may be consuming meat from cattle that have been fed genetically modified feed. If you are still consuming milk, it is preferable to acquire it from grass-fed animals and ensure it is organic. There are plant-based milk alternatives that can provide the calcium we require without the growth hormone, antibiotics, and genetic modification.

5. **Be wary of soy products** – Only consume organically sourced soy and research the controversies surrounding the hormones that soy contains. If in doubt, leave it out.

6. **Remove cosmetic toxins** – Use toiletries and cosmetics free from parabens, SLS, artificial colours, preservatives, and fragrances. To prevent burning and skin damage, it would be preferable to cover up rather than use sunscreen, because the chemicals in sunscreen are potentially harmful and can be absorbed into the bloodstream. However, a small amount of sun exposure is the quickest way to acquire essential vitamin D, so sensible sun exposure is very beneficial. Stay away from synthetic air fresheners, as they contain chemicals that have the potential to irritate our airways and cause inflammation.

7. **Fizzy and high energy drinks** – These products contain particularly high quantities of refined sugars that can feed fungal growth. Low calorie or sugar-free drinks will usually contain artificial sweeteners that may cause inflammation. Many cans are also lined with BPA, the plastic hormone disrupter that can leach into the contents of the can and cause inflammation.

8. **Go easy on the salt** – It can be an instigator of inflammation and cell damage when taken to excess – it may be preferable to increase potassium and magnesium levels instead. If you do consume salt, ensure it is not highly refined table salt, choose natural sea or rock salts, high in minerals.

9. **Understand oils,** trans fats, hydrogenation, and the correct balance of Omega-3 and -6:
   - **Trans fats** are oils that become altered when heated, and are no longer recognisable by the body as food. Some oils, such as rapeseed, have a high burning temperature, so they don't become damaged and do not turn into trans fats when used for cooking. Oils with a low burning point, such as virgin olive oil, sunflower oil, and flaxseed oil, turn into trans fats even at low temperatures. Trans fats are not well absorbed and cause systemic inflammation. Margarine is highly processed, can contain trans fats, and can be homogenised, resulting in products that cause inflammation. An option that avoids the risk of inflammation is to steam vegetables, or to fry them using water instead of oil.
   - **Homogenisation** is a process in which the fat in butter, margarine, and milk has been pressurised to form unnaturally

compressed molecules, to give consistency to products. The problem is that these molecules can pass directly into the bloodstream without being broken down first. This can cause damage to arteries, instigates inflammation, and may increase cholesterol levels within the blood.

- **Omega fatty acids** can be found in seaweed supplements, fish and vegetable oils. Fish provides a ratio of 4/1 in favour of omega-3 over omega-6 fatty acids. Most vegetable oils contain a ratio of at least 1/6 in favour of omega-6. Our cells do not know how to process this ratio. Omega-6 blocks the receptor sites for omega-3, which causes inflammation and stops the cell from gaining the omega-3 it needs. Sadly most fish now contain dangerous levels of mercury, which needs to be taken into account when considering this source of omega-3. Flaxseed is one of the few non-animal foods that provides the ideal balance of omega-3s and -6s. To obtain the full benefit that flaxseeds can provide, rather than relying on unstable oil, sprinkle organic ground flaxseed on cereal. Rapeseed oil appears to have the best omega ratio of all vegetable oils and has the added advantage of a very high burning point, so it won't turn into trans fat when used for cooking. Nuts and avocados are good natural sources of oil; just be sure to determine which ratio of omega-3 to -6 they contain. There are three types of omega-3: ALA, EPA and DHA. EPA and DHA are the most beneficial, as ALA needs to be converted into DHA before it can be used, and the conversion rate to DHA is often low. Vegans can obtain DHA from seaweed supplements.

Everyday toxins to avoid:

Below is just a small sample of the toxins we are regularly exposed to. There are many more contained within cosmetics and our environment, most of which can lead to cell damage and persistent inflammation. Educating ourselves about toxins, and doing our best to limit our exposure is of paramount importance:

Mercury blocks the absorption of zinc,[679] which is essential for immune system function. *Candida albicans* absorbs mercury and releases it as a toxin. Mercury is a dangerous neurotoxin and can be found in fish, tooth fillings, energy-saving bulbs, and even some vaccines (as Thimerosal).

Fluoride, which is added to toothpaste and water, is classed as a neurotoxin and causes inflammation which damages neurons:

> '...In 2006, we did a systematic review and identified five industrial chemicals as developmental **neurotoxicants**: lead, methylmercury, polychlorinated biphenyls, arsenic, and toluene. Since 2006, epidemiological studies have documented six additional developmental neurotoxicants — manganese, *fluoride*, chlorpyrifos, dichlorodiphenyltrichloroethane, tetrachloroethylene, and the polybrominated diphenyl ethers. We postulate that even more neurotoxicants **remain undiscovered**.'
>
> <u>The Lancet Neurology</u> 2014 [146]

Another study performed by *Harvard School of Public Health* concluded:

> '...children in high-fluoride areas had significantly **lower IQ scores** than those who lived in low-fluoride areas.
>
> Conclusions: The results support the possibility of an adverse effect of **high fluoride exposure on children's neurodevelopment**. Future research should include detailed individual-level information on prenatal exposure, neurobehavioral performance, and covariates for adjustment.'
>
> <u>Harvard School of Public Health</u> 2012 [147]

Fluoride exposure can result in a condition called fluorosis, which ironically results in the yellowing of teeth and tooth decay – its use in the water supply and toothpaste is highly questionable, given that there is no conclusive evidence to confirm that it provides any benefit to teeth. It can be found in teas, soups, and many foods in higher concentrations. The currently accepted safe consumption level is one part per million parts of water (1 ppm). Fluoride toothpaste contains over 1,100 ppm. Just one accidental swallowing of toothpaste will result in a toxic exposure above the safe level. This is why toothpaste carries medical warnings against ingesting it.

4-MeI is the colouring agent used in most soft drinks and provides a potential cancer risk to humans:

*'In 2007, a federal government study concluded that 4-MeI **caused cancer in mice** and the International Agency for Research on Cancer determined the chemical to be "**possibly carcinogenic to humans**" in 2011.*

*Caramel colour is the single most used food colouring in the world, according to a 2013 report from market research firms Mintel and Leatherhead Food Research. "There's no reason why consumers should be exposed to an **avoidable and unnecessary risk that can stem from colouring food brown**".'*

<u>*consumerreports.org*</u> ***2014*** [148]

Carrageenan is used as a thickening agent and preservative in many products such as milkshakes and meat. It is a stomach irritant and a known cause of inflammation. Some animal studies have observed colitis-like disease and tumour promotion. A study contained within this article concludes:

*'"Because of the acknowledged carcinogenic properties of degraded carrageenan in animal models and the cancer-promoting effects of under-graded carrageenan in experimental models, **the widespread use of carrageenan in the Western diet should be reconsidered**".'*

<u>***Research Review*** *2001*</u> [075]

MSG (Monosodium Glutamate), the additive used to increase the intensity of flavour in many foods, should also be researched and it's consumption re-considered for any cancer patient. A study in 2007 concluded that it should be withdrawn from the food chain:

*'**Chronic inflammation** is a common theme in a variety of disease pathways, including autoimmune diseases. The pathways of chronic inflammation are well illustrated by non-alcoholic steatohepatitis (**NASH**), which is of a serious concern due to its increasing prevalence in the Westernised world… NASH may ultimately lead to the development of hepatocellular carcinoma [**liver cancer**]. We previously reported that injection of **monosodium glutamate (MSG)** in ICR mice leads to the development of **significant inflammation**, central obesity, and type 2 diabetes.*

*By 6 and 12 months of age, all MSG-treated mice developed NAFLD and **NASH-like** histology, respectively. In particular, the* *murine steatohepatitis at 12 months was virtually undistinguishable from **human NASH**... We submit that MSG treatment of mice induces obesity and diabetes with steatosis and steatohepatitis resembling human NAFLD and NASH with preneoplastic lesions [**pre-cancerous lumps**]. These results take on considerable significance in light of the widespread usage of dietary MSG and we suggest that **MSG should have its safety profile re-examined** and be potentially **withdrawn from the food chain.**'*

Journal of Autoimmunity 2007 [149]

Bisphenol A (BPA) is a known endocrine disrupter and causes hormonal imbalance and is linked with cancer.[668] BPA is found in most plastics and can leach into food and drink, posing a potential health risk. Aluminium is very reactive, especially with fizzy and acidic soda drinks. To prevent the leaching of heavy metals into food, most aluminium cans, including tinned food, are lined with BPA. Most people are unaware of the level at which BPA pervades our lives, and of how it finds its way into our food supply. The main problem is that it accumulates within us over time, so limiting our exposure is critical. Even till receipts are coated with BPA, posing a potential risk of BPA absorption through the skin. Stainless steel containers and glass jars appear to be the safest option for storing food to ensure BPA contamination does not occur.

Glyphosate is partly responsible for the destruction of the beneficial soil microbiome and harms the human gut microbiome – both have negative implications for our health:

*'Contrary to the current widely-held **misconception** that glyphosate is relatively harmless to humans, the available evidence shows that **glyphosate may rather be** the **most important factor** in the development of **multiple chronic diseases** and conditions that have become prevalent in Westernised societies.'*

This article goes on to say:

*'Roundup® [which contains glyphosate] kills plants by interfering with a biochemical pathway involved with synthesis of amino acids, called the **shikimate pathway**. This pathway is not found in humans, therefore it was assumed that glyphosate does not harm humans. **The pathway is found in bacteria**, however, and*

> **humans depend on bacteria in the gastrointestinal (GI) tract to synthesize the essential amino acids.'**
>
> <u>The Cornucopia Institute</u> **2014** [122]

According to studies, glyphosate damages the microbiome in the soil, and also within our gut when we consume the crops that have absorbed it. A recent 2018 landmark trial against Monsanto, and its glyphosate herbicide, has resulted in the jury finding Monsanto guilty of negligence in relation to a link to cancer.[518]

Unfortunately, there are many more toxins to consider. It's worthwhile spending a little time researching the extent of the toxic chemicals we are routinely exposed to. You may be surprised at the quantity of compounds and the level of damage they can inflict upon the body – everyday compounds that we assume are perfectly safe.

Closing comments:

Cancer is more than just a warning that your health has been compromised, and that a lifestyle re-evaluation is urgently required. Yes it is scary, as it forces us to come face to face with our ultimate fear; but within the process of contemplating our own mortality, can develop a renewed vigour for life, an awakening if you will. Cancer, with all its negative connotations, forces us to re-evaluate how we conduct ourselves in this fragile but beautiful world, and in doing so can, if we let it, galvanise a re-ignition of our soul that can encourage us to be extra-ordinary, and live our best life. I think Sophie Sabbage said it best when she stated:

> *"I have cancer, but cancer does not have me."*
>
> *– Sophie Sabbage*

While in the darkness we all have the ability to find ourselves, and be born again anew, this is not the end. With the new interpretation of cancer presented within this book comes renewed hope, and an additional tool with which to address the disease. With the very real possibility that an underlying mechanism behind cancer has been identified, if not 'the' mechanism, you are provided with the information that allows you to take back some semblance of control, and may ultimately result in a vastly improved survival outcome.

Afterword

Beginning, middle, and a promising future...

This project has been quite the journey. I initially set out to spend just two years researching the disease. Never did I envisage dedicating eight years of my life to this project, nor that it would culminate in a landmark event that would see leading experts evaluate my research in an online debate, with over 200 medical professionals in the audience also interacting with proceedings. While having my model of cancer validated in this way is a remarkable achievement, and is a milestone reached, this is just the beginning.

The hope now is to disseminate the Cell Suppression model far and wide to stimulate much needed debate. For too long, dogma seems to have dominated the narrative on cancer within mainstream medical circles, to the detriment of cancer patients, it would seem. A return to objective scientific discourse is urgently required and well overdue. This innovative new way of looking at cancer can help to further drive a much-needed conversation between scientists, clinicians and patients, as the Metabolic Theory has, and continues to encourage. Through open discussion of new ideas and evidence that challenges current paradigms, we can better determine the mechanisms that underlie the disease, and so improve survival outcomes for people with cancer. Open, objective debate is, after-all, the foundational principle of science. Dogmatic belief in one theory, and a dismissive attitude towards other perspectives, is not only unscientific, but it stifles progress. It's not science if it can't be questioned, which is why I allowed my thinking to be scrutinised in the very public and open manner I did, at the *Cancer Through Another Lens* event, held on the 12th February 2023. As Albert Einstein once stated:

"The important thing is to never stop questioning."
- Albert Einstein

The other remarkable aspect of this journey, given the acceptance of my ideas, is that I'm not a scientist, I'm a graphic designer from the UK. I taught myself everything I now know about cancer through studying thousands of scientific papers, the many theories that exist, and countless hours listening to lectures, and studying many other aspects of health and disease. I've always had a passion for health, biology and problem-solving, and at 28 I developed the motivation to turn my attention towards cancer. It was at this age that I was diagnosed with skin cancer, which I'd caught early and had surgically removed.

At the time of my diagnosis I was devastated, and wanted to know why and how it had occurred. Unfortunately my doctor and oncologist were unable to clarify which DNA genes had become mutated, apparently I was just 'unlucky'. This vague explanation was not acceptable to me, I wanted to know more so that I could prevent a similar diagnosis occurring in the future. And so I set off on a journey of research to initially uncover more about my particular cancer, the DNA genes involved, and why I'd developed the disease at such an early age. My research continued with vigour a while later when a close friend was diagnosed with cervical cancer at the age of 30.

She unfortunately passed away a year after her initial diagnosis. During that year and the extensive research I had performed, it became apparent that there were serious flaws in the medical system, and the view of the disease adopted by the medical establishment – there were a number of serious anomalies indicating that cancer was not being driven by DNA mutations. Given the other theories that existed, it became clear that the underlying mechanism of cancer was still to be determined. Having committed myself to this research, I vowed to keep going so that my friend's death would not be in vain.

The initial desire was to document my immediate findings in a book that I could provide to family and friends. The aim was to provide them with the beneficial information I had already uncovered, to enable them to make more informed decisions pending a diagnosis.

As I continued my research, I became more drawn in to the detail, and intrigued by the notion that the underlying cause of the disease was still unknown. Eight years later and here I am, a new theory written, accepted as being credible by cancer experts, and a book published on the subject.

This is quite remarkable considering I don't have a medical qualification. Sometimes I have to pinch myself to make sure I'm not dreaming, at which point I remember the long hours of extensive research, often till 3am, the frustration in having to work to earn money to pay the bills, which prevented me from focusing on the project full time, and all the stress associated with living on such a tight budget. Losing friendships, due to the obsessive nature of my study, was not a highlight looking back, but it was necessary, and reaffirms why I have achieved what I have so far.

But what sets me apart from most scientists? I truly couldn't say, I had a normal upbringing by anyone's standards, although I've always been perceptive, creative and interested in problem solving. I was only ever going to choose a career in one of two disciplines, something arty, or science-based, preferably biological. Maybe choosing the former developed my ability to think on a more creative level, honing my analytical and problem solving skills, making me a good candidate to challenge convention; after all, that's what designers do.

This maybe where my non-science background, particularly my graphic design training, may have been of great benefit during the problem-solving process, enabling me to address the issue of cancer from a unique perspective. Within a design environment we are required to dismiss our initial ideas, and to constantly challenge our thinking to come up with novel approaches. Going out on a limb, attempting to develop a new never-before-created design, and not being afraid of the criticism if it doesn't work, becomes second nature. Furthermore, a graphic designer needs to be both creative, and orderly, during the problem-solving process and execution those ideas. This background freed me from cognitive constraints, allowing me to explore possibilities that others may routinely dismiss. I was able to utilise a level of creative freedom that doesn't seem available to most scientists – this ultimately enabled me to view cancer through a different lens, while applying a structured approach to evidence-based data collection and analysis.

> *"To raise new questions, new possibilities, to regard old problems from a new angle, requires creative imagination and marks real advance in science." - **Albert Einstein***

Moreover, I wasn't under the normal pressure from industry to conform to accepted ways of thinking, or the group think that can occur. I wasn't under pressure to accept the established view that DNA mutations are driving the disease, as many medical students seem to be. This freedom, and creative thought process, emboldened me to look at all aspects of health, to see if I could draw a different conclusion from the same published scientific data. It also enabled me to question and scrutinise the dominant theories without bias, or allegiance to any one particular viewpoint.

I think part of the problem with medical science is that each medical discipline has become segregated and compartmentalised, which is understandable given the sheer complexity involved. It seems to be frowned upon for a scientist to stray into the speciality of another, which is required in order to solve a complex problem such as cancer, because invariably, it involves many different aspects of health and biology – genetics, metabolism, immunology, biochemistry etcetera etcetera.

Ultimately, it was this objective approach to research – while not being aligned with any theory or school of thought – that led me to search for and identify a different, but significant factor, that could explain the Warburg effect, which could then provide an entirely new interpretation of cancer. I found that the same scientific data used to support other theories, could also be interpreted differently. For example, anti-fungal drugs have shown great promise in cancer studies. This is thought to be due to these drugs acting directly upon particular pathways that the cancer cell utilises, because the overarching school of thought on cancer, is that it develops through cell malfunction, where the cell itself is to blame for generating the disease. This does not leave much scope for creative thought. Alternatively, that same anti-fungal drug could be affecting an intracellular fungal pathogen that has the capacity to suppress the pathways in question. Eliminating the fungal pathogen would elicit a change that makes it seem as though the drug is directly affecting said pathways, especially if the influence of the fungal pathogen hasn't been considered.

A similar argument can be made for many off-label drugs that appear to show efficacy against the disease – such as Metformin, Mebendazole, Tamoxifen, Lovastatin and even Doxycycline – in addition to their primary role, they all possess anti-fungal properties and have been shown to kill common fungal pathogens. All I've done here is to apply my design process. I've suspended my thinking, blocked out the noise and assumptions made by others, to reset my mind to work from a clean slate, so to speak. The aim is to allow myself to establish a new pattern of thinking that deviates from pre-conditioned thought pathways. This enabled me to ask a daring question that challenged the consensus view: could those anti-fungal drugs be acting upon a fungal pathogen?

I think too often we can get caught up in the whirlwind that is life and may allow our thought processes to be subconsciously influenced by established ideas – it is in our nature to want to fit in with the group, we are after all, social animals. My training allowed me to reset my thinking and not be afraid of being seen as an outcast, which is what happens when you question or challenge any sort of consensus view.

Hopefully, I've been able to introduce new insight that can stimulate debate to consider a different perspective, and further our understanding of the disease. While I've covered a lot of ground over my eight years of research, there are still aspects of cancer I would like to address, such as the *Abscopal effect*, which is where other tumours in the body are reduced, and may disappear, when the focus of treatment is only on the primary tumour mass – a reduction in the primary tumour using radiotherapy for instance, can trigger a reduction in other tumours that have metastasised, without them being treated. I have by no means answered all the questions associated with the disease, and no doubt I've generated more. But at some point I had to stop, and declare I had enough evidence to present this model for deeper analysis and consideration by the medical community. This is an ongoing project that I hope the public, and scientists alike, will engage in, because cancer is our collective enemy – it does not discriminate, we are all susceptible.

Given my non-traditional research background, and limited funding, I can only take this line of scientific enquiry so far. It is now within the hands of scientists and clinicians – who are far more capable and skilled – to test this model with a view to verifying it's concepts, and ultimately, establishing an improved treatment approach that can significantly increase patient survival. Of course, there is always the danger that new information that challenges established views can be ignored and side-lined, which has often been the case throughout medical history. This is where you, the public, can have a positive influence within the cancer industry. One major force for change in the world is public pressure. If enough of the public become aware of this new model of cancer, and push these ideas forward into the realm of oncology through sheer determination to be informed on the subject, then even the most hardy of scientists determined to only focus on DNA mutations as a cause of the disease, will be forced to consider this different perspective. And that can only be a good thing for cancer science and patient outcomes.

In conclusion:

In light of all the evidence provided, I conclude that the DNA, Stem Cell, and Metabolic Theories explain significant factors associated with cancer development – but rather than detailing the cause of the disease, they describe the symptoms that occur.

It would seem there is an additional factor that has been overlooked, and a more straightforward explanation. While toxin exposure, nutrient deficiency, and immune weakness create the environment in which tumours can form, tumours cannot develop without the additional influence of a pathogenic micro-organism. A tumour arises due to a failure of damaged cells to eliminate opportunistic pathogens that take advantage of damaged tissue. Cancer, therefore, is a terrain-based disease that is immune system related, suppressive, domineering, and opportunistic in nature, and fungal in origin.

Appendix A

T he *'Cancer Through Another Lens'* event 2023

As I mentioned in the *preface* and in the *afterword* above, on the 12th February 2023 I took part in a six hour webinar where I presented my new cancer model to a panel of 10 cancer experts, and around 200 medical professionals present in the audience. The aim was to have an objective scientific debate between different experts to assess the new model of cancer I would put forward. My three 40 minute presentations were punctuated with 26 polls that allowed the expert panel, and audience, to provide a confidence vote on specific statements I made that reflected the new perspective I was proposing. It was a resounding success. Details of the event can be found on the *Yes To Life* cancer charity website – www.yestolife.org. A summary of the event can also be found on the *Alliance for Natural Health* website, written by Dr Robert Verkerk PhD. Below are the credentials of the expert panellists who attended the event to evaluate the model of cancer I put forward.

Biographies of expert panel members:

The expert evaluation panel consisted of four cancer scientists, three cancer clinicians, and three expert cancer patients. As you can see, these are heavy-weight cancer experts.

EXPERT SCIENTIST PANEL:

Professor Michael Lisanti *MD-PhD FRSA FRSB FRSC:*

Professor Lisanti graduated *Magna Cum Laude* in Chemistry at *New York University*, and went on to obtain MD-PhD degrees at *Cornell University Medical College in Cell Biology and Genetics*. From 1992-96, he was a *Skeggs Fellow* at the *Whitehead Institute for Biomedical Research at the Massachusetts Institute of Technology* (MIT). Then followed several distinguished appointments at the *Albert Einstein College of Medicine* and the *Kimmel Centre* in 2006, following which Professor Lisanti was selected for the leadership of the *Program in Molecular Biology and Genetics of Cancer*. In 2009, he became the Chair of the *Department of Stem Cell Biology and Regenerative Medicine at Thomas Jefferson University*. Other previous posts include *Editor-in-Chief* of the *American Journal of Pathology*, and the *Muriel Edith Rickman Chair of Breast Oncology*. Professor Lisanti left the US to continue his research in the UK. He joined the *Breakthrough Breast Cancer Research Unit* in 2012 at *The University of Manchester*, as *Professor of Cancer Biology*. He is currently the *Chair of Translational Medicine at Salford University* and is listed amongst the *Top 100 Most-Cited Researchers in Biochemistry and Biology*. He has a Hindex of 175, with nearly 110,000 citations, and has published > 578 papers. For the fields of Biology & Biochemistry, Professor Lisanti's laboratory is currently ranked number 1 in England, number 2 in the UK, and number 39 world-wide. Professor Lisanti has been an active research scientist for more than 35 years and is well known for many important discoveries in the field of cancer, including the *Reverse Warburg Effect*. In 2015, his laboratory developed a new therapeutic approach for eradicating cancer stem cells (CSCs), with simple FDA-approved antibiotics. More recently, in 2021, his team identified high mitochondrial ATP production as a biomarker of "stemness" and metastatic potential, in aggressive cancer cells.

EXPERT SCIENTIST PANEL:

Dr J William LaValley *MD:*

Dr LaValley is a physician in Austin, Texas and in Nova Scotia, Canada. He is medically licensed by the *Texas Medical Board* (TMB) and the *College of Physicians and Surgeons of Nova Scotia* (CPSNS) from 1988 to present. He has clinical expertise as a *Functional Integrative Medicine physician*, treating patients for over 34 years, and as a professional consultant to other physicians since the mid 1990's. Over two decades, Dr LaValley has developed advanced data-mining tools to access the molecular biology of cancer   peer-reviewed   published   literature,   and genomics/transcriptomics/proteomic databases, to search, curate, develop and update rigorous, evidence-based Molecular Integrative Oncology treatment interventions using anti-cancer natural products and re-purposed pharmaceuticals in addition to – not instead of – conventional oncology chemotherapy, targeted biologics and/or radiation therapy. Dr LaValley has been appointed by the *Canadian Federal Minister of Health to the Expert Advisory Committee* (EAC) of the *Natural Health Products Directorate* (NHPD) for the development of *Regulations for Natural Health Products* (NHPs) in Ottawa, Canada. He has served in the antecedent *Natural Health Products Advisory Panel* and *National Transition Team* – for the *Office of Natural Health Products, Therapeutic Products Directorate, Health Protection Branch, Health Canada,* and also as a member of the *Canadian National Advisory Group on Complementary and Alternative Medicine, Health Promotion and Programs Branch, Health Canada.*

EXPERT SCIENTIST PANEL:
Professor Brigitte König *PhD:*
Brigitte König is *Professor of Medical Microbiology and Virology, Infectious Immunology and Infectious Epidemiology.* She has degrees in Biology, Chemistry and Medicine, and a PhD in *Medical Microbiology and Infectious Immunology.* She has served as *Deputy Director* of the *Institute of Medical Microbiology and Epidemiology of Infectious Diseases at Leipzig University* and as *Head of the Department of Molecular Microbiology, Diagnostics and Biotechnology at the Otto von Guericke University in Magdeburg.* She has been responsible for the quality management of the *Institute of Medical Microbiology of the Otto von Guericke University* and the *Medical Faculty of Leipzig.* Professor König founded the *Magdeburg Molecular Detections laboratory* (MMD) in 2008; she is its Managing Director. MMD is located in Magdeburg, Germany. It works closely with the *Medical Faculty* of the *University of Magdeburg* and is dedicated to 'putting together the puzzle'of a patient's results to help detect the underlying causes of their health issues. She has written five books and nine book chapters, as well as publishing 130 peer-reviewed articles as first author and 503 peer-reviewed scientific articles. Professor König has a *Certificate in Management Studies from the University of Hagen.* She has professional memberships with the *European Society of Clinical Microbiology and Infectious Diseases,* the *DGHM (German Society for Hygiene and Microbiology)* and the *DGFI (German Society for Infectious Diseases).* She is the recipient of several prestigious

awards, including a *Postdoctoral Fellow Award* from the *American Society of Microbiology*.

EXPERT SCIENTIST PANEL:
Dr Ahmed Elsakka:

Dr El-Sakka graduated from *Faculty of Medicine, Alexandria University* to take up a 3 year neurosurgery residency. He then acquired a post-graduate diploma in *Neuro-metabolism* from *Johns Hopkins Hospitals*, researching the underlying metabolism affecting refractory epileptic patients. This work made clear to him the impact that a ketogenic diet can have on cellular energetics, including cancer cell metabolism. He pursued a career as a Research Fellow in *Cancer Molecular Biology and Metabolism at Boston College*, USA, working alongside Prof Thomas Seyfried, with whom he co-authored many scientific papers. Dr EL-Sakka continued his studies into cancer at a submolecular level, resulting in a *Postgraduate Diploma in Clinical Applied Biochemistry from Harvard School of Medicine*, a *Postgraduate Diploma in Epigenetics and Gene Expression from Melbourne University*, and a *Postgraduate Diploma of Clinical Nutrition and Metabolisms from National Nutritional Institute, Cairo*. He also obtained his *Laser Practice License Certificate* for the use of class 3b and class 4 laser in Photobiomodulation and Photodynamic Therapy (PDT) and Laser Ablation. Currently, Dr El-Sakka is *Senior Researcher and Medical Director of the Egyptian Foundation for Research and Community Development*, applying the science of clinical metabolism, cancer metabolism and clinical applied biochemistry to develop better outcomes and quality of life for cancer patients, and the optimisation of conventional therapies.

EXPERT CLINICIANS PANEL:
Dr Penny Kechagioglou *MBBS (Honours) MRCP CCT (Clin Onc) MPH MBA Clinical oncologist:*

Dr Kechagioglou is a *Senior Consultant Clinical Oncologist* who is practising at *NHS University Hospitals Coventry and Warwickshire*. She has experience in advanced radiotherapy techniques for breast cancer including proton therapy, personalised chemotherapy and immunotherapy treatments based on genomic testing, as well as integrative oncology (complementary therapies and lifestyle medicine). After graduating from *Cardiff University* with Honours in 2003, Dr Kechagioglou completed her general medical training in the UK leading to the *MRCP award* (2006). During her specialist training, Dr Kechagioglou worked in Scotland, London and Athens and she obtained her *CCT in Clinical Oncology* in 2010. Dr Kechagioglou currently serves as the *Chief Clinical Information and Deputy Chief Medical Officer at UHCW*. She is a *Trustee of Penny Brohn UK* and *CoppaFeel* cancer charities, and Co-chair of the *British Society for Integrative Oncology*. She has served in various leadership roles including as *Chief Medical Officer at GenesisCare UK*, as *Clinical Governance lead* in the NHS and as CQC advisor. Dr Kechagioglou is passionate about quality in healthcare, integrative oncology and offering patient choice to care and is recently being awarded a senior fellow in the faculty of leadership and management.

EXPERT CLINICIANS PANEL:
Dr Nasha Winters *ND FABNO:*

Dr Nasha Winters started naturopathic medical school five years after receiving a terminal diagnosis of cancer. After qualifying, the opportunity arose to support someone with cancer and this led to her working with thousands of cancer patients over many years. The programme she developed incorporated lab testing, molecular profiling, tissue assays, epigenetic testing, and more, and then metabolically support the body's terrain with oxidative therapy, therapeutic diet, stress reduction, and other therapies. Decades of experience with patients led to the writing of *The Metabolic Approach to Cancer*, and over the last few years, she has travelled extensively to speak about the metabolic approach to cancer to physicians. She currently offers doctor-to-doctor consultations as a way to support physicians to implement the metabolic approach. Dr Winters is currently focused on opening *The Metabolic Terrain Institute of Health*, a comprehensive non-profit metabolic oncology hospital and research institute in the US where the best that standard of care has to offer and the most advanced integrative therapies will be offered. This facility will be in a residential setting, against a backdrop of regenerative farming, green building and restorative amenities, EMF mitigation and retreat, as well as state of the art medical technology and individualised data assessment to employ the right therapies at the right time to improve patient outcomes.

EXPERT CLINICIANS PANEL:
Dr Sean Devlin *DO MD(H) HMD MS:*

Dr Sean Devlin is a board-certified Family Physician and board eligible in Emergency Medicine. He is also board-certified and fellowship-trained in Anti-Aging and Regenerative Medicine and fellowship-trained in

Integrative Cancer Therapeutics. Dr Devlin holds a *Masters Degree* in Biochemistry and has pursued doctoral studies in Pharmacology with an emphasis on the evaluation of novel antineoplastic agents. During his tenure as a PhD student he uncovered a variety of novel research on the endocannabinoid system and its relationship with the parasympathetic nervous system. Dr Devlin has travelled extensively, working with cancer physicians and researchers nationally and internationally in an effort to better understand cancer and its treatment. He currently teaches for and works with the *AAAAM Integrative Cancer Therapeutics Fellowship* and Masters degree programme through the *University of South Florida*. Dr Devlin is published in the Townsend Letter, a lead article entitled "Medical Use of Cannabinoids, Going Beyond THC"as well as the "Six Pillars of Integrative Oncology".

EXPERT PATIENT PANEL:
Jane McLelland:

Jane McLelland is winner of the *Lifetime Achievement Award 2019 'Amazing Women Global'* for unsung heroines, awarded for her work educating and helping cancer patients since 2003, as well as author of *How to Starve Cancer*. She trained as a *Chartered Physiotherapist*, gaining a distinction in her exams and winning the *Sarah Leeson Memorial Award* for the most promising student. After qualifying she worked in the NHS and private practice for 12 years specialising in Neurology and then Orthopaedics after which she left the profession to pursue more entrepreneurial endeavours. From 1994 until 2004, Jane faced two aggressive cancers with metastatic spread, both classed as 'terminal'. Using her medical knowledge and researching heavily, she put together a cancer-starving formula, using natural therapies, exercise and diet. When she developed a second cancer, leukaemia – the result of chemotherapy and radiotherapy – she received for her first cancer, and with nothing to lose, she put together a unique cocktail of old drugs. This proved to be more powerful than she could have hoped. Since her remarkable recovery, Jane has been a staunch supporter of 'off label' drugs for cancer therapy (medicines used for other conditions than their approved licence), and leads a Facebook group with 65 thousand members. She is campaigning for off-label drugs to be recognised as effective cancer treatment, and has visited parliament, helping to change legislation for 'off patent' and 'off label' drugs. She continues to push for the vast Cancer Drug Fund to be used to investigate these—something cancer charities are failing to do.

EXPERT PATIENT PANEL:
Daniel Stanciu *PhD*:

Daniel Stanciu is a scientist located in Eindhoven, the Netherlands. He holds a PhD in *Experimental Physics* (magneto-optics), obtained at *Nijmegen University*, the Netherlands. During his academic activity, Daniel has made breakthrough discoveries in Physics, demonstrating something that was 'known' to be impossible: switching magnets by light with ultrafast (femtosecond) lasers. His discoveries have been recognised via the *Spinoza Prize* and today have become a major research area in physics, addressed by research centres worldwide. As a result, Daniel has a portfolio of highly cited scientific publications and has been awarded multiple scientific prizes around the world. Due to family members being diagnosed with aggressive cancer, Daniel's life took a major turn. Since 2013, Daniel has intensively researched the academic field for potential solutions to cancer. In order to share with the world his findings and help others, Daniel founded *Cancer Treatments Research* in 2015, which today is a website visited by more than half a million patients, scientists and medical doctors each year. In 2017, he founded *MCS Foundation for Life*, a non-profit organisation, focused on supporting the translation of valuable academic findings in oncology, to the clinical space. At the end of 2019, Daniel founded *MCS Formulas*, a food supplement company with the goal of generating financial support for academic findings that have the potential to improve and extend the life of cancer patients. MCS Formulas donates 50% of its profits to academic research. During his more than 7 years' activity in the oncology area, Daniel has collaborated with numerous scientists, medical doctors and patients around the world. The results of some of this work has also been published in academic oncology journals. Daniel has dedicated his life to contributing towards a better life for cancer patients.

EXPERT PATIENT PANEL:
Mark Sean Taylor:

Mark Taylor is the *Founder of Patient Led Oncology*, a movement set up to improve human data, access, safety, costs and the experience of an integrative cancer journey for patients and their caregivers. He blogs about his findings and progress through the *Patient Led Oncology Trials* Facebook group. Using a combination of patient and clinic collaboration, exceptional responder analysis, as well as through studying the latest clinical research, they communicate a view on the best path to integrate conventional oncology with the vast ever-growing range of non-standard care options. Mark is an advisor to the *Valencia Clinic of Integrative Oncology* in Spain, *ImunoMedica in Romania* and the *Art of Healing Cancer Centre in India*. Mark has a degree in *Maths, Operational Research, Statistics and Economics* from the *University of Warwick,* and an *MBA* from *The University of Hong Kong*. A former *Fintech Director* at a large international bank, he is also working on bringing business and technology concepts to willing Integrative Oncology clinics around the world.

Appendix B

F**urther reading and resources:**

To supplement the information contained within this book, I recommend at the very least, that you consider watching and reading the following excellent resources:

- **The Cancer Whisperer** by Sophie Sabbage, in this book Sophie does an incredible job in providing the strategies that can help cancer patients cope mentally with a cancer diagnosis and turn it round to their advantage.[687] *ISBN-13 978-1473637962.*

- **The Metabolic Approach to Cancer** by Dr Nasha Winters and Jess Kelley provides a clinicians understanding of targeting cancer metabolism. It covers the terrain of the body and is a great addition to Jane McLellands book, as it discusses how to achieve optimum metabolic health in general as well as with cancer. *ISBN-13 978-1603586863.*

- **How to Starve Cancer** is a book by Jane McLelland which explains how she conquered terminal cancer using a combination of conventional treatment, off-patent drugs, diet, and alternative treatments aimed at targeting metabolic pathways as described by the Metabolic Theory. She provides a practical approach to treatment using her 'metro map' system, which can aid you in creating a strategy to target energy pathways to starve the disease.

Her Facebook group is also a great resource.[449] *ISBN-13 978-0951951736.*

* **Tripping Over the Truth** by Travis Christofferson is a layman's interpretation of the Metabolic Theory. It explains the role that a faulty energy system plays in tumour growth and details why DNA is not the cause of the disease, and catalogues the history of cancer science in a way that is easy to understand. *ISBN-13 1603589352.*

* **anti cancer** is a book by Dr David Servan-Schreiber that highlights the benefits of diet against cancer using the latest scientific evidence.[566] *ISBN-13 978-0452295728.*

* **How Not to Die** is a book by Dr Michael Greger, a renowned physician who brings together the latest scientific findings, showing how a whole-foods plant-based diet can prevent and even reverse the 15 leading causes of disease, including cancer. *ISBN-13 978-1509852505.*

* **The Cancer Revolution** is a book written by Patricia Peat, and endorsed by the UK cancer charity *Yes To Life*. It specifically deals with complimentary and alternative treatments in order to provide clear advice on the options that are available. *ISBN-13 978-1526200327.*

* **Curing cancer with carrots** is a book that details how Ann Cameron cured herself of cancer by juicing 5lbs of carrots daily. This was achieved after surgery had failed with the tumours returning and without chemotherapy or radiotherapy treatment. Carrots contain effective anti-fungal compounds. *ISBN-13 978-0692521762*

* **Surviving Terminal Cancer** is a documentary that charts the remarkable story of Professor Ben Williams' approach to solving his incurable brain cancer. Professor Williams has also written a book under the same title.[322, 324] *ISBN-13 978-1477496510.*

* **Yes To Life** is an established cancer charity that seeks to provide additional information to that provided by conventional medicine. It's goal is to bring together the best of complimentary and conventional medicine to improve patient outcomes and support cancer patients in their time of need. It was *Yes To Life* who worked tirelessly with me for over a year to organise and run the very successful and groundbreaking *Cancer Through Another Lens* webinar held on the 12th February 2023. This landmark event brought together scientists, clinicians and expert cancer patients,

to assess the credibility of the model of cancer laid out within this book. Their dedication to aid people with cancer is exemplary. I cannot recommend this charitable organisation highly enough.

- **Patient Led Oncology Trials Group** is a Facebook group created by Mark Sean Taylor. It is both a resource for cancer patients to discuss cancer-related issues surrounding potential treatment options, and seeks to extract data from cancer patients regarding the treatments they are using to see if this data can shed light on the most effective treatments available.
- **Cancer treatment research** is an initiative setup by Daniel Stanciu Ph.D that seeks to fund research into off-label treatments that show promise against cancer. His website provides a wealth of researched information: www.cancertreatmentresearch.com
- **Interconnected** hosted by Dr Pedram Shojai is a documentary series that deals with the latest science regarding health and disease with a particular focus on the microbiome.[761]

It may also be beneficial to study the many lectures that can be found online, particularly Professor Thomas Seyfried's work, and Professor Max Wicha's lecture *Cancer Stem Cells: New Frontier in Cancer Research*,[178] where he explains the role of cancer stem cells, and highlights they are resistant to chemotherapy.

Medical corruption, scientific malfeasance, and your health:

Unfortunately, there is a dark side to medicine that many would rather ignore, but ignore it at your peril. I do not wish to dwell on the influence of vested interests and corruption within the medical industry, but it is something that everyone should be aware of, as it pervades every aspect of medicine and can negatively impact patient outcomes.

My extensive research has highlighted that, sadly, it is no longer beneficial to place all our faith in the medical industry when it comes to making health decisions, as the practice of medicine has been deeply compromised by private corporations and other vested interests that tend to seek a profitable outcome over and above patient care. [250, 289, 291, 292, 317, 341, 354, 358, 360, 367, 368, 369, 435, 480, 500, 537, 586, 618, 657, 688, 689, 690, 748, 767]

While most medical professionals are dedicated to your well-being, the medical system, and the guidelines they are forced to work within, are less than ideal, and in many cases are inadequate when it comes to protecting the patient from harm or malfeasance. Even some well-established and well-meaning cancer charities fall foul of a system that is rife with 'corporate' science that cannot be trusted to be accurate, or information that is outdated and misleading at best, or simply incorrect.

My concern is that the public are too trusting of medical authorities and medicine in general, meaning that many are unaware of the controversies that blight the industry and may do us more harm than good. For this reason, and to gain some much needed insight, I recommend the following resources:

- **Deadly medicines and organised crime: How big pharma has corrupted healthcare** by Peter C Gotezsche, provides a damning indictment of the corrupt influence permeating throughout the medical industry. *ISBN-13 978-1846198847*
- **Death by medicine** by Gary Null, details the level of adverse events to drugs and other medical interventions. *ISBN-13 978-1607660026*
- **What doctors don't know about the drugs they prescribe** is a short Ted talk by Dr Ben Goldacre. He briefly highlights the fraud associated with evidence-based medicine and how easy it is to manipulate scientific studies to fit a desired outcome that is often geared towards profit over patient care. www.youtube.com/watch?v=RKmxL8VYy0M
- **The Truth About Cancer: A Global Quest** by Ty Bollinger is a remarkable nine-part documentary series covering all aspects of cancer, including nutritional health and the medical industry.[262]
- **The C Word** is a documentary that sheds light on the relationship between poor diet, sugar and the development of cancer. It provides critical insight into the lifestyle that may have led to the disease, and identifies positive changes to aid a healthier way of living with one eye on cancer prevention.
- **WHAT THE HEALTH** is also a documentary that deals with nutrition and the impact of the food and the drug industry.
- **Food Matters** is an evidence-based nutritional documentary.
- **The Game Changers** is a documentary created by James Cameron that highlights the health benefits of a plant-based diet and attempts to debunk some myths associated with the meat-heavy diet that Western countries have adopted.

Hallmarks of cancer update – New dimensions:

In a recent update to the hallmark list (January 2022) Douglas Hanahan provides four additional conditions, effectively increasing the official hallmarks from 10 to 14.[811] While these are not explicitly discussed within this book, as they are yet to be accepted as hallmarks by the medical community, and as they are only intended as associated conditions that scientists should consider investigating, I will address them only briefly here to illustrate that this new Cell Suppression model has already accounted for them. These four additional conditions are:

1. **Unlocking phenotypic plasticity** (stem cells)
2. **Non-mutational epigenetic reprogramming** (external influences)
3. **Polymorphic microbiomes** (micro-organism influence)
4. **Senescent cells** (dormant cells)

1 – Unlocking phenotypic plasticity. This refers to the ability of cells to undergo an epithelial to mesenchymal transition (EMT), where they acquire stem-cell-like properties. These cells are able to emit a changeable phenotype. It's good to see the role of cancer stem cells acknowledged here, which will hopefully lead to recognition of their role in chemotherapy resistance and metastasis, so that treatments can be adapted accordingly. I cover cancer stem cells and the EMT event extensively, showing how fungal pathogens interact to facilitate such plasticity.

2 – Non-mutational epigenetic reprogramming. This refers to external environmental influences, such as diet, stress, exercise and toxins that can alter DNA gene expression to benefit a cancerous outcome, without causing a mutation. The Cell Suppression model within this book explores these issues by discussing the external influences that can influence the disease in both a positive or negative way (outside influences that change DNA expression). Primarily it is the control of the pathogen over the cell, that explains why the odd behaviour of the cell does not correlate with any particular mutation – pathogen control explains non-mutational epigenetic reprogramming.

3 – Polymorphic microbiomes. This refers to the influence of micro-organisms in relation to the development and progression of cancer. It is an acknowledgement of the recent evidence showing that micro-organisms are not mere bystanders, but play an integral role that's yet to be defined. The focus on micro-organisms is the essence of the Cell Suppression model, in which attention has been primarily focused on fungal pathogens, so it is fair to say that this additional hallmark has been covered in detail. Arguably, I could have given more attention to the diversity of different microbial populations and their symbiotic interactions, to determine their overall affect on disease progression; however, this level of detail would probably have required another book, and further fresh thinking.

4 – Senescent cells. This refers to cells that lie dormant. They do not die when they should and they do not grow or proliferate either. This may be a reflection of the level of damage cells have received whereby their DNA and cell machinery is no longer physically capable of operating in any functional capacity. These cells are clearly problematic in that they shouldn't be present in the first place, and will add to the tumour mass. They also appear to increase inflammation so are not completely benign. The Cell Suppression model doesn't directly address these cells, but it does discuss how several different immune cells, such as T-cells, neutrophils and macrophages become dormant when exposed to the toxins released by fungal pathogens, as well as the build-up of lactic acid and iron. These essentially cause senescence of some cells, which may explain why up to 50% of a tumour mass can be comprised of macrophage immune cells.

In summary, all four additions to the hallmark list are already largely addressed within the Cell Suppression model.

Appendix C

Controversies and counter-arguments:

During the course of my research and interactions with medical professionals, several controversies and counter-arguments have been put forward that may at first appear to discount the Cell Suppression model, and in particular, that micro-organisms are driving the disease. Here, I have addressed some key issues, no doubt there will be more.

Tamoxifen:

You may have wondered why I discuss Tamoxifen in a positive light, as it has been reported to cause problems with prolonged use and is also associated with an increased risk of developing other hormone-related cancers, such as endometrial and uterine cancers.[457, 768] I've used it to show its short-term effectiveness to highlight its anti-fungal properties as well as the fungal and estrogen link to cancer. The problem with Tamoxifen use appears to be related to its over-use and to the estrogen promoting effects it has on other cells.[768]

Tamoxifen is used in breast cancer because in this tissue it blocks estrogen – which stimulates fungal growth. Unfortunately, it acts like estrogen in endometrial and uterine cells, which may help to stimulate fungal pathogens. One would hope that it's anti-fungal properties would also inhibit fungal pathogen survival in endometrial and uterine cells – but this effect may be mitigated by the resistance to drugs that fungal pathogens can develop through estrogen-related mechanisms.[023] This has led to an increased risk of uterine and endometrial cancer when used for a long period.[768]

Moreover, using any antimicrobial drug for extended periods will lead to other complications and cell damage. This is because man-made anti-fungal drugs are toxic to human cells, and Tamoxifen has been shown to possess strong anti-fungal properties. Prolonged use means that fungi will also develop resistance to the drug. With this in mind, many breast cancer patients are given Tamoxifen not to cure the disease but as a preventative agent after surgery to stop breast cancer from returning. This anti-fungal drug is usually prescribed for years at a time, much longer than it should be. This encourages fungi to develop resistance to the drug in the same manner over-use of antibiotics lead to bacterial resistance.

We don't use antibiotics to prevent bacterial infections by taking them for years at a time, so we shouldn't use anti-fungals this way either, especially if they stimulate estrogen in other cells that are prone to developing cancer. Furthermore, persistent low levels of estrogen have been shown to generate insulin resistance.[580] Insulin resistance increases glucose levels within the blood, thus helping to feed both cancer and the fungus.

Dr Tullio Simoncini:

Dr Tullio Simoncini is an Italian medical doctor who concluded that cancer is caused by a fungus. While I welcome that a medical professional has noticed the indisputable link between cancer and fungi, our theories bear **no relation** to one another, other than the proposition that fungi are involved.

Dr Simoncini asserts that cells grow around a fungal colony to contain it and that this protective growth is the tumour. For me, the evidence does not confirm this; instead, the Cell Suppression concept I've proposed asserts that the cause of tumour growth, and cancer, occurs when fungi invade damaged cells leading to the suppression of cell functions, with the aim of sustaining access to nutrients. It is this cell manipulation that is responsible for tumour growth. The presence of the pathogen results in the abnormal metabolic shift to glycolysis that ultimately drives cell division and prevents cell death.

Dr Simoncini advocates sodium bicarbonate as a treatment as it's a well-known anti-fungal agent and alkalising substance. However, he was struck off the medical register by the Italian medical board for his views regarding fungus as the underlying cause, and for providing sodium bicarbonate as a treatment solution. I do not advocate sodium bicarbonate as a treatment solution. Although the independent study below indicates that administering sodium bicarbonate in a safe manner appears to have a beneficial effect:

> *'In support of the functional importance of our findings, oral administration of **sodium bicarbonate** was sufficient to increase peritumoral pH and **inhibit tumour growth** and **local invasion** in a preclinical model, supporting the acid-mediated invasion hypothesis.'*
>
> <u>Cancer Research</u> **2013** [334]

Voriconazole and skin cancer:

Not all anti-fungal drugs show benefit, and in some instances seem to stimulate cancer. Some may suggest that this confirms that fungi aren't an underlying cause of the disease. For instance, the anti-fungal drug *Voriconazole* actually increases the risk of Squamous cell carcinoma (skin cancer).[869] But this interpretation assumes that Voriconazole is effective against all fungi – 100% of the time, that resistance to the drug isn't an issue, and fails to acknowledge how the toxicity of the drug itself generates inflammation within the area of concern.

Moreover, the retrospective study linking Voriconazole to increased skin cancer risk, was looking at transplant patients whose immune systems are already compromised,[869] and where the risk of cancer is at least 3 fold higher compared with the healthy population (as discussed in Chapter 10). Significantly, side effects from Voriconazole show it as a skin irritant, which would generate the inflammation within the skin required to aid fungal infection, especially if a fungal pathogen present at the time isn't affected by Voriconazole.

So, when we consider that not all fungi are killed by this drug, that resistance to the drug is also likely in some fungal species, then it becomes understandable to see why Voriconazole may cause skin cancer, especially when it was being studied in transplant patients with weak immune systems, and when the drug itself causes damage and inflammation to the skin layer that cancer forms within. The cancer that this drug encourages, under these conditions may be caused by a fungal species that isn't affected by the drug, which would allow a particular type of fungal pathogen to dominate this tissue. The irritation to the skin, caused by the drug, would explain why it promotes the disease by enabling the unaffected fungal pathogen(s) on the skin to gain access to the cells that are inflamed. This by no means establishes a rebuttal of the theory presented within this book.

As I've shown, the intricate detail is nuanced, it would be short-sighted to draw such a reductive conclusion, dismissing an entire theory in the process, on the outcome of one anti-fungal drug study under these conditions.

Fluconazole – regular use in leukaemia patients:

I've previously been asked the question: "*if cancer is caused by fungal pathogens, and Fluconazole is an anti-fungal drug that is regularly provided to leukaemia patients during a bone marrow transplant, why doesn't it cure their disease?*" The inference here is that fungi cannot be the cause of cancer because Fluconazole doesn't cure leukaemia patients.

Firstly, this claim is based upon the flawed premise that Fluconazole can kill all fungal pathogens 100% of the time. Fluconazole does not target all known fungal pathogens. If leukaemia is caused by one that isn't affected by Fluconazole – *Aspergillus* species for instance – then this would explain why. Secondly, resistance to the limited number of anti-fungals we have to offer, is now an emerging problem, could resistance to Fluconazole also play a part?

Thirdly, leukaemia develops from abnormally functioning stem cells within the bone marrow. Stem cells are proficient at expelling toxins compared to regular cells. Any intracellular fungal pathogen residing within these stem cells will benefit from a higher level of protection against toxic anti-fungal drugs, which can explain why these drugs may not be effective for leukaemia.

Fourthly, in order to ensure the immune system does not reject a bone marrow transplant, drugs are used to suppress the immune system. This increases the risk of bacterial and fungal infection, which will likely benefit fungal pathogens despite Fluconazole being administered, and especially as anti-bacterial drugs are also used to prevent bacterial infections, which would further compromise the immune system, and the beneficial bacteria that would normally keep fungal pathogens under control. Moreover, antibacterial drugs are damaging to mitochondria, which also compromises cell defence mechanisms.

Fifthly, over 95% of micro-organisms are yet to be identified. Moreover, some bacteria work synergistically with fungal pathogens. Bacteria have been known to neutralise drug compounds, as Ravid Straussman discovered during his research into drug effectiveness against cancer cells. This sparked his later research that led to the discovery that fungal pathogens are present in all cancers. Could such a bacteria neutralise the effectiveness of Fluconazole, resulting in a level of protection for the fungal pathogen? I'm speculating on this last point, but these are all important and plausible considerations that highlight the complexities involved. It's never as black and white as some would like to claim, and certainly the failure of a drug that doesn't target all fungal pathogens, is not a blanket confirmation that fungal pathogens are not an underlying cause of cancer.

Germ free mice and spontaneous cancer:

Germ free mice, are mice carefully bread to be sterile – free of micro-organisms; or at least those we know of. Some of these mice have been known to spontaneously develop tumours, even though no microbes are claimed to be present. This appears to contradict the view that micro-organisms, fungi in particular, are driving cancer. The germ-free mouse model was conceived a long time ago. The model for determining whether a mouse was germ free or not, was largely based on culture samples (micro-organisms grown in the lab), as well as microscopy (viewing samples through a microscope).

The problem, though, is that most micro-organisms living within animals, cannot be cultured within a lab because they simply do not grow under lab conditions:

> *'Molecular methods have revealed that most environmental* **microorganisms grow poorly, if at all**, *in artificial media, and that many of those that do grow require specialized media and/or atmospheres.'*

> <u>Gut Microbes</u> **2015** [911]

Viewing diseased tissue, or other samples under a microscope, is an extremely complex process and is limited by the experience of the histopathologist. Samples may miss an area containing micro-organisms. So the two main methods for testing tissue to identify micro-organisms is not exactly accurate. The problem today is that surprisingly, these same limited methods of detection remain in place, not much has changed:

> *'Today, surprisingly,* **little has changed**. *The methods for sterilizing isolators and equipment (ie, chemicals, steam, or irradiation) and the methods used for detecting contamination*

> *(direct **microscopy** and **culture** of samples on laboratory media),*
> *which were established by Reyniers et al, are **remarkably similar***
> *to those used in today's germ free facilities.'*
>
> <u>Gut Microbes</u> **2015** [911]

This begs the question: how can we ensure mice are germ-free when we are still using methods that cannot detect all micro-organisms? In fact, the germ-free mice that appear to spontaneously develop cancer, have been found to contain particular virus particles within those tumours, prompting the conclusion that germ-free mice are not free of viruses.[912]

Recent advancements in genetic sequencing means that we can now identify the DNA of micro-organisms within any given sample through PCR testing, which is now being used to determine germ-free status alongside the traditional methods mentioned above, in order to bolster confidence in the screening process.[911]

But even PCR testing has its limits. This study shows that it cannot identify micro-organisms that exist in colonies smaller than a particular detection range:

> *'In summary, the results of the current study showed that while*
> ***culture, Gram stain** [microscopy], and **PCR** are all **fairly***
> ***accurate** in detecting bacterial contamination of isolators, **none** of*
> *the screening assays, including qPCR **were able to detect fewer***
> ***than** 105 cfu/g of feces. This, then, leaves open the 70- year-old*
> *question of whether or not germ free animals can be contaminated*
> *by poorly colonizing bacterial species that are present **below the***
> ***limit of detection of our assays**.'*
>
> <u>Gut Microbes</u> **2015** [911]

Aside from the fact that culture, microscopy, and PCR testing are unable to detect all micro-organisms that are present, we should also consider that we have yet to discover the vast majority of micro-organisms that exist. In other words, our current knowledge, and technology, cannot be said to identify all germs. As James Reyniers, the father of germ-free mice models, once said:

> *"The so-called germ-free animal is germ free **only within the***
> ***limits** of the techniques used to determine its freedom from*
> *microbic contamination."*
>
> <u>Gut Microbes</u> **2015** [911]

In other words, germ-free doesn't actually mean 100% germ free, rather, these mice are germ-free only within the limitations of the technology, testing facilities in use, and our ability to detect the less that 5% of micro-organisms that we actually know about. It's not unsurprising then, to consider that unknown micro-organisms / fungal pathogens, that we have yet to identify, and cannot detect with our current technology, could be driving the cancers present in these mice.

Appendix D

Glossary

General terms

Tumour
An abnormal lump or swelling. A tumour can be benign (harmless) or malignant (a danger to life).

Cancer
A malignant tumour capable of unlimited growth and metastasis (invading and spreading to new tissue).

Carcinogen
A cancer-causing substance or agent.

Carcinogenesis
Defines the initiation of a tumour. It refers to the process by which a normal cell is converted into a cancer cell.

Cytology
The study of cells.

Micro-organism
A microscopic organism that may exist in its single-cell form or in a colony of cells. These include archaea, bacteria, fungi, and viruses.

Cell
The basic structural, functional, and biological unit of all known living organisms.

Prokaryote
Is a single-celled organism with simple cell structures, and primarily takes the form of bacteria.

Eukaryote
Is a single-celled or multi-celled organism, that contains a more complex cell structure, it includes a nucleus, mitochondria and other important organelles. Nearly all other organisms, such as fungi, plants, animals and humans, are made from Eukaryotic cells.

Epithelial cell	Epithelial cells offer a protective layer for the organs they encase. An example would be the epidermis, the outermost layer of the skin. Epithelial cells constitute up to 85% of all cancers that exists and represent carcinoma's.
Endothelial cells	Cells that line the interior surface of blood vessels and lymphatic vessels.
Cytoplasm	The liquid-like substance within a living cell, excluding the nucleus.
Cytosol	The aqueous component of the cytoplasm of a cell, within which various organelles and particles are suspended.
Nucleus	A membrane-enclosed organelle that houses the genetic code. It contains our DNA (nDNA).
DNA	A thread-like chain of nucleotides carrying our genetic instructions used in the growth, development, functioning, and reproduction of all known living organisms. (Deoxyribonucleic acid)
Chromosomes	Capsules that house the thread-like structure of DNA. Chromosomes reside within the nucleus.
Aneuploidy	A damaged or abnormal number of chromosomes.
Methylation	Required for all essential chemical reactions within the body. It relates to the addition of a methyl group to many chemical compounds.
Organelle	A specialised sub-unit within a cell that has a specific function.
Mitochondrion	A double-membrane-bound organelle living within the cytoplasm. Among other things, it deals with generating cell energy and controls cell death and growth mechanisms, as well as the generation of free radicals and antioxidants. It has a bacterial ancestry and has DNA of its own (mtDNA) separate to the DNA found within the nucleus.
Phenotype	The characteristics, behaviours, and output of an organism or cell. A phenotype results from the expression of an organism's genetic code, its genotype, the influence of environmental factors, and the interactions between the two.
Purinergic signalling	Communication between cells when under threat where ATP is used as a communication molecule.
Stem cell	A unspecialised cell that can give rise to one or more different types of specialised cells such as skin or liver cells. It can regenerate itself indefinitely.

Differentiation	The act of a stem cell morphing into or creating a specialised type of cell, such as a skin or liver cell.
Dedifferentiation	The act of a specialised cell, such as a skin or liver cell, morphing back into a cell that has stem-cell-like qualities.
Ligand	A binding molecule, usually found on the surface of cells.
Free radical	An atom or group of atoms that has at least one unpaired electron and is therefore unstable and highly reactive.
Antioxidant	A molecule that inhibits the oxidation of other molecules by neutralising free radicals.
Glutathione	The master antioxidant that neutralises free radicals and helps to remove toxins. It is partly created from glutamine.
Superoxide Dismutase	A natural antioxidant that neutralises free radicals.
In Vitro	Studies performed on cells in a Petri dish, outside of their normal biological context.
In Vivo	Studies performed in living organisms, including humans.
Oocyte	An immature egg cell of the animal ovary. In humans, one oocyte matures during the menstrual cycle, becoming an ootid and then an ovum.
Exosome	Exosomes are membrane-bound extracellular vesicles that are produced in the endosomal compartment of most eukaryotic cells. They are used for cell-to-cell communication and the sharing of nutrients as well as RNA and DNA. They appear to have a similar structure, and function, to that of viruses.
Phagosome	Is an internal cell vesicle (compartment) that has been used to contain pathogens within a cell. Pathogens are killed within these vesicles.
Fibroblast	Creates collagen and the extracellular matrix which is the structural framework for animal tissue, they are the most common cells of connective tissue. They play a critical role in wound healing.
Energy metabolism	**Cell energy creation.**
ATP	Adenosine Triphosphate. The energy currency of the cell.
Mitochondria	The energy-creating bacteria that combines oxygen and glucose to form ATP energy.
Glucose	A simple sugar.

Carbohydrate	A complex form of sugar or starch which can be broken down into glucose to be used to create energy.
TCA cycle	A series of chemical reactions used to release stored energy through the oxidation of Acetyl CoA derived from food. Also referred to as the 'citric acid cycle'.
Cori cycle	The conversion of lactate back to glucose via gluconeogenesis (lactate conversion to glucose) within the liver.
Gluconeogenesis	The creation of glucose from protein (glutamine) and lactate. It is usually performed in the liver but can be created in the kidneys, or instigated by fungi.
Glyoxylate cycle	An energy process present within fungi that allows the conversion of fat into glucose.
Glutaminolysis	A series of biochemical reactions where the amino acid glutamine is broken apart to create other substrates such as glutamate, aspartate, pyruvate, lactate, alanine and citrate.
Acetyl CoA	A molecule that participates in biochemical reactions related to energy metabolism within the TCA cycle.
Glycolysis	The initial step of energy metabolism that occurs within the cytosol where glucose is converted to pyruvate. Pyruvate can then be kept in the cytosol or transferred to mitochondria to create ATP energy depending upon the availability of oxygen.
Aerobic	With oxygen.
Anaerobic	Without oxygen.
Aerobic respiration	Energy production via mitochondria using oxygen. It produces 36 ATP units of energy per glucose molecule converted.
Anaerobic glycolysis	Energy production without oxygen using glycolysis within the cytosol – also known as 'fermentation' and can be referred to as 'anaerobic respiration'. It produces 2 ATP units of energy per glucose molecule converted.
Aerobic glycolysis	The abnormal use of glycolysis (fermentation) to create energy in the presence of oxygen – also referred to as the 'Warburg effect'.
The Warburg effect	Abnormal energy production in the form of aerobic glycolysis when oxygen is present and available for mitochondria to use. Named after Otto Warburg who discovered this anomaly in cancer cells.
Reverse Warburg effect	Where cells external to the tumour, such as fibroblasts, excrete lactate, and where cells of the tumour use this

	lactate for fuel within the TCA cycle found within mitochondria.
OXPHOS	The term used to describe the metabolic pathway in which cells use enzymes to oxidize nutrients within mitochondria, thereby releasing ATP energy.
Reactive Oxygen Species	Free radicals that are released due to stress caused by various insults such as toxins, micro-organisms, and radiation that threaten the cell. This reactive response is often referred to as oxidative stress or ROS, and is instigated by mitochondria.
Oxidative stress	A state of cellular stress that results in cells releasing large amounts of free radicals in a defensive response. Often referred to as Reactive Oxygen Species.
mSLP	Mitochondrial Substrate-level Phosphorylation, refers to the ability of mitochondria to ferment glutamine without the need to use oxygen.
Lactate	The waste byproduct of glycolysis where glucose is converted into pyruvate and lactate.
Glutamine	An amino acid used to create protein. It can be converted to glucose via gluconeogenesis, or lactate via glutaminolysis.
Cachexia	Wasting syndrome, loss of weight and muscle mass.
Arginine	An amino-acid/protein used for several cell functions including the creation of nitric oxide. It is required by immune cells and fuels fungal aggression.
Arginine auxotrophy	The loss of ASS1 expression which inhibits the ability of the cell to convert aspartate into arginine.
Nitric Oxide	A form of free radical generated from arginine.
Arginase-1	An enzyme that breaks-down arginine.
CYP1B1	An enzyme that is capable of metabolising many chemicals for use within the cell, including toxins and beneficial salvestrol plant-antibiotic compounds.
Apoptosis	**Programmed cell death.**
Necrosis	Unplanned cell death caused by external factors.
P53 gene	Regulates cell death and repair processes.
RAS gene	Regulates cell growth.
BRCA gene	Linked to DNA and mitochondrial DNA repair. Also linked to many cancers including breast cancer.
Caspase	Plays an essential role in cell death and inflammation.
Bcl-2	Promotes or prevents cell death by blocking or allowing the release of cytochrome c from mitochondria.

Cytochrome C	Instigates apoptosis (cell death) when released from mitochondria.
Angiogenesis	**Blood vessel growth.**
Hypoxia	A condition where the body, or a region of the body, is deprived of an adequate oxygen supply at the tissue level.
HIF1a	The activity of this gene increases when oxygen is lacking (known as hypoxia). It instigates the production of lactate dehydrogenase which increases lactate production and lactic acid accumulation. This denotes a switch in the energy system to glycolysis.
LDH	Increased activity indicates a switch in cell energy. Lactate is used as fuel when oxygen isn't present. This results in lactic acid production.
VEGF	This pathway generates new blood vessels known as angiogenesis. Lactic acid production stimulates this growth factor.
Lysis	Lysis is the breaking down of the membrane of a cell, often by pathogens, leading to the compromise of cell integrity resulting in cell death.
Metastasis	**The spread of a tumour to a distant location within the body.**
E-cadherin	A cell adhesion molecule important in the act of binding cells together.
MMP-9	Proteins of the matrix metalloproteinase (MMP) family are involved in the breakdown of extracellular matrix in normal physiological processes, such as embryonic development, reproduction, and tissue remodelling, as well as in disease processes, such as arthritis and metastasis.
Malignant	The transition from a benign tumour to its aggressive disease-causing phase.
Hypoglycaemic	Low blood sugar levels.

Appendix E

INDEX

References

001 – Jeffrey L Arnold, MD, FACEP. '*Chemical Warfare.*' November 2019.
www.emedicinehealth.com/chemical_warfare/article_em.htm#risk_of_exposure_to_c
hemical_weapons

002 – NCI staff. '*Antioxidants accelerate the growth and invasiveness of tumours in Mice.*'
National Cancer Institute. November, 2015. www.cancer.gov/news-events/cancer-
currents-blog/2015/antioxidants-metastasis

003 – Zosia Chustecka. '*Antioxidants Appear to Be Harmful in Cancer Patients.*' Medscape. July
2014. https://www.medscape.com/viewarticle/828132

004 – Peter Tarr. '*Scientists propose how antioxidants can accelerate cancers and why they don't
protect against them.*' Cold Spring Harbo Laboratory. 2014.
https://www.cshl.edu/scientists-propose-how-antioxidants-can-accelerate-cancers-
and-why-they-dont-protect-against-them/

005 – Garagnani, Paolo et al. '*The three genetics (nuclear DNA, mitochondrial DNA, and gut
microbiome) of longevity in humans considered as metaorganisms.*' BioMed research
international. 2014. doi:10.1155/2014/560340

006 – Kara Rogers. '*Mitochondrion.*' Encyclopedia Britannica. September 2019.
www.britannica.com/science/mitochondrion

007 – Thomas N. Seyfried et al. '*Cancer as a metabolic disease: implications for novel
therapeutics.*' Carcinogenesis. December, 2013. doi.org/10.1093/carcin/bgt480

008 – Thomas N. Seyfried. '*Cancer as a Metabolic Disease: On the Origin, Management, and
Prevention of Cancer.*' 2012. ISBN: 978-0-470-58492-7

009 – A.P. John. '*Dysfunctional mitochondria, not oxygen insufficiency, cause cancer cells to
produce inordinate amounts of lactic acid: the impact of this on the treatment of cancer.*' Med
Hypotheses. 2001. doi.org/10.1054/mehy.2001.1335

010 – Brenda Murray, D.J. Wilson. '*A study of metabolites as intermediate effectors in
angiogenesis.*' Angiogenesis. 2001. doi: 10.1023/a:1016792319207

011 – Baumann F et al. '*Lactate promotes glioma migration by TGF-beta2-dependent regulation of
matrix metalloproteinase-2.*' Neuro Oncol. August, 2009. doi: 10.1215/15228517-2008-106

012 – Thomas Seyfried. '*Cancer as a metabolic disease.*' Boston College. March 2015.
www.youtube.com/watch?v=SEE-oU8_NSU.

013 – NIHvcast. '*A Mitochondrial Etiology of Metabolic and Degenerative Diseases, Cancer and
Aging.*' https://oir.nih.gov/wals/2013-2014/mitochondrial-etiology-metabolic-
degenerative-diseases-cancer-aging

014 – Gaude, Edoardo, and Christian Frezza. '*Defects in Mitochondrial Metabolism and
Cancer.*' Cancer & Metabolism. 2014. doi: 10.1186/2049-3002-2-10

015 – Weigl, Stefania, et al. '*Mitochondria and Familial Predisposition to Breast Cancer.*' Current Genomics. 2013. doi: 10.2174/1389202911314030005

016 – Maniccia, Anna W et al. '*Mitochondrial Localization, ELK-1 Transcriptional Regulation and Growth Inhibitory Functions of BRCA1, BRCA1a and BRCA1b Proteins.*' Journal of cellular physiology. 2009. doi: 10.1002/jcp.21708

017 – Ben Goldacre. '*Battling bad science*'. TED. September 2011. www.youtube.com/watch?v=h4MhbkWJzKk

018 – Professor Paul Davies. '*Cancer from a physicist's perspective: a new theory of cancer.*' New Scientist. National Cancer Institute. June 2013. https://www.youtube.com/watch?v=yoQYh0qPtz8.

019 – Beric R. Henderson, '*The BRCA1 Breast Cancer Suppressor: Regulation of Transport, Dynamics, and Function at Multiple Subcellular Locations.*' Scientifica. 2012. doi:10.6064/2012/796808

021 – Stella Ibata-Ombetta et al. '*Candida albicans Phospholipomannan Promotes Survival of Phagocytosed Yeasts through Modulation of Bad Phosphorylation and Macrophage Apoptosis.*' J. Biol. Chem. 2003. doi:10.1074/jbc.M210680200

023 – Xiaoqian Zhang, Michael Essmann, Edward T. Burt, Bryan Larsen. '*Estrogen Effects on Candida albicans: A Potential Virulence-Regulating Mechanism.*' J Infect Dis. 2000. doi:10.1086/315406

024 – Georgina Cheng et al. '*Cellular and Molecular Biology of Candida albicans Estrogen Response.*' Eukaryotic Cell. January, 2006. doi:10.1128/EC.5.1.180-191.2006

027 – Inflammation and fungal toxins (mycotoxins): Environmental and Occupational Hazards – University of Minnesota

028 – CHOO, Z.W. et al. '*A Comparative Histopathological Study of Systemic Candidiasis in Association with Experimentally Induced Breast Cancer.*' Oncology Letters. 2010. doi: 10.3892/ol_00000039

029 – '*Cancer and mold toxins.*' James L. Schaller, MD, MAR. December 2019. www.personalconsult.com/articles/moldandbiotoxins/cancerandmoldtoxins.html

031 – Bennett, J. W., and M. Klich. '*Mycotoxins.*' Clinical Microbiology Reviews. 2003. doi: 10.1128/CMR.16.3.497-516.2003

032 – Seyfried Thomas N. '*Cancer as a Mitochondrial Metabolic Disease.*' Frontiers in Cell and Developmental Biology. 2015. doi=10.3389/fcell.2015.00043

033 – Sameer Agnihotri et al. '*TM-02 Identification of the azole class of anti-fungals as potent inhibitors of Hexokinase II mediated tumour metabolism in glioblastoma.*' Neuro Oncol. 2014. doi:10.1093/neuonc/nou278.2

034 – Ranjini Raghunath. '*Oral anti-fungal drug can treat skin cancer in patients, study shows.*' Stanford Medicine – News Center. February 2014. http://med.stanford.edu/news/all-news/2014/02/oral-anti-fungal-drug-can-treat-skin-cancer-in-patients-study-shows.html

038 – Susan G. Komen. '*Tamoxifen.*' Cleveland Clinic. Accessed 9/23/2013. https://my.clevelandclinic.org/health/drugs/9785-tamoxifen

039 – '*Tamoxifen kills fungus cells and may prevent them from causing disease.*' News Medical Life Sciences. July 2009. https://www.news-medical.net/news/20090720/Tamoxifen-kills-fungus-cells-and-may-prevent-them-from-causing-disease.aspx

041 – '*Injected Bacteria Shrink Tumors in Rats, Dogs and Humans.*' Johns Hopkins Medicine. August 2014. www.hopkinsmedicine.org/news/media/releases/injected_bacteria_shrink_tumors_in_rats_dogs_and_humans

043 – Fresco P, et al. '*The anticancer properties of dietary polyphenols and its relation with apoptosis.*' Curr Pharm Des. Jan, 2010. doi: 10.2174/138161210789941856

044 – Kanti Bhooshan Pandey and Syed Ibrahim Rizv. *'Plant polyphenols as dietary antioxidants in human health and disease.'* Oxidative Medicine and Cellular Longevity. 2009. doi: 10.4161/oxim.2.5.9498

045 – Alyssa M. Voss, M.P.H. *'Cancer Risk Among Immunosuppressed Populations.'* Division of Cancer Epidemiology and Genetics, NCI, July 2012. https://dceg.cancer.gov/news-events/news/2012/immunosuppressed-populations

046 – J Adami et al. *'Cancer risk following organ transplantation: a nationwide cohort study in Sweden.'* British Journal of Cancer. September, 2003. doi:10.1038/sj.bjc.6601219

047 – W. Lajean Chaffin et al. *'Cell Wall and Secreted Proteins of Candida albicans: Identification, Function, and Expression.'* Microbiol Mol Biol Rev. March 1998. 62(1): 130–180:

048 – *'Candida albicans can sense immune status of host cells and evade them.'* News Medical Life Sciences. February 2012. https://www.news-medical.net/news/20120223/Candida-albicans-can-sense-immune-status-of-host-cells-and-evade-them.aspx

050 – Claudia Jiménez-López, Michael C. Lorenz. *'Fungal Immune Evasion in a Model Host–Pathogen Interaction: Candida albicans Versus Macrophages.'* PLOS Pathogens. November, 2013. doi: 10.1371/journal.ppat.1003741

051 – Héctor M et al. *'Recognition and Blocking of Innate Immunity Cells by Candida albicans Chitin.'* Infect. Immun. May, 2011. doi:10.1128/IAI.01282-10

052 – Brown, Gordon D. et al. *'Dectin-1 Is A Major B-Glucan Receptor On Macrophages.'* The Journal of Experimental Medicine. 2002. doi: 10.1084/jem.20020470

053 – Shen, Hui et al. *'Abolishing Cell Wall Glycosylphosphatidylinositol-Anchored Proteins in Candida albicans Enhances Recognition by Host Dectin-1.'* Infection and immunity. 2015. doi:10.1128/IAI.00097-15

054 – Lee-Ann H et al. *'Helicobacter pylori Disrupts NADPH Oxidase Targeting in Human Neutrophils to Induce Extracellular Superoxide Release.'* J Immunol. 2005. doi:10.4049/jimmunol.174.6.3658

055 – Saharuddin B Mohamad et al. *'Tumor cell alpha-N-acetylgalactosaminidase activity and its involvement in GcMAF-related macrophage activation.'* Comparative Biochemistry and Physiology Part A: Molecular & Integrative Physiology. May, 2002. doi:10.1016/S1095-6433(01)00522-0

056 – *'Nagalase in the Blood.'* European Laboratory of Nutrients, Health Diagnostics and Research Institute. January 2020. http://www.hdri-usa.com/tests/nagalase/

057 – Wang, A M, D Schindler, and R Desnick. *'Schindler Disease: The Molecular Lesion in the Alpha-N-Acetylgalactosaminidase Gene That Causes an Infantile Neuroaxonal Dystrophy.'* Journal of Clinical Investigation, November, 1990. doi: 10.1172/JCI114901

058 – Weignerová L, Filipi T, Manglová D, Kren V. *'Induction, purification and characterization of alpha-N-acetylgalactosaminidase from Aspergillus Niger.'* Appl Microbiol Biotechnol. July, 2008. doi: 10.1007/s00253-008-1485-3

059 – Hisashi Ashida et al. *'Molecular Cloning of cDNA Encoding α-N-Acetylgalactosaminidase from Acremonium sp. and its Expression in Yeast.'* Archives of Biochemistry and Biophysics. Volume 384, Issue 2, Pages 305–310. December, 2000. doi:10.1006/abbi.2000.2114

060 – Ehsan Saburi et al. *'Is α-N-acetylgalactosaminidase the key to curing cancer? A mini-review and hypothesis.'* JBUON. 2017. ISSN: 1107-0625, online ISSN: 2241-6293.

061 – Reticker-Flynn, N., Malta, D., Winslow, M. et al. *'A combinatorial extracellular matrix platform identifies cell-extracellular matrix interactions that correlate with metastasis.'* Nat Commun. 2012. doi.org/10.1038/ncomms2128

063 – Luciana Kohatsu et al. *'Galectin-3 Induces Death of Candida Species Expressing Specific β-1,2-Linked Mannans.'* J Immunol. 2006. doi:10.4049/jimmunol.177.7.4718.

REFERENCES

064 – Bertram JS. *'The molecular biology of cancer.'* Mol Aspects Med. 2000. doi: 10.1016/s0098-2997(00)00007-8

065 – *'Antioxidant Supplementation in Cancer: Potential Interactions with Chemotherapy & Radiation Therapy.'* Myrna Brind Center of Integrative Medicine. July 2006.

068 – *'More evidence that exercise prevents cancer.'* Prevent Disease. http://preventdisease.com/home/tips42.shtml

069 – *'Types of cancer'* – Cancer Research UK. https://www.cancerresearchuk.org/what-is-cancer/how-cancer-starts/types-of-cancer#carcinomas

070 – William A. Freed-Pastor and Carol Prives. *'Mutant p53: one name, many proteins.'* Genes Dev. June, 2012. doi:10.1101/gad.190678.112

071 – Jia-Sheng Wang, John D Groopman. *'DNA damage by mycotoxins.'* Johns Hopkins University. 1999. doi:10.1016/S0027-5107(99)00017-2

072 – Vaughn, Allyson E., and Mohanish Deshmukh. *'Glucose Metabolism Inhibits Apoptosis in Neurons and Cancer Cells by Redox Inactivation of Cytochrome c.'* Nature cell biology 10.12 (2008): 1477–1483. PMC. Web. 14 Aug. 2015.

074 – Annie N et al. *'Red meat-derived glycan promotes inflammation and cancer progression.'* PNAS. January 2015. doi.org/10.1073/pnas.1417508112.

075 – Joanne K. Tobacman. *'Review of Harmful Gastrointestinal Effects of Carrageenan in Animal.'* College of medicine, University of Iowa. Research review. Environ Health Perspect, 2001. www.ncbi.nlm.nih.gov/pmc/articles/PMC1242073/pdf/ehp0109-000983.pdf

077 – Morgan G1, Ward R, Barton M. *'The contribution of cytotoxic chemotherapy to 5-year survival in adult malignancies.'* Clinical Oncology (Royal College Radiologist – Great Britian). 2004 Dec;16(8):549-60. doi: 10.1016/j.clon.2004.06.007

079 – Bergh J, Jönsson PE, Glimelius B, Nygren P; SBU-group. *'A systematic overview of chemotherapy effects in breast cancer.'* Acta Oncol. 2001;40(2-3):253-81. doi: 10.1080/02841860151116349 or doi.org/10.1080/02841860120784

080 – Bria E et al. *'Magnitude of benefit of adjuvant chemotherapy for non-small cell lung cancer: meta-analysis of randomized clinical trials.'* Lung Cancer. 2009 Jan;63(1):50-7. doi: 10.1016/j.lungcan.

081 – María Salazar et al. *'Cannabinoid action induces autophagy-mediated cell death through stimulation of ER stress in human glioma cells.'* The Journal of Clinical Investigation 2009;119(5):1359–1372. doi:10.1172/JCI37948.

082 – Turner CE, Elsohly MA. *'Biological activity of cannabichromene, its homologs and isomers.'* J Clin Pharmacol. 1981 Aug-Sep. doi: 10.1002/j.1552-4604.1981.tb02606.x

083 – Ramer R et al. *'Cannabidiol inhibits lung cancer cell invasion and metastasis via intercellular adhesion molecule-1.'* FASEB J. 2012 April. doi: 10.1096/fj.11-198184.

084 – McAllister, Sean D. et al. *'Pathways Mediating the Effects of Cannabidiol on the Reduction of Breast Cancer Cell Proliferation, Invasion, and Metastasis.'* Breast cancer research and treatment 129.1 (2011): 37–47. doi: 10.1007/s10549-010-1177-4

088 – Life Science. *'Sativex - Commercialised cannabis.'* www.leafscience.com/2017/11/02/what-is-sativex-nabiximols/

089 – University News. *'Tea tree oil offers hope to skin cancer patients.'* The University of Western Australia. June 2010.

090 – Anna Mertas et al. *'The Influence of Tea Tree Oil (Melaleuca alternifolia) on Fluconazole Activity against Fluconazole-Resistant Candida albicans Strains.'* BioMed Research International, vol. 2015, Article ID 590470, 9 pages, 2015. doi:10.1155/2015/590470

091 – Johansson NL, Pavia CS, Chiao JW. *'Growth inhibition of a spectrum of bacterial and fungal pathogens by sulforaphane, an isothiocyanate product found in broccoli and other cruciferous vegetables.'* Planta Med. 2008;74(7):747-750. doi:10.1055/s-2008-1074520

092 – Yanyan Li et al. '*Sulforaphane, a Dietary Component of Broccoli/Broccoli Sprouts, Inhibits Breast Cancer Stem Cells: Study*.' Clinical Cancer Research, Vol. 16, No. 9; May 1, 2010. doi: 10.1158/1078-0432.CCR-09-2937. Source article: University of Michigan Comprehensive Cancer Center.

093 – Amini, Afshin et al. '*Cytotoxic Effects of Bromelain in Human Gastrointestinal Carcinoma Cell Lines (MKN45, KATO-III, HT29-5F12, and HT29-5M21)*.' OncoTargets and therapy 6 (2013): 403–409. doi: 10.2147/OTT.S43072

094 – B. López-García, M. Hernández andB.S. Segundo. '*Bromelain, a cysteine protease from pineapple (Ananas comosus) stem, is an inhibitor of fungal plant pathogens*.' Letters in Applied Microbiology. Volume 55, Issue 1, pages 62–67, July 2012. doi: 10.1111/j.1472-765X.2012.03258.x

095 – San-Lang Wang et al. '*Reclamation of chitinous materials by bromelain for the preparation of antitumor and antifungal materials*.' Bioresource Technology. July, 2008. doi.org/10.1016/j.biortech.2007.08.035.

097 – Christine M. Kaefer and John A. Milner. '*Herbs and Spices in Cancer Prevention and Treatment*.' Herbal Medicine: Biomolecular and Clinical Aspects. 2nd edition. https://www.ncbi.nlm.nih.gov/books/NBK92774/

098 – Jayaraj Ravindran et al. '*Curcumin and Cancer Cells: How Many Ways Can Curry Kill Tumor Cells Selectively?*' The AAPS Journal. September 2009. Volume 11, Issue 3, pp 495-510. doi: 10.1208/s12248-009-9128-x

099 – Dorrah Deeb et al. '*Curcumin sensitizes prostate cancer cells to tumor necrosis factor–related apoptosis-inducing ligand/Apo2L by inhibiting nuclear factor-κB through suppression of IκBα phosphorylation*.' Mol Cancer Ther. July 2004. 3:803-812

100 – Kumar, Awanish et al. '*Curcumin Targets Cell Wall Integrity via Calcineurin-Mediated Signaling in Candida albicans*.' Antimicrobial Agents and Chemotherapy 58.1 (2014): 167–175. doi: 10.1128/AAC.01385-13

101 – Winston J Craig. '*Health-promoting properties of common herbs*.' The American Journal of Clinical Nutrition. September 1999. doi.org/10.1093/ajcn/70.3.491s

102 – S.T. Pai andM.W. Platt. '*Anti-fungal effects of Allium sativum (garlic) extract against the Aspergillus species involved in otomycosis*.' Letters in Applied Microbiology. January 1995. doi: 10.1111/j.1472-765X.1995.tb00397.x

103 – Brian A Schaefer et al. '*Salvestrol and the CYP1B1 enzyme found in cancer cells: Case studies with salvestrol treatment*' OrthoKennis www.orthokennis.nl/artikelen/salvestrol-case-studies-2012-(english)

104 – Franco-Molina, Moisés A et al. '*Antitumor Activity of Colloidal Silver on MCF-7 Human Breast Cancer Cells*.' Journal of Experimental & Clinical Cancer Research: CR 29.1 (2010): 148. doi: 10.1186/1756-9966-29-148

105 – T N Seyfried et al. ''*Role of glucose and ketone bodies in the metabolic control of experimental brain cancer*.' British Journal of Cancer (2003) 89, 1375–1382. doi:10.1038/sj.bjc.6601269

106 – Catherine Paddock, Ph.D. '*Prolonged fasting 're-boots' immune system. Three-day fast protected cancer patients from toxic chemo effects*.' Medical News Today. June 2014. www.medicalnewstoday.com/articles/277860

110 – Fazlia Shireen, Sunayana Manipal, D Prabu. '*Anti-fungal activity of Aloe vera: In vitro study*.' SRM Journal of Research in Dental Sciences, 2015, vol 6, issue 2, page: 92-95. doi: 10.4103/0976-433X.155464.

111 – Teresa Pecere, M et al. '*Is a New Type of Anticancer Agent with Selective Activity against Neuroectodermal Tumors*.' Cancer Research. June 2000. 60:2800-2804

112 – M. R. Saini et al. '*Anti-Tumor Activity ofAloe vera Against DMBA/Croton Oil-Induced Skin Papillomagenesis in Swiss Albino Mice.*' Journal of Environmental Pathology, Toxicology and Oncology. doi: 10.1615/JenvironPatholToxicolOncol.v29.i2.60

113 – Media centre. '*Cancer rate increase.*' World Health Organisation. 2003. www.who.int/mediacentre/news/releases/2003/pr27/en/

115 – '*NIH researchers conduct first genomic survey of human skin fungal diversity – Microbiome.*' National Institute of Health. May 2013.

116 – Anne Ringgaard. '*Giant study links C-sections with chronic disorders.*' Science Nordic. December 2014. https://sciencenordic.com/birth-c-section-children/giant-study-links-c-sections-with-chronic-disorders/1411238

117 – Ed Yong. '*How Breast Milk Engineers a Baby's Gut (and Gut Microbes).*' National Geographic. February 2014. www.nationalgeographic.com/science/phenomena/2014/02/03/how-breast-milk-engineers-a-babys-gut-and-gut-microbes/

119 – El-Nezami, Hani et al. '*Binding Rather Than Metabolism May Explain the Interaction of Two Food-Grade Lactobacillus Strains with Zearalenone and Its Derivative A-Zearalenol.*' Applied and Environmental Microbiology 68.7 (2002): 3545–3549. PMC. Web. 15 Aug. 2015. doi: 10.1128/AEM.68.7.3545-3549.2002

120 – James E. Galagan et al. '*Plant pathogenesis and the relationship with the microflora.*' Genome Res. 2005. 15: 1620-1631. doi: 10.1101/gr.3767105

121 – Nic Flemming. '*Plants Communicate Using An Internet Of Fungus.*' BBC. November 2014. http://www.bbc.com/earth/story/20141111-plants-have-a-hidden-internet

122 – Pamela Coleman, PhD, Farm and Food Policy Analyst. '*Gut-Wrenching: New Studies Reveal the Insidious Effects of Glyphosate.*' The Cornucopia Institute, March 2014. www.cornucopia.org/2014/03/gut-wrenching-new-studies-reveal-insidious-effects-glyphosate/

123 – '*Toxic UK: pesticide levels in our food are rising.*' Natural Health News. August 2013. www.naturalhealthnews.uk/food/2013/08/toxic-uk-pesticide-levels-in-our-food-are-rising/

124 – '*Is our food becoming less nutritious?*' The Gaurdian May 2005. www.theguardian.com/lifeandstyle/2005/may/15/foodanddrink.shopping3

125 – Cheng, Shih-Chin et al. '*Interplay between Candida albicans and the Mammalian Innate Host Defense.*' Infection and Immunity. August 2015. 80.4 (2012): 1304–1313. PMC. doi: 10.1128/IAI.06146-11

126 – Gary P. Moran et al. '*Comparative Genomics and the Evolution of Pathogenicity in Human Pathogenic Fungi.*' Eukaryotic Cell. January 2011. 10:1 34-42; Accepted manuscript posted online 12 November 2010, doi:10.1128/EC.00242-10.

127 – Vatansever, Fatma et al. '*Antimicrobial Strategies Centered around Reactive Oxygen Species – Bactericidal Antibiotics, Photodynamic Therapy and beyond.*' FEMS microbiology reviews 37.6 (2013): 955–989. PMC. Web. 15 Aug. 2015.

128 – Pat Thomas. 'Is our food becoming less nutritious?' Natural Health News. October 2015. www.naturalhealthnews.uk/article/is-our-food-becoming-less-nutritious/

129 – Marta Stanzani et al. '*Aspergillus fumigatus suppresses the human cellular immune response via gliotoxin-mediated apoptosis of monocytes.*' Blood Mar 2005, 105 (6) 2258-2265; doi: 10.1182/blood-2004-09-3421.

130 – Melanie Wellington et al. '*Suppresses Production of Reactive Oxygen Species in Phagocytes.*' Infect. Immun. January 2009 vol.77 no. 1 405-413. doi: 10.1128/IAI.00860-08

131 – Paul Hinson. '*Andrew Scarborough: the story of the man who beat cancer using a Paleo Keto diet.*' KetoForHealth.org. 2020. https://www.ketoforhealth.org/articles/679-andrew-scarborough-the-story-of-the-man-who-beat-cancer-using-paleo-keto-diet

132 – Christopher Wanjek. '*Deadly Heart Disease May Hitch a Ride on Dust Storms.*' Live Science. May 2014. www.livescience.com/45716-kawasaki-heart-disease-airborne-dust.html

133 – Shi-Min Yuan. "*Fungal Endocarditis.*" Brazilian journal of cardiovascular surgery. Vol. 31,3 (2016): 252-255. doi:10.5935/1678-9741.20160026

134 – Honor Whiteman. '*Fungus may cause symptoms of Parkinson's disease*'. Medical News Today. November 2013. https://www.medicalnewstoday.com/articles/268848.php

135 – Janaina de Cássia Orlandi Sardi et al. '*A Mini Review of Candida Species in Hospital Infection.*' Trop Med Surg. 2013. 1:5. doi.org/10.4172/2329-9088.1000141.

136 – Mazaheritehrani, Sala, Orsi, Neglia, Morace, Blasi, Cermelli. '*Human pathogenic viruses are retained in and released by Candida albicans bio-film in vitro.*' Virus Res. 2014 Jan 22;179:153-60. doi: 10.1016/j.virusres.2013.10.018.

137 – Santhoshkumar Muthu, Brindha Durairaj. '*Evaluation of Antimicrobial and anti-fungal Properties of Annona muricata Leaf Extracts.*' Br J Med Health Res. 2015; 2(3).

139 – Torres, María P. et al. Graviola: '*A novel promising natural-derived drug that inhibits tumorigenicity and metastasis of pancreatic cancer cells in vitro and in vivo through altering cell metabolism.*' Cancer Letters, Volume 323, Issue 1, 29 – 40. doi.org/10.1016/j.canlet.2012.03.031

140 – Gatenby RA, Silva AS, Gillies RJ, Frieden BR. '*Adaptive therapy.*' Cancer Res. 2009 Jun 1;69(11):4894-903. doi: 10.1158/0008-5472.CAN-08-3658. PMID: 19487300; PMCID: PMC3728826.

142 – Orjan Hallberg, M.Sc. e.e., consultant and Olle Johansson, Assoc. Professor. '*Cancer Trends During the 20th Century.*' Journal of Australian College of Nutritional & Environmental Medicine Vol. 21 No. 1; April 2002. www.avaate.org/IMG/pdf/HALLBERG_JOHANSSON_-_CANCER_TRENDS_DURING_THE_20TH_CENTURY.pdf

143 – '*Child cancers steadily rising.*' Children with Cancer UK. www.childrenwithcancer.org.uk/childhood-cancer-info/childhood-cancer-facts-figures/

144 – Liza Oates et al. '*Reduction in urinary organophosphate pesticide metabolites in adults after a week-long organic diet.*' Environmental Research, Volume 132, July 2014, Pages 105–111. doi:10.1016/j.envres.2014.03.021

146 – Philippe Grandjean, Philip J Landrigan. '*Fluoride – Neurobehavioural effects of developmental toxicity.*' The Lancet Neurology. Volume 13, No. 3, p330–338, March 2014. doi.org/10.1016/S1474-4422(13)70278-3.

147 – Choi, Anna L. et al. "*Developmental Fluoride Neurotoxicity: A Systematic Review and Meta-Analysis.*" Environmental Health Perspectives 120.10 (2012): 1362–1368. PMC. Web. 16 Aug. 2015. doi: 10.1289/ehp.1104912

148 – '*Popular Soda Ingredient Poses Cancer Risk to Consumers:*' www.consumerreports.org/cro/news/2014/01/caramel-color-the-health-risk-that-may-be-in-your-soda/index.htm

149 – Yuko Nakanishi et al. '*Monosodium glutamate (MSG): A villain and promoter of liver inflammation and dysplasia.*' Journal of Autoimmunity Volume 30, Issues 1–2, February–March 2008, Pages 42–50. doi:10.1016/j.jaut.2007.11.016.

150 – Vatansever F et al. '*Antimicrobial strategies centered around reactive oxygen species - bactericidal antibiotics, photodynamic therapy, and beyond.*' FEMS Microbiol Rev. 2013 Nov;37(6):955-89. doi: 10.1111/1574-6976.12026.

152 – Emma Smith. *'Sugar and cancer – what you need to know.'* Cancer Research UK: Science blog, Cancer Research UK, 2020. https://news.cancerresearchuk.org/2020/10/20/sugar-and-cancer-what-you-need-to-know/

155 – Marcovitch, Harvey. *"Editors, publishers, impact factors, and reprint income."* PLoS medicine. October 2010. doi:10.1371/journal.pmed.1000355

156 – Dr. Richard Horton. Offline: *'What is medicine's 5 sigma?'* The Lancet.com. www.thelancet.com/pdfs/journals/lancet/PIIS0140-6736(15)60696-1.pdf

157 – Kahlin Cheung-Ong, et al. *'DNA-Damaging Agents in Cancer Chemotherapy.'* Serendipity and Chemical Biology: Chemistry and Biology Volume 20, Issue 5, 23 May 2013, Pages 648–659. doi:10.1016/j.chembiol.2013.04.007

158 – Swift, Lucy H., and Roy M. Golsteyn. *'Genotoxic Anti-Cancer Agents and Their Relationship to DNA Damage, Mitosis, and Checkpoint Adaptation in Proliferating Cancer Cells.'* International Journal of Molecular Sciences 15.3 (2014): 3403–3431. doi: 10.3390/ijms15033403

159 – Lee, Changhan, and Valter Longo. *'Dietary restriction with and without caloric restriction for healthy aging.'* F1000Research vol. 5 F1000 Faculty Rev-117. 29 Jan. 2016. doi:10.12688/f1000research.7136.1

164 – Harith Rajagopalan & Christoph Lengauer. *'Progress Aneuploidy and cancer.'* Nature 432, 338-341 (18 November 2004). doi:10.1038/nature03099; Published online 17 November 2004

165 – Li, Ruhong et al. *'Aneuploidy vs. Gene Mutation Hypothesis of Cancer: Recent Study Claims Mutation but Is Found to Support Aneuploidy.'* Proceedings of the National Academy of Sciences of the United States of America 97.7 (2000): 3236–3241. Print.

166 – Hassan Malekinejad et al. *'Exposure of Oocytes to the Fusarium Toxins Zearalenone and Deoxynivalenol Causes Aneuploidy and Abnormal Embryo Development in Pigs'.* Biol Reprod November 2007 77 (5) 840-847; published ahead of print July 25, 2007, doi:10.1095/biolreprod.107.062711.

167 – Siegfried Knasmuller et al. *'Structurally Related Mycotoxins Ochratoxin A, Ochratoxin B, and Citrinin Differ in Their Genotoxic Activities and in Their Mode of Action in Human-Derived Liver (HepG2) Cells: Implications for Risk Assessment.'* Nutrition and Cancer. Volume 50, Issue 2, 2004. doi: 10.1207/s15327914nc5002_9

168 – E Pfeiffer, K Gross, and M Metzler. *'Aneuploidogenic and clastogenic potential of the mycotoxins citrinin and patulin.'* Carcinogenesis (1998) 19 (7): 1313-1318 doi:10.1093/carcin/19.7.1313.

169 – Ann S. Wilson et al. *'DNA hypomethylation and human diseases.'* Biochimica et Biophysica Acta (BBA) - Reviews on Cancer. Volume 1775, Issue 1, January 2007, Pages 138–162. doi:10.1016/j.bbcan.2006.08.007

170 – *'Methylation – A Simple Explanation.'* Healthier Talk.com https://healthiertalk.com/methylation-simple-explanation-0101/

171 – Christman, Judith K. et al. *'Methyl deficiency, DNA methylation, and cancer: Studies on the reversibility of the effects of a lipotrope-deficient diet.'* Journal of Nutritional Biochemistry, Volume 4, Issue 12, 672 – 680. doi.org/10.1016/0955-2863(93)90106-7

172 – Elsie Wainfan and Lionel A Poirier. *'Methyl Groups in Carcinogenesis: Effects on DNA Methylation and Gene Expression.'* Cancer Research. April, 1992 52:2071s-2077s PMID: 1544143

173 – E Anyanwu. *'The validity of the environmental neurotoxic effects of toxigenic moulds and mycotoxins.'* The Internet Journal of Toxicology. Volume 5 Number 2. 2007

175 – Melanie Ehrlich. *'DNA methylation in cancer: too much, but also too little.'* Oncogene. August, 2002. doi:10.1038/sj.onc.1205651

176 – Jane E. Visvader & Geoffrey J. Lindeman. *'Cancer stem cells in solid tumours: accumulating evidence and unresolved questions.'* Nature Reviews Cancer. October, 2008. doi:10.1038/nrc2499

177 – Video lecture. *'Cancer Stem Cells: The Origin of Cancer.'* Irving Weissman, professor of developmental biology at Stanford University Medical Center 2009. www.youtube.com/watch?v=vAA5wbo9xJI

178 – Video lecture. *'Cancer Stem Cells'* Max Wicha, M.D. March 2013. www.youtube.com/watch?v=AG22BEXscQE

179 – Video lecture. *'Cancer Stem Cells: 'A New Target in the Fight Against Cancer'* by Dr Robert Weinberg. https://www.youtube.com/watch?v=Nou8VWpWba4

183 – Kenyon SH, Nicolaou A, Gibbons WA. *'The effect of ethanol and its metabolites upon methionine synthase activity in vitro.'* Alcohol. May, 1998. doi.org/10.1016/S0741-8329(97)00134-1

184 – Gainza-Cirauqui ML et al. *'Production of carcinogenic acetaldehyde by Candida albicans from patients with potentially malignant oral mucosal disorders.'* J Oral Pathol Med. 2013. doi: 10.1111/j.1600-0714.2012.01203.x

186 – Gregory D. Kirk, et al. *'HIV Infection Is Associated with an Increased Risk for Lung Cancer, Independent of Smoking.'* Clin Infect Dis. 2007. doi:10.1086/518606

187 – Silverberg, Michael J. et al. *'HIV Infection and the risk of cancers with and without a known infectious cause.'* AIDS. 2009. doi:10.1097/QAD.0b013e3283319184

188 – Birkeland, S. A. et al. *'Cancer risk after renal transplantation in the nordic countries, 1964–1986.'* Int. J. Cancer. 1995. doi:10.1002/ijc.2910600209.

189 – Lindelöf, B. et al. *'Incidence of skin cancer in 5356 patients following organ transplantation.'* British Journal of Dermatology. 2000. doi:10.1111/j.1365-2133.2000.03703.x

190 – National Cancer Institute. *'Antioxidants Accelerate the Growth and Invasiveness of Tumors in Mice.'* November 12, 2015 by NCI Staff

191 – Ingrid E Frohner et al. *'Candida albicans cell surface superoxide dismutases degrade host-derived reactive oxygen species to escape innate immune surveillance.'* Mol Microbiol. January, 2009. doi:10.1111/j.1365-2958.2008.06528.x

192 – Purzycki CB, Shain DH. *'Fungal toxins and multiple sclerosis: a compelling connection.'* Brain Res Bull. 2010. doi:10.1016/j.brainresbull.2010.02.012

193 – Milton White. *'Ascospore-O, Oxidant, Host Assistance – The Pathway to Carcinogenesis.'* Medical hypotheses issue: 4, volume: 50, year: 1998, pages: 339 – 345

194 – Melissa Conrad Stöppler, William C. Shiel Jr., MD, FACP, FACR MD. *'Genetic Disease.'* Medicinenet.com. https://www.medicinenet.com/genetic_disease/article.htm

195 – Omotayo O. Erejuwa, Siti A. Sulaiman and Mohd S. Ab Wahab. *'Effects of Honey and Its Mechanisms of Action on the Development and Progression of Cancer.'* Molecules. 2014. doi:10.3390/molecules19022497

196 – Agustine Nengsih Fauzi' Mohd. Nor Norazmi' Nik Soriani Yaacob. *'Tualang honey induces apoptosis and disrupts the mitochondrial membrane potential of human breast and cervical cancer cell lines.'* Food and Chemical Toxicology. April, 2011. doi.org/10.1016/j.fct.2010.12.010

197 – Abdulmlik A Ghashm et al. *'Antiproliferative effect of Tualang honey on oral squamous cell carcinoma and osteosarcoma cell lines.'* BMC Complementary and Alternative Medicine. 2010. doi:10.1186/1472-6882-10-49

198 – Author Rose Cooper, PhD, PGCE, BSc, is reader in Microbiology, University of Wales Institute, Cardiff. *'Using honey to inhibit wound pathogens 2008.'* Nursing Times; 104: 3, 46–49.

199 – Ali Reza Khosravi et al. '*Fungicidal potential of different Iranian honeys against some pathogenic Candida species.*' Journal of Apicultural Research. 2008. doi:10.1080/00218839.2008.11101471

200 – Noori AL-Waili et al. '*Differences in Composition of Honey Samples and Their Impact on the Antimicrobial Activities against Drug Multiresistant Bacteria and Pathogenic Fungi.*' Archives of medical research. May, 2013. doi.org/10.1016/j.arcmed.2013.04.009

201 – *The RAS gene.* NCI Dictionary of Cancer Terms. www.cancer.gov/publications/dictionaries/cancer-terms/def/ras-gene-family

202 – '*What are genes.*' American Cancer Society. Last Medical Review: 06/25/2014

203 – Human disease and conditions forum. '*Fungal disease.*' www.humanillnesses.com/original/E-Ga/Fungal-Infections.html

204 – Levrero M et al. '*The p53/p63/p73 family of transcription factors: overlapping and distinct functions.*' J Cell Sci. 113 (Pt 10):1661-70. May 2000.

205 – Karna, Prasanthi et al. "*Benefits of Whole Ginger Extract in Prostate Cancer.*" The British journal of nutrition. February, 2012. doi:10.1017/S0007114511003308

206 – D Tagoe et al. '*A Comparison Of The Antimicrobial (anti-fungal) Properties Of Garlic, Ginger And Lime On Aspergillus Flavus, Aspergillus Niger And Cladosporium Herbarum Using Organic And Water Base Extraction Methods.*' The Internet Journal of Tropical Medicine. 2009. doi:10.3923/rjmp.2011.281.287

208 – '*How a plant's anti-fungal defence may protect against cancer.*' Cancer Research UK. Press release. February 2002. www.cancerresearchuk.org/about-us/cancer-news/press-release/2002-02-26-how-a-plants-anti-fungal-defence-may-protect-against-cancer

209 – Gerry Potter. '*Breakthroughs in the Quest to Cure Cancer.*' De Montfort University slideshow presentation. www.slideshare.net/gerrypotter52/breakthroughs-in-the-quest-to-cure-cancer

212 – Emmanuelle Passegué. '*Metabolism Defines Stem Cells.*' Cell Stem Cell. December, 2014. doi:10.1016/j.stem.2014.11.013

213 – Vicki Brower. '*Back to Nature: Extinction of Medicinal Plants Threatens Drug Discovery.*' JNCI J Natl Cancer Inst. 2008. doi: 10.1093/jnci/djn199

215 – '*Cancer facts and figures 2018.*' American Cancer Society. www.cancer.org/research/cancer-facts-statistics/all-cancer-facts-figures/cancer-facts-figures-2018.html

219 – People against childhood cancers (PAC2). '*Childhood Cancer – Long-Term Outcomes (Sept 2015 Update)*' *http://curechildhoodcancer.ning.com/forum/topics/currentlongtermoutcomes*

223 – Stephen Devries, MD et al. '*A Deficiency of Nutrition Education in Medical Training.*' The American Journal of Medicine. April, 2014. doi.org/10.1016/j.amjmed.2014.04.003

224 – Ball, Lauren et al. "*Nutrition in Medical Education: Reflections from an Initiative at the University of Cambridge.*" Journal of Multidisciplinary Healthcare. May, 2014. doi: 10.2147/JMDH.S59071

225 – Dr. Michael Greger. '*How Not to Die.*' Google. NYC. https://www.youtube.com/watch?v=7rNY7xKyGCQ&nohtml5=False

226 – DEAN ORNISH et al. '*Intensive Lifestyle Changes May Affect the Progression of Prostate Cancer.*' Journal of Urology. September, 2005. doi:10.1097/01. ju.0000169487.49018.73

227 – Barnard RJ et al. '*Effects of a low-fat, high-fiber diet and exercise program on breast cancer risk factors in vivo and tumor cell growth and apoptosis in vitro.*' Nutr Cancer. 2006. doi: 10.1207/s15327914nc5501_4

228 – '*Tangerine peel 'kills cancer'.* BBC news. Wednesday, 12 September 2007, 09:42 GMT 10:42 UK. http://news.bbc.co.uk/1/hi/health/6987200.stm

229 – M Guzmán et al. '*A pilot clinical study of Δ^9-tetrahydrocannabinol in patients with recurrent glioblastoma multiforme.*' British Journal of Cancer. 2006. doi:10.1038/sj.bjc.6603236

230 – Sánchez et al. '*Inhibition of glioma growth in vivo by selective activation of the CB(2) cannabinoid receptor.*' Cancer Res. 2001 Aug 1;61(15):5784-9. PMID: 11479216

231 – Paola Massi et al. '*Antitumor Effects of Cannabidiol, a Nonpsychoactive Cannabinoid, on Human Glioma Cell Lines.*' JPET. March, 2004. doi.org/10.1124/jpet.103.061002

232 – Sofía Torres et al. '*A Combined Preclinical Therapy of Cannabinoids and Temozolomide against Glioma.*' Mol Cancer Ther. January, 2011. doi:10.1158/1535-7163.MCT-10-0688

233 – Whyte DA et al. '*Cannabinoids inhibit cellular respiration of human oral cancer cells.*' Pharmacology. 2010. doi: 10.1159/000312686

234 – McAllister SD et al. '*Pathways mediating the effects of cannabidiol on the reduction of breast cancer cell proliferation, invasion, and metastasis.*' Breast Cancer Res Treat. 2011. doi: 10.1007/s10549-010-1177-4

235 – Nasser MW et al. '*Crosstalk between chemokine receptor CXCR4 and cannabinoid receptor CB2 in modulating breast cancer growth and invasion.*' PLOS ONE. 2011. doi: 10.1371/journal.pone.0023901

236 – María M Caffarel et al. '*Cannabinoids reduce ErbB2-driven breast cancer progression through Akt inhibition.*' Molecular Cancer. 2010. doi: 10.1186/1476-4598-9-196

238 – Ramer R et al. '*Cannabidiol inhibits lung cancer cell invasion and metastasis via intercellular adhesion molecule-1.*' FASEB J. 2012. doi:10.1096/fj.11-198184

239 – A Preet et al. '*Tetrahydrocannabinol inhibits epithelial growth factor-induced lung cancer cell migration in vitro as well as its growth and metastasis in vivo.*' Oncogene. 2008. doi:10.1038/sj.onc.1210641

240 – Anna Wagstaff. '*Jim Watson: DNA revealed the causes, it may never reveal a cure.*' Cancer world.net. September 2013. https://cancerworld.net/cover-story/jim-watson-dna-revealed-the-causes-it-may-never-reveal-a-cure/

241 – Sarah Boseley. '*Worldwide cancer cases expected to soar by 70% over the next 20 years.*' The Guardian UK. 2014.

242 – '*Incidence rates for all cancers combined have increased – Statistics.*' Cancer Research UK. www.cancerresearchuk.org/health-professional/cancer-statistics/incidence/age#collapseZero

244 – Sarah Knapton. '*Let's stop trying to cure cancer, says cancer professor.*' The Telegraph UK 2016. www.telegraph.co.uk/science/2016/03/15/lets-stop-trying-to-cure-cancer-says-cancer-professor/

246 – Charlie Cooper. '*The tipping point? Half of people now survive cancer diagnosis.*' The Independent. April 2014. https://www.independent.co.uk/life-style/health-and-families/health-news/the-tipping-point-50-per-cent-of-people-now-survive-cancer-diagnosis-9298682.html

248 – Wendy Warner, Kellyann Petrucci. '*Avoid sugar, an immune suppressor to boost immunity.*' Boosting your immunity For Dummies. www.dummies.com/health/avoid-sugar-an-immune-suppressor-to-boost-immunity/

249 – Albert Sanchez et al. '*Role of sugars in human neutrophilic phagocytosis 1, 2.*' Am J Clin Nutr. November, 1973. doi: 10.1093/ajcn/26.11.1180

250 – Moynihan, Ray. "*Who Pays for the Pizza? Redefining the Relationships between Doctors and Drug Companies. 1: Entanglement.*" BMJ: British Medical Journal 326.7400 (2003): 1189–1192. Print.

251 – *'Whistleblowers reveal FDA exacerbated Vioxx scandal.'* Oursourcing-Pharma.com. 19 July 2008. www.outsourcing-pharma.com/Article/2005/05/30/Whistleblowers-reveal-FDA-exacerbated-Vioxx-scandal

252 – Centers for Disease Control and Prevention. *'Change in US death rates by cause, 1950 and 2005. 1950 Mortality Data* - CDC/NCHS, NVSS. 2008.' https://duckduckgo.com/?q=CDC+Change+in+US+death+rates+by+cause%2C+1950+and+2005.&t=opera&iax=images&ia=images&iai=https%3A%2F%2Fimage.slidesharecdn.com%2Fanticanceractivitystudies-111201084417-phpapp01%2F95%2Fanticancer-activity-studies-4-728.jpg%3Fcb%3D1322731355

253 – Leyi Li, Michele C. Connelly, Cynthia Wetmore, Tom Curran, James I. Morgan. *'Mouse Embryos Cloned from Brain Tumors.'* Cancer Res Jun 2003 (63) (11) 2733-2736;

255 – Weidong Zhu et al. *'EGFR and HER2 receptor kinase signaling mediate epithelial cell invasion by Candida albicans during oropharyngeal infection.'* August, 2012. doi: 10.1073/pnas.1117676109

256 – Phan QT et al. *'Als3 is a Candida albicans invasin that binds to cadherins and induces endocytosis by host cells.'* PLoS Biol. 2007. doi:10.1371/journal.pbio.0050064

257 – DARLINGTON, C D. *'The plasmagene theory of the origin of cancer.'* British journal of cancer. 1948. doi:10.1038/bjc.1948.17

258 – Travis Christofferson. *'Tripping over the truth – The return of the metabolic theory of cancer illuminates a new and hopeful path to a cure.'* 2014. ISBN 9781500600310

259 – Charlotte Tobitt. *'Journalists claim alternative Covid-19 news has been 'censored' to create 'one official narrative.'* July 26th 2021. Press Gazzette. https://pressgazette.co.uk/journalists-claim-alternative-covid-19-news-censorship-create-one-official-narrative/

260 – Leah Barkoukis. *'The single most qualified' mRNA expert censored after discussing concerns over vaccine.'* June 24th 2021, Townhall. https://townhall.com/tipsheet/leahbarkoukis/2021/06/24/the-single-most-qualified-mrna-expert-censored-after-discussing-concerns-over-vaccines-n2591500

261 – *'War on cancer: 3BP and the metabolic approach to cancer: a visit with Peter Pedersen and Young Hee Ko..'* The Free Library. 2013 The Townsend Letter Group 14 Dec. 2016 www.thefreelibrary.com/War+on+cancer%3a+3BP+and+the+metabolic+approach+to+cancer%3a+a+visit+with...-a0332893717

262 – Ty Bolinger. *'The Truth About Cancer – a Global Quest.'* 9 part documentary series.

263 – Clarke L. *'Covid-19: Who fact checks health and science on Facebook?'* BMJ 2021; 373 :n1170 doi:10.1136/bmj.n1170

264 – Holenarasipur (HR) R. Vikram, M.D. *'Emerging Fungal Infection Mimics Gastrointestinal Cancer – Mayo Clinic.'* YouTube Published on 27 Mar 2012. www.youtube.com/watch?v=7P56JbKCtZM

265 – Jazz Shaw. *'Scientists suing Biden admin over Covid info censorship.'* HotAir, August 8th, 2022. https://hotair.com/jazz-shaw/2022/08/08/scientists-suing-biden-admin-over-covid-info-censorship-n488161

266 – Cliff Leaf, David Agus, MD, J. Craig Venter, Ph.D. *'How biology and big data converge in the medicine world.'* Fortune Magazine. 2015. https://www.youtube.com/watch?v=fDSQMeRgZHM

267 – Prof. Simon Carding. *'Gut bacteria and mind control: to fix your brain, fix your gut!'* FoodResearch 2015. Institute of Food Research and Norwich Medical School at the University of East Anglia.

268 – Kat Arney. *'Why are men more likely to die from cancer?'* Cancer Research UK 2009. https://scienceblog.cancerresearchuk.org/2009/06/15/why-are-men-more-likely-to-die-from-cancer/

269 – Wiley-Blackwell. *'Women have stronger immune systems than men - and it's all down to X-chromosome related microRN.'* ScienceDaily, 28 September 2011 - www.sciencedaily.com/releases/2011/09/110927192352.htm

270 – Mayo Clinic. *'Mayo Clinic Discovers One Mechanism For Why Men And Women Differ In Immune Response.'* ScienceDaily, 10 November 2004- www.sciencedaily.com/releases/2004/11/041108015954.htm

271 – Wang K et al. *'Dual anti-fungal properties of cationic antimicrobial peptides polybia-MPI: membrane integrity disruption and inhibition of bio-film formation.'* Peptides. June, 2014. doi: 10.1016/j.peptides.2014.03.005

272 – By Michelle Roberts. *Wasp venom 'a weapon against cancer'*. Health editor, BBC News online September 2015. https://www.bbc.co.uk/news/health-34115112

273 – Dandawate PR et al. *'Targeting cancer stem cells and signalling pathways by phytochemicals: Novel approach for breast cancer therapy.'* Semin Cancer Biol. 2016. doi: 10.1016/j.semcancer.2016.09.001

274 – Centers for Disease Control and Prevention. *'Gastrointestinal Basidiobolomycosis -- Arizona, 1994-1999.'* August 1999 / 48(32);710-713

275 – Cornelius J. Clancy, M. Hong Nguyen. *'Finding the "Missing 50%" of Invasive Candidiasis: How Nonculture Diagnostics Will Improve Understanding of Disease Spectrum and Transform Patient Care.'* Clin Infect Dis. 2013. doi:10.1093/cid/cit006

276 – *'Exploring Diagnostic Accuracy in Cancer: A Nationwide Survey of 400 Leading Cancer Specialist.'* National Coalition on Health Care, Best Doctors, 2012.

277 – *'Micro-organisms.'* University of Leicester UK. 2000 www.le.ac.uk/se/centres/sci/selfstudy/eco7.htm

280 – Guarner, Jeannette, and Mary E. Brandt. *"Histopathologic Diagnosis of Fungal Infections in the 21st Century."* Clinical Microbiology Reviews. November, 2016. doi: 10.1128/CMR.00053-10

282 – Singh G, Lakkis CL, Laucirica R, Epner DE. *'Regulation of prostate cancer cell division by glucose.'* J Cell Physiol. 1999. doi: 10.1002/(SICI)1097-4652(199909)180:3<431::AID-JCP14>3.0.CO;2-O

284 – Alyssa Kneller. *'White blood cells are picky about sugar.'* Whitehead Institute. Study citation – Ifat Rubin-Bejerano, Claudia Abeijon, Paula Magnelli, Paula Grisafi & Gerald Fink. *'Phagocytosis by human neutrophils is stimulated by a unique fungal cell wall component.'* Cell Host & Microbe. July, 2007. doi:10.1016/j.chom.2007.06.002

286 – JitkaY. Sagiv, et al. *'Phenotypic Diversity and Plasticity in Circulating Neutrophil Subpopulations in Cancer.'* Cell Reports. February, 2015. doi:dx.doi.org/10.1016/j.celrep.2014.12.039

287 – Fernando F. Gazzoni et al. *'Fungal diseases mimicking primary lung cancer: radiologic - pathologic correlation.'* Mycoses. October, 2013. doi:10.1111/myc.12150

288 – Nikolic DM. *'Effects of Candida on insulin secretion of human adult pancreatic islets and possible onset of diabetes.'* Br J Biomed Sci. 2014. doi:10.1080/09674845.2014.11669968

289 – Zlata Rodionova. *'Pfizer fined record £84.2m for overcharging NHS 2600%.'* INDEPENDENT, Wednesday 7th Decempber 2016.

291 – Gary Null, Valerie Van Cleve. *'Death by Medicine.'* 2011. https://www.youtube.com/watch?v=DSVFz06rPAs https://www.imdb.com/title/tt1776887/

292 – Christopher J.L. et al. *'Ranking 37th — Measuring the Performance of the U.S. Health Care System.'* N Engl J Med. 2010 doi: 10.1056/NEJMp0910064

293 – Lansdown AB. *'Silver in health care: antimicrobial effects and safety in use.'* Curr Probl Dermatol. 2006. doi: 10.1159/000093928

294 – *'Rhizopus.'* Go pets America. www.gopetsamerica.com/bio/fungi/rhizopus.aspx

295 – Tsujimoto Y. *'Role of Bcl-2 family proteins in apoptosis: apoptosomes or mitochondria?'* Genes Cells. November, 1998. doi: 10.1046/j.1365-2443.1998.00223.x

296 – Gordon Pedersen Ph.D. and Keith Moeller. *'Silver Sol Improves Wound Healing: Case Studies In the Use of Silver Sol in Closing Wounds (Including MRSA), Preventing Infection, Inflammation and Activating Stem Cells.'* https://healthy-living.org/~rxsilver/Pedersen-Silver-Sol-Wound-Healing-MRSA.pdf

297 – Judith K. Christman, Mei-Ling Chen et al. *'Methyl deficiency, DNA methylation, and cancer: Studies on the reversibility of the effects of a lipotrope-deficient diet.'* The Journal of Nutritional Biochemistry Volume 4, Issue 12, Pages 672-680. December, 1993. doi.org/10.1016/0955-2863(93)90106-7

298 – Joan Boren et al. *'Gleevec (STI571) Influences Metabolic Enzyme Activities and Glucose Carbon Flow toward Nucleic Acid and Fatty Acid Synthesis in Myeloid Tumour Cells.'* The Journal of Biological Chemistry. October 2001. doi: 10.1074/jbc.M105796200

299 – Hans Prenen et al. *'Imatinib Mesylate Inhibits Glucose Uptake in Gastrointestinal Stromal Tumor Cells by Downregulation of the Glucose Transporters Recruitment to the Plasma Membrane.'* American Journal of Biochemistry and Biotechnology. 2005. doi: 10.3844/ajbbsp.2005.95.102

300 – Hirsch, Heather A. et al. *'Metformin Selectively Targets Cancer Stem Cells, and Acts Together with Chemotherapy to Block Tumor Growth and Prolong Remission.'* Cancer research 69.19: 7507–7511. October, 2009. doi: 10.1158/0008-5472.CAN-09-2994

301 – Viollet, Benoit et al. *'Cellular and Molecular Mechanisms of Metformin: An Overview.'* Clinical Science. March, 2012. doi:10.1042/CS20110386

302 – Wang Z et al. *'Glycolysis inhibitor 2-deoxy-D-glucose suppresses carcinogen-induced rat hepatocarcinogenesis by restricting cancer cell metabolism.'* Mol Med Rep. March, 2015. doi: 10.3892/mmr.2014.2945

303 – Berger, Abi. *'Positron Emission Tomography.'* BMJ: British Medical Journal 326.7404 (2003): 1449. Print.

304 – Roberts, D J, and S Miyamoto. *"Hexokinase II integrates energy metabolism and cellular protection: Akting on mitochondria and TORCing to autophagy."* Cell death and differentiation. 2015. doi:10.1038/cdd.2014.173

305 – N El Mjiyad et al. *'Sugar-free approaches to cancer cell killing.'* Oncogene. 2011. doi:10.1038/onc.2010.466

306 – Changhan Lee et al. *'Reduced Levels of IGF-I Mediate Differential Protection of Normal and Cancer Cells in Response to Fasting and Improve Chemotherapeutic Index.'* Therapeutics, Targets, and Chemical Biology. February, 2010. doi:10.1158/0008-5472.CAN-09-3228

307 – Yandong Shi Et al. *'Starvation-induced activation of ATM/Chk2/p53 signaling sensitizes cancer cells to cisplatin.'* BMC Cancer. 2012 doi: 10.1186/1471-2407-12-571

308 – *'How Herceptin Works.'* BreastCancer.ORG. www.breastcancer.org/treatment/targeted_therapies/herceptin

309 – Soto, Ana M., and Carlos Sonnenschein. *'The Tissue Organization Field Theory of Cancer: A Testable Replacement for the Somatic Mutation Theory.'* BioEssays: news and reviews in molecular, cellular and developmental biology 33.5 (2011): 332–340. December, 2016. doi:10.1002/bies.201100025

310 – Ron Milo, Rob Phillips. *'How quickly do different cells in the body replace themselves?'* Cell biology by the numbers. http://book.bionumbers.org/how-quickly-do-different-cells-in-the-body-replace-themselves/

311 – *'Prostate Cancer In-Depth Report.'* The New York Times. Nytimes.com. www.nytimes.com/2016/09/15/health/prostate-cancer.html

312 – *'Cancer registration statistics, England, 2013.'* Office for National Statistics. webarchive.nationalarchives.gov.uk/20160106061903/http://www.ons.gov.uk/ons/dcp171778_409714.pdf.

313 – *'Causes of multiple sclerosis.'* National Health Service website UK 2018. https://www.nhs.uk/conditions/multiple-sclerosis/causes/

314 – F. Batmanghelidj, M.D. *'The body's many cries for water.'* 3rd edition. ISBN: 0-9702458-8-2

316 – BBC. *'Curry spice kills cancer cells.'* http://news.bbc.co.uk/1/hi/health/8328377.stm

317 – Allen Frances. *'Why are most cancer drugs so Expensive and so ineffective?'* The Huffington Post. October 2016.

321 – *'Fungal Meningitis.'* Centres for Disease Control and Prevention. www.cdc.gov/meningitis/fungal.html

322 – Ruth Wood. *'The professor who 'cured' his cancer with a cocktail of everyday pills and 20 years on remains disease free.'* The Telegraph. February 2015.

323 – Pantziarka, Pan et al. *'Repurposing Drugs in Oncology (ReDO)-itraconazole as an anti-cancer agent.'* Ecancermedicalscience. April, 2015. doi:10.3332/ecancer.2015.521

324 – Waking Giant Productions. *'Surviving Terminal Cancer.'* Survivingtermingalcancer.com

325 – Lois Rogers. *'Could these cheap drugs hold a cure for cancer?'* The Telegraph. January 2017. https://www.telegraph.co.uk/health-fitness/body/crowdfunding-cure-cancer/

327 – Jeevitha B. Patil, Jinhee Kim, G.K. Jayaprakasha. *'Berberine induces apoptosis in breast cancer cells (MCF-7) through mitochondrial-dependent pathway.'* European Journal of Pharmacology. October, 2010. doi.org/10.1016/j.ejphar.2010.07.037

328 – Kris Gunnars, BSc. *'Berberine – A Powerful Supplement With Many Benefits.'* healthline. January 2017.

329 – Sun, Yiyi; Xun, Keli; Wang, Yitao; Chen, Xiuping. *'A systematic review of the anticancer properties of berberine, a natural product from Chinese herbs.'* Anti-Cancer Drugs. October, 2009. doi:10.1097/CAD.0b013e328330d95b

330 – Jack Woodfield. *'Diabetes drug metformin can block the growth of cancer, researchers report.'* Diabetes.co.uk. December 2016. https://www.diabetes.co.uk/news/2016/dec/diabetes-drug-metformin-can-block-the-growth-of-cancer,-researchers-report-97361523.html

331 – David Robert Grimes. *'Tackling cancer treatment myths, from clean eating to cannabis.'* The Guardian. January 2017.

334 – Estrella V et al. *'Acidity generated by the tumor microenvironment drives local invasion.'* Cancer Res. March, 2013. doi: 10.1158/0008-5472.CAN-12-2796

338 – Aditya Bardia, MD, MPH et al. *'Efficacy of Antioxidant Supplementation in Reducing Primary Cancer Incidence and Mortality: Systematic Review and Meta-analysis.'* Mayo Clinic Proceedings. January, 2008. doi.org/10.4065/83.1.23

339 – Druesne-Pecollo et al. *'Beta-carotene supplementation and cancer risk: a systematic review and metaanalysis of randomized controlled trials.'* Int. J. Cancer. 2010. doi:10.1002/ijc.25008

340 – Robert A. Weinberg. *'The biology of cancer'.* Jun 2013. ISBN: 9780815342205

341 – *'Life expectancy vs. health expenditure over time, 1970-2014.'* https://ourworldindata.org/grapher/life-expectancy-vs-health-expenditure

342 – Bruce N. Ames. *'DNA damage from micronutrient deficiencies is likely to be a major cause of cancer.'* Mutation Research/Fundamental and Molecular Mechanisms of Mutagenesis. April, 2001. doi.org/10.1016/S0027-5107(01)00070-7

343 – Amuthan, Govindasamy et al. *'Mitochondria-to-Nucleus Stress Signaling Induces Phenotypic Changes, Tumour Progression and Cell Invasion.'* The EMBO Journal. February, 2017. doi: 10.1093/emboj/20.8.1910

344 – M Guha et al. *'Mitochondrial retrograde signaling induces epithelial–mesenchymal transition and generates breast cancer stem cells.'* Oncogene advance online publication. November, 2013. doi:10.1038/onc.2013.467

345 – *How Cancer Spreads (Metastasis).* Cancer Quest. Winship Cancer Institute. www.cancerquest.org/cancer-biology/metastasis

346 – Pärnänen P, Meurman JH, Sorsa T. *'The effects of Candida proteinases on human proMMP-9, TIMP-1 and TIMP-2.'* Mycoses. 2011. doi:10.1111/j.1439-0507.2010.01889.x

348 – Dr. Andreas Eenfeldt, MD. *'Using a ketogenic diet to stop brain tumour growth.'* Diet Doctor. July 2016. https://www.dietdoctor.com/pablo-27-beats-cancer-using-ketogenic-diet – Plymouth Herald www.plymouthherald.co.uk/news/local-news/man-brain-tumour-cut-out-316430

349 – Dana White. *'A second chance at health.'* Westchester magazine 2015

350 – *'The Royal Society biography of John Dick.'* (Establishing the existence of cancer stem cells 1994). https://royalsociety.org/people/john-dick-11333/

351 – Rhona Finkel. *'8 FDA Approved Drugs That Were Pulled From The Market.'* Drugsdb.com. October 2012.

353 – *'How science goes wrong.'* The Economist. October 2013. www.economist.com/leaders/2013/10/21/how-science-goes-wrong

354 – *'Vitamin cartel fined for price fixing.'* The Guardian. November 2001.

355 – Damian Carrington. *'UN experts denounce 'myth' pesticides are necessary to feed the world.'* The Guardian. March 2017. www.theguardian.com/environment/2017/mar/07/un-experts-denounce-myth-pesticides-are-necessary-to-feed-the-world

356 – *'The Naga gene.'* Intogen.org. DNA sequencing database.

357 – *'Genomic Data Commons Data Portal.'* National Cancer Institute. February, 2021. https://portal.gdc.cancer.gov

358 – Laura A. Stokowski. *'Who Believes That Medical Error Is the Third Leading Cause of Hospital Deaths?'* Medscape. May 2016. www.medscape.com/viewarticle/863788_3

360 – Gary Nulls. *'Death by Medicine.'* Life Extension magazine. March 2004. www.lifeextension.com/magazine/2006/8/report_death

361 – M.W. White. *'Cancer: the role of oxygen in fungal-induced carcinogenesis.'* Medical Hypotheses. October, 2000. doi.org/10.1054/mehy.2000.1056

362 – Alison Phillips. *'I gave my dying son cannabis to ease his cancer symptoms and he made a miracle recovery.'* Mirror.co.uk. 2017. https://www.mirror.co.uk/news/uk-news/i-gave-dying-son-cannabis-10103387#comments-section

363 – Rima Obeid. *'The Metabolic Burden of Methyl Donor Deficiency with Focus on the Betaine Homocysteine Methyltransferase Pathway.'* Nutrients. 2013. doi:10.3390/nu5093481

364 – Changhan Lee et al. *'Fasting Cycles Retard Growth of Tumors and Sensitize a Range of Cancer Cell Types to Chemotherapy.'* Science Translational Medicine. March, 2012. doi:10.1126/scitranslmed.3003293

365 – Susannah Cahalan. *'Medical studies are almost always bogus.'* New York Post. May 6, 2017, 1:04pm. https://nypost.com/2017/05/06/medical-studies-are-almost-always-bogus/

366 – Yan Jiang et al. *'A Sucrose-Enriched Diet Promotes Tumorigenesis in Mammary Gland in Part through the 12-Lipoxygenase Pathway.'* Cancer Research. January, 2016. doi: 10.1158/0008-5472.CAN-14-3432

367 – Paul Flynn MP (Newport, West). *'Timely reform, but will it go far enough?'* www.paulflynnmp.co.uk/SpotlightMHRA.htm

368 – Richard Brook (Mind). *'Upset and angry at lack of action.'* Panorama, BBC 2004. http://news.bbc.co.uk/1/hi/programmes/panorama/3710380.stm

369 – House of Commons Health Committee report 2005. *'The Influence of the Pharmaceutical Industry'*. 2005.
https://publications.parliament.uk/pa/cm200405/cmselect/cmhealth/42/42.pdf

370 – Cancer Research UK. 'Cake bake fundraising.' Cancer Research UK November, 2022.
www.cancerresearchuk.org/sites/default/files/bake_sale_0.pdf

376 – Hiddink GJ, Hautvast JG, van Woerkum CM, Fieren CJ, van 't Hof MA. *'Nutrition guidance by primary-care physicians: perceived barriers and low involvement.'* Eur J Clin Nutr. 1995 Nov;49(11):842-51

377 – Ball LE, Hughes RM, Leveritt MD. *'Nutrition in general practice: role and workforce preparation expectations of medical educators.'* Aust J Prim Health. 2010. doi: 10.1071/PY10014

378 – Han SL, Auer R, Cornuz J, Marques-Vidal P. *'Clinical nutrition in primary care: An evaluation of resident physicians' attitudes and self-perceived proficiency.'* Clin Nutr ESPEN. October, 2016. doi: 10.1016/j.clnesp.2016.06.005

379 – Denis Campbell. *'Doctors know too little about nutrition and exercise'*. The Guardian. October 2016.

380 – Chemo.com. *'Anthracyclines.'* http://chemoth.com/types/anthracyclines

381 – Chi V. Dang1. *'Links between metabolism and cancer.'* Genes & Development. 2012. doi: 10.1101/gad.189365.112

382 – Besedovsky, Luciana, Tanja Lange, and Jan Born. *'Sleep and Immune Function.'* Pflugers Archiv. June, 2017. doi: 10.1007/s00424-011-1044-0

383 – Jason Karp PhD. *'The Three Metabolic Energy Systems.'* Ideafit.com. 2009.
www.ideafit.com/personal-training/the-three-metabolic-energy-systems/

384 – The Institute of Cancer Research. *'Abiraterone: a story of scientific innovation and commercial partnership.'* May 2014.
www.icr.ac.uk/news-features/latest-features/abiraterone-a-story-of-scientific-innovation-and-commercial-partnership

385 – Jenny Hope, James Chapman. *'Breast cancer drug 'is best for 20 years'*. Mail online.
www.dailymail.co.uk/health/article-115350/Breast-cancer-drug-best-20-years.html

386 – HGH. *'Immune system and testosterone deficiency.'* May 2020.
www.hgh.biz/blog/testosterone/immune-system-and-testosterone-deficiency/

387 – Debora Mackenzie. *'Why do women keep taking HRT despite breast cancer risks?'* NewScientist 2016. https://www.newscientist.com/article/2102063-why-do-women-keep-taking-hrt-despite-breast-cancer-risks/

388 – Clancy, S. *'DNA damage & repair: mechanisms for maintaining DNA integrity.'* Nature Education 1(1):103 (2008). https://www.nature.com/scitable/topicpage/dna-damage-repair-mechanisms-for-maintaining-dna-344/

389 – Nicola Traverso, Roberta Ricciarelli, Mariapaola Nitti, et al., *'Role of Glutathione in Cancer Progression and Chemoresistance.'* Oxidative Medicine and Cellular Longevity. 2013. doi:10.1155/2013/972913

390 – Vicent Ribas, Carmen García-Ruiz and José C. Fernández-Checa. *'Glutathione and mitochondria.'* Front. Pharmacol. July, 2014. doi.org/10.3389/fphar.2014.00151

391 – Lucia Coppo, Pietro Ghezzi. *'Thiol regulation of pro-inflammatory cytokines and innate immunity:protein S-thiolation as a novel molecular mechanism.'* Biochemical Society Transactions. October, 2011. doi: 10.1042/BST0391268

392 – Environmental Working Group. *'Body Burden: The pollution in newborns.'* EWG 2005.
www.ewg.org/research/body-burden-pollution-newborns

393 – Sarah Knapton. *'Chemotherapy may spread cancer and trigger more aggressive tumours, warn scientists.'* The Telegraph 2017.

394 – George S. Karagiannis et al. *'Neoadjuvant chemotherapy induces breast cancer metastasis through a TMEM-mediated mechanism.'* Science Translational Medicine. July, 2017. doi: 10.1126/scitranslmed.aan0026

395 – Brücher BL, Jamall IS. *'Somatic Mutation Theory – Why it's Wrong for Most Cancers.'* Cell Physiol Biochem. 2016. doi.org/10.1159/000443106

397 – Elisa Robles-Escajeda et al. *'Analysis of the cytotoxic effects of ruthenium–ketoconazole and ruthenium–clotrimazole complexes on cancer cells.'* Cell Biology and Toxicology. December 2013, Volume 29, Issue 6, pp 431–443

398 – Mary Strasberg Rieber et al. *'Tumor apoptosis induced by ruthenium(II)-ketoconazole is enhanced in nonsusceptible carcinoma by monoclonal antibody to EGF receptor.'* IJC. November, 2004. doi.org/10.1002/ijc.20415

399 – Yuan-Soon Ho et al. *'Molecular mechanisms of econazole-induced toxicity on human colon cancer cells: G0/G1 cell cycle arrest and caspase 8-independent apoptotic signaling pathways.'* Food and Chemical Toxicology. October, 2005. doi.org/10.1016/j.fct.2005.04.002

400 – Chih-HsiungWu et al. *'Antitumor Effects of Miconazole on Human Colon Carcinoma Xenografts in Nude Mice through Induction of Apoptosis and G0/G1 Cell Cycle Arrest.'* Toxicology and Applied Pharmacology. April 2002. doi.org/10.1006/taap.2002.9352

401 – Yuan-SoonHo et al. *'Ketoconazole-Induced Apoptosis through P53-Dependent Pathway in Human Colorectal and Hepatocellular Carcinoma Cell Lines.'* Toxicology and Applied Pharmacology. 1998. doi.org/10.1006/taap.1998.8467

402 – Sobecks R et al. *'Imidazole anti-fungals Miconazole and Econazole induce apoptosis in mouse lymphoma and human T cell leukemia cells: regulation by Bcl-2 and potential role of calcium.'* Cell Death and Differentiation. July 1996, 3(3):331-337. PMID: 17180102

403 – Baker, Stuart G. *'A Cancer Theory Kerfuffle Can Lead to New Lines of Research.'* JNCI Journal of the National Cancer Institute. February, 2015. doi:10.1093/jnci/dju405

404 – İyikesici M et al. *'Efficacy of Metabolically Supported Chemotherapy Combined with Ketogenic Diet, Hyperthermia, and Hyperbaric Oxygen Therapy for Stage IV Triple-Negative Breast Cancer.'* Cureus. July, 2017. doi:10.7759/cureus.1445

405 – David Perlmutter MD. *'The Empowering Neurologist - David Perlmutter, MD and Dr. Thomas Seyfried.'* David Perlmutter YouTube channel 2017. *www.youtube.com/watch?v=Mlpx9yyk1Fw*

406 – Thomas N Seyfried and Laura M Shelton. *'Cancer as a metabolic disease.'* Nutrition & Metabolism. 2010. doi: 10.1186/1743-7075-7-7© Seyfried and Shelton; licensee BioMed Central Ltd.

407 – H.V.M.N. *'An Alternative View of Cancer ft. Thomas Seyfried || Episode 27.'* Youtube channel HVMN. https://www.youtube.com/watch?v=rDM5TS4tGT4

408 – *'Apoptosis vs Necrosis.'* July 2020. www.diffen.com/difference/Apoptosis_vs_Necrosis

409 – Sharon Begley. *'Health Officials find first cases of new super-bug in US.'* Stat news. November 4th 2016.

411 – Isabella Nikolic. *'Terminally-ill British mother, 40, who kept her lung cancer secret from her young daughter shocks medics after tumour shrinks by 75% following alternative treatment in Mexico.'* Mailonline. 23rd March 2019

413 – Steinshamn, S and A Waage. *'Tumor necrosis factor and interleukin-6 in Candida albicans infection in normal and granulocytopenic mice.'* Infection and Immunity. 1992. doi: 10.1128/IAI.01041-09

414 – Moaz M.Choudhary et al. *'Interleukin-6 role in head and neck squamous cell carcinoma progression.'* World Journal of Otorhinolaryngology-Head and Neck Surgery. June, 2016. doi.org/10.1016/j.wjorl.2016.05.002

415 – Randa Akel, MD, Mazen Kurban, MD, Ossama Abbas, MD. '*CD47 expression for in situ and invasive cutaneous epithelial lesions.*' JAAD. August, 2016. doi.org/10.1016/j.jaad.2016.03.011

417 – Yang J, Liu X et al. '*Prevention of apoptosis by Bcl-2: release of cytochrome c from mitochondria blocked.*' Science. 1997 Feb 21;275(5303):1129-32. PMID: 9027314.

418 – BBC Bitesize. '*Cell Respiration.*' www.bbc.co.uk/education/guides/zcxrd2p/revision/3

419 – Seema Gupta et al. '*Metabolic Cooperation and Competition in the Tumor Microenvironment: Implications for Therapy.*' Front. Oncol. April, 2017. doi.org/10.3389/fonc.2017.00068

421 – Toby Leigh. '*Good news for Pablo in unconventional brain tumour battle. IvyBridge & South Brent Gazette.*' Thursday 14th September 2017

422 – Kat Arney. '*Cannabis, cannabinoids and cancer – the evidence so far.*' Cancer Research UK science blog. July 12th 2012.

423 – Gill, Sean E., and William C. Parks. '*Metalloproteinases and Their Inhibitors: Regulators of Wound Healing.*' The international journal of biochemistry & cell biology. September, 2017. doi: 10.1016/j.biocel.2007.10.024

424 – News Medical. '*Neutrophils linked to growth and spread of cancer.*' September 2, 2011. www.news-medical.net/news/20110902/Neutrophils-linked-to-growth-and-spread-of-cancer.aspx

425 – David Kadosh, Jose L. Lopez-Ribot. '*Candida albicans: Adapting to Succeed.*' Cell Host & Microbe. November, 2013. doi: 10.1016/j.chom.2013.10.016

426 – C. Orian Truss, M.D. '*Metabolic Abnormalities in Patients with Chronic Candidiasis The Acetaldehyde Hypothesis.*' Orthomolecular.org. www.orthomolecular.org/library/jom/1984/pdf/1984-v13n02-p066.pdf

428 – Caroline Schild-Poulter. University of Western Ontario. '*Why cancer cells just won't die: Researcher identifies protein which regulates cell suicide.*' ScienceDaily. 10 December 2009. www.sciencedaily.com/releases/2009/12/091209114158.htm

429 – Zvi Granot and Jadwiga Jablonska. '*Distinct Functions of Neutrophil in Cancer and Its Regulation. Mediators of Inflammation.*' Volume 2015, Article ID 701067, 11 pages. doi.org/10.1155/2015/701067

430 – James Hamblin. '*1,458 Bacteria Species 'New to Science' Found in Our Belly Buttons.*' The Atlantic. December 2012. https://www.theatlantic.com/health/archive/2012/12/1-458-bacteria-species-new-to-science-found-in-our-belly-buttons/266360/

431 – '*Cancer drug Herceptin can prolong sufferers' lives.*' Mirror.co.uk. February 2012. www.mirror.co.uk/news/uk-news/cancer-drug-herceptin-can-prolong-311035

432 – F. Polet, O. Feron. '*Endothelial cell metabolism and tumour angiogenesis: glucose and glutamine as essential fuels and lactate as the driving force.*' Journal of Internal medicine. February, 2013. doi: 10.1111/joim.12016

433 – Independent.co.uk. '*10 Persistent myths about cancer that are false.*' October 2015. www.independent.co.uk/lifestyle/health-and-families/features/10-persistent-myths-about-cancer-that-are-false-a6709496.html

434 – Express.co.uk. '*Preventions, cures and causes: Top 10 cancer myths debunked.*' October 2015. Article source: Cancer Research UK Science blog. *https://www.express.co.uk/life-style/health/468697/Top-10-cancer-myths-debunked*

435 – Ben Kentish. '*Cancer drug price rises 15-fold as owner raises cost for ninth time in four years.*' Independent.co.uk December 2017.

436 – Hou, Yilin et al. '*High Glucose Levels Promote the Proliferation of Breast Cancer Cells through GTPases.*' Breast Cancer: Targets and Therapy 9 (2017): 429–436. PMC. Web. 29 Dec. 2017.

437 – Cheryl Hague. *'Grandmother says she has almost beat cancer thanks to cannabis oil as she urges government to act.'* Daily Record.co.uk December 2017.

440 – Tech. *'Cannabis Treatment For Brain Cancer Begins First Human Trials.'* Leaf Science November 2013. www.leafscience.com/2013/11/12/cannabis-treatment-brain-cancer-begins-first-human-trials/

442 – P.C. Calder, P. Yaqoob. *'Glutamine and the immune system.'* Amino Acids. 1999. doi.org/10.1007/BF01366922

443 – Satyajit Dutta et al. *'Glutamic acid as anticancer agent: An overview.'* Saudi Pharmaceutical Journal. January, 2018. doi: 10.1016/j.jsps.2012.12.007

445 – *'What causes cancer cachexia?'* Cancer Cachexia Hub. www.cancercachexia.com/what-causes-cancer-cachexia#biblio4

446 – *Corticosteroids and Diabetes.* Diabetes.co.uk. https://www.diabetes.co.uk/diabetes-medication/costicosteroids-and-diabetes.html

447 – Sanford-Burnham Medical Research Institute. *'How cancer cells rewire their metabolism to survive.'* Sciencedaily.com. January 31, 2013. www.sciencedaily.com/releases/2013/01/130131144427.htm

448 – Keneth C.H. et al. *'Cancer Cachexia: Mediators, Signaling, and Metabolic Pathways.'* Cell Metabolism. 2012. doi.org/10.1016/j.cmet.2012.06.011

449 – Jane McLelland. *'How to Starve Cancer.'* ISBN: 978-0-9519517-1-2 www.howtostarvecancer.com

450 – University of Salford. *'Vitamin C and antibiotics: A new one-two 'punch' for knocking-out cancer stem cells.'* ScienceDaily. ScienceDaily, 12 June 2017. www.sciencedaily.com/releases/2017/06/170612094405.htm

451 – Press release. *'Study confirms long-term benefit of anastrozole to stop breast cancer returning.'* Cancer research UK. December 2010. www.cancerresearchuk.org/about-us/cancer-news/press-release/2010-12-01-study-confirms-long-term-benefit-of-anastrozole-to-stop-breast-cancer-returning

452 – Prof Jack Cuzick, Phd, et al. *'Effect of anastrozole and tamoxifen as adjuvant treatment for early-stage breast cancer: 10-year analysis of the ATAC trial.'* The Lancet Oncology. November, 2010. doi.org/10.1016/S1470-2045(10)70257-6

453 – *'Arimidex and immune system suppression.'* Breast Cancer.Org community. https://community.breastcancer.org/forum/78/topics/694669. October 2007.

454 – Lu, Q., Yue, W., Wang, J. et al. *'The effects of aromatase inhibitors and antiestrogens in the nude mouse model.'* Breast Cancer Res Treat. 1998. doi.org/10.1023/A:1006004930930

455 – Allen D, Wilson D, Drew R, Perfect J. *'Azole anti-fungals: 35 years of invasive fungal infection management.'* Expert Rev Anti Infect Ther. June 2015. doi:10.1586/14787210.2015.1032939

456 – Eric Bakker N.D. *'Connection Between Chronic Yeast Infections and Hormonal Imbalance.'* Yeast infection.org. July 6th 2015. https://www.yeastinfection.org/connection-between-chronic-yeast-infections-and-hormonal-imbalance/

457 – David H. Philips. *'Understanding the genotoxicity of tamoxofen.'* Carcinogenesis. June, 2001. doi.org/10.1093/carcin/22.6.839

458 – Susie East. *'How fungi kill millions globally.'* CNN 27th September 2016. http://edition.cnn.com/2016/09/27/health/deadly-fungal-infections/index.html

459 – *'The largely unknown health epidemic affecting almost all Americans.'* Body Ecology. https://bodyecology.com/articles/unknown_health_epidemic.php

460 – Krzysztof Piotr Michalak et al. *'Key Roles of Glutamine Pathways in Reprogramming the Cancer Metabolism.'* Oxidative Medicine and Cellular Longevity. 2015. doi:10.1155/2015/964321

461 – Stephanie Pappas. *'There might be 1 trillion species on earth.'* Live Science. May 5th 2016. www.livescience.com/54660-1-trillion-species-on-earth.html

462 – Katharina S. Kuhn, et al. *'Glutamine as indispensable nutrient in oncology: experimental and clinical evidence.'* European Journal of Nutrition. June, 2010. doi: 10.1007/s00394-009-0082-2

463 – The Expert Committe on Pesticide Residues in Food (PriF) Annual Report 2016. www.gov.uk/government/uploads/system/uploads/attachment_data/file/655035/expert-committee-pesticide-residues-food-annual-report-2016.pdf

464 – Barry J. Marshall Biographical. *'The Nobel Prize in Physiology or Medicine 2005.'* Nobelprize.org 2005. https://www.nobelprize.org/prizes/medicine/2005/summary/

465 – J Cole Aidan, Nicole R Priddee, and James J McAleer. *'Chemotherapy causes cancer! A case report of therapy related acute myeloid leukaemia in early stage breast cancer.'* Ulster Med J. 2013 May; 82(2): 97–99. PMCID: PMC3756867.

466 – *'Cancer Survival Statistics.'* Cancer Research UK 2011. www.cancerresearchuk.org/health-professional/cancer-statistics/survival. May 2020.

467 – Thomas Hoffman. *'Scientists: we will never find a cure for cancer.'* ScienceNordic. November 11, 2016.

469 – Zach Klein. The Scientist (2015) Medical Marijuana. *Www.mechoulamthescientist.com*

470 – *University of Michigan Health System. 'Finding Key To Cancer Drug Gleevec's Limitations.' ScienceDaily. ScienceDaily, 7 August 2009.* www.sciencedaily.com/releases/2009/08/090805084953.htm

471 – Hans Prenen et al. *'Imatinib Mesylate Inhibits Glucose Uptake in Gastrointestinal Stromal Tumor Cells by Downregulation of the Glucose Transporters Recruitment to the Plasma Membrane'.* American Journal of Biochemistry and Biotechnology. 2005. doi:10.3844/ajbbsp.2005.95.102

472 – Tanveer Mann. *'Mother claims cannabis oil cured her breast cancer for just £100.'* Metro.co.uk February 2018.

473 – *'Cannabis oil Cures 8 month old infant of cancer, dissolving large inoperable tumour in 8 months.'* Cannabis News World. March 2018. https://cannabisnewsworld.com/2018/03/07/cannabis-oil-cures-8-month-old-infant-of-cancer-dissolving-large-inoperable-tumor-in-8-months-health-times/

474 – *'All cancers combined incidence trends over time by age.'* Cancer Research UK. All Cancers Excluding Non-Melanoma Skin Cancer (ICD-10 C00-97 Excl C44), European Age-Standardised Incidence Rates, By Age, UK, 1993-2015

475 – Cancer registration statistics, England Statistical bulletins. Office for National Statistics. www.ons.gov.uk/peoplepopulationandcommunity/healthandsocialcare/conditionsan ddiseases/bulletins/cancerregistrationstatisticsengland/previousReleases

476 – Kaoru Sugimoto, Sean P. Gordon and Elliot M. Meyerowitz. *'Regeneration in plants and animals: dedifferentiation, transdifferentiation, or just differentiation?'* Trends in Cell Biology. April, 2011. doi:10.1016/j.tcb.2010.12.004

477 – Ella Sparrenius Waters. *'Pesticides on a plate.'* Pesticide Action NetworkUK. https://issuu.com/pan-uk/docs/pesticides_on_a_plate

478 – Sheila Dillon. *'We learn nothing about nutrition, claim medical students'.* BBC Health, 25th March 2018. www.bbc.co.uk/news/health-43504125.

480 – Richard D. Lyons. *'Ousted F.D.A Chief Charges 'Pressure' From Drug Industry.'* The New York Times. December 30th 1969. Page 1, continued on page 13, column 1. https://timesmachine.nytimes.com/timesmachine/1969/12/31/81561101.pdf

481 – Kendel Stewart MD. *'Methyl-deficiency: The missing component to Neurological and Immunological Recovery.'* Presentation from American Acadamy of Anti-Ageing

Medicine World Congress in Las Vegas, NV. Dec. 12, 2012.
www.neurobiologix.com/v/Files/Methylation%20Deficiency%20by%20Dr.%20Kendal
%20Stewart.pdf

482 – Siddhartha Mukerjee. *'The Emperor of All Maladies: A Biography of Cancer'*. Scribner. 16th November 2010. ISBN 978-1-4391-0795-9

483 – Lauren Pecorino. *'Molecular Biology of Cancer: Mechanisms, Targets, and Therapeutics'*. Third Edition. University of Greenwich. Oxford University Press. 2012. ISBN 978-0-19-957717-0

484 – Karsten Bartels, Almut Grenz, and Holger K. Eltzschig. *'Hypoxia and inflammation are two sides of the same coin.'* PNAS. November, 2013. doi.org/10.1073/pnas.1318345110

485 – Eugene D. Weinberg. *'Iron availability and infection, Biochimica et Biophysica Acta (BBA) - General Subjects.'* Volume 1790, Issue 7, 2009, Pages 600-605,ISSN 0304-4165. doi.org/10.1016/j.bbagen.2008.07.002.

486 – Roberta J. Ward et al. *'Iron and the immune system.'* J Neural Transm. 2011. doi.org/10.1007/s00702-010-0479-3

487 – Ricardo S. Almeida et al. *'The Hyphal-Associated Adhesin and Invasin Als3 of Candida albicans Mediates Iron Acquisition from Host Ferritin.'* PLOS Pathogens. November, 2008. doi.org/10.1371/journal.ppat.1000217

488 – Torti, Suzy V., and Frank M. Torti. *'Iron and Cancer: More Ore to Be Mined.'* Nature reviews. May, 2013. doi: 10.1038/nrc3495

489 – John J. Bullen, Henry J. Rogers, Paul B. Spalding, C. Gillon Ward. *'Natural resistance, iron and infection: a challenge for clinical medicine.'* Journal of Medical Microbiology. March, 2006. doi: 10.1099/jmm.0.46386-0

490 – Ernest M. Walker, Jr. and Sandra M. Walker. *'Review: Effects of Iron Overload on the Immune System.'* Annals of Clinical & Laboratory Science, vol. 30, no 4, 2000. www.annclinlabsci.org/content/30/4/354.full.pdf

491 – Shinya Toyokuni. *'Iron overload as a major targetable pathogenesis of asbestos-induced mesothelial carcinogenesis.'* Redox Report. 2013. doi:10.1179/1351000213Y.0000000075

492 – L. Mascitelli, M.R. Goldstein. *'Inhibition of iron absorption by polyphenols as an anti-cancer mechanism.'* QJM: An International Journal of Medicine. May 2011. doi.org/10.1093/qjmed/hcq239

493 – Helmholtz Association of German Research Centres. *'Iron Induces Death In Tumor Cells.'* ScienceDaily. ScienceDaily, 13 March 2009. <www.sciencedaily.com/releases/2009/03/090311103607.htm>.

494 – Narendra P. Singh, Henry C. Lai. *'Artemisinin Induces Apoptosis in Human Cancer Cells.'* Anticancer Research. July-August 2004. doi:10.1371/journal.pone.0019804

495 – Woong Nam DDS, MSD et al. *'Effects of artemisinin and its derivatives on growth inhibition and apoptosis of oral cancer cells.'* Head and Neck. December, 2006. doi.org/10.1002/hed.20524

496 – Shinya Toyokuni. *'Role of iron in carcinogenesis: Cancer as a ferrotoxic disease. Cancer Science.'* January, 2009. doi.org/10.1111/j.1349-7006.2008.01001.x

497 – Ricardo S. Almeida, Duncan Wilson, Bernhard Hube. *'Candida albicans iron acquisition within the host.'* FEMS Yeast Research. October, 2009. doi.org/10.1111/j.1567-1364.2009.00570.x

498 – Jenny Hope. *'Most cancers are 'caused by bad luck – not lifestyle': Scientists claim 65% of cases are down to random mistakes in genes that we can do nothing about'*. MailOnline, January, 2015. www.dailymail.co.uk/news/article-2893932/Most-cancers-caused-bad-luck-not-lifestyle-Scientists-claim-65-cases-random-mistakes-genes-about.html

499 – Genkinger JM, Koushik A. *'Meat Consumption and Cancer Risk.'* PLoS Med. 2007. doi.org/10.1371/journal.pmed.0040345

500 – Dr Richard J. Albin. *'The Great Prostate Mistake.'* The New York Times. March 2010. www.nytimes.com/2010/03/10/opinion/10Ablin.html

501 – Pallab Sanpui, et al. *'Induction of Apoptosis in Cancer Cells at Low Silver Nanoparticle Concentrations using Chitosan Nanocarrier.'* ACS Appl. Mater. Interfaces. 2011. doi: 10.1021/am100840c

503 – Takashi Matsuura et al. *'Effect of salivary gland adenocarcinoma cell-derived α-N-acetylgalactosaminidase on the bioactivity of macrophage activating factor.'* March, 2004. doi.org/10.3892/ijo.24.3.521

504 – Douglas Hanahan, Robert A.Weinberg. *'Hallmarks of Cancer: The Next Generation.'* Cell. March, 2011. doi.org/10.1016/j.cell.2011.02.013

507 – Cowan, Marjorie Murphy. *'Plant Products as Antimicrobial Agents.'* Clinical Microbiology Reviews 12.4 (1999): 564–582. Print. PMID: 10515903

510 – Damian Carrington. *'Avoiding meat and dairy is 'single biggest way' to reduce your impact on Earth.'* The Guardian. 2018. www.theguardian.com/environment/2018/may/31/avoiding-meat-and-dairy-is-single-biggest-way-to-reduce-your-impact-on-earth.

511 – Mandal, Manisha Deb, and Shyamapada Mandal. *'Honey: Its Medicinal Property and Antibacterial Activity.'* Asian Pacific Journal of Tropical Biomedicine. August, 2018. doi.org/10.1016/S2221-1691(11)60016-6

512 – Daniel. *'Itraconazole: An Anti-fungal drug with anti-cancer properties.'* Cancer Treatment Research.com 2016. https://www.cancertreatmentsresearch.com/itraconazole/

513 – Lockhart NR, et al. *'Itraconazole therapy in a pancreatic adenocarcinoma patient: A case report.'* June, 2015. doi: 10.1177/1078155215572931

514 – *Hepatotoxicity from Chemotherapy treatment.* www.mesotheliomaweb.org/hepatoxicity.htm

515 – https://thriva.co (Thriva a blood testing company)

516 – Liver function tests. British Liver Trust. https://www.britishlivertrust.org.uk/liver-information/tests-and-screening/liver-function-tests/

518 – Patrick Greenfield. *'Monsanto ordered to pay $289 million as jury rules weedkiller caused man's cancer.'* The Guardian. Saturday 11th August 2018. www.theguardian.com/business/2018/aug/10/monsanto-trial-cancer-dewayne-johnson-ruling

519 – Drugs.com. *'Morphine.'* 2017. https://www.drugs.com/morphine.html

520 – Cell Press. *'High doses of vitamin C to improve cancer treatment passes human safety trial.'* ScienceDaily. ScienceDaily, 30 March 2017. <www.sciencedaily.com/releases/2017/03/170330142341.htm>.

522 – AnneLe et al. *'Glucose-Independent Glutamine Metabolism via TCA Cycling for Proliferation and Survival in B Cells.'* Cell Metabolism. January, 2012. doi.org/10.1016/j.cmet.2011.12.009

525 – Young Ko. *'3BP.'* KoDiscovery. https://www.kodiscovery.org/

527 – Jo Lewis. *'Organic food linked to cancer prevention.'* Soil Association, 22 October 2018. www.soilassociation.org/news/2018/october/22/organic-food-linked-to-cancer-prevention/?fbclid=IwAR0C67Ra_zG-FVhCnfBfQ0mJPRKyd1Xe8iQ0tYu1U_UU8cHYT1eSUkDeUhk

528 – Press Office. *'Organic vs non-organic food'.* Newcastle University, 8 October 2015. www.ncl.ac.uk/press/articles/archive/2015/10/organicvsnon-organicfood/

529 – Lu, Jianrong et al. *'The Warburg effect in tumor progression: mitochondrial oxidative metabolism as an anti-metastasis mechanism.'* Cancer letters vol. 356,2 Pt A (2014): 156-64. [anoikis] http://europepmc.org/backend/ptpmcrender.fcgi?accid=PMC4195816&blobtype=pdf

530 – George Monbiot. *'The best way to save the planet? Drop meat and dairy.'* The Guardian. Friday 8th June 2018. www.theguardian.com/commentisfree/2018/jun/08/save-planet-meat-dairy-livestock-food-free-range-steak

531 – *'Facts on Animal Farming and the Environment.'* Onegreenplanet.org. www.onegreenplanet.org/animalsandnature/facts-on-animal-farming-and-the-environment/

532 – Omer Faruk Tekbas et al. *'Melatonin as an antibiotic: New insights into the actions of this ubiquitous molecule.'* Journal of pineal research. April, 2008. doi:10.1111/j.1600-079X.2007.00516.x

533 – Fatma Pehlivan Karakas, et al. *'Antibacterial and antitumor activities of melatonin hormone.'* Spatula DD. 2013. doi 10.5455/spatula.20130422052142

534 – Glenister, Rachael et al. *'Therapeutic actions of melatonin on gastrointestinal cancer development and progression.'* Translational gastrointestinal cancer vol. 2013. doi:10.3978/j.issn.2224-4778.2012.08.03

535 – Malhotra, Samir et al. *'The therapeutic potential of melatonin: a review of the science.'* MedGenMed: Medscape general medicine vol. 6,2 46. 14 Apr. 2004. www.researchgate.net/publication/8443872_The_Therapeutic_Potential_of_Melatonin_A_Review_of_the_Science

536 – Meg Tirrel. *'The world spent this much on cancer drugs last year.'* CNBC. 2 June 2016. www.cnbc.com/2016/06/02/the-worlds-2015-cancer-drug-bill-107-billion-dollars.html

537 – Lenzer J. *'What Can We Learn from Medical Whistleblowers?'* PLoS Med. 2005. doi.org/10.1371/journal.pmed.0020209

538 – Vighi, G et al. *'Allergy and the gastrointestinal system.'* Clinical and experimental immunology vol. 153 Suppl 1,Suppl 1 (2008): 3-6.

539 – Mayo Clinic. *'Mayo Clinic Study Implicates Fungus As Cause Of Chronic Sinusitis.'* ScienceDaily. ScienceDaily, 10 September 1999.

540 – NHS. *'Sinusitis infection.'* December 2017. https://www.nhs.uk/conditions/sinusitis-sinus-infection/

541 – *'Sinusitis.'* BUPA. May 2020. www.bupa.co.uk/health-information/lungs-breathing/sinusitis

543 – Elisabeth Streit, et al. *'Multi-Mycotoxin Screening Reveals the Occurrence of 139 Different Secondary Metabolites in Feed and Feed Ingredients '* MDPI. Toxins. 2013. doi:10.3390/toxins5030504

544 – Keuk-Jun Kim et al. *'Anti-fungal activity and mode of action of silver nano-particles on Candida albicans.'* BioMetals. April, 2009. doi: 10.1007/s10534-008-9159-2

545 – Mao L, et al. *'Melatonin suppression of aerobic glycolysis (Warburg effect), survival signalling and metastasis in human leiomyosarcoma.'* J Pineal Res. 2016. doi: 10.1111/jpi.12298

546 – Hevia D, et al. *'Melatonin uptake through glucose transporters: a new target for melatonin inhibition of cancer.'* J Pineal Res. March, 2015. doi: 10.1111/jpi.12210

547 – Salk, Jesse J et al. *'Mutational heterogeneity in human cancers: origin and consequences.'* Annual review of pathology vol. 5 (2010): 51-75. doi:10.1146/annurev-pathol-121808-102113

548 – Sze-Ue Luk, et al. *'Chemopreventive Effect of PSP Through Targeting of Prostate Cancer Stem Cell-Like Population.'* PLOS ONE. May, 2011. doi:10.1371/journal.pone.0019804

549 – Ting-Li Han, et al. *'The metabolic basis of Candida albicans morphogenesis and quorum sensing.'* Fungal Genetics and Biology. 48 (2011) 747–763. www.thecandidadiet.com/wp-content/uploads/research/metabolic-basis-of-candida-morphogenesis-and-quorum-sensing.pdf

550 – Sarah Constantin. '3-Bromopyruvate.' 2018.
www.sarah-constantin.org/blog/2018/1/14/3-bromopyruvate

551 – Ko YH, et al. 'Advanced cancers: eradication in all cases using 3-bromopyruvate therapy to deplete ATP.' Biochem Biophys Res Commun. November, 2004.
doi.org/10.1016/j.bbrc.2004.09.047

552 – Lis, Paweł et al. 'Screening the yeast genome for energetic metabolism pathways involved in a phenotypic response to the anti-cancer agent 3-bromopyruvate.' Oncotarget. 2016. doi: 10.18632/oncotarget.7174

553 – Mariusz Dylag, et al. '3-Bromopyruvate: A novel anti-fungal agent against the human pathogen Cryptococcus neoforman.' Biochemical and Biophysical Research Communications. May, 2013. doi.org/10.1016/j.bbrc.2013.02.125

554 – IzabelaSadowska-Bartosz, et al. 'Anticancer agent 3-bromopyruvic acid forms a conjugate with glutathione.' Pharmacological Reports. April, 2016.
doi.org/10.1016/j.pharep.2015.11.007

555 – Niedźwiecka, Katarzyna et al. 'Glutathione may have implications in the design of 3-bromopyruvate treatment protocols for both fungal and algal infections as well as multiple myeloma.' Oncotarget. 2016. doi: 10.18632/oncotarget.11592

556 – Shoshan, M.C. '3-bromopyruvate: Targets and outcomes.' Journal of Bioenergetics and Biomembranes. 2012. doi: 10.1007/s10863-012-9419-2

557 – Blue Zones. 'The Okinawa Diet: Eating and Living to 100.' May 23, 2017.
www.bluezones.com/2017/05/okinawa-diet-eating-living-100/?fbclid=IwAR1y-Jz7LRrc6g9Oe4vkA9ez-alZgtwdD1OtZ1Tvz_4ZnDqT_sW8XORzHqY

558 – Phillips RL. 'Role of lifestyle and dietary habits in risk of cancer among seventh-day adventists.' Cancer Res. 1975 Nov;35(11 Pt. 2):3513-22.

559 – Tantamango-Bartley, Yessenia et al. 'Vegetarian diets and the incidence of cancer in a low-risk population.' Cancer epidemiology, biomarkers & prevention: a publication of the American Association for Cancer Research, cosponsored by the American Society of Preventive Oncology. 2012. doi:10.1158/1055-9965.EPI-12-1060

560 – Ashleigh R. Poh and Matthias Ernst. 'Targeting Macrophages in Cancer: From Bench to Bedside.' Frontiers in Oncology. March, 2018. doi.org/10.3389/fonc.2018.00049

561 – Caulin, Aleah F and Carlo C Maley. 'Peto's Paradox: evolution's prescription for cancer prevention.' Trends in ecology & evolution vol. 26,4 (2011): 175-82.

562 – Filler, Scott G and Donald C Sheppard. 'Fungal invasion of normally non-phagocytic host cells.' PLoS pathogens. 2006. doi:10.1371/journal.ppat.0020129

563 – A. I. Medeiros, et al. 'Histoplasma scpsulatum Inhibits Apoptosis and Mac-1 Expression in Leucocytes.' Scandinavian Journal of Immunology. September, 2002.
doi.org/10.1046/j.1365-3083.2002.01142.x

564 – Moyes, David L et al. 'Candida albicans-epithelial interactions and pathogenicity mechanisms: scratching the surface.' Virulence. 2015. doi:10.1080/21505594.2015.1012981

565 – C. Cunha Villar, J. Chukwuedum Aniemeke, X-R Zhao, G. Huynh-Ba. 'Induction of apoptosis in oral epithelial cells by Candida albicans.' Mol Oral Microbiol. December, 2012. doi: 10.1111/j.2041-1014.2012.00648.x

566 – Dr David Servan-Schreiber. 'anti cancer, a new way of life.' 2011 ISBN: 978-0-718-15684-8

567 – Matt McGrath. 'UN: Growing threat to food from decline in bio-diversity.' 2019.
www.bbc.co.uk/news/science-environment-47308235

569 – Hereditary Diffuse Gastric Cancer. Cancer.Net. 2017. https://www.cancer.net/cancer-types/hereditary-diffuse-gastric-cancer

570 – Amy Stettner, MS, CGC. 'CDH1 Mutations.' No Stomach For Cancer. May 2020.
www.nostomachforcancer.org/about/hereditary-diffuse-gastric-cancer/genetics/cdh1-mutations

571 – C. C. Villar, H. Kashleva, C. J. Nobile, A. P. Mitchell, A. Dongari-Bagtzoglou. '*Mucosal Tissue Invasion by Candida albicans Is Associated with E-Cadherin Degradation, Mediated by Transcription Factor Rim101p and Protease Sap5p*'. Infection and Immunity. April, 2007. doi.org/10.1128/IAI.00054-07

572 – Kumamoto, Carol A. '*Inflammation and gastrointestinal Candida colonization.*' Current opinion in microbiology. 2011. doi: 10.1016/j.mib.2011.07.015

573 – Giulia Enders. '*GUT, the inside story of our body's most under-rated organ.*' ISBN: 9781911344773

574 – Sophie Jamieson. '*Majority of supermarket meat comes from animals fed on GM crops.*' Telegraph. 23rd February 2016.

577 – Ben Goldacre. '*What doctors don't know about the drugs they prescribe.*' TED. 2012. www.youtube.com/watch?v=RKmxL8VYy0M

578 – Max Roser and Hanna Ritchie. '*Cancer.*' Our World in Data. March 2018. https://ourworldindata.org/cancer

579 – '*White blood cell count decreased with Arimidex – from FDA reports.*' www.ehealthme.com/ds/arimidex/white-blood-cell-count-decreased/. 2019.

580 – Krithika Subramanian, PH.D. '*Insulin resistance and Estrogen*' www.livestrong.com/article/412793-insulin-resistance-estrogen/ May, 2018.

581 – Arthur I.CederbaumabCharles S.LieberabEmanuelRubinab. '*The effect of acetaldehyde on mitochondrial function.*' Archives of biochemistry and Biophysics. March, 1974. doi.org/10.1016/0003-9861(74)90231-8

582 – Dr Russell Ackoff. '*Systems thinking.*' 2015. https://www.youtube.com/watch?v=EbLh7rZ3rhU

583 – Pećina-Slaus, Nives. '*Tumor suppressor gene E-cadherin and its role in normal and malignant cells.*' Cancer cell international. October, 2003. doi:10.1186/1475-2867-3-17

584 – Ron Smits et al. '*E-cadherin and Adenomatous Polyposis Coli Mutations Are Synergistic in Intestinal Tumour Initiation in Mice.*' Gastroenterology. 2000. doi.org/10.1053/gast.2000.18162

585 – Koji Aoki, Makoto M. Taketo. '*Adenomatous polyposis coli (APC): a multi-functional tumor suppressor gene.*' Journal of Cell Science. 2007. doi:10.1242/jcs.03485

586 – '*AG Grewal Files Antitrust Lawsuit Against Twenty Generic Drug Companies, Alleging Conspiracy to Raise Prices on Over 100 Drugs.*' May 12, 2019. Office of the Attorney General. USA. https://www.nj.gov/oag/newsreleases19/pr20190512a.html

587 – Cheng JC, Qiu X,Chang HM, Leung PC. '*HER2 mediates epidermal growth factor-induced down-regulation of E-cadherin in human ovarian cancer cells.*' Biochemical Biophysical Research Communications. April, 2013. doi:10.1016/j.bbrc.2013.03.062

588 – Alejandra Borunda. '*First global look finds most rivers awash with antibiotics.*' National Geographic May 29, 2019. www.nationalgeographic.com/environment/2019/05/hundreds-of-worlds-rivers-contain-dangerous-levels-antibiotics/

589 – Behind The Bench Staff. '*Antibiotics in our Water Supply – Are we Polluting the Element of Life?*' 2016. https://www.thermofisher.com *to provide children's medical services.*' Mainl online. June 2018

590 – Daleen Totten. 'Global cancer researcher Professor Dan Burke on the benefits of Salvestrols.' Natural Medicine World. July 14th 2017. www.youtube.com/watch?v=2pzm0qdxWeM

592 – Weill Cornell Medicine. '*Scientists identify immune cells that keep gut fungi under control.*' ScienceDaily, 11 January 2018. www.sciencedaily.com/releases/2018/01/180111155030.htm

593 – *Crohn's disease*. NHS UK. June 9th 2019. https://www.nhs.uk/conditions/Crohns-disease/

594 – Kim, Eun Ran, and Dong Kyung Chang. *'Colorectal cancer in inflammatory bowel disease: the risk, pathogenesis, prevention and diagnosis.'* World journal of gastroenterology. 2014. doi:10.3748/wjg.v20.i29.9872

595 – GASTRIC (Global Advanced/Adjuvant Stomach Tumor Research International Collaboration) Group, Paoletti X et al. *'Benefit of adjuvant chemotherapy for resectable gastric cancer: a meta-analysis.'* JAMA. May, 2010. doi: 10.1001/jama.2010.534

596 – newswise.com. *'Unhealthy gut promotes breast cancer's spread, study finds.'* 2019 - Melanie R Rutkowski et al. *'Pre-existing commensal dysbiosis is a host-intrinsic regulator of tissue inflammation and tumor cell dissemination in hormone receptor-positive breast cancer.'* Cancer Res. 2019. doi: 10.1158/0008-5472.CAN-18-3464

597 – Lorenz, Michael C, and Gerald R Fink. *'Life and death in a macrophage: role of the glyoxylate cycle in virulence.'* Eukaryotic cell. 2002. doi:10.1128/ec.1.5.657-662.2002

598 – Kaleta, Christoph et al. *'In silico evidence for gluconeogenesis from fatty acids in humans.'* PLoS computational biology. 2011 doi:10.1371/journal.pcbi.1002116

599 – Galgóczy L, Nyilasi I, Papp T, Vágvölgyi C. *'Statins as anti-fungal agents.'* World J Clin Infect Dis. 2011. doi: 10.5495/wjcid.v1.i1.4

601 – Naomi Imatome-Yun. *'How does fat affect insulin resistance and diabetes?'* April 2016. www.forksoverknives.com/fat-insulin-resistance-blood-sugar/#gs.m913iz.

602 – Kathleen Doheny. *'The link between high blood glucose and high infection risk.'* 2015. www.endocrineweb.com/news/diabetes/16186-link-between-high-blood-glucose-high-infection-risk.

603 – Cutruzzolà Francesca et al. *'Glucose Metabolism in the Progression of Prostate Cancer.'* Frontiers in Physiology. 2017. doi=10.3389/fphys.2017.00097

604 – Barrie, Allison M et al. *'Dramatic response to Laetrile and cannabidiol (CBD) oil in a patient with metastatic low grade serous ovarian carcinoma.'* Gynecologic oncology reports. May, 2019. doi:10.1016/j.gore.2019.05.004

605 – Elena Fernández-Arenas et al. *'Integrated Proteomics and Genomics Strategies Bring New Insight into Candida albicans Response upon Macrophage Interaction.'* Molecular & Cellular Proteomics March, 2007. doi: 10.1074/mcp.M600210-MCP200

606 – Cordero, P et al. *'Fat-to-glucose interconversion by hydrodynamic transfer of two glyoxylate cycle enzyme genes.'* Lipids in health and disease. December, 2008. doi:10.1186/1476-511X-7-49

607 – Aggarwal BB1, Kumar A, Bharti AC. *'Anticancer potential of curcumin: preclinical and clinical studies.'* Anticancer Res. 2003 Jan-Feb;23(1A):363-98.

608 – Galdiero MR, Garlanda C, Jaillon S, Marone G, Mantovani A. *'Tumor associated macrophages and neutrophils in tumor progression.'* Journal of Cell Physiology. July, 2013. doi: 10.1002/jcp.24260

609 – Polet.F, Feron.O. *'Endothelial cell metabolism and tumour angiogenesis: glucose and glutamine as essential fuels and lactate as the driving force.'* Journal of Internal Medicine. December, 2012. doi.org/10.1111/joim.12016

610 – Mitochondria. The Human Protein Atlas. www.proteinatlas.org/humanproteome/cell/mitochondria#function

611 – Hirpara, Ankit et al. *"Speciation Theory of Carcinogenesis Explains Karyotypic Individuality and Long Latencies of Cancers."* Genes. August, 2018. doi:10.3390/genes9080402

612 – Timothy M. Tucey et al. *'Glucose Homeostasis Is Important for Immune Cell Viability during Candida Challenge and Host Survival of Systemic Fungal Infection.'* Cell Metabolism. 2018. doi.org/10.1016/j.cmet.2018.03.019

613 – Ballou, Elizabeth R et al. *'Lactate signalling regulates fungal β-glucan masking and immune evasion.'* Nature microbiology. December, 2016. doi:10.1038/nmicrobiol.2016.238

614 – Pradhan, Arnab et al. *'Hypoxia Promotes Immune Evasion by Triggering β-Glucan Masking on the Candida albicans Cell Surface via Mitochondrial and cAMP-Protein Kinase A Signaling.'* mBio. 2018. doi:10.1128/mBio.01318-18

616 – Caroline J. Barelle, et al. *'Niche-specific regulation of central metabolic pathways in a fungal pathogen.'* Cellular Microbiology. 2006. doi.org/10.1111/j.1462-5822.2005.00676.x

617 – Mihra S. Taljanovic, Imran M. Omar, Kevin B. Hoover, and Tyson S. Chadaz. *'Musculoskeletal Imaging Volume 2'* 2019 (page 121, chapter 91, Fungal and Higher Bacterial Infections) ISBN-10: 019093817X, ISBN-13: 978-0190938178

618 – Davis Courtney et al. *'Availability of evidence of benefits on overall survival and quality of life of cancer drugs approved by European Medicines Agency: retrospective cohort study of drug approvals.'* BMJ. 2017. doi.org/10.1136/bmj.j4530

619 – Ladin Daniel A., Soliman Eman, Griffin LaToya, Van Dross Rukiyah. *'Preclinical and Clinical Assessment of Cannabinoids as Anti-Cancer Agents.'* Frontiers in Pharmacology. 2016. doi=10.3389/fphar.2016.00361

621 – Russo, J, and Irma H Russo. *'The role of estrogen in the initiation of breast cancer.'* The Journal of steroid biochemistry and molecular biology. 2006. doi:10.1016/j.jsbmb.2006.09.004

623 – Kristine Krafts M.D. *'How do steroids inhibit the immune system.'* Pathology Student. 2010. www.pathologystudent.com/how-do-steroids-inhibit-the-immune-response/

624 – Nathaniel Parish Flannery. *'Monsanto's Pesticide Problems Raise Awareness about Corporate Environmental Responsibility.'* Forbes. 2011.

625 – Julie Wilson. *'Superbugs to Kill More People than Cancer if Industrial Agriculture Doesn't Ditch Antibiotics and Pesticides.'* Organic Consumers Association. 2019. www.organicconsumers.org/blog/superbugs-kill-more-people-cancer-if-industrial-agriculture-doesnt-ditch-antibiotics-and

626 – Li Ma et al. *'Control of Nutrient Stress-Induced Metabolic Reprogramming by PKCζ in Tumorigenesis.'* Cell. 2013. doi: 10.1016/j.cell.2012.12.028

627 – James Masuoka. *'Surface Glycans of Candida albicans and Other Pathogenic Fungi: Physiological Roles, Clinical Uses, and Experimental Challenges.'* Clinical Microbiology Reviews. 2004. doi: 10.1128/CMR.17.2.281-310.2004

628 – Michael Irving. *'New study suggests antibiotics can weaken the immune system.'* New Atlas. 2017. https://newatlas.com/antibiotics-counteract-immune-system/52457/

629 – Jason H. Yang et al. *'Antibiotic-Induced Changes to the Host Metabolic Environment Inhibit Drug Efficacy and Alter Immune Function.'* Cell Host & Microbe. 2017. doi.org/10.1016/j.chom.2017.10.020

630 – Ephrat Livni. *'The Japanese practice of 'forest bathing' is scientifically proven to improve your health.'* 2016. https://qz.com/804022/health-benefits-japanese-forest-bathing/

631 – Li Q et al. *'A forest bathing trip increases human natural killer activity and expression of anti-cancer proteins in female subjects.'* J Biol Regul Homeost Agents. 2008. doi: 10.1177/03946320070200S202

632 – Rossella Russo et al. *'Exploitation of Cytotoxicity of Some Essential Oils for Translation in Cancer Therapy.'* Hindawai. 2015. doi.org/10.1155/2015/397821

633 – Mahmoud M Suhail et al. *'Boswellia sacra essential oil induces tumor cell-specific apoptosis and suppresses tumor aggressiveness in cultured human breast cancer cells.'* BMC Complement Altern Med. 2011. doi: 10.1186/1472-6882-11-129.

634 – Jorge Domínguez-Andrés, et al. *'Rewiring monocyte glucose metabolism via C-type lectin signaling protects against disseminated candidiasis.'* PLOS Pathogens. 2017. doi.org/10.1371/journal.ppat.1006632

635 – Hideki Makinoshima. *'Signaling through the Phosphatidylinositol 3-Kinase (PI3K)/Mammalian Target of Rapamycin (mTOR) Axis Is Responsible for Aerobic Glycolysis mediated by Glucose Transporter in Epidermal Growth Factor Receptor (EGFR)-mutated Lung Adenocarcinoma.'* The Journal of Biological Chemistry. 2015. doi: 10.1074/jbc.M115.660498.

636 – Cheng, Shih-Chin et al. *'mTOR- and HIF-1α-mediated aerobic glycolysis as metabolic basis for trained immunity.'* Science (New York, N.Y.). 2014. doi:10.1126/science.1250684

637 – Volling K, et al. *'Phagocytosis of melanized Aspergillus conidia by macrophages exerts cytoprotective effects by sustained PI3K/Akt signalling.'* Cellular Microbiology. 2011. doi: 10.1111/j.1462-5822.2011.01605.x

638 – Morgensztern, Daniel, McLeod, Howard L. *'PI3K/Akt/mTOR pathway as a target for cancer therapy.'* Anti-Cancer Drugs: September 2005 - Volume 16 - Issue 8 - p 797-803. doi: 10.1097/01.cad.0000173476.67239.3b

639 – Jones, William, and Katiuscia Bianchi. *'Aerobic glycolysis: beyond proliferation.'* Frontiers in immunology. May, 2015. doi:10.3389/fimmu.2015.00227

640 – Nicci Owusu-Brackett et al. *'Role of PI3K/AKT/mTOR in Cancer Signaling.'* Predictive Biomarkers in Oncology. December, 2018. doi.org/10.1007/978-3-319-95228-4_20.

641 – UT Southwestern Medical Center. *'Fasting kills cancer cells of most common type of childhood leukemia, study shows.'* ScienceDaily. 12 December 2016. www.sciencedaily.com/releases/2016/12/161212133654.htm

642 – Knvul Sheikh. *'In the pancreas, common fungi may drive cancer'*. The New York Times. October 3rd, 2019.

643 – Michael Greger M.D. *'How Not to Die'*. Pan books 2015. ISBN 978-1-5098-5250-5.

645 – Lu, Jianrong et al. *'The Warburg effect in tumor progression: mitochondrial oxidative metabolism as an anti-metastasis mechanism.'* Cancer letters. 2015. doi:10.1016/j.canlet.2014.04.001

646 – Alistair J.P.Brown. *'Metabolism impacts upon Candida immunogenicity and pathogenicity at multiple levels.'* Science Direct. November, 2014. doi.org/10.1016/j.tim.2014.07.001

647 – Moyes, David L et al. *'Protection against epithelial damage during Candida albicans infection is mediated by PI3K/Akt and mammalian target of rapamycin signaling.'* The Journal of infectious diseases. June, 2014. doi:10.1093/infdis/jit824

648 – Brian A Schaefer et al. *'Cancer and Related Case Studies Involving Salvestrol and CYP1B1.'* JOM. Number, 2012. doi=10.1.1.835.9436&rep=rep1&type=pdf http://citeseerx.ist.psu.edu/viewdoc/download?

649 – Gerry Potter et al. *'Salvestrols: A new perspective in nutritional research.'* Journal of Orthomolecular Medicine Volume 22, No. 1, 2007. www.orthomolecular.org/library/jom/2007/pdf/2007-v22n01-p039.pdf

650 – Lefèvre, Lise et al. *'LRH-1 mediates anti-inflammatory and antifungal phenotype of IL-13-activated macrophages through the PPARγ ligand synthesis.'* Nature communications. April, 2015. doi:10.1038/ncomms7801

651 – Amandine Gales et al. *'PPARγ Controls Dectin-1 Expression Required for Host Antifungal Defense against Candida albicans.'* PLOS Pathogens. January, 2010. doi.org/10.1371/journal.ppat.1000714

652 – *'Manuka Honey.'* Memorial Sloan Kettering Cancer Centre. January 2017. www.mskcc.org/cancer-care/integrative-medicine/herbs/manuka-honey

653 – VIB. *'Scientists reveal the relationship between sugar, cancer.'* ScienceDaily. ScienceDaily, 13 October 2017. <www.sciencedaily.com/releases/2017/10/171013103623.htm>.

654 – Yun, Jihye et al. *'Vitamin C selectively kills KRAS and BRAF mutant colorectal cancer cells by targeting GAPDH.'* Science (New York, N.Y.). 2015. doi:10.1126/science.aaa5004

655 – Julia Bradshaw. '*UK set for cannabis boom as GW Pharma storms ahead.*' The Telegraph. February 2017. www.telegraph.co.uk/business/2017/02/11/uk-set-cannabis-boom-gw-pharma-storms-ahead/

656 – Gina Kolata. '*Advances elusive in the drive to cure cancer.*' The New York Times, April 2009. www.nytimes.com/2009/04/24/health/policy/24cancer.html?_r=0

657 – Donald Light. '*New Prescription Drugs: A major health risk with few offsetting advantages.*' Harvard University, Edmond J. Safra Center for Ethics. June 2014. https://ethics.harvard.edu/blog/new-prescription-drugs-major-health-risk-few-offsetting-advantages

658 – Jaiswal, Siddhartha et al. '*CD47 is upregulated on circulating hematopoietic stem cells and leukemia cells to avoid phagocytosis.*' Cell. 2009. doi:10.1016/j.cell.2009.05.046

660 – '*Environmental Topics and Essays – Sustainable vs Conventional Agriculture.*' Stony Brook University. 2019. https://you.stonybrook.edu/environment/sustainable-vs-conventional-agriculture/

661 – Lamb, Rebecca et al. '*Antibiotics that target mitochondria effectively eradicate cancer stem cells, across multiple tumor types: treating cancer like an infectious disease.*' Oncotarget vol. 6,7 (2015): 4569-84. doi:10.18632/oncotarget.3174

662 – Alina Bradford. '*What is Estrogen?*' Live Science. May 2017. www.livescience.com/38324-what-is-estrogen.html

663 – Sofia La Vecchia, Carlos Sebastian. '*Metabolic pathways regulating colorectal cancer initiation and progression*'. Science Direct. May, 2019. doi.org/10.1016/j.semcdb.2019.05.018

664 – Chi V. Dang. '*Links between metabolism and cancer.*' Genes & Development. 2012. doi:10.1101/gad.189365.112

665 – Pedro Escoll, Carmen Buchrieser. '*Metabolic reprogramming of host cells upon bacterial infection: Why shift to a Warburg-like metabolism?*' The FEBS Journal. March, 2018. doi.org/10.1111/febs.14446

667 – Catharine Paddock, PH.D. '*Fungi from the gut can promote cancer in the pancreas.*' October 2019. Medical News Today. www.medicalnewstoday.com/articles/326565.php#1

668 – University of Texas at Arlington. '*BPA linked to breast cancer tumour growth.*' ScienceDaily. ScienceDaily, 6 March 2014. www.sciencedaily.com/releases/2014/03/140306163359.htm

669 – Lars P. Christensen. '*Aliphatic C(17)-polyacetylenes of the falcarinol type as potential health promoting compounds in food plants of the Apiaceae family.*' Recent Patents on Food Nutrition and Agriculture. January, 2011. doi:10.2174/2212798411103010064

670 – Gaziano R, et al. '*Antifungal activity of Cardiospermum halicacabum L (Sapindaceae) against Trichophyton rubrum occurs through molecular interaction with fungal Hsp90.*' Drug Design, Development and Therapy. 2018. doi.org/10.2147/DDDT.S155610

671 – Ann Cameron. '*Curing Cancer with Carrots.*' 2015. Amazon. ISBN: 9780692521762

673 – Tomova, Aleksandra et al. '*The Effects of Vegetarian and Vegan Diets on Gut Microbiota.*' Frontiers in nutrition. April, 2019. doi:10.3389/fnut.2019.00047

674 – Ahmad, A., Ormiston-Smith, N. & Sasieni, P. '*Trends in the lifetime risk of developing cancer in Great Britain: comparison of risk for those born from 1930 to 1960.*' British Journal of Cancer. 2015. doi.org/10.1038/bjc.2014.606

675 – Cancer Research UK. '*Change in cancer incidence rates since the early 1990s*'. 2020. www.cancerresearchuk.org/health-professional/cancer-statistics/incidence/all-cancers-combined#heading-Zero

676 – Valter D. Longo, Mark P. Mattson. *'Fasting: Molecular Mechanisms and Clinical Applications.'* Cell Metabolism. 2014. doi.org/10.1016/j.cmet.2013.12.008 www.sciencedirect.com/science/article/pii/S1550413113005032

677 – Nana-Maria Grüning, et al. *'Pyruvate kinase triggers a metabolic feedback loop that controls redox metabolism in respiring cells.'* Cell Metabolism. 2011. doi.org/10.1016/j.cmet.2011.06.017

678 – Verdegem, Dries et al. *'Endothelial cell metabolism: parallels and divergences with cancer cell metabolism.'* Cancer & metabolism. September, 2014. doi:10.1186/2049-3002-2-19

679 – Dufault, R., Schnoll, R., Lukiw, W.J. et al. *'Mercury exposure, nutritional deficiencies and metabolic disruptions may affect learning in children.'* Behavioral and Brain Functions. 2009. doi.org/10.1186/1744-9081-5-44

680 – XiQian, ReemAboushoush, Cherylvan de Wetering, et al. *'IL-1/inhibitory κB kinase ε–induced glycolysis augment epithelial effector function and promote allergic airways disease.'* Journal of Allergy and Clinical Immunology. August, 2018. doi.org/10.1016/j.jaci.2017.08.043

681 – Geisler, J. *'Differences between the non-steroidal aromatase inhibitors anastrozole and letrozole--of clinical importance?.'* British journal of cancer. 2011. doi:10.1038/bjc.2011.58

683 – Kip Anderson, Keegan Kuhn. *'What The Health.'* https://www.whatthehealthfilm.com

684 – Rice University. *'Biologists ID defense mechanism of leading fungal pathogen.'* EurekAlert! June 2004. https://www.eurekalert.org/pub_releases/2004-06/ru-bid062504.php

685 – Wachtler B, Citiulo F, Jablonowski N, Forster S, Dalle F, et al. *'Candida albicans-Epithelial Interactions: Dissecting the Roles of Active Penetration, Induced Endocytosis and Host Factors on the Infection Process.'* PLOS ONE. April, 2012. doi:10.1371/journal.pone.0036952

686 – Lev Ginzburg, Mark Colyvan. *'Ecological Orbits: How Planets Move and Populations Grow.'* Oxford University Press, 2004. ISBN: 0198037546 https://books.google.co.uk/books/about/Ecological_Orbits.html?id=9pZfyyRP0ccC&redir_esc=y

687 – Sophie Sabbage. *'The Cancer Whisperer.'* Coronet 2017. ISBN: 1473637961

688 – Sarah Bosely. *'Drug companies pay doctors £40m for travel and expenses.'* The Guardian. 2013. www.theguardian.com/society/2013/apr/05/drug-companies-pay-doctors-40m

689 – Fiona MacDonald. *'This is the sickening amount pharmaceutical companies pay top journal editors.'* Science Alert. April, 2018. https://www.sciencealert.com/how-much-top-journal-editors-get-paid-by-big-pharma-corrupt#

690 – Jessica J Liu. *'Payments by US pharmaceutical and medical device manufacturers to US medical journal editors: retrospective observational study.'* BMJ. 2017. doi.org/10.1136/bmj.j4619

691 – Fiona MacDonald. *'Peter Higgs says he wouldn't have predicted the Higgs Boson in today's academic climate.'* Science Alert. October, 2016. https://www.sciencealert.com/peter-higgs-says-he-wouldn-t-have-predicted-the-higgs-boson-in-today-s-academic-climate

692 – Jackson, Brendan R et al. *'On the Origins of a Species: What Might Explain the Rise of Candida auris?'* Journal of fungi (Basel, Switzerland). July, 2019. doi:10.3390/jof5030058

693 – Bensasson, Douda et al. *'Diverse Lineages of Candida albicans Live on Old Oaks.'* Genetics. 2019. doi:10.1534/genetics.118.301482

694 – Gabaldón, Toni, and Cécile Fairhead. *'Genomes shed light on the secret life of Candida glabrata: not so asexual, not so commensal.'* Current genetics. 2019. doi:10.1007/s00294-018-0867-z

695 – Fiona Macdonald. *'It's official: A brand-new human organ has been classified. Science Alert.'* January 2017. www.sciencealert.com/it-s-official-a-brand-new-human-organ-has-been-classified

696 – Rachael Rettner. *'Meet your Interstitium, a newfound organ.'* Live Science. March 2018. www.livescience.com/62128-interstitium-organ.html

697 – Chen Yuxin, Zhou Zhongyang, Min Wang. *'Mitochondria, Oxidative Stress and Innate Immunity.'* Frontiers in Physiology. 2018. doi=10.3389/fphys.2018.01487

698 – Dhermendra K Tiwari, Takashi Jin, J. Behari. *'Dose-dependent in-vivo toxicity assessment of silver nanoparticle in Wistar rats.'* Toxicology mechanisms and Methods. November, 2010. doi.org/10.3109/15376516.2010.529184

699 – Seltenrich, Nate. *'Nanosilver: weighing the risks and benefits.'* Environmental health perspectives. 2013. doi:10.1289/ehp.121-a220

700 – Cancer Research UK. *'How chemotherapy works.'* June, 2020. /www.cancerresearchuk.org/about-cancer/cancer-in-general/treatment/ chemotherapy/how-chemotherapy-works

701 – Cancer.net editorial board. *'Understanding statistics use to guide prognosis and evaluate treatment.'* Cancer.net. March, 2020. www.cancer.net/navigating-cancer-care/cancer-basics/understanding-statistics-used-guide-prognosis-and-evaluate-treatment

702 – Kevin C. Oeffinger, M.D., et al. *'Chronic health conditions in adult survivors of childhood cancer.'* The New England Journal of Medicine. October, 2006. doi:10.1056/NEJMsa060185

703 – Ann C. Mertens, Qi Liu, Joseph P. Neglia, et al. *'Cause-Specific Late Mortality Among 5-Year Survivors of Childhood Cancer: The Childhood Cancer Survivor Study.'* JNCI: Journal of the National Cancer Institute. October, 2008. doi.org/10.1093/jnci/djn310

704 – Cure Search. *'5-year survival rate.'* June, 2020. https://curesearch.org/5-Year-Survival-Rate

705 – William Reville. *'Do synthetic chemicals in our environment threaten our future?'* University College, Cork. June, 2020. http://undersci.ucc.ie/wp-content/uploads/sites/12/2014/11/synthetic_chemicals_envir onment.pdf

706 – Eileen Uribe-Querol and Carlos Rosales. *'Neutrophils in Cancer: Two sides of the same coin.'* Journal of Immunology Research. December, 2015. doi.org/10.1155/2015/983698

707 – Mowaffaq Adam Ahmed Adam, et al. *'Effects of different mycotoxins on humans, cell genome and their involvement in cancer (Review).'* Oncology Reports. February, 2017. doi.org/10.3892/or.2017.5424

708 – Marcos, Caroline M et al. *'Anti-Immune Strategies of Pathogenic Fungi.'* Frontiers in cellular and infection microbiology. November, 2016, doi:10.3389/fcimb.2016.00142

709 – Amin, Shayista et al. *'Melanin dependent survival of Apergillus fumigatus conidia in lung epithelial cells.'* International journal of medical microbiology. 2014. doi:10.1016/j.ijmm.2014.04.009

710 – Coller, Hilary A. *'Is cancer a metabolic disease?'* The American journal of pathology. 2014. doi:10.1016/j.ajpath.2013.07.035

711 – Jeff Charles Kremer, et al. *'Arginine deprivation inhibits the Warburg effect and upregulates glutamine anaplerosis and serine biosynthesis in ASS1-deficient cancers.'* Cell Reports. January, 2016. doi.org/10.1016/j.celrep.2016.12.077

712 – Ene, Iuliana V et al. *'Growth of Candida albicans cells on the physiologically relevant carbon source lactate affects their recognition and phagocytosis by immune cells.'* Infection and immunity. January, 2013. doi:10.1128/IAI.01092-12

713 – J. Carlos Aledo, and Alicia Esteban del Valle. *'Glycolysis in Wonderland: The importance of energy dissipation in metabolic pathways.'* Universidad de Malaga. Spain. July, 2020. http://atarazanas.sci.uma.es/docs/tesisuma/16638244.pdf

714 – Julie A. Wasylnka, Margo M. Moore. '*Aspergillus fumigatus conidia survive and germinate in acidic organelles of A549 epithelial cells.*' Journal of Cell Science. 2003. doi: 10.1242/jcs.00329

715 – Jiménez-López, Claudia et al. '*Candida albicans induces arginine biosynthetic genes in response to host-derived reactive oxygen species.*' Eukaryotic cell. January, 2013. doi:10.1128/EC.00290-12

716 – Fu, Yaojie et al. '*The reverse Warburg effect is likely to be an Achilles' heel of cancer that can be exploited for cancer therapy.*' Oncotarget. May, 2017. doi:10.18632/oncotarget.18175

717 – Patil T R et al. '*Antimicrobial potential of Metformin.*' International Journal of Pharmacognosy and Phytochemical Research. 2018. doi:10.25258/phyto.10.7.2

718 – Meherunisa, Sapna Jaiswal, Vikas Seth. '*Study of Metformin effect on antimicrobial property.*' International Archives of BioMedical and Clinical Research. September, 2018. doi:10.21276/iabcr.2018.4.3.00
https://iabcr.org/index.php/iabcr/article/download/412/389/

719 – Bio-Cancer Treatment International. '*BCT-100 in Arginine Auxotrophic Cancers, Arginine and Arginine Auxotrophic Cancers.*' July, 2020. www.bio-cancer.com/science/

720 – Fuming Qui, et al. '*Arginine starvation impairs mitochondrial respiratory function in ASS1-deficient breast cancer cells.*' Science Signal. April, 2014. doi:10.1126/scisignal.2004761

721 – Cheng, Chun-Ting et al. '*Arginine starvation kills tumour cells through aspartate exhaustion and mitochondrial dysfunction.*' Communications biology. October, 2018. doi:10.1038/s42003-018-0178-4

722 – Jeanette Wagener, et al. '*Candida albicans Chitin Increases Arginase-1 Activity in Human Macrophages, with an Impact on Macrophage Antimicrobial Functions.*' mBio. January, 2017. doi: 10.1128/mBio.01820-16

723 – Asano, K et al. '*Constitutive and inducible nitric oxide synthase gene expression, regulation, and activity in human lung epithelial cells.*' Proceedings of the National Academy of Sciences of the United States of America. 1994. doi:10.1073/pnas.91.21.10089

724 – Anna-Maria Dietl, et al. '*Arginine Auxotrophy Affects Siderophore Biosynthesis and Attenuates Virulence of Aspergillus fumigatus.*' Genes. 2020. doi.org/10.3390/genes11040423

725 – Miethke, Marcus, and Mohamed A Marahiel. '*Siderophore-based iron acquisition and pathogen control.*' Microbiology and molecular biology reviews: MMBR. 2007. doi:10.1128/MMBR.00012-07

726 – Joseph E. Qualls, et al. '*Sustained generation of nitric oxide and control of mycobacterial infection requires argininosuccinate synthase 1.*' Cell Host & Microbe. September, 2012. doi.org/10.1016/j.chom.2012.07.012

727 – Cao, Yu et al. '*L-Arginine supplementation inhibits the growth of breast cancer by enhancing innate and adaptive immune responses mediated by suppression of MDSCs in vivo.*' BMC cancer. June, 2016. doi:10.1186/s12885-016-2376-0

728 – Noel, Brianna et al. '*Role of natural compounds in preventing and treating breast cancer.*' Frontiers in bioscience (Scholar edition) vol. 12 137-160. 1 Mar. 2020

729 – Scorzoni Liliana, et al. '*Antifungal Therapy: New Advances in the Understanding and Treatment of Mycosis.*' Frontiers in Microbiology. 2017. doi=10.3389/fmicb.2017.00036

730 – Douglas Marvel, Dmitry I. Gabrilovich. '*Myeloid-derived suppressor cells in the tumor microenvironment: expect the unexpected.*' The Journal of Clinical Investigation. 2015. doi.org/10.1172/JCI80005

731 – Futagami, A., Ishizaki, M., Fukuda, Y. et al. '*Wound Healing Involves Induction of Cyclooxygenase-2 Expression in Rat Skin.*' Laboratory Investigation. 2002. doi.org/10.1097/01.LAB.0000035024.75914.39

732 – Umansky, Viktor et al. '*The Role of Myeloid-Derived Suppressor Cells (MDSC) in Cancer Progression.*' Vaccines. 2016. doi:10.3390/vaccines4040036

733 – Rodríguez, Paulo C, and Augusto C Ochoa. '*Arginine regulation by myeloid derived suppressor cells and tolerance in cancer: mechanisms and therapeutic perspectives.*' Immunological reviews. 2008. doi:10.1111/j.1600-065X.2008.00608.x

734 – Suman Ghosh et al. '*Arginine-Induced Germ Tube Formation in Candida albicans Is Essential for Escape from Murine Macrophage Line RAW 264.7.*' Infection and Immunity. March, 2009. doi: 10.1128/IAI.01452-08

735 – Geiger, Roger et al. '*L-Arginine Modulates T Cell Metabolism and Enhances Survival and Anti-tumor Activity.*' Cell. 2016. doi:10.1016/j.cell.2016.09.031

736 – Chitty, Jessica L, and James A Fraser. '*Purine Acquisition and Synthesis by Human Fungal Pathogens.*' Microorganisms. June, 2017. doi:10.3390/microorganisms5020033

737 – M. O. F. Fasoli and D. Kerridge. '*Uptake of pyrimidines and their derivatives into Candida glabrata and Candida albicans.*' Microbiology Society. August, 1990. doi.org/10.1099/00221287-136-8-1475

738 – '*The Urea Cycle Enzyme ASS1 Regulates Pyrimidine Synthesis in Tumors.*' Cancer Discovery. January, 2016. doi: 10.1158/2159-8290.CD-RW2015-222

739 – Sullivan, Lucas B et al. '*Supporting Aspartate Biosynthesis Is an Essential Function of Respiration in Proliferating Cells.*' Cell. 2015. doi:10.1016/j.cell.2015.07.017

740 – Anne Marie Helmenstine, Ph.D. '*The difference between purines and pyrimidines.*' ThoughtCo. March, 2019. https://www.thoughtco.com/purines-and-pyrimidines-differences-4589943

741 – Nagamani, Sandesh C S, and Ayelet Erez. '*A metabolic link between the urea cycle and cancer cell proliferation.*' Molecular & cellular oncology vol. 3,2 e1127314. February, 2016. doi:10.1080/23723556.2015.1127314

742 – Long, Yan et al. '*Arginine deiminase resistance in melanoma cells is associated with metabolic reprogramming, glucose dependence, and glutamine addiction.*' Molecular Cancer Therapeutics. 2013. doi:10.1158/1535-7163.MCT-13-0302

743 – Shan, Yan-Shen et al. '*Argininosuccinate synthetase 1 suppression and arginine restriction inhibit cell migration in gastric cancer cell lines.*' Scientific reports. April, 2015. doi:10.1038/srep09783

744 – Barbara Delage et al. '*Arginine deprivation and argininosuccinate synthetase expression in the treatment of cancer.*' International Journal of Cancer. April, 2010. doi.org/10.1002/ijc.25202

745 – Barbone D et al. '*Analysis of Gene Expression in 3D Spheroids Highlights a Survival Role for ASS1 in Mesothelioma.*' PLOS ONE. March, 2016. doi.org/10.1371/journal.pone.0150044

746 – Rogers LC, Van Tine BA. '*Innate and adaptive resistance mechanisms to arginine deprivation therapies in sarcoma and other cancers.*' Cancer Drug Resist. 2019. doi.org/10.20517/cdr.2019.49

747 – R. J. Tesi. '*MDSC; the most important cell you have never heard of.*' Trends in Pharmacological Sciences. December, 2018. doi.org/10.1016/j.tips.2018.10.008

748 – Dr Marcia Angel. '*The truth about the drug companies.*' The New York Review of Books. July, 2004. www.nybooks.com/articles/2004/07/15/the-truth-about-the-drug-companies/?pagination=false

749 – Hicks, Amy M et al. '*Transferable anticancer innate immunity in spontaneous regression/complete resistance mice.*' Proceedings of the National Academy of Sciences of the United States of America. 2006. doi:10.1073/pnas.0602382103

750 – Yun-Gi Kim, et al. *'Gut Dysbiosis Promotes M2 Macrophage Polarization and Allergic Airway Inflammation via Fungi-Induced PGE2.'* Cell Host & Microbe. January, 2014. doi.org/10.1016/j.chom.2013.12.010

751 – Balaji Pathakumari, Guanzhao Liang, Weida Liu. *'Immune defence to invasive fungal infections: A comprehensive review.'* Biomedicine and Pharmacotherapy. 130. 110550. doi:10.1016/j.biopha.2020.110550.

752 – Potter, G. Patterson, L. Wanogho, E. et al. *'The cancer preventative agent resveratrol is converted to the anticancer agent piceatannol by the cytochrome P450 enzyme CYP1B1.'* Br J Cancer. 2002. doi.org/10.1038/sj.bjc.6600197

753 – Aayush Kukreja, Neha Wadhwa and Archana Tiwari. *'Therapeutic role of resveratrol and piceatannol in disease prevention.'* Journal of Blood disorders & Transfusion. 2014. doi: 10.4172/2155-9864.1000240

754 – Lee, J., Lee, D.G. *'Novel Antifungal Mechanism of Resveratrol: Apoptosis Inducer in Candida albicans.'* Curr Microbiol. 2015. doi.org/10.1007/s00284-014-0734-1

755 – Agnès Coste, et al. *'IL-13 Attenuates Gastrointestinal Candidiasis in Normal and Immunodeficient RAG-2–/– Mice via Peroxisome Proliferator-Activated Receptor-γ Activation.'* The Journal of Immunology. April, 2008. doi:10.4049/jimmunol.180.7.4939

756 – Li, Fei et al. *'Potential role of CYP1B1 in the development and treatment of metabolic diseases.'* Pharmacology & Therapeutics. 2017. doi:10.1016/j.pharmthera.2017.03.007

757 – Cnris Kresser. *'Treating Methylation: Are we over-supplementing?'* Kresser Institute. June, 2017. https://kresserinstitute.com/treating-methylation-supplementing/

758 – Andreas Kühbacher, Helena Henkel, Philip Stevens et al. *'Central Role for Dermal Fibroblasts in Skin Model Protection against Candida albicans.'* The Journal of Infectious Diseases. June 2017, Pages 1742–1752. doi.org/10.1093/infdis/jix153

759 – Keith I.BlockaCharlotteGyllenhaalaLeroyLowe et al. *'Designing a broad-spectrum integrative approach for cancer prevention and treatment.'* Seminars in Cancer Biology. Vol. 35, pages S276-S304. December 2015. doi.org/10.1016/j.semcancer.2015.09.007

760 – Cristina Sanchez Ph.D. *'Antitumour effect of cannabinoid-based therapies related to subtypes of breast cancer.'* Medicinal Genomics. December 2018. www.youtube.com/watch?v=KQUSoIJkaWg

761 – Dr Pedram Shojai. *'Interconnected'*. 2020 https://secure.interconnectedseries.com/eg/trailer

762 – Zheng, Jie. *'Energy metabolism of cancer: Glycolysis versus oxidative phosphorylation (Review).'* Oncology letters. doi:10.3892/ol.2012.928

763 – Shiratori, R., Furuichi, K., Yamaguchi, M. et al. *'Glycolytic suppression dramatically changes the intracellular metabolic profile of multiple cancer cell lines in a mitochondrial metabolism-dependent manner.'* Scientific Reports, 9, 18699. December, 2019. doi.org/10.1038/s41598-019-55296-3

764 – Abena Nsiah-Sefaa, Matthew McKenzie. *'Combined defects in oxidative phosphorylation and fatty acid β-oxidation in mitochondrial disease.'* Biosci Rep. April, 2016; 36 (2): e00313. doi.org/10.1042/BSR20150295

765 – Gaber El-Saber Batiha et al. *'The Pharmacological Activity, Biochemical Properties, and Pharmacokinetics of the Major Natural Polyphenolic Flavonoid: Quercetin.'* Foods. March 2020. 9(3), 374; doi.org/10.3390/foods9030374

766 – Abd, El-Baky Rehab Mahmoud, Dalia Mohamed Mohamed Abo El Ela, and Gamal Fadl Mamoud Gad. *'N-acetylcysteine Inhibits and Eradicates Candida albicans Biofilms.'* American Journal of Infectious Diseases and Microbiology 2.5 (2014): 122-130. DOI:10.12691/ajidm-2-5-5

767 – Paul Flynn MP. Westminster Hall. 10th November 2004. MHRA debate. https://publications.parliament.uk/pa/cm200304/cmhansrd/vo041110/halltext/41110h01.htm

768 – American Cancer Society. 'Tamoxifen'. November, 2020. www.cancer.org/cancer/breast-cancer/treatment/hormone-therapy-for-breast-cancer.html

769 – Thomas N. Seyfried, Gabriel Arismendi-Morillo, Purna Mukherjee, Christos Chinopoulos. '*On the Origin of ATP Synthesis in Cancer.*' iScience. Volume 23, Issue 11, 2020, 101761, ISSN 2589-0042. doi.org/10.1016/j.isci.2020.101761.

770 – Weng, Ml., Chen, Wk. et al. '*Fasting inhibits aerobic glycolysis and proliferation in colorectal cancer via the Fdft1-mediated AKT/mTOR/HIF1α pathway suppression.*' Nat Commun (2020). doi.org/10.1038/s41467-020-15795-8

771 – Iñigo San-Millán, George A. Brooks. '*Reexamining cancer metabolism: lactate production for carcinogenesis could be the purpose and explanation of the Warburg Effect.*' Carcinogenesis. February, 2017. doi.org/10.1093/carcin/bgw127

772 – Martinez-Outschoorn, Ubaldo E et al. '*Oxidative stress in cancer associated fibroblasts drives tumor-stroma co-evolution: A new paradigm for understanding tumor metabolism, the field effect and genomic instability in cancer cells.*' Cell cycle (Georgetown, Tex.) vol. 9,16 (2010): 3256-76. doi:10.4161/cc.9.16.12553

773 – Care Oncology Clinic. 2021. https://careoncologyclinic.com/what-is-the-coc-protocol/

774 – Ke Xu, et al. '*Glycolysis fuels phosphoinositide 3-kinase signaling to bolster T cell immunity.*' Science. 22 Jan 2021. 405-410. doi: 10.1126/science.abb2683

775 – Memorial Sloan-Kettering Cancer Centre. '*Sloan Kettering Institute Scientists Solve a 100-Year-Old Mystery about Cancer.*' January, 2021. www.mskcc.org/news/sloan-kettering-institute-scientists-solve-100-year-old-mystery-about?utm_source=Twitter&utm_medium=Organic&utm_campaign=012121MingLi-100-year-old-mystery&utm_content=Research&fbclid=IwAR0M7HU24J6RTLBXnBHJ48B05cpYACMLgIUJtHhFbuP7WsM5Z-0IXO-AE5A

776 – Lawrence A. Donehower,Thierry Soussi, et al. '*Integrated Analysis of TP53 Gene and Pathway Alterations in The Cancer Genome Atlas.*' Cell Reports, Elsevier. July, 2019. doi.org/10.1016/j.celrep.2019.07.001

777 – L Bishop, E., Ismailova, A., Dimeloe, S., Hewison, M. and White, J.H. '*Vitamin D and Immune Regulation: Antibacterial, Antiviral, Anti-Inflammatory.*' JBMR Plus, 2021. 5: e10405. doi.org/10.1002/jbm4.10405

778 – Thomas M. Ashton, W. Gillies McKenna, Leoni A. Kunz-Schughart and Geoff S. Higgins. '*Oxidative Phosphorylation as an Emerging Target in Cancer Therapy.*' Clin Cancer Res. June, 2018. (24) (11) 2482-2490. doi:10.1158/1078-0432.CCR-17-3070

779 – Zheng, J."*Energy metabolism of cancer: Glycolysis versus oxidative phosphorylation (Review)*". Oncology Letters 4.6 (2012): 1151-1157. doi.org/10.3892/ol.2012.928

780 – Johns Hopkins drug discovery. '*Glutamine antagonist*'. March 2021. https://drugdiscovery.jhu.edu/our-projects/glutamine-antagonist/

781 – Oncology Central. '*Targeting metabolic pathways: why are we missing a trick in cancer treatment?*' July, 2015. https://www.oncology-central.com/targeting-metabolic-pathways-why-are-we-missing-a-trick-in-cancer-treatment/

782 – Andrea Miró-Canturri, Rafael Ayerbe-Algaba and Younes Smani. '*Drug Repurposing for the Treatment of Bacterial and Fungal Infections.*' Front. Microbiol. January, 2019. doi.org/10.3389/fmicb.2019.00041

783 – Rana Muhsin Khalaf et al. '*Investigation of the antifungal activity of some non-antifungal drugs in clinical isolates of otomycosis: In vitro study.*' IASJ February, 2021. www.iasj.net/iasj/download/2c8f56ad6f5acaa5

784 – Press release. '*Vitamin D dials down the aggression in melanoma cells.*' Cancer Research UK. November, 2019. www.cancerresearchuk.org/about-us/cancer-news/press-release/2019-11-06-vitamin-d-dials-down-the-aggression-in-melanoma-cells

785 – Health News Review. '*Reporting the findings: Absolute vs relative risk.*' March, 2021. www.healthnewsreview.org/toolkit/tips-for-understanding-studies/absolute-vs-relative-risk/?fbclid=IwAR02IUaYCITetbbVStJHnKD0ZYds5z2AmOo_Pq_hXtQJwHkw4GWSGuYUN40

786 – Vanderbilt University Medical Center. '*Study revises understanding of cancer metabolism.*' EurekAlert. April, 2021. www.eurekalert.org/pub_releases/2021-04/vumc-sru040521.php?fbclid=IwAR3scr_DCB-9F5QYXzNL4YBmXv7RakX0jOFeNGzrFthDvEyy0Rld121cJTs#.YHOvAb_7EpU.facebook

787 – ISB. '*Cancer Treatment: A Systems Approach.*' ISB. April, 2021. https://isbscience.org/news/2014/05/12/cancer-treatment-a-systems-approach/

788 – Pelicano, H., Martin, D., Xu, RH. et al. '*Glycolysis inhibition for anticancer treatment.*' Oncogene 25, 4633–4646 (2006). doi.org/10.1038/sj.onc.1209597

790 – Rui-hua Xu, et al. '*Inhibition of Glycolysis in Cancer Cells: A Novel Strategy to Overcome Drug Resistance Associated with Mitochondrial Respiratory Defect and Hypoxia.*' Cancer Res. January 15 2005 (65) (2) 613-621

791 – E.O. da Silva, A.P.F.L. Bracarense and I.P. Oswald. '*Mycotoxins and oxidative stress: where are we?*' World Mycotoxin Journal, 2018; 11 (1): 113-133. www.wageningenacademic.com/doi/epdf/10.3920/WMJ2017.2267

792 – Manosha Perera, Nezar Noor Al-hebshi, Irosha Perera, et al. '*A dysbiotic mycobiome dominated by Candida albicans is identified within oral squamous-cell carcinomas.*' Journal of Oral Microbiology, 9:1, (2017). doi:10.1080/20002297.2017.1385369

793 – Galloway-Peña JR, Kontoyiannis DP. '*The gut mycobiome: The overlooked constituent of clinical outcomes and treatment complications in patients with cancer and other immunosuppressive conditions.*' PLoS Pathog 16(4): e1008353, (2020). doi.org/10.1371/journal.ppat.1008353

794 – Harvard Health Publishing. '*Understanding antioxidants*'. Harvard Medical School. January 2019. www.health.harvard.edu/staying-healthy/understanding-antioxidants

795 – Alessandro Fiori, Patrick Van Dijck. '*Potent Synergistic Effect of Doxycycline with Fluconazole against Candida albicans Is Mediated by Interference with Iron Homeostasis.*' Antimicrobial Agents and Chemotherapy. June, 2021. doi.org/10.1128/AAC.06017-11

796 – Tarcieli Pozzebon Venturini, Abdullah M.S. Al-Hatmi, Luana Rossato, et al. '*Do antibacterial and antifungal combinations have better activity against clinically relevant fusarium species? in vitro synergism.*' International Journal of Antimicrobial Agents, Volume 51, Issue 5, 2018, Pages 784-788, ISSN 0924-8579. doi.org/10.1016/j.ijantimicag.2017.10.017.

797 – Rigaud, Vagner O C et al. '*Stem Cell Metabolism: Powering Cell-Based Therapeutics.*' Cells vol. 9,11 2490. 16 Nov. 2020. doi:10.3390/cells9112490

798 – Chinopoulos, Christos, and Thomas N Seyfried. '*Mitochondrial Substrate-Level Phosphorylation as Energy Source for Glioblastoma: Review and Hypothesis.*' ASN neuro vol. 10 (2018): 1759091418818261. doi:10.1177/1759091418818261

799 – Sam Apple. '*An old idea, Revived: Starve cancer to death.*' NYTimes.com. May 2016. www.nytimes.com/2016/05/15/magazine/warburg-effect-an-old-idea-revived-starve-cancer-to-death.html

801 – Ricardo S. Almeida, Duncan Wilson, Bernhard Hube. '*Candida albicans iron acquisition within the host.*' FEMS Yeast Research, Volume 9, Issue 7, November 2009, Pages 1000–1012. doi.org/10.1111/j.1567-1364.2009.00570.x

802 – Santarpia, Libero et al. '*Targeting the MAPK-RAS-RAF signaling pathway in cancer therapy.*' Expert opinion on therapeutic targets vol. 16,1 (2012): 103-19. doi:10.1517/14728222.2011.645805

803 – Julian R Naglik, Sarah L Gaffen, Bernhard Hube. '*Candidalysin: discovery and function in Candida albicans infections.*' Current Opinion in Microbiology, Volume 52, 2019, Pages 100-109, ISSN 1369-5274, doi.org/10.1016/j.mib.2019.06.002.

804 – Kim, A., Im, M., Yim, NH. et al. '*Reduction of metastatic and angiogenic potency of malignant cancer by Eupatorium fortunei via suppression of MMP-9 activity and VEGF production.*' Sci Rep 4, 6994 (2014). doi.org/10.1038/srep06994

805 – Anna Azvolinsky. '*Insulin resistant metastatic breast cancer patients fare worse*'. Cancer Network. June, 1st, 2014. https://www.cancernetwork.com/view/insulin-resistant-metastatic-breast-cancer-patients-fare-worse

806 – Burzawa, Jennifer K et al. '*Prospective evaluation of insulin resistance among endometrial cancer patients.*' American journal of obstetrics and gynecology vol. 204,4 (2011): 355.e1-7. doi:10.1016/j.ajog.2010.11.033

807 – Xin Guo, Honggui Li, Hang Xu, et al. '*Glycolysis in the control of blood glucose homeostasis*'. Acta Pharmaceutica Sinica B, Volume 2, Issue 4, 2012, Pages 358-367, ISSN 2211-3835, doi.org/10.1016/j.apsb.2012.06.002.

808 – Yalcin, A et al. '*6-Phosphofructo-2-kinase (PFKFB3) promotes cell cycle progression and suppresses apoptosis via Cdk1-mediated phosphorylation of p27.*' Cell death & disease vol. 5,7 e1337. 17 Jul. 2014, doi:10.1038/cddis.2014.292

809 – Ho, J., Camilli, G., Griffiths, J.S., Richardson, J.P., Kichik, N. and Naglik, J.R. '*Candida albicans and candidalysin in inflammatory disorders and cancer.*' Immunology, 162: 11-16. (2021). doi.org/10.1111/imm.13255

810 – M Vadovics, N Igaz, R Alföldi, et al. '*Candida albicans enhances the progression of oral squamous cell cancrinoma in vitro and in vivo.*' bioRxiv 2021.03.31.437836. doi:org/10.1101/2021.03.31.437836 Now accepted for publication in mBio (23/01/2022).

811 – Douglas Hanahan. '*Hallmarks of Cancer: New Dimensions.*' Cancer Discovery. Review. January, 2022. doi:10.1158/2159-8290.CD-21-1059

812 – Serrano-Gomez, S.J., Maziveyi, M. & Alahari, S.K. '*Regulation of epithelial-mesenchymal transition through epigenetic and post-translational modifications.*' Mol Cancer 15, 18 (2016). doi.org/10.1186/s12943-016-0502-x

813 – Kalluri, Raghu, and Robert A Weinberg. '*The basics of epithelial-mesenchymal transition.*' The Journal of clinical investigation vol. 119,6 (2009): 1420-8. doi:10.1172/JCI39104

814 – Islam, M.T., Mishra, S.K., Tripathi, S. et al. '*Mycotoxin-assisted mitochondrial dysfunction and cytotoxicity: Unexploited tools against proliferative disorders.*' IUBMB Life, 70: 1084-1092. (2018) doi.org/10.1002/iub.1932

815 – Pyo MC, Choi I-G, Lee K-W. '*Transcriptome Analysis Reveals the AhR, Smad2/3, and HIF-1α Pathways as the Mechanism of Ochratoxin A Toxicity in Kidney Cells.*' Toxins. 2021; 13(3):190. doi.org/10.3390/toxins13030190

816 – Proal AD, VanElzakker MB. '*Pathogens Hijack Host Cell Metabolism: Intracellular infection as a Driver of the Warburg Effect in Cancer and Other Chronic Inflammatory Conditions.*' Immunometabolism. 2021;3(1):e210003. doi.org/10.20900/immunometab20210003

817 – Angel Gonzalez, Carlos Pelleschi Taborda. '*Pathogenesis of dimorphic fungal infections.*' Frontiers Research Topics. Frontiers Media SA. Pg 92-93. (6ᵗʰ January, 2022). ISBN: 2889719707, 9782889719709 https://books.google.co.uk/books?id=ZPFXEAAAQBAJ&source=gbs_navlinks_s

818 – Wu, F., Yang, J., Liu, J. et al. '*Signaling pathways in cancer-associated fibroblasts and targeted therapy for cancer.*' Sig Transduct Target Ther 6, 218 (2021). doi.org/10.1038/s41392-021-00641-0

819 – Smith, Gillian et al. '*Mutations in APC, Kirsten-ras, and p53--alternative genetic pathways to colorectal cancer.*' Proceedings of the National Academy of Sciences of the United States of America vol. 99,14 (2002): 9433-8. doi:10.1073/pnas.122612899

820 – Laiza Angela De Medeiros Nunes Da Silva, Pamella De Pinho Montovani, et al. '*Oral Paracoccidioidomycosis referred as an oral cancer: case report.*' Oral Surgery, Oral Medicine, Oral Pathology and Oral Radiology, Volume 130, Issue 3, 2020, Page e162, ISSN 2212-4403. doi.org/10.1016/j.oooo.2020.04.248.

821 – Jef Akst. '*Cancer's Microbes.*' TheScientist Digest, pg 15. March 2022. www.the-scientist.com/ts-digest/view/cancer-s-microbes-3-2?page=14&utm_campaign=ts_daily_newsletter_2022&utm_medium=email&_hsmi=206987022&_hsenc=p2ANqtz-99qGcrNQFs2aWKzdG8SOBvHQqjOysGuHfCMhSz2d5u1dUpC9jYrzq2rymSj8PUHjuDHzVHSNWhcqSx0w0rWqJo599Ljg&utm_content=206987022&utm_source=hs_email

822 – Luan, C., Xie, L., Yang, X. et al. '*Dysbiosis of Fungal Microbiota in the Intestinal Mucosa of Patients with Colorectal Adenomas.*' Sci Rep 5, 7980 (2015). doi.org/10.1038/srep07980

823 – Esfahani, Ava Nasr et al. '*Antifungal effect of Atorvastatin against Candida species in comparison to Fluconazole and Nystatin.*' Medicine and pharmacy reports vol. 92,4 (2019): 368-373. doi:10.15386/mpr-1209

824 – Zhong, Mengya et al. '*Candida albicans disorder is associated with gastric carcinogenesis.*' Theranostics vol. 11,10 4945-4956. 5 Mar. 2021, doi:10.7150/thno.55209

825 – Mishra, Kirtishri et al. '*Symbiosis and Dysbiosis of the Human Mycobiome.*' Frontiers in microbiology vol. 12 636131. 22 Sep. 2021, doi:10.3389/fmicb.2021.636131

826 – Travis Christofferson. '*Healthy conversations with Travis Christofferson and guest, Jason Fung MD.*' StageZero Life Sciences, YouTube. Dec, 2021. (37:50) www.youtube.com/watch?v=v6KqBYiMZmc

827 – Farhad, Mohammad et al. '*The role of Galectin-3 in modulating tumor growth and immunosuppression within the tumor microenvironment.*' Oncoimmunology vol. 7,6 e1434467. 20 Feb. 2018, doi:10.1080/2162402X.2018.1434467

828 – Emerit J, Beaumont C, Trivin F. '*Iron metabolism, free radicals, and oxidative injury.*' Biomed Pharmacother. 2001 Jul;55(6):333-9. doi: 10.1016/s0753-3322(01)00068-3. PMID: 11478586.

829 – Cruzat, V.; Macedo Rogero, M.; Noel Keane, K.; Curi, R.; Newsholme, P. '*Glutamine: Metabolism and Immune Function, Supplementation and Clinical Translation.*' Nutrients 2018, 10, 1564. doi.org/10.3390/nu10111564

830 – Hoffman, R.M. '*Is DNA methylation the new guardian of the genome?*' Mol Cytogenet 10, 11 (2017). doi.org/10.1186/s13039-017-0314-8

831 – Garbe, E., Vylkova, S. '*Role of Amino Acid Metabolism in the Virulence of Human Pathogenic Fungi.*' Curr Clin Micro Rpt 6, 108–119 (2019). doi.org/10.1007/s40588-019-00124-5

832 – Endicott, M., Jones, M. & Hull, J. '*Amino acid metabolism as a therapeutic target in cancer: a review.*' Amino Acids 53, 1169–1179 (2021). doi.org/10.1007/s00726-021-03052-1

833 – Parkhitko, Andrey A et al. '*Methionine metabolism and methyltransferases in the regulation of aging and lifespan extension across species.*' Aging cell vol. 18,6 (2019): e13034. doi:10.1111/acel.13034

834 – Lam, Gretl BA; Fontaine, Rocky CHT; Ross, Frank L. MD; Chiu, Ernest S. MD. '*Hyperbaric Oxygen Therapy: Exploring the clinical evidence.*' Advances in Skin & Wound Care: April 2017 – Volume 30 - Issue 4 - p 181-190. doi: 10.1097/01.ASW.0000513089.75457.22

835 – Goerger, Elsa et al. '*Anti-infective therapy without antimicrobials: Apparent successful treatment of multidrug resistant osteomyelitis with hyperbaric oxygen therapy.*' IDCases vol. 6 60-64. 28 Sep. 2016. doi:10.1016/j.idcr.2016.09.008

836 – Bentur Y1, Shupak A, Ramon Y et al. '*Hyperbaric oxygen therapy for cutaneous/soft-tissue zygomycosis complicating diabetes mellitus.*' Plastic and Reconstructive Surgery. 01 Sep 1998, 102(3):822-824 doi:10.1097/00006534-199809030-00030 PMID: 9727450

837 – García-Covarrubias L1, Barratt DM, Bartlett R et al. '*Invasive aspergillosis treated with adjunctive hyperbaric oxygenation: a retrospective clinical series at a single institution.*' Southern Medical Journal. April 2001;95(4):450-6. PMID:11958246

838 – Chen, SY., Tsuneyama, K., Yen, MH. et al. '*Hyperbaric oxygen suppressed tumor progression through the improvement of tumor hypoxia and induction of tumor apoptosis in A549-cell-transferred lung cancer.*' Sci Rep 11, 12033 (2021). doi.org/10.1038/s41598-021-91454-2

839 – Endicott, M., Jones, M. & Hull, J. '*Amino acid metabolism as a therapeutic target in cancer: a review.*' Amino Acids 53, 1169–1179 (2021). doi.org/10.1007/s00726-021-03052-1

840 – Jenkinson HF, Douglas LJ. '*Interactions between Candida Species and Bacteria in Mixed Infections.*' In: Brogden KA, Guthmiller JM, editors. Polymicrobial Diseases. Washington (DC): ASM Press; 2002. Chapter 18. Available from: www.ncbi.nlm.nih.gov/books/NBK2486/

841 – Hannah Devlin. '*Top oncologist to study effect of diet on cancer drugs.*' The Guardian. 6th July 2018. www.theguardian.com/science/2018/jul/06/top-oncologist-to-study-effect-of-diet-on-cancer-drugs

842 – Kumwenda P, Cottier F, Hendry AC, et al. '*Estrogen promotes innate immune evasion of Candida albicans through inactivation of the alternative complement system.*' Cell Rep. 2022 Jan 4;38(1):110183. doi: 10.1016/j.celrep.2021.110183. PMID: 34986357; PMCID: PMC8755443.

843 – Patrick Vandeputte, Selene Ferrari, Alix T. Coste, '*Antifungal Resistance and New Strategies to Control Fungal Infections.*' International Journal of Microbiology, vol. 2012, Article ID 713687, 26 pages, 2012. doi.org/10.1155/2012/713687

844 – Cancer Research UK. '*Hodgkin lymphoma risk.*' October 2022. www.cancerresearchuk.org/health-professional/cancer-statistics/statistics-by-cancer-type/hodgkin-lymphoma/risk-factors#heading-Zero

845 – Esther Landhuis. '*Cancer cells cast a sweet spell on the immune system.*' SceinceNews.org. March, 2017. www.sciencenews.org/article/cancer-cells-cast-sweet-spell-immune-system

846 – Gina Kolata. '*Cancer drug proves to be effective against multiple tumours.*' The New York Times. June, 2017. www.nytimes.com/2017/06/08/health/cancer-drug-keytruda-tumors.html

847 – Ren, Y., Qian, Y., Ai, L. et al. '*TRAPPC4 regulates the intracellular trafficking of PD-L1 and antitumor immunity.*' Nat Commun 12, 5405 (2021) doi.org/10.1038/s41467-021-25662-9

848 – Wang, X, Zhao, W, Zhang, W, Wu, S, Yan, Z. '*Candida albicans induces upregulation of programmed death ligand 1 in oral squamous cell carcinoma.*' J Oral Pathol Med. 2022; 51(5): 444- 453. doi:10.1111/jop.13298

849 – Eszter Lazar-Molnar, Attila Gacser et al. '*The PD-1/PD-L costimulatory pathway critically affects host resistance to the pathogenic fungus Histoplasma capsulatum.*' PNAS, 2007. doi/10.1073/pnas.0711918105

850 – Marcos Duarte Guimaraes, Edson Marchori and Myrna Cobos Barco Godoy. '*Fungal infection mimicking lung cancer: A potential cause of misdiagnosis.*' American Journal of Roentgenology. 2013;201: W364-W364. 10.2214/AJR.13.10568

851 – Ma H, Croudace JE, Lammas DA, May RC. '*Direct cell-to-cell spread of a pathogenic yeast.*' BMC Immunol. 2007 Aug 16;8:15. doi: 10.1186/1471-2172-8-15. PMID: 17705831; PMCID: PMC1976318.

852 – Chang YC, Stins MF, McCaffery MJ et al. '*Cryptococcal yeast cells invade the central nervous system via transcellular penetration of the blood-brain barrier. Infect Immun.*' 2004 Sep;72(9):4985-95. doi: 10.1128/IAI.72.9.4985-4995.2004. Erratum in: Infect Immun. 2004 Nov;72(11):6753. Paul-Satyasee, Maneesh [corrected to Paul-Satyaseela, Maneesh]. PMID: 15321990; PMCID: PMC517459.

853 – Davy James. '*Can common antibiotics eradicate cancer cells?*' Pharmacy Times. February, 2015. www.pharmacytimes.com/view/can-common-antibiotics-eradicate-cancer-cells

854 – Zhou S, Wang F, Wong ET, et al. '*Salinomycin: a novel anti-cancer agent with known anti-coccidial activities.*' Curr Med Chem. 2013;20(33):4095-101. doi: 10.2174/15672050113109990199. PMID: 23931281; PMCID: PMC4102832.

855 – Gao Y, Shang Q, Li W, Guo W, et al. '*Antibiotics for cancer treatment: A double-edged sword.*' J Cancer. 2020 Jun 28;11(17):5135-5149. doi: 10.7150/jca.47470. PMID: 32742461; PMCID: PMC7378927.

856 – Norma Erickson, Peter H Deusberg, PhD. '*What if HPV does NOT cause cervical cancer?*' SaneVax, Inc. January, 2015. https://sanevax.org/hpv-not-cause-cervical-cancer/

857 – Lian Narunsky-Haziza, Gregory D. Sepich-Poore, et al. '*Pan-cancer analyses reveal cancer-type-specific fungal ecologies and bacteriome interactions.*' Cell. September, 2022. doi.org/10.1016/j.cell.2022.09.005

858 – Mary Ann Liebert. '*Map of links between cancers and fungi created.*' Inside Precision Medicine. September, 2022. https://www.insideprecisionmedicine.com/topics/patient-care/fungal-diseases/map-of-links-between-cancers-and-fungi-created/

859 – Mun-Keat Looi. '*The human microbiome: Everything you need to know about the 39 trillion microbes that call our bodies home.*' BBC Science Focus. July, 2020. www.sciencefocus.com/the-human-body/human-microbiome/

860 – Epilepsy Society. '*Ketogenic diet.*' Epilepsy Society. April, 2019. https://epilepsysociety.org.uk/about-epilepsy/treatment/ketogenic-diet

861 – Lemons JM, Feng XJ, Bennett BD et al. '*Quiescent fibroblasts exhibit high metabolic activity.*' PLoS Biol. 2010 Oct 19;8(10):e1000514. doi: 10.1371/journal.pbio.1000514. PMID: 21049082; PMCID: PMC2958657

862 – Fatica EM, DeLeonibus GA, House A, et al. '*Barth Syndrome: Exploring Cardiac Metabolism with Induced Pluripotent Stem Cell-Derived Cardiomyocytes.*' Metabolites. 2019 Dec 17;9(12):306. doi: 10.3390/metabo9120306. PMID: 31861102; PMCID: PMC6950123.

863 - Amy E Baek. '*Bacteria benefit tumour cells.*' Science Signaling. April, 2022 doi: 10.1126/scisignal.abq4492

864 – Gunjan Sinha. '*Bacteria in tumours may promote cancer.*' Science. November, 2022. doi: 10.1126/science.adf8541

865 – Niño, J.L.G., Wu, H., LaCourse, K.D. et al. *'Effect of the intratumoral microbiota on spatial and cellular heterogeneity in cancer.'* Nature (2022). doi.org/10.1038/s41586-022-05435-0

866 – Seyfried TN, Chinopoulos C. *'Can the Mitochondrial Metabolic Theory Explain Better the Origin and Management of Cancer than Can the Somatic Mutation Theory?'* Metabolites. 2021 Aug 25;11(9):572. doi: 10.3390/metabo11090572. PMID: 34564387; PMCID: PMC8467939.

867 – Tae Kim. *'Goldman Sachs asks in biotech research report: "Is curing patients a sustainable business model?"'* CNBC. April, 2018. https://www.cnbc.com/2018/04/11/goldman-asks-is-curing-patients-a-sustainable-business-model.html

868 – Felty Q, Roy D. *'Estrogen, mitochondria, and growth of cancer and non-cancer cells.'* J Carcinog. 2005 Jan 15;4(1):1. doi: 10.1186/1477-3163-4-1. PMID: 15651993; PMCID: PMC548143.

869 – Tang H, Shi W, Song Y, Han J. *'Voriconazole exposure and risk of cutaneous squamous cell carcinoma among lung or hematopoietic cell transplant patients: A systematic review and meta-analysis.'* J Am Acad Dermatol. 2019 Feb;80(2):500-507.e10. doi: 10.1016/j.jaad.2018.08.010. Epub 2018 Aug 18. PMID: 30130598.

870 – NICE. *'Voriconazole'.* National Institute for Health and Care Excellence. November, 2022. https://bnf.nice.org.uk/drugs/voriconazole/

871 – Currie E, Schulze A, Zechner R, Walther TC, Farese RV Jr. *'Cellular fatty acid metabolism and cancer.'* Cell Metab. 2013 Aug 6;18(2):153-61. doi: 10.1016/j.cmet.2013.05.017. Epub 2013 Jun 20. PMID: 23791484; PMCID: PMC3742569.

872 – Kennedy KM, Scarbrough PM, Ribeiro A, et al. *'Catabolism of exogenous lactate reveals it as a legitimate metabolic substrate in breast cancer.'* PLoS One. 2013 Sep 12;8(9):e75154. doi: 10.1371/journal.pone.0075154. PMID: 24069390; PMCID: PMC3771963.

873 – Galal AM, Ross SA, Jacob M, ElSohly MA. *'Antifungal activity of artemisinin derivatives.'* J Nat Prod. 2005 Aug;68(8):1274-6. doi: 10.1021/np050074u. PMID: 16124777.

874 – Juteau F, Jerkovic I, Masotti V, et al. *'Composition and antimicrobial activity of the essential oil of Artemisia absinthium from Croatia and France.'* Planta Med. 2003 Feb;69(2):158-61. doi: 10.1055/s-2003-37714. PMID: 12624823.

875 – Fan J, Kamphorst JJ, Mathew R, et al. *'Glutamine-driven oxidative phosphorylation is a major ATP source in transformed mammalian cells in both normoxia and hypoxia.'* Mol Syst Biol. 2013 Dec 3;9:712. doi: 10.1038/msb.2013.65. PMID: 24301801; PMCID: PMC3882799.

876 – Robert K. Naviaux. *'Metabolic features of the cell danger response.'* Mitochondrion, Volume 16, 2014, Pages 7-17, ISSN 1567-7249, doi.org/10.1016/j.mito.2013.08.006.

877 – Sonnenschein C, Soto AM. *'Somatic mutation theory of carcinogenesis: why it should be dropped and replaced.'* Mol Carcinog. 2000 Dec;29(4):205-11. doi: 10.1002/1098-2744(200012)29:4<205::aid-mc1002>3.0.co;2-w. PMID: 11170258.

878 – Gilbert AS, Wheeler RT, May RC. *'Fungal Pathogens: Survival and Replication within Macrophages.'* Cold Spring Harb Perspect Med. 2014 Nov 10;5(7):a019661. doi: 10.1101/cshperspect.a019661. PMID: 25384769; PMCID: PMC4484954.

879 – Crunkhorn, S. *'Targeting cancer cell metabolism in glioblastoma.'* Nat Rev Cancer 19, 250 (2019). https://doi.org/10.1038/s41568-019-0139-3

880 – Fu, X., Guo, J., Finkelbergs, D. et al. *'Fungal succession during mammalian cadaver decomposition and potential forensic implications.'* Sci Rep 9, 12907 (2019). doi.org/10.1038/s41598-019-49361-0

881 – Soto-Heredero G, Gómez de Las Heras MM, et al. *'Glycolysis - a key player in the inflammatory response.'* FEBS J. 2020 Aug;287(16):3350-3369. doi: 10.1111/febs.15327. Epub 2020 Apr 27. PMID: 32255251; PMCID: PMC7496292.

882 – Vyas S, Zaganjor E, Haigis MC. *'Mitochondria and Cancer.'* Cell. 2016 Jul 28;166(3):555-566. doi: 10.1016/j.cell.2016.07.002. PMID: 27471965; PMCID: PMC5036969.

883 – Zong WX, Rabinowitz JD, White E. *'Mitochondria and Cancer.'* Mol Cell. 2016 Mar 3;61(5):667-676. doi: 10.1016/j.molcel.2016.02.011. PMID: 26942671; PMCID: PMC4779192.

884 – Santiago-Tirado FH, Onken MD, Cooper JA, Klein RS, Doering TL. *'Trojan Horse Transit Contributes to Blood-Brain Barrier Crossing of a Eukaryotic Pathogen.'* mBio. 2017 Jan 31;8(1):e02183-16. doi: 10.1128/mBio.02183-16. PMID: 28143979; PMCID: PMC5285505.

885 – Artiukh L, Povnitsa O, Zahorodnia S, Pop CV, Rizun N. *'Effect of Coated Silver Nanoparticles on Cancerous vs. Healthy Cells.'* J Toxicol. 2022 Oct 8;2022:1519104. doi: 10.1155/2022/1519104. PMID: 36254120; PMCID: PMC9569232.

886 – Afrin S, Giampieri F, Gasparrini M, et al. *'The inhibitory effect of Manuka honey on human colon cancer HCT-116 and LoVo cell growth. Part 1: the suppression of cell proliferation, promotion of apoptosis and arrest of the cell cycle.'* Food Funct. 2018 Apr 25;9(4):2145-2157. doi: 10.1039/c8fo00164b. PMID: 29645049.

887 – Ravid Straussman Lab. *'The Tumour Microbiome.'* Weizmann Institute of Science. 2023. www.weizmann.ac.il/mcb/Straussman/research-activities/tumor-microbiome

888 – Aikun Fu, Bingqing Yao, Tingting Dong et al. *'Tumor-resident intracellular microbiota promotes metastatic colonization in breast cancer.'* Cell. Volume 185, Issue 8, 2022. ISSN 0092-8674. doi.org/10.1016/j.cell.2022.02.027

889 – Medical College of Georgia at Augusta University. *"Antibiotics may impact cancer treatment efficacy."* ScienceDaily. ScienceDaily, 3 March 2018. www.sciencedaily.com/releases/2018/03/180303090356.htm

890 – Ningna Weng, Zhe Zhang, Yunhan Tan, et al. *'Repurposing antifungal drugs for cancer therapy.'* Journal of Advanced Research, 2022. ISSN 2090-1232. doi.org/10.1016/j.jare.2022.08.018

891 – Angus Chen. *'Fungi find their way into cancer tumors, but what they're doing there is a mystery.'* STAT news. January, 2023. www.statnews.com/2022/09/30/fungi-found-in-cancer-tumors-but-why-is-a-mystery/

892 – Jean-Paul Latge. *'The cell wall: a carbohydrate armour for the fungal cell.'* Molecular Microbiology. 2007. doi:10.1111/j.1365-2958.2007.05872.x

893 – Danielle Underferth. *'H.pylori and your stomach cancer risk.'* The University of Texas MD Anderson Cancer Center. April 2021. www.mdanderson.org/cancerwise/h--pylori-and-your-stomach-cancer-risk.h00-159460056.html

894 – Donald Maxwell Parkin. *'The global burden of infection-associated cancers in the year 2002.'* International Journal of Cancer. Jan, 2006. doi.org/10.1002/ijc.21731

895 – Takenaka, Y., Fukumori, T. & Raz, A. *'Galectin-3 and metastasis.'* Glycoconj J 19, 543–549 (2002). doi.org/10.1023/B:GLYC.0000014084.01324.15

896 – Wraith DC. *'The Future of Immunotherapy: A 20-Year Perspective.'* Front Immunol. 2017 Nov 28;8:1668. doi: 10.3389/fimmu.2017.01668. PMID: 29234325; PMCID: PMC5712390.

897 – Gordon, D., Resio, B. & Pellman, D. *'Causes and consequences of aneuploidy in cancer.'* Nat Rev Genet 13, 189–203 (2012). https://doi.org/10.1038/nrg3123

898 – One Health: *'Fungal Pathogens of Humans, Animals, and Plants: Report on an American Academy of Microbiology Colloquium held in Washington, DC, on October 18, 2017.'* Washington (DC): American Society for Microbiology; 2019. Available from: www.ncbi.nlm.nih.gov/books/NBK549988/ doi: 10.1128/AAMCol.18Oct.2017

899 – Bradbury Science Museum. *'How many species of fungi are there?'* Bradbury Science Museum, article. January, 2018.
www.lanl.gov/museum/news/newsletter/2018/01/fungi.php

900 – *Microbiology by numbers*. Nat Rev Microbiol 9, 628 (2011). doi.org/10.1038/nrmicro2644

901 – Oncology Nursing News. *'The link between gastric ulcers and stomach cancer.'* Oncology Nursing News. June, 2014. www.oncnursingnews.com/view/the-link-between-gastric-ulcers-and-stomach-cancer

902 – Mot AI, Liddell JR, White AR, Crouch PJ. *'Circumventing the Crabtree Effect: A method to induce lactate consumption and increase oxidative phosphorylation in cell culture.'* Int J Biochem Cell Biol. 2016 Oct;79:128-138. doi: 10.1016/j.biocel.2016.08.029. Epub 2016 Aug 30. PMID: 27590850.

903 – Jessica Watson. *'Inflammatory markers explained.'* NIHR Applied Research Collaboration West. May 2022. https://arc-w.nihr.ac.uk/news/inflammatory-markers-explained/

904 – Yes To Life. *'Cancer through another lens.'* Yes To Life.org. 12th February, 2023. https://yestolife.org.uk/event/cancer-through-another-lens/?ch=past

905 – Navdeep S. Chandel, Ph.D. David A. Tuveson, M.D., Ph.D. *'The promise and perils of antioxidants for cancer patients.'* N Engl J Med 2014; 371:177-178. doi: 10.1056/NEJMcibr1405701

906 – Daniel S, Ph.D. *'Modulating the Yin and Yang energy fo cells to fight cancer: Pro-oxidant strategy.'* CancerTreatmentResearch.com. January, 2021. www.cancertreatmentsresearch.com/modulating-the-yin-and-yang-energy-of-cells-to-fight-cancer-pro-oxidant-strategy/?highlight=super%20antioxidants

907 – Toren Finkel. *'Signal transduction by reactive oxygen species.'* J Cell Biol (2011) 194 (1): 7-15. doi.org/10.1083/jcb.201102095

908 – Bouayed J, Bohn T. *'Exogenous antioxidants--Double-edged swords in cellular redox state: Health beneficial effects at physiologic doses versus deleterious effects at high doses.'* Oxid Med Cell Longev. 2010 Jul-Aug;3(4):228-37. doi: 10.4161/oxim.3.4.12858. PMID: 20972369; PMCID: PMC2952083.

909 – Rob Verkerk. *'Cancer through another lens.'* Alliance for Natural Health International. 15th February, 2023. www.anhinternational.org/news/cancer-through-another-lens/

910 – Yes To Life. *'Cancer through another lens.'* Yes To Life. 12th February, 2023. https://yestolife.org.uk/event/cancer-through-another-lens/

911 – Clinton A Fontaine, Anna M Skorupski, Chriss J Vowles, et al. *'How free of germs is germ-free? Detection of bacterial contamination in a germ free mouse unit.'* Gut Microbes, 6:4, 225-233, doi: 10.1080/19490976.2015.1054596

912 – DEHARVEN E. *'VIRUS PARTICLES IN THE THYMUS OF CONVENTIONAL AND GERM-FREE MICE.'* J Exp Med. 1964 Nov 1;120(5):857-68. doi: 10.1084/jem.120.5.857. PMID: 14247725; PMCID: PMC2137866.

913 – Sameer AS, Nissar S. *'Toll-Like Receptors (TLRs): Structure, Functions, Signaling, and Role of Their Polymorphisms in Colorectal Cancer Susceptibility.'* Biomed Res Int. 2021 Sep 12;2021:1157023. doi: 10.1155/2021/1157023. PMID: 34552981; PMCID: PMC8452412.

914 – Pradere JP, Dapito DH, Schwabe RF. *'The Yin and Yang of Toll-like receptors in cancer.'* Oncogene. 2014 Jul 3;33(27):3485-95. doi: 10.1038/onc.2013.302. Epub 2013 Aug 12. PMID: 23934186; PMCID: PMC4059777.

915 – Sonnenschein C, Soto AM. *'Somatic mutation theory of carcinogenesis: why it should be dropped and replaced.'* Mol Carcinog. 2000 Dec;29(4):205-11. doi: 10.1002/1098-2744(200012)29:4<205::aid-mc1002>3.0.co;2-w. PMID: 11170258.

916 – Connie M. Krawczyk, Thomas Holowka, Jie Sun et al. *'Toll-like receptor–induced changes in glycolytic metabolism regulate dendritic cell activation.'* Blood (2010) 115 (23): 4742–4749. doi.org/10.1182/blood-2009-10-249540

917 – Khalid O. Alfarouk1, Daniel Verduzco, Cyril Rauch, et al. *'Glycolysis, tumor metabolism, cancer growth and dissemination. A new pH-based etiopathogenic perspective and therapeutic approach to an old cancer question.'* Oncoscience. 2014. Vol.1, No.12. doi.org/10.18632/oncoscience.109

918 – Vu K, Buckley BJ, Bujaroski RS, Blumwald E, Kelso MJ, Gelli A. *'Antifungal activity of 6-substituted amiloride and hexamethylene amiloride (HMA) analogs.'* Front Cell Infect Microbiol. 2023 Feb 16;13:1101568. doi: 10.3389/fcimb.2023.1101568. PMID: 36923593; PMCID: PMC10009331.

919 – Aaron Kheriaty. MD. Twitter. April 12th 2023. https://twitter.com/akheriaty/status/1645937691920568320? s=43&t=K7yxC7_YmO0qqpXj0mVeTw&utm_source=substack&utm_medium=email

920 – John Kay. *'Science is the pursuit of the truth, not consensus.'* John Kay. 2007. www.johnkay.com/2007/10/10/science-is-the-pursuit-of-the-truth-not-consensus/

921 – Mark J. Perry. *'Michael Chrichton explains why there is 'no such thing as consensus science.''* AEI. December 2019. www.aei.org/carpe-diem/michael-crichton-explains-why-there-is-no-such-thing-as-consensus-science/

922 – Dr Nash Winters, Jess Kelley. *'The Metabolic Approach to Cancer.'* Chelsea Green Publishing. May 2017. *ISBN-13 978-1603586863*

923 – NCI staff. *'For women with Breast Cancer, regular exercise may improve survival.'* National Cancer Institute. May 2020. https://www.cancer.gov/news-events/cancer-currents-blog/2020/breast-cancer-survival-exercise

924 – Torti SV, Manz DH, Paul BT, Blanchette-Farra N, Torti FM. *'Iron and Cancer.'* Annu Rev Nutr. 2018 Aug 21;38:97-125. doi: 10.1146/annurev-nutr-082117-051732. PMID: 30130469; PMCID: PMC8118195.

925 – Pânzariu, AT., Apotrosoaei, M., Vasincu, I.M. et al. *'Synthesis and biological evaluation of new 1,3-thiazolidine-4-one derivatives of nitro-L-arginine methyl ester.'* Chemistry Central Journal 10, 6 (2016). doi.org/10.1186/s13065-016-0151-6

926 – Zhang, Q., Liu, F., Zeng, M. et al. *'Drug repurposing strategies in the development of potential antifungal agents.'* Appl Microbiol Biotechnol 105, 5259–5279 (2021). doi.org/10.1007/s00253-021-11407-7

927 – Yuan Gao1,2, Hui Li1, Shuyuan Liu1, Xiang Zhang3, Shujuan Sun. *'Synergistic effect of fluconazole and doxycycline against Candida albicans biofilms resulting from calcium fluctuation and downregulation of fluconazole-inducible efflux pump gene overexpression.'* Journal of Medical Microbiology. July 2014, Vol 63, Issue 7. doi.org/10.1099/jmm.0.072421-0

Amendment: Total number of references remaining after editing: 814

Made in the USA
Las Vegas, NV
10 October 2024

96595452R00339